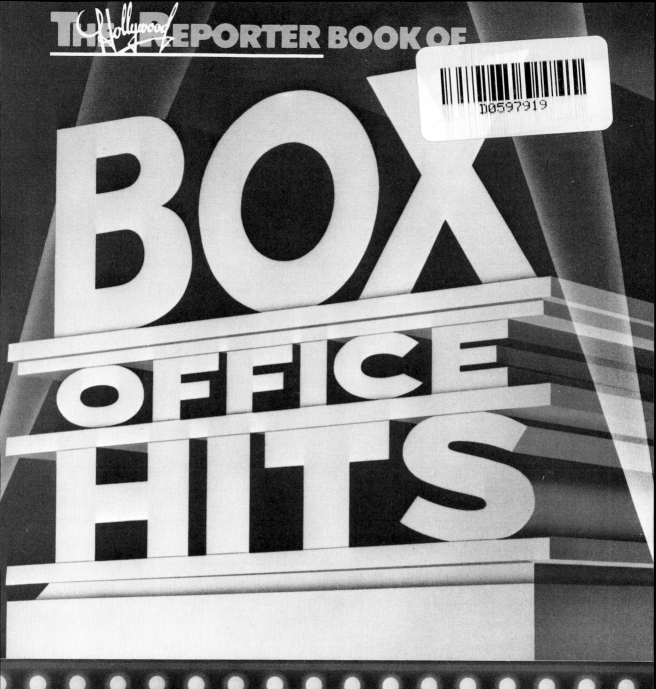

THE HOLLYWOOD REPORTER BOOK OF

BOX OFFICE HITS

SUSAN SACKETT

BILLBOARD BOOKS
An imprint of Watson-Guptill Publications/New York

D0597919

Research Assistant: Marcia Rovins
Senior Editor: Tad Lathrop
Assoc. Editor: Fred Weiler
Book and Jacket Design: Bob Fillie
Jacket Illustration: David Myers
Production Manager: Ellen Greene

First published 1990 by Billboard Books, an imprint of
Watson-Guptill Publications, a division of Billboard Publications, Inc.
1515 Broadway, New York, NY 10036.

Library of Congress Cataloging-In-Publication Data

Sackett, Susan.
    The Hollywood reporter book of box office hits / Susan Sackett.
       p.   cm.
    Includes bibliographical references.
    ISBN 0-8230-7549-4
    1. Motion pictures—United States—History.   2. Motion pictures—
United States—Awards.   3. Motion pictures—United States—
Statistics.   4. Film credits—United States.   I. Title.
PN1993.5.U6S18   1990
    791.45'75'0973—dc20   89-48076
                                                    CIP

Manufactured in the United States of America
First Printing, 1990

1 2 3 4 5 6 7 8 9 / 95 94 93 92 91 90

To Fred Bronson, for many reasons.

ACKNOWLEDGMENTS

This book could probably not have been written if I lived in Albuquerque, or Sioux Falls, or even my former hometowns of New Haven and Palm Beach. Because of my proximity to the resources available only in the Southern California area, I was able to acquire the mountain of material needed in researching this project. Chief mountaineer and research assistant Marcia Rovins deserves my greatest thanks for her help, her patience, and her friendship in keeping me centered when I was awash in a sea of facts, reviews, articles, tapes, and computer diskettes. This book truly could not have happened if it wasn't for Marcia.

Also worthy of special praise, for her unquestioning eagerness as well as her uncanny knowledge of glitchy computers, is my assistant, Jana Wallace. Besides typing innumerable drafts of the manuscript when the computer seemed determined to thwart her attempts, Jana and her friend (and mine) Joseph Kerezman were kind enough to supply my video habit with many much-needed tapes of movies on cable channels I don't receive. Thanks, guys.

Also thanks to Andy Davis for his helping me cope with the computer age.

Special thanks, too, to Lynne Kortidis, who spent many hours helping compile the definitive list of top hits, a two-month-long project itself! (Lynne's reward for her hard work was a visit to Hollywood's Cinerama Dome, where I made her endure the rollercoaster ride in *This is Cinerama*'s 1989 re-release—the motion-sickness-prone Lynne kept her eyes tightly closed.)

Marvin Paige, long-time friend and business associate, was kind enough to allow me access to his archives during my search for black-and-white stills. Thanks, Marvin, Snooper, and Nicole.

Richard Arnold, Denny Arnold, and Cass Paley were also instrumental in lending me many of the videocassettes I needed to view, and for this I offer my special thanks.

Eddie Brandt's video store in North Hollywood (especially Donovan and Heidi), 20/20 Video, and Music Plus Video in

Studio City were also helpful in finding rare tapes for my research, and deserve a mention of thanks.

Cheryl Blythe deserves a mention for her support and help in answering many questions with her special knowledge.

Also to Rich Kelley, my video repairer, for keeping my VCR up and running.

Thanks to Ori Seron, April Sackett, and Judy Maher for their help in acquiring stills for the book; Ernie Over, for his research help; John Ginelli at *The Hollywood Reporter* library, for his invaluable assistance in obtaining reviews; and the staff of the Burbank Public Library, for their patience and assistance.

A special word of gratitude and love to my friend Fred Bronson, for his introducing me to the good people at Billboard Publications and for his support in this project and in my life.

As always, my boss, lifelong mentor, and friend, Gene Roddenberry, deserves my special thanks and love for his understanding and for allowing me extra time off during our active shooting of the TV series "Star Trek: The Next Generation."

Finally, no amount of thanks is sufficient for my editors at Billboard Books, Tad Lathrop and Fred Weiler, who never once lost their tempers, no matter what seemingly insurmountable (to me) problems I threw their way.

The following people at the Hollywood studios that made all of it possible deserve a word of gratitude for their assistance:

COLUMBIA: Ivy Orta, Terry Saevig.

DISNEY: Jeffrey Katzenberg, Leonard Nimoy, Terry Press, Susan Salazar, Cindy George, Miriam Estany.

PARAMOUNT: Deborah Rosen, Maggie Young, Diane Isaacs, Michael Kochman, Vanessa Fleming, Gregg Brilliant, Antony Davies, Gregg Brooks.

TWENTIETH CENTURY-FOX: Shary Klamer.

TURNER ENTERTAINMENT: Diana Brown, Steve Snyder.

MGM/UNITED ARTISTS: Joan Pierce.

UNIVERSAL: Tony Sauber, Nancy Cushing-Jones.

WARNER BROS.: Judy Singer (especially helpful—thanks!)

CONTENTS

1 9 8 9   A N D
T H E   1 9 9 0 s

INTRODUCTION

It seemed like a dream assignment. Imagine—watching movies and getting paid for it! All I had to do was find a list of the top five films for each of the last 50 years, rent the cassettes, and settle down in my favorite chair to a marathon of celluloid and magnetic tape.

I love movies, especially those of the '30s and '40s, and had established credit at all the video shops in town ("Name? Credit card numbers? Driver's license? First-born child we can take hostage if you lose the tape?") Many rainy weekends had been spent watching Hollywood classics and munching popcorn with one of my dogs curled up next to me. This would be fun—and easy.

Actually, it *was* easy watching the films, once I was able to determine which were on the list. I live in Hollywood (well, Los Angeles, really; nobody actually *lives* in Hollywood). So it seemed a simple thing to call upon my many friends in "the industry" and get a list of the top-grossing films of all time, by year, and wow! Crank up the microwave—here comes Orville Redenbacher! Problem was, no such list existed. Oh, there had been a few brave attempts at Top Ten lists, or lists of films that had made megabucks in the last 15 years. But to my surprise, no one had pulled together a list of the top films, year by year, and certainly not one going back 50 years.

I began combing through charts of films and discovered that the most complete figures available were not *grosses*, but *rentals*. At first, I thought this must have something to do with videocassettes and how much money they made from people who rented them, but I soon learned that the term *rental* had nothing whatsoever to do with tapes and video. The most accurate records I was able to locate are those which are reported annually in that old industry bible, *Variety*. And for the most part, this is the source of the dollar figures in this book.

What is the difference between grosses and rentals?

Most of us are more familiar with *gross* figures. These are the actual dollars taken in at the box office. (If a ticket cost $6.00 and Theater A sells 1000 seats one weekend, it would gross $6,000.) These are all added together, for a total gross. The highest *grossing* film of all time (not counting inflation) was *E.T.: The Extraterrestrial*, which grossed $700,000,000. (Okay, math fans, how many tickets did *E.T.* sell to reach this figure?)

Rental figures, however, are considerably lower, and represent the amount of money paid to the distributors of a film (usually a motion picture studio has its own distribution arm) by those who rent a film (generally a movie theater). Rentals are also a more accurate picture of how much a film has earned. The amount *E.T.* has made in domestic (U.S. and Canada) rentals is $228,600,000.

Once I figured out which films would be included in this book, the next step was actually *viewing* them. Surprisingly, about nine out of ten films which are included in this book are available on videocassette. Most of the others appear regularly on local and cable television channels such as HBO, Cinemax, Disney Channel, Showtime, The Movie Channel, and American Movie Classics. Thus, armed with stacks of cassettes and my trusty bag of popcorn, I began what turned out to be one of the great adventures of my life. For the next several months, I howled with laughter, cried myself silly, shook with fear, fell in love, fought several wars, traveled to outer space, and occasionally snoozed—all in front of the 40-inch big-screen TV (highly recommended for home viewing). I hired a research assistant and bombarded her with questions like "How do they train cats for the movies?" "What was the name of the mechanical shark in Jaws?" "What was the real Annie Oakley like?" "What was the true story of the Alamo, and did Davy Crockett really look like John Wayne?" and my favorite, "What ever became of _____?" It was a truly educational experience, but most of all, a great deal of fun.

It is important to bear in mind that although some of the dollar figures for films back in the '40s are well under $10,000,000, inflation must always be taken into account. You cannot, for instance, compare a 1940 film like *Boom Town*, at $4,500,000, with something like 1984's *The Karate Kid*, at $43,500,000. While the latter would appear to have earned nearly ten times the amount of the 1940 film, you could also buy a very comfortable house in 1940 for around $5,000. Of course, there is no exact formula for computing the box office inflation factor— these days, ticket prices are hitting the $7.00 range and climbing all too rapidly. Some megahits play on thousands of screens across the country simultaneously, and the population of North America has more than doubled since the '40s. All of these factors should be kept in mind when you compare rental figures.

For its annual report on rental figures, *Variety*'s cut-off point is $4,000,000; they only include films which earned at least that amount. And studios didn't keep complete records of their take from rentals in the early '40s. Generally, ranking the films by rental figures was no problem for those years, since the big hits made quite a bit of money. However, 1939, 1940, and 1941 had several gaps in the list. Joel Finler's book *The Hollywood Story* was particularly helpful in filling these positions for 1939 and 1940, but 1941 proved to be particularly elusive.

By combing through reel after reel of microfilm at the Motion Picture Academy Library, plus searching through old volumes of such '40s publications as *Motion Picture Daily, Film Daily, Film Yearly Almanac,* and *Interna-*

tional Motion Picture Almanac, I was able to compile a list of the top-*grossing* films of 1941, although dollar figures were not always indicated. Some of the studios were able to supply approximate figures, but most admitted that they couldn't give definite amounts. I finally settled on $1,500,000 as the best estimate for these films, a figure based on all the above sources plus some very tentative nods from the studios themselves. For 1939, 1940, and 1941, those films "tied" with the $1,500,000 amount appear in alphabetical order, as do 1949's *Jolson Sings Again* and *The Sands of Iwo Jima*, which both made $5,000,000 in rentals.

This book is intended as a companion to your own movie viewing, whether it's on your VCR, in a multiplex cinema, or at a 3,000-seat theater with 70-millimeter and Dolby stereo. So settle back, dim the lights, and let's go to a movie!

SUSAN SACKETT
Studio City, California
November, 1989

1939

Nineteen thirty-nine! Mention that year to any movie-goer who hasn't been living in an ice cave on Pluto and he or she is sure to blurt out "Oh, yes! *Gone With the Wind*" or even "*The Wizard of Oz.*" But to film lovers around the world, 1939 was *the* year for movies . . . many people claim that we've been on a downhill slide ever since.

There were 400 movies made in 1939, and the average American went to church every Sunday and to the movies three times a week. There were 15,115 movie theaters, but only 14,952 banks. That year (some use the term "watershed") saw the release of over a dozen films which now, 50 years later, we nostalgically refer to as "classics." Audiences were treated to the likes of *The Hunchback of Notre Dame*, with Charles Laughton and Maureen O'Hara; *Raffles*, starring David Niven and Olivia de Havilland; *Destry Rides Again*, with Marlene Dietrich and James Stewart; *Mr. Smith Goes to Washington*, another Jimmy Stewart winner; *Ninotchka*, starring Greta Garbo and Melvyn Douglas; *The Private Lives of Elizabeth and Essex*, with Bette Davis, Errol Flynn, and Olivia de Havilland; *Goodbye, Mr. Chips*, with Robert Donat and Greer Garson; *Only Angels Have Wings*, with Cary Grant, Jean Arthur, and Rita Hayworth; *Stanley and Livingstone*, with Spencer Tracy and Sir Cedric Hardwicke; *Dark Victory*, one of Bette Davis' finest; John Ford's classic Western, *Stagecoach*; Judy Garland and Mickey Rooney in the box office hit *Babes in Arms*; and, of course, Judy's most memorable performance of all, as Dorothy in *The Wizard of Oz*.

It would have been a memorable bumper crop if these, plus a handful of other classics, had been the full legacy of 1939. But then, two weeks before the year drew to a close, one final film was released. And it more than fulfilled the prediction of one reviewer that this picture was "likely to perform some record-breaking feats of box office magic."

1

GONE WITH THE WIND

METRO-GOLDWYN-MAYER
$77,641,106

On December 15, 1939, *Gone With the Wind* premiered.

The long-awaited event was treated like a local holiday. In fact, the governor of Georgia declared one, and the mayor of Atlanta, where the film had its premiere, held a three-day festival. The theater, which seated only 2,500 people, sold tickets for this once-in-a-lifetime event for 10 dollars apiece, a hefty price, considering that tickets usually went for 25 cents.

With tickets costing only two bits, it's easy to see why the film's producer, David O. Selznick, was concerned about making back the $3,900,000 in production costs. That's a lot of quarters. Yet he needn't have worried. For nearly 35 years thereafter, *GWTW* held the number-one position, earning over *25 times* its initial outlay. This would be equivalent to a film costing $40,000,000 today—not an uncommon figure for a "special effects"-type film of the '80s—making over *one billion dollars* in rentals!

The critics, not surprisingly, were unanimous in their praise. *The Hollywood Reporter* reviewer said: "This is more than the greatest motion picture which ever was made. It is the ultimate realization of the dreams of what might be done in every phase of film wizardry, in production, performance, screen writing, photography, and every other of the multitude of technical operations which enter into the making of a picture." *Variety* called it "one of the truly great films, destined for record-breaking box-office business everywhere." And while *The New York Times* thought the film was "a handsome, scrupulous and unstinting version of the 1,037 page novel," the reviewer also pulled his punches by asking, "Is it the greatest motion picture ever made? Probably not . . ." Today, of course, many film historians beg to differ.

Gone With the Wind is often noted as one of the most mystery-shrouded films of the century. All kinds of myths and legends were born when Margaret Mitchell's book first appeared in 1936. After millions had read the book and she had sold the rights to Selznick for $50,000 (eventually he gave her another $50,000, the first amount seem-

ing so inadequate to him), more rumors began. To this day, many of these still persist. For example, it is a commonly held belief that she envisioned Clark Gable in the part of Rhett Butler when she wrote the novel.

Actually, Margaret Mitchell Marsh began the novel in 1926, while bedridden from an ankle injury. Having read every book in the Atlanta public library, she decided to follow through with her husband's suggestion that she write one of her own. She began the task that would take her 10 years to complete—but wrote the last chapter first! And in 1926, Clark Gable was an obscure actor touring in stock companies. It is very

Screenplay by Sidney Howard

Based on the novel by Margaret Mitchell

Produced by David O. Selznick

Directed by Victor Fleming

CAST

Scarlett O'Hara	Vivien Leigh
Rhett Butler	Clark Gable
Ashley Wilkes	Leslie Howard
Melanie Hamilton	Olivia de Havilland
Mammy	Hattie McDaniel
Prissy	Butterfly McQueen

ACADEMY AWARD NOMINATIONS

13 nominations, 8 wins

*Best Picture
 Best Actor (Clark Gable)
*Best Actress (Vivien Leigh)
*Best Supporting Actress (Hattie McDaniel)
 Best Supporting Actress (Olivia de Havilland)
*Best Director (Victor Fleming)
*Best Screenplay (Sidney Howard)
*Best Color Cinematography
*Best Interior Decoration
 Best Sound Recording
 Best Original Score
*Best Film Editing
 Best Special Effects

William Cameron Menzies was awarded a special plaque for outstanding achievement in the use of color for the enhancement of dramatic mood.

doubtful she had ever heard of him.

Another rumor that crops up frequently is that she never even wrote the book; this is a kind of "Shakespeare syndrome" that frequently surrounds unknown writers who produce bestsellers. Friends who visited her never saw her working on a manuscript. This is because she was secretive about her work, writing the book on pieces of paper which she would stuff into envelopes. Whenever friends dropped by, she would hide these under the sofa cushions. Later, she moved the stacks of envelopes into closets, never seriously intending to publish the novel. When she finally did turn the manuscript over to a publisher, it consisted of a mass of paper squeezed into a suitcase, untitled and lacking a complete first chapter. And Margaret, now having second thoughts, cabled the publisher, "Please send manuscript back. I've changed my mind." Fortunately, he ignored her request.

Mitchell overcame her shyness at least long enough to attend *Gone With the Wind*'s premiere in Atlanta. In fact, one of the classic comments about the film has been attributed to her. *Hollywood Anecdotes* reports that after watching the high crane shot of the Atlanta station where Scarlett attends the wounded and dying Confederate troops, Mitchell turned to Clark Gable and whispered, "Mah Gawd, if we'd o' had as many soldiers as that, we'd o' won the woah!"

From the day the cameras began rolling on the film production, the rumor mills also began to turn. In an oft-recounted story, the search for the perfect Scarlett O'Hara had been conducted all over the country, and Selznick had interviewed 1,400 actresses. The most extensive screen tests in the history of motion pictures were made for this role. Sixty actresses tested, with 165,000 feet of film shot, costing $105,000 (enough to shoot a minor movie in those days). A nationwide poll of movie fans showed their first choice to be Bette Davis (43 percent), second was Katharine Hepburn (14 percent), Norma Shearer was third (12 percent), Miriam Hopkins fourth (6 percent), and miscellaneous other actresses received the remainder of the public's votes.

Ignoring the public, Selznick had selected the three screen tests he liked best—those of Joan Bennett, Jean Arthur, and Paulette Goddard. Yet Scarlett O'Hara had still not been cast when the first scene—the burning of Atlanta—was filmed. As the old teardown sets on the backlot (including the native fortress/gate from 1933's *King Kong*) were consumed by flames, Selznick is said to have been introduced to a charming young lady who was a visitor on the set. This little-known English actress named Vivien Leigh so bedazzled him with her face aglow in the firelight that he immediately agreed with his brother Myron, who introduced him to Vivien with those now-immortal words, "I want you to meet Scarlett O'Hara!" The possibility that this story was concocted by the publicity department was never denied by David O. Selznick, who when interviewed later would only comment, "You may be right."

And for what turned out to be the most memorable role in movie history, Vivien Leigh received the paltry sum of $15,000 for her performance.

There was never any doubt in Selznick's or the public's mind, however, about who would play the role of Rhett Butler. Once the book was published, Clark Gable was the only actor ever seriously considered. Yet Gable himself almost turned down the role. According to *Academy Award Winners*, the actor's initial reaction was, "I don't want the part for money, chalk or marbles"— but a $2,500 weekly paycheck, plus $100,000 bonus, probably went a long way towards changing his mind. Later Gable disclosed the real reasons for his hesitation: "I was scared when I discovered that I had been cast by the public. I felt that every reader would have a different idea as to how Rhett should be played on the screen, and I didn't see how I could please everybody."

Keeping track of the film's writers and directors soon became as much a public pastime as guessing who would be Scarlett. At least 10 writers worked on the screenplay. Although Sidney Howard was credited and received the Oscar for Best Screenplay, other drafts were written by F. Scott Fitzgerald, Jo Swerling, Ben Hecht, John Balderston, John Van Druten, and Michael Foster. Selznick himself did the final rewrites. Three directors also had a hand in the production. George Cukor was on the set the first day, January 26, 1939. Three weeks later he was fired, according to some, at the behest of Clark Gable. His replacement was Victor Fleming, who received full screen credit, although having just completed *The Wizard of Oz*, Fleming eventually succumbed to sheer exhaustion, leaving the final week's shooting to Sam Wood (*Goodbye, Mr. Chips*).

One line that presented a bit of a problem to all the scriptwriters is that immortal one delivered by Rhett Butler at the story's end, "Frankly, my dear, I don't give a damn." Audiences familiar with Mitchell's book were placing bets as to whether the line would be allowed. Although today there is probably nothing that can't and hasn't been said on screen, audiences' easily outraged ears were protected in those days by a Hollywood censorship bureau known as the Hays Office. In 1922, former Postmaster General Will Hays was appointed president of the Motion Picture Producers and Distributors of America. This self-regulatory board immediately compiled a list of 11 "don'ts" and 25 "be carefuls." This later became known as the Motion Picture Production Code, and was with us through the '60s.

Although the word "damn" was a big no-no, it had gotten by the censors at least three times in the past. In 1932, Emma Dunn exclaimed, "Well, I'll be damned" in *Blessed Event*, and Fred Stone had cursed on screen by saying "Damn you" in *Alice Adams*, a 1935 film. "Damn" was uttered by both Leslie Howard and Marie Lohr in *Pygmalion* (1938).

Somehow, these precedents didn't seem to count, and the Hays Office stubbornly refused to let the word remain in the script. In an impassioned letter, Selznick pleaded with Hays:

> "The word as used in the picture is not an oath or a curse . . . The omission of this line spoils the punch at the very end of the picture and on our very fade-out gives an impression of unfaithfulness after three hours and forty-five minutes of extreme fidelity to Miss Mitchell's work . . ."

Hays finally relented, but fined Selznick $5,000 for having violated the Production Code.*

On November 7, 1976, *Gone With the Wind* had another debut, this time on the small screen. Again, records were set. Aired in two parts, the first part scored a Nielsen rating of 47.6 (47.6 percent of all sets were tuned to the

---

*However, the word "miscarriage" was strictly *verboten*, and the book's sentence "Cheer up, maybe you'll have a miscarriage" was revised in the film to "Cheer up, maybe you'll have an accident."

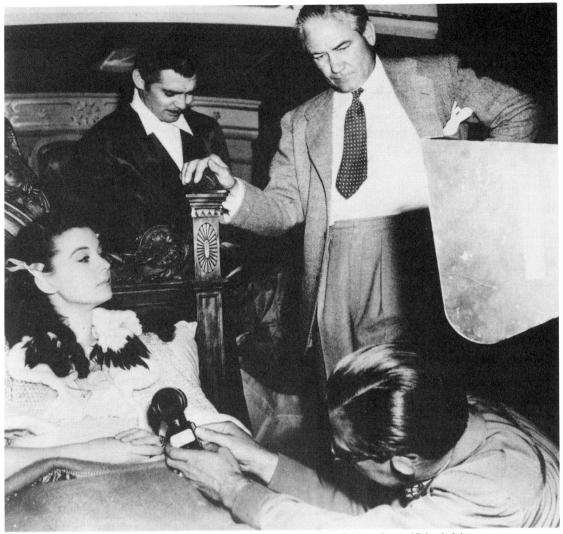

Clark Gable and director Victor Fleming (right) watch as a technician takes a light reading on Vivien Leigh.

film) and a 65 share (65 percent of all sets turned on were tuned to *GWTW*). The second day's showing had equally impressive numbers. In 1978, CBS paid $35 million to MGM for the rights to televise *GWTW* 20 times over the next 20 years, the highest fee ever paid for TV rights to a movie.

Since then, *Gone With the Wind* has become available for viewing in our living rooms at any time on videocassette. Yet in 1989, a restored print of the film began breaking box office records all over again when it was released to the theaters.

Ted Turner, the controversial Atlanta businessman who had bought the MGM film library in 1985, spent two years and $250,000 restoring the print for its 50th anniversary re-release. The premiere screening at the 5,874-seat Radio City Music Hall in New York was a sellout, with seats going for $12.50 apiece (cheap, by the Atlanta 1939 premiere prices). On hand then, as she had been 50 years before, was Butterfly McQueen ("Prissy"), one of the film's few surviving cast members.

Nearly all of the cast of *Gone With the Wind* are themselves gone.

Clark Gable ("Rhett Butler") died of a heart attack in 1960.

Vivien Leigh ("Scarlett O'Hara"), plagued by tuberculosis and physical exhaustion through much of her career, died in 1967.

Leslie Howard ("Ashley Wilkes") was killed in a plane crash in 1943 on a secret mission for the British government.

Hattie McDaniel ("Mammy"), the first black Oscar winner, died in 1952.

Margaret Mitchell was hit by a car and died in 1949.

David O. Selznick died in 1965.

Sidney Howard won an Oscar posthumously for Best Screenplay. He died in August, 1939, when he was crushed to death by a tractor at his Massachusetts home.

THE WIZARD OF OZ
METRO-GOLDWYN-MAYER
$4,544,851

HAD *GONE WITH THE WIND* never been made, 1939 would still have been a wonderful year to be a moviegoer. Even as *Gone With the Wind* was being completed, MGM released what has since become one of the best-loved films of all time.

Initially, *The Wizard of Oz* was a flop. Costing $2,777,000, it took over 20 years to earn back its money. Part of the problem was that its early audience consisted almost entirely of children, and children's tickets were generally half-price or less. It wasn't until NBC and later CBS bought the film for television that MGM began to show a substantial profit.

It opened in New York on August 17 to huge lines and critical acclaim. *The Hollywood Reporter* noted that people began lining up at 5:30 A.M. and that by 8:00 there were 15,000 people standing four abreast. *The Hollywood Reporter* called the film an artistic hit.

In 1900, L. Frank Baum published his book, *The Wizard of Oz*, and in 1925, Chadwick Pictures produced a silent version of it, marked by Oliver Hardy's portrayal of the Tin Woodman. In 1938, MGM purchased the rights to the children's story from Samuel Goldwyn for $75,000.

From the beginning, MGM's production was plagued with problems, not the least of which was the casting of the lead character, Dorothy. Studio chief Louis B. Mayer wanted that box office-drawing moppet, Shirley Temple, who, at nine years old, was just the right age. But she was under contract to 20th Century-Fox, and Darryl F. Zanuck refused to loan her out. MGM took stock of its own contract players and came up with a second choice—16-year-old Judy Garland (who ended up having her breasts taped flat each morning by the wardrobe department in order to appear as childlike as possible).

Other problems beset the cast. Buddy Ebsen was set as the Tin Man. Scenes with him in the role were shot for two weeks, and then he collapsed, hospitalized from an allergic reaction to the aluminum dust they had used to powder his face and give the Tin Man his silvery appearance. He was re-

Screenplay by Noel Langley, Florence Ryerson, and Edgar Allan Woolf

Adaptation by Noel Langley

From a book by L. Frank Baum

Songs written by E. Y. Harburg and Harold Arlen

Produced by Mervyn LeRoy

Directed by Victor Fleming

CAST

Dorothy	Judy Garland
Prof. Marvel (The Wizard)	Frank Morgan
Hunk (The Scarecrow)	Ray Bolger
Zeke (The Cowardly Lion)	Bert Lahr
Hickory (The Tin Woodman)	Jack Haley
Glinda (The Good Witch)	Billie Burke
Miss Gulch (The Wicked Witch)	Margaret Hamilton

ACADEMY AWARD NOMINATIONS

6 nominations, 2 wins*

Best Picture
Best Color Cinematography
Best Interior Decoration
*Best Song ("Over the Rainbow," music by Harold Arlen, words by E.Y. Harburg)
*Best Original Score
Best Special Effects

Judy Garland received a special award for her outstanding performance as a screen juvenile during the past year (miniature statuette).

placed by Jack Haley in what became his most famous role.

Margaret Hamilton, who appears as the Wicked Witch of the West (total time on the screen: 12 minutes), ended up bedridden for six weeks after receiving severe burns on her hand during the broomstick-burning sequence.

There were production problems as well. After five weeks of filming at a cost of $80,000, a lavish musical number called "The Jitter Bug" was

dropped after the first preview. (Recently, this "lost" footage has been restored on the laser-disk and home video versions.) Louis Mayer wanted to remove the song "Over the Rainbow," but fortunately, this was one decision by the studio boss that didn't stand.

Like *Gone With the Wind*, *The Wizard of Oz* also had its share of writers and directors. In all, 10 writers took turns working on the script. The number of writers seems odd by today's standards, but back then, studios hired writers by the ream and sat them down in a room where they wrote more or less on an assembly-line basis. Directors were frequently replaced as well, and *Wizard* had four. Richard Thorpe started it off, working for two weeks, and then was replaced by George Cukor, who lasted three days. Victor Fleming came in and worked four months, long enough to wind up with his name on the screen. When he was hired away by David O. Selznick to direct *Gone With the Wind*, the studio brought in King Vidor, who directed the final ten days—sort of like a chief surgeon asking a less skilled doctor to "close" following an operation.

On November 3, 1956, a milestone in the saga of *The Wizard of Oz* was reached. For the first time, the movie was shown on television. With this first appearance on CBS, a whole new generation discovered the magic of Oz. By 1989, with the thirty-first airing, it had been calculated that the movie had been seen in more than 473,000,000 households since its first telecast.

In 1989, MGM/UA Home Video released a 50th Anniversary videocassette of *The Wizard of Oz*. The newly-restored print features the Kansas scenes in warm sepia tones (as originally shown in 1939), not the more familiar black and white. But best of all, people can now see on their home TV monitors what has never been shown in movie theaters before. A series of special clips give audiences a look at the long-lost "Jitter Bug" number, a Ray Bolger/"Scarecrow" dance sequence, and some of the Buddy Ebsen footage.

There really is "no place like home."

THE HUNCHBACK OF NOTRE DAME

RKO
$1,500,000

"**W**HY WAS I not made of stone like thee?"

With these plaintive words, one of the most memorable films of any decade draws to a close. Based on the classic novel by Victor Hugo, *Hunchback* had been made as a silent film in 1923 with the "Man of a Thousand Faces," Lon Chaney. Many thought this performance would never be equaled. But Charles Laughton managed to make the hunchbacked Quasimodo not only monstrous, but pitiably human. What could be more moving or dramatic than when he lifts Esmerelda (Maureen O'Hara, in her American screen debut), gleefully bellowing "Sanctuary! Sanctuary!"?

Playing the role of the deformed bellringer was no easy task. Although Laughton's make-up had been lightened from the 34 pounds that Chaney wore to a mere six, it was still a chore for Perc Westmore's assistant, make-up artist Gordon Bau, who spent five-and-a-half hours each day applying a sponge-rubber right cheek and false eye socket which covered Laughton's own right eye. The RKO special effects department even found a way to make this false eye open and blink on cue. So realistic was the effect that *Variety* warned moviegoers in its review of *The Hunchback of Notre Dame*, "Charles Laughton's grotesque makeup . . . is not exactly palatable for patrons sensitively inclined."

This film enjoys immense popularity even today, to the extent that it is a mainstay of many independent television stations—in one week it was listed three times on three different stations. With the advent of the controversial process of colorization, many people who would not normally watch a black-and-white film (for reasons unfathomable) will be pleased to note that this movie is not hurt one bit by the colorization process. In fact, the colorization actually enhances the exterior shots, especially the marketplace with its bright blue sky (although, like most colorized pictures, the clothing all too often seems to run to tans and greens).

Screenplay by Sonya Levien

Adaptation by Bruno Frank

From a novel by Victor Hugo

Produced by Pandro S. Berman

Directed by William Dieterle

CAST

The Hunchback . . . . Charles Laughton
Frollo . . . . Sir Cedric Hardwicke
Clopin . . . . Thomas Mitchell
Esmeralda . . . . Maureen O'Hara
Gringoire . . . . Edmond O'Brien

ACADEMY AWARD NOMINATIONS

2 nominations, no wins

Best Sound Recording
Best Score

④

JESSE JAMES

20TH CENTURY-FOX
$1,500,000

"After the tragic War Between the States, America turned to the winning of the West. The symbol of this era was the building of the transcontinental railroads. The advance of the railroads was, in some cases, predatory and unscrupulous . . . It was this uncertain and lawless age that gave the world, for good or ill, its most famous outlaws, the brothers Frank and Jesse James."

—PROLOGUE

IN THE LATE '30s, the "A" Western made a comeback, and each studio rushed their own box office hopeful into production. None was more successful than Fox's *Jesse James*, which boasted a top cast with Tyrone Power and Henry Fonda, as well as the prestigious director Henry King. Portraying the outlaw as a Robin Hood of the Old West,

Power was the first in a long line of future Jesses, among them Lawrence Tierney, MacDonald Carey, Audie Murphy, Robert Wagner, and Dale Robertson. But the plum role here was that of brother Frank, aptly played by Fonda. So well-received was his characterization that a year later a sequel was made, *The Return of Frank James*, with Fonda reprising his part.

The making of *Jesse James* was fraught with mishaps. Henry Fonda suffered powder burns on his leg when his horse reared and his gun accidentally fired its blanks. Tyrone Power stepped on broken glass while surfing on the Elk River and sliced open his foot. Lon Chaney, Jr. sprained his ankle in a fall. The next day, the cinch on his saddle snapped and he took a spill that left him unconscious. But much worse was the death of a horse in the scene in

which a stuntman covering for Power rides his horse over a cliff.

Horses don't take kindly to jumping off cliffs, so a slide was constructed and covered with vegetation. At the last minute, a crew member drew aside a blanket and the horse went over. But the horse slipped, injured itself on landing in the lake, and drowned. A second take with a second horse was more successful: the stuntman separated from the horse, but reseated himself underwater, and both emerged from the lake unscathed.

The public outcry was so enormous that Hollywood arranged for the American Humane Association to become the official watchdog for animals used by the industry. Fifty years later, there is still an AHA rep on the set when animal actors are in use. Perhaps *Jesse James* did some good after all.

Screenplay by Nunnally Johnson

Based on historical data assembled by Rosalind Shaffer and Jo Frances James

Produced by Darryl F. Zanuck

Directed by Henry King

CAST

Jesse James	....	Tyrone Power
Frank James	....	Henry Fonda
Zerelda (Zee)	....	Nancy Kelly
Will Wright	....	Randolph Scott

MR. SMITH GOES TO WASHINGTON
COLUMBIA
$1,500,000

NINETEEN THIRTY-NINE was a busy year for James Stewart—he made five films in all. But unquestionably, the best of them was *Mr. Smith Goes to Washington*. Stewart was 31 years old when he was signed to star as the wide-eyed, idealistic young senator from Wisconsin who single-handedly takes on a corrupt Congress.

The film opened to a storm of controversy. After a disastrous premiere in Washington, D.C. to a room packed with Supreme Court justices, cabinet members, senators, and other political dignitaries, the picture was lambasted by the local press. Director Frank Capra was labeled a traitor, along with Columbia Pictures president Harry Cohn. Cohn received an urgent cablegram from the United States ambassador to England, Joseph P. Kennedy, saying that *Mr. Smith* ridiculed democracy, could be construed by our European allies as pro-Axis, and thus should be withdrawn from European distribution. Members of the U.S. Senate had even harsher words, crying "It stinks!" and "I've never seen a member

Screenplay by Sidney Buchman

Based on a story by Lewis R. Foster

Produced and directed by Frank Capra

CAST

Saunders	Jean Arthur
Jefferson Smith	James Stewart
Senator Joseph Paine	Claude Rains
Jim Taylor	Edward Arnold
Governor Hopper	Guy Kibbee

ACADEMY AWARD NOMINATIONS

11 nominations, 1 win*

Best Picture
Best Actor (James Stewart)
Best Supporting Actor (Harry Carey)
Best Supporting Actor (Claude Rains)
Best Director (Frank Capra)
*Best Original Story (Lewis R. Foster)
Best Screenplay
Best Interior Decoration
Best Sound Recording
Best Score
Best Film Editing

as dumb as that boy!" The ultimate epithet was hurled by one member of Congress, who labeled the film "just something from Hollywood."

But the majority of the media loved the film. *The Hollywood Reporter* headlined: "'MR. SMITH' GOES TO TOWN; DUE FOR BOXOFFICE SUCCESS," and went on to say that "Frank Capra has another smash hit . . . James Stewart is the perfect choice for the role . . . under Frank Capra's guidance, Stewart turns in the finest performance of his career . . ." *The New York Times*' reviewer was equally generous with his praise: "[Capra] has paced it beautifully and held it in perfect balance . . . James Stewart is a joy for this season, if not forever. He has too many good scenes, but we like to remember the way his voice cracked when he got up to read his bill . . ." No Method acting here—Jimmy Stewart hired a doctor who sprayed his throat periodically with bichloride of mercury in order to

hoarsen his voice in that famous scene.

The film was so successful that it spawned a number of imitators, including a short-lived television series starring Fess Parker (September, 1962 to March, 1963), and a Tom Laughlin movie vehicle, *Billy Jack Goes to Washington* (1977).

But perhaps the highest tribute that could be paid to a film was one given by a former actor . . . who also happens to be a former President. Ronald Reagan, when asked to reflect on the film that most affected his life, cited *Mr. Smith Goes to Washington*. He said: "When Jimmy Stewart walked the halls of the Capitol building, I walked with him. When he stood in awe of that great man at the Lincoln Memorial, I bowed my head too. When he stood in the Senate chamber and refused to knuckle under to the vested interests, I began to realize, through the power of motion pictures, one man can make a difference."

1940–1949

The film industry had peaked in 1939. Not that it was all downhill from there, but there would never be another year with so many memorable films. With half of Europe overrun by Hitler, the motion picture industry, dependent on foreign revenue for much of its income, began to feel the pinch well before the rest of the United States. In January, 1940, there were 17,000 movie houses in the U.S., 36,000 in Europe, and 7,000 in the Far East. As World War II cut deeply into the revenue, studio output declined drastically, in some cases by one-third.

It would be nearly two years before the Yanks entered the war, but Hollywood went to war even sooner, and continued producing films of that genre throughout the decade and well into the '50s. We would not recover quickly.

With so many of our men and boys overseas, it's not too surprising that the top box office draws were mostly male. A survey by *Variety* showed that the top stars of the early '40s were Clark Gable, Mickey Rooney, Spencer Tracy, Errol Flynn, Bette Davis, and Gary Cooper. Bing Crosby, Cary Grant, and an emerging box office star named John Wayne would dominate the second half of the decade.

PINOCCHIO
WALT DISNEY PRODUCTIONS
$32,957,000

WALT DISNEY premiered *Snow White and the Seven Dwarfs* in 1937 and established his reputation as one of the true geniuses of the century. This first feature-length animation created a new genre and paved the way for the many Disney classics that would follow.

The first of these was *Pinocchio*. Production began in 1937, with an unprecedented budget of $2,600,000. Taking inflation into account, it would require $50,000,000 to produce today.

The story of Pinocchio was written by Carlo Lorenzini (*nom de plume*: C. Collodi) and first published in Rome in 1881. Translations appeared in over 200 languages and dialects. Staff members called Walt's attention to the story, originally written in installments for a weekly magazine. He liked it and felt that the characters were perfect for the medium of animation because of their fanciful qualities.

Particularly memorable among these characters is Jiminy Cricket, Pinocchio's mentor. His rendition of "When You Wish Upon a Star" has become an anthem for all things Disneyana. Years later, the Academy Award-winning song struck a chord in the heart of director Steven Spielberg, who used it to inspire awe in *Close Encounters of the Third Kind*.

An interesting commentary on Collodi's times can be found in the characterization of the whale, Monstro, whose very name evokes his station in life. To environmentally conscious audiences of the '80s and '90s, it seems unbelievable that these gentle giants of the sea could have been given such bad press. Not since Moby Dick had a whale been viewed with this much fear and malevolence.

The original C. Collodi story of "Pinocchio" had been written in installments, and rambled through a wide range of adventures. One of the first tasks of the Disney writers was to narrow the tale down to a cohesive plot while still maintaining the spirit of the original narrative.

In true Disney fashion, more than 750 artists, 80 musicians, 1,500 shades of color, and 1,000,000 drawings were involved in bringing *Pinocchio* to life on the screen. The animation staff on the

Disney lot was quickly expanded from 300 to nearly 2,000 animators and artists. New ways of handling paints and pastels were explored and developed; complex airbrush and drybrush techniques were created, as the need arose, by the highly imaginative Disney artists.

Use of the multiplane camera, still in its infancy, enhanced the realism, but gave creator Walt Disney financial nightmares. For example, the "truck" shot in which the camera pans the sleeping village and ducks between buildings and down the street to focus on Jiminy Cricket, used dozens of planes for the 3-D effect and ran up a bill of $25,000 for just 30 seconds of footage.

Pinocchio himself was drastically changed from the book's concept of the puppet who wants to be a real little boy. In Collodi's story, the puppet listens to the cricket who wants to be his conscience, squashes him with his foot, and goes out into the world as a juvenile delinquent. Very un-Disney.

Pinocchio's voice was supplied by child actor Dick Jones, who at the time had already appeared in almost 40 Westerns. Billed as "Little Dickie Jones," he had been discovered at age five by Hoot Gibson. After appearing in a string of "B" Westerns, Jones moved on to such major productions as *Mr.*

Smith Goes to Washington, Destry Rides Again,* and *Virginia City*. A radio-show veteran, he found doing the voice for Pinocchio similar to performing on radio. According to a Disney press release, "We had a script and would read right into the microphone. They had an 8-millimeter camera that they used to photograph my lips as I spoke, so the animators could make Pinocchio's lip movements as realistic as possible." In order to encourage himself to "get into the part," Jones recorded his dialogue dressed in a Pinocchio costume complete with blue short pants, suspenders, a white shirt with a fluffy collar on it, and a cap with a feather. Forty-seven years later, Charles Fleischer used the same technique on another Disney film when he donned a rabbit suit to record his dialogue as the title character in *Who Framed Roger Rabbit*.

Pinocchio premiered on February 7, 1940, marred by a publicity stunt that backfired. The gimmick itself was bizarre: Disney studios hired 11 midgets dressed in Pinocchio costumes and placed them atop the theater marquee, where they were instructed to frolic about. Around lunchtime, some kind soul sent up some refreshments, including a couple of quarts of liquor. By mid-afternoon, the merry Pinocchios were frolicking stark naked, belching loudly and shooting craps on the marquee. Police were summoned and carted off the jolly lads in pillowcases.

Despite this incident, reviews were excellent. *The Hollywood Reporter* called it a "screen triumph; Walt Disney's Masterpiece . . . when one enters the land of enchantment under the guidance of Walt Disney, the magic wand is in the hands of the supreme master. . . . so completely charming and delightful that there is profound regret when it reaches the final fadeout." *The New York Times* called *Pinocchio* "the best cartoon ever made," and *Variety* termed it "perfection in animation and photographic effects."

But it is the audiences in the long run who are the critics. And audiences all over the world have fallen in love with the little wooden puppet, making it one of the most beloved films of all time.

From the story by C. Collodi

Produced by Walt Disney

Directed by Ben Sharpsteen and
   Hamilton Luske

VOICES

Pinocchio	Dick Jones
Geppetto	Christian Rub
Jiminy Cricket	Cliff Edwards
The Blue Fairy	Evelyn Venable

ACADEMY AWARD NOMINATIONS

2 nominations, 2 wins*

*Best Song ("When You Wish Upon a
   Star," music by Leigh Harline,
   words by Ned Washington)
*Best Original Score

②

FANTASIA
WALT DISNEY PRODUCTIONS
$28,660,000

It WAS a great year for Walt Disney. Following close on the heels of his Pinocchio success, the studio released *Fantasia*, which took three years and $2,280,000 to make. Walt collaborated with conductor Leopold Stokowski, and the film was originally planned as a short subject. Eventually, Walt and Stokowski agreed on a full-length concert feature, and a program was selected. Works illustrated were Bach's "Toccata and Fugue in D Minor," Tchaikovsky's "The Nutcracker Suite," Stravinsky's "The Rite of Spring," Beethoven's "Pastoral Symphony," Ponchielli's "Dance of the Hours," Moussorgsky's "Night on Bald Mountain," Schubert's "Ave Maria," and the most memorable number, Dukas' "The Sorcerer's Apprentice."

Walt Disney's lovable Mickey Mouse was chosen to represent the Sorcerer. The little guy had come a long way since he appeared in the first sound cartoon, *Steamboat Willie*, in 1928. In fact, Mickey almost didn't get off the ground back then. MGM's Louis B. Mayer refused to put the young Disney under contract after seeing a preview of his first Mickey cartoon, fearing that pregnant women would be frightened of a 10-foot-high rodent on the screen.

Other segments of *Fantasia* proved equally imaginative. The Bach Fugue is particularly vivid, opening with images fading into an undulating, abstract sea of rolling, pitching colors dotted with gem-like sparkles. The Fugue builds into swirling circles of vaporous clouds rising into pillars, climaxing with a red-fire sun outlining the silhouette of the conductor. The number became an unintentional hit with latent flower children who toked up and turned on to its re-release in the late '70s.

For the Igor Stravinsky "The Rite of Spring" segment, Disney consulted with paleontologists from Cal Tech and assembled a herd of pet iguanas and a baby alligator so animators could study their movements. Dinosaurs were a particular fascination for Disney; not only were they used in *Fantasia*, but they were the centerpiece of the Ford exhibit Disney designed for the 1964 World's Fair, as well as in a diorama at Disneyland and at the Exxon "Energy"

exhibit at Epcot Center in Florida. Despite the lavish treatment given his work, however, Stravinsky is said to have despised the battling dinosaurs and Stokowski's conducting with equal vehemence.

The Hays Office managed to earn its keep on this Disney animated feature when Disney animators drew bare-breasted female centaurs in Beethoven's "Pastoral Symphony" segment. The Office insisted that the "centaurettes" be completely redrawn with flowers hiding the offending area.

The film opened to mixed reviews, with most critics unsure of what to make of this innovation. It didn't do very well in its initial run, and it wasn't until re-release in the '70s with a new 70-millimeter print and Dolby stereo sound system that *Fantasia* became a box office hit.

Based on original soundtrack by Leopold Stokowski

Conducted by Irwin Kostal

Produced by Walt Disney

Directed by Samuel Armstrong, James Algar, Bill Roberts, Paul Satterfield, Hamilton Luske, Jim Handley, Ford Beebe, T. Hee, Norm Ferguson, and Wilfred Jackson

ACADEMY AWARD NOMINATIONS

In 1941, the Academy of Motion Picture Arts and Sciences awarded Leopold Stokowski and his associates a certificate for their unique achievement in the creation of a new form of visualized music.

That same year, Walt Disney, William Garity, John N. A. Hawkins, and the RCA Manufacturing Company received a certificate from the Academy for their outstanding contribution to the advancement of the use of sound in motion pictures through the production of *Fantasia*.

Walt Disney was also awarded the Irving G. Thalberg Memorial Award in 1941.

BOOM TOWN
METRO-GOLDWYN-MAYER
$4,586,415

ONE OF THE HOTTEST casts ever to appear in a '40s film—Clark Gable, Spencer Tracy, Claudette Colbert, and Hedy Lamarr—made *Boom Town* a powerhouse at the box office, which was exactly what MGM was banking on. These were the most popular stars at the beginning of the decade, and the studio would probably have had a hit no matter what the quartet had appeared in. *Time* noted, "Like most movies that are built on the theory that four stars are better than one, *Boom Town* is not so much a picture as a series of personal appearances." Had Disney's *Pinocchio* and *Fantasia* not enjoyed such prosperity from their many re-releases over the years, *Boom Town* would certainly be considered the number-one film for 1940.

The story is a simple one—environmentally disinterested "wildcat" oil drillers find love and big bucks in the West Texas oil fields, a premise that would again be used successfully in the 1956 hit film *Giant*. State-of-the-art special effects of oil-well gushers and spectacular fires caught the attention of the Motion Picture Academy, which nominated *Boom Town* for a Special Effects Oscar. (Watch for Mickey Rooney's father, vaudeville entertainer Joe Yule, in the minor role of "Ed Murphy.")

Female audience members were swooning by now over Clark Gable, lately of *Gone With the Wind*. Ironically, Gable himself was the son of an Ohio farmer-turned-oil-driller. In 1915, at the age of 14, he left school to work in a tire factory in nearby Akron. There he saw his first play and was hooked. Stock company bit parts followed. An MGM screen test found him turned down by that studio, as well as by Warner Bros. Producer Darryl F. Zanuck declared, "His ears are too big. He looks like an ape." He was eventually signed by MGM, and it was on a loanout to Columbia that the highly successful *It Happened One Night* (1934) was made. Gable and co-star Claudette Colbert both won Academy Awards for their roles. *Boom Town* marked their first screen reunion, much to the delight of movie audiences.

Screenplay by John Lee Mahin

Based on "A Lady Comes to Burkburnett" by James Edward Grant

Produced by Sam Zimbalist

Directed by Jack Conway

CAST

Big John McMasters	Clark Gable
Square John Sand	Spencer Tracy
Betsy Bartlett	Claudette Colbert
Karen Vanmeer	Hedy Lamarr
Luther Aldrich	Frank Morgan

ACADEMY AWARD NOMINATIONS

2 nominations, no wins

Best Cinematography
Best Special Effects

④

REBECCA
SELZNICK/UNITED ARTISTS
$1,500,000

"Last night I dreamt I went to Manderley again."
—OPENING LINE

EVEN AS David O. Selznick was shooting his masterpiece, *Gone With the Wind,* the obsessed producer was simultaneously working on another project that he was sure would top the story of Scarlett and Rhett (as if anything ever could!). He was convinced that he had all the ingredients, and had that first picture never been made, he would surely have been remembered for *Rebecca.* For it, too, is a masterpiece in its own right.

It was Alfred Hitchcock's first American film. In 1939, the successful British director, having gained a reputation for making chilling suspense films, left his native land at Selznick's behest to film Daphne du Maurier's atmospheric tale

---

Screenplay by Robert E. Sherwood and Joan Harrison

Adaptation by Philip MacDonald and Michael Hogan

From the novel by Daphne du Maurier

Produced by David O. Selznick

Directed by Alfred Hitchcock

CAST

Maxim de Winter	Laurence Olivier
Mrs. de Winter	Joan Fontaine
Jack Flavell	George Sanders
Mrs. Danvers	Judith Anderson
Giles	Nigel Bruce

ACADEMY AWARD NOMINATIONS

11 nominations, 2 wins*

*Best Picture
  Best Actor (Laurence Olivier)
  Best Actress (Joan Fontaine)
  Best Supporting Actress
    (Judith Anderson)
  Best Director (Alfred Hitchcock)
  Best Screenplay
*Best Cinematography, Black and White
  Best Interior Decoration, Black and White
  Best Original Score
  Best Film Editing
  Best Special Effects

---

of the "second Mrs. de Winter" (we never learn her name, Rebecca being the name of the deceased first Mrs. de Winter). In true Hitchcockian style, we are shown how the power of the dead can affect the living, a theme Hitch successfully explored in his later box office hits *Spellbound, Psycho,* and another marriage of Hitchcock with du Maurier storytelling, *The Birds.*

Casting Laurence Olivier and Joan Fontaine in the lead roles contributed to the box office success. Fontaine, in her first major role, was a big draw for fans curious to see the latest David O. Selznick "discovery," and the role established her as a major star (the following year, she won the Academy Award for Hitchcock's *Suspicion*).

Hitchcock cast Leo G. Carroll in the minor part of "Dr. Baker." Five years later, the director again used Carroll as a doctor with a much more important role in the thriller *Spellbound.* (Television audiences may recognize Leo G. Carroll as "Mr. Waverly" from the '60s series "The Man From U.N.C.L.E.")

Critics were lavish in their praise of the British director. *Variety* hailed the film as "an artistic success" while noting that its box office draw might be limited. *The New York Times* called *Rebecca* "an altogether brilliant film, haunting, suspenseful, handsome and handsomely played."

Alfred Hitchcock continued to be one of the most successful directors of all time, with a career spanning 53 years—from the 1923 British film *Always Tell Your Wife,* to the 1976 hit *Family Plot.* He died in 1980 at the age of 81.

SANTA FE TRAIL
WARNER BROS.
$1,500,000

"The United States Military Academy—West Point. When the gray cradle of the American Army was only a small garrison with few cadets, but under a brilliant commandant named Robert E. Lee, it was already building for the defense of a newly-won nation in a new world."
—PROLOGUE

THE STORY of West Point graduates assigned to Ft. Leavenworth, Kansas, actually has nothing to do with Santa Fe (although the railroad ends and the Santa Fe Trail begins in Leavenworth—a minor plot point). The title misleads, for this is actually about the abolitionist leader John Brown, played to the hilt by Raymond Massey as an insane religious zealot on a "mission from God."

Audiences didn't seem to mind that Hollywood had once again rewritten the history books. This time, they took all the important generals of the Civil War—Jeb Stuart (Errol Flynn), George Custer (Ronald Reagan), Phil Sheridan, James Longstreet, George Pickett, and John B. Hood—made them the West Point graduating Class of '54 (that's 1854), and set them on the trail of John Brown (whose body did not yet lie a-moulderin' in the grave, although the generals were working on that).

Santa Fe Trail was directed by one of the most renowned directors of the '40s, a Hungarian named Michael Curtiz (who later directed *Casablanca*). He was notorious for murdering the English language, as well as having a bad habit of mixing his casts' real names with those of their characters. Thus Raymond Massey became "Joe Brown" (a popular comedian of that time), Errol Flynn was dubbed "Earl Flint," and Reagan became "Ron Custard."

While most of the critics had a field day with the historical inaccuracies, audiences loved the film. *Variety* noted that "some historians may find fault with the way John Brown is pictured," while *The New York Times* called *Santa Fe Trail* "the biggest non-sequitur of the season, from the directional, historical and titular point of view."

Ron Custard went on to become President of the United States.

Director Michael Curtiz (second from left) sets up a shot as Olivia de Havilland (center) prepares to cue other actors.

Screenplay by Robert Buckner

Produced by Robert Fellows

Directed by Michael Curtiz

CAST

Jeb Stuart	. . . .	Errol Flynn
Kit Carson Halliday	. . .	Olivia de Havilland
John Brown	. . . .	Raymond Massey
George Custer	. . . . . .	Ronald Reagan
Tex Bell	. . . .	Alan Hale

1

SERGEANT YORK

WARNER BROS.
$6,135,707

"We are proud to present this picture and are grateful to the many heroic figures still living, who have generously consented to be portrayed in its story. To their faith and ours that a day will come when men will live in peace on earth, this picture is humbly dedicated."

—PROLOGUE

OUT OF THE Tennessee mountains came a simple, pacifistic man whose religious upbringing taught him that killing was wrong. But the Army thought differently, and the young conscientious objector Alvin C. York, already a crack shot with rifle and pistol, was denied the exemption he desperately wanted. As a corporal in the Infantry, he took part in the Argonne-Meuse offensive in France, and on October 8, 1918, he single-handedly crushed a German machine-gun nest, killing 25 soldiers and taking 132 prisoners. Having proved himself an effective killing machine, this World War I "Rambo" was made a sergeant and awarded the Croix de Guerre, France's highest honor, as well as the Congressional Medal of Honor.

In 1941, at a time when America's thoughts were turning more and more to the possibility of involvement in another deadly world war, Warner Bros. chose to make *Sergeant York,* a film about this number-one hero of the First World War. It was not really what you would call a recruitment film, but did a great deal more than any "Uncle Sam wants you" movie to sound the reveille and send home its patriotic message. *Variety* called the film "as timely as a White House fireside chat, a moving and effective presentation in thrilling entertainment terms of what is meant by 'the American way of life.' . . . Gary Cooper appears in the title role for which he seems singularly suited and well chosen."

It was not an accident that Gary Cooper was given this part. In 1940, Jesse Lasky bought the rights to York's life story, and the war hero agreed to let Lasky film it after being convinced that it would inspire a new generation of soldiers. But York insisted that he oversee the production, that his wife be played by a demure young lady and not a Hollywood sex goddess (Joan Leslie got the part), and that Gary Cooper play York. Cooper later won the Academy Award for Best Actor in this role (and a second Oscar for Best Actor in 1952 in *High Noon*). The actor also received the "Distinguished Citizenship Medal" from the Veterans of Foreign Wars, a ceremony with the real Alvin York in attendance.

Director Howard Hawks had no problems with the casting of Coop as Sgt. York. In fact, he considered it a stroke of luck. "You'd watch him do a scene," Hawks later said, according to *All-Time Box-Office Hits*, "and you'd go home worrying about whether you had it. And then you'd look next day at the rushes—and there was more there than you wanted in the first place."

Again, as with many films of the '30s and '40s, a team of writers worked to turn this into a memorable screenplay. The script was based on the diary of Sergeant York himself as edited by Tom Skeyhill. The teams of Abem Finkel and Harry Chandlee, Howard Koch and John Huston were credited with the writing chores.

Especially noteworthy here is the musical score. Listen carefully and you'll hear, very subtly, the strains of "Give Me That Old Time Religion" used to underscore the scene whenever Walter Brennan appears on the screen as the pastor, or when York is torn between his religious teachings and his duty to his country.

Another familiar member of the cast is a very young June Lockhart, who plays York's sister Rosie. Television fans will remember her as Timmy's mom on "Lassie," as well as the mother on "Lost in Space."

York married in 1919 and settled on a farm donated to him by the state of Tennessee. He established the York Foundation and a Bible school, and donated his share of royalties from the movie to that school. For years, the IRS claimed they were owed several thousand dollars in income tax on the money that he earned from the film, but in 1961 a public subscription cleared his debt. York died on Sept. 2, 1964, at the age of 76.

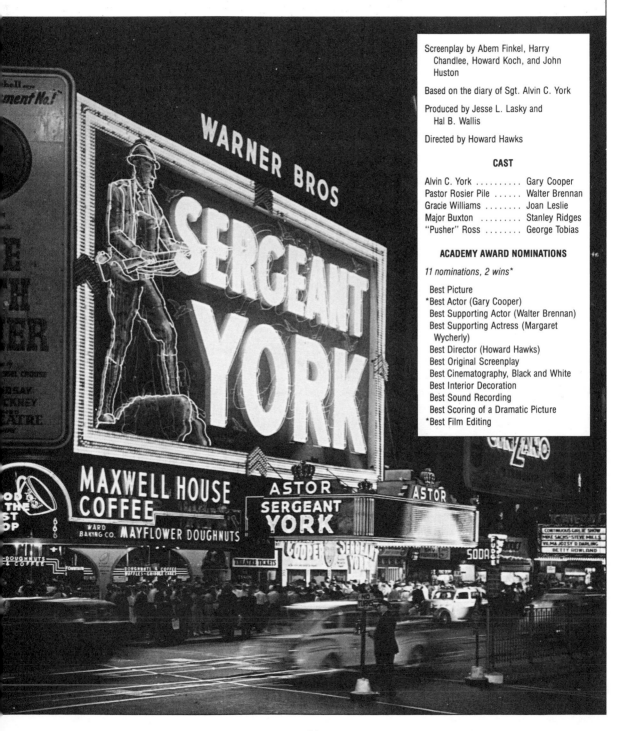

Screenplay by Abem Finkel, Harry
Chandlee, Howard Koch, and John
Huston

Based on the diary of Sgt. Alvin C. York

Produced by Jesse L. Lasky and
Hal B. Wallis

Directed by Howard Hawks

CAST

Alvin C. York . . . . Gary Cooper
Pastor Rosier Pile . . . . . . Walter Brennan
Gracie Williams . . . . Joan Leslie
Major Buxton . . . . Stanley Ridges
"Pusher" Ross . . . . George Tobias

ACADEMY AWARD NOMINATIONS

11 nominations, 2 wins*

Best Picture
*Best Actor (Gary Cooper)
Best Supporting Actor (Walter Brennan)
Best Supporting Actress (Margaret
    Wycherly)
Best Director (Howard Hawks)
Best Original Screenplay
Best Cinematography, Black and White
Best Interior Decoration
Best Sound Recording
Best Scoring of a Dramatic Picture
*Best Film Editing

(2)

DIVE BOMBER
METRO-GOLDWYN-MAYER
$1,500,000*

JUST FOUR MONTHS before the Japanese attack at Pearl Harbor, in August, 1941, *Dive Bomber* was released. It was another "recruitment" film, depicting the brave men who took off from carrier decks to fly bombing missions. The picture was made with the cooperation of the United States Navy and a bunch of technical advisors, duly thanked in the credits. But the real heroes of the film are naval flight surgeons, to whom the picture is dedicated "in recognition of their heroic efforts to solve the immensely difficult problems of aviation medicine."

While this film could be called the *Top Gun* of its day, it is certainly dated. Today's audience may enjoy watching this as a curiosity piece—the "modern" equipment has an ancient, historical appearance. The directing is very static and the "wipe" technique between

scenes is overdone. It is startling, too, to see how frequently all the doctors take cigarette breaks, lighting up whenever the tension mounts. One surgeon even offers a cigarette to a dying patient so his last moment on Earth will be a pleasant one!

The film starred Errol Flynn, an Australian national who became a naturalized American citizen in 1942. He was every man's vision of the dashing young Naval officer/surgeon. Ironically, Flynn made no effort whatsoever to take part in the war, unlike many Hollywood stars of the day.

Co-starring as an old-line pilot is Fred MacMurray, a dashing leading actor of the '40s. Born in Kankakee, Illinois in 1908, MacMurray began his career as a saxophonist, and by the '30s he had signed with Paramount, playing the lead in a variety of films. He

found his forté in comedy, and today's audiences probably best remember MacMurray as a staple of the '60s Walt Disney comedies, as well as the star of the TV series "My Three Sons."

An unintentional laugh comes for today's audience when a character named "Lucky" remarks that he's just been transferred to San Diego from Pearl Harbor. With that attack still four months away, he was aptly named.

---

*Positions 2, 3, 4, and 5 are "guestimates" based on figures reported for high-ranking films early in the '40s. Since records weren't kept for films which were not re-released (and therefore brought in rentals of less than $4,000,000, *Variety*'s cut-off), these figures are derived from compilations of reports in the trade papers as well as raw estimates from the studios themselves. The films 2 through 5 all earned roughly the same amount, and appear in alphabetical order.

Screenplay by Frank Wead and
  Robert Buckner

From a story by Frank Wead

Produced by Hal B. Wallis

Directed by Michael Curtiz

CAST

Doug Lee	....	Errol Flynn
Joe Blake	....	Fred MacMurray
Dr. Lance Rogers	....	Ralph Bellamy
Linda Fisher	....	Alexis Smith
Art Lyons	....	Robert Armstrong

ACADEMY AWARD NOMINATIONS

1 nomination, no wins

Best Cinematography, Color

HONKY TONK
METRO-GOLDWYN-MAYER
$1,500,000*

ELIZABETH COTTON (LANA TURNER) after a kiss: *"I want you to stay away from me."*

"CANDY" JOHNSON (CLARK GABLE): *"No you don't. Why don't you jump in and get wet all over."*

It WAS SCENES like this, between two of the biggest stars of the '40s, that MGM was counting on to make *Honky Tonk* a box office bonanza, and they weren't disappointed. Fans weren't disappointed, either. If the plot seemed familiar—the story of a gambling-hall hustler (Gable) and his sparring partner and eventual wife—that was because it was derivative of many an Old West yarn.

When *Honky Tonk* opened, however, most reviewers ignored the thin plot about an Old West con artist "fleecing the sheep" and moved on to the chemistry between Miss Turner and Mr. Gable. Said *The New York Times:* "Miss Turner is not only beautifully but ruggedly constructed . . . Mr. Gable snarls, wrinkles his eyes and occasion-

ally becomes condescendingly tender, but usually he keeps his chin well out in front. One could hear rapturous sighs all over the Capitol mezzanine yesterday. . . . Miss Turner gives a competent, if limited performance and Mr. Gable again shows off his muscles." *Newsweek* also thought the virtues of the two leads were the film's strong points, terming *Honky Tonk* "a horse opera without the horses," and adding that MGM's main purpose in making the film seemed to be the "glamor

merger" of Gable with Turner and "the promise of exciting and unpredictable variations on the tender passion."

Honky Tonk's producer, Pandro S. Berman, was one of the most ubiquitous filmmakers of all times. His work spanned four decades, with his name appearing on dozens of important movies, including *The Gay Divorcee, Top Hat, The Hunchback of Notre Dame, National Velvet, The Three Musketeers, Father of the Bride, Ivanhoe, The Blackboard Jungle, Tea and Sympathy, The Brothers Karamazov, Butterfield 8,* and many others.

This movie was really a lark for Berman. The casting of Frank Morgan as Judge Cotton, father of Lana Turner's character, was not unusual since he was a Metro contract player. And when it came time to select his wardrobe, he was attired in almost the exact same outfit he wore in *The Wizard of Oz.* Add to that Gable's character looking like Rhett Butler, and we get something akin to *Gone With the Wind* meets *The Wizard of Oz.*

Screenplay by Marguerite Roberts and John Sanford

Produced by Pandro S. Berman

Directed by Jack Conway

CAST

"Candy" Johnson	Clark Gable
Elizabeth Cotton	Lana Turner
Judge Cotton	Frank Morgan
"Gold Dust" Nelson	Claire Trevor
Mrs. Varner	Marjorie Main

*Rough estimate. See footnote on p. 32.

THE PHILADELPHIA STORY

METRO-GOLDWYN-MAYER
$1,500,000*

FOUR-TIME Academy Award winner Katharine Hepburn is one of the true legends of Hollywood. She arrived in California from her native Hartford, Connecticut in 1932 and immediately began shocking the community by wearing slacks (then referred to as "men's pants"), driving a station wagon—classified at the time as a "truck" for lack of a better descriptive term—and sitting on curbstones, since studios didn't provide benches for stars whose feet hurt. She was unique and headstrong, a lot like her character "Tracy Lord" in *The Philadelphia Story*.

The story centers on a Philadelphia "Main Liner" (wealthy woman) played by Katharine Hepburn. On the eve of her wedding to hubby number two, she must fend off the advances of her ex, C. K. Dexter Haven (the ever-dashing Cary Grant). At the same time, she develops an infatuation with an amorous reporter, played by Jimmy Stewart.

Screenplay by Donald Ogden Stewart

From the play by Philip Barry

Produced by Joseph L. Mankiewicz

Directed by George Cukor

CAST

C. K. Dexter Haven .. Cary Grant
Tracy Lord .... Katharine Hepburn
Macaulay Connor .... James Stewart
Elizabeth Imbrie ..... Ruth Hussey
George Kittredge .... John Howard

ACADEMY AWARD NOMINATIONS

*6 nominations, 2 wins**

Best Picture
*Best Actor (James Stewart)
Best Actress (Katharine Hepburn)
Best Supporting Actress (Ruth Hussey)
Best Director (George Cukor)
*Best Screenplay (Donald Ogden Stewart)

Film had a pre-release of limited showing in December, 1940, which qualified it for the 1940 Academy Awards. Officially, however, the movie wasn't released until January 10, 1941, as per a Theatre Guild agreement, so as not to conflict with the road-show performances.

This *ménage à quatre* delighted audiences anxious to see which suitor would win the blue-blooded hand of Miss Hepburn.

A highly successful Broadway play, *The Philadelphia Story* was still playing in road companies when the film was released. Having optioned the film rights when signing for the stage play, Miss Hepburn had secured the part for herself, along with rights of approval on director and co-star.

Hepburn had performed the part hundreds of times, a distinct advantage when it came to putting the play on film. Still, director George Cukor found working with her difficult. "I have no pedestal for Miss Hepburn," he wrote in *The Hollywood Reporter* shortly after the film's completion. "She can be wrong. She can be difficult. We have had our arguments. But Miss Hepburn can most sincerely be judged by the almost tearful affection with which the crew regarded her at the completion of *The Philadelphia Story*."

The film was even more successful than the play, and it didn't hurt that her two co-stars were Cary Grant and Jimmy Stewart. For his performance as the love-struck reporter, Stewart received an Oscar. At his father's request, the young actor shipped the award back to his hardware store in Pennsylvania, where it was displayed in the front window for 20 years.

Years later, Stewart, who has often been called one of the greatest American actors of all time, commented on his seemingly effortless acting technique in an interview on the television magazine show "Entertainment Tonight": "You try to go through and do this part and not have the acting show."

Jimmy Stewart's performance certainly captured the attention of the critics. *The Hollywood Reporter* remarked: "How that boy does troupe. Nobody in pictures . . . that we have ever seen could have given Macaulay Connor what that role required, and his performance meant so much to that of Miss Hepburn."

In 1956 *High Society*, a Cole Porter musical version, was produced. It starred Grace Kelly, Frank Sinatra, and Bing Crosby, and while popular, it didn't match the success of the original.

---

*Rough estimate. See footnote on p. 32.

A YANK IN THE R.A.F.

20TH CENTURY-FOX
$1,500,000*

THIS WAS another timely war film released just prior to the United States' involvement in World War II—only three months before Pearl Harbor. The film stars Tyrone Power as an American flyer eager to get into the thick of it, and like *Sergeant York*, released that same year, the film did much to heighten war fever.

The story centers on Power's character, a cocky young American flier who ferries a bomber to England, then runs into an old flame (Grable) who's a dancer in a London nightclub. He joins up with the R.A.F. to be near her, but soon finds himself involved in bombing missions over the Continent.

A great deal of attention went into the movie's authenticity. For the Battle of Dunkirk sequence, the English Channel was re-created on 27 acres of backlot. Much actual battle footage was included. Britain's Royal Air Force gave its complete cooperation and made possible the filming of the aerial scenes in the production. There is one par-

ticularly well-done dog-fight sequence in which the plane-filled air seems to be abuzz with a giant swarm of gnats. Twentieth Century-Fox had originally

---

Screenplay by Darrell Ware and
   Karl Tunberg

From a story by Melville Crossman

Produced by Darryl F. Zanuck

Directed by Henry King

CAST

Tim Baker . . . . Tyrone Power
Carol Brown . . . . Betty Grable
Wing Commander
Morley . . . . John Sutton
Roger Pillby . . . . Reginald Gardiner
Corporal Harry Baker . Donald Stuart

ACADEMY AWARD NOMINATIONS

1 nomination, no wins

Best Special Effects

---

planned to shoot its own aerial footage, and two studio cameramen were sent aloft with a defending squadron. Tragically, their plane was shot down during a dog fight, and both cameramen were killed.

In an early version shown to preview audiences, the producers had Tyrone Power losing Betty Grable (whose beautiful legs are spotlighted as often as possible) to John Sutton. The original version also had Power's character killed in action. The British were frantic and asked Zanuck to revise the ending. They didn't care who got Grable, but they didn't want other potential American recruits to be discouraged from joining the R.A.F. A new ending was filmed, and Power lived and got the girl.

When the United States finally did enter the war, Lieutenant Tyrone Power, USMC, flew missions in the Pacific, transporting supplies to Saipan and Okinawa.

---

*Rough estimate. See footnote on p. 32.

1942

BAMBI
WALT DISNEY PRODUCTIONS
$47,265,000

WALT DISNEY had begun work on *Bambi* in 1937, right after *Snow White and the Seven Dwarfs*. But the project had several setbacks, including the high cost of making the film of Felix Salten's successful book.

From its inception, Walt wanted *Bambi* to be different from the cartoon style of its predecessors. "I respect nature very much, and by watching and observing the habits of creatures of nature, man can learn a lot," Walt stated in a press release. To ensure authenticity, Walt (he preferred to be addressed by his first name) hired top artists and instructors and brought them to the studio to lecture his animators on animal drawing and anatomy. An actual deer carcass was brought in so the animators could dissect it and study the ligaments and musculature. Two live fawns were sent to the studio courtesy of the Maine Development Commission. Appropriately dubbed "Bambi" and "Faline," they were kept in a pen outside the animation building. Later a menagerie of two skunks, birds, squirrels, chipmunks, and rabbits were added to the Disney on-lot zoo.

One of the studio's biggest concerns from the start was how to superimpose personalities on realistically-drawn animal characters and still maintain their believability. Whereas the animal characters in *Snow White* and *Pinocchio* had been cartoon-like, Bambi and his friends were anthropomorphic, animals with human traits, intended to be taken seriously by the audience.

The animators solved this problem by paring dialogue down to a compact 900-word script. Great care was taken in animating the mouths of the creatures so that they moved in a manner suggesting delivery of dialogue while mimicking true animal movement.

To further add to the realism, Disney animators studied up on child behavior and development, learning to adapt the expressions of human toddlers to the various animals. This also proved helpful in establishing the personalities of the young animals.

Additional research was required for the forest backgrounds that would be the setting for *Bambi*, and the studio sent artist Jake Day on a photographic safari to the Maine woods. Day spent five months sketching and photographing the Kadahdin wilderness in the Baxter Game Preserve. His volumes of meticulously detailed sketches and photos were used not only for *Bambi*, but later became the basis for Disney's award-winning series of True-Life Adventures, documentary movie shorts depicting various nature themes.

It is the animated characters themselves who take center stage: Bambi, the little fawn who grows to be a great forest prince; Thumper, his rabbit pal who manages to say all the wrong things; Flower, the shy skunk; and a score of quintessential big-Disney-eyed forest critters.

Although no voice credits were given to the youngsters who portrayed Bambi and his playmates, Walt Disney Studios later released the name of the child who read the part of Thumper. Peter Behn was only four years old when he came in to audition for the part. The son of a veteran Hollywood screenwriter, Peter was first brought in to vocalize the bunny family for the scene in which Bambi learns to walk. According to a Disney press release, when Peter said, "Did the young prince fall down?" someone whispered, "Get the kid out of here; he can't act." The production staff listened to the tapes later and discovered Peter had the perfect voice for Thumper. It took some scrambling to locate him after his dismissal the previous day.

Bambi is essentially a children's story, and even today eager parents will rush off to the latest re-release, or sit restless youngsters down in front of the TV set, plop a cassette in the VCR, and catch a few moments' peace. Yet there is something very adult about the underlying themes in the film. Early on, young Bambi is warned by his mother to take care when "Man [is] in the forest." Later the fawn is orphaned when hunters (Man) shoot and kill her. Was there ever a sadder murder on screen? Mercifully, Disney didn't dwell on this scene, and quickly followed it with a song and the promise of Spring. Still later, in some of the most exciting animation ever created, a fire roars through the forest. The cause: Man. The point couldn't have been better made if the film had been produced by the Sierra Club.

Most audiences, including the critics, saw it as just plain exciting entertainment, which it definitely is. *The Hollywood Reporter* said: "The feature is by far the most realistic achievement of the Disney merchants of magic. It likewise boasts the most beautiful effects these master artists have as yet created . . . it is more like a fine painting artfully lit and hung, actually a work of love by craftsmen who have remained young in heart. It will make millions happy and bring millions to the box office."

Actually, the film didn't do well in its initial release, and it took many years for it to turn a profit. Bob Thomas' *Walt Disney* quotes Disney as saying: "I think back to 1942 when we released that picture and there was a war on, and nobody cared much about the love life of a deer, and the bankers were on my back. It's pretty gratifying to know that *Bambi* finally made it."

In 1942, Walt Disney halted his feature filmmaking. He chose to use the studio for working on government films to help with the war effort. *Bambi* would be his last commercial effort for the duration of the war.

From the novel by Felix Salten

Story adaptation by Larry Morey

Produced by Walt Disney

Directed by David D. Hand

VOICE

Thumper . . . . Peter Behn*

ACADEMY AWARD NOMINATIONS

3 nominations, no wins

Best Sound Recording
Best Song ("Love Is a Song That Never Ends," music and words by Frank Churchill and Edward Plumb)
Best Scoring of a Dramatic or Comedy Picture

---

*While no voice credits are given in the film, "it is known," according to *The Disney Films*, "that Peter Behn did the voice of Thumper."

② MRS. MINIVER
METRO-GOLDWYN-MAYER
$5,390,009

"This story of an average English middle-class family begins with the summer of 1939: when the sun shone down on a happy, careless people, who worked and played, reared their children and tended their gardens in that happy, easy-going England that was so soon to be fighting desperately for her way of life and for life itself."
—OPENING CRAWL

OF ALL THE FILMS made about and during World War II, *Mrs. Miniver* had the most impact. Winston Churchill wrote to Louis B. Mayer, saying its propaganda was worth a hundred battleships. The American public ate it up;

Screenplay by Arthur Wimperis, George Froeschel, James Hilton, and Claudine West

From the novel by Jan Struther

Produced by Sidney Franklin

Directed by William Wyler

CAST

Mrs. Miniver . . . . Greer Garson
Clem Miniver . . . . Walter Pidgeon
Carol Beldon . . . . Teresa Wright
Lady Beldon . . . . Dame May Whitty
Foley . . . . Reginald Owen

ACADEMY AWARD NOMINATIONS

12 nominations, 6 wins*

*Best Picture
  Best Actor (Walter Pidgeon)
*Best Actress (Greer Garson)
  Best Supporting Actor (Henry Travers)
*Best Supporting Actress (Teresa Wright)
  Best Supporting Actress (Dame May Whitty)
*Best Director (William Wyler)
*Best Screenplay (Arthur Wimperis, George Froeschel, James Hilton, and Claudine West)
*Best Cinematography, Black and White
  Best Sound Recording
  Best Film Editing
  Best Special Effects

Greer Garson gave the longest acceptance speech ever made at an Oscar ceremony—it lasted over an hour.

the film did much to increase the empathy of Americans for their English allies besieged by Hitler's "blitz." And in its portrayal of the brave English woman and her family adjusting to the day-to-day problems of coping with the war, *Mrs. Miniver* served as an inspiration to Americans fearful that their lives might one day be similarly disrupted.

The film had an impact on the Germans, too. Hitler's henchman Goebbels cited the film as "an exemplary propaganda film for the German industry to copy." Churchill ordered leaflets of the film's inspirational closing speech dropped behind enemy lines. The message, delivered by Henry Wilcoxon as the Vicar, is nearly as rousing as Lincoln's Gettysburg Address:

"This is not only a war of soldiers in uniform. It is a war of the people, of *all* the people, and it must be fought not only on the battlefield, but in the cities and in the villages; in the factories and on the farms; in the homes and in the heart of every man, woman and child who loves freedom . . . this is the people's war . . . fight it with all that is in us, and may God defend the right."

Thus stirred, the people sing "Onward Christian Soldiers" in the bombed-out cathedral, followed by a chorus of "Pomp and Circumstance"—familiar to many Americans as a graduation song.

In case you missed the message, the end slide announces: "America needs your money. Buy defense bonds and stamps every pay day."

Mrs. Miniver turned out to be the most financially successful film of 1942, and it was only because of re-releases of *Bambi* that it did not achieve number-one status in the long run. In 1950, a sequel, *The Miniver Story*, was produced. It bombed (no pun intended), unable to capture the mood, or the need, of the original.

YANKEE DOODLE DANDY

WARNER BROS.
$4,719,681

"Ladies and gentlemen, my mother thanks you, my father thanks you, my sister thanks you, and I thank you."
—GEORGE M. COHAN

IN A YEAR laden with war movies, *Yankee Doodle Dandy*, the musical biography of George M. Cohan, gave film audiences a chance to catch their breath. Yet even this movie had an inspirational "let's go get 'em" message with rousing patriotic renditions of "You're A Grand Old Flag" and "Over There" (". . . and we won't come back till it's over, over there!"). *Time* noted that the song "is enough to send movie audiences straight off to battle."

Maybe so, but mainly it sent them straight to the box office. And reason number one was the new singing and dancing sensation James Cagney. His performance as Cohan made him the first actor to receive an Academy Award for a musical performance.

It seems almost inevitable that George M. Cohan would become the subject of an autobiographical film. The celebrated actor, singer, dancer, songwriter, playwright, and screenwriter was one of the most gifted talents of the early 20th century. He was born on the 3rd (not the 4th) of July in 1878 to an Irish family originally named Keohane. By the time of his death in 1942, he had written over 500 songs, created 41 musicals and plays, and produced 130 others.

It was Cohan himself that insisted Cagney play him. Audiences remembered Jimmy Cagney as the tough who smashes Mae Clarke in the face with a grapefruit in *The Public Enemy* (Warner Bros., 1931). But Cohan was familiar with Cagney as an ex-Broadway hoofer, and Cagney spent four months in rehearsals, perfecting the "hitch" and other mannerisms which would become the mainstay of future impressionists. And it didn't come easy—he sprained his ankle twice while perfecting a Cohan-esque stiff-legged dancing style.

Like George M. Cohan, whose family formed the act "The Four Cohans," Cagney managed to bring his own family members into the act. His brother, William, associate-produced many of his films, including this one, and his sister Jeanne acted and likewise appeared in *Yankee Doodle Dandy*.

On April 10, 1968, the highly successful play *George M!*, the musical account of the life of Cohan, premiered on Broadway, and ran for many years. Joel Grey and Bernadette Peters starred in this tribute to Cohan, replete with all his famous tunes.

On July 4, 1985, *Yankee Doodle Dandy* had the dubious honor of being the first computer-colorized film released when entrepreneur Ted Turner, who owns 3,500 films of the MGM library,* premiered the movie on his Turner Broadcasting System. It opened a floodgate that eventually saw the issue of colorization being debated before a congressional committee, with many directors and stars opposed to the practice on the grounds that it diminishes the visual quality of films which were intended to be seen only in black and white. The controversy continues today, with the only resolution in the hands of the television viewer, who has the option of turning off all color on his TV set and viewing the film in its original monochrome hues.

---

*MGM bought the rights to many early Warner Bros. and RKO films, which Turner acquired with his purchase of the MGM library.

Screenplay by Robert Buckner and Edmund Joseph

From original story by Robert Buckner

Produced by Hal B. Wallis

Directed by Michael Curtiz

CAST

George M. Cohan	James Cagney
Mary Cohan	Joan Leslie
Jerry Cohan	Walter Huston
Sam Harris	Richard Whorf
Fay Templeton	Irene Manning

ACADEMY AWARD NOMINATIONS

8 nominations, 3 wins*

Best Picture
*Best Actor (James Cagney)
Best Supporting Actor (Walter Huston)
Best Director (Michael Curtiz)
Best Original Story
*Best Sound Recording
*Best Scoring of a Musical Picture
Best Film Editing

1942

RANDOM HARVEST
METRO-GOLDWYN-MAYER
$4,665,501

IT WAS THE YEAR of Greer. Following her success as Mrs. Miniver, Greer Garson starred in the melodramatic hit, *Random Harvest*, which had critics rushing to their thesauruses, making lists of superlatives. Gushed *The Hollywood Reporter:* "One of the truly fine motion pictures of this or any year . . . an emotional experience of rare quality. Rave press notices cannot fail to greet the excellence of its production, direction, performances and craftsmanship, for there can be no fault to find with any phase of the great, enduring love story it stirringly brings to life." Not only the critics, but audiences, too, were enthralled by this romantic story of a man who marries while suffering from amnesia, only to get his memory back, return to his former life, and become amnesic about his wife. This soap-operatic premise was actually the basis of a major novel by James Hilton (author of *Lost Horizon*, among other classics), and film audiences, eager for

Screenplay by Claudine West, George Froeschel, and Arthur Wimperis

Based on the novel by James Hilton

Produced by Sidney Franklin

Directed by Mervyn LeRoy

CAST

Charles Rainier	Ronald Colman
Paula	Greer Garson
Dr. Jonathan Benet	Philip Dorn
Kitty	Susan Peters
Dr. Sims	Henry Travers

ACADEMY AWARD NOMINATIONS

7 nominations, no wins

Best Picture
Best Actor (Ronald Colman)
Best Supporting Actress (Susan Peters)
Best Director (Mervyn LeRoy)
Best Writing, Screenplay
Best Interior Decoration, Black and White
Best Scoring of a Dramatic or
    Comedy Picture

Sidney Franklin, who produced the two Garson movies of 1942 (*Mrs. Miniver* and *Random Harvest*), received the Academy's Irving G. Thalberg Memorial Award.

a reprieve from war films, made *The Hollywood Reporter's* box office prediction a reality.

Kudos went to Greer Garson, with much of the attention centering on her legs, which made their first (and tasteful) appearance in this film. *Time* went so far as to say, "*Random Harvest* . . . is distinguished by (1) a moving love story, (2) the unveiling of Miss Garson's interesting legs." And *The New York Times* noted that "[Miss Garson] is modestly permitted to show off her dimpled knees." With all this attention showered upon Garson's gams, it's a wonder these critics were even aware of Ronald Colman's fine co-starring performance. His role as the World

War I shell-shocked amnesia victim was certainly one of his most memorable, and once the reviewers recovered from the sight of his leggy co-star, they had equal praise for Colman. The Academy confirmed this by honoring him with a nomination for Best Actor.

One of the most dashing heroes of the '30s and '40s, Ronald Colman first began his career in silent films. With his mellow, British-accented voice, he moved easily to "talkies," starring in a number of memorable films such as *Arrowsmith* (1931), *A Tale of Two Cities* (1935)—in which he utters those unforgettable lines, " 'Tis a far, far better thing I do than I have ever done . . ." —and *Lost Horizon* (1937).

CASABLANCA
WARNER BROS.
$4,145,178

"Play it, Sam. Play 'As Time Goes By.' " —INGRID BERGMAN

"You've played it for her, you can play it for me. Play it!" —HUMPHREY BOGART

EVERYBODY COMES TO RICK'S. That was the unproduced play that became the immensely successful movie *Casablanca.* The title change by producer Hal Wallis was fortuitous: just as the film was being released in November of 1942, the Allies serendipitously landed in Axis-occupied Casablanca, and the North African city's name was suddenly ubiquitous.

Other changes occurred which no doubt helped *Casablanca* become one of the favorite films of all time. As in *Gone With the Wind*, this picture owes a lot to the chemistry between the two leads, Humphrey Bogart and Ingrid Bergman. But these two great stars were not always everyone's first choice. Some of the names kicked around by Wallis and director Mike Curtiz were Ann Sheridan, Hedy Lamarr, and Michele Morgan for "Ilsa," and George Raft and Ronald Reagan for "Rick."

The Germans considered this a propaganda film, and it wasn't until after World War II that it was allowed to play in Germany. Even then, the censors took a scissor to it and deleted 20 minutes of footage. All references to Nazis were axed, including all of Conrad Veidt's scenes as a Nazi high commander.

In 1987, for a private showing at the Rio Film Festival, Joao Luiz Albuquerque re-edited a print and changed the ending to show Ingrid Bergman not getting on the plane, but coming back into the arms of Bogey. ("We'll always have Paris . . . and Casablanca"?)

Many remakes have been attempted, but none have ever been successful. Back in 1943, a sequel was planned and a writer put under contract, but it was nixed almost immediately. A 1955 television series made a brief appearance on ABC, with Charles McGraw recreating the role of Rick, but it didn't last more than seven months.

In 1983, the British Film Institute polled its members on the 30 best movies of all time. Out of a total of 2,000 films nominated, *Casablanca* was overwhelmingly the number-one choice.

Today *Casablanca* has the honor of being the most often-repeated movie on U.S. television, according to a recent survey conducted by *TV Guide*.

And you'd think that with a film this popular, people would know that no one in the movie ever says, "Play it *again*, Sam."

Screenplay by Julius J. Epstein, Philip G. Epstein, and Howard Koch

From a play by Murray Burnett and Jean Alison

Produced by Hal B. Wallis

Directed by Michael Curtiz

CAST

Rick . . . . Humphrey Bogart
Ilsa Lund . . . . Ingrid Bergman
Victor Laszlo . . . . Paul Henreid
Capt. Louis Renault . Claude Rains
Major Straseer . . . . . Conrad Veidt
Señor Ferrari . . . . . . Sydney Greenstreet
Ugarte . . . . Peter Lorre

ACADEMY AWARD NOMINATIONS

8 nominations, 3 wins*

*Best Picture
  Best Actor (Humphrey Bogart)
  Best Supporting Actor (Claude Rains)
*Best Director (Michael Curtiz)
*Best Screenplay (Julius J. Epstein, Philip G. Epstein, and Howard Koch)
  Best Cinematography, Black and White
  Best Scoring of a Dramatic or Comedy Picture
  Best Film Editing

Hal B. Wallis was honored with the Irving G. Thalberg Memorial Award.

Award nominations were for the year 1943, although the film was released in a limited run in November, 1942.

◥◤ 1 ◥◤
THIS IS THE ARMY
WARNER BROS.
$8,301,000

THOUSANDS OF Americans had already seen *This is the Army* as a touring road show conceived to make money for the Army Relief Fund. In fact, the combined efforts of film and play netted that fund $10,000,000.

Basically an all-soldier revue, the stage show's 350 soldiers appear in the film along with an all-star Warner Bros. cast. The movie is comprised of a string of production numbers featuring singing and dancing soldiers. Many of the numbers are memorable, including songstress Kate Smith greeting the audience with, "Hello, everybody. It is my privilege to introduce a new song— 'God Bless America.' "

It's a beautiful number, guaranteed to send a tear down the cheek of nearly any American seeing it today. In fact, it has often been suggested that should "The Star Spangled Banner" ever be replaced as a national anthem, Irving Berlin's tune would be a suitable substitute.

But the best number in the whole movie comes when the audience is treated to none other than composer Irving Berlin himself, decked out in his old World War I doughboy uniform, gently singing a version of his own song, "Oh, How I Hate to Get Up in the Morning." An amusing anecdote has it that as this bit was being filmed, someone on the set remarked, "If the fellow who wrote this song could hear this guy sing it, he'd roll over in his grave."

When Kate Smith sings her "God Bless America" number, there is a montage showing Americans in their homes, thinking about their sons at war, going about their daily lives. And in one home sits Ronald Reagan, reading *Variety*. Future president Reagan (billed in the credits as *Lieutenant* Ronald Reagan) had a fairly large part in this film as the son of a theatrical producer (played by George Murphy).

Mostly, though, *This is the Army* is a vaudeville show with the emphasis on song and dance, featuring a few dreadfully boring comedy routines. One spectacular number is a minstrel show featuring the tune "Mandy." With a giant banjo in the background, tap dancers in blackface are partnered with black women—who turn out to be guys

in drag. Seen today, the whole number is really a sad commentary on the racism that was so acceptable in those days. There were racial clichés aplenty, right down to a tap-dancing black unit of soldiers.

The Navy wasn't left out either. There is a big production number with a Navy battleship on stage. Not to be outdone, the Army Air Corps bit has a plane on stage with turning propellers.

Critics couldn't praise it enough. *Variety* wrote: "After the history of World War II is written, the Warner Bros. filmization will stand out like the Empire State Bldg. amidst the many other highlights in the motion picture industry's contributions to the home front and war front. It's that kind of all-embracing job. . . ." They summed up with the trademark showbiz term, "It's socko!" *The New York Times'* reviewer agreed, calling *This is the Army* "buoyant, captivating, as American as hot dogs or the Bill of Rights . . . it is, from beginning to end, a great show . . . A bouquet to Warner Brothers who have waived all profits in the venture."

Following the film's release, the touring company continued to perform for live audiences, heading overseas to Great Britain, and then to combat areas of Europe, the Near East, and the Pacific. Having been seen by 2,500,000 American soldiers, the show closed in Honolulu on October 22, 1945. For his contribution, Irving Berlin was decorated with the Medal of Merit by General George C. Marshall.

Born Israel Isidore Baline in Russia on May 11, 1888, Berlin and his Jewish parents fled the *pogroms* when he was five, settling in New York's Lower East Side. By the time he was a teenager, he was a singing waiter selling songs on the side. His first big hit was "Alexander's Ragtime Band" (1911), and in the course of his career, he composed over 1,000 tunes. His songs had such a familiarity about them that many thought they were old American folk songs. Among his best-known ones are "White Christmas," "Blue Skies," "Easter Parade," and "There's No Business Like Show Business." When he passed away in 1989 at the age of 101, he was mourned as a national hero.

Screenplay by Casey Robinson and
Capt. Claude Binyon

Based on the stage presentation by
Irving Berlin

Produced by Jack L. Warner and
Hal B. Wallis

Directed by Michael Curtiz

CAST

Jerry Jones . . . . George Murphy
Eileen Dibble . . . . . . Joan Leslie
Maxie Twardofsky . . George Tobias
Sergeant McGhee . . Alan Hale
Eddie Dibble . . . . Charles Butterworth

ACADEMY AWARD NOMINATIONS

3 nominations, 1 win*

Best Interior Decoration, Color
Best Sound Recording
*Best Scoring of a Musical Picture

FOR WHOM THE BELL TOLLS

PARAMOUNT
$7,100,000

"Any man's death diminishes me because I am involved in Mankind: and therefore never send to know for whom the bell tolls. It tolls for thee." —OPENING CARD (FROM A POEM BY JOHN DONNE)

PRODUCED at the height of the American involvement in World War II, the screen version of Ernest Hemingway's novel about an American fighting with Spanish Civil War soldiers is a faithful adaptation, retaining much of the original dialogue of the novel. Still, *For Whom the Bell Tolls* did not meet with unanimous critical acclaim when it was translated into a nearly three-hour-long film. While *The Hollywood Reporter* called the production "breath-taking" and *Variety* termed it "one of the important pictures of all time," *Newsweek* noted that "the film leaves a good deal to be desired," and the *New York Telegram* told its readers that the "dialogue runs on and on and drags the story to temporary halts . . . People simply talk too much."

Concerned about potential box office mishaps, Paramount began heavily playing up the now-famous sleeping bag

---

Screenplay by Dudley Nichols

From the novel by Ernest Hemingway

Produced and directed by Sam Wood

CAST

Robert Jordan	Gary Cooper
Maria	Ingrid Bergman
Pablo	Akim Tamiroff
Pilar	Katina Paxinou
Anselmo	Vladimir Sokolof

ACADEMY AWARD NOMINATIONS

9 nominations, 1 win*

Best Picture
Best Actor (Gary Cooper)
Best Actress (Ingrid Bergman)
Best Supporting Actor (Akim Tamiroff)
*Best Supporting Actress (Katina Paxinou)
Best Cinematography, Color
Best Interior Decoration, Color
Best Scoring of a Dramatic or Comedy Picture (Victor Young)
Best Film Editing

---

scene. At a time when the Hays Office insisted that even married couples have twin beds and that one foot must rest on the floor at all times, the idea of having Gary Cooper's and Ingrid Bergman's unmarried characters share a sleeping bag was downright scandalous. Compared to today's see-all bedroom scenes, this is pretty much G-rated, but in those days, what you *didn't* see was sometimes even better, and the audience filled in the rest with their libidinous imaginations.

Paramount had invested $2,000,000 in faithfully re-creating Hemingway's novel, so it is no wonder they were concerned. The studio strove for authenticity. When costume designer

Edith Head needed a tough, well-weathered outfit for Ingrid Bergman, she selected an old pair of men's trousers and a shirt from the extras' wardrobe. Producer/director Sam Wood was incensed and ordered Miss Head to custom-design a new costume. She did—copying the clothes exactly, then bleaching and redying them to look worn. When the California mountains in the background looked too lush and green to double for the rugged hills of Spain, the set designers sprayed gray paint over the landscape, even uprooting wildflowers to keep the scenery from being too pretty for the Technicolor camera.

THE OUTLAW

RKO
$5,075,000

NOT TOO MANY people remember this as a film about the life of William Bonney—a.k.a. Billy the Kid. It could hardly be termed "biographical," even though the story did have some elements of historical accuracy, such as lawman Pat Garrett's pursuit of the murderous Billy, and the young criminal's teaming up with "Doc" Holliday, an old-time gunman and former friend of Garrett. But with most of the historical facts rather clouded, this is far from a film biography. Alas, *The Outlaw* will always be remembered for Jane Russell's bustline.

When the film was released in 1943, it didn't have time to generate much business before it was pulled from release. A subsequent release in 1946 of the Howard Hughes film saw it being pulled after a week, thanks to its being banned by the censors of the Hays Office. It was finally allowed to be seen in 1947, by which time Hughes had launched a massive advertising campaign with the much-publicized photo of Jane Russell lolling in a haystack.

Actually, she never really does much lolling in the hay. The scene goes like this:

RIO

Let me go!

BILLY

Hold still lady or you won't have much dress left.

(ripping sounds)

RIO

Let me go!

All this takes place in shadow, but you get the idea.

Then there's the famous sequence where Rio (Russell) is nursing the wounded Billy back to health. When he suffers a chill, the resourceful Rio uses her body heat to warm him up ("You can bring a minister here in the morning if it'll make you feel better about it.").

Most of the attention was centered on the aforementioned chest of Jane Russell. Joseph Breen of the Hays Office wrote: "I have never seen anything quite so unacceptable as the shots of the breasts of the character of Rio . . . Throughout almost half the picture the girl's breasts, which are quite large and prominent, are shockingly uncovered."

Perhaps audiences agreed. They returned again and again to be shocked by Miss Russell's assets, making a pile of money for Hughes and Company.

Screenplay by Jules Furthman

Produced and directed by Howard Hughes

CAST

Rio	Jane Russell
Billy	Jack Buetel
Pat Garrett	Thomas Mitchell
Doc Holliday	Walter Huston

THE SONG OF BERNADETTE

20TH CENTURY-FOX
$5,000,000

"For those who believe in God, no explanation is necessary. For those who do not believe in God, no explanation is possible."

—OPENING CARD

Aₗₜₕₒᵤ𝒈ₕ ᴛʜᴇʀᴇ ᴡᴇʀᴇ undoubtedly many in the audience who did not agree with the film's opening card, most people were able to dismiss this presumptuous introductory statement and enjoy the film on a dramatic level.

The tale of the young peasant French girl, Bernadette Soubirous, who has a vision of "The Lady" and later becomes a nun, is by now a familiar one, since the spring water of Lourdes has become revered by Catholics and other believers as the site of miracle cures.

Based on the best-selling novel by Franz Werfel, the film introduced 23-year-old Jennifer Jones in the title role "by arrangement with David O. Selznick." (Selznick later came to a different sort of arrangement with the lovely Miss Jones—following their divorces, the two were married in 1949.) It proved to be a fortuitous choice when the ingenue grabbed an Oscar for her performance.

The reviews were mixed. *The Hollywood Reporter* called it a "great spir-

Screenplay by George Seaton

From the novel by Franz Werfel

Produced by William Perlberg

Directed by Henry King

CAST

Bernadette Soubirous . . Jennifer Jones
Dean Peyramale . . . . . . Charles Bickford
Antoine Nicolau . . . . . . William Eythe
Prosecutor Dutour . . . . . Vincent Price
Dr. Dozous . . . . Lee J. Cobb

ACADEMY AWARD NOMINATIONS

12 nominations, 4 wins*

Best Picture
*Best Actress (Jennifer Jones)
Best Supporting Actor (Charles Bickford)
Best Supporting Actress (Gladys Cooper)
Best Supporting Actress (Anne Revere)
Best Director (Henry King)
Best Screenplay
*Best Cinematography, Black and White
*Best Interior Decoration, Black and White
Best Sound Recording
*Best Scoring of a Dramatic or Comedy Picture
Best Film Editing

itual masterpiece . . . Jennifer Jones proves to be the perfect choice for Bernadette, and she gives a beautiful, moving performance of rare sincerity . . . It is doubly a remarkable work being her first important screen role." But *The New York Times* thought it was "tedious and repetitious; it lingers too fondly over images that lack visual mobility, and it goes in for dialectic discourse that will clutter and fatigue the average mind."

Jennifer Jones was an unknown at the time, and little publicity preceded her debut. The idea was to have her appear as pure as her character. She wore a minimum of make-up and simple peasant dress to further enhance her virginal appearance. In actuality, however, she had been married to Robert Walker since 1939, and the couple had a son, Robert Walker, Jr.

In another odd bit of casting, sexy actress Linda Darnell appears (unbilled) as the Virgin Mary. Hollywood being short on virgins, they had to make do with whomever was available.

Vincent Price does an admirable job as the adversarial Imperial Prosecutor bent on thwarting all claims of Bernadette's vision. Today, that actor is still playing the villain.

STAGE DOOR CANTEEN
UNITED ARTISTS
$4,339,532

DURING World War II, there was a real Stage Door Canteen in New York City (and a Hollywood Canteen on the West Coast). In time, each of these entertainment centers had a film based on it. The movies were basically an excuse to gather up famous Hollywood stars who each night dished up hot meals and entertainment to our boys before they shipped off to war. Appearing at various times throughout the film (don't blink, you'll miss them) were:

Judith Anderson	Gypsy Rose Lee
Kenny Baker	Alfred Lunt
Tallulah Bankhead	Harpo Marx
Ralph Bellamy	Elsa Maxwell
Edger Bergan & Co.	Yehudi Menuhin
Ray Bolger	Ethel Merman
Ina Clair	Paul Muni
Katharine Cornell	Merle Oberon
Gracie Fields	George Raft
Lynn Fontanne	Lanny Ross
Helen Hayes	Martha Scott
Katharine Hepburn	Ethel Waters
Hugh Herbert	Johnny
Jean Hersholt	Weissmuller
George Jessel	Ed Wynn

Screenplay by Delmer Daves

Produced by Sol Lesser

Directed by Frank Borzage

CAST

Eileen	Cheryl Walker
"Dakota" Ed Smith	William W. Terry
Jean	Marjorie Riordan
"California"	Lon McCallister
Ella Sue	Margaret Early

ACADEMY AWARD NOMINATIONS

2 nominations, no wins

Best Song ("We Mustn't Say Good Bye,"
  music by James Monaco,
  words by Al Dubin)
Best Scoring of a Musical Picture

and 38 "other celebrated artists from Stage, Screen and Radio." As if that weren't enough, there were bands, big bands . . . as in Count Basie, Xavier Cougat, Benny Goodman, Kay Kyser, Guy Lombardo, and Freddie Martin.

This movie was filmed at a time when the words "We're in a war and we've got to win" were able to rouse the emotions of the audience. They may sound simplistic, but those were simpler times, and simple words sufficed. The soldiers and their girls were facing the very real and frightening prospect that they might never return.

In addition to featuring a heavy dose of production numbers with song and dance, this musical revue had a wisp of a plot about romance between the non-movie-star canteen workers and the servicemen visiting the famous New York rendezvous. The use of unknowns as the GIs and their gals was intended to give audiences people to whom they could relate. Besides, nearly every available professional talent was already doing a solo performance in one of the movie's big numbers. Although this could have been the "big break" many actors dream of, not one future "star" emerged from the pack of unknowns.

The film is enjoying new popularity on cable television, and is frequently shown on Nickelodeon's "Nick at Night." It's well worth a look.

1

GOING MY WAY
PARAMOUNT
$6,500,000

HIS FULL NAME was Charles Francis Patrick O'Malley. He was the kindest, singingest priest to ever grace the screen. And sing he did. One of the decade's best songs (and a number-one hit at that) came from *Going My Way*, a catchy tune called "Swinging on a Star." It won a well-deserved Oscar. Not so memorable was the title song, also sung by the old crooner himself. Can anyone hum a few bars of "Going My Way"? Thought not. It's no wonder Father O'Malley has to struggle with music publishers to get it noticed (watch for William Frawley, Fred Mertz of TV's "I Love Lucy," in the role of his publisher).

Bing Crosby, Father O'Malley's alter ego, couldn't read a note of music. But that didn't stop him from becoming one of the most beloved singers of this century. He was born Harry Crosby on May 2, 1904, in Tacoma, Washington, and changed his name to Bing (after "The Bingville Bugle," a Sunday comic section in the his hometown newspaper). In 1929, he earned $100 for appearing in a film with Douglas Fairbanks, for which he received no billing. Known mostly as a radio star, he received his big break in 1932, appearing in *The Big Broadcast*.

But he came into his own as an actor with *Going My Way*. Although both

Spencer Tracy and James Cagney were approached to play the part, neither was available. It was then that director Leo McCarey decided to offer Bing his first dramatic role. He seemed to be born to the part. According to his brother Bob, interviewed for a 1989 PBS television special, "He played Bing Crosby, 'cause he went to Jesuit school all his life." It was a role that Bing embraced with his whole life, embodying the values he had grown up with, his deep religious conviction, his innate Irish charm—all combining to make his Academy Award performance an American classic.

During the war, metal was in short supply, and Oscar statuettes were

made of plaster (they were later replaced with the real thing). Bing reportedly decapitated his plaster award one day while practicing his golf swing in the living room.

Co-star Barry Fitzgerald also turned in an Oscar-winning performance. *Life* Magazine told readers to catch "a wonderful Irishman named Barry Fitzgerald. His performance is one of the half-dozen finer things seen in motion pictures. . . ." *The Hollywood Reporter* also sang his praises, declaring, "Barry Fitzgerald gives a truly brilliant performance every foot of the way . . . he is a joy. . . ." He received an unprecedented two nominations for the same picture—Best Actor and Best Supporting Actor (the Academy subsequently changed the rules to prevent this sort of double indemnity).

Barry Fitzgerald's portrayal of a gruff, stubbornly aging old priest was a perfect contrast for Crosby's easygoing characterization. Fitzgerald was born William Joseph Shields on May 10, 1888 in Dublin, Ireland. His early years

saw him as a stage performer in Dublin, where he changed his name to a more Irish-sounding one; this also avoided confusion with his brother Arthur Shields, himself an actor. He made his film debut in Hitchcock's British film, *Juno and the Paycock* (1930), and landed in Hollywood in the late '30s, where he honed his portrayals of whimsical Irishmen to the brink of near-caricatures. Among his most notable films were *Bringing Up Baby* (1938), *How Green Was My Valley* (1941), *None But the Lonely Heart* (1944), *Duffy's Tavern* (1945), *Welcome Stranger* (1947), and *The Quiet Man* (1952). He died in 1961 at the age of 73.

Fitzgerald's competition in the Best Actor category included his own co-star, Bing Crosby, as well as Charles Boyer, Cary Grant, and Alexander Knox. In the Supporting Actor contest, however, he took home the prized Oscar after overcoming a field of talented actors that included Hume Cronyn, Claude Rains, Clifton Webb, and Monty Woolley.

Risë Stevens is the only cast member whose appearance in this film seems a bit contrived: her true bailiwick was as a star of the Metropolitan Opera. That's exactly how she's introduced in the picture, and her voice is obligingly showcased with her renditions of "Ave Maria," an aria from "Carmen," and the title song.

Despite tough competition at the Academy Award ceremony for 1944—nominated films were *Double Indemnity, Gaslight, Since You Went Away,* and *Wilson*—*Going My Way* had no trouble finding the Best Picture Oscar going its way, along with many others, for a total of seven for this audience-pleasing film. Leo McCarey proved that like Fitzgerald, he had the luck of the Irish, and received an award for Best Director. A former silent-film director, he was never comfortable with the written word. Often while rehearsing a scene, he would tell his actors, "Forget the script and just talk it through." He usually preferred to have the cast ad-lib scenes during filming, giving scriptwriters nightmares.

On October 3, 1962, ABC premiered a television series of *Going My Way*. It starred Gene Kelly as Father Chuck O'Malley and Leo G. Carroll as a crusty old pastor named Father Fitzgibbon. Kelly neither sang nor danced, but the show survived on the airwaves for a year. The 1944 film will survive, with the luck of the Irish, forever.

Screenplay by Frank Butler and
  Frank Cavett

From a story by Leo McCarey

Produced and directed by Leo McCarey

CAST

Father Chuck O'Malley .. Bing Crosby
Jenny Linden .... Risë Stevens
Father Fitzgibbon ...... Barry Fitzgerald
Ted Haines Jr. .... James Brown
Carol James .... Jean Heather

ACADEMY AWARD NOMINATIONS

10 nominations, 7 wins*

*Best Picture
*Best Actor (Bing Crosby)
 Best Actor (Barry Fitzgerald)
*Best Supporting Actor (Barry Fitzgerald)
*Best Director (Leo McCarey)
*Best Writing, Original Story (Leo
  McCarey)
*Best Screenplay (Frank Butler and
  Frank Cavett)
 Best Cinematography, Black and White
*Best Song ("Swinging on a Star,"
  music by Jimmy Van Heusen,
  words by Johnny Burke)
 Best Film Editing

This was the last comedy to win the award for Best Picture until Billy Wilder's *The Apartment* in 1960.

1944

MEET ME IN ST. LOUIS

METRO-GOLDWYN-MAYER
$5,132,202

BASED ON a series of stories by Sally Benson that appeared in the *New Yorker*, and that were later published as a book, *Meet Me in St. Louis* has the feeling of a stage musical. The original book, a collection of reminiscences, had warmth, charm, period costumes, a loving family—and the 1903 Louisiana Purchase Exposition (World's Fair). Producer Arthur Freed (*The Wizard of Oz*) called the book to director Vincent Minnelli's attention, and Minnelli jumped at the chance to direct. Twenty-one-year-old Judy Garland was set to star. Her last picture, *Presenting Lily Mars*, hadn't clicked with the public, and she wanted to move into more adult roles. A year after completing the film, she divorced husband David Rose and married Minnelli, with whom she had fallen in love while working on the movie.

If the film has the look of a musical*, it is because Minnelli spent his early years as a designer and art director for stage. With its series of family incidents centering around the Smith home, *Meet Me In St. Louis* was the

Screenplay by Irving Brecher and
  Fred F. Finklehoffe

From the book by Sally Benson

Produced by Arthur Freed

Directed by Vincente Minnelli

CAST

Esther Smith	Judy Garland
"Tootie" Smith	Margaret O'Brien
Mrs. Anna Smith	Mary Astor
Rose Smith	Lucille Bremer
John Truett	Tom Drake

ACADEMY AWARD NOMINATIONS

4 nominations, no wins

Best Screenplay
Best Cinematography, Color
Best Song ("The Trolley Song," music and
  words by Hugh Martin and Ralph Blane)
Best Scoring of a Musical Picture

Margaret O'Brien received a miniature statuette as Outstanding Child Actress of 1944.

perfect film for his talents.

Fans of Judy Garland will no doubt think of this as *her* picture. She sings nearly as much as she did in *The Wizard of Oz*, such tunes as the title song, "The Boy Next Door," "Have Yourself a Merry Little Christmas" (which became a number-one record), and "The Trolley Song" ("Clang, clang, clang," and so forth). It's always a treat to audiences, even today.

If ever there was a scene-stealer, though, it was Margaret O'Brien, who was seven years old when this movie was made. The juvenile actress received second billing, and it was well deserved. Her character, Tootie, is a somewhat morbid little creature who lops off the heads of her "snowpeople" and buries her "dead" dolls in their own cemetery. One scene called for Margaret to cry her heart out, something she usually could do on cue. For some reason, however, she was being stubborn and not a tear would flow. Vincent Minnelli solved the problem. He told

her that there was a little dog which was going to be shot, and it was going to suffer terribly, "and then," Minnelli said, "THE DOG IS GOING TO DIE!" Tears began flooding down Margaret's face, Minnelli told the assistant director to roll the cameras, and they got the scene in one take. "I went home feeling like a monster," Minnelli later recalled in his book, *I Remember It Well*. "I marvel that Margaret didn't turn out to be one too. That sort of preparation struck me as most unhealthy."

It's curious that this movie ends with almost the exact same words as does *The Wizard of Oz*, with Judy Garland delivering the closing lines. When the family finds out that they won't have to move to New York, Judy remarks about how wonderful it will be to stay "Right here where we live. Right here in St. Louis." There's still no place like home.

---

*Forty-five years later, *Meet Me in St. Louis* finally did arrive on the Broadway musical stage, where it opened in the fall of 1989.

SINCE YOU WENT AWAY
UNITED ARTISTS
$4,924,756

IF JUDY GARLAND was growing up over at MGM, David O. Selznick decided that Shirley Temple could have a whole new career as an adult actress, too. He cast her in a somewhat shallow part as the younger sister of Jennifer Jones in *Since You Went Away* (based on the book by Margaret Wilder)—his $2,400,000, nearly three-hour-long tribute to American families coping at home with the realities of World War II. It was a noble try, but Shirley's days as a box office draw were over.

Selznick was still obsessed with trying to top *Gone With the Wind*, and he billed *Since You Went Away* as "an epic of the homefront." He spent 127 days filming the production—only 10 days less than the record set by *Gone With the Wind*. He added popular stars to the cast, like Claudette Colbert, Joseph Cotten, Jennifer Jones, and her soon-to-be ex-husband Robert Walker. Crit-

ics and audiences agreed he had a success. But another *GWTW*? Never!

Part of the reason this film is so dated is its view of the world at that time. In one scene, a police officer stops Claudette Colbert and Joseph Cotten, and on learning that Cotten is shipping out, says, "Get one of them Japs for me" as he tugs upwards on the corners of his eyelids while all enjoy a hearty laugh. This sort of racism, so acceptable at the time, can only make today's audiences squirm uncomfortably. To drive the message home, strains of "America the Beautiful," "Home Sweet Home," and even the words on the Statue of Liberty ("Give me your tired, your poor . . .") constantly remind us what we were fighting for. In this war story about the

people back home and how their lives are disrupted, virtually every moviegoer at the time could identify with the situations portrayed—the husband or boyfriend going away, ration coupons, the dreaded telegram from the U.S. War Department. But it doesn't evoke these emotions when viewed today. We can only watch it as a sentimental curiosity piece and shake our heads.

Still, Selznick had given the film his all. True to his legendary pursuit of perfection, Selznick requested detailed sketches from the art department, and over 1,500 scenes were drawn. In his quest for a certain scene with a particular background, Selznick sent a memo to the art department. It stated simply: "Please get me 500 sunsets."

Screenplay by David O. Selznick

From the book by Margaret Buell Wilder

Produced by David O. Selznick

Directed by John Cromwell

CAST

Anne Hilton	Claudette Colbert
Jane Hilton	Jennifer Jones
Lt. Tony Willett	Joseph Cotten
Bridget "Brig" Hilton	Shirley Temple
Col. Smollett	Monty Woolley
The Clergyman	Lionel Barrymore
William G. Smollett II	Robert Walker
Emily Hawkins	Agnes Moorehead
Fidelia	Hattie McDaniel

ACADEMY AWARD NOMINATIONS

9 nominations, 1 win*

Best Picture
Best Actress (Claudette Colbert)
Best Supporting Actor (Monty Woolley)
Best Supporting Actress (Jennifer Jones)
Best Cinematography, Black and White
Best Interior Decoration, Black and White
*Best Scoring of a Dramatic or Comedy Picture (Max Steiner)
Best Film Editing
Best Special Effects

30 SECONDS OVER TOKYO
METRO-GOLDWYN-MAYER
$4,471,080

In 1942, men under the command of then-Colonel James H. Doolittle flew a dramatic air raid on Japan. Two years later, this event was brought to the screen, with Spencer Tracy as Doolittle (he did little, too; it was basically a guest appearance) and Van Johnson, Robert Walker, and Robert Mitchum as some of the young fliers. The story follows the lives of a group of volunteer Air Force fliers through their training in B-52 bombers, followed by their transfer to a Naval aircraft carrier and their startling discovery that they are on a secret mission to bomb Japan. From there we pursue the saga of Captain Ted Lawson, played by Van Johnson, as he and his crew crash-land their fighter on the coast of China.

The picture is noted for its outstanding special effects, state-of-the art work which won *30 Seconds* an Academy Award. One of the most noteworthy achievements was the model of the aircraft carrier *Hornet*, which had a flight deck 54 feet long, too big to maneuver in a 300-square-foot studio tank. To solve this problem, A. Arnold Gillespie, the model's designer, built it on hydraulic ramps which he could use to simulate the rolling and pitching effect of ocean waves on a carrier.

Although no one would ever accuse this of being an anti-war or isolationist film, the screenwriter, Dalton Trumbo, did manage to work in some bits of dialogue that were about as liberal as one dared get. "I don't like killing people," remarks one sailor, "but it's a case of drop a bomb on them, or pretty soon they'll drop one on [my wife] Ellen."

Both audience and critics gave *30 Seconds* their nod of approval. *The New York Times* said: "The true and tremendous story . . . is told with magnificent integrity and dramatic eloquence . . . as a drama of personal heroism, it is nigh the best yet made in Hollywood . . . the film has the tough and literal quality of an Air Force documentary." Pictures like this did much to bolster the morale of those on the home front. *30 Seconds Over Tokyo* had a documentary quality to it, to the extent that *The Hollywood Reporter* called the movie "more than one of the greatest war pictures ever made . . . it is an all-time winner."

Screenplay by Dalton Trumbo

Based on the book by Capt. Ted W. Lawson and Robert Considine

Produced by Sam Zimbalist

Directed by Mervyn LeRoy

CAST

Lieut. Col. James H. Doolittle	Spencer Tracy
Ted Lawson	Van Johnson
David Thatcher	Robert Walker
Ellen Lawson	Phyllis Thaxter
Bob Gray	Robert Mitchum

ACADEMY AWARD NOMINATIONS

2 nominations, 1 win*

Best Cinematography, Black and White
*Best Special Effects

THE WHITE CLIFFS OF DOVER
METRO-GOLDWYN-MAYER
$4,045,250

"I have loved England, dearly and deeply,
Since the first morning, shining and pure,
The white cliffs of Dover, I saw rising steeply
Out of the sea that once made her secure . . .
I have loved England, and still as a stranger
Here is my home, and I still am alone."

—OPENING NARRATION

THE RECITATION of the above poem by the film's heroine, sensitively portrayed by Irene Dunne, opens *The White Cliffs of Dover*. The movie was loosely based on Alice Duer Miller's poem, which had been a best-seller and was well known to audiences on both sides of the Atlantic. Throughout the film, Dunne continues to narrate with additional poetry written especially for the picture by Robert Nathan, and with lots of patriotic music like "When Johnny Comes Marching Home Again," this wartime film struck the proper chord with moviegoers.

Those viewing this film for the first time will probably be listening for strains of the familiar tune which begins, "There'll be bluebirds over /The white cliffs of Dover." Forget it. That song is not from this movie.

One of the things that this picture had going for it was that it was strongly a "woman's film," something badly needed amidst all the shoot-'em-up war movies of the times. Although set against the backdrop of England's valiant war efforts, the picture held actual war scenes to a minimum. Told in retrospect, the story concerns an American woman caught in the throes of war. Her original two-week tour in 1914 ends with a romance and eventual marriage to a titled Englishman. He dies in the First World War, but her love affair continues—with England. Their son, a baby when Dad went off to war, then goes on to fight in the Second World War.

A highlight for today's audience are the sequences of child actress Elizabeth Taylor flirting with young Roddy McDowall. She was just beginning to become known to audiences, and her most famous film as a child, *National Velvet*, was also released in 1944.

The "white cliffs" themselves have become a sort of national symbol of England—a landmark easily spotted during a Channel crossing, just as the Statue of Liberty symbolizes approach to the United States by sea. The cliffs are made from calcium and limestone deposits, layed down over the eons by sea creatures and left high and dry as the Channel retreated to a lower depth. (Similar strata on the French side confirm that in prehistoric times, a land connection between the two countries existed.) During World War II, the towering chalk cliffs presented a highly visible target to the Germans, who constantly shelled them. Subterranean caves and tunnels in the cliffs, once used by smugglers, also served as shelters during the war.

Screenplay by Claudine West, Jan Lustig, and George Froeschel

Based on the poem by Alice Duer Miller

Produced by Sidney Franklin

Directed by Clarence Brown

CAST

Susan Ashwood	Irene Dunne
Sir John Ashwood	Alan Marshal
John Ashwood II (as a boy)	Roddy McDowall
Hiram Porter Dunn	Frank Morgan
Sam Bennett	Van Johnson

ACADEMY AWARD NOMINATIONS

1 nomination, no wins

Best Cinematography, Black and White

THE BELLS OF ST. MARY'S
RKO
$8,000,000

WOULDN'T IT BE GREAT if we could all "Just dial 'O' for 'O'Malley'"? Bing Crosby's revival of the kindly priest we first grew to love in *Going My Way* outshone his performance in that first film. All the ingredients are there—the struggling young student who may miss graduation, the ailing nun (sweetly portrayed by Ingrid Bergman), and, of course, the priest with a heart of gold. Makes you wish you had a clergyman like Bing for your very own.

When Ingrid sings a little Swedish ditty, then is joined by Bing to sing the title song, it's the highlight of the film. And during the final scene between the two, when Ingrid's heart is breaking, there was not a dry hanky left in the house.

The take at the box office was phenomenal. This sequel had the unique privilege of being the first film to actually outgross its predecessor. It was RKO's most profitable hit so far.

Relying more on characterization than plot, the narrative is reinforced through a number of unrelated episodes, with Bing and Ingrid the unifying forces throughout. There is the story of a schoolgirl who may not be able to graduate; there's the crusty old industrialist who is finally persuaded to turn benefactor; there are songfests (naturally) with the Sisters gathered around the piano, and one of the best scenes in the picture—a group of uninhibited, unrehearsed five-year-olds who re-enact the Story of Christmas. Since *The Bells of St. Mary's* appeared just in time for the holiday season, the sketch was a natural. Bobby Dolan, son of the picture's musical director, doubles as the Narrator and Joseph. His wheezing, ad-libbed lines are classic: "Oh, this is Mary and I'm Joseph and we came to Bethlehem to see if we can have some place . . . find some place to stay. And that's all you have to know really." In the stable, an angel perches atop a ladder, surrounded by wise men and shepherds, while an 18-month-old, playing the Christ Child, waves to the audience from a clothes basket. This was all improvised by a group of kindergartners based on a rough idea given them by director Leo McCarey, who told *Time* Magazine that "it was

one of the most difficult sequences I ever directed."

Many critics were enthusiastic, but others found fault with the absence of Barry Fitzgerald. Comparisons with *Going My Way* were inevitable. *The New York Times* said that "Sister Benedict has not the veracity of her counterpart character which was played by Barry Fitzgerald. She is much too precisely sugar-coated, too eagerly contrived . . . although a plenteous and sometimes winning show [*Bells*] lacks the charm of its predecessor—and that comparison cannot be escaped." But *The Hollywood Reporter*'s reviewer disagreed: "The first question that will be instantly asked is how does 'Bells of St. Mary's' compare with 'Going My Way.' Both reflect the same simple sincerity of inspired entertainment. Both are tremendous credits to everyone who had a hand in the filming—actually proud credits to the entire motion picture industry . . . Bing Crosby's Father O'Malley is a casual joy and Ingrid Bergman's Sister Superior a portrait of quiet depth, highlighted by a sparkling sense of humor."

A true multiple talent (rare for those days), producer-director Leo McCarey is said to have based the original story of *The Bells of St. Mary's* on the real-life character of his aunt, Sister Mary Benedict of the Immaculate Heart Convent in Hollywood.* He also co-authored (with Dudley Nichols) the screenplay from his original story.

The Bells of St. Mary's is a staple of independent television stations, especially around Christmastime. A word of caution: the colorized version of this film leaves much to be desired. In the graduation sequence, for instance, the person in charge of the computer adding the color seems to have gone wild, giving the girls dresses of chartreuse, hot peach, bright yellow, and other Day-Glo colors. Best to turn your color control down all the way and spare yourself this travesty.

---

*There was also a real-life counterpart to Father O'Malley. Father Eugene O'Malley, a Chicago priest, directed the Old St. Mary's Church choir for more than 40 years until his death in 1989.

Screenplay by Dudley Nichols

Produced and directed by Leo McCarey

CAST

Father O'Malley .... Bing Crosby
Sister Benedict .... Ingrid
　　　　　　　　　　　　Bergman
Mr. Bogardus .... Henry Travers
Patsy .... Joan Carroll
Patsy's Mother .... Martha Sleeper

ACADEMY AWARD NOMINATIONS

8 nominations, 1 win*

Best Picture
Best Actor (Bing Crosby)
Best Actress (Ingrid Bergman)
Best Director (Leo McCarey)
*Best Sound Recording
Best Song ("Aren't You Glad You're You,"
　music by Jimmy Van Heusen, words by
　Johnny Burke)
Best Scoring of a Dramatic or Comedy
　Picture
Best Film Editing

LEAVE HER TO HEAVEN

20TH CENTURY-FOX
$5,500,000

THE OPENING SEQUENCE of *Leave Her to Heaven* consists of the pages of a book being turned as credits appear. This is appropriate for two reasons: one of the central characters is a writer, and the film was based upon a book which chalked up sales of over a million copies while staying on the best-seller list for 12 months. Audiences were familiar with the tale of the obsessively jealous woman who does her best (including murder) to try to spend some quality time with her gregarious husband.

Leave Her to Heaven's story is set against a background of several architectural achievements—the Santa Fe ranch house, whose look is so sought after today, is likely to send modern homebuilders to their drafting tables. There's also a beautiful Bar Harbor, Maine, mansion, and some stunning scenic vistas.

Many of the critics seemed to confuse actress Gene Tierney—who faithfully portrayed the book's misguided anti-heroine and won an Oscar nomination—with "Ellen Berent," a deliberately shallow character who was

Screenplay by Jo Swerling

Based on the novel by Ben Ames Williams

Produced by William A. Bacher

Directed by John M. Stahl

CAST

Ellen	Gene Tierney
Richard	Cornel Wilde
Ruth	Jeanne Crain
Russell Wuinton	Vincent Price
Mrs. Berent	Mary Philips

ACADEMY AWARD NOMINATIONS

4 nominations, 1 win*

Best Actress (Gene Tierney)
*Best Cinematography, Color
Best Interior Decoration, Color
Best Sound Recording

jealousy personified. *Time* stated: "No amount of strenuous plot trouble—or even a long fall down a flight of steps—seems to jar Gene Tierney's smooth deadpan. Walking or sleeping, in ec-

stasy or anger, joy or sorrow, her pretty, composed features seem to be asking the single, gamin-and-spinach question: 'Huh?'" And *The New York Times* seemed to be saying "shoot the messenger," claiming that "Miss Tierney's petulant performance of this vixenish character is about as analytical as a piece of pin-up poster art. It is strictly one-dimensional, in the manner of a dot on an I."

The *Times* reporter didn't have any kind words for the other members of the cast, either. He saw Cornel Wilde as "equally restricted as her curiously over-powered spouse." Jeanne Crain was "colorless and wooden" and Vincent Price, Mary Philips, and Darryl Hickman were said to "mechanically play [their] roles." The reviewer did, however, enjoy the sets.

The fault may have been in the script. As the prosecuting attorney, Vincent Price's character is emotional and badgering—more a *per*secuting attorney. And the defense attorney should have been disbarred for putting up with this without so much as an "Objection!"

SPELLBOUND
UNITED ARTISTS
$4,970,583

THERE ARE MANY reasons why *Spellbound* became Alfred Hitchcock's most profitable film of the decade. Among them were Ingrid Bergman—who at first turned Hitch down because she thought the script was implausible—and handsome newcomer Gregory Peck as her patient/lover, a twosome that audiences found irresistible.

Peck, suffering from amnesia, believes he has committed a murder, but cannot remember the circumstances. Ingrid Bergman, as his psychiatrist, falls in love with him while trying to unlock the secrets of his tortured mind, certain he could not have committed such a crime. The solution to the film's mysteries stems from the analysis of one of Peck's recurring dreams—one of the most memorable dream sequences in cinematic history.

In an attempt to capture the "vividness of dreams," Hitchcock hired artist Salvador Dali to design the sequence. Dali proffered more than a hundred sketches and five paintings. The surrealistic number opens with four hundred human eyes glaring down from

Screenplay by Ben Hecht

Based on the novel *The House of Dr. Edwardes* by Francis Beeding

Produced by David O. Selznick

Directed by Alfred Hitchcock

CAST

Dr. Constance Peterson	Ingrid Bergman
J. B.	Gregory Peck
Matron	Jean Acker
Harry	Donald Curtis
Miss Carmichael	Rhonda Fleming

ACADEMY AWARD NOMINATIONS

6 nominations, 1 win*

Best Picture
Best Supporting Actor (Michael Chekhov)
Best Director (Alfred Hitchcock)
Best Cinematography, Black and White
*Best Scoring of a Dramatic or Comedy Picture
Best Special Effects

black velvet drapes, which are sliced by a woman with a pair of huge scissors. There is a giant pair of pliers chasing Gregory Peck up the side of a pyramid. Ingrid Bergman is draped in a Grecian gown with a crown on her head and an arrow through her neck. The statue breaks open and ants stream forth from her face. Selznick despised the sequence, and the 20-minute segment was trimmed down to a few moments.

The other treat for audiences in this suspense drama came near the movie's end. With true Hitchcockian flair, the director photographs from the POV (point of view) of the gunman. We follow the gun as it points at Bergman, but then, the gun is turned and aimed directly at the camera—and the audience. In a surprise that had people gasping in their seats, the gun fires at *us* in a sudden burst of red color (a moment easily captured by freezing frame on a VCR). This startling use of *two frames* of color ("Did I really see that?") in the original black-and-white print had audiences returning for a second look.

ANCHORS AWEIGH
METRO-GOLDWYN-MAYER
$4,778,679

1945

THIS FILM marked the first major appearance of Frank Sinatra, who was then riding the crest of a teen heart-throb wave. Frankie really got to demonstrate his talent, singing and dancing with Gene Kelly, and keeping pace with the professional hoofer quite well.

In this classic screen musical, Sinatra and Kelly are sailors on liberty in Hollywood. Sinatra is a shy Brooklyn boy who's coached on picking up girls by self-assured Kelly. Both end up falling for the same gal—the aunt of a youngster (Dean Stockwell) who is ga-ga over the Navy. There's a subplot about getting the object of their affections (Kathryn Grayson) an audition with conductor Jose Iturbi, which gives the film one of its biggest musical moments. Anyone familiar today with Los Angeles' Hollywood Bowl will enjoy a look at that famous site before acoustical superstructures were added, and the production number in the film is a spectacular one featuring row after row of precocious children whose piano lessons paid off. It's gimmicky but clever.

The highlight of *Anchors Aweigh*, though, is the musical fairy-tale number called "The King Who Couldn't Dance," with Gene and his animated-mouse

Screenplay by Isobel Lennart

Suggested by a story by Natalie Marcin

Produced by Joe Pasternak

Directed by George Sidney

CAST

Joseph Brady	Gene Kelly
Susan Abbott	Kathryn Grayson
Clarence Doolittle	Frank Sinatra
Donald Martin	Dean Stockwell
Girl From Brooklyn	Pamela Britton

ACADEMY AWARD NOMINATIONS

4 nominations, 1 win*

Best Picture
Best Cinematography, Color
Best Song ("I Fall in Love Too Easily,"
  music by Jule Styne, words by
  Sammy Cahn)
*Best Scoring of a Musical Picture

partner Jerry (of the "Tom and Jerry" cartoons) interacting on screen. Although it broke new ground as the first Technicolor live-animated interaction, this technique, so highly touted in 1988 with *Who Framed Roger Rabbit*, was actually not an innovation at all. As early as 1909, French artist Emil Cohl pioneered the first use of matte photography to combine live action and animation in *Clair de Lune Espanol/ Man in the Moon*. Later, the famous cartoonist Max Fleischer (creator of Betty Boop) animated a black-and-white series called "Out of the Inkwell" in which he appeared with the characters as he drew them. But this beautiful

Technicolor sequence in *Anchors Aweigh* served as a launching pad for such treats to follow as *Song of the South, Mary Poppins*, and, of course, *Roger Rabbit*.

Also a treat is the appearance of eight-year-old Dean Stockwell as a scene-stealing lad hung up on joining the Navy. Stockwell went on to a successful film career which is stronger than ever these days. In 1988, he played the part of Howard Hughes in the Paramount film *Tucker* and received an Academy Award nomination for Best Supporting Actor for his role in *Married to the Mob*. He also co-starred in the television series "Quantum Leap."

THE VALLEY OF DECISION

METRO-GOLDWYN-MAYER
$4,566,374

1945

ANOTHER FILM based on a bestselling novel (written by Marcia Davenport), this is a Cinderella love story of an Irish girl of the 1870s (Greer Garson) who works as a servant in the home of a Pittsburgh steel-mill boss (Donald Crisp), and subsequently falls in love with his son, played by Gregory Peck. Paul Scott (Peck) must not marry beneath his station, of course, and she is forced to watch him endure a loveless marriage. The film ends with the promise that at least she and Paul can share an unconsummated love.

Just to complicate things, there is a *Romeo and Juliet* subplot—Pat Rafferty (Lionel Barrymore), father of Mary (Greer Garson), lost both his legs in an accident at the Scott Mill and is psychopathic in his hatred of the senior Scott (father of the man Mary loves). There was irony in Barrymore's playing this role; in 1938, at the age of 60, the actor was partially paralyzed by a combination of arthritis and a leg injury, but managed to continue his acting career even though confined to a wheel chair.

Newcomer Gregory Peck captured the immediate attention of the critics, appearing here in an early screen performance. *Variety* wrote: "Gregory Peck, playing opposite as Paul Scott, is standout. He has the personality and ability to command and hold attention in

any scene." *Newsweek* chimed in: "Gregory Peck impersonates the intense young steel man with both the authority and the romantic appeal the role requires . . . the onetime guide at Radio City in New York is established as one of Hollywood's outstanding leading men."

The Valley of Decision was only Peck's third screen appearance; *Spellbound*'s release later in 1945 would see this now-legendary actor on the road to one of Hollywood's most successful acting careers of all time. Peck is one of those rarities among old-time Hollywood actors—a California native who didn't change his name. Born Eldred Gregory Peck on April 5, 1916 in La Jolla, California, Peck graduated from San Diego State and studied pre-med at

the University of California, but soon discovered he had more interest in acting. He enrolled in New York's Neighborhood Playhouse, making his Broadway debut in 1942 in *The Morning Star*. Barred from military service due to an old spinal injury during a college rowing match, he soon discovered that Hollywood was his for the taking, with many leading men away overseas serving in the armed forces. His handsome looks, warm voice, and natural acting ability have seen Peck through a career now entering its sixth decade. Among his most memorable films are *The Yearling* (1946) and *Gentleman's Agreement* (1947)—both Oscar-nominated performances—and *To Kill a Mockingbird* (1962), for which he won an Academy Award.

Screenplay by John Meehan and Sonya Levien

Based on the novel by Marcia Davenport

Produced by Edwin H. Knopf

Directed by Tay Garnett

CAST

Mary Rafferty	Greer Garson
Paul Scott	Gregory Peck
William Scott	Donald Crisp
Pat Rafferty	Lionel Barrymore
Jim Brennan	Preston Foster

ACADEMY AWARD NOMINATIONS

2 nominations, no wins

Best Actress (Greer Garson)
Best Scoring of a Dramatic or Comedy Picture

SONG OF THE SOUTH

WALT DISNEY PRODUCTIONS
$29,228,717

"Out of the humble cabin, out of the singing heart of the Old South, have come the tales of Uncle Remus, rich in simple truths, forever fresh and new."
—PROLOGUE

Z IP-A-DEE-DOO-DAH! What a treat this movie was for kids and adults alike. The war was over and Walt Disney was back doing what he did best—making movies with family appeal. And *Song of the South* had all the right ingredients: child actors, a kindly old storyteller, lots of animated critters, and songs— really fun songs, like the Academy Award-winning "Zip-A-Dee-Doo-Dah" and nine other tunes. (Of the film's 95 minutes, 90 of them are enhanced by music.)

The movie was based on the tales of Uncle Remus, by Joel Chandler Harris, written in the late 1800s. Walt Disney had enjoyed these stories as a boy and had frequently thought about the possibility of turning them into a motion picture. He chose James Baskett, a black actor with years of stage and radio experience, to play the part of Uncle Remus. Baskett was only 41, but

Screenplay by Dalton Reymond, Morton Grant, and Maurice Rapf

From an original story by Dalton Reymond

Animated episodes based on "Uncle Remus" stories by Joel Chandler Harris

Produced by Walt Disney

Directed by Wilfred Jackson (Animation) and Harve Foster (Live Action)

CAST

Uncle Remus	James Baskett
Johnny	Bobby Driscoll
Sally	Ruth Warwick
Ginny	Luana Patten
Aunt Tempy	Hattie McDaniel

ACADEMY AWARD NOMINATIONS

2 nominations, 1 win*

*Best Song ("Zip-A-Dee-Doo-Dah," music by Allie Wrubel, words by Ray Gilbert)
Best Scoring of a Musical Picture

James Baskett received a special award (statuette) for portraying Uncle Remus, "storyteller to the children of the world."

Although officially released in November, 1946, *Song of the South* was submitted to the Academy for consideration as a 1947 release.

his portrayal of the elderly, white-haired Uncle Remus was so convincing and endearing that the Motion Picture Academy awarded him an honorary Oscar "for his able and heart-warming characterization of Uncle Remus, friend and storyteller to the children of the world." In addition to his role as the kindly yarn spinner, Baskett performed the voices of Brer Fox and a butterfly in the animated sequences.

Brer Rabbit, Brer Fox, and Brer Bear ("Brer" is a contraction for "brother") were some of Disney's most memorable animated characters, and their stories account for 30 percent of the film's 95 minutes. Disney animators worked for almost two years on the cartoon sequences, which are cleverly combined with live action for the most sustained interaction between the two to that time.

In years to come, Walt Disney would become noted for his ability to single out acting talent in children (remember Hayley Mills and Annette?), and *Song of the South* saw him signing his studio's first young contract players. Seven-year-old Luana Patten was a child model who performed for the cameras for the first time in this picture, while nine-year-old Bobby Driscoll was a veteran of four previous films. Both became Disney stars. They were re-teamed in *So Dear to My Heart, Melody Time,* and *Fun and Fancy Free.* Bobby went on to do *Treasure Island**, while Luana starred in *Johnny Tremain* and *Follow Me, Boys,* all for Disney.

Reviews were mixed. Most critics much preferred the animation to the humans. *The New York Times* noted that "the ratio of 'live' to cartoon action is approximately two to one—and that is approximately the ratio of its mediocrity to charm." *Time* wrote: "Artistically, *Song of the South* could have used a much heavier helping of cartooning. Technically, the blending of two

---

*Bobby Driscoll never managed to make it as an adult actor. In 1961 he had drug problems, and was jailed for various offenses. He suffered a heart attack in 1968 and was found dead in an abandoned tenement. He was 31.

movie mediums is pure Disney wizardry. Ideologically, the picture is certain to land its maker in hot water. Tattered ol' Uncle Remus, who cheerfully 'knew his place' in the easygoing world of late 19th Century Georgia . . . is a character bound to enrage all educated Negroes, and a number of damyankees."

And therein lay the rub. The National Urban League, quoted in *Time,* called the movie "another repetition of the perpetuation of the stereotype casting of the Negro in the servant role, depicting him as indolent, one who handles the truth lightly." And the National Association for the Advancement of Colored People (NAACP), though finding "remarkable artistic merit" in the film, deplored the "impression it gives of an idyllic master-slave relationship which is a distortion of the facts."

It is important to acknowledge these comments, but a few corrections are in order. The story does not depict slav-

ery in the South, but rather takes place *after* the Civil War. The film was far less degrading to blacks than was, say, *Gone With the Wind.* According to Leonard Maltin's *The Disney Films,* a Disney representative noted at the time that Walt "was not trying to put across any message but was making a sincere effort to depict American folklore, to put the Uncle Remus stories into pictures." It should also be pointed out that Uncle Remus is the only sympathetic adult character in the film. The children's white mother comes off as a short-tempered, closed-minded bitch; Uncle Remus emerges as the film's true hero.

But the bottom line on this film can be measured at the box office. The fourth successful re-release of *Song of the South* came in 1986, and millions more dollars were earned for the studio, making this the number-one film released in 1946, more than 40 years ago. Disney must have done *something* right.

THE BEST YEARS OF OUR LIVES

RKO
$11,300,000

*" 'The Best Years of Our Lives' is
one of the best pictures of our lives."*
—VARIETY

IT WAS A PICTURE perfectly suited to its time. The "our" referred to in the title will not have the same meaning and effect on today's generation, but in 1946, this was *the* film of that generation. Based on the novel *Glory for Me*, by MacKinlay Kantor (most famous for his later novel, *Andersonville*), this remarkable film addresses the question of what happens to three typical veterans returning to their middle-America hometown after the war.

What is so amazing about this film, viewing it from the perspective of our present insecurity about nuclear war, is the maturity for that time. Observe this dialogue between son and father, one of the soldiers becoming re-acquainted with his teenager:

SON
Say, you were at Hiroshima,

Screenplay by Robert E. Sherwood

From the novel *Glory For Me*
by MacKinlay Kantor

Produced by Samuel Goldwyn

Directed by William Wyler

CAST

Milly Stephenson .... Myrna Loy
Al Stephenson .... Fredric March
Fred Derry .... Dana Andrews
Peggy Stephenson ...... Teresa Wright
Marie Derry .... Virginia Mayo
Homer Parriah .... Harold Russell

ACADEMY AWARD NOMINATIONS

8 nominations, 7 wins*

**Best Picture
**Best Actor (Fredric March)
**Best Supporting Actor (Harold Russell)
**Best Director (William Wyler)
**Best Screenplay (Robert E. Sherwood)
  Best Sound Recording
**Best Scoring of a Dramatic or
  Comedy Picture
**Best Film Editing

Harold Russell was awarded a special statuette in addition to his regular Oscar.

---

weren't you Dad? Did you happen to notice any effect of radioactivity on the people who survived the blast?

FATHER
No, I didn't. Should I have?

SON
Well, we've been having lectures in atomic energy at school, and Mr. McLaughlin, he's our physics teacher, he says that we've reached a point where the whole human race has either got to find a way to live together or else . . .

FATHER
Or else . . .?

SON
That's right. Or else. Because when you combine atomic energy with the jet propulsion and radar and guided missiles, just think . . .

This, from a film made less that a year

after we nuked Hiroshima and Nagasaki. It seems curious that this concept was so long overlooked and that it has taken nearly 45 years for us to begin to move toward the goals set forth here.

Most people remember *The Best Years of Our Lives* for the performance of double amputee Harold Russell. Russell was a Canadian paratrooper who lost both hands in a grenade explosion. The performance (his first) won him an Academy Award as Best Supporting Actor, as well as a special Academy Award "for bringing hope and courage to his fellow veterans." He is the only actor ever to win *two* Oscars for the same role. In 1949, he published his autobiography, *Victory in My Hands*. Later he became a business executive, and in 1964 he was appointed by President Johnson as chairman of the President's Committee on Hiring the Handicapped. His only other film was a brief appearance in *Inside Moves* (1981).

DUEL IN THE SUN

SELZNICK
$11,300,000

DAVID O. SELZNICK continued trying to top himself. Each time he produced a picture, he was convinced that *this* was the masterpiece that would go beyond *Gone With the Wind*. He wrote the screenplay for *Duel in the Sun* from an adaptation of the novel by Niven Busch and cast his paramour Jennifer Jones opposite hunky Gregory Peck in the leading roles. He spent over $8,000,000 filming and promoting the movie, making it the costliest to that date. It had magnificent cinematography of gorgeous Western landscapes. It had a majestic score by Dimitri Tiomkin, the John Williams of his day (or perhaps John Williams is the Dimitri Tiomkin of today).

Duel made money, but it was no *GWTW*. For all its excellent production values, it was, in fact, a "horse opera," a big-budgeted, glorified Western. Never mind—the audiences loved it.

Screenplay by David O. Selznick

Adaptation by Oliver H. P. Garrett

From the novel by Niven Busch

Produced by David O. Selznick

Directed by King Vidor

CAST

Pearl Chavez	Jennifer Jones
Lewt McCanles	Gregory Peck
Jesse McCanles	Joseph Cotten
Senator McCanles	Lionel Barrymore
Mrs. McCanles	Lillian Gish

ACADEMY AWARD NOMINATIONS

2 nominations, no wins

Best Actress (Jennifer Jones)
Best Supporting Actress (Lillian Gish)

They came to see he-man Peck in the role of anti-hero, and St. Bernadette (see p. 46) as a half-breed tramp, clawing their way through the dirt toward each other at picture's end, each having fatally shot the other. For this scene, the picture earned the nickname *Lust in the Dust*.

Critics had a field day. *Variety* called *Duel* "raw, sex-laden, western pulp fiction . . . rarely has a film made such frank use of lust and still been cleared for showings." The sex was fairly tame by today's standards, but audiences then weren't used to seeing such things at the corner Bijoux. *Time* magazine quipped that "with all their frenzied galloping, *Duel's* horses run a poor second to Sex (Jennifer Jones) . . . The audience eventually learns . . . that Illicit Love doesn't really pay in the long run, but for about 134 minutes it has appeared to be loads of fun."

4

THE JOLSON STORY
COLUMBIA
$7,600,000

Screenplay by Stephen Longstreet

Adaptation by Harry Chandler and Andrew Solt

Produced by Sidney Skolsky

Directed by Alfred E. Green

CAST

Al Jolson . . . . Larry Parks
Julie Benson . . . . Evelyn Keyes
Steve Martin . . . . William Demarest
Tom Baron . . . . . . Bill Goodwin
Cantor Yoelson . . Ludwig Donath

ACADEMY AWARD NOMINATIONS

6 nominations, 2 wins*

Best Actor (Larry Parks)
Best Supporting Actor (William Demarest)
Best Cinematography, Color
*Best Sound Recording
*Best Scoring of a Musical Picture
Best Film Editing

ONCE A TOP STAR, Al Jolson was 60 when his film biography, *The Jolson Story*, was released by Columbia. He begged Columbia boss Harry Cohn for a chance to play himself, but Cohn refused and instead signed small-time Hollywood actor Larry Parks. On the basis of this successful film, both men's popularity soared, with Jolson being rediscovered by a whole new generation.

The film was peppered with Jolson's memorable songs—25 in all were used, and Larry Parks lip-synched to the original Jolson recordings. Only in the "Swanee" sequence did Jolson actually appear (he can be seen in a long shot).

The real Al Jolson was born Asa Yoelson, a talented cantor's son determined to make it big. The film portrays him as a youngster befriended by a fiddling, tumbling vaudevillian named Steve Martin (no relation to the modern actor/comedian of that name) who becomes his mentor, and from the first moment he performs, he's hooked. Actually, "hooked" is a good word to describe his obsession with his work as portrayed here—singing is an addiction, and Jolson is an addict.

Jolson himself is best remembered for his appearance in what is often touted as "the first talkie"—*The Jazz Singer*. Originally, *The Jazz Singer* was to star George Jessel, but he demanded $10,000 more than the $30,000 Warner Bros. offered him. Eddie Cantor, the next choice, insisted the role should only be played by Jessel. Jolson received $75,000 when Jack Warner capitulated to his salary demands.

In actuality, there were several talking pictures which preceded *The Jazz Singer*. The idea of talking pictures was investigated as early as 1896, with a presentation in Germany of film with synchronized discs. The first sound-on-film was actually achieved in 1910 by Eugene Lauste, who held the first patent. By the early '20s, there were several demonstrations of sound-on-film in limited presentations. When *The Jazz Singer* arrived in 1927, it was the first talking *feature* film, although the process was sound-on-disc, rather than on film. Most of the movie was actually silent, with exactly 354 words being spoken, including the immortal "Wait a minute. You ain't heard nothin' yet!"

BLUE SKIES
PARAMOUNT
$5,700,000

HEY KIDS! Let's put on a show! We'll put on some great production numbers with a lot of recycled Irving Berlin tunes like "A Pretty Girl Is Like a Melody" (previous films: *The Great Ziegfeld, Alexander's Ragtime Band*) and "Heat Wave" (*As Thousands Cheer, Alexander's . . .*). Then, we'll get Fred Astaire and Bing Crosby, (wow!) together in the same movie. We'll get Fred to dance to "Puttin' on the Ritz," maybe get Bing to do "White Christmas." Lots of pretty chorines, of course. A plot? Naa, who needs one? This picture can't miss.

Of course, no one actually said those words . . . not exactly. But you could almost hear the wheels turning in the corporate heads at Paramount, and this picture, they were pleased to announce, helped pull them out of the financial doldrums—along with *The Paleface*, it became the biggest color hit of the decade. It helped put a few pennies in Bing's pocket, too. He was already on a winning streak at the box office with *Going My Way* (p. 48) and *The Bells of St. Mary's* (p. 54). According to *Time* Magazine that year, he grossed $1,500,000 in income.

There is certainly nothing lacking in the musical department. The movie featured 22 Irving Berlin songs, including "Always," "Say It Isn't So," "All By

Screenplay by Arthur Sheekman

Adaptation by Allan Scott

From an original idea by Irving Berlin

Produced by Sol C. Siegel

Directed by Stuart Heisler

CAST

Johnny Adams	Bing Crosby
Jed Potter	Fred Astaire
Mary O'Hara	Joan Caulfield
Tony	Billy DeWolfe

ACADEMY AWARD NOMINATIONS

2 nominations, no wins

Best Song ("You Keep Coming Back Like a Song," words and music by Irving Berlin)

Best Scoring of a Musical Picture

Myself," "Everybody Step," "How Deep Is the Ocean," "You'd Be Surprised," "See You in C-u-b-a," and "A Couple of Song and Dance Men." This last number pulls a real switch, with Astaire singing and Bing dancing. In a comment to *Time* Magazine, Astaire noted: "Bing is a wonderful performer. His dancing tickles me to death. But if I said he was a good dancer, it would be the same as Bing calling me a good singer."

Blue Skies received mixed reviews. *Newsweek* dubbed it "Blue Hokum" and said that "the only fly in this ointment is a ho-hum story—and add a 'k' if you play anagrams." *The Hollywood Reporter* tempered its enthusiasm for the film

with caution: "No one writes better hit tunes than Berlin, and no one better can be found to sing them than Crosby or dance to them than Astaire. It is a combination that nobody can beat. Yet strangely enough the picture leaves something to be desired . . . a lack of spark, vivacity or spirit."

The thread of a plot has Crosby and Astaire competing for the same girl while Bing strives to improve his career as a nightclub owner, eventually losing, then regaining, the lady in question. But most people will look past this soap-opera story and just enjoy the Crooner and Hoofer doing what they're best noted for; on that level, this is a sure-fire piece of entertainment.

WELCOME STRANGER
PARAMOUNT
$6,100,000

"**I**F IT AIN'T BROKE, don't fix it."

Paramount seemed to be ignoring the old adage when they decided to re-team *Going My Way* stars Bing Crosby and Barry Fitzgerald. The producers had them trade in their clerical collars for doctors' stethoscopes, took them out of the parish, and sent them off to a small town in Maine. Now free of his vows of chastity, Bing was even given a girl (Joan Caulfield) to woo.

Luckily for Paramount, the ploy worked, and the movie became the top grosser for the year. There were many really fine moments, like Bing and Barry fishing together—classic stuff. Along the way there were hay rides and square dances, and an appendectomy for Fitzgerald's character, who demanded a local anesthetic and a bank of mirrors so he could back-seat-drive Crosby's performance.

What there was of a plot had Jim Pearson (Bing Crosby) making an obvious play for the pretty school teacher Trudy (Joan Caulfield) at a barn dance-going away party for Doc McRory (Fitzgerald). Later, Bing helps Fitzgerald outwit the Chamber of Commerce president, who is trying to block his bid for superintendent of the town's new hospital. The more casual Crosby gets, the more crotchety and quarrelsome Fitzgerald becomes—indeed, they are almost self-parodies throughout the good-natured bantering. Typical patter: "One hundred and eighty thousand doctors in the United States and I have to get you!" bemoans Fitzgerald with the arrival of "Der Bingle."

Bing's musical performance needed no supervision. Four songs by Johnny Burke and James Van Heusen were added for spice (although this movie is really no more of a "musical" than *Going My Way*). Most memorable are "Make Mine Country Style" and Bing's crooning of "My Heart Is a Hobo." (For the record, the other two songs were "Smile Right Back at the Sun" and "As Long as I'm Dreaming.")

It was really Bing Crosby's year—for the 12th year in a row, he was ranked among the top 10 box office draws (number 3 for 1947), not bad for a man of 43. And since Bing's "Father O'Malley" image seemed to carry over into whatever he did, even into his personal life, the critics gave a gentle nod of approval to this film. *Time* deemed *Welcome Stranger* "as pleasantly relaxed as Crosby's singing . . ."; *The Hollywood Reporter* described it as "sparkling fun"; and *The New York Times* called the film "as genial as the day is long—just the kind of picture that is nice to have around."

Co-starring with Bing and Barry was an actress who was becoming well-known to audiences of the day, although her name is little-remembered today. Joan Caulfield was a former model who had been playing ingenues on Broadway before entering motion pictures in the mid-'40s. Paramount signed her to a "we'll make you a star" contract, and for a while it seemed this promise was to be fulfilled. Early films included *Duffy's Tavern* (1945), *Blue Skies* (1946), *Monsieur Beaucaire* (1946), *Dear Wife* (1950), and *The Rains of Ranchipur* (1955). In 1950, she married producer Frank Ross and announced her retirement from film (they divorced in 1960). She did, however, make appearances in several more movies, especially Westerns like *Cattle King* (1963), *Red Tomahawk* (1967), *Buckskin* (1968), and *Pony Express Rider* (1976). She also starred in two television series, "My Favorite Husband" (1953–55) and "Sally" (1957–58).

Watch for an appearance by Robert Shayne as the town's petulant pharmacist. Fans of early television will recognize him as "Inspector Henderson" of "Superman" fame.

Screenplay by Arthur Sheekman

Adaptation by Arthur Sheekman and
 N. Richard Nash

From a story by Frank Butler

Produced by Sol C. Siegel

Directed by Elliott Nugent

CAST

Jim Pearson	Bing Crosby
Trudy	Joan Caulfield
Dr. Joseph McRory	Barry Fitzgerald
Emily	Wanda Hendrix
Bill Walters	Frank Faylen

1947

THE EGG AND I

UNIVERSAL-INTERNATIONAL
$5,500,000

"I'll bet you think an egg is something you casually order for breakfast. Well I did once. But that was before the egg and I."
—CLAUDETTE COLBERT'S OPENING SPEECH

IN ONE OF THE MORE clever openings of '40s film, we hear the sound of a rooster crowing, but it quickly becomes apparent that this sound is actually the steam whistle on a locomotive. Claudette Colbert's character "Betty" delivered the above narration, and audiences knew immediately that they were in for two hours of fun.

The Egg and I is certainly that . . . and more. The film has a lot to say about the friendship and support of neighbors, about the struggles and hardship found among farming people. The film, based on the autobiographical best-seller by Betty MacDonald, has Bob (Fred MacMurray) taking his wife Betty (Colbert) away from her familiar city life, and setting up a country chicken ranch. (Apparently, women had

Screenplay by Chester Erskine and Fred F. Finklehoffe

From the novel by Betty MacDonald

Produced by Chester Erskine and Fred F. Finklehoffe

Directed by Chester Erskine

CAST

Betty	Claudette Colbert
Bob	Fred MacMurray
Ma Kettle	Marjorie Main
Harriet Putnam	Louise Allbritton
Pa Kettle	Percy Kilbride

ACADEMY AWARD NOMINATIONS

1 nomination, no wins

Best Supporting Actress (Marjorie Main)

no say in those days, doing whatever their husbands demanded of them.) Brave soul, she does her darndest to adjust. Help comes in the form of "Ma and Pa Kettle," characters played by

Marjorie Main and Percy Kilbride, respectively, who were introduced in this picture and subsequently went on to make one "Kettle" film a year until 1957.

These characters are really *caricatures* of rural people—sincere, honest, uneducated, but full of nurturing warmth. When Ma Kettle sets the table for dinner for 12 young-un's, she merely sweeps her arm across the clutter on the table to make room for the clean dishes. Disgusting? Yes. But she's so full of love for her brood that it's hard to criticize her. And when she makes room for one more mouth to feed (Betty), your heart goes out to her. But then, she's already got such a big one.

The old "fixer-upper" theme set forth in this film has since become a frequent one in comedy films. A year later, *Mr. Blandings Builds His Dream House* found Cary Grant hard at work with hammer and nails, and the '80s saw a revival of the theme with *The Money Pit* and *Baby Boom*.

UNCONQUERED
PARAMOUNT
$5,250,000

"At the forks of the Ohio stands an American city, a colossus of steel, whose mills and furnaces bring forth bone and sinew for a nation. Not so long ago a lonely outpost guarded this very spot. It was called Fort Pitt . . . men kept coming west, some to build their own fortunes, even at the price of Indian wars—others to build a nation—even at the price of their own lives. These are the unconquered, who push ever forward the frontiers of man's freedom." —PROLOGUE

ALTHOUGH he touted it as a historical film, *Unconquered*'s director, Cecil B. DeMille, was more interested in doing what he did best—making a sweeping piece of screen entertainment. He only halfway succeeded.

Listed in the film's opening credits is Chief Iron Eyes Cody, as "Indian language advisor." A full-blooded Cherokee, Iron Eyes himself makes a brief appearance in *Unconquered* as "Red Corn." Born in Oklahoma in 1907, he entered show business at an early age, touring with circuses and Wild West shows. He has appeared in numerous films and TV episodes and acted as technical advisor on many others. His acting career was still going strong in 1989, spanning over 70 years as a professional.

Too bad Iron Eyes wasn't consulted

Screenplay by Charles Bennett, Fredric M. Frank, and Jesse Lasky, Jr.

Based on the novel by Neil H. Swanson

Produced and directed by Cecil B. DeMille

CAST

Capt. Christopher
Holden . . . . Gary Cooper
Abby Hale . . . . Paulette Goddard
Martin Garth . . . . Howard Da Silva
Guyasuta, Chief
of the Senecas . . . . Boris Karloff
Jeremy Love . . . . Cecil Kellaway

ACADEMY AWARD NOMINATIONS

1 nomination, no wins

Best Special Effects

on more than language, since this movie is one long racial cliché. First there's Boris Karloff in the role of Guyasuta, chief of the Senecas, and DeMille's own daughter, Katherine, as the chief's crafty daughter. Then there's the dialogue. Gary Cooper was forced to deliver lines like "This is greater than you or me or both of us" and "White Man's medicine is strong. Nothing can stop them." The oft-cited reason for our pushing aside the aborigines, our "manifest destiny," is expressed when Cooper notes:

"People like the Salters [home steaders] can never be stopped . . . Indians can kill them and run them off, but more will keep

coming. The Salters are the New World, unconquered, unconquerable because they're strong and free—because they have faith in themselves and in God."

Fortunately, attitudes have changed in Hollywood, and there are now organizations of Native American actors which are more effective than Iron Eyes was allowed to be. But in the '40s, this view of Indians was more than acceptable; it was the norm.

Despite its problems, *Unconquered* is still good entertainment, a colorful drama in the DeMille tradition. For this reason, it is worth a watch whenever it appears on TBS and other cable stations.

④

LIFE WITH FATHER
WARNER BROS.
$5,057,000

ONE OF THOSE rare stories suitable for nearly every conceivable medium, *Life with Father* began as a best-selling book of sketches, reminiscences by Clarence Day, Jr. of his 1880s adolescence. In 1939, Howard Lindsay and Russell Crouse adapted the material into a play that ran on Broadway for a record eight years. Hot on the heels of that success was this film version, released in 1947, starring William Powell as Clarence, Sr., the blustering paterfamilias with a heart of custard creme, and Irene Dunne as his patient yet unobtrusively independent wife Vinnie.

That the book/play/movie was created from a string of "day in the life" events is evident in the loosely connected incidents that comprise this film. We see Clarence, Jr., buying a new suit (against Father's approval); the family trying to hire a new maid; Clarence, Jr., falling in love with a beautiful young lady played by Elizabeth Taylor; Vinnie struggling through a near-fatal illness; and, of course, Vinnie

Screenplay by Donald Ogden Stewart

From the play by Howard Lindsay and Russell Crouse

Based on the writings of Clarence Day, Jr.

Produced by Robert Buckner

Directed by Michael Curtiz

CAST

Father .... William Powell
Vinnie .... Irene Dunne
Mary .... Elizabeth Taylor
Rev. Dr. Lloyd .... Edmund Gwenn
Cora .... ZaSu Pitts

ACADEMY AWARD NOMINATIONS

4 nominations, no wins

Best Actor (William Powell)
Best Cinematography, Color
Best Art Direction-Set Decoration, Color
Best Scoring of a Dramatic or
   Comedy Picture

persisting in getting the ever-stubborn Clarence, Sr., to be baptized.

One of the Day boys, John, is played by Martin Milner, who later went on to star in the '60s TV series "Route 66" and "Adam 12."

Also credited is Mrs. Clarence Day, who served as Technical Advisor.

ZaSu Pitts, who plays Cora, had co-starring roles in the late '50s and early '60s with Gale Storm on "Oh! Susanna" and "The Gale Storm Show." Her last film appearance was in 1963, in *It's a Mad Mad Mad Mad World*. She died of cancer the year that film was released, at the age of 65.

Life With Father found new life on prime-time television a few years later. The thirty-minute sitcom premiered on CBS on Nov. 22, 1953, and lasted until July 5, 1955, with Leon Ames portraying Clarence Day, Sr., Lurene Tuttle as Vinnie, and a variety of different actors as the children. The TV version had the honor of being the first live color series on network television originating in Hollywood.

FOREVER AMBER

20TH CENTURY-FOX
$5,000,000

WRITTEN IN 1945, Kathleen Winsor's 956-page novel sold over 3,000,000 copies and still holds up as a good read today. Fox bought the book and spent over $6,000,000 getting it on film, an unheard-of sum. But although it became a top moneymaker for the year, it lost money for the studio.

Part of the high cost was due to a number of problems. Darryl F. Zanuck hired and then fired John Stahl as director. He found his replacement in Otto Preminger, who hated the book. Zanuck reminded him of his option contract, which still had six years to run. Preminger agreed, but not until the young English actress Peggy Cummins was also fired. He wanted Lana Turner, but Zanuck insisted on Linda Darnell; Preminger yielded, but only if her hair were dyed.

Preminger spent recklessly. The Great Fire of London sequence was shot five times until the director was satisfied that he had it right—and not until the Beverly Hills Fire Department had rushed to the lot, called in by anxious neighbors at 3:00 A.M. when filming took place.

The book had the dubious honor of being literally "banned in Boston," and the Catholic Legion of Decency demanded a screening before giving the film its official recommendation.

In the story, Amber, a poor, ambitious 17th-century peasant, does a lot of bed-hopping until she eventually gains favor in the court of Charles II. She's the quintessential flirt who makes Scarlett O'Hara seem like a shrinking violet. At the initial screening, the Legion of Decency first asked that the title be changed, then demanded that all love scenes be cut at the point where the lips are about to touch. There were other equally absurd demands. Preminger refused, and the film was officially banned, the Legion calling it "a glorification of immorality and licentiousness." This was followed by a message from Francis Cardinal Spellman, Archbishop of New York, advising that "Catholics may not see [*Forever Amber*] with a safe conscience." The message was to be read at all masses in the archdiocese on Sunday.

The picture was recalled, cuts were made, and the Legion gave the film a tenuous approval. But *Forever Amber* never recouped its expenses.

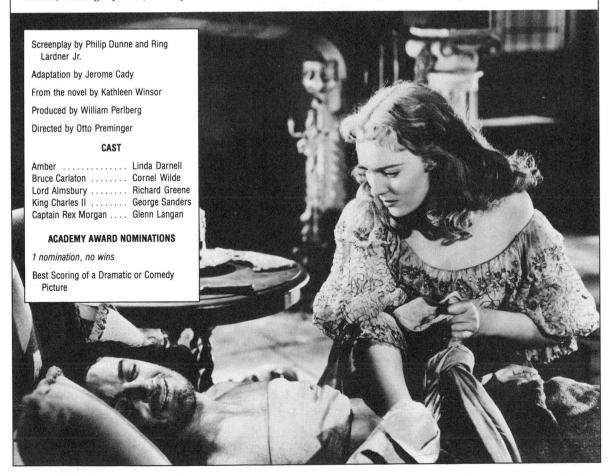

Screenplay by Philip Dunne and Ring Lardner Jr.

Adaptation by Jerome Cady

From the novel by Kathleen Winsor

Produced by William Perlberg

Directed by Otto Preminger

CAST

Amber	Linda Darnell
Bruce Carlaton	Cornel Wilde
Lord Almsbury	Richard Greene
King Charles II	George Sanders
Captain Rex Morgan	Glenn Langan

ACADEMY AWARD NOMINATIONS

1 nomination, no wins

Best Scoring of a Dramatic or Comedy Picture

THE RED SHOES
RANK-ARCHERS/EAGLE-LION
$5,000,000

"The growing popularity of the bal-let in Britain has been a post-war phenomenon and undoubtedly in-fluenced [Michael] Powell and [Emeric] Pressburger to produce this, their last for Rank. Although good ballet is assured boxoffice in London and possibly other big cities, its popularity in small towns and country districts is dubious. And in America, too, it will proba-bly only attract a limited audience."
—*VARIETY*

HAPPILY, *Variety* was wrong. *The Red Shoes* has to be considered a high point in cinema, not only because it has made so much money, and is a perennial favorite, but because it got off the ground (so to speak) at all. Movies were supposed to be funny, or scary, or shoot-'em-ups, or tense thrillers. But ballet? That was considered (and by many still is) highbrow "culture," cer-tainly not mainstream fare for ex-hibitors.

But this film had a lot going for it, starting off with the beautiful female ballet-star-turned-actress, Moira Shearer. The daughter of a Scottish civil engineer, Moira had her first dancing lessons at six and made her professional debut with the Interna-tional Ballet at 15. At 16, she joined Sadler's Wells Ballet. Six years later, at the age of 22, she was signed for *The Red Shoes*, a role which demanded not only perfect dance skills, but a consid-erable amount of acting. *The Red Shoes* is a play-within-a-play; it's the story of a dancer torn between two possessive men, as well as her career. The high-light, of course, is the performance (20 minutes long, complete with special effects) of Hans Christian Andersen's fairy tale, also titled *The Red Shoes*.

Most critics chose to ignore the rather melodramatic story, instead showering praise on Miss Shearer. *The New York Times* noted: "As the leading ballerina and the romantic heroine of the film, Moira Shearer is amazingly accomplished and full of a warm and radiant charm." *Newsweek* also com-mented on the young ballerina: "Per-haps Miss Shearer, an attractive 22-year-old redhead, is a little too sweet and starry-eyed to make the tragic

Vicky's fate completely credible. Never-theless, the Covent Garden ballet star proves that she is a promising actress as well as a graceful and appealing dancer."

So much attention was heaped upon Moira Shearer that she resisted sug-gestions that she dance in other screen presentations. The 1950 edition of *Cur-rent Biography* quoted her as saying: "I am not ready to find satisfaction in the cinema because there I would not know how to strive for perfection. Perfection is what we strive for constantly in the ballet." She returned to Sadler's Wells for a few years, but again danced on the screen in *Tales of Hoffman* (1951). She later made a few non-ballet films, but retired in the early '60s after marrying broadcaster and novelist Ludovic Kennedy.

The picture also garnered critical praise for its fine production values, including the excellent music and Tech-nicolor cinematography. One outstand-ing sequence has a point-of-view shot from the angle of the dancer's head, spinning as she "spots" (focuses on a distant point so as not to become dizzy) in the "Swan Lake" number.

J. Arthur Rank (the "Rank" in "Rank-Archers/Eagle-Lion") was born in 1888, the heir to a flour and milling fortune. His first venture into the world of films was producing promotional religious films for the Methodist Church during the '30s. The British film magnate (later given the honorary title of "Lord") parlayed this modest start in films into a virtual monopoly on the British motion picture industry; by the mid-'40s, his Rank Organisation was involved in all aspects of filmmaking, including production, processing, dis-tribution, and exhibition. At one time, his company owned more than half of all British studios and over 1,000 theaters. He died in 1972 at the age of 84.

"The Archers" was the name of the production company directly involved with this British production; the open-ing of *The Red Shoes* features the Rank logo (a man striking a gong), followed by an archery target pierced by numer-ous arrows, all to the accompaniment of trumpet fanfare. "Eagle-Lion" was the company that released this film in the United States.

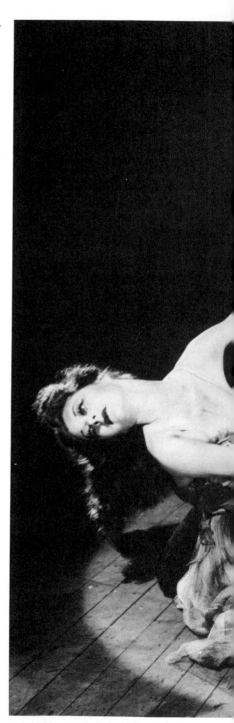

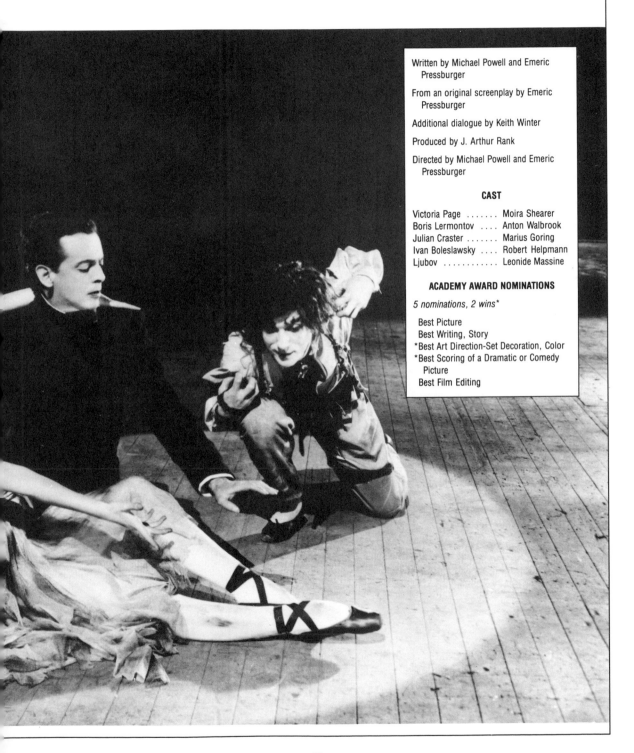

Written by Michael Powell and Emeric Pressburger

From an original screenplay by Emeric Pressburger

Additional dialogue by Keith Winter

Produced by J. Arthur Rank

Directed by Michael Powell and Emeric Pressburger

CAST

Victoria Page	Moira Shearer
Boris Lermontov	Anton Walbrook
Julian Craster	Marius Goring
Ivan Boleslawsky	Robert Helpmann
Ljubov	Leonide Massine

ACADEMY AWARD NOMINATIONS

5 nominations, 2 wins*

Best Picture
Best Writing, Story
*Best Art Direction-Set Decoration, Color
*Best Scoring of a Dramatic or Comedy Picture
Best Film Editing

RED RIVER
UNITED ARTISTS
$4,506,825

RED WAS CERTAINLY the color for 1948. Following in *The Red Shoes'* footsteps, *Red River* generated big business at the box office. Much of its strength lay in its production values—there was beautiful photography of sprawling Western vistas; a full and rich musical score by Dimitri Tiomkin, who by now was famous for his Westerns; plus a top-notch cast, including "The Duke," John Wayne, and a promising young newcomer, Montgomery Clift.

Critics praised just about everything and everybody. John Wayne, of course, had long been identified with Westerns—starting with *The Big Trail* in 1930—but many reviewers took special notice of Clift (it was his second film). *The Hollywood Reporter* called his performance "a decisive bid for important screen stardom. . . . with his charm, unaffected style and winning personality, [Clift] is a bet if ever one has

shown up in Hollywood." *Variety* called the young actor "a sympathetic personality that invites audience response. He reads the Garth character with an instinctive, nonchalant underplaying that is sock."

Clift's role was a pivotal one as the adopted son of Wayne's character; eventually there is a showdown between father and son in the film's dramatic climax, with both Wayne and Clift exhibiting their acting talent in this emotionally charged scene.

Ironically, Wayne was not Howard Hawks' first choice for the lead in *Red River*. Gary Cooper was the man Hawks had in mind, but Coop turned down the part because he didn't like the ruthless nature of the character of Tom Dunson. Montgomery Clift, however, was always Hawks' first choice for the part of Matt Garth. Eventually, Hawks signed Clift to a five-picture

deal, but *Red River* was the only picture they ever did together.

The sequence most frequently recalled is the cattle drive over the newly-opened Chisholm Trail, and the resulting stampede. To make the cattle appear to be stampeding and trampling the carefully-placed stuntmen, cameras were undercranked* to emphasize the speed of the running animals, which were being frightened by off-camera wranglers. It took 10 days of film, using 15 cameras, 35 wranglers, and thousands of head of cattle. Seven men were injured during the filming.

*Undercranking is a process of shooting at less than the normal 24 frames per second. When the film is shown, the action appears speeded up. Silent films were shot at 18 frames per second, which is why when they're shown with modern projection equipment, the people always seem to be running.

Screenplay by Borden Chase and Charles Schnee

From a magazine story "The Chisholm Trail" by Borden Chase

Produced and directed by Howard Hawks

CAST

Thomas Dunson ..... John Wayne
Matthew Garth .... Montgomery Clift
Tess Millay .... Joanne Dru
Groot .... Walter Brennan
Fen .... Colleen Gray

ACADEMY AWARD NOMINATIONS

2 nominations, no wins

Best Writing, Story
Best Film Editing

THE PALEFACE
PARAMOUNT
$4,500,000

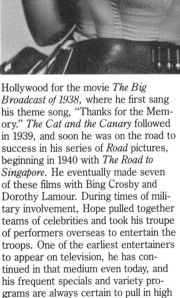

BOB HOPE'S first color picture was *The Paleface*, and it became his biggest box office success. In addition to Hope, the film had cowboys, Indians, and Howard Hughes' discovery from *The Outlaw*, Jane Russell, as Calamity Jane. All the ingredients were there, and the burlesque, a send-up of the classic "shoot out on Main Street" films like *The Virginian*, opened in time for Christmas and continued to pull in big bucks long after the holiday season.

The most notable thing about this picture, aside from the snappy dialogue bantered between Russell and Hope, is the the hit song the film introduced. "Buttons and Bows" won an Oscar for its composers, Jay Livingston and Ray Evans. In the movie, Bob Hope sings it, lip-synching and faking accompaniment on a concertina. The song went to the top of the charts and became a number-one record, but not as sung by Hope. Leaving nothing to chance, the composers insisted that Dinah Shore be signed as the singer, and her recording became a smash hit. Livingston and Evans had many famous tunes in the decades that followed, including "Tammy," "Que Sera Sera," and the familiar themes to television's "Bonanza" and "Mr. Ed."

Bob Hope had been making films for many years and was a perennial favorite even back then. A successful radio career in New York brought him to

Hollywood for the movie *The Big Broadcast of 1938*, where he first sang his theme song, "Thanks for the Memory." *The Cat and the Canary* followed in 1939, and soon he was on the road to success in his series of *Road* pictures, beginning in 1940 with *The Road to Singapore*. He eventually made seven of these films with Bing Crosby and Dorothy Lamour. During times of military involvement, Hope pulled together teams of celebrities and took his troupe of performers overseas to entertain the troops. One of the earliest entertainers to appear on television, he has continued in that medium even today, and his frequent specials and variety programs are always certain to pull in high ratings.

Although *The Paleface* was a comedy and did not strive for authenticity, it is interesting to note that Iron Eyes Cody (see *Unconquered*, page 69) played the part of "Chief Iron Eyes" and a Native American by the name of Chief Yowlachie appears as "Chief Yellow Feather."

If you have a VCR and rent the videocassette of *The Paleface*, you can witness for yourself how stunt doubles are effectively used in movie making. Watch the scene where the dental patient slugs "Painless Potter" (Hope) and you'll see why doubles are filmed in long shots. The man doing the flip over the counter is a terrible likeness of Bob Hope—freeze-frame just as he begins his stunt. Notice how, when he completes the back flip, the pile of towels hides him. A few seconds pass, and up pops Hope, who had been waiting behind the towels. Of course, this scene, and thousands of others like it, were never meant to be seen this way by anybody except the film editor, and in the theatrical runs there was never any chance of these things being caught.

A sequel, *Son of Paleface*, followed in 1951, with much of the same cast—plus singing cowboy Roy Rogers—but its success couldn't match the original. In 1962, Don Knotts starred in a remake, *The Shakiest Gun in the West*.

Screenplay by Edmund Hartmann and Frank Tashlin

Produced by Robert L. Welch

Directed by Norman Z. McLeod

CAST

"Painless"
Peter Potter . . . . Bob Hope
Calamity Jane . . . . Jane Russell
Terris . . . . Robert Armstrong
Pepper . . . . Iris Adrian
Toby Preston . . . . Robert Watson

ACADEMY AWARD NOMINATIONS

1 nomination, 1 win*

*Best Song ("Buttons and Bows," music by Jay Livingston, words by Ray Evans)

THE THREE MUSKETEERS

METRO-GOLDWYN-MAYER
$4,306,876

Actually, there are *four*, not three, musketeers in Alexandre Dumas' classic novel, but poor D'Artagnan always seems to be left out of the total. And if you take into account the number of times this book has been made into film and television versions, well, there have been *hundreds* of musketeers. Edison made a version way back in 1911, so everything else has to be considered a remake. These came in 1913, 1914, 1921 (the famous Douglas Fairbanks version), 1935 (Paul Lukas), 1939 (Don Ameche and the Ritz Brothers!), this 1948 edition, as well as two back-to-back Richard Lester productions starring Michael York—*The Three Musketeers* and *The Four* (yes, count 'em, four) *Musketeers*.

Several elements distinguish the 1948 production, such as the lavish sets and use of color; Lana Turner as "Lady de Winter"; a fine performance by a young Angela Lansbury (of TV's "Murder, She Wrote" fame); plus June Allyson, Van Heflin, Frank Morgan, Gig Young, Reginald Owen, Vincent Price—the list goes on and on. But the best thing about this film is the actor playing D'Artagnan—the great hoofer, Gene Kelly. Gene really knew how to buckle a swash (or is it swash a buckle?).

Although critics were not in accord about the film's total merits (most found it uneven or too long), they were unanimous in their praise for Kelly. Said *The New York Times*: "Not since Douglas Fairbanks swung through the air with magic ease and landed on balconies and beefsteaks has a fellow come along who compares with that robustious actor in vitality and grace . . . what's more, he looks good in plush costumes." And *Variety* agreed: "There are acrobatics by Gene Kelly that would give the late great Douglas Fairbanks pause. His first duel with Richelieu's cohorts is almost ballet, yet never loses the feeling of swaggering swordplay. It is a masterful mixture of dancing grace, acro-agility and sly horseplay . . ."

Many of the exteriors were shot on the back lot of MGM. There is a small bridge noticeable in the European village set which was used in dozens of MGM movies. You'll see this same bridge frequently in MGM television series of the '60s and '70s, notably "Combat" and "The Man From U.N.C.L.E." (currently being seen in re-runs).

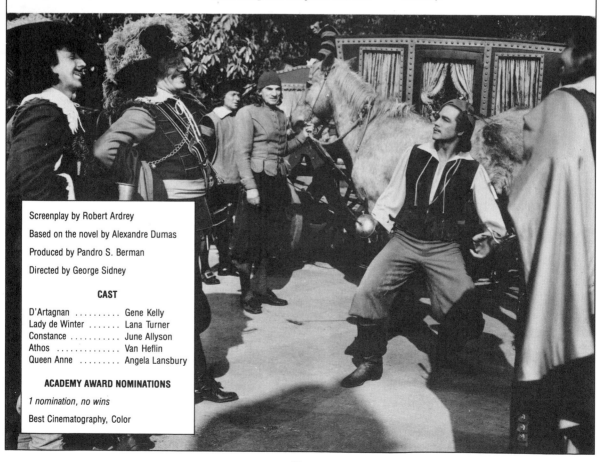

Screenplay by Robert Ardrey

Based on the novel by Alexandre Dumas

Produced by Pandro S. Berman

Directed by George Sidney

CAST

D'Artagnan . . . . Gene Kelly
Lady de Winter . . . . Lana Turner
Constance . . . . June Allyson
Athos . . . . Van Heflin
Queen Anne . . . . Angela Lansbury

ACADEMY AWARD NOMINATIONS

1 nomination, no wins

Best Cinematography, Color

JOHNNY BELINDA
WARNER BROS.
$4,266,000

BROUGHT TO THE SCREEN from a moderately successful 1940 play by Elmer Harris, *Johnny Belinda* was a milestone picture. It is the story of an uncultured little waif, deaf and unspeaking from birth, dwelling among the simple fishing and farming folk of Prince Edward Island, Canada. It marked the first time on the screen that an actress neither spoke nor heard. Signed to play the part of the deaf girl was Jane Wyman, married at the time to Ronald Reagan. Miss Wyman spent a year studying for the part and six months in actual preparation. From a technical advisor, she learned signing and lip reading. The intense preparation was indicated as one of the reasons for the breakup of the Reagan-

Screenplay by Irmgard von Cube and
  Allen Vincent

From the stage play by Elmer Harris

Produced by Jerry Wald

Directed by Jean Negulesco

CAST

Belinda .... Jane Wyman
Dr. Robert
Richardson .... Lew Ayres
Black McDonald ..... Charles Bickford
Aggie .... Agnes Moorehead
Locky .... Stephen McNally

ACADEMY AWARD NOMINATIONS

12 nominations, 1 win*

Best Picture
Best Actor (Lew Ayres)
*Best Actress (Jane Wyman)
Best Supporting Actor (Charles Bickford)
Best Supporting Actress (Agnes
  Moorehead)
Best Director (Jean Negulesco)
Best Writing, Screenplay
Best Cinematography, Black and White
Best Art Direction-Set Decoration,
  Black and White
Best Sound Recording
Best Scoring of a Dramatic or
  Comedy Picture
Best Film Editing

Jerry Wald (producer) won the Irving G.
Thalberg Memorial Award.

Wyman marriage shortly after the release of the film.

When it came time to film *Johnny Belinda*, Jane realized that something was missing—she could still hear, while her character could not. To enhance her performance, she had plastic, wax, and cotton earplugs made to block out all sound while she was working. And the film crew developed a set of signs with which to communicate with the actress.

Jane Wyman was born Sarah Jane Fulks in 1914. While still very young, her mother toted her off to Hollywood, hopeful that she would become a child star. When that didn't happen, Sarah Jane returned to her homestate University of Missouri. Work in radio followed, and she finally landed some bit parts in Hollywood. It took ten years until her career began to take off with major parts in *The Lost Weekend* and *The Yearling*. This led to her being offered the role of "Belinda," which in turn won her the Oscar.

Producer Jerry Wald took great care to ensure authenticity in the film. To duplicate the rugged Nova Scotia setting, he took his cameras to the jagged California coastal area of Fort Bragg and Mendocino, 200 miles north of San Francisco. The area, noted for its fog, winds, and rain, was the perfect location, and saved the studio the considerable money it would have cost to shoot in Canada.

Attention was paid to the small details, too, like wardrobe and hair. To achieve the dinginess that was needed for Belinda's simple clothing, the costumes were soaked and scrubbed and beaten for weeks with rocks. Belinda's haircut was the result of period studies of hundreds of magazine photos of the 1900s "bowl over the head" look.

All these elements contributed to box office success, along with the recognition the film received from critics, the Academy, and moviegoers alike. Today it is well-deserving of the term "classic."

SAMSON AND DELILAH

PARAMOUNT
$11,500,000

"Before the dawn of history, ever since the first man discovered his soul, he has struggled against the forces that sought to enslave him . . ." —Prologue, Narrated by Cecil B. DeMille

Sex, biblical pageantry, spectacle—stir rapidly, add Cecil B. DeMille, and voilà—instant box office blockbuster.

With those ingredients and more, *Samson and Delilah* became the number-one film of 1949, netting Paramount its biggest take of the '40s. Part of the reason was the cast. Brawny, beefy Victor Mature was the "and more" for the ladies in the audience. He was the hunk of the year and can easily be seen as a "Rambo" prototype by today's audiences, right down to the sweatband. As he swings the ass's jawbone, crushing all foes, it seems likely that Sylvester Stallone had to have had this image in mind when he created his "Rambo" character, who bears more than a passing resemblance to Victor Mature. Overwhelmed by the attention afforded him by the *femmes*, Mature relinquished his title as "America's Number One Sweater Boy." *Hollywood Legends* quoted him as stating at the time that "I can't help it if I've got something more. I'm tired of being nothing but a male strip-teaser."

As one-half of the title role, Mature's Samson was up to his ass's jawbone in women. Hedy Lamarr, at age 36, seemed a bit old for the part of Delilah, but even more bizarre was the casting of Angela Lansbury as her older sister Semadar, since she was only 24.

Notable among others in the cast was George Reeves in the minor part of the "Wounded Messenger." Reeves, television fans will recall, later became a muscle man in his own right when he landed the part of "Superman." The one-time wrestler seemed to have a promising acting career in the late '30s, but his film roles were basically supporting ones, including a brief but memorable cameo as one of the Tarleton twins in *Gone With the Wind*. Reeves also appeared in *From Here to*

Screenplay by Jesse L. Lasky, Jr. and Frederic M. Franc

From original treatments by Harold Lamb and Vladimir Jabotinsky

Produced and directed by Cecil B. DeMille

CAST

Delilah	Hedy Lamarr
Samson	Victor Mature
The Saran of Gaza	George Sanders
Semadar	Angela Lansbury
Ahtur	Henry Wilcoxon

ACADEMY AWARD NOMINATIONS

5 nominations, 2 wins*

Best Cinematography, Color
*Best Art Direction-Set Decoration, Color
Best Scoring of a Dramatic or Comedy Picture (Victor Young)
*Best Costume Design, Color
Best Special Effects

Samson and Delilah was released at Christmastime in 1949, but was submitted to the Academy for consideration as a 1950 release.

Cecil B. DeMille picked up an honorary Academy Award statuette as a "distinguished motion picture pioneer, for thirty-seven years of brilliant showmanship."

Eternity (p. 107). He starred as the "Man of Steel" in the weekly "Superman" television series from 1951 to 1957, and the handsome actor eventually found himself typecast after this long TV stint as "Superman." It eventually became too much for him to cope with, and Reeves took his own life in 1959.

DeMille, of course, was the acknowledged master of Biblical epic, having already made one version of *The Ten Commandments* in 1923 (another would follow in the '50s), as well as other religious spectacles such as *The King of Kings*, *The Sign of the Cross*, and *The Crusades*. Of his 18 sound films, 12 are built around historical situations. *Samson and Delilah* helped kick off the '50s trend of Biblical spectaculars.

While DeMille excelled at managing crowd scenes, he was lax in other areas, for example, the unconvincing scene where Samson has to wrestle with and kill the lion. The poor beast was noticeably tranquilized into la-la-land while Samson appeared to vanquish the animal, complete with dubbed roars. Like "Superman," he bends rather fake-looking steel (or iron) in his bare hands. And the effect of his pulling down the temple would have been more believable if it had not been supported by two tiny pillars.

Critics were mixed in their appraisal of *Samson and Delilah*. *Time* noted that "even lovers of cinematic art who recognize *Samson and Delilah* as a run-of-DeMille epic should enjoy it as a simple-minded spree. In its way, it is as

much fun as a robust, well-organized circus." Puns on DeMille's name abounded, as in *The New York Times'* review: "If ever there was a movie for DeMillions, here it is . . . Victor Mature as Samson is a dashing and dauntless hunk of man . . . Hedy Lamarr as Delilah is a sleek and bejeweled siren whose charms have a strictly occidental and twentieth-century grace and clarity . . ."

In 1984, *Samson and Delilah* was remade as a movie for television, with Antony Hamilton as the strongman and Belinda Bauer as the Philistine temptress. Shown occasionally for late-night viewing, it is worth catching for a special reason—the part of Samson's father was played by Victor Mature, still going strong after all those years.

② BATTLEGROUND
METRO-GOLDWYN-MAYER
$5,051,143

WHEN SOMEONE first proposed *Battleground* to MGM's Louis B. Mayer, he turned it down, convinced that the public wanted no more war movies. But in 1948, a deal was made which saw Dore Schary arriving as boss of the studio. The first thing he did was dust off the *Battleground* script, purchased from Howard Hughes when Schary was at RKO. (Hughes also believed people were tired of war films and had refused to make the movie.) With the public having recovered sufficiently from its World War II shell shock, the picture proved a box office sensation.

Much of its success must be attributed to director William Wellman, coupled with a strong Oscar-winning script by Robert Pirosh. The message of the film about men fighting the Battle of the Bulge is delivered by Leon Ames, in the role of the Chaplain. It sums up America's feelings about the war and why we fought, but also sounds the alarm about the perceived menace of Red Communism, of grave concern at the time.

"Was this trip necessary? . . . Nobody wanted this war but the Nazis. A great many people tried to deal with them. Millions have died for no other reason except that the Nazis wanted them dead. In the final showdown there was nothing left to do except to fight. There's a great lesson in this. And those of us who learned it the hard way aren't going to forget it. We must never again let any force dedicated to a super race or super idea or super anything become strong enough to impose itself upon a free world. We must be smart enough and tough enough in the beginning to put out the fire before it starts spreading . . . yes, this trip was necessary."

The all-star cast included Van Johnson, John Hodiak, Ricardo Montalban, George Murphy, James Whitmore, and Jim Arness (later "James" Arness of TV's "Gunsmoke").

Battleground won unanimous critical acclaim. *Variety* called it "the first great picture to come out of Hollywood treating with World War II . . . a fine, mature war picture of smash proportions for audience and boxoffice impact." *The Hollywood Reporter* termed the film "eloquent and compelling . . . the war picture for which the industry and the public have been waiting. It is a strong, realistic and gripping drama."

Screenplay by Robert Pirosh

Produced by Dore Schary

Directed by William A. Wellman

CAST

Holley	Van Johnson
Rodrigues	Ricardo Montalban
Jarvess	John Hodiak
"Pop" Stazak	George Murphy
Jim Layton	Marshall Thompson

ACADEMY AWARD NOMINATIONS

6 nominations, 2 wins*

Best Picture
Best Supporting Actor (James Whitmore)
Best Director (William A. Wellman)
*Best Story and Screenplay (Robert Pirosh)
*Best Cinematography, Black and White
Best Film Editing

JOLSON SINGS AGAIN
COLUMBIA
$5,000,000

1949

W HEN JOLSON sang again, so too did Columbia Pictures. Betting that the public would return to the theaters for a sequel to the first successful film, Columbia re-teamed Larry Parks as Al Jolson and William Demarest as his pal Steve Martin.

It is surprising that this picture did so well. There was very little original new material, with much of the film devoted to recapping *The Jolson Story* through the overdone technique of newspaper clippings.

The film begins where the first picture ended, establishing Jolson as a successful entertainer, obsessed with adulation from his audiences. Everything else in his life, from his marriage and family life to his health, is subjugated to his love of the applause ringing in his ears. In a way, the movie becomes a documentary of *The Jolson Story*, showing Al Jolson (Larry Parks) standing with the production crew and watching as his life story is being made. There is a particularly interesting sequence in which Larry Parks, playing Jolson, meets Larry Parks (played by Larry Parks). It's not nearly as confusing on the screen as it sounds, and must be seen to be appreciated for the clever bit of writing that it is.

There are so many clips from the first film that they seem almost like filler. As the sequel recounts the details from that movie, it nearly catches up with itself . . . a situation which is narrowly avoided.

Screenplay by Sidney Buchman

Produced by Sidney Buchman

Directed by Henry Levin

CAST

Al Jolson . . . . Larry Parks
Ellen Clark . . . . Barbara Hale
Steve Martin . . . . William Demarest
Cantor Yoelson . . . . . . Ludwig Donath

ACADEMY AWARD NOMINATIONS

3 nominations, no wins

Best Story and Screenplay
Best Cinematography, Color
Best Scoring of a Musical Picture

Despite the inevitable comparisons to the original film, *Jolson Sings Again* has some enjoyable moments, most of them coming from the original recordings of Jolson tunes, lip-synched by Parks. Since the first picture, Jolson had staged a comeback and audiences delighted to the soundtrack of favorites like "California, Here I Come," "Red, Red Robin," "Sonny Boy," and, of course, "Mammy."

Although he had found a new generation of fans following the success of the biographical films *The Jolson Story* and *Jolson Sings Again*, Al Jolson's comeback was short-lived. In 1950, a year after the latter picture was released, Jolson set off on a trip to Korea to entertain the U.S. troops stationed there during the Korean War. Shortly after returning home, he died of a heart attack.

THE SANDS OF IWO JIMA

REPUBLIC
$5,000,000

"To the United States Marine Corps, whose exploits and valor have left a lasting impression on the world and in the hearts of their countrymen. Appreciation is gratefully acknowledged for their assistance and participation which made this picture possible."
—DEDICATION

ONE OF THE MOST profound bits of philosophy ever to be expressed in any motion picture came, surprisingly, from this war film which dramatizes the raising of the flag over Iwo Jima during World War II.

Two soldiers are discussing their plight. One asks, "What's war?" The other replies, "Trading real estate for men."

Oversimplification? Yes. True? You bet. If the film said nothing else for its 110 minutes, it would be worthy of a place in movie history for having the fortitude to sum up the senselessness of war. But the line is buried in the midst of all the action and blood-and-guts that brings in audience dollars; moviegoers are not likely to line up for a "preachy" war movie, although most fans don't have any objection to some serious statements being made on the subject of war, as long as there's plenty

of action. *The Hollywood Reporter* reviewer was quick to point out that there was something more happening here for those who cared (and many certainly did): "It is obvious that the picture industry is not shirking its responsibilities. To meet the public half way it is necessary to camouflage documentation and social content as entertainment. 'Sands of Iwo Jima' accomplishes this to near perfection."

The Sands of Iwo Jima has long been acknowledged as one of the best war movies ever made. *Variety* noted: " 'Sands of Iwo Jima' is a real war story. There is no half way about it. The picture uses footage actually shot during combat and weaves it, with tremendous effect, into a gripping, dramatic and tragic story." And *TV Guide* calls the picture "the granddaddy of all those basic-training-to-battlefield war stories." Director Allan Dwan superbly blended his staged battle scenes with actual war footage, and the picture benefitted enormously from the acting of John Wayne, who at 42 was voted America's number-one box office star for the year, the fourth year in a row he

had made the top 10. The star's popularity contributed to the box office success, making Republic's costliest production ever also its most profitable .

Others in the cast in minor roles were Martin Milner as "Pvt. Mike McHugh" and Richard Webb as "Pfc. Shipley." Milner, whose part in *Sands* consisted of only two lines, later co-starred in TV's "Route 66" and "Adam 12." Webb went on to TV fame as the star of "Captain Midnight."

The highlight of the movie is the flag-raising over Iwo Jima. Most of the audience was familiar with the famous photo of six Marines placing the American flag atop the newly secured Mount Suribachi. Actually, this famous picture was done as a "photo opportunity" restaged for the camera since a first, smaller flag had been raised in the same spot earlier in the day on Feb. 23, 1945. Joe Rosenthal captured the second, more dramatic moment on film and received a Pulitzer Prize for the picture. Of the six Marines who participated in the second flag-raising, only three survived to leave the island after further skirmishes with the Japanese.

Screenplay by Harry Brown and James Edward Grant

Based on a story by Harry Brown

Produced by Edmund Grainger

Directed by Allan Dwan

CAST

Sergeant Stryker . . . . John Wayne
Pfc. Conway . . . . John Agar
Allison Bromley . . . . Adele Mara
Corporal Thomas . . . . Forrest Tucker
Pfc. Ragazzi . . . . Wally Cassell

ACADEMY AWARD NOMINATIONS

4 nominations, no wins

Best Actor (John Wayne)
Best Writing, Story
Best Sound Recording
Best Film Editing

I WAS A MALE WAR BRIDE

20TH CENTURY-FOX
$4,100,000

THE TITLE says it all. The "I" in this case was a Frenchman named Henri Rochard, who wrote the original first-person story. However, most moviegoers tend to forget the name of the character and instead remember the film's final (and best) moments when Cary Grant, as the hapless Rochard, dons his gay apparel in order to slip aboard a shipful of war brides. It seems the sexist War Department forgot to provide for *male* spouses of female military personnel married overseas, and in this case, a picture *is* worth a thousand words (see photo illustration).

Grant plays French Captain Rochard, who is assigned to track down a famous German lens grinder and persuade him to work for the French, rather than the German black-marketeers. His as-sistant is an American WAC lieutenant, played by Ann Sheridan, who has worked with him before and calls him a "human octopus with hands." Naturally,

Screenplay by Charles Lederer, Leonard Spigelgass, and Hagar Wilde

From a story by Henri Rochard

Produced by Sol C. Siegel

Directed by Howard Hawks

CAST

Henri Rochard	Cary Grant
Lt. Catherine Gates . . .	Ann Sheridan
WACs	Marion Marshall, Rudy Stuart
Capt. Jack Rumsey . . .	William Neff

they fall in love and marry, making for the "war bride" problem.

Cary Grant and Ann Sheridan romped their way through a lot of interesting German locations (Bad Nauheim and Frankfurt) which showed the effects of Allied bombing. Grant, a former acrobat, did all his own stunts, one notably dangerous one involving climbing onto a guardrail which swings up in the air. By the time of this film, however, Grant was noted for his light, comedic roles, and although some found it difficult to accept an Englishman playing the part of the French captain, his action was praised by nearly all the critics. It is impossible to imagine anyone else playing the role.

The comedy film is frequently seen on the American Movie Classics cable channel.

With the advent of the Fifties came the demise of the motion picture theater as the sole bastion of on-screen entertainment. The reason could be summed up in one word: television. The medium was first publicly demonstrated at the New York World's Fair in 1939; by the end of World War II, there were still only 6,500 sets in existence, most of these still in bars. By 1950, the number had climbed to 11,000,000.

All of a sudden, millions of moviegoers—*ticket-buyers*—were staying home to watch Uncle Miltie in a dress. Attendance fell from 80,000,000 a week in 1946 to only 60,000,000 in 1950, and kept dropping. Something had to be done.

Television was here to stay, and there was nothing the movie industry could do to change that. But the challenge had been presented, and the studios responded. In an attempt to woo audiences away from the hypnotic eye of the cathode-ray tube, studios produced more and more epics—Biblical films, historical themes, musicals with lavish casts, and, in the words of *Silk Stockings* (1957), "glorious Technicolor, breathtaking CinemaScope and stereophonic sound."

It worked, and people began returning to theaters as box office figures surged ever higher.

CINDERELLA
WALT DISNEY PRODUCTIONS
$41,087,000

ACCORDING TO *The Guinness Book of Movie Facts and Feats*, there have been 84 productions of *Cinderella*, ranging from an 1898 film from England called *Cinderella and the Fairy Godmother*, to everything from cartoons, live-action, ballets, operas, parodies, and even porn films. *Cinderella*, in fact, has been remade more times than any other story. There were two "Cinderella" films released the year Walt Disney brought his creation to the screen—the "also-ran" was a live-acted version from Estela Film in Spain. Walt had nothing to worry about. Thanks to numerous re-releases, the Disney classic went on to become the second-highest-grossing all-animated film ever made (*Bambi* being the first).

Cinderella was Disney's first attempt at traditional feature-length animation since *Bambi*, eight years earlier. A team of 750 animators and writers spent nearly six years adapting the story of the scullery maid who becomes the belle of the ball and marries Prince Charming. Disney chose to adapt Charles Perrault's 17th-century French fable, although variations of the Cinderella story have in fact been found in the folklore of the ancient Egyptians, Romans, and even American Indians.

The final days of World War II found Walt Disney Studios in a financial crunch. During the war, the Disney animators had devoted much of their energy to government training films, patriotic short subjects, and episodic animated packages like *Make Mine Music* and *Fun and Fancy Free*. Now Walt was anxious to make another full-length animated fairy tale. The task of creating a believable and empathetic heroine was essential to the success of *Cinderella*. According to a studio press release, Walt told his animators, "I want to be hit right here in the heart. You have to pull for her and feel for her." Although publicly, Walt Disney professed that *Bambi* was his all-time favorite, it was well known that he had a soft spot for *Cinderella*, occasionally referring to it as another favorite. The scene that he liked best was supposedly the one in which Cinderella gets her gown. In an interview with a Disney publicist, Marc Davis, one of Disney's trusty "nine old men," reported that Walt identified with Cinderella because he, too, came from very humble beginnings.

In traditional Disney fashion, the team made a number of changes, adding to and improving on the original story. Among these changes was the transformation of the Fairy Godmother from an old hag (as depicted in Perrault's original) to the grandmotherly character we see in the film. And the original's fur slipper had by now evolved into a glass model, so Disney chose to go along with this version.

But perhaps the best of these additions was a memorable musical score written by Mack David, Jerry Livingston, and Al Hoffman. The six

Story by William Peet, Ted Sears,
   Erdman Penner, Winston Hibler,
   and Harry Reeves

Based on a fairy tale by Charles Perrault

Produced by Walt Disney

Directed by Wilfred Jackson, Hamilton
   Luske, and Clyde Geronimi

VOICES

Cinderella . . . . Ilene Woods
Prince Charming . . . . William Phipps
Stepmother . . . . Eleanor Audley
Fairy Godmother . . . . Verna Felton

ACADEMY AWARD NOMINATIONS

3 nominations, no wins

Best Sound Recording
Best Song ("Bibbidi-Bobbidi-Boo,"
   music and words by Mack David,
   Al Hoffman, and Jerry Livingston)
Best Scoring of a Musical Picture

songs composed by the trio were "So This Is Love," "A Dream Is a Wish Your Heart Makes," "Cinderella," "The Work Song," "Sing, Sweet Nightingale," and the one which earned them the Oscar nomination for Best Song—"Bibbidi-Bobbidi-Boo." The *Cinderella* record album released that year became the number-three top-selling soundtrack for 1950.

Many memorable Disney characters made their debut in this one hour, 14-minute animated feature. The title character, with her blond hair and graceful movements, embodied the universal ideal of the "Cinderella" character created 300 years earlier by Perrault. Her "wicked" stepmother and jealously abusive stepsisters, Anastasia and Drizella, also evoked most people's childhood concepts from the original fable. The King is depicted as a well-meaning but anxious parent, while

Prince Charming is the incarnation of his name. Rounding out the human cast was an additional Disney creation, the Prince's faithful "foot-servant," the Grand Duke.

Among the featured animated animals are a crafty cat called Lucifer, a helpful dog named Bruno, and a group of resident mice with names like Jaq, Gus-Gus, Luke, Mert, Bert, Suzy, Perla, and Blossom. Their voices, part of the Academy Award–nominated sound recording, are played at high speed, so that they sound a lot like (but actually pre-date) "Alvin and the Chipmunks."

Radio star Ilene Woods provided the voice of Cinderella, while actress Eleanor Audley (who later did the voice of Maleficent in Disney's *Sleeping Beauty*) spoke the part of the Wicked Stepmother. Most notable, however, was the singing voice of Prince Charming—

that of talk-show host Mike Douglas (another actor did the speaking part).

To bring Cinderella to life, the animators were provided with a source of inspiration—a live model, 18-year-old actress Helen Stanley, who was photographed in various graceful poses. The animators then studied blow-ups of her photo sessions to achieve the right feeling in their drawings. This technique was so successful that Disney used it in *Sleeping Beauty* (again with Miss Stanley) and other animated features.

Cinderella had frequent theatrical re-releases, the last one taking place in 1987. In 1988, the Walt Disney Company finally brought *Cinderella* out on videocassette, where it soared to the top of the charts, remaining there for many weeks. At the Disney Company, at least, they all lived happily ever after.

KING SOLOMON'S MINES
METRO-GOLDWYN-MAYER
$5,586,000

HOLLYWOOD CONTINUED in its tradition of turning to other media for film inspiration, and in 1950, every one of the top five films was derived from another source.

H. Rider Haggard's *King Solomon's Mines* had been a very popular book ever since it was published in 1885. The first film version came in 1937, starring (Sir) Cedric Hardwicke. But Hollywood likes to top itself, and the 1950 spectacular produced by MGM had Technicolor cameras and crew, plus Deborah Kerr, Stewart Granger, and Richard Carlson, trekking 25,000 miles to Tanganyika (Tanzania), Uganda, Kenya, and Belgian Congo (Zaire) to get it all on film. The magnificent shots of Africa's wildlife—lions, giraffes, crocodiles, antelope—served as stock footage for many an MGM film to follow. Tragically, an elephant hunt was part of the script, and although this caused nary an eyebrow to be raised in those pre-conservation-conscious days, it is the one painful moment for today's viewers, aware of the plight of a species being poached to the brink of extinction.

Screenplay by Helen Deutsch

Based on the novel by H. Rider Haggard

Produced by Sam Zimbalist

Directed by Compton Bennett and Andrew Marton

CAST

Elizabeth Curtis	Deborah Kerr
Allan Quatermain	Stewart Granger
John Goode	Richard Carlson
Smith	Hugo Haas
Eric Masters	Lowell Gilmore

ACADEMY AWARD NOMINATIONS

3 nominations, 2 wins*

 Best Picture
*Best Cinematography, Color
*Best Film Editing

The film made good use of the local tribes, and the credits listed several Watusi natives. Then-president of Uganda Godfrey Binaisa was also given a bit part, and he would later appear in *The African Queen*.

Stewart Granger starred as the legendary Allan Quatermain. Like so many screen personalities, British-born Granger originally had a different name—James Stewart—which he changed to avoid confusion with the American actor by that name. In the '30s and '40s, Granger became a matinee idol in England. His early films included British pictures such as *So This is London* (1939), *Waterloo Road* (1945), and *Captain Boycott* (1947). In 1950, MGM signed him to a seven-year contract. *King Solomon's Mines* was the first of many adventure movies he made for the studio.

As in *Red River*, there is a stampede scene, shot with undercranked cameras to make the animals seem to run faster. To the *Variety* reviewer, it was the highlight: "The standout sequence is the animal stampede, minutes long, that roars across the screen to the terrifying noise of panic-driven hoofbeats."

In 1985 there was yet another remake, starring Richard Chamberlain and John Rhys-Davies, in an attempt to capture the *Indiana Jones* crowd. It wasn't nearly as successful.

ANNIE GET YOUR GUN
METRO-GOLDWYN-MAYER
$4,919,394

METRO'S FIRST ATTEMPT at bringing a popular stage musical to the screen proved highly successful—*Annie Get Your Gun* was the studio's first big musical hit since 1945's *Anchors Aweigh*. Although it was Ethel Merman who first belted out Irving Berlin's hit theme from this play—"There's No Business Like Show Business"—her screen replacement Betty Hutton did a credible job and won the approving nod of the critics. *The Hollywood Reporter* lauded her performance: "For Betty Hutton, charged with the difficult and challenging job of playing one of the greatest parts ever handed a popular singer and chanting a score without peer, the role of 'Annie' is the opportunity of a lifetime. How she is ever going to top it is a problem she will have to take up with her agent and advisors. For us and for the public, her performance ranks as an all-time great in motion picture annals."

The songs were the real stars of the show—great Irving Berlin showstoppers, all. In addition to "There's No Business Like Show Business" (sung by Betty three times, in three different costumes), there was "The Girl That I Marry," "You Can't Get a Man with a

Gun," and "They Say It's Wonderful."

The screenplay was written by Sidney Sheldon, later better known as a popular novelist. Sheldon's career dates back to the early '40s, when he began as a $24-a-week reader for Universal Studios. In 1947 he won an Oscar for his original screenplay of *The Bachelor and the Bobby Soxer*. His bestselling novels of the '70s included *The Other Side of Midnight* and *Bloodline*, both of which were made into films.

Although portrayed as a tomboy in the movie, the real Annie Oakley was a quiet homebody who enjoyed doing needlepoint. Born in Darke County, Ohio, she learned to shoot at age eight in order to provide for her family. As in the movie, at 15 she defeated Frank Butler in a sharpshooting contest, and by age 16 she had married him. She joined Buffalo Bill's Wild West show and, with her husband as her manager, toured with that company for 16 years. Standing only five feet tall, she was

dubbed "Little Sure Shot" by Chief Sitting Bull, also in Buffalo Bill's show, and she proved her talent by shooting a dime out of Butler's hand and a cigarette out of the mouth of German Crown Prince Wilhelm. During World War I, she gave shooting exhibitions and instruction to American soldiers.

Her life was much happier than that of the woman who played her on screen. *The Hollywood Reporter* was right—the part was a tough act for Betty Hutton to follow. Hutton had one other success, starring in *The Greatest Show On Earth* (see page 100), but she walked out of a Paramount contract in 1952 over a dispute in which she demanded that her husband be assigned to direct her films. Only one minor film offer followed, and in 1967, having made and lost $10,000,000, she filed for bankruptcy. She married and divorced five times, and eventually ended up as a cook in a Rhode Island Catholic rectory.

Screenplay by Sidney Sheldon

From the play by Herbert Fields and Dorothy Fields

Music and lyrics by Irving Berlin

Produced by Arthur Freed

Directed by George Sidney

CAST

Annie Oakley . . . . Betty Hutton
Frank Butler . . . . Howard Keel
Buffalo Bill . . . . Louis Calhern
Sitting Bull . . . . J. Carrol Naish
Pawnee Bill . . . . Edward Arnold

ACADEMY AWARD NOMINATIONS

4 nominations, 1 win*

Best Cinematography, Color
Best Art Direction-Set Decoration, Color
*Best Scoring of a Musical Picture
Best Film Editing

1950

CHEAPER BY THE DOZEN
20TH CENTURY-FOX
$4,425,000

Based on the best-selling novel by Frank B. Gilbreth, Jr. and his sister Ernestine Gilbreth Carey, *Cheaper By the Dozen* is the story of their father, Frank, Sr., a motion-study expert trying to run his household brood of 12 children as efficiently as one would run a factory. Set in the 1920s, it is plotless and episodic, in some ways reminiscent of *Life With Father*, and the hilarious results were just what was needed to convince families that "Movies are better than ever" (quoth 20th Century-Fox). They turned their television sets off and made this charming film a box office hit.

The movie stars Clifton Webb as the proud and persistent Frank Gilbreth, and audiences of the time were familiar with him for his creation of the character of "Mr. Belvedere," which had already made him immensely popular. His first appearance as the pompous babysitter had been only two years earlier, and he became subsequently typecast, appearing in several more "Belvedere" films. (Years later, "Mr. Belvedere" became a popular TV se-

ries starring Christopher Hewett.)

Jeanne Crain stars as the oldest sister, and she is given much more to do than in *Leave Her to Heaven*, where she served basically as "set dressing."

Reviews were mixed, with most critics picking up on the lack of real plot while generally praising the film's cast. *The Hollywood Reporter* described the picture as "glib, provocative entertainment." Of Clifton Webb, the trade

Screenplay by Lamar Trotti

Based on the novel by Frank B. Gilbreth, Jr., and Ernestine Gilbreth Carey

Produced by Lamar Trotti

Directed by Walter Lang

CAST

Frank Bunker Gilbreth ..	Clifton Webb
Ann Gilbreth	Jeanne Crain
Mrs. Lillian Gilbreth	Myrna Loy
Libby Lancaster	Betty Lynn
Dr. Burto	Edgar Buchanan

paper remarked: " 'Cheaper by the Dozen' will go a long way toward implementing the strong hold he already maintains on the affection of the public." But *Time* Magazine disagreed, calling the film a "string of mild, rambling anecdotes" and claiming that Clifton Webb was miscast as head of the Gilbreth household: "It is not much more fun than leafing through somebody else's family album . . . the result is seldom comic and never moving."

The main reason for this negativity seems to be that critics were too familiar with "Mr. Belvedere," unable to separate the performance of Webb as Gilbreth from his more familiar characterization of Belvedere. Today's audiences, however, free from that stereotyping, can enjoy this film and Webb's portrayal in the spirit it was intended.

A 1952 sequel, *Belles on Their Toes*, had Myrna Loy returning as Mrs. Gilbreth, along with Jeanne Crain as her now mature daughter. As usual, the sequel couldn't match the success of the original.

FATHER OF THE BRIDE
METRO-GOLDWYN-MAYER
$4,054,405

"I would like to say a few words about weddings."
—SPENCER TRACY'S
OPENING LINES

ANOTHER BEST-SELLING novel made the successful transition to the screen with the release of *Father of the Bride.* Although there were many fine actors in the cast, including Joan Bennett, Don Taylor, Billie Burke, and Leo G. Carroll, the film is best remembered for the two in the title: the Father, played by Spencer Tracy; and the Bride, played by Elizabeth Taylor.

Some people might find *Father of the Bride.* This look at the white, middle-class traditional American family of the '50s, the kind of family that gathered every evening for dinner around the dining-room table, has a "Father Knows Best" quaintness about it, and today's viewers may find these images of '50s pre-marital social rituals something of a museum piece. Still, there is enough fine acting and direction to give any modern audience viewing pleasure. Particularly enjoyable are the opening scenes of Spencer Tracy, awash in a sea of post-wedding-reception debris, recounting the sorry lot of the bride's father.

Screenplay by Frances Goodrich and
   Albert Hackett

Based on the novel by Edward Streeter

Produced by Pandro S. Berman

Directed by Vincente Minnelli

CAST

Stanley T. Banks .... Spencer Tracy
Ellie Banks .... Joan Bennett
Kay Banks .... Elizabeth Taylor
Buckley Dunstan .... Don Taylor
Doris Dunstan .... Billie Burke
Mr. Massoula .... Leo G. Carroll

ACADEMY AWARD NOMINATIONS

3 nominations, no wins

Best Picture
Best Actor (Spencer Tracy)
Best Screenplay

As the narrator, Tracy/Father treats us to his wit with such gems as: "An experienced caterer can make you ashamed of your house in fifteen minutes" and "Given enough ointment, there's always a fly. Given enough presents, there's bound to be a stinker." The latter remark refers to one of the wedding gifts, a plaster figurine of a lady with a clock in her stomach.

Elizabeth Taylor is a standout in this, her first mature role since the '40s films in which she played second banana to horses and dogs. Her first appearance in bridal gown is a memorable cinematic effect. Director Vincente Minnelli strategically placed four mirrors to catch her in a multiple shot, and it's very effective.

Minnelli's technique throughout much of this film is a simple one. He filmed most of his scenes as master shots (i.e., the whole scene rather than close-ups or smaller groups broken down). By locking down his camera, he

let the drama play out in front of it. There are several of these long "takes" without cutaways: the wedding rehearsal, the chaos of the reception being set up at the house . . . all done without change of set-up. The effect is a "you are there" feeling.

MGM tried to catch lightning in a bottle twice, with a sequel film the next year called *Father's Little Dividend,* this time with Tracy as an expectant grandfather. It was well received, but didn't match the box office success of its predecessor.

A television series based on the film was produced by CBS and ran from September, 1961 to September, 1962. It starred Leon Ames (who had also played the lead in the TV series "Life With Father").

In 1989, there was some talk in Hollywood of a remake of *Father of the Bride* being prepped, although no mention was made of who would reprise the Tracy/Taylor roles.

QUO VADIS?
METRO-GOLDWYN-MAYER
$11,901,662

"**Q**UO VADIS . . . whither goest thou?" Or, as modern English would have it, "Where are you going?" The answer for MGM was simple—straight to the bank. Even at a reported cost of $7,000,000, making it the most expensive film to date, the studio still came away with a huge profit. Metro had managed to place three of its releases in the top five in 1950, and they equaled that record in 1951—a feat they have not duplicated since.

Quo Vadis? was a Biblical epic set in Rome during Nero's reign. Everything about it was lavish—the sets, the costumes, the score—and it lured people out of their living rooms and away from their TVs in droves, the crowd scenes at the box office rivaling those on the screen. They came to see Peter Ustinov as Nero fiddle while Rome burned. They came to see 30,000 extras on 55 sets wearing a record 32,000 costumes. They came to watch starving lions chow down on hapless Christians. They came to be dazzled, and they were.

Peter Ustinov was perfectly cast as the sybaritic, egomaniacal Nero, a villainous, somewhat Hitleresque caricature whom audiences, with the horrors of the Second World War still vivid in their minds, could boo and hiss with unrestrained glee. *Variety* accused the actor of "scenery-chewing" and *The New York Times* claimed that "Peter Ustinov plays [Nero] in a manner to elevate Charles Laughton as a master of restraint in the role . . . [his] mouthing and screaming . . . become the most monotonous and vexing things in the film." Yet in retrospect, Ustinov's performance in *Quo Vadis?* is now seen as the quintessential Nero.

The London-born actor has made a living at unusual characterizations. Born in 1921 to a journalist-father of Russian descent and an artist-mother of French descent, Ustinov's early training was for the London stage. He made his acting debut at the age of 17, and later perfected his craft on stage and on the British and American screens. He won Academy Awards for *Spartacus* (1960) and *Topkapi* (1964). In 1961, the multi-talented Ustinov wrote, produced, directed, and starred in *Romanoff and Juliet*, and in 1962 he

produced, directed, co-scripted, and starred as Captain Edward Fairfax Vere in *Billy Budd*. His other films include *Blackbeard's Ghost* (as Captain Blackbeard, 1968), *Hammersmith Is Out* (also directed; 1972), *Logan's Run* (1976), and *The Thief of Baghdad* (1979). Ustinov continues working in film and television, recently writing and narrating a multi-part documentary entitled *Peter Ustinov's Russia*.

One of the minor parts in *Quo Vadis?*, that of Ursus the Slave, was played by an ex-pugilist named Buddy Baer. (Not unintentionally, his character's name, "Ursus," means "bear" in Latin.) He was the brother of famed prizefighter Max Baer, the former heavyweight champion of the world (1934), who also appeared in films. His nephew, Max Baer, Jr., appeared in the television series "The Beverly Hillbillies." Buddy also played a giant in *Jack and the Beanstalk* (1952).

In making this epic, MGM turned again to the classics, this time the novel by Henryk Stenkiewicz, which had served as the basis for two earlier productions of *Quo Vadis?*, one in 1912

and again in 1924.

Filming the spectacular took six months, although it was in the pre-production stages for nearly three years. The entire facilities of Rome's Cinecitta studios were given over to the production. In addition to hiring the thousands of extras (one of whom was an unknown 15-year-old named Sophia Loren), director Mervyn LeRoy scouted all over Europe for the lions required, finally securing the necessary 63 cats from circuses. To simulate realism, LeRoy resorted to stuffing empty clothing with meat, making it appear that the lions were eating actual people. Close-ups were handled with fake lions attacking the extras.

For the burning of Rome sequence (yes, Nero fiddled), a miniature city was constructed, although it could hardly be called that. It consisted of several hundred scaled-down buildings on two acres of ground.

Critics roared with approval. *The Hollywood Reporter* used a banner headline in announcing the cinematic triumph:

MGM'S 'QUO VADIS' COLOSSAL
INDUSTRY'S GREATEST SPECTACLE SUPERB DRAMA AND EXCELLENT ENTERTAINMENT—SHOULD RUN BIGGEST GROSSES EVERYWHERE

The paper's reviewer noted that the press screening "left most of those in attendance limp in their astonished enthusiasm," and described the film as "the real gigantic king of all pictures, the most expensive, the largest cast, the most tremendous display of scenic, wardrobe and color investiture ever known in our business."

Not even *Gone With the Wind* had left people gasping that hard. In fact, MGM tried very hard to promote *QV* as the greatest thing since *GWTW*, taking out a three-page trade ad telling exhibitors, "The quickest way to understand *Quo Vadis'* business is to compare it with *Gone With the Wind*." *The Hollywood Reporter* continued the comparison, stating, "If *Quo Vadis* wins the best picture Oscar, it'll be the second Technicolor item to do so, first being *GWTW*."

Strangely, it won nary a one.

Screenplay by John Lee Mahin, S. N. Behrman, and Sonya Levien

Based on the novel by Henryk Stenkiewicz

Produced by Sam Zimbalist

Directed by Mervyn LeRoy

CAST

Marcus Vinicius	Robert Taylor
Lygia	Deborah Kerr
Petronius	Leo Genn
Nero	Peter Ustinov
Poppaea	Patricia Laffan

ACADEMY AWARD NOMINATIONS

8 nominations, no wins

Best Picture
Best Supporting Actor (Leo Genn)
Best Supporting Actor (Peter Ustinov)
Best Cinematography, Color
Best Art Direction-Set Decoration, Color
Best Scoring of a Dramatic or Comedy Picture
Best Film Editing
Best Costume Design, Color

ALICE IN WONDERLAND
WALT DISNEY PRODUCTIONS
$7,196,000

L EWIS CARROLL'S book *Alice in Wonderland* was a project that had interested Walt Disney since 1933, when he considered a possible live-action film with Mary Pickford. Walt had always been fond of the Carroll story; back in the '20s, when he was beginning to experiment with animation, he had created a marriage of cartoon and live action in his *Alice in Cartoonland* series of shorts, with a live little girl playing in a cartoon world. In 1937, he produced a Carroll-inspired short called *Thru the Mirror*, with Mickey Mouse. Walt also thought about starring Ginger Rogers as a live Alice in a cartoon Wonderland, but he eventually dropped the idea of a live-action character, feeling the results would be disappointing.

Production finally began on an all-animated feature in 1946, and it took nearly five years and $3,000,000 to bring it to the screen. The results were disappointing both financially (it initially lost $1,000,000) and critically, and Walt found himself making apologies for it.

Much of the criticism was directed at the lack of respect for the "classics," since the Disney team had taken the liberty of reshuffling the story, adding bits and pieces from *Through the Looking Glass*, as Alice strolled "through her dream world to the accompaniment of ballads and musical nonsense" (*Variety*).

Musical nonsense? Among the songs which went unheralded at the time were tunes which have become classics today. Most notable is the White Rabbit intoning "I'm Late" and the wonderful Mad Tea Party number, "The Unbirth-

day Song." Even *Variety* couldn't deny the loveliness of "All in the Golden Afternoon," with its singing flowers, terming the number a "standout." Other songs included "Very Good Advice," "In a World of My Own," "The Walrus and the Carpenter," "The Caucus Race," "March of the Cards," and "Painting the Roses Red," all by Bob Hilliard and Sammy Fain. Still others songs were contributed by the teams of Mack David, Al Hoffman, and Jerry Livingston, and by Oliver Wallace and Ted Sears.

In this hybrid of *Through the Looking Glass* and *Alice in Wonderland*, Alice follows the white rabbit and falls down the rabbit hole, where she has adventures in a surrealistic setting, encountering Tweedledee and Tweedledum; the dope-smoking caterpillar whose words form letters in the air; the smile, tail, and occasionally all of the Cheshire Cat; the Mad Hatter and March Hare; and, of course, the King and Queen of Hearts ("Off with her head!").

The voices of the characters were a clever piece of casting; most memorable were Sterling Holloway as the "Cheshire Cat," Ed Wynn as "The Mad Hatter," and Jerry Colonna as "The March Hare."

Though not nearly as successful as other Disney animated features, *Alice* eventually made back its money, and more. Certainly, nothing for Walt Disney to apologize for.

From a story by Lewis Carroll

Produced by Walt Disney

Directed by Clyde Geronimi, Hamilton Luske, and Wilfred Jackson

VOICES

Alice	Kathryn Beaumont
Mad Hatter	Ed Wynn
Caterpillar	Richard Haydn
Cheshire Cat	Sterling Holloway
March Hare	Jerry Colonna

ACADEMY AWARD NOMINATIONS

1 nomination, no wins

Best Scoring of a Musical Picture

SHOW BOAT

METRO-GOLDWYN-MAYER
$5,533,000

"Ol' Man River, he just keeps rollin' along."

WHEN JEROME KERN first approached novelist Edna Ferber back in 1926 with the idea of adapting her novel *Show Boat* into a musical, she thought he was insane. She could hardly envision her story of a Mississippi river showboat of the late 19th century as a stage show, yet it proved to be one of the most successful ones ever. Produced by impresario Florenz Ziegfeld, *Show Boat* ran two years on Broadway, then toured the world for several more.

What convinced Miss Ferber? Jerome Kern played "Ol' Man River" for her (lyrics by Oscar Hammerstein II). She is quoted in *The New Complete Book of the American Musical Theatre* as saying: "My hair stood on end, the tears came to my eyes, and I breathed like a heroine in a melodrama. This was great music. This was music that would

Screenplay by John Lee Mahin

Based on the musical play by Jerome Kern and Oscar Hammerstein II

From the novel by Edna Ferber

Produced by Arthur Freed

Directed by George Sidney

CAST

Magnolia Hawks . . . . . . Kathryn Grayson
Julie Laverne . . . . Ava Gardner
Gaylord Ravenal . . . . . . Howard Keel
Capt. Andy Hawks . . . . Joe E. Brown
Ellie May Shipley . . . . . Marge Champion

ACADEMY AWARD NOMINATIONS

2 nominations, no wins

Best Cinematography, Color
Best Scoring of a Musical Picture

outlast Jerome Kern's day and mine." She was correct. Kern's immortal hymn to the Mississippi is so remarkably close to a true Negro spiritual that many feel it must be an American folk song.

The tune must be considered the highlight of the MGM movie version, too—in fact, all the Kern/Hammerstein songs were popular enough to make the soundtrack album the number-one seller for 1951. Also contributing to the film's success was a fine cast, including Howard Keel (of *Annie Get Your Gun* fame), Kathryn Grayson, and Ava Gardner, who did her own singing for "Bill," although her voice was dubbed for the torch-sung "Can't Help Lovin' Dat Man." Dancing by Marge and Gower Champion added to the appeal.

The show's popularity is still evident today, with frequent revivals by touring companies and dinner theaters. If you can't catch a live performance of this "classic," the film is just the ticket.

DAVID AND BATHSHEBA

20TH CENTURY-FOX
$4,720,000

"Three thousand years ago, David and Bathsheba ruled over the united tribes of Israel. This story of King David's reign is based on one of the world's oldest historical narratives written by an anonymous chronicler in the Second Book of Samuel of the Old Testament."
—PROLOGUE

INSPIRED BY the phenomenal success of Paramount's *Samson and Delilah*, Fox decided to jump on the Biblical bandwagon that would become so crowded during the '50s. The studio entered the race with Gregory Peck and Susan Hayward as *David and Bathsheba*. Since Biblical works were usually free of harsh censorship (you can't rewrite the word of God, after all), the film was full of lust, adultery, murder—all the good stuff. Moviegoers didn't object, and since *Quo Vadis?* would not be released for nearly three more months, there was little competition in that genre for the box office dollars.

The story of David and Bathsheba is drawn from the pages of the Old Testament, Second Book of Samuel,

with Peck as the shepherd/song composer/King of Israel, and Hayward as the notoriously beautiful and sexy Bathsheba. Problem: she's already married. Solution: send her hubby off to war, where, hopefully, he'll be killed (he

---

Screenplay by Philip Dunne

Produced by Darryl F. Zanuck

Directed by Henry King

CAST

David	Gregory Peck
Bathsheba	Susan Hayward
The Prophet Nathan . .	Raymond Massey
Uriah the Hittite	Kieron Moore
Michal	Jayne Meadows

ACADEMY AWARD NOMINATIONS

5 nominations, no wins

Best Story and Screenplay
Best Cinematography, Color
Best Art Direction-Set Decoration, Color
Best Scoring of a Dramatic or
  Comedy Picture
Best Costume Design, Color

---

is). The Hollywood ending is a bit more upbeat than the original story; producers seemed more concerned about box office than total Biblical accuracy.

By the end of the year, Susan Hayward was voted the number-one female box office star, with Gregory Peck in the number-two spot (his fourth year in the top 10). Rounding out the excellent cast were Raymond Massey as the prophet Nathan, Francis X. Bushman as King Saul, and Jayne Meadows as Michal.

The critics adored *David and Bathsheba*. *The New York Times* called it "a reverential and sometimes majestic treatment of chronicles that have lived three millennia . . . in concerning itself with an ageless romance, 'David and Bathsheba' admirably achieves its goal." And *The Hollywood Reporter* predicted a "sure box office hit . . . a big, luxurious, spectacular production that should promote big ticket sales . . ."

One point of interest is the depiction of the Ark of the Covenant. The design is virtually the same as in the 1981 hit film, *Raiders of the Lost Ark*, both having been drawn from the illustrations of medieval scholars.

5

THE GREAT CARUSO
METRO-GOLDWYN-MAYER
$4,531,000

"A man thinks he has a voice. The truth is, the voice has a man."

THE ABOVE LINE from *The Great Caruso* was not only true of the man portrayed in this musical biography, but was also true of Mario Lanza, the singer and actor who played the part of Enrico Caruso.

Mario's father owned a wholesale grocery business, but at night he escaped from the reality of his Philadelphia tenement neighborhood by playing opera records. By the time Mario (born Alfredo Cocozza) was 10, he knew several by heart. Yet, it wasn't until he was 20 years old that he finally sang. "Sitting in my father's room listening to Caruso sing 'Ch'ella mi creda' from Puccini's *Girl of the Golden West,* I suddenly opened my mouth and began to sing with him," Lanza told a reporter, according to the book *Hollywood Legends.* The voice definitely had a man. His father, moved to tears, insisted that young Mario study voice, and eventually the young man sang in summer festivals and other appearances. MGM signed him to a film contract following World War II, and he reached his peak in *The Great Caruso,* playing the legendary singer.

The film, suggested by Dorothy Car-uso's biography of her husband, is packed with operatic music from all the greats—Verdi, Puccini, Bach, Rossini, Ponchielli, Herbert, and DeCurtis. The oft-criticized American public, supposedly so lowbrow in its tastes, made the soundtrack album the number-three hit of the year, and a single from the album, "The Loveliest Night of the Year," was a number-three hit.

Mario Lanza wasn't the only actor to play *The Great Caruso* in 1951. That same year, there was an Italian film based on the life of the famous singer, titled *Enrico Caruso, Legend of a Voice.* The film starred Ermanno Randi, but was never any real competition for the Lanza vehicle, and quickly faded from sight.

A few other films followed for Mario Lanza—*Because You're Mine, The Student Prince* (voice only), and one or two others—but Lanza's volatile personality, coupled with an alcohol and drug problem and chronic obesity, helped ruin his career as well as his health. He died of a heart attack, in Rome, at the age of 38.

Screenplay by Sonya Levien and
 William Ludwig

Suggested by the biography of Enrico
 Caruso by Dorothy Caruso

Produced by Joe Pasternak

Directed by Richard Thorpe

CAST

Enrico Caruso	Mario Lanza
Dorothy Benjamin	Ann Blyth
Louise Heggar	Dorothy Kirsten
Maria Selka	Jarmila Novotna
Carlo Santi	Richard Hageman

ACADEMY AWARD NOMINATIONS

3 nominations, 1 win*

**Best Sound Recording
 Best Scoring of a Musical Picture
 Best Costume Design, Color

THIS IS CINERAMA

CINERAMA RELEASING CORPORATION (CRC)
$15,400,000

"Ladies and gentlemen, this is CINERAMA!"
—LOWELL THOMAS

IT STARTS WITH a basic 35-millimeter screen. Lowell Thomas, famed world traveler, narrates a very long black-and-white documentary on the history of art, from early cave paintings through 19th-century attempts at motion pictures. We are given the impression that all that has gone before had but one goal to attain—the miraculous achievement Thomas has been leading up to for ten tedious minutes—Cinerama! With a sudden smash cut to full color, the screen suddenly widens to three times its previous size as we enter a roller coaster, go up the ramp, then find ourselves hurtling at breakneck speed back down to a chorus of screams from the unseen patrons (we're in the front car) in the most memorable and famous point-of-view shot of all time.

Ask anyone what they know or remember about Cinerama and they will inevitably tell you, "The roller coaster ride." This sequence would be considered tame today by a generation raised on the great special effects of films like *Star Wars*, but seen as a museum piece, it is easy to understand why people were so enthralled.

To begin with, it was a big screen, a very big screen—certainly bigger than the tiny TVs in people's living rooms. It was not the first time wide-screen had been attempted, however. Back in 1896, an Englishman named Birt Acres shot a local regatta in 70-millimeter, but he soon abandoned the use of wide-gauge film as too costly. In 1929, *Fox Movietone Follies* became the first wide-screen 70-millimeter feature film shown in New York, but it was a curiosity, not ready for mass distribution.

Cinerama was developed by Frederick Waller of Huntington, New York. His original idea was to use 11 16-millimeter projectors to cover a vast area of screen. There were numerous technical problems at first, but eventually he was successful.

Through three separate 27-millimeter lenses—each of which roughly resembled the lens of a human eye—the Cinerama cameras took three pictures simultaneously on three separate rolls of film. Set at 48-degree angles to each other, each lens covered precisely one-third of the entire picture—the one on the right photographing the left third, the one on the left photographing the right third, and the one in the center shooting straight ahead. A single rotating shutter assured simultaneous exposures on each of the films, while single focus and diaphragm controls adjusted the settings on all three lenses at the same time. The footage was then shown in the theater by three projectors, producing a wider-than-average image. These projectors, grounded in concrete, were locked together by motors that automatically kept the three images in perfect synchronization on the screen. Tiny comb-like bits of steel were fitted into each projector at the side of the film gate. Jiggling up and down along the edges of the film at high speed, they fuzzed the edges of the pictures to minimize the lines between them. Oversized reels which fed film to the Cinerama projectors held 7,500 feet (50 minutes' worth) of film. It was a cumbersome process at best, by today's standards, but the novelty was just what was needed to compete with television.

Audiences ate it up. Tickets were on a reservations-only basis, often sold out weeks in advance. *This Is Cinerama* ran more than two years in New York alone, and played in limited engagements around the country. Only 47 theaters in the world were able to show Cinerama, with its 97-foot-wide screen and special equipment. Had even more theaters been able to make the equipment conversion, the film undoubtedly would have made even more millions.

The medium was definitely the message. There was absolutely no story in *This Is Cinerama*. In addition to the roller coaster, the audience watched a ballet, a helicopter ride over Niagara Falls, and a church organ service (with a locked-off camera, making for one of the dullest segments ever put on film—audiences, however, were enchanted). A gondola ride in Venice, bagpipes in Scotland, the Vienna Boy's Choir, and a bullfight in Spain, plus a ho-hum segment at Florida's Cypress Gardens, were all on the program. There were two excellent numbers. The first was a visit to La Scala Opera House in Italy, where we witnessed a spectacular performance of *Aida* with what seemed like half of Italy in the chorus. The second was the film's final segment, which featured a stirring flyover of the United States, including forests, wheatfields, the Golden Gate, and the Grand Canyon, all set to the music of the Mormon Tabernacle Choir.

This is the sort of film that will never be seen again by most people, since it is not suitable for release on videocassette. In 1988, there was a reissue of *This Is Cinerama* at Los Angeles' Cinerama Dome—a theater which claims to have never actually shown a film in Cinerama, and normally runs only modern blockbuster hits like *E.T.* and *Who Framed Roger Rabbit*. Most of the people in the audience were either film students or older couples, there to recapture some of the thrill they felt when Lowell Thomas first said those magic words.

Illustration from the *This is Cinerama* program booklet shows how Fred Waller's three-camera, three-projector process works.

Developed by Fred Waller

Stereophonic sound concept by Hazard Reeves

Produced by Merian C. Cooper and Robert L. Bendick

Narrated by Lowell Thomas

ACADEMY AWARD NOMINATIONS

1 nomination, no wins

Best Scoring of a Dramatic or Comedy Picture

Producer Merian C. Cooper received an honorary statuette "for his many innovations and contributions to the art of motion pictures."

Fred Waller was presented with a special Oscar "for designing and developing the multiple photographic and projection systems which culminated in Cinerama."

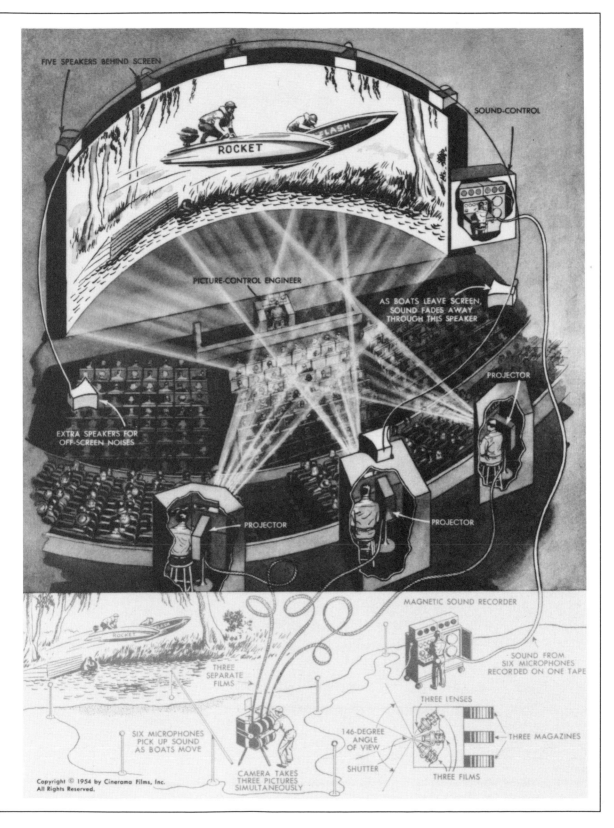

FIVE SPEAKERS BEHIND SCREEN

SOUND-CONTROL

ROCKET

PICTURE-CONTROL ENGINEER

AS BOATS LEAVE SCREEN, SOUND FADES AWAY THROUGH THIS SPEAKER

PROJECTOR

EXTRA SPEAKERS FOR OFF-SCREEN NOISES

PROJECTOR

PROJECTOR

MAGNETIC SOUND RECORDER

THREE SEPARATE FILMS

SOUND FROM SIX MICROPHONES RECORDED ON ONE TAPE

THREE LENSES

SIX MICROPHONES PICK UP SOUND AS BOATS MOVE

146-DEGREE ANGLE OF VIEW

THREE MAGAZINES

CAMERA TAKES THREE PICTURES SIMULTANEOUSLY

SHUTTER

THREE FILMS

THE GREATEST SHOW ON EARTH

PARAMOUNT
$14,000,000

"This is the story of the biggest of the big tops and the men and women who fight to make it to The Greatest Show on Earth."
—OPENING NARRATION

CECIL B. DEMILLE was 70 when he directed his 69th film. He proved he was still the master of the spectacle when he took his camera crew on the road to follow the Ringling Bros. and Barnum & Bailey circus to its winter headquarters in Sarasota, Florida. The movie was the perfect vehicle for the untiring showman—as *Time* put it, "a mammoth merger of two masters of malarkey for the masses: P. T. Barnum and Cecil B. DeMille."

In some ways, *The Greatest Show on Earth* seemed almost like a documentary, with DeMille's own narration telling us of the 58,000 pounds of fireproof canvas used to make up the Big Top. Over 60 circus acts paraded through the scenario—elephants, aerialists, sword swallowers, clowns, dogs, seals, lions and tigers and bears, oh, my! The man didn't miss a trick.

Of course, there was an excellent

Screenplay by Fredric M. Frank, Barre Lyndon, and Theodore St. John

From a story by Frank Cavett, Fredric M. Frank, and Theodore St. John

Produced and directed by Cecil B. DeMille

CAST

Holly	Betty Hutton
Sebastian	Cornel Wilde
Brad	Charlton Heston
Phyllis	Dorothy Lamour
"Buttons," a Clown	James Stewart

ACADEMY AWARD NOMINATIONS

5 nominations, 2 wins*

*Best Picture
Best Director (Cecil B. DeMille)
*Best Writing, Motion Picture Story (Frank Cavett, Frederic M. Frank, and Theodore St. John)
Best Film Editing
Best Costume Design, Color

Cecil B. DeMille was honored with the Irving G. Thalberg Memorial Award.

cast, too, with Charlton Heston (here in only his second film) and Betty Hutton, doing an outstanding follow-up to her *Annie Get Your Gun* performance. The expert intercutting of her own close-ups and her stunt double's performances on the trapeze are totally convincing.

And then there was Jimmy Stewart as Buttons, the doctor-turned-fugitive-clown whom we never see out of make-up. It was a dream come true for Stewart, who had always wanted to play such a part. In a recent television interview, he recalled a telegram he had sent DeMille. "I had never met Cecil B. DeMille. . . and I just said, 'Mr. DeMille, could you possibly find a place for me as a clown in your picture?' and

two days later he wrote me back, and he said, 'You're in!' "

One of the most memorable sequences is the train wreck. To achieve the special effect, a derailment of miniature trains was filmed, then skillfully interwoven with footage of full-scale models of upended individual cars. The rest is pure DeMille.

Uncredited were cameo appearances by Bob Hope and Bing Crosby, who appear as spectators in the audience, contentedly munching popcorn.

An ABC television series of *The Greatest Show on Earth* appeared in September, 1963, and lasted for one year. It starred Jack Palance and Stu Erwin, and featured regular performers from Ringling Bros. circus.

THE SNOWS OF KILIMANJARO

20TH CENTURY-FOX
$6,500,000

"Kilimanjaro is a snow-covered mountain 19,710 feet high and is said to be the highest mountain in Africa. Close to the western summit there is a dry and frozen carcass of a leopard. No one has explained what the leopard was seeking at that altitude."

—OPENING NARRATION

THE ABOVE OPENING to the film version of Ernest Hemingway's short story "The Snows of Kilimanjaro" is also the riddle that the central character, Harry Street, must solve. The leopard comes to represent Harry's own drive as a writer, a quest that impels him to struggle toward seemingly unattainable heights. Never mind if you miss the symbolism. It's still an epic film (did Hollywood make anything else in the '50s?) which reunited Gregory Peck with Susan Hayward—*David and Bathsheba* together again. Also adding spice to the cast was Ava Gardner as Peck's first love.

Screenplay by Casey Robinson

Based on short story by
Ernest Hemingway

Produced by Darryl F. Zanuck

Directed by Henry King

CAST

Harry	Gregory Peck
Helen	Susan Hayward
Cynthia	Ava Gardner
Countess Liz	Hildegarde Neff
Uncle Bill	Leo G. Carroll

ACADEMY AWARD NOMINATIONS

2 nominations, no wins

Best Cinematography, Color
Best Art Direction-Set Decoration, Color

Screenwriter Casey Robinson described the script to *Time* as "one-third Hemingway, one-third [Darryl F.] Zanuck, and one-third myself." And he didn't seem concerned that critics might attack him for changing to the traditional Hollywood "happy ending" in which Peck's character gets to live rather than meet the death Hemingway chose for him. Most critics allowed him to get away with it, and audiences didn't protest either.

The African footage—which led *The New York Times* to dub *Snows* "an eye-filling film"—was shot by a second unit dispatched to the continent to film wildlife and panoramic scenery, while the live action was done in Hollywood and on location nearby. A technique called "rear projection" was used for the scene where Gregory Peck shoots a rhinoceros. The African unit filmed the charging rhino on location, with someone shooting the poor beast dead for the benefit of the camera. Back on the Fox soundstage, that footage was then projected on the screen behind Peck, who at the proper moment aimed his blank-loaded rifle at the screen and fired.

④

IVANHOE
METRO-GOLDWYN-MAYER
$6,258,000

"In the 12th Century, at the close of the Third Crusade to free the Holy Land, a Saxon knight called Wilfred of Ivanhoe undertook a private crusade of his own. . . [Richard the Lionhearted's] disappearance had dealt a cruel blow to his unhappy country already in turmoil from the bitter conflict between Saxon and Norman."
—OPENING NARRATION

ENTER IVANHOE, in the person of Robert Taylor, a handsome young actor whom audiences proclaimed the number-three box office star of the year (his fifth year on the list). And at his side was another (though unrelated) Taylor, Elizabeth, in her first big box office hit since *Father of the Bride*.

While this wasn't a Biblical epic, it felt like it. There were battles, great tournaments on colorfully draped horses; there were lavish costumes, great scenery, and lots of extras, this time played by Britons in their native land. Producer Pandro S. Berman was proud of the fact he had saved MGM $650,000 by shooting on location in England's MGM facility there, and since three of the stars were British

born (Ms. Taylor, Joan Fontaine, and George Sanders all had British parentage), there was little problem with work permits for the cast.*

Second-unit direction was done by Yakima Canutt, who was noted for his work not only as a director but also as

---

Screenplay by Noel Langley

Adaptation by Aeneas MacKenzie

Produced by Pandro S. Berman

Directed by Richard Thorpe

CAST

Ivanhoe . . . . Robert Taylor
Rebecca . . . . Elizabeth Taylor
Rowena . . . . Joan Fontaine
De Bois-Guilbert . . . . George Sanders
Wamba . . . . Emlyn Williams

ACADEMY AWARD NOMINATIONS

3 nominations, no wins

Best Picture
Best Cinematography, Color
Best Scoring of a Dramatic or
  Comedy Picture

---

an actor and stuntman. In *Gone With the Wind*, for example, he was the Yankee deserter shot in the face by Scarlett O'Hara. During his career as second-unit director, he filmed backgrounds and long shots for such other box office hits as *Ben-Hur* (1959), *Spartacus* (1960), *El Cid* (1961), and *How the West Was Won* (1962).

It is interesting to note that Elizabeth Taylor played a Jewish girl in this film, although she was not raised in that faith. Seven years after *Ivanhoe*'s release, she converted to Judaism. According to Ms. Taylor, in her book *Elizabeth Takes Off*, "It had absolutely nothing to do with my past marriage to Mike [Todd] or my upcoming marriage to Eddie Fisher, both of whom were Jewish. It was something I had wanted to do for a very long time."

In 1957, *Ivanhoe* became a British-produced television series starring Roger Moore, who later made "The Saint"-hood before being drafted into James Bond-age. The 30-minute program ran for a year in syndication.

---

*British labor laws insist that casting be done with British actors unless just cause can be shown for importing foreign talent.

HANS CHRISTIAN ANDERSEN

RKO
$6,000,000

"Kaye is Andersen."
—*THE HOLLYWOOD REPORTER*

AND LUCKY for RKO that he was, too. In taking Danny Kaye out of his customary comedian-entertainer roles and putting him into the part of the beloved Danish storyteller, producer Samuel Goldwyn and director Charles Vidor gave children around the world the best Christmas present ever. For it is Danny's interaction with the youngsters in this movie that gives the film its magic, as every child who has ever seen it can attest. Many years later, when Danny Kaye was working with UNICEF and needy children worldwide, it became apparent that he was truly gifted when it came to dealing with kids.

Kaye's rare talent permeates every inch of this picture. Whether it's singing one of the movie's many memorable songs to a group of children, or telling a Hans Christian Andersen story to them, it is Danny's movie all the way.

There are many charming songs. Among the most memorable are "No

Screenplay by Moss Hart

From a story by Myles Connolly

Words and music by Frank Loesser

Produced by Samuel Goldwyn

Directed by Charles Vidor

CAST

Hans Christian Andersen	Danny Kaye
Niels	Farley Granger
Doro	Renee Jeanmaire
Peter	Joey Walsh
Otto	Phillip Tonge

ACADEMY AWARD NOMINATIONS

6 nominations, no wins

Best Cinematography, Color
Best Art Direction-Set Decoration, Color
Best Sound Recording
Best Song ("Thumbelina," music and
   words by Frank Loesser)
Best Scoring of a Musical Picture
Best Costume Design, Color

Two People," "Anywhere I Wander," "Inch Worm," "Ugly Duckling," "Copenhagen," "Thumbelina," and, of course, the title song. The album became the number-two selling soundtrack of the year.

As popular as the film was in the United States, it was without honor in Andersen's homeland. The Danes condemned it even before it had opened there on the basis that most of the film about their beloved storyteller was also a fairy tale. But when it finally opened in Denmark eight months after its American debut, the critics lauded Danny Kaye, and Denmark's biggest newspaper avowed that "it contains both poetry and art." Danish Queen Ingrid herself attended opening night, and that ended any doubt—*Hans Christian Andersen* was at last welcomed home.

This movie should be mandatory viewing for every child, or anyone who's ever been a child. Be sure to watch for it around holiday time, when many television stations offer it as a special treat.

PETER PAN
WALT DISNEY PRODUCTIONS
$24,532,000

1953

"You can fly, you can fly, you can fly!"

He flew, he wore a feathered cap, and he refused to grow up. He touched the child in all of us, brought to us by none other than that perennial child himself, Walt Disney.

When *Peter Pan* first flew across movie screens in 1953 straight into the hearts of the audience, the Disney factory had again found gold. The plot centers on Peter Pan, The Boy Who Never Grew Up, who travels to Never Never Land with the Darling children and does battle with Captain Hook and his pirates. Many re-releases of the animated feature have since followed, including the most recent one in the summer of 1989, which found Peter Pan, Wendy, John, Michael *et al.* earning their keep once again for Uncle Walt's company.

Yet Walt Disney himself was not particularly pleased with the film. He found Peter a rather cold character, one with whom he did not feel comfortable. Fortunately, several generations of children disagreed.

Back in 1939, Walt had optioned *Peter Pan* from the Hospital for Sick Children, in London, to whom Sir James M. Barrie had bequeathed ownership rights. (Until June, 1989, all for-profit productions of *Peter Pan* had to be cleared through this licensee.) When Disney took on the task of bringing the play to the screen, he tried to approximate what he felt Barrie himself might have done if animation had been at the playwright's command when his version opened in 1904. The original play directions and annotated scripts gave Disney many ideas during the three years it took to complete the $4,000,000 production.

During preparation, Walt had every one of his top animators, background painters, and character developers—over 100 artists—working on the project. More than 500,000 separate drawings were made, with more than 900 painted backgrounds, an all-time feature cartoon record to that date.

Traditionally, Peter Pan has always been played by a female. However, Walt chose Bobby Driscoll, veteran of a number of Disney films (*Song of the*

Margaret Kerry as a live model for Tinker Bell for the Disney animators.

South, So Dear to My Heart, and *Treasure Island*), to do the voice of Peter, breaking with that tradition, although the animated figure of the boy is basically androgynous.

The most drastic changes were in the character of Tinker Bell. On stage, Tink had always been portrayed as a beam of light. For his version, Disney chose to depict the pixie as a tiny humanoid with wings. If there is a scene-stealer in the movie, Tinker Bell is it. She flirts, she pouts, she even preens in front of a mirror, showing concern that she's gaining weight in the hips. When Wendy says she wants to give Peter a kiss, the little charmer literally flies into a tizzy. And at one point, Tinker Bell tries to find a way to seal Wendy's doom. Yet audiences loved this tiny vixen. Animator Marc Davis, one of the original "nine old men" who created many of the Disney animated classics, recalled to *Premiere* Magazine: "I hear from a lot of people how crazy they were about that little character. She was kind of sexy, and I think there was an appeal in that." Quite possibly true, since the artist used a live 18-year-old model named Margaret Kerry to pose for sketches of Tinker Bell. Kerry had been a child actress as well, appearing under her given name of Peggy Lynch in four *Little Rascal* featurettes.

Although no voice was necessary for Tink, who never speaks, actors were required for the other parts. Noteworthy are Kathryn Beaumont as the voice of Wendy (she spoke for Alice in 1951's *Alice in Wonderland*), and actor Hans

From a play by J. M. Barrie

Produced by Walt Disney

Directed by Hamilton Luske, Clyde Geronimi, and Wilfred Jackson

VOICES

Peter Pan	Bobby Driscoll
Wendy	Kathryn Beaumont
Captain Hook and George Darling	Hans Conried
Mary Darling	Heather Angel
Smee	Bill Thompson

Conried, who read for Mr. Darling and Captain Hook.

Several teams of songwriters helped to create the music. Most famous were Sammy Cahn and Sammy Fain, who wrote "The Elegant Captain Hook," "What Makes the Red Man Red," "You Can Fly," and "Your Mother and Mine." Songs by other writers include "A Pirate's Life," "Tee Dum, Tee Dee," and the memorable "Never Smile at a Crocodile."

When Walt Disney opened his first theme park, Disneyland, in 1955, one of the rides in "Fantasyland" was a "Peter Pan" adventure. Originally conceived as an experience for the younger set, it is not unusual today to find more adults than kids lined up for as long as 30 minutes to board a Pirate Ship and set sail over London with the words, "Come on everybody. Here we go-o-o-o!"

Roland Dupree and Kathy Beaumont model for Disney artists.

THE ROBE
20TH CENTURY-FOX
$17,500,000

"Rome. Master of the Earth, in the eighteenth year of the Emperor Tiberius, our legions stand guard on the boundaries of civilization . . . we have reached the point where there are more slaves in Rome than citizens . . ."
—OPENING NARRATION

LONG AFTER the silly plot about a curse on Christ's crucifixion garment had been forgotten, *The Robe* took its place in cinematic history as the first movie in CinemaScope. With the gauntlet having been thrown down by the novelty of Cinerama, every studio in town rushed to achieve its own big-screen miracle in order to lure in the couch potatoes. Like Cinerama, Cin-

Screenplay by Philip Dunne

Adaptation by Gina Kaus

From the novel by Lloyd C. Douglas

Produced by Frank Ross

Directed by Henry Koster

CAST

Marcellus Gallio	Richard Burton
Diana	Jean Simmons
Demetrius	Victor Mature
Peter	Michael Rennie
Caligula	Jay Robinson

ACADEMY AWARD NOMINATIONS

5 nominations, 2 wins*

Best Picture
Best Actor (Richard Burton)
Best Cinematography, Color
*Best Art Direction-Set Decoration, Color
*Best Costume Design, Color

An Honorary Award (statuette) went to 20th Century-Fox "in recognition of their imagination, showmanship and foresight in introducing the revolutionary process known as CinemaScope."

A statuette also went to Professor Henri Chretien, Earl Sponable, Sol Halprin, Lorin Grignon, Herbert Bragg, and Carl Faulkner of 20th Century-Fox Studios "for creating, developing and engineering the equipment, processes and techniques known as CinemaScope."

emaScope offered a wider screen, 68 feet wide and 24 feet high, but simplified the process by requiring only a single camera and single projector. Virtually any exhibitor could utilize the system, promising more dollars in their coffers.

With *The Robe*, 20th Century-Fox made good that promise. In the true tradition of the Biblical epic genre, the $5,000,000 production (the most expensive one of the year) had it all. Based on Lloyd Douglas's best-selling novel, there were lavish Technicolor sets and costumes, pomp and pageantry, gladiatorial contests, and a soaring musical score. The fact that handsome young actor Richard Burton played opposite beautiful young actress Jean Simmons didn't hurt, either. The film set a New York box office record, grossing close to $3,500,000 in the first 12 days.

The film's title refers to the crucifixion garment worn by Jesus. Richard Burton, as a Roman tribune assigned to carry out the crucifixion, wins Christ's robe in a game of dice. But for his "sin," he suffers from the delusion that he is cursed by the robe, deteriorating into mental agony, eventually vindicat-

ing himself by conversion and defense of his new-found faith. Although most critics found the acting and storyline only mediocre, they were unanimous in their praise of Fox's new wide-screen process. *The Hollywood Reporter* went to a banner headline:

CINEMASCOPE, 'ROBE' TRIUMPH
PREMIERE CROWDS THRILLED
IN N.Y. BY FIRST FILM MADE
IN REVOLUTIONARY PROCESS

Publisher W. R. Wilkerson continued by saying that "CinemaScope arrived at the Roxy Theatre here last night with a bang that must certainly have been heard all over the amusement world. All the hopes and promises of 20th-Fox have been fulfilled with the presentation of 'The Robe' in a medium that holds promise of revolutionizing the making of films and their presentation throughout the world."

With success like this, Fox couldn't wait to try for more, and a year later released a sequel, *Demetrius and the Gladiators*, with Victor Mature re-creating his role from *The Robe*. The sequel fell short of the mark, and the film only did about a third of the business of its predecessor.

FROM HERE TO ETERNITY
COLUMBIA
$12,200,000

"I never knew it could be like this."
—DEBORAH KERR TO
BURT LANCASTER

THE LINE WAS pure corn, but it was dialogue like this, along with the famous beach scene (SHE: "I've got a bathing suit under my dress." HE: "Me too.") that drew the fans to the theaters and gave Columbia a bona fide entry into the 1953 box office sweepstakes. The excellent production values made this film the most honored one in over a decade, taking top honors at the Oscars against contenders that included *The Robe, Shane, Julius Caesar,* and *Roman Holiday.* And in a year of widescreen epics, *From Here to Eternity* was shown in basic 35-millimeter, and in black and white at that.

Adapted from the novel by James Jones, the story concerns the lives of several soldiers stationed in Honolulu just prior to the bombing of Pearl Harbor. Montgomery Clift plays a former boxer who once blinded a sparring partner and refuses to fight again, even if it means humiliation. There are several levels of storytelling here, with Clift's sergeant (Burt Lancaster) involved with the neglected wife (Deborah Kerr) of the base's captain (Philip Ober).

Aside from the good filmmaking, the picture is also remembered for the

Screenplay by Daniel Taradash

Based on the novel by James Jones

Produced by Buddy Adler

Directed by Fred Zinnemann

CAST

Sgt. Milton Warden . . . Burt Lancaster
Robert E. Lee Prewitt . . Montgomery Clift
Karen Holmes . . . . Deborah Kerr
Angelo Maggio . . . . . . Frank Sinatra
Alma (Lorene) . . . . Donna Reed

ACADEMY AWARD NOMINATIONS

13 nominations, 8 wins*

*Best Picture
 Best Actor (Burt Lancaster)
 Best Actor (Montgomery Clift)
 Best Actress (Deborah Kerr)
*Best Supporting Actor (Frank Sinatra)
*Best Supporting Actress (Donna Reed)
*Best Director (Fred Zinnemann)
*Best Screenplay (Daniel Taradash)
*Best Cinematography, Black and White
*Best Sound Recording
 Best Scoring of a Dramatic or
  Comedy Picture
*Best Film Editing
 Best Costume Design, Black and White

This film won the most Academy Awards for any picture since *Gone With the Wind*.

controversy surrounding its casting. Deborah Kerr won her role as the Captain's wife after Joan Crawford fought with the studio over her wardrobe. Columbia boss Harry Cohn wanted Robert Mitchum in the part eventually played by Lancaster. He had Aldo Ray in mind for "Robert E. Lee Prewitt," a part that went to Montgomery Clift. Eli Wallach was signed for the role of "Maggio" but subsequently withdrew in favor of Frank Sinatra, who had pressured Harry Cohn until the mogul relented.

Rumors abounded that it was Sinatra's ties to the Mafia that clinched the part for him, a point which became a scenario in another book and film, *The Godfather.* Sinatra, however, denied any outside pressure, and indeed had applied enough of his own. His singing career had been on hold due to some throat problems, and he was anxious to get back into the public eye. Leaving wife Ava Gardner on location in Africa, he flew to Hollywood and screen-tested for the part. When Wallach bowed out, Frank got the role. Although he only received a reported salary of $8,000, he was ecstatic.

In 1979, a six-hour "From Here to Eternity" television miniseries ran on NBC. A ratings success, the network tried it as a weekly series the following August, but it survived only a month.

"Shane! Come back!"

BRANDON DE WILDE'S plaintive call at the end of *Shane* goes unacknowledged, as our hero rides off into the sunset. But the audience heard the call, and returned to the box office again and again, giving Paramount not only a big hit but a film that has become a classic in the Western genre. It was a truly "adult" Western, a trend that was quickly copied by television when "Gunsmoke" hit the airwaves two years later.

Based on the novel by Jack Schaefer, this film had a lot going for it, not the least of which was the beautiful scenery of Wyoming's Grand Tetons National Park.

Blatantly obvious in its symbolism, *Shane* brings together the forces of good (blond-headed Alan Ladd) and evil (dark-complected, black-outfitted Jack Palance—billed as *Walter* Jack Palance) for the eternal showdown.

There's never a doubt that we are watching a morality play, with its lessons to be taught, among them: "A gun is a tool . . . no better, no worse than any other tool—an ax, a shovel, or anything. A gun is as good or as bad as the man using it."

But don't get the impression that the movie is bogged down in preaching; it isn't. There's action, for instance, in what has to be the quintessential barroom brawl, a sequence that lasts a full eight minutes on screen. Fine performances were turned in by Ladd, Palance, Van Heflin as the boy's father, and Jean Arthur as Heflin's wife, who has an eye for the drifter Shane. But the old Hollywood adage about never working with children or dogs applies here (there's one of each), with Brandon de Wilde stealing many a scene. As *The New York Times* pointed out: "It is Master de Wilde with his bright face, his clear voice and his resolute boyish ways who steals the affections of the audience and clinches 'Shane' as a most unusual film."

De Wilde was born into a theatrical family and came to the Broadway stage at the age of nine in *The Member of the Wedding.* Following *Shane* and an Oscar nomination, he starred in his own TV series in the 1953–54 season ("Jamie"). He later appeared in films like *Blue Denim* and *Hud,* but met with a tragic end in 1972 in a car accident at the age of 29.

In 1966, ABC attempted a television series of *Shane.* It had a fine cast, including David Carradine and Jill Ireland, but it lasted only three months.

Screenplay by A. B. Guthrie Jr.

Based on the novel by Jack Schaefer

Additional dialogue by Jack Sher

Produced and directed by George Stevens

CAST

Shane	Alan Ladd
Mrs. Starrett	Jean Arthur
Mr. Starrett	Van Heflin
Joey Starrett	Brandon de Wilde
Wilson	Jack Palance

ACADEMY AWARD NOMINATIONS

6 nominations, 1 win*

Best Picture
Best Supporting Actor
  (Brandon de Wilde)
Best Supporting Actor (Jack Palance)
Best Director (George Stevens)
Best Writing, Screenplay
*Best Cinematography, Color

HOW TO MARRY A MILLIONAIRE
20TH CENTURY-FOX
$7,300,000

IF THIS MOVIE were being made today, the title might be "How to *Become* a Millionaire," and would probably end up something like the Melanie Griffith film, *Working Girl*. Today's '90s women don't dream about marrying money, they find ways to earn it.

But in the '50s, times were different, and it was with great pride that Fox trotted out its second CinemaScope picture of the year. The light comedy was just the thing to offset that studio's other centerpiece, *The Robe*. Audiences were now primed for the wide screen, and Fox wasn't about to let them down.

Among the film's assets were its three female stars: Lauren Bacall, noted for "The Look" and her deep, sexy voice; Betty Grable, the World War II pinup girl admired for her sexy legs; and Marilyn Monroe, the 26-year-old blonde bombshell who was famous for her sexy . . . everything.

The movie itself was a delight. There were beautiful sets, and attractive costumes by Bill Travilla in a fashion-show sequence that is still modern-looking by today's standards. There was clever "in" dialogue, with producer-screenwriter Nunnally Johnson poking fun at his real-life cast. At one point, Lauren Bacall's character says, "I've always liked older men. Look at Roosevelt, look at Churchill, look at that old fellow, what's his name in *African Queen*—absolutely crazy about him." Then there is the banter between Betty Grable and Fred Clark:

BETTY
Good old Harry James.

FRED
Really, how can you tell?

BETTY
Because it *is* Harry James.

RADIO ANNOUNCER
You're listening to the music of Ziggy Colombo.

BETTY
Turn that liar off!

These very inside jokes were easily-understood details of the private lives of two of the film's stars—Humphrey Bogart was the "what's his name" star married to Lauren Bacall, and Harry James, "Ziggy Colombo," was the husband of Betty Grable. It was little bits like this that kept the audience coming back for more. And as if the feminine scenery weren't enough, Fox made sure to use real locations, from the New York skyline to the snow-covered timberland of Maine.

In 1958, Fox tried a syndicated television show based on this picture. It starred a promising newcomer, Barbara Eden, but like so many prior attempts to translate hit movies into TV shows, it lasted only a season.

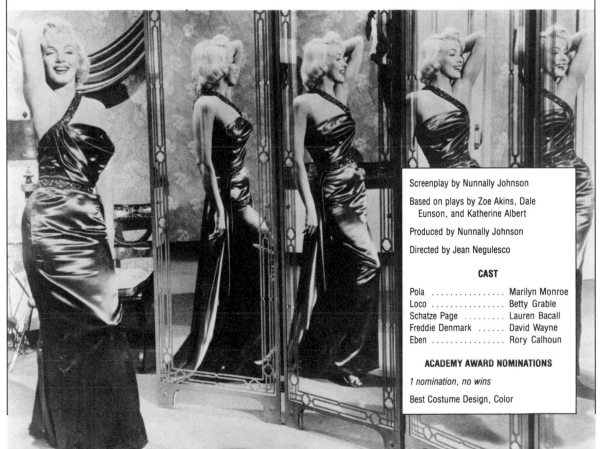

Screenplay by Nunnally Johnson

Based on plays by Zoe Akins, Dale Eunson, and Katherine Albert

Produced by Nunnally Johnson

Directed by Jean Negulesco

CAST

Pola	Marilyn Monroe
Loco	Betty Grable
Schatze Page	Lauren Bacall
Freddie Denmark	David Wayne
Eben	Rory Calhoun

ACADEMY AWARD NOMINATIONS

1 nomination, no wins

Best Costume Design, Color

1954

WHITE CHRISTMAS
PARAMOUNT
$12,000,000

CHRISTMAS IN October? It must have felt like it at Paramount Pictures when they released the movie *White Christmas* and the box office dollars began to chime like Yuletide bells.

How could they miss? Not only did the movie have stars Bing Crosby, Danny Kaye, Rosemary Clooney, and Vera-Ellen, but it had something even more wonderful.

VistaVision. Paramount's answer to Fox's CinemaScope, virtually indistinguishable from the other widescreen format. And what better way to introduce this modern miracle of the moviehouse than to use proven material?

By now, Bing Crosby and the song "White Christmas" were synonymous—the holiday and the crooner were Siamese twins, joined at the warbling throat. The song harkens back to a 1942 musical, *Holiday Inn,* when Bing first sang "White Christmas." It won an Oscar for its composer, Irving Berlin, who presented it to himself onstage—the only person ever to do

Screenplay by Norman Krasna and Melvin Frank

Music and lyrics by Irving Berlin

Produced by Robert E. Dolan

Directed by Michael Curtiz

CAST

Bob Wallace . . . . Bing Crosby
Phil Davis . . . . Danny Kaye
Betty . . . . Rosemary Clooney
Judy . . . . Vera-Ellen
General Waverly . . . . . Dean Jagger

ACADEMY AWARD NOMINATIONS

1 nomination, no wins

Best Song ("Count Your Blessings Instead of Sheep," words and music by Irving Berlin)

Danny Kaye received an Honorary Award (statuette) "for his unique talents, his service to the Academy, the motion picture industry, and the American people."

that. Berlin was entitled: "White Christmas" went on to become the best-selling record of all time, with over 30,000,000 copies sold to date. Even so, the story is told of how Berlin paced the halls during the filming of *White Christmas,* nervous about how Bing would perform it this time, until Crosby told him to go back to his office and relax.

A couple of other memorable tunes rounded out the musical program. "Sisters" has become a classic since it was introduced in this picture. Best of all is the send-up treatment given to it by Crosby and Kaye in drag. Other musical numbers include "The Best Things Happen While You're Dancing," "Count Your Blessings," and reprises from earlier Berlin hits—"The Old Man" and "Mandy."

For the record, there was a plot, but it seemed incidental to the songs. Bing, Danny, Rosie, and Vera-Ellen depart warm, balmy Florida for a New England ski lodge at Christmastime, dreaming of all the snow they'll soon

20,000 LEAGUES UNDER THE SEA

WALT DISNEY PRODUCTIONS
$11,267,000

"Got a whale of a tale to tell you . . ."

IT WAS ONLY fitting that Walt Disney be the one to bring Jules Verne's classic undersea tale, *20,000 Leagues Under the Sea*, to the screen. The two men had much in common, both being among the greatest visionaries of their times. Writing this adventure in 1869, Verne described the forerunner of the modern *nuclear* submarine, as well as predicting the aqualung. It wasn't until decades later that these things came to pass.

Verne's visions were never in better hands. For years, MGM had been toying with the idea of bringing this story to the screen, but it never got off the drawing boards. When Walt's idea

men suggested they produce an underwater adventure, he decided to purchase the property from Metro. The film was given the big-budget treatment, with $5,000,000 being spent in bringing Captain Nemo and the Nautilus to life. Much of the money went to secure a top cast, including James Mason as the farsighted but demented captain, along with Kirk Douglas, Peter Lorre, and Paul Lukas.

But most of the budgetary demands were for the sets and special effects. A 200-foot-long model of the submarine was built, and although much of the underwater footage was shot on location in the clear, fish-laden waters of Nassau, a great deal of photography had to be done under studio-controlled

conditions. To facilitate this, Disney built an entirely new soundstage at the Burbank studios, housing a 90-by-165-foot tank 12 feet deep.

Still more money was spent in filming the attack by a giant squid in the newly-built tank. It cost $200,000 and took eight days to film the sequence, the costliest scene in the movie.

The investment paid off. *20,000 Leagues Under the Sea* did well at the box office, especially with the younger set, and the critics acclaimed it as well. *Variety* called the film "a very special kind of picture making, combining photographic ingenuity, imaginative story telling and fiscal daring . . . ultra high box-office around the world."

A prediction worthy of Verne himself.

Sketch for the original poster of Walt Disney's *20,000 Leagues Under the Sea*.

Screenplay by Earl Felton

Based on the story by Jules Verne

Produced by Walt Disney

Directed by Richard Fleischer

CAST

Ned Land	Kirk Douglas
Captain Nemo	James Mason
Professor Arronnax	Paul Lukas
Conseil	Peter Lorre
Mate on Nautilus	Robert J. Wilke

ACADEMY AWARD NOMINATIONS

3 nominations, 2 wins*

*Best Art Direction-Set Decoration, Color
Best Film Editing
*Best Special Effects

find. Unfortunately, there isn't any when they arrive at the inn—the ski tow is being used to dry the wash in the warm air. And wouldn't you know it, Bing and Danny's old army general is the unfortunate new owner of the inn, and because there's no snow, business is terrible. No problem for these song-and-dance men and women. Let's put on a show, round up the general's old division, and fill this puppy up to the rafters—surprise the old coot, watch him fight back the tears. Of course, it works, and of course, it snows flakes the size of tennis balls, just in time for the holidays.

Critics were definitely snowed by the production's music, Technicolor, and lavish choreographed routines coming at them in VistaVision. *The New York Times* wrote: "The colors on the big screen are rich and luminous, the images are clear and sharp . . . director

Michael Curtiz has made his picture look good." *The Hollywood Reporter* immediately sized up the box office potential, offering these words of advice: "The exceptional theatre operator . . . will spare no effort to let all veterans of World War II know that this is their picture."

The film went over well with nearly everyone, not just veterans, and for the 12th year in a row, Bing Crosby was voted among the top 10 box office stars, this time perched squarely at the top. Not far behind was his co-star, Danny Kaye, at number three.

Kaye had a prolific film career both prior to and following his performance in *White Christmas*. Born David Daniel Kaminski in 1913 in Brooklyn, he was a garment center tailor's son who quit school at 13 to learn comedy as a busboy in upstate New York's "Borscht Belt." Vaudeville and nightclub work

followed, and by 1939 he had landed a part in a Broadway review. In 1943, after Kaye had made a few two-reelers, Samuel Goldwyn signed him to appear in his comedies; soon a succession of films followed, including *Up in Arms* (1944), *Wonder Man* (1945), *The Secret Life of Walter Mitty* (1947), *The Inspector General* (1949), *Hans Christian Anderson* (1952; see page 103), and *Knock on Wood* (1953). Following *White Christmas*, Kaye made the popular films *The Court Jester* (1956) and *The Five Pennies* (1959). In the '60s, he had his own successful TV variety program, which won him both an Emmy and a Peabody Award. Work with UNICEF, more Broadway musical performances, and some hands-on experiences conducting the New York Philharmonic and other symphony orchestras rounded out his prolific career. He died in 1987 at the age of 74.

REAR WINDOW

PARAMOUNT
$9,812,271

ALFRED HITCHCOCK'S *Rear Window* has become one of the most written about, studied, dissected, and analyzed films in cinematic history. It purports to be a simple story: a man (James Stewart) is confined to a wheelchair and uses the time to witness the everyday life in his Greenwich Village apartment courtyard. Chief among his observations: the murder of one of his neighbors.

The film can be viewed from almost as many angles as Stewart's courtyard. It is at once a comedy, a mystery, a psychological drama, a love story, social commentary—the list is long enough to have led to several in-depth studies of the classic film. But most of all, it is what it is supposed to be: *entertainment*, the kind only the "master of the macabre" could give us.

Hitchcock had a habit of reusing the same actors in his films. In addition to *Rear Window*, Jimmy Stewart appeared in Hitch's *The Rope* (1948), *The Man Who Knew Too Much* (1956), and *Vertigo* (1958); Stewart's co-star, Grace Kelly, was cast in two additional Hitchcockian thrillers—*Dial M for Murder*

(1954) and *To Catch a Thief* (1955).

Most critics never thought of Grace Kelly as an acting powerhouse, although she won the 1954 Oscar for *The Country Girl*. But Hitchcock was said to have used her for her "sexual elegance" along with her humor,

---

Screenplay by John Michael Hayes

From a short story by Cornell Woolrich

Produced and directed by Alfred Hitchcock

CAST

Jeff	James Stewart
Lisa Fremont	Grace Kelly
Thomas J. Doyle	Wendell Corey
Stella	Thelma Ritter
Lars Thorwald	Raymond Burr

ACADEMY AWARD NOMINATIONS

4 nominations, no wins

Best Director (Alfred Hitchcock)
Best Screenplay
Best Cinematography, Color
Best Sound Recording

---

warmth, and serenity. (A few years later, Prince Rainier of Monaco agreed—he married her and made her his Princess Grace in the oft-told Hollywood fairy-tale-come-true.)

Also noteworthy in the cast is Raymond Burr as the man who chops his wife up into cutlets. (Fortunately, this is never actually seen on screen.) Burr is familiar to television audiences for his portrayals of "Perry Mason" and "Ironside," but in 1954, he was virtually unknown to the public. He had appeared in a few films as the "heavy," but his name was not a household word. Only 37 years old when he was cast as the murderer in *Rear Window*, he was too young-appearing for the part as it was written, so Hitchcock had his hair died gray.

Rear Window sat on the shelf for 30 years after its initial release, finally reappearing on the big screen in 1984 and eventually on videocassette. When it was re-released, it opened a legal can of worms having to do with copyright law and its effects on the estates of deceased writers. These issues are still being resolved in the courts.

1954

(4)

THE CAINE MUTINY

COLUMBIA
$8,700,000

"There has never been a mutiny on a ship of the United States Navy. The truths of this film lie not in its incidents but in the way a few men meet the crisis of their lives . . ."
—PROLOGUE

IT IS FORTUNATE that this film opens with that disclaimer. So convincing is the movie based upon Herman Wouk's Pulitzer Prize-winning novel, that audiences unfamiliar with the book thought they were seeing a re-enactment of fact.

Producer Stanley Kramer insisted on the disclaimer, stating this was his own idea and not a requirement dictated by the United States Navy. Ever since the film was announced as a project by Columbia, rumors abounded that the Navy had been at odds with the studio, first saying they might permit filming but only if the story was not labeled a "mutiny," later insisting the producers eliminate the character of Captain Queeg, the neurotic skipper. Columbia and Kramer got frequent coverage in the press by squelching these rumors, giving the film some good advance publicity.

When the picture was finally released, the rumors still abounded, but they only added to the attraction at the box office. Even *Newsweek* commented: "There must be something basically healthy about a nation whose armed services not only permit but abet the production of such clinically observant films as 'From Here to Eternity' and 'The Caine Mutiny.' . . ." The reviewer then praised all involved, summing up by calling *The Caine Mutiny* "one of the year's best films, with a half dozen of the year's best performances."

Most outstanding was the work of Humphrey Bogart. It was a dramatic triumph for the actor most noted for playing gangsters and scoundrels. It was his last great role—less than three years later, Bogey died of cancer.

Other memorable performances were turned in by Jose Ferrer, Van Johnson, Fred MacMurray, and E. G. Marshall as the judge advocate. Marshall seemed to be born to the bar—he later went on to star as an attorney on the TV show "The Defenders" (CBS, 1961–1965).

In 1988, *The Caine Mutiny* was remade as a movie for television, so be sure to check listings carefully before watching or taping to determine which version is being broadcast.

Screenplay by Stanley Roberts

From the novel by Herman Wouk

Produced by Stanley Kramer

Directed by Edward Dmytryk

CAST

Captain Queeg	Humphrey Bogart
Lieut. Barney Greenwald	Jose Ferrer
Lieut. Steve Maryk ...	Van Johnson
Lieut. Tom Keefer	Fred MacMurray
Ensign Willie Keith ...	Robert Francis

ACADEMY AWARD NOMINATIONS

7 nominations, no wins

Best Picture
Best Actor (Humphrey Bogart)
Best Supporting Actor (Tom Tully)
Best Screenplay
Best Sound Recording
Best Scoring of a Dramatic or Comedy Picture
Best Film Editing

THE GLENN MILLER STORY
UNIVERSAL-INTERNATIONAL
$7,590,994

GLENN MILLER and his Orchestra rode the crest of a wave of big bands in the '30s and '40s whose popularity set millions of young people dancing to the "swing" beat. When Miller died in 1944 while serving in Europe as the Army Air Force's bandmaster, a generation mourned him. That a biographical film of his life would be made was only a question of time.

In Jimmy Stewart, Universal found the perfect actor to play the mild-mannered, spectacled bandleader. To prepare for the role, Stewart signed on with a trombone tutor named Joe Yukl, but was soon fired as a pupil when it was discovered he really had no aptitude for the "bone." Stewart said that the sounds emanating from the instrument so upset Yukl that he had taken to kicking his dog. A solution was found when Stewart plugged up the

mouthpiece and maneuvered the slide to approximate the correct positions. It worked, even fooling some professional musicians.

Stewart's portrayal of the bandleader was so effective, in fact, that Miller's mother sent her compliments to the actor, although, as Stewart told *KCET* Magazine, "she was sorry that I wasn't better looking."

Music was the focal point, of course, with guest appearances by many popular stars of the era, including Louis Armstrong, Gene Krupa, and the Modernaires. Credited with "Musical Adaptation" was Henry Mancini, with one of his earliest screen credits.

The "Tuxedo Junction" number in which Stewart as Miller conducts his orchestra at a motion picture "scoring" session is quite accurate, giving viewers a good behind-the-scenes look at

how a real session takes place. Only in the last few years has the method of scoring changed—instead of a large screen running a black-and-white print with cues for the conductor, many modern studios now use TV monitors to roll film-on-tape, a much more inexpensive procedure. And of course there is *instant* tape playback today, rather than the "wax" they promised Glenn Miller "after lunch."

Nino Tempo, who had the number-one record "Deep Purple" with sister April Stevens in 1963, appears in a bit part. Glenn Miller's friend Chummy MacGregor served as technical advisor on the film, here played by Harry Morgan (credited as "Henry" Morgan). Television fans of "M*A*S*H" may recognize him as Colonel Potter, although he is quite a bit younger here. There's no mistaking that voice, though.

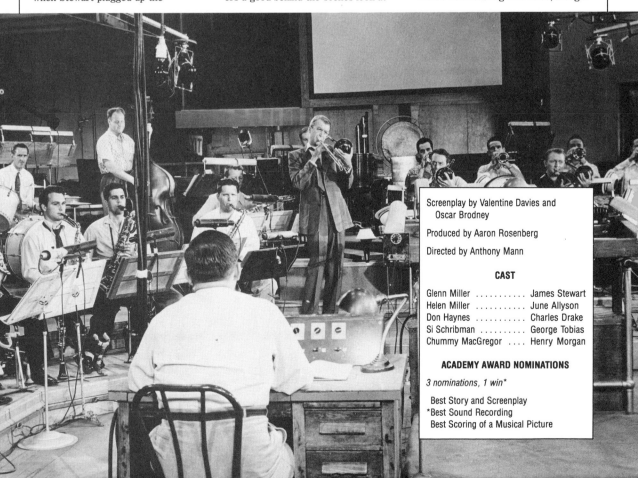

Screenplay by Valentine Davies and
Oscar Brodney

Produced by Aaron Rosenberg

Directed by Anthony Mann

CAST

Glenn Miller	....	James Stewart
Helen Miller	....	June Allyson
Don Haynes	....	Charles Drake
Si Schribman	....	George Tobias
Chummy MacGregor	....	Henry Morgan

ACADEMY AWARD NOMINATIONS

3 nominations, 1 win*

Best Story and Screenplay
*Best Sound Recording
Best Scoring of a Musical Picture

1

LADY AND THE TRAMP
WALT DISNEY PRODUCTIONS
$40,249,000

"In the whole history of the world, there is but one thing that money cannot buy, to wit—the wag of a dog's tail."

—JOSH BILLINGS

ONE EVENING after a long day at his drawing board back in 1925, Walt Disney had forgotten a dinner engagement, so he brought home a peace offering to his bride—a puppy in a hat box. The image stayed in his mind, and in 1937 he began plans for an animated adventure about a sedate cocker spaniel. About the same time, he read a short story by Ward Greene called "Happy Dan, the Whistling Dog." When Walt joked about how the two dogs should get together, Greene wrote a story called "Happy Dan, the Whistling Dog, and Miss Patsy, the Beautiful Spaniel." Several interruptions later, the tale evolved into the now-famous *Lady and the Tramp*, one of the most beloved and enduring of the Disney classics.

One of the qualities that is so impressive about this movie is how the story is told from a dog's point of view. Anyone who has ever been owned by a dog will understand. For instance, Lady refers to her humans as "Jim Dear" and "Darling"—after all, that's what they call each other. And the cartoon is packed with commentary on human life. "Remember," cautions Jock in his Scottie's burr, "they're only humans

after all." Tramp, who describes himself as "footloose and collar-free," dismisses apes as "too closely related to humans." And then there's the wonderful dialogue about babies:

> LADY
> What's a baby?
>
> JOCK
> Well, they resemble humans.
>
> BLOODHOUND
> But I'd say a mite smaller.
>
> JOCK
> Aye, and they walk on all fours.
>
> BLOODHOUND
> And if I remember correctly, they beller a lot.
>
> JOCK
> Aye, and they're expensive. You'll no' be permitted to play with it.
>
> BLOODHOUND
> But they're mighty sweet.
>
> JOCK
> And verra, verra soft, Tramp. Just a cute little bundle . . . of trouble. They scratch, pinch, pull ears.

Aside from the love story between the two title dogs, all sorts of canine characters cavort in this animated feature (the first ever made in Cinema-Scope). There's a Russian wolfhound who quotes Gorky, the German-accented Dachsie, and the sultry ex-show-dog named Peg, whose voice was provided by songstress Peggy Lee.* Miss Lee also co-wrote five of the film's songs, including the jazzy number "He's a Tramp." Additionally, she provided the voices for three other characters.

As with the live-animal studies for *Bambi*, plenty of pooches were paraded through Disney's Burbank studio for the animators to study and sketch. Their thorough understanding of how dogs react and move is clearly evident to any dog owner.

Story by Erdman Penner, Joe Rinaldi, Ralph Wright, and Don DaGradi

Based on an original story by Ward Greene

Songs written by Peggy Lee, Sonny Burke, and Walt Disney

Produced by Walt Disney

Directed by Hamilton Luske, Clyde Geronimi, and Wilfred Jackson

VOICES

Darling, Peg, Si, and Am .	Peggy Lee
Lady	Barbara Luddy
Tramp	Larry Roberts
Jock, Bull, Dachsie	Bill Thompson
Trusty	Bill Baucon

---

*In 1988, Peggy Lee filed a $25,000,000 suit against Walt Disney Productions, saying that in violation of her contract, the company had not secured her approval prior to releasing the videocassette version of *Lady and the Tramp*.

CINERAMA HOLIDAY

CINERAMA RELEASING CORPORATION (CRC)
$12,000,000

Cinerama was still big cinema in 1955. When the process was first mass-shown in 1952 (see page 98), it made box office history with its "Hey, look what we can do" production. So it isn't surprising that the producers wanted to show more of their stuff before the novelty wore off.

Producer Louis de Rochemont found a unifying thread this time for the basic travelogue format, choosing a honeymooning couple from Kansas City and a young couple from Zurich, Switzerland, and putting them on the road for a *Cinerama Holiday*. The results? Your basic travelogue.

The "exchange student"-type film saw the Swiss couple, Fred and Beatrice Troller of Zurich, touring the U.S. on a Vespa motorbike, exploring the likes of such far-West sights as Las Vegas, an Apache Indian Reservation, and a cocktail lounge atop San Francisco's Mark Hopkins Hotel. From the Top o' the Mark to the top of the Alps, we find the Americans, John and Betty Marsh, skiing and bobsledding, making full use of the Cinerama process à la the roller-coaster sequence from the first film. They then proceed to Paris to see High Mass at Notre Dame, the boulevards, the Louvre, and the ballet. The picture ends with the four travelers back in New York at a performance of Cinerama. For the finale, there is a fireworks display with the American flag, the Statue of Liberty, and the Eiffel Tower.

The couples were non-professionals, carefully selected from screen tests. When not skipping about the globe sightseeing, the foursome compare cultures. "Does John really do the

THE **2**ND CINERAMA PRESENTATION

Based on "America Through a French Looking Glass" by Renee & Pierre Gosset

Narration written by John Stuart Martin

Adaptation by Otis Carney and Louis de Rochemont III

Produced by Louis de Rochemont

Directed by Robert Bendick and Philippe de Lacy

Narrated by Martin Weldon

dishes?" asks the Swiss Mrs. "Well, under pressure and without enthusiasm, he'll do some of them sometimes. Doesn't Fred?" The Alpine hausfrau is aghast. "I should say not! That's my domain!" So much for the status of women in the '50s.

Cinerama was no longer the darling of the critics, although there was general praise for the content as "a good travelogue/documentary." But on closer inspection, the process wasn't as perfect as had once been thought. *The Hollywood Reporter,* for instance, noted that "there seem to have been some

improvements in Cinerama since it was first introduced, but the lines dividing the three pictures still are there, though less visible; and in some scenes the jiggling of the two side pictures in opposite directions to the center picture is distracting and annoying. Also, the center panel often is a different color shade than the two side panels."

But for the uncritical eye of movie audiences, *Cinerama Holiday* was still a good ride even without a roller coaster, and they made it the top film of the year (surpassed in re-releases by *Lady and the Tramp*).

MISTER ROBERTS
WARNER BROS.
$8,500,000

THE STORY OF *Mister Roberts* successfully navigated the waters from best-seller to stage hit to screen success, but there were some land mines along the way. John Ford was signed to direct the film based on Thomas Heggen's novel and Joshua Logan's play. Ford refused to direct unless Henry Fonda, who had already played the part on stage over a thousand times, was signed to reprise the role of Lieutenant (j.g.) Roberts (Warner Bros. wanted either William Holden or Marlon Brando). But all was not roses even after the studio capitulated, and Ford feuded with Fonda, the director eventually leaving after the first week's filming. Mervyn LeRoy was quickly drafted to fill his shoes, and the two received a Hollywood rarity—a shared directing credit.

The play was transplanted to the screen virtually intact from its familiar play form, and audiences were well acquainted with the voyages of the USS *Reluctant*, affectionately called "The Bucket," as she slogged through the backwaters of the Pacific with her vital cargo of toothpaste and toilet paper. It was practically a foregone conclusion that this would be a big hit, if not the biggest hit that year. Aside from Fonda, there was an equally fine cast including James Cagney as the crusty ship's captain; William Powell as the doctor (famous for his grain alcohol/Coke/iodine/hair tonic cocktails); and young Jack Lemmon as Ensign Pulver, "easily the most engaging of Hollywood's new comedians" (*Time* Magazine). The Academy thought so, too, and awarded him the Oscar.

Life Magazine awarded the coveted cover spot to Henry Fonda, proclaiming "*Mister Roberts* is finally a movie." The great publicity meant more dollars in Warner Bros.' coffers as rave reviews continued. *The New York Times* announced: "Now hear this! Another 21-gun salute is hereby accorded 'Mister Roberts' . . . to 'Mister Roberts' and all hands involved in one of the season's greatest pleasures: 'Well done!'"

In 1964, an inevitable sequel was attempted. *Ensign Pulver* starred Robert Walker, Jr. (son of Jennifer Jones and Robert Walker), and featured Walter Matthau, Burl Ives, and Tommy Sands. The film also had a pack of future big stars like Jack Nicholson, James Farentino, Larry Hagman, and James Coco. But *Ensign Pulver* lacked the warm appeal of the original. So, too, did a "Mister Roberts" television series starring Roger Smith. It survived a year on NBC (1965–66).

Screenplay by Frank Nugent and
    Joshua Logan

Based on the play by Thomas Heggen and
    Joshua Logan

From the novel by Thomas Heggen

Produced by Leland Hayward

Directed by John Ford and Mervyn LeRoy

CAST

Lieutenant Roberts . . . . . . Henry Fonda
The Captain . . . . James Cagney
Doc . . . . William Powell
Ensign Pulver . . . . Jack Lemmon
Lt. Ann Girard . . . . Betsy Palmer

ACADEMY AWARD NOMINATIONS

3 nominations, 1 win*

Best Picture
*Best Supporting Actor (Jack Lemmon)
Best Sound Recording

4

BATTLE CRY
WARNER BROS.
$8,100,000

"They call me Mac. The name's not important. It's January, 1942. Marine outposts all over the world have fallen to the Japanese. Our ranks are empty and ill equipped. We need help. And from every part of the country, kids are answering the call."

—OPENING NARRATION

Even though the war had been over for ten years, *Battle Cry* was Warner Bros.' first successful war picture. Taking a gamble on Leon Uris' best-selling 1953 novel, the studio found that the war still meant big business at the box office.

Basically a boot-camp-to-battlefield "recruitment" film, *Battle Cry* follows a platoon of baby-faced Marine recruits through basic training to their assignments in World War II in the Pacific. Along the way, the boys become men, drinking and barroom brawling, as well as falling for women in their base of

operations—in this case, New Zealand. The film climaxes with the bloody invasion of the beaches of Saipan.

As with any good drama, it was the

Screenplay by Leon M. Uris

Based on the novel by Leon M. Uris

Directed by Raoul Walsh

CAST

Major Huxley	Van Heflin
Andy	Aldo Ray
Kathy	Mona Freeman
Pat	Nancy Olson
Sergeant Mac	James Whitmore

ACADEMY AWARD NOMINATIONS

1 nomination, no wins

Best Scoring of a Dramatic or
  Musical Picture

---

characters that appealed to the audience. The well-stratified cast included James Whitmore as the inevitable Old Sarge, Van Heflin as the colonel with the soft heart beneath a skin of steel, and Tab Hunter as a young collegian-turned-leatherneck. Nancy Olson provided the love interest for another young recruit played by Aldo Ray. Also in the cast were Fess Parker (of "Davy Crockett" fame), William Campbell (who would later became popular with "Star Trek" fans for having guest-starred in two episodes), and Anne Francis (another science-fiction favorite, from *Forbidden Planet*).

Excellent reviews brought encouraging news to exhibitors who were advised to count on huge takes. They weren't disappointed. *The Hollywood Reporter* headlined "'BATTLE CRY' REAL BIG ONE HEADED FOR B.O. BONANZA," while *Variety* predicted "good box office expectations."

War was indeed big business.

OKLAHOMA!
MAGNA THEATRE CORPORATION
$7,100,000

"Oh, what a beautiful morning!"

AND OH, WHAT a beautiful matinee and evening performance as well. 30,000,000 theatergoers had already seen the Rodgers and Hammerstein musical, which had been appearing on stages for over five years. The eagerly-awaited film version delivered all that had been promised, and more.

It couldn't miss. Joseph M. Schenck, an independent producer recently resigned from Fox, formed Magna Theatre Corporation and promptly became one of the few independent producer/distributors ever to have a top-five film. His firm spent $5,000,000 to bring *Oklahoma!* to the big screen—and big it was. Much of the hoopla centered around Magna's new process, Todd-AO (named for developer Mike Todd and the *A*merican *O*ptical Company). The wider- and deeper-than-normal screen went Cinerama one better—it didn't have seams. Magna Theatre Corporation's process would be successfully used in 1956 for Mike Todd's *Around the World in 80 Days.*

In many ways, *Oklahoma!*'s arrival

Screenplay by Sonya Levien and
  William Ludwig

From the Theatre Guild Production

Book and lyrics by Oscar Hammerstein II

Music by Richard Rodgers

Based on a play by Lynn Riggs

Produced by Arthur Hornblow, Jr.

Directed by Fred Zinnemann

CAST

Curly	Gordon MacRae
Laurey	Shirley Jones
Aunt Ellen	Charlotte Greenwood
Will Parket	Gene Nelson
Ado Annie	Gloria Grahame

ACADEMY AWARD NOMINATIONS

4 nominations, 2 wins*

  Best Cinematography, Color
*Best Sound Recording
*Best Scoring of a Musical
  Best Film Editing

was reminiscent of the excitement surrounding *Gone With the Wind.* For the New York City premiere, the city held a parade for visiting Oklahoma officials and dignitaries, with Oklahoma governor Raymond Gary in the lead atop his white horse. Right behind him was a cavalcade of surreys "with the fringe on top," riding up Broadway, eventually arriving at the Rivoli Theatre, where the contingency was welcomed by composers Richard Rodgers and Oscar Hammerstein II.

But the movie's the thing, and fans of the play were not disappointed in the screen version. *Oklahoma!* has often been termed an American opera/ballet. The memorable music sung so richly by Gordon MacRae and Shirley Jones, coupled with the staginess of the production, is operatic in style, while the surrealistic dream sequence can only be termed balletic. This gives an unevenness to the film, which alternates between a location picture with beautiful exteriors to one which is very much bound to the soundstage, with an obvious painted backdrop. Never mind, it's not meant to be reality (after all, how many people go around bursting into song?). Audiences loved it, coming back for more "corn as high as an elephant's eye." With its success at the box office, the movie *Oklahoma!* took its rightful place next to the stage play *Oklahoma!* as an American classic.

THE TEN COMMANDMENTS
PARAMOUNT
$43,000,000

"Those who see this motion picture produced and directed by
CECIL B. DEMILLE
will make a pilgrimage over the very ground that Moses trod more than 3,000 years ago."
—OPENING CREDIT

AND IT CAME TO PASS, that the legend named DeMille brought forth the most ambitious, most successful picture of his career. For DeMille, now age 75, it would also be his last. But what a finale! The legacy of *The Ten Commandments* may not last 3,000 years, but the film will certainly be around for decades to come.

This was actually a remake of the 1923 version of the film, also by De-Mille. But now, with $13,500,000 at his command, DeMille showed the world how to make an epic. In the '50s era of Biblical extravaganzas, *The Ten Com-*

mandments became the touchstone, surpassing those that preceded it as well as those to follow.

Ten years in the planning, three years in research and preliminary exploration, three in the writing—the film required the longest shooting schedule up to that time. Much of the footage was shot on location in the Middle East and on the Sinai Peninsula, DeMille having insisted that as many actual locales as possible be used. Over 25,000 extras took direction from the master as he perched atop his platform, happy to once again be in his element.

Much of the budget went for special effects. Most memorable of these was the parting of the Red Sea. To get the effect, shots of the actual Red Sea were matched with shots of dump tanks pouring huge amounts of water into a Paramount tank set. When the footage

was reversed, the waters seemed to part. The careful blending of these two shots produced the desired effect. The combined footage took 18 months to film, at a cost of $1,000,000.

An important part of the special effects was the use of animation. Animated "fire" was drawn to represent the finger of God burning the Commandments onto the tablets. Compare this technique with the use of similar animation in recent special effects films like *Raiders of the Lost Ark* and *Star Trek V*, and you'll appreciate how ahead of its time *Commandments* was.

Critics marveled at the film, predicting success. *Variety* speculated that "the boxoffice returns will be mountainous . . . Biblical entries of the past have won marked public endorsement and this one tops them all. Its theme, its photographic magnificence and the truly powerful publicity campaign must mean that 'Ten Commandments' will run on and on."

A year later, the film had been seen by 21,900,000 people in 800 United States cities, and had *grossed* $26,500,000. Since the ratio of grosses to rentals generally runs 2:1, this was approximately the break-even point for Paramount. From then on, it was all gravy.

A good deal of credit for the film's success must also be given to Charlton Heston, with his portrayal of Moses one of the most outstanding characterizations in cinematic history. Heston was, and to many *is*, Moses—he is still sometimes jokingly referred to by the prophet's name. Garnering much of the attention was co-star Yul Brynner, whose shaved head and exotic looks had made him Hollywood's newest sex symbol. *Redbook* called him "the most exciting male on the screen since Rudolph Valentino." Brynner, whose newly released film version of his successful musical, *The King and I* (for which he would receive the year's Best Actor award), had made him a familiar face to audiences, received critical acclaim as Egyptian pharaoh Ramses II.

The last shot of the last picture of DeMille's career was taken on the director's birthday. According to an interview in Paul Boller's *Hollywood Anecdotes* with the late Yul Brynner, DeMille seemed reluctant to call it a wrap. "I could see he just didn't want to get off that boom. His one regret, I think, was that he didn't die as he finished the film. He was so sad. He kept trying to think of another shot when it was really over."

With that in mind, the picture's final card seems doubly meaningful. DeMille opted to omit the traditional "The End" for this:

"So it was written, so it shall be done."

Screenplay by Aeneas MacKenzie, Jesse L. Lasky, Jr., Jack Gariss, and Frederic M. Frank

Produced and directed by Cecil B. DeMille

CAST

Moses	. . . .	Charlton Heston
Nefertiti	. . . .	Anne Baxter
Rameses	. . . .	Yul Brynner
Sephbra	. . . .	Yvonne DeCarlo
Sethi	. . . .	Sir Cedric Hardwicke

ACADEMY AWARD NOMINATIONS

7 nominations, 1 win*

Best Picture
Best Cinematography, Color
Best Art Direction-Set Decoration, Color
Best Sound Recording
Best Film Editing
Best Costume Design, Color
*Best Special Effects

AROUND THE WORLD IN 80 DAYS
UNITED ARTISTS
$23,120,000

IN BRINGING Jules Verne's classic novel to the screen, Mike Todd, the irrepressible showman, produced his first—and only—motion picture. All producers should be so lucky.

The movie to end all movies was a celluloid three-ring circus. His oversized Todd-AO screen was front and center, of course. And with a subject like The World, the possibilities were endless. But what brought this picture to life was the balance that he struck between his forte—showmanship—and engrossing cinematic entertainment. Todd is credited with creating the "cameo" appearance, and practically everyone who had a Screen Actors Guild card appeared in this movie. His cast read like a who-was-who of Hollywood. Anchored by David Niven, Cantinflas, and Shirley MacLaine (as an Indian Princess, yet!), the parade included: Charles Boyer, Joe E. Brown, John Carradine, Charles Coburn, Ronald Colman, Noel Coward, Marlene Dietrich, Sir John Gielgud, Hermione Gingold, Trevor Howard, Buster Kea-

---

Screenplay by S. J. Perelman

Based on the novel by Jules Verne

Produced by Michael Todd

Directed by Michael Anderson

CAST

Phileas Fogg . . . . David Niven
Passepartout . . . . Cantinflas
Princess Aouda . . . . . . Shirley MacLaine

ACADEMY AWARD NOMINATIONS

8 nominations, 5 wins*

*Best Picture
  Best Director (Michael Anderson)
*Best Screenplay-Adapted (James Poe,
  John Farrow, and S. J. Perelman)
*Best Cinematography, Color
  Best Art Direction-Set Decoration, Color
*Best Scoring of a Dramatic or Comedy
  Picture (Victor Young)
*Best Film Editing
  Best Costume Design, Color

After a career with 22 nominations, composer Victor Young finally won an Oscar, posthumously—for Best Scoring.

---

ton, Peter Lorre, Robert Morley, Edward R. Murrow, George Raft, Cesar Romero, Frank Sinatra, and Red Skelton. Theater patrons had to return several times just to play "How many stars can you spot?"

Extras? Todd gave new meaning to the word, using 68,894 of them, if you can believe the press releases, plus more animals than any other picture ever made—7,959 of them, including 800 horses, 950 burros, 2,448 American bison, and 3,800 Rocky Mountain sheep.

The film took 34 directors 160 days to make on 112 locations and 140 sets in 13 countries. The wardrobe department spent $410,000 on 74,685 costumes. Still, the total budget came in at a mere $6,000,000, prompting Todd to quip to *Time*, "I'm ashamed to admit it, it cost so little. Take *The Ten Commandments*. That cost $1,000,000 a commandment."

To ensure box office success, Mike Todd guided the film's exhibition with diligence. He sent a manual to each theater, outlining procedures for organizing the reserved seating, ticket pricing, and scheduling of two performances per day. With a running time of

nearly three hours, Todd didn't want any anxious patrons watching the clock, and had theater owners remove any illuminated ones near the screen. In keeping with presenting his film in the tradition of a Broadway show, ticket holders received programs; popcorn and other munchies were verboten.

On the first anniversary of *Around the World in 80 Days*, Mike Todd hosted a party for 20,000 of his most intimate friends, where he announced his next project. It was to be a lavish picturization of Cervantes' *Don Quixote*, for which the showman had already begun construction of an exact replica of a 17th-century Spanish town. The centerpiece was to be Mrs. Todd, Elizabeth Taylor. Todd never got the chance to fulfill this fantasy. In 1958, on his way to receive an award as "Showman of the Year," his private plane crashed in the New Mexico desert, killing all aboard. The plane's name was the "Lucky Liz."

In 1989, a six-part TV mini-series of "Around the World in 80 Days" was broadcast on NBC. It starred Pierce Brosnan, Peter Ustinov, and Eric Idle, but pulled in only mediocre ratings. Mike Todd's legacy was in no jeopardy.

3

GIANT

WARNER BROS.
$14,000,000

W HEN EDNA Ferber wrote her novel *Giant* in 1952, she couldn't have chosen a more fitting title. In the decade of the mastodon movie, this sprawling Texas saga of greed, lust, family strife, and social conflict lasting 197 minutes did everything to live up to its name.

It had a giant cast. Elizabeth Taylor proved her mettle to critics, whose attention she caught by handling the mature role with confidence and intelligence. Rock Hudson's role as cattle baron Bick Benedict was his first important one, and some later called it his best performance (it won him an Oscar nomination). *Newsweek* noted that "Rock Hudson as her rancher-husband is gigantic, relaxed, rocklike indeed, and right for the part."

The scope of the film is giant in itself. The saga of the Benedict family begins with Rock Hudson as a rugged Texan rancher married to an elegant society girl (Elizabeth Taylor). Together they raise their brood (watch for young actor Dennis Hopper as Jordan Benedict III; Hopper later became the director/star of *Easy Rider* [see page 206]). Both Hudson and Taylor do admirable jobs with their characters' evolution and progressive aging over

Screenplay by Fred Guiol and Ivan Moffat

Based on the novel by Edna Ferber

Produced by George Stevens and Henry Ginsberg

Directed by George Stevens

CAST

Leslie Benedict	Elizabeth Taylor
Bick Benedict	Rock Hudson
Jett Rink	James Dean
Luz Benedict	Carroll Baker
Vashti Snythe	Jane Withers

ACADEMY AWARD NOMINATIONS

10 nominations, 1 win*

Best Picture
Best Actor (Rock Hudson)
Best Actor (James Dean)
Best Supporting Actress (Mercedes McCambridge)
*Best Director (George Stevens)
Best Screenplay-Adapted
Best Art Direction-Set Decoration, Color
Best Scoring of a Dramatic or Comedy Picture
Best Film Editing
Best Costume Design, Color

the 25-year span of the film. There is also a controversial (especially for its time) subplot dealing with racism against Mexicans, a theme that had been traditionally taboo in filmmaking.

Most film buffs, however, recall *Giant* as the last performance of James Dean. He had honed his "lonely rebel" character to perfection, and in the role of Jett Rink, he created one of the screen's most unforgettable personifications. *Time* called his acting "a streak of genius," adding: "He has caught the Texas accent to nasal perfection, and has mastered the lock-hipped, high-heeled stagger of the wrangler . . . the actor is able to press an amazing variety of subtleties into the mood of the moment, to achieve what is certainly the finest piece of atmospheric acting seen on screen since Marlon Brando and Rod Steiger did their 'brother scene' in *On the Waterfront*."

James Dean never lived to learn about the Oscar nomination he so deservingly received for his performance. Two weeks after his last scene in *Giant* was filmed, he was killed in a highway crash while driving his Porsche to a racing competition. He was only 24 years old.

SEVEN WONDERS OF THE WORLD

CINERAMA RELEASING CORPORATION (CRC)

$12,500,000

NINETEEN FIFTY-SIX was the year of numbers. Of the top five films, three had numerals in their titles. There were 10 commandments, 80 days in which to go around the world, and a lucky 7 (for CRC, at least) Wonders of the World.

Actually, Lowell Thomas' camera crews found themselves unable to stop at seven, and in preparing this latest entry in the Cinerama saga, his crews trekked hundreds of thousands of miles, shooting as many feet of film as they globetrotted through 32 countries for the two-hour movie. Alas, the Cinerama crews were several thousand years too late to capture all Seven Wonders of the Ancient World. (These were comprised of the Hanging Gardens of Babylon, the Colossus of Rhodes, the Statue of Olympian Zeus, the Pharos Lighthouse of Alexandria, the Tomb of King Mausolus, the Temple of Diana at Ephesus, and the Sphinx and Pyramid of Cheops—the oldest man-made object in the world.)

Since the only remaining Wonder of the ancient world's famous collection is Egypt's Sphinx and Pyramid of Cheops, Thomas decided to go in search of some modern wonders. The triple bank of Cinerama cameras recorded an impressive collage of footage of such far-flung places as New York City, Rio de Janeiro, the Sahara Desert, East Africa, the Taj Mahal in India, Mt. Fuji in Japan, Italy's Leaning Tower of Pisa, the Parthenon, and Mt. Sinai (a popular site for films this year, it would seem). And of course there were the obligatory crowd-pleasing scenes of spectacular American scenery, the Cinerama finale this time showcasing flybys of the Grand Canyon, Niagara Falls, and the redwoods of Yosemite.

Set amidst this vast array of scenery was one unusual segment done in

Rome. Pope Pius XII had expressed interest in the Cinerama process when the films were screened at La Scala in Milan, and the production team was only too happy to oblige when His Holiness requested a part in this latest venture. The platform housing the cameras was placed a mere two feet from the balcony the Pope would use to bless the audience gathered in St. Peter's Square. Right on cue, the Pope hit his mark and delivered his blessing. The nervous Cinerama crew was delighted, and was about to wrap when the Pope's advisors suggested another take. They felt the bright lights and cameras had made the Pontiff a bit nervous, so to the surprise of the throng below, the Pope did "take two." Later, the Pope joked with the crew, "Ah, you Americans, you always want two to make sure."

Seven Wonders of the World was the last of the Cinerama travelogues, and it wasn't until 1962 that moviegoers would see a new film using that three-camera process, this time with a plot (see *How the West Was Won*, page 160).

Scenario by Prosper Buranelli and
   William Lipscomb

Produced by Lowell Thomas

Directed by Ted Tetzlaff, Andrew Marton,
   Tay Garnett, Paul Mantz, and Walter
   Thompson

Narrated by Lowell Thomas

THE KING AND I

20TH CENTURY-FOX
$8,500,000

Rodgers and Hammerstein's delightful score saw people returning to box offices again and again, eager to sing along with such tunes as "Shall We Dance?," "Getting to Know You," "Whistle a Happy Tune," "We Kiss in a Shadow," and "Hello, Young Lovers." Fans also made the album the number-one seller of the year. Point of trivia: Yul Brynner's looks and charm must have distracted the person in charge of on-set wardrobe, because when Yul Brynner sings "A Puzzlement," some shots show him with an earring, some without.

Fox hoped it had at last found the elusive key to making television spin-offs from movies when they signed Yul Brynner to reprise his "King of Siam" role (sans singing) for a TV series on CBS. It debuted in September, 1972, and made it all the way to December, three months later. The movie version, and Yul, will always remain King.

Screenplay by Ernest Lehman

Music by Richard Rodgers

Book and lyrics by Oscar Hammerstein II

From the musical play based on the book *Anna and the King of Siam* by Margaret Landon

Produced by Charles Brackett

Directed by Walter Lang

CAST

Anna	Deborah Kerr
The King	Yul Brynner
Tuptim	Rita Moreno
Kralahome	Martin Benson
Lady Thiang	Terry Saunders

ACADEMY AWARD NOMINATIONS

9 nominations, 5 wins*

  Best Picture
*Best Actor (Yul Brynner)
  Best Actress (Deborah Kerr)
  Best Director (Walter Lang)
  Best Cinematography, Color
*Best Art Direction-Set Decoration, Color
*Best Sound Recording
*Best Scoring of a Musical Picture
*Best Costume Design, Color

YUL BRYNNER. The Asian-born actor of Gypsy extraction made 1956 *his* year. He appeared in three films, two of them in the top five (*The Ten Commandments* and *The King and I*), and fans voted him King of the Box Office as well.

Brynner was not the first one to play the Siamese King. In 1946, Fox had produced *Anna and the King of Siam*, a straight drama taken from Margaret Landon's fictionalized biography (which was in turn based on Anna Leonowens' autobiography). In that film, Rex Harrison played King to Irene Dunne's Anna. Gertrude Lawrence was enchanted with the picture and secured the rights so that she could play Anna in a musical version. Rodgers and Hammerstein set to work writing the now-memorable music, and an unknown Brynner was cast as the King for the

stage version. When Fox decided to bring the well-known musical to the screen 10 years later, there was never any doubt about the man who would be king. Critics sang his praises; *Variety* noted that "the larger exposure via the film medium should make Brynner an international personality . . ." Deborah Kerr, as the properly English schoolteacher, was the perfect foil for Brynner. Her singing voice had to be dubbed by Marni Nixon, a chanteuse who would later make a career of dubbing on-screen singing for less gifted actresses. *Variety* commented that Kerr's voice was "ghosted so well that it is hard to believe that it is not Miss Kerr," and credited Kerr with portraying Anna with "charm and understanding and, when necessary, the right sense of comedy."

Along with the two top stars,

THE BRIDGE ON THE RIVER KWAI
COLUMBIA
$17,195,000

COLUMBIA PICTURES, distributors of British-made *The Bridge on the River Kwai*, went firmly to the top of the 1957 box office with the film. Even though the profits had to be split with British producer Sam Spiegel, there was plenty to spare, since cost of the movie was only $3,000,000.

The producers' money was well spent. Not only did they get a wide-screen, sweeping drama about British prisoners in a Japanese POW camp in the jungles of Burma, but along the way they managed to secure seven Oscars.

The scope of this film is the stuff of love affairs between Academy members and the motion picture screen. It had excellent production values—cast, crew, special effects, sound, cinematography, location sets, and score.

Made entirely on location in the jungles of what is now Sri Lanka, much of the low cost was due to the use of Ceylonese labor, elephants, and materials, during the year the crew spent there. In fact, director David Lean's wife thought he spent too much time on the picture and sued him for divorce on the grounds of desertion.

Among the Academy Awards was one for writing—Best Screenplay Based on Material from Another Medium. Novelist Pierre Boulle was named as the winner, and indeed it is his name that appears in the credits. But in fact the screenplay had been co-scripted by Carl Foreman and Michael Wilson. Why were their names omitted? The late '40s and early '50s was the time of Senator Joseph McCarthy's

hearings to rout the "Red Menace" in our midst (with that infamous question, "Are you now or have you ever been a member of the Communist Party?"). These witch hunts extended to the literati and film community, and several Hollywood actors, producers, directors, and writers were either jailed or blacklisted. Two such blacklisted scribes were Foreman and Wilson, whose names were deliberately omitted from the credits. Only later, when this absurd paranoia subsided, were they able to come forward and publicly take credit for their superb screenplay.

Topping the cast was a British actor known mostly to patrons of "art houses." Alec Guinness, portraying the tough, disciplinarian English colonel who defies his captors, garnered a

Director David Lean (left) and Alec Guinness relax a moment during the location filming of *The Bridge on the River Kwai*.

Screenplay by Pierre Boulle

Based on the novel by Pierre Boulle

Produced by Sam Spiegel

Directed by David Lean

CAST

Shears	William Holden
Colonel Nicholson	Alec Guinness
Major Warden	Jack Hawkins
Colonel Saito	Sessue Hayakawa
Major Clipton	James Donald

ACADEMY AWARD NOMINATIONS

*8 nominations, 7 wins**

*Best Picture
*Best Actor (Alec Guinness)
 Best Supporting Actor
  (Sessue Hayakawa)
*Best Director (David Lean)
*Best Screenplay Based on Material from
  Another Medium (Pierre Boulle)
*Best Cinematography
*Best Score
*Best Film Editing

great deal of critical attention in this picture, the turning point in his career. Said *The New York Times*: "Alec Guinness does a memorable—indeed a classic—job in making the ramrod British colonel a profoundly ambitious type . . . He gives one of the most devastating portraits of a militarist that we have ever seen." Kudos also went to his Japanese adversary, Sessue Hayakawa, a former silent screen star, whom *The Times* labeled "superb."

But *The Bridge on the River Kwai* is David Lean's picture all the way, and all critics were quick to point out that although the film runs about two and three-quarter hours, the director achieved such intensity that it seems like only an hour or so.

In striving for authenticity, Lean chose not to use miniatures for his special effects. Instead, he had a real bridge built, at a cost of $250,000. From the Ceylon Government Railway he purchased six old coaches and an ancient locomotive once belonging to a maharajah; these were also destroyed as the train crossed the bridge.

The "Colonel Bogie March," the film's famous theme song whistled by the stalwart soldiers, became a hit record, and soon other movies began writing marketable theme songs into their scripts.

In 1989, a film entitled *The Return from the River Kwai* was completed. Distribution was halted while the courts decided whether or not Leisure Time Productions, the film's producers, would have to delete the words "River Kwai" from its title, since it is *not* a sequel to *The Bridge*.

PEYTON PLACE
20TH CENTURY-FOX
$11,500,000

THE TEMPERATURE wasn't the only thing that was hot in the summer of '57 as 3,000,000 people toted copies of Grace Metalious' steamy novel *Peyton Place* to their favorite beach spots. And when Fox bought the film rights to the best-seller, no one thought that her novel could be filmed without cutting most of the sex out of it. They were wrong.

When *Peyton Place* hit the screens at Christmas, the majority of the scenes of suicide, abortion, adultery, rape, and murder were still intact. The film flew in the face of the by-now-impotent censors, and that was just fine with the paying public, who couldn't wait to see it all discussed up on the bigger-than-life CinemaScope screen.

It wasn't all no-holds-barred, however. Compared to today's Peeping-Tom camera with its almost clinical shots of sex acts, this was quite tame; not exactly *Bambi*, but tame. Set in 1941, in a small New Hampshire town (beautifully doubled here by Camden, Maine), some taboos had yet to be broken in screen dialogue. Four-letter words beginning with "f" were certainly not a part of this film's vocabulary. Nor, oddly, was the word "abortion." When the town doctor performs that then-illegal operation, he tells someone, "I

assisted her in a miscarriage." You may recall that Clark Gable wasn't even allowed to say *that* no-no back in '39.

Screenplay by John Michael Hayes

From the novel by Grace Metalious

Produced by Jerry Wald

Directed by Mark Robson

CAST

Constance . . . . Lana Turner
Selena Cross . . . . Hope Lange
Michael Rossi . . . . Lee Philips
Dr. Swain . . . . Lloyd Nolan
Lucas Cross . . . . Arthur Kennedy
Norman Page . . . . Russ Tamblyn

ACADEMY AWARD NOMINATIONS

9 nominations, no wins

Best Picture
Best Actress (Lana Turner)
Best Supporting Actor (Arthur Kennedy)
Best Supporting Actor (Russ Tamblyn)
Best Supporting Actress (Hope Lange)
Best Supporting Actress (Diane Varsi)
Best Director (Mark Robson)
Best Screenplay Based on Material from Another Medium
Best Cinematography

We'd come a long way, baby.

Casting had much to do with the film's success. Lana Turner finally played an adult role, as the mother of a teenager. Lloyd Nolan, Arthur Kennedy, Leon Ames, and a pre-"Bonanza" Lorne Greene completed the adult roster, while a crop of newcomers—Hope Lange, Russ Tamblyn, Diane Varsi, and David Nelson (yes, Ozzie and Harriet's boy)—proved their professionalism.

In true Hollywood style, Fox came up with a sequel in a 1961 movie called *Return to Peyton Place*. Most people didn't want to.

But most surprising of all was what happened seven years after the film was released. Finally, 20th Century-Fox found the perfect vehicle for a television spinoff. "Peyton Place" went on ABC in September, 1964, and continued to run for five seasons. It was the original nighttime soap. The show made stars out of two of its cast, Mia Farrow and Ryan O'Neal, and had a stock of other prestigious actors like Leslie Nielsen, Barbara Parkins, Lee Grant, John Kerr, Wilfred Hyde-White, Lana Wood, Leigh Taylor-Young, Gena Rowlands, Barbara Rush, and Dan Duryea. It was not until June 2, 1969, that *Peyton Place* ran its full course.

SAYONARA

WARNER BROS.
$10,500,000

"The pleasure does not lie in the end itself. It's the pleasurable steps to that end." —ORIENTAL WISDOM AS QUOTED IN *SAYONARA*

BASED ON James Michener's 1954 novel about American servicemen on leave in Japan during the Korean War, *Sayonara* is very much a modern *Madame Butterfly.* The tragedy centers on the theme of interracial love and marriage, something with which Michener had first-hand experience. In 1955, shortly after the novel's publication, Michener married his third wife, Mari Yoriko Sabusawa, an American of Japanese extraction.

In the film—which opens with a less-than-memorable title song by Irving Berlin—Major Gruver, played by Marlon Brando, comes face to face with his own prejudices, gradually understanding that love is more than skin deep. What we see is something akin to a religious conversion as he rushes to Red Button's character's defense. His conversion is complete when he meets and falls in love with a beautiful dancer. From a writing perspective, this is a model script: we have a central character who learns, grows, and eventually changes by story's end. Paul Osborn did an admirable job of translating Michener's novel to the screen and was rewarded with an Oscar.

Both Brando and Buttons were lauded by the press for their fine performances. *The Hollywood Reporter* commented: "Brando has done something in this picture that is seen so rarely that it is especially notable. He has undertaken to portray a drastic change in character and he brings it off with conviction and resolution." Until this film, Red Buttons was known primarily as a comedian. With this dramatic debut, *Variety* noted: "The performance [director Joshua Logan] gets out of Buttons, deeply moving in its sincerity, should raise the erstwhile air comic to entirely new stature. In this 'straight' part, he's excellent and his devotion and final desperation ring completely true."

Buttons' ill-fated Japanese wife was played by newcomer Miyoshi Umeki (familiar to later TV audiences as Mrs. Livingston on "The Courtship of Eddie's Father"), who was discovered singing in a San Fernando Valley nightclub. Her film debut was honored by the Academy with an Oscar—rare for a first performance.

Screenplay by Paul Osborn

Based on the novel by James A. Michener

Produced by William Goetz

Directed by Joshua Logan

CAST

Major Gruver . . . . Marlon Brando
Hana-ogi . . . . Miiko Taka
Kelly . . . . Red Buttons
Katsumi . . . . Miyoshi Umeki
Eileen Webster . . . . Patricia Owens

ACADEMY AWARD NOMINATIONS

10 nominations, 4 wins*

 Best Picture
 Best Actor (Marlon Brando)
*Best Supporting Actor (Red Buttons)
*Best Supporting Actress (Miyoshi Umeki)
 Best Director (Joshua Logan)
 Best Screenplay Based on Material from
   Another Medium
 Best Cinematography
*Best Art Direction-Set Decoration
*Best Sound
 Best Film Editing

4

OLD YELLER

WALT DISNEY PRODUCTIONS
$10,050,000

WALT DISNEY proved that he knew how to make a tear-jerker with *Old Yeller*. It's a charming story about a boy and his dog, but the master storyteller also gave us a basic human tale blending fun, laughter, love, adventure—and tragedy. Most people will think of this as a children's tale, but many a kid learned about real life and grew up a tad or two after watching this film.

For his story, Walt turned to an acclaimed novel by Fred Gipson, who collaborated on the screenplay with William Tunberg. Gipson described *Old Yeller* as fiction based on fact. "My grandfather owned a big yellow stray dog who could throw wild range cattle and who once rescued him from a meat-eating hog," he recounted.

The film introduced Tommy Kirk and Kevin Corcoran, two young players who were put under Disney contract and appeared in numerous films to follow. Jeff York, Chuck Connors (former baseball star and "The Rifleman" of TV fame), and Beverly Washburn rounded out the cast.

But this was really a picture about animals and *their* relationships. The title dog was played by "Spike," who was rescued by trainer Frank Weatherwax from a Van Nuys, California, animal shelter. He paid $3.00 for his future star. Weatherwax invested $20,000 and four years in training time before Disney cast Spike as "Old Yeller." Other animals in the cast weren't that easy to come by. Where do you find a red-eyed wild boar? Disney wranglers located a herd with

Screenplay by Fred Gipson and William Tunberg

Based on the book by Fred Gipson

Produced by Walt Disney

Directed by Robert Stevenson

CAST

Mrs. Coates	Dorothy McGuire
Mr. Coates	Fess Parker
Travis Coates	Tommy Kirk
Arliss Coates	Kevin Corcoran
Mr. Searcy	Jeff York
Mr. Sanderson	Chuck Connors
Lisbeth Searcy	Beverly Washburn

four-inch tusks in the back country of central California. Buzzards had to be shipped from Florida, reptiles from Texas and Arizona, squirrels from Kentucky. A pregnant cow was located, and obliged the Disney crew by giving birth to her calf on cue.

The script called for Spike/Yeller to fight with a 500-pound bear, and the battle took place without any harm to either animal. For months, Spike was introduced to his wrestling partner Doug, a nine-year-old movie bear. They learned to play-fight, later re-creating such a scene for the cameras. Appropriate growls and yelps were all added by the sound department for effectiveness, and the animals, closely supervised by an American Humane Association representative, emerged without a single scratch.

But it is the film's sad ending that is remembered by most. Walt argued for realism. "This is a Texas farm in 1869 and the dog has rabies; there's no way he can be saved. You gotta shoot him . . . The kids'll cry, but it's important for them to know that life isn't all happy endings." Who said only kids would cry?

RAINTREE COUNTY
METRO-GOLDWYN-MAYER
$5,962,839

"War is the most monstrous of man's illusions. Any idea worth anything is worth not *fighting for."*
—WALTER ABEL

GEMS LIKE the above line of dialogue notwithstanding, *Raintree County* was a costly, overly long picture which MGM hoped would be a Northern *Gone With the Wind.* It cost $5,000,000 to make, barely breaking even.

Based on Ross Lockridge, Jr.'s, 1947 best-seller, the film starred Elizabeth Taylor and Montgomery Clift, along with Eva Marie Saint, Lee Marvin, Rod Taylor, Agnes Moorehead, and Walter Abel. (In the part of a Southern officer who dies at the end, there's a feller named DeForest Kelley, whom "Star Trek" fans later came to know as Dr. "Bones" McCoy.)

Montgomery Clift plays an idealistic Hoosier shortly before the outbreak of the American Civil War. But the story concerns the internal conflicts of the characters more than the War Between the States; Clift's character is driven by a need to find the legendary raintree and the secret of life it is reported to contain. Elizabeth Taylor plays his troubled wife, whose obsessive belief that she is part Negro leads her to insanity. These stories are played out against historical events such as the election of Abraham Lincoln, the Northern aboli-

tion movement, the secession of the South, and briefly, the Civil War.

The novel on which *Raintree Country* was based was Lockridge's first and only one. The English teacher from Indiana had labored on his tome for seven years, completing it in 1948 when he was 33. It was an immediate best-seller and a Book-of-the-Month-Club selection. But the novel had taken its toll on its author: two months after the book appeared, the father of four committed suicide.

Most of the success at the box office must be attributed to the cast. People would probably have come to see Elizabeth Taylor recite the Yellow Pages. Critics disagreed over the effectiveness of her performance. *Variety* termed her work as Clift's ditsy Southern-belle wife "a firm portrayal," while *The New York Times* seems to have confused the character with the characterization: "Miss Taylor's daughter of the Deep South is a vain, posey, shallow young thing whose only asset is her beauty." *The Hollywood Reporter,* however, called this Taylor's finest performance, one that "shows that this legendary beauty can be a really good actress if she desires . . ."

During the production, Elizabeth Taylor gave a dinner party attended by Montgomery Clift. On his drive home, the inebriated actor had a near-fatal car accident and was rushed to the hospital. His slashed face and internal injuries caused production on *Raintree County* to be shut down for two months. He was left with permanent facial scarring, and during the following years, there were rumors of heavy alcohol and drug abuse. He died of a heart attack in 1966 at the age of 45.

Screenplay by Millard Kaufman

Based on the novel by Ross Lockridge Jr.

Produced by David Lewis

Directed by Edward Dmytryk

CAST

John Wickliff Shawnessy	Montgomery Clift
Susanna Drake	Elizabeth Taylor
Nell Gaither	Eva Marie Saint
Jerusalem Webster Stiles	Nigel Patrick
Orville "Flash" Perkins	Lee Marvin
T. D. Shawnessy	Walter Abel

ACADEMY AWARD NOMINATIONS

4 nominations, no wins

Best Actress (Elizabeth Taylor)
Best Art Direction-Set Decoration
Best Score
Best Costume Design

SOUTH PACIFIC
20TH CENTURY-FOX
$17,500,000

"You've got to be carefully taught."
—LYRIC FROM "YOU'VE
GOT TO BE TAUGHT"

FOR THE YEAR 1958, Hollywood turned to Broadway. Every one of the top five films that year had been adapted from a successful Broadway play or musical. The feeling seemed to be that if it made money on the stage, go with the film. The public confirmed that attitude, spending their box office dollars on two musicals, two comedies, and one drama.

The most successful of these was *South Pacific*, the James Michener musical adapted from his book *Tales of the South Pacific*. Again, as in *Sayonara* the previous year, the talents of director Joshua Logan were brought to a Michener property, and again the book dealt with interracial relationships. While *South Pacific* was not actually a "message" movie, the statement made by the above lyrics was the play/movie's theme in a nutshell—you have to be taught to hate all the people your relatives hate.

Although *South Pacific* was a morality play, its main emphasis was on the wonderful music of Rodgers and Hammerstein—songs like "I'm Gonna Wash That Man Right Out of My Hair," "Some Enchanted Evening," "Younger Than Springtime," "Happy Talk," "Bloody Mary," and "Bali Ha'i." Joshua Logan had brought the first version of the show to the stage in 1949, when World War II was not yet a distant memory, and the story may have had more immediacy then. Still, audiences had been humming the popular tunes for nine years when the movie hit the screens in Todd-AO and stereophonic sound, and Fox's $6,000,000 investment paid off handsomely.

Presentation in movie theaters was, as with many spectacular '50s films, "an event." People booked in advance for the privilege of seeing this film lasting two hours and 51 minutes, with a 15-minute intermission. No one seemed to mind the length. In fact, the film proved such a success in London that it played at the same movie house there for four years.

Success came for many reasons. In addition to the love stories, there was much comic relief, as well as beautiful settings. When Mitzi Gaynor washes that man right out of her hair, she does so on one of Kauai's (Hawaii) most beautiful beaches.

While the public took *South Pacific*'s screen version to their hearts, many of the critics didn't, finding fault with the cast (they missed Mary Martin and Ezio Pinza from the Broadway version), the length, the colors, and so on. *Time* found the film "about as tastelessly impressive as a ten-ton marshmallow" but then went on to predict that "nevertheless, it will probably run almost as long as it did on Broadway . . . and it seems sure to make yet another bale of kale . . ."

Cast in the leads were Mitzi Gaynor as Nurse Nellie Forbush and Rossano Brazzi as her French suitor. Brazzi was a particularly puzzling choice, since although the Italian film star had caught the attention of the American public in *The Barefoot Contessa* (1954), his vocals for *South Pacific* all had to be dubbed by Giorgio Tozzi. Others in the cast included Ray Walston, who later starred as TV's "My Favorite Martian," and in bit parts, Doug McClure (later star of TV's "The Virginian") and Ron Ely (later TV's "Tarzan").

Much of the film's controversy centered on director of photography Leon Shamroy's unorthodox use of color gels to establish "mood" with each use of song. Many found this technique distracting or annoying. When the film was released, Shamroy defended the process, telling *Newsweek*: "My interpretation of the South Pacific was like Gauguin painted it. I also wanted to create a change of pace. You have to think of the audience's restlessness watching the same thing for three hours. You have to change the atmosphere. So I shot the musical parts as a fantasy by sliding colored gelatin filters across the lens." The D.P.'s peers at the Academy obviously enjoyed these innovations—they gave Shamroy an Oscar nomination.

This technique may have given audiences a break then, but the color variations are jarring today when viewing this movie on a television set via VCR—one has the urge to continually fiddle with the color adjustments.

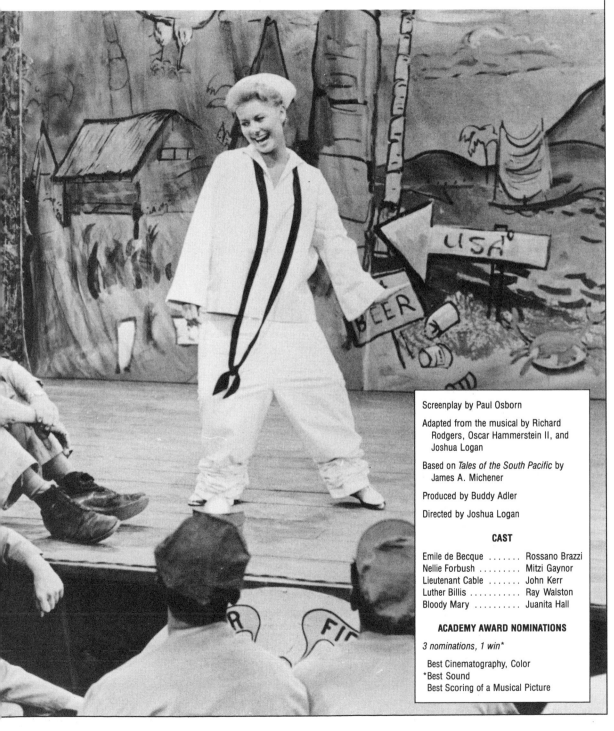

Screenplay by Paul Osborn

Adapted from the musical by Richard Rodgers, Oscar Hammerstein II, and Joshua Logan

Based on *Tales of the South Pacific* by James A. Michener

Produced by Buddy Adler

Directed by Joshua Logan

CAST

Emile de Becque	Rossano Brazzi
Nellie Forbush	Mitzi Gaynor
Lieutenant Cable	John Kerr
Luther Billis	Ray Walston
Bloody Mary	Juanita Hall

ACADEMY AWARD NOMINATIONS

3 nominations, 1 win*

Best Cinematography, Color
*Best Sound
Best Scoring of a Musical Picture

AUNTIE MAME
WARNER BROS.
$9,300,000

"Life is a banquet, and most poor suckers are starving to death."
—ROSALIND RUSSELL

PATRICK DENNIS' semi-autobiographical book about his eccentric (to say the least) Auntie Mame remained on the best-seller list for 112 weeks, so it was only natural that it be converted into a play. And, as we've seen, successful plays beget successful motion pictures. With an audience pre-sold on the farce, how could it miss?

It was the role of a lifetime, and Rosalind Russell will always be remembered as Auntie Mame. She had already perfected her portrayal of the kind-hearted kook on the Broadway stage as she romped through 639 performances. And since the play/film is basically a one-woman *tour de force*, most of the glory went to Miss Russell as well. One reason Miss Russell was able to pull it off so brilliantly was the warmth and humanism she brought to her character, who would otherwise come off as an egocentric airhead.

Roger Smith, who played the part of her grown nephew Patrick, is best remembered as having co-starred in the television series "77 Sunset Strip," which went on the air three months before the release of *Auntie Mame*. (Those readers too young to remember that show will probably know him as the husband of performer Ann-Margret.)

Another television regular, Fred Clark, appeared in *Auntie Mame* as Mame's no-nonsense banker. Clark was also familiar to TV audiences of the '50s as "Harry Morton" on "The Burns and Allen Show." Coincidentally, he played an accountant on that program.

Contributing to the popularity of this movie were the clever sets. Mame's apartment is almost a character itself. One of the most unforgettable moments comes when she is trying to destroy her nephew's relationship, and the fun she has with the barber-chair-like sofas which rise ceilingward. It's totally unbelievable, and yet the total absurdity of the scene works beautifully.

In 1966, Broadway was again treated to the outrageous aunt, this time in the musical *Mame*. It starred Angela Lansbury (who won a Tony Award) and ran for 1,508 performances, an even more impressive record than its predecessor.

Less impressive was the 1974 movie version of *Mame* starring Lucille Ball. Audiences loved Lucy, but not this musical fiasco.

Screenplay by Betty Comden and Adolph Green

Based on the novel by Patrick Dennis

Stage adaptation by Jerome Lawrence and Robert E. Lee

Directed by Morton DaCosta

CAST

Mame	Rosalind Russell
Beauregard Burnside . .	Forrest Tucker
Vera Charles	Coral Browne
Mr. Babcock	Fred Clark
Patrick Dennis	Roger Smith
Agnes Gooch	Peggy Cass

ACADEMY AWARD NOMINATIONS

6 nominations, no wins

Best Picture
Best Actress (Rosalind Russell)
Best Supporting Actress (Peggy Cass)
Best Cinematography, Color
Best Art Direction-Set Decoration
Best Film Editing

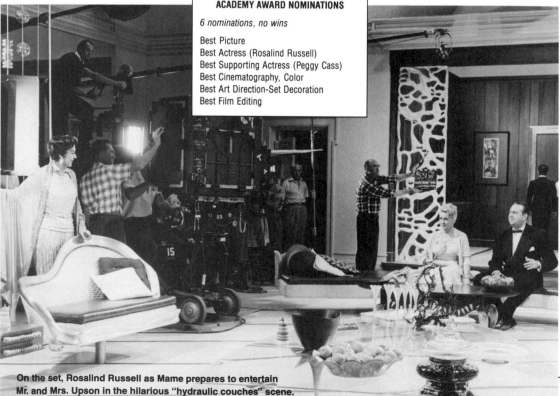

On the set, Rosalind Russell as Mame prepares to entertain Mr. and Mrs. Upson in the hilarious "hydraulic couches" scene.

CAT ON A HOT TIN ROOF

METRO-GOLDWYN-MAYER
$8,785,162

WHEN TENNESSEE Williams' stage play was brought to the screen, audiences eagerly rushed to see whether it would remain intact, since the drama unabashedly dealt with what were considered very "adult" topics—greed, lust, latent homosexuality—set to the tune of four-letter words so much a part of the Southern dramatist's realistic vocabulary. Much of this was indeed toned down for the screen, but the dramatic impact was still very much in evidence. Even more enticing to paying audiences were the fine performances of its lead actors—Elizabeth Taylor, Paul Newman, and Burl Ives.

Ms. Taylor almost didn't get the part. When MGM bought the film rights to the play, they had Grace Kelly in mind. But by the time cameras were ready to roll, Grace had landed another part, that of Princess of Monaco.

Just as Elizabeth Taylor was finishing the opening sequences of *Cat*, her husband Mike Todd was killed in a plane crash (see page 124). In the "show must go on" tradition, she worked throughout her grief, turning in an intense performance which drew raves from the critics. *Newsweek* wrote: "Elizabeth Taylor, who never has been known as a dramatic star of

particularly commanding stature, is more than satisfactory as Maggie the Cat, the first role she has been given

---

Screenplay by Richard Brooks and James Poe

Based on the play by Tennessee Williams

Produced by Lawrence Weingarten

Directed by Richard Brooks

CAST

Maggie	Elizabeth Taylor
Brick	Paul Newman
Big Daddy	Burl Ives
Gooper	Jack Carson
Big Mama	Judith Anderson

ACADEMY AWARD NOMINATIONS

6 nominations, no wins

Best Picture
Best Actor (Paul Newman)
Best Actress (Elizabeth Taylor)
Best Director (Richard Brooks)
Best Screenplay Based on Material from Another Medium
Best Cinematography, Color

---

which is not bigger-than-life. Her ably modulated performance suggests a promising future that could extend long after the bloom is off the rose."

Ever since the death of Todd, Ms. Taylor had been comforted by his best friend, Eddie Fisher. Although married to Debbie Reynolds at the time (the "perfect Hollywood couple," proclaimed the press), Fisher suddenly dumped Debbie for Liz. A few months later, Eddie Fisher became the fourth husband of Elizabeth Taylor.

The press also took notice of Paul Newman as Maggie's latent homosexual husband, Brick. *Variety* noted: "Newman again proves to be one of the finest actors in films, playing cynical underacting against highly developed action. His command of the articulate, sensitive sequences is unmistakable, and the way he mirrors his feelings is basic to every scene."

Burl Ives was the only actor who had appeared in the original Broadway version of this film; forevermore he would be the embodiment of "Big Daddy." The one-time banjo-pickin' balladeer received kudos from the critics. Also released in 1958 was *The Big Country*; Ives won an Academy Award for Best Supporting Actor in that picture.

NO TIME FOR SERGEANTS

WARNER BROS.
$7,500,000

Yᴇᴛ ᴀɴᴏᴛʜᴇʀ Broadway hit made it to the screen in this comedy about a farmboy turned flyboy. The movie is based on Ira Levin's (later of *Rosemary's Baby* fame) popular play, which in turn was based on Mac Hyman's best-seller. Andy Griffith created the stage role and re-created it quite successfully in the movie.

The North Carolina native was born to play the wide-eyed draftee, whose character is not so much dumb as literal-minded in a Gracie Allenesque way. Two years later, some clever people saw the potential in Andy, and the actor took his rightful place in Mayberry on the weekly television program "The Andy Griffith Show." And since Andy had become the respectable sheriff, his hayseed character from *No Time for Sergeants* was subdivided. The "gaaaaaah-ly" that we heard so frequently from Gomer Pyle in the weekly TV series was lifted straight out of the mouth of Private Will Stockdale in *No Time for Sergeants*.

Andy also recruited actor Don Knotts from this movie's cast (listed in the film's credits as "Manual Dexterity Corporal").

Three other cast members also went on to star or co-star in television shows. Nick Adams became "The Rebel" in 1959; Will Hutchins landed the

Screenplay by John Lee Mahin	
From the play by Ira Levin	
Based on the novel by Mac Hyman	
Produced and directed by Mervyn LeRoy	

CAST

Will Stockdale	Andy Griffith
Sergeant King	Myron McCormick
Ben	Nick Adams
Irvin	Murray Hamilton
General Bush	Howard Smith
Manual Dexterity Corporal	Don Knotts

lead in "Sugarfoot" back in 1957 and had just completed that show's first season when he filmed *Sergeants*; and Jamie Farr, who plays an uncredited co-pilot in this film, later became Corporal Maxwell Klinger on TV's "M*A*S*H."

Although it was popular at the time of release, this film seems slow and a bit of the humor dated when viewed on videocassette. Particularly ludicrous is the sequence where Andy and his buddy jump from an airplane over Yucca Flats immediately after a brush with an A-Bomb test, and they calmly converse while descending through a fallout cloud! No one thought this odd in those days, particularly the unsuspecting military, whose tests were carried on with virtually no protection for nearby spectators.

As you have probably guessed, a television series of "No Time for Sergeants" appeared in September, 1964. It ran for a year on ABC with Sammy Jackson playing the Griffith-created role of Private Stockdale.

GIGI

METRO-GOLDWYN-MAYER
$7,321,423

SOMEHOW IT SEEMS unfitting that *Gigi* was number five for 1958 and not number one, since this musical film has stood the test of time much better than *South Pacific*. It proved to be the favorite film of the Motion Picture Academy for that year, when it received an all-time high number of Oscars—nine all told. And the *My Fair Lady*-like story of the tomboyish French girl blooming into lovely young womanhood continues to charm audiences as much today as it did over thirty years ago.

Gigi began with the pen of French novelist Colette, who wrote it when

---

Screenplay by Alan Jay Lerner

Based on the novel by Colette

Lyrics by Alan Jay Lerner

Music by Frederick Loewe

Produced by Arthur Freed

Directed by Vincente Minnelli

CAST

Gigi . . . . Leslie Caron
Honore Lachaille . . . . . Maurice Chevalier
Gaston Lachaille . . . . . Louis Jourdan
Mme. Alvarez . . . . Hermione Gingold
Liane D'Exelmans . . . . Eva Gabor

ACADEMY AWARD NOMINATIONS

9 nominations, 9 wins*

*Best Picture
*Best Director (Vincente Minnelli)
*Best Screenplay Based on Material from
   Another Medium (Alan Jay Lerner)
*Best Cinematography, Color
*Best Art Direction—Set Decoration
*Best Song ("Gigi," music by Frederick
   Loewe, words by Alan Jay Lerner)
*Best Scoring of a Musical Picture
*Best Film Editing
*Best Costume Design

Maurice Chevalier won an Honorary Award (statuette) "for his contributions to the world of entertainment for more than half a century."

Gigi swept the Oscars, setting a new record for most Awards won.

---

she was 70. In 1950, a French movie version was made, and was soon followed by a non-musical Broadway play with a young unknown by the name of Audrey Hepburn. Then, in 1957, producer Arthur Freed (*The Wizard of Oz*) and director Vincente Minnelli (*Meet Me in St. Louis*) hit upon the idea of a musical. They immediately turned to Alan Jay Lerner and Frederick Loewe, the musical pair behind *My Fair Lady*, still in its unprecedented Broadway run.

Some called the result a *My Fair Gigi*, with many of the songs nearly paraphrases of those from the first musical. Compare, for example, *My Fair Lady*'s "The Rain in Spain" with *Gigi*'s "The Night They Invented Champagne," or Henry Higgins' musings in "I've Grown Accustomed to Her Face" with Louis Jordan's longing for "Gigi." Even the critics noticed the similarities. As *The New York Times* wrote, "There won't be much point in anybody trying to produce a film of 'My Fair Lady' for awhile, because Arthur

Freed has virtually done it with 'Gigi' . . ." (The producers of *My Fair Lady* must have been reading *The Times*, because it took six more years for that play to become a film.)

Chemistry was a key element in the success of *Gigi*. The cast worked well in pairs—Maurice Chevalier opposite Hermoine Gingold; Leslie Caron with Louis Jordan—and occasional mixes of the above created whole new recipes for fun and song. Yet it is ironic that with all the Oscars this great musical won, not one of the film's fine cast walked away with an Award (although Maurice Chevalier received an honorary Oscar).

Leslie Caron was born near Paris to a French father and an American-born mother, a former dancer. She studied ballet, and at age 16 was discovered in a local company by Gene Kelly; he later selected her to co-star in *An American in Paris* (1951), thus launching her film career. She is still working today, making occasional TV appearances.

BEN-HUR

METRO-GOLDWYN-MAYER
$36,992,088

1959

"EXTRAORDINARY, OF GREATER DIMENSIONS THAN ANY FILM OF OUR TIME."
—*THE HOLLYWOOD REPORTER*

METRO MADE a go-for-broke move in 1959. The financially ailing studio sank $15,000,000 into a remake of an old film based on an even older novel. The film was *Ben-Hur*, considered a "spectacular" back in 1921 when the Cinematograph Corporation spent $600,000 to acquire the rights to General Lew Wallace's 1880 novel. Produced in 1926 by MGM, the silent film cost $4,000,000, starred Ramon Novarro and Francis X. Bushman, and by 1936 had grossed $10,000,000 for the studio. This proven property sitting in their Culver City vaults seemed the perfect vehicle for a remake, especially in the wide-screen, religious-epic epoch of the 1950s. Leo tossed back his mane and gave one last roar. It was the roar heard 'round the world.

Ben-Hur was the most expensive film ever made at the time of its release. It took five years of preparation, six and one-half months of shooting in Italy at the Cinecitta studios, and nine months of editing in Hollywood to produce the three hour, 37-minute movie.

Screenplay by Karl Tunberg

From the novel by Gen. Lew Wallace

Produced by Sam Zimbalist

Directed by William Wyler

CAST

Judah Ben-Hur . . . . Charlton Heston
Quintus Arrius . . . . Jack Hawkins
Messala . . . . Stephen Boyd
Esther . . . . Haya Harareet
Sheik Ilderim . . . . Hugh Griffith

ACADEMY AWARD NOMINATIONS

12 nominations, 11 wins*

*Best Picture
*Best Actor (Charlton Heston)
*Best Supporting Actor (Hugh Griffith)
*Best Director (William Wyler)
 Best Screenplay Based on Material from Another Medium
*Best Cinematography, Color
*Best Art Direction-Set Decoration, Color
*Best Sound
*Best Scoring of a Dramatic or Comedy Picture
*Best Film Editing
*Best Costume Design, Color
*Best Special Effects

Vital statistics: 50,000 extras, 100,000 costumes, 300 sets. The chariot race, the film's most famous sequence, required six months of planning and two months to shoot, at a cost of $1,000,000, making it the most expensive 11 minutes moviegoers had ever seen. The film won enough Academy Awards to sink a Roman galley: 11—count 'em—11, more than any film before or since.

Producer Sam Zimbalist (who died of a heart attack before the film was completed) assembled some of the greatest talents in Hollywood. For his director, he chose William Wyler, whose credits included *Mrs. Miniver* and *The Best Years of Our Lives* (and in 1966, *Funny Girl*); the script was written by Karl Tunberg, with assistance from S. N. Behrman, Gore Vidal, and Christopher Fry. According to *Time*, the lines "sometimes sing with good rhetoric and quiet poetry." And for the title role, who else but Charlton Heston, late of Mt. Sinai, whom someone once called "Hollywood's resident epic hero"? Other fine cast members included Stephen Boyd as Ben-Hur's nemesis Messala, plus Jack Hawkins, Haya Harareet, Martha Scott, Sam Jaffe, and an odd assortment of several dozen credited speaking parts such as

"Rower No. 42," "Rower No. 28," and "Leper."

Stephen Boyd's biggest film was *Ben-Hur*. Born William Millar in Belfast on July 4, 1928, the actor began his stage career in childhood, and arrived in Canada when he was 18, performing on radio and in summer stock. He toured the States with a stock company in 1950, and set his sights on an acting career there. His first film break came in England, with *An Alligator Named Daisy* (1955). He also appeared in *The Man Who Never Was* (1956) and a few others before his co-starring role as Messala in *Ben-Hur*. He was featured in *Fantastic Voyage* (1966) and *The Bible* (as Nimrod; 1966), but never really had another role with the importance of Messala. In the early '70s, Boyd appeared mainly in low-budget Spanish films. He died in 1977, at the age of 49.

For this most spectacular of films there was without a doubt *the* most spectacular of scenes—the chariot race. Producer Sam Zimbalist selected Andrew Marton to direct this sequence, since Marton had successfully worked with William Wyler on the Dunkirk segment in *Mrs. Miniver*. Marton began by securing the necessary horses. The race was to be run by nine chariots drawn by four horses each, but he actually used doubles and "understudy" teams, for a total of 82 horses, all obtained in Yugoslavia. Months were spent rehearsing the teams on a duplicate race track. Chuck Heston already was a skilled rider from experience in Westerns, and his strong hands and shoulder muscles gave him an advantage. Stephen Boyd had a much rougher time of it, with his hands constantly blistered and bloody. In the filming, Heston and Boyd did all their own chariot driving except for two stunts. One stunt which Boyd did, for a close-up of him being dragged under his chariot, left him battered and bruised.

There were some accidents, although despite rumors to the contrary, there were no fatalities. Once a couple of chariots smashed into two cameras as they came out of a turn. The other serious accident occurred when stuntman Yakima Canutt's 22-year-old son Joe bounced his chariot, sailing into the air. As he landed, his chariot flipped him into a head-stand and he was thrown out between the horses. He instinctively grabbed the cross-bar, dragging behind it. Amazingly, he required only four stitches on his chin, and returned to work the same day.

It is scenes like the above, with their attention to perfection, that made *Ben-Hur* the darling of the critics and public alike. It marked the end of an era, the last of the epic blockbusters—and MGM's last number-one film to the present time.

SLEEPING BEAUTY
WALT DISNEY PRODUCTIONS
$21,998,000

THERE MUST BE a plaque somewhere on the Walt Disney lot memorializing 1959. With three of the top films of that year bearing the familiar flourish of the "Walt Disney" signature, 1959 can only be called "The Year of Disney." Together, *Sleeping Beauty*, *The Shaggy Dog*, and *Darby O'Gill and the Little People* netted $42,651,000—a fine pot of gold under the Disney rainbow.

The best and most successful of the year's trio was *Sleeping Beauty*, the classic story of the young princess and her narcoleptic kingdom, the struggle for good and evil, and her eventual winning of the charming Prince Phillip.

This was also the most elaborate (read: expensive) of the Disney animated features. Preliminary work on *Sleeping Beauty* began in 1950 and went into full production in 1953, but was delayed with the development and opening of the Disneyland theme park. The film was released in wide-screen Technirama-70 at a cost of $6,000,000—nothing to yawn at there. (Only one other Disney animated feature has ever used this process: *The Black Cauldron* [1985].) Artists found the technique difficult to work with, complaining about working in a "letterbox" format, trying to balance the action in the center of the screen while filling the sides with more supporting characters.

Walt wanted to adapt Tchaikovsky's "Sleeping Beauty Ballet" for the musical score, so the studio's top composer, George Bruns, was dispatched to West Germany, where the music was recorded in six-channel stereo by the Berlin Symphony Orchestra. Additionally, lyrics were added to the main theme—"Once Upon a Dream"—and some new (not very memorable) songs were created.

As in other Disney animated features with human characters, live models were used to aid the artists. For Princess Aurora (the title slumberer), veteran actress Helen Stanley posed, cavorted, waltzed, and snoozed for the artists. In an interview at the time, Ms. Stanley remarked: "We rehearsed the big waltz sequence for three days before we shot it. I had to wear a specially made costume and a cumbersome wig, plus learn all the dialogue." No mention was made of how she survived the sleeping segments.

The voice of Ms. Beauty was supplied by soprano Mary Costa, who went on to a successful operatic career following her vocal appearance in *Sleeping Beauty*. Recently she learned of the huge, uh, royalties earned by the videocassette sales, and has filed suit, claiming her 1952 contract entitles her to a piece of the Disney pie. Yawn.

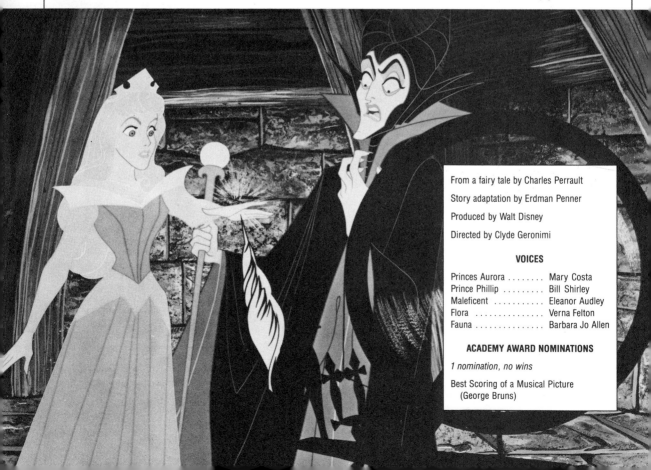

From a fairy tale by Charles Perrault

Story adaptation by Erdman Penner

Produced by Walt Disney

Directed by Clyde Geronimi

VOICES

Princes Aurora . . . . Mary Costa
Prince Phillip . . . . Bill Shirley
Maleficent . . . . Eleanor Audley
Flora . . . . Verna Felton
Fauna . . . . Barbara Jo Allen

ACADEMY AWARD NOMINATIONS

1 nomination, no wins

Best Scoring of a Musical Picture (George Bruns)

THE SHAGGY DOG

WALT DISNEY PRODUCTIONS
$12,317,000

"In canis corpore transmuto."
—SECRET SPELL

Don't say the above words unless you are seriously interested in spending a good part of your life as a shape-shifter . . . to wit: a shaggy English sheepdog. While the incantation (translation: "I change into the body of a dog") is likely to produce laughs from the Pope and a few other Latin buffs, it was certainly a successful chant for the folks at Disney, where it translated into "big box office bucks."

Since the '30s, Walt Disney had been planning a film based on the novel *The Hound of Florence* by Felix Salten (author of *Bambi*). The project lapsed during the war, and in 1957 Walt proposed it to ABC as a television series. The network turned it down as being too far-fetched, so Walt went back to his original idea of a feature. He chose to have it shot in black and white, rather than color, reasoning that color would add a disturbing note of reality to the supernatural comedics. (Today, however, colorized versions have been made available by Disney Studios.)

Although basically a kid's picture, the film did well with a wide-ranging audience. Part of the reason is the broad appeal of the cast, comprised of child star Kevin "Moochie" Corcoran, some teens, and a few mostly misguided adults. For this slapstick comedy, Disney re-teamed Tommy Kirk and Kevin Corcoran, the brothers in *Old Yeller*, in

Screenplay by Bill Walsh and
Lillie Hayward

Suggested by *The Hound of Florence* by
Felix Salten

Produced by Walt Disney

Directed by Charles Barton

CAST

Wilson Daniels	Fred MacMurray
Frieda Daniels	Jean Hagen
Wilby Daniels	Tommy Kirk
Moochie Daniels	Kevin Corcoran
Buzz Miller	Tim Considine
Allison D'Allessio	Annette Funicello

another dog tale. Fred MacMurray was cast as the canine-o-phobic father in the film, and soon found he had a whole new career as a Disney character actor, going on to star in a succession of Disney hits such as *The Absent-Minded Professor* and *Son of Flubber*. Annette Funicello, fresh out of Mouseketeer ears, made her motion picture debut in this production at the age of 16, and she, too, went on to appear in other Disney films, as well as all those Frankie Avalon beach movies.

But the real star of the show was the dog himself. The three-year-old sheep-dog was actually a non-pro belonging to a clerk for the California State Highways. Trainers Bill Koehler and Hal Driscoll spent three months prepping the pooch named Sam (renamed "Shaggy" by the Disney staff) for his first starring role. Although it may appear as if a person is dressed in a

dog suit, the director seldom used a human double, with Sam doing nearly all of his own stunts. One particularly clever bit involved the dog driving a hot-rod convertible. To get the scene, Koehler and Driscoll had mittens put over Sam's feet, and at the command "Feet up," the dog obediently placed his paws on the wheel. Thongs were used to anchor the mittens in the steering position. On the other side of the car, a man crouched to reach a synchronized steering wheel, driving the car while looking through a viewing slot. The effect was realistic, making it appear that the dog was actually driving the car.

The Disney Studios managed to get some mileage out of a couple of sequels—*The Shaggy DA* (1976) and *The Return of the Shaggy Dog* (Made-for-TV, 1987). The original, though, is still the best.

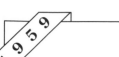

OPERATION PETTICOAT
UNIVERSAL-INTERNATIONAL
$9,321,555

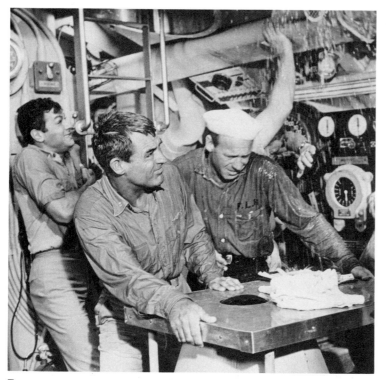

IT IS HARD to believe that a comedy about a pink submarine with a cargo of women and toilet paper could be based on fact, but that was the claim made by story writers Paul King and Joseph Stone.

It seems that the United States, for a time, had a bright red sub, the *Sea Dragon*, operating in the Pacific; an explosion near her berth had blistered her surface paint, eventually reducing it to the red priming coat. The USS *Skipjack* got into a bureaucratic hassle with its requisitions for toilet paper. Two pregnant natives of the Solomon Islands gave birth aboard the USS *Geta*, attended by nuns, who'd also been evacuated. Nurses were evacuated onto U.S. ships from islands after the fall of Manila. The USS *Bowfin* accidentally torpedoed a *bus* filled with Japanese sailors. Armed with these historical facts, King and Stone finally convinced producer Robert Arthur to make this unlikely movie.

The teaming of Cary Grant with

Tony Curtis proved to be pure inspiration for Universal-International in this high comedy about the war we didn't find so funny until films like this were made. The story is narrated by Grant, reading to us from the USS *Sea Tiger* captain's journal (a format later used successfully in the television series "Star Trek," which opened each week with excerpts from the Captain's log). But that's about as serious as the film ever gets. Most of this farce deals with Grant's conniving junior officer, played by Tony Curtis, and his attempts to scrounge supplies for the submarine, include a much-needed supply of sexy nurses. Appropriately risqué (for that time) humor abounds, and this early Blake Edwards hit shows the director's skill and promise in directing the type of farcical comedy which has continued to delight audiences through several decades.

Cary Grant garnered the lion's share of critical approval. *Variety* called Grant "a living lesson in getting laughs with-

out lines." *The Hollywood Reporter* also noted this aspect of Grant's performance: "Though he gets many laughs, Cary plays an essentially straight part, and theatrical pros will recognize it as one of the trickiest acting jobs of his long and brilliant career."

Tony Curtis' career was barely underway at the time. Curtis, né Bernard Schwartz, had been signed by Universal as a contract player in 1949 after paying his dues in the Catskills' "Borscht Belt" and on Broadway, but the studio hadn't found the right vehicle to showcase his talents. He was still basically a "pretty-boy" type when signed to do *Operation Petticoat* (although an appearance in *The Defiant Ones* the previous year had already won him a Best Actor nomination). Critics began to sit up and take notice, *Variety* stating that: "Tony Curtis is a splendid foil [for Cary Grant], one of the two or three best young comedians around, and his different style of playing meshes easily with Grant's."

Other lesser-known cast members who would go on to greater things included Marion Ross as one of the nurses (she became Mrs. Cunningham on TV's "Happy Days"), and Gavin MacLeod as one of the crew (he later became captain of "The Love Boat").

Screenplay by Stanley Shapiro and Maurice Richlin

Based on a story by Paul King and Joseph Stone

Produced by Robert Arthur

Directed by Blake Edwards

CAST

Comdr. Matt Sherman ... Cary Grant
Lieut. Nick Holden ..... Tony Curtis
Dolores Crandall .... Joan O'Brien
Barbara Duran .... Dina Merrill
Ernest Hunkle .... Gavin MacLeod
Ruth Colfax .... Marion Ross

ACADEMY AWARD NOMINATIONS

1 nomination, no wins

Best Story and Screenplay Written Directly for the Screen

DARBY O'GILL AND THE LITTLE PEOPLE

WALT DISNEY PRODUCTIONS
$8,336,000

"My thanks to King Brian of Knocknasheega and his Leprechauns, whose gracious co-operation made this picture possible. —Walt Disney"
—OPENING CARD

CLEVER, THAT Uncle Walt. In opening his film about the legendary wee folk of Ireland and the human who encounters them, the producer established the "authentic" feeling he wanted to give the picture. True, the credits do list a technical advisor named Michael O'Herlihy, but he was more an expert in Irish lore and a dialogue coach, and not an actual leprechaun himself.

To give this live-acted film (one of Disney's best) even more clout, the special effects were carefully planned and executed by Peter Ellenshaw, whom the studio had used as a matte artist on *20,000 Leagues Under the Sea*. Under his direction, a huge

Throne Room set was designed for *Darby* so that certain scenes could be shot without any special process. Darby and the Little People were all full-size human beings; the apparent difference in their scale was an optical illusion created by their distances relative to the camera. The enormous set required so much light to maintain the depth of field that at one point the production blacked out a portion of Burbank.

The entire picture was filmed on Disney's Burbank lot and on two Southern California ranches, with the beautiful scenery of Ireland being filmed by a second unit. This footage was later combined with the matte paintings and live sequences to obtain the overall effect.

Cast in the title role was 73-year-old Irish actor Albert Sharpe, who had retired since his appearance in 1954 in

MGM's *Brigadoon*. Disney's casting people tracked him down in his ivy-covered cottage near Belfast and convinced him to play the feisty old Shanachie (storyteller) who matches wits with the King of the Leprechauns.

The part of the young Irish romantic lead went to a Scotsman, however. Connery—Sean Connery. Two years before he became James Bond, while still virtually unknown in America, the young actor was spotted by Disney's casting people while he was working in Britain on a Paramount film, *Another Time, Another Place*. In *Darby*, not only did Connery get the girl, but he won her heart with his rendition of "Pretty Irish Girl," his first—and last—screen song. Director Robert Stevenson contemplated dubbing him, but the duet with co-star Janet Munro remained on the soundtrack and was later released as a single in Britain.

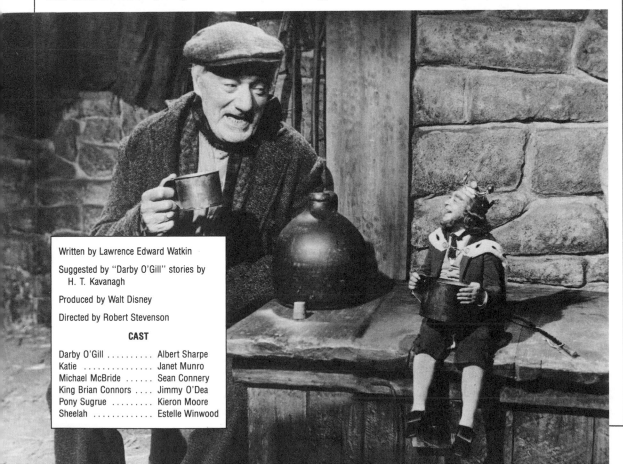

Written by Lawrence Edward Watkin

Suggested by "Darby O'Gill" stories by
  H. T. Kavanagh

Produced by Walt Disney

Directed by Robert Stevenson

CAST

Darby O'Gill	Albert Sharpe
Katie	Janet Munro
Michael McBride	Sean Connery
King Brian Connors	Jimmy O'Dea
Pony Sugrue	Kieron Moore
Sheelah	Estelle Winwood

1960 – 1969

Throughout the Sixties, Hollywood, still clinging to familiarity, found sustenance in proven success formulas. Musicals were a mainstay, spearheaded by classical Broadway fare like *West Side Story, The Music Man, My Fair Lady, The Sound of Music, Funny Girl*, and *Hello, Dolly!.* Biblical epics were history except for *Spartacus* and *The Bible*, and a new genre, the "historical epic," made an entrance. These epics included *Exodus, The Alamo, The Guns of Navarone, El Cid, How the West Was Won, The Longest Day, Lawrence of Arabia, Cleopatra, A Man for All Seasons*, and *The Dirty Dozen.*

The films of the Sixties were becoming more permissive in their content and language. Nudity began appearing not only in bawdy films like *Tom Jones*, but in classics like *Romeo and Juliet.* The 70-millimeter camera now went everywhere, especially into the bedroom.

With Hollywood's new permissiveness came a new rating system for movies. Established in 1968 to advise parents in planning film attendance by their offspring, this rating system, in a slightly modified form, is still with us today. The Motion Picture Association of America (MPAA), under the leadership of president Jack Valenti, established the following letter guidelines:

G   Suggested for GENERAL audiences.
M   Suggested for MATURE audiences
    (parental discretion advised).
R   RESTRICTED—Persons under 16 not admitted
    unless accompanied by parent or adult guardian.
X   Persons under 16 not admitted.

The Hayes Office and its censorship were gone, but so was Hollywood's age of innocence. This new rating system brought with it an implied censorship: if a distributor didn't like a rating a film received, it was up to the studio or producer to make appropriate changes in the film. If not, a whole set of ticket-purchasers might be eliminated—box office disaster.

1

SWISS FAMILY ROBINSON

WALT DISNEY PRODUCTIONS
$20,178,000

OF ALL THE Walt Disney live-acted films, this was certainly one of the most difficult ever undertaken. In searching for the proper remote desert island, the Disney scouts selected Tobago, part of Trinidad in the West Indies. The island was a treasure-trove of all things tropical: sun, sand, colorful water, palm trees—and hurricanes. After spending a fortune constructing sheet-metal soundstages, the crew was hit by Hurricane Edith, one of the biggest storms ever to strike Tobago. It flooded the stage and washed out the treehouse and other sets. They couldn't shoot for weeks, during which time the crew not only reconstructed the sets, but helped the islanders rebuild their homes destroyed by the storm.

The story called for a large treehouse for the Robinson family, and the crew built the most elaborate one imaginable. It was such a hit that Disney decided to have it duplicated for Disneyland. Visitors to that park and to Walt Disney World's Magic Kingdom can climb through the tri-level chalet with its family room and two bedrooms. All the details were reproduced in the 70-foot-high treehouse, including the sailcloth curtains and cracked mirror. A waterfall-operated waterwheel feeds a storage barrel through a system of buckets and bamboo plumbing.

One of the great challenges to the production crew was the large assortment of animals needed, and *Swiss Family Robinson* holds the record for variety. More than 200 birds and animals were used in the six months of filming. Among the members of the

Disney menagerie were ostriches, zebras, anacondas, monitor lizards, iguanas, monkeys, tigers, cheetahs, hyenas, alligators, dogs, goats, a cow, an elephant, and a mule, plus a large variety of tropical birds, fowl, and a couple of dozen vultures.

An excellent cast helped make this film a hit at the box office—again, with an eye to appeal to all age groups. The cast included the third appearance of Kevin Corcoran and Tommy Kirk paired as brothers (by now, *they* even thought they were related); John Mills, renowned British actor, as papa Robinson (although Disney fans couldn't help but think of him as *Hayley's* father); Dorothy McGuire as the mother (she'd been the mother of the young boys in *Old Yeller*); James MacArthur, Helen Hayes' son, who at the time was starring in

"Hawaii Five-O" (playing Danno, as in "Book him, Danno"); Janet Munro, who had co-starred in the Disney hit *Darby O'Gill and the Little People* the previous year; and Sessue Hayakawa, the heavy from *The Bridge on the River Kwai,* as the Pirate Chief. This basically recycled group always worked well for Disney, with the audience not seeming to mind the same "family" appearing in film after film.

John Mills was one of the most illustrious actors ever to appear in a Disney film. The English-born performer made his professional debut as a chorus boy in a London revue in 1929 at the age of 21. By 1932, he was landing roles in films. His career would see him making nearly a hundred pictures in all, including *The Chalk Garden* (with Hayley, 1963) and *Ryan's Daughter,* for which he won the Academy Award (1970). His daughter Juliet Mills is also an actress. Mills died in 1982, at the age of 74.

While some critics were upset at the license taken by the Disney gang with the 147-year-old tale by Johann Wyss, most gave *Swiss Family Robinson* a nod of approval for its fine production val-

Screenplay by Lowell S. Hawley

Based on the novel by Johann Wyss

Produced by Bill Anderson

Directed by Ken Annakin

CAST

Father	John Mills
Mother	Dorothy McGuire
Fritz	James MacArthur
Ernst	Tommy Kirk
Roberta	Janet Munro
Francis	Kevin Corcoran
Kuala	Sessue Hayakawa

ues and stunning visual imagery. While *Variety* praised the cinematography and the Technicolor views of Tobago, the trade paper lambasted the film for its lack of realism: "Huge boulders and logs dispatched downhill by the Robinsons at their corsair adversaries are so obviously cardboard that the scene just about lapses into sheer slapstick for everyone but tots." When the film opened on December 23, *The New York Times* gave it a terrific notice, writing that "any parent who denies it to the kids deserves to be shipwrecked on a remote island, at least till the new year."

For the Disney organization, *Swiss Family Robinson* was the gift that keeps on giving. Walt Disney Productions had a loss of $1,500,000 during 1960, but the year ended on a happy note, and thanks to re-releases, this movie became one of the studio's most successful films ever.

PSYCHO
PARAMOUNT/UNIVERSAL
$11,200,000

"I am to provide the public with beneficial shocks. Civilization has become so protective that we're no longer able to get our goose bumps instinctively. The only way to remove the numbness and revive our moral equilibrium is to use artificial means to bring about the shock. The best way to achieve that, it seems to me, is through a movie."
—ALFRED HITCHCOCK,
QUOTED IN *THE FILMS OF ALFRED HITCHCOCK*

WITHOUT A DOUBT, *Psycho* is one of the scariest pieces of celluloid make-believe to ever run through a projector. Yet Hitch himself saw the picture as a *humorous* film, his idea of the blackest of black comedies. Some joke. After viewing this film, no one would ever feel quite safe in the shower again. And it is not known whether or not the motel business fell off after the film's release, but you can bet that anyone who owned one named "Bates" quickly changed it.

Much of the shock value of this picture comes from Hitchcock's use of black and white. The director himself selected the monochrome tones because he felt that the bloody shower scene would be *too* realistic for his audience. If anyone should ever decide to colorize this picture (and undoubtedly that day will come) you might be wise to listen to the maestro's warning and turn down the color control, or face the consequences.

Suspense was heightened by the music Hitchcock selected. With the only soundtrack ever to be composed entirely of strings, composer Bernard Herrmann gave the director the "black-and-white music" he sought. The shrieking of the violins coupled with the stabbing in the shower scene make for a moment that virtually every film historian has termed "classic."

Actually, the shower scene was shot with doubles for both stars Anthony Perkins and Janet Leigh. Perkins was in New York rehearsing for a play when the scene was filmed in Hollywood, and he never actually wielded the knife in this sequence. And Janet Leigh also used a body double since partial nudity was used, and stars very seldom did their own nude scenes in those days. Most disillusioning of all, no real blood was used. Instead, chocolate sauce was seen flowing out of the body and down the drain! Black and white does have its advantages.

Although the knife never actually makes bodily contact in the shower scene, our minds tell us differently. This sequence set the pace for later violent films of the decade, such as *Bonnie and Clyde*.

Sequels? It took a while, but in 1983 Anthony Perkins reprised his role as Norman Bates in *Psycho II*. It did surprisingly well, so Universal (owner of all Hitchcock properties) did still another sequel, appropriately titled *Psycho III* (1986) with Anthony Perkins not only acting, but directing the film. It was a dismal failure, but Universal continues to get mileage out of Norman Bates and his mother—in 1987, NBC aired a two-hour pilot film for a proposed series named "Bates Motel," starring Bud Cort.

Screenplay by Joseph Stefano

Based on the novel by Robert Bloch

Produced and directed by Alfred Hitchcock

CAST

Norman Bates .... Anthony Perkins
Marion Crane .... Janet Leigh
Lila Crane .... Vera Miles
Sam Loomis .... John Gavin
Milton Arbogast .... Martin Balsam

ACADEMY AWARD NOMINATIONS

4 nominations, no wins

Best Supporting Actress (Janet Leigh)
Best Director (Alfred Hitchcock)
Best Cinematography, Black and White
Best Art Direction-Set Decoration,
   Black and White

SPARTACUS
UNIVERSAL-INTERNATIONAL
$10,300,454

IN SPENDING $12,000,000 on the making of *Spartacus*, Universal-International was banking on the two top box office stars of the year—Tony Curtis (number one) and Kirk Douglas (number two)—to draw people into the theaters for the latest entry in the Biblical-spectacular genre that had been so popular in the '50s. Although far from a flop, the film failed to break even, and it would be a decade more before Universal again had a top-five hit.

Kirk Douglas himself was the film's executive producer, and was particularly drawn to the theme of the film. In *The Films of the Sixties*, Douglas is quoted as saying: "I tended to be attracted to roles of people fighting society. The focus is on a man bucking the system and getting destroyed in the process." Not only was this to be the theme of many a film to come during the decade, but it would be mirrored with the unrest that was to sweep America during the '60s.

For his screenwriter, Douglas selected Dalton Trumbo, one of the so-called "Hollywood Ten" who was sentenced to a year in jail in 1950 for

---

Screenplay by Dalton Trumbo

Based on the novel by Howard Fast

Produced by Edward Lewis

Directed by Stanley Kubrick

CAST

Spartacus	Kirk Douglas
Crassus	Laurence Olivier
Antoninus	Tony Curtis
Varinia	Jean Simmons
Gracchus	Charles Laughton
Batiatus	Peter Ustinov
Caesar	John Gavin

ACADEMY AWARD NOMINATIONS

6 nominations, 4 wins*

**Best Supporting Actor (Peter Ustinov)
**Best Cinematography, Color
**Best Art Direction-Set Decoration, Color
 Best Scoring of a Dramatic or
  Comedy Picture
 Best Film Editing
**Best Costume Design, Color

---

refusing to testify before House Committee on Un-American Activities. The blacklisted writer had been forced to work under a pseudonym since his release from jail, and the man who had written *30 Seconds Over Tokyo* was reduced to writing a string of "B" movies. In 1957, under the name of Robert Rich, Trumbo won an Oscar for his script of *The Brave One*. And with his work on *Spartacus*, he was able to put the dreaded blacklist behind him.

It was an excellent script, not just because it made use of the wide screen and spectacular visual events in its storytelling, but also because of the fine dialogue, as illustrated by this exchange between Antoninus (Tony Curtis) and Spartacus (Kirk Douglas):

ANTONINUS
Are you afraid to die, Spartacus?

SPARTACUS
No more than I was to be born.

Interesting little bit of philosophy, profound in its simplicity.

So there were thousands of extras who made the gladiatorial halftime look like Super Sunday as Roman legions marched before their leaders. And the all-star cast didn't hurt, either—names like Laurence Olivier, Jean Simmons, Charles Laughton, Peter (can't have a film about Rome without him) Ustinov, John Gavin, and many more known and unknown actors, including a couple of the Canutt boys, Tap and Joe (who also appeared in *Ben-Hur*).

Stanley Kubrick did an excellent job as director, although he was frustrated over his lack of control. Nevertheless, the avant-garde director won praise from the critics. According to *Variety*, "The individual who emerges above all is Director Kubrick. At 31, and with only four other pix behind him . . . Kubrick has out-DeMilled the old master in spectacle, without ever permitting the story or the people who are the core of the drama to become lost in the shuffle. He demonstrates here a technical talent and comprehension of human values."

Spartacus is frequently shown on independent television stations, generally over a two-day period due to its 184-minute length. (Originally it was 196 minutes long, but has been trimmed by twelve minutes.) Although its theme is by no means revolutionary today, *Spartacus* still stands as a tribute to the soul's yearning for freedom—written by a man who ought to know.

EXODUS
UNITED ARTISTS
$8,331,582

LEON URIS' novel *Exodus* was a best-seller's best-seller. After 80 weeks on the list and sales upwards of 4,000,000 copies, it arrived on the (wide) screen amidst much well-deserved fanfare. Since filming was done on location in Israel and Cyprus, producer Otto Preminger was able to bring in this 212-minute epic for a cost of only $4,000,000, cheap for a film of this scope. There were the usual thousands of extras—this film claimed to have 45,000 of them—plus a moving script by previously blacklisted "Hollywood Ten" writer Dalton Trumbo. *Spartacus* had not yet been released, and Preminger was actually the first one to give Trumbo a chance to write under his own name once again.

Preminger's casting choices were unusual, since most of the major roles of Jews were played by non-Jews. Paul Newman was selected for the part of Ari Ben Canaan, a hero in the Mosaic tradition, and it is hard to imagine anyone else in the part; Eva Marie Saint is a perfect counterpoint as the WASPish love interest whom he wins over to his cause; Sal Mineo, an Italian-American, was so convincing in his portrayal of the zealous young Jewish terrorist that he won an Academy Award nomination; and even 14-year-old Jill Haworth as Karen was effective as a Nordic Jewish refugee (although she could have used a dialogue coach).

Exodus received generally favorable critical acclaim, although most critics found it overly long. *The New York Times* called the film "a dazzling, eye-filling, nerve-tingling display of a wide variety of individual and mass reactions to awesome challenges and, in some of its sharpest personal details, a fine reflection of experience that rips the heart."

Although the production team did its best to try to please both the Arabs and Jews in Israel by constantly rewriting the script during filming, there were still complaints from both groups. Both Otto Preminger and Paul Newman received threatening letters while on location. Perhaps that is to be expected of any political film. Still, the message of *Exodus* is one that should be heeded by all warring factions. At the end of the picture, Ari Ben Canaan buries two dead patriots—Arab and Jew—in a common grave. In one of the film's most poignant moments, he says: "The dead always share the earth in peace; and that's not enough. It's time for the living to have a turn. The day will come when Arab and Jew will share in a peaceful life this land that they have always shared in death."

Nearly 30 years have passed since those lines were written, but unfortunately, not much has changed in the Mideast. The Arab-Israeli conflict is flaring to this day, a bit of Hollywood irony, since so many films involving recent history are usually out of date shortly after their release.

Screenplay by Dalton Trumbo

Based on the novel by Leon Uris

Produced and directed by Otto Preminger

CAST

Ari Ben Canaan	Paul Newman
Kitty Fremont	Eva Marie Saint
General Sutherland	Ralph Richardson
Major Caldwell	Peter Lawford
Barak Ben Canaan	Lee J. Cobb
Dov Landau	Sal Mineo

ACADEMY AWARD NOMINATIONS

3 nominations, 1 win*

Best Supporting Actor (Sal Mineo)
Best Cinematography, Color
*Best Scoring of a Dramatic or Comedy Picture (Ernest Gold)

THE ALAMO

UNITED ARTISTS
$7,918,776

IT'S AMAZING that John Wayne could pass himself off as Davy Crockett, when every child over the age of eight knew that the "king of the wild frontier" looked exactly like Fess Parker. That actor had popularized the frontier hero (and struck terror into the hearts of raccoons everywhere) six years earlier in the Walt Disney version of *Davy Crockett.* Now The Duke was proclaiming himself heir to "old Betsy" and the coonskin cap.

What's truly amazing is that *The Alamo,* directed by Wayne himself, proved a huge financial success. The drawing power of John Wayne was, like the star, bigger than life.

In a year when longer equaled better, *The Alamo* was a hot contender, ringing in at just under 200 minutes. All the epic trappings were there: the 1,500 horses, the $1.5-million reproduction of the Alamo and surrounding village, the wide-screen Todd-AO treatment, and the all-star cast—including Richard Widmark, Laurence Harvey, Richard Boone, Chill Wills, and, for the Dick Clark/bubblegum set, Philadelphia's own Frankie Avalon (without Annette).

According to historians, Davy Crockett didn't die in battle at the Alamo at all, but was taken prisoner. Brought before Santa Anna, he tried to save his neck by claiming he was a tourist who had sought refuge in the Alamo. The Mexican general was unconvinced, and had Crockett and his fellow prisoners run through with sabers. This film, however, portrays the story in the romanticized "they all died at the Alamo" version which most audiences believe is the truth.

Screenplay by James Edward Grant

Produced and directed by John Wayne

CAST

Col. David Crockett ... John Wayne
Col. James Bowie .... Richard Widmark
Col. William Travis .... Laurence Harvey
Smitty .... Frankie Avalon
Capt. James Bonham .. Patrick Wayne
Flaca .... Linda Cristal
Gen. Sam Houston ... Richard Boone

ACADEMY AWARD NOMINATIONS

7 nominations, 1 win*

Best Picture
Best Supporting Actor (Chill Wills)
Best Cinematography, Color
*Best Sound
Best Song ("The Green Leaves of Summer," music by Dimitri Tiomkin, words by Paul F. Webster)
Best Scoring of a Dramatic or Comedy Picture (Dimitri Tiomkin)
Best Film Editing

The best part of the film comes when John Wayne gives his Big Speech. It's so Waynesque, it seems like it might have been written as a parody of the actor, but it's meant to be taken quite seriously:

"I want ya to listen tight. I'm talkin' about all people everywhere . . . that's what's important . . . to feel useful in this old world, to hit a lick against what's wrong or to say a word for what's right even tho' ya get walloped for saying that word. Now, I may sound like a Bible-beater yellin' up a revival at a river crossing camp. But that don't change the truth none. There's right and there's wrong, and ya gotta do one or the other. Ya do the one and yer living; ya do the other and ya may be walkin' around, but yer dead as a beaver hat."

Yes, he was an actor delivering lines, but he believed in those words, and, as it did with another well-known conservative actor, the Republican party tried to convince him to run for office. "I can't afford the cut in salary," Wayne once said, "and who would vote for an actor anyway?" Perhaps not too many, but the citizens of Republican-dominated Orange County honored Wayne after he passed away many years later by naming their local airport after him.

101 DALMATIANS
WALT DISNEY PRODUCTIONS
$38,562,000

N O ONE COULD tell a dog story, shaggy or otherwise, like Walt Disney. After successes like *Old Yeller*, *Lady and the Tramp*, and *The Shaggy Dog*, Walt again turned to the canine kingdom for his next feature-length animated movie. You say you want dogs? Okay, here's *one hundred and one* of them, all adorable and cuddly, with lots of spots, and the ability to make their master a big pile of box office kibble (at $38,500,000 in rentals to date, that's close to $400,000 per puppy).

Based on the book *The Hundred and One Dalmatians* by Dodie Smith, this film represented a significant departure from previous Disney animated fare in several respects. Unlike most of its predecessors, the story was not derived from a classic fairy tale and took place in a contemporary setting instead of in a magical or fantasy world. It's a tale of dognapping by one of the meanest villainesses ever created, Disney or otherwise. Cruella De Vil is a

candidate for animal rights activists' dartboard of the month. With her deathmask-like face and fondness for wearing fur, she plans the demise of the innocent Dalmatian puppies whose spotted skins she sees as potential coat material ("Poison them, drown them, bash them in the head"). She makes the Wicked Witch in *Snow White* look like a Sunday School teacher.

The fact that audiences identify with the dogs and not the humans in this and other Disney stories is not by accident. The stories are told from the anthropomorphized animal's point of view, emphasized by such comments as "At times she seems almost canine!" (a high compliment) and Pongo's calling his human his "pet."

As with other animated Disney movies about animals, lots of dog models were brought to the studio to be photographed for the artists. As Frank Thomas, one of the Disney animators, explained in a Disney press

release at the time: "The Dalmatians were complicated and tough to draw because of their sleek short-haired bodies. The character design required accurately drawn bones, muscles and structure instead of a more caricatured approach." Another Disney animator, Eric Larson, was responsible for the sequence in which the puppies watch TV. To capture the feeling, according to the same release, he pictured them as a bunch of kids in front of the set. "I just thought of what regular kids would do as they watched TV . . . one of the pups sits directly in front of the set blocking everyone else's view. Another is constantly hungry. It was a lot of fun doing that scene."

At the time of its initial release, *101 Dalmatians* introduced a revolutionary new process—Xerox photography, an electromagnetic technique for transferring animators' drawings directly to cels. It saved an enormous amount of time and money, especially in scenes in

which dozens of puppies fill the screen, each of them peppered with spots. The Xerox camera allowed the artists to animate one small group of puppies, then repeat this group across the entire surface, being careful that the scene did not appear too mechanical. Disney statisticians are fond of noting that there are exactly 6,469,952 spots on the backs of the dogs and puppies in 113,760 frames of film ("Pongo" has 72, "Perdita" has 68, and each pup sports 32 spots). Without the Xerox process, we'd probably still be waiting for the first showing of this movie.

Great care went into the selection of the vocal actors for the leading dog and human roles. Rod Taylor is the voice of Pongo. A popular star of science fiction films in the '50s and '60s, the Australian-born actor is best known for his starring roles in *The Birds* and *The Time Machine*.

For Cruella De Vil, the Disney team chose Betty Lou Gerson, who had previously provided the voice-over narration for *Cinderella*. Her impression of the wicked dognapper sounded quite a bit like Tallulah Bankhead, which delighted the producers. She also obliged the animators by modeling for them, slinking around the studio while they photographed and sketched the lean, high-cheekboned actress. As Ms. Gerson said in Disney's press release, "The character you see on the screen is a fairly accurate caricature of me—

Story by William Peet

Based on the book by Dodie Smith

Produced by Walt Disney

Directed by Wolfgang Reitherman, Hamilton S. Luske, and Clyde Geronimi

VOICES

Pongo	Rod Taylor
Cruella De Vil	Betty Lou Gerson
Roger	Ben Wright
Anita	Lisa Davis
Horace	Fred Worlock
Jasper	J. Pat O'Malley

except for the white streak in Cruella's hair."

Variety called the film "a painstaking creative effort and certainly a valuable and welcome addition to the current theatrical scene," adding that "children are certain to get a big kick out of it." *The New York Times* admitted that "even with a lady Lucifer hell-bent for their hides, those Dalmatians are a friendly lot worth knowing." *Time* described the feature as "one of the nicest things that have happened so far this year to dog's best friend: a full-length animated cartoon that should please just about everybody but cats . . . the wittiest, most charming, least pretentious cartoon feature Walt Disney has ever made."

101 Dalmatians has been re-released twice to date: in 1969, and again in 1985. Each time, a new generation of children have taken their parents to see this Disney classic, and it should soon be available on videocassette for your *dogs'* home viewing. Try not to let them crowd in front of the set.

②

WEST SIDE STORY
UNITED ARTISTS
$19,645,570

WILLIAM SHAKESPEARE. Leonard Bernstein. Robert Wise. An unlikely trio to produce a Broadway/motion picture hit? Certainly, the Bard would have been delighted to see what had become of his Capulets and Montagues in modern times. And that is just what choreographer-director Jerome Robbins thought when he translated Shakespeare's classic *Romeo and Juliet* into a Puerto Rican–American gang fight on the mean streets of Manhattan's Upper West Side. When the musical opened in September, 1957, it shattered the mold for Broadway musicals. Three record-breaking years later, it would repeat the magic on the motion picture screen.

The translation to film cost $6,000,000 but more than tripled that amount in profit on a domestic level (and even more when worldwide distribution is considered). At the helm of the expensive production was Robert Wise, a director noted for his sense of artistry and economy of filming. The studio wanted Robbins as co-director, and Wise did his best to work with him. Robbins' only prior film work was the staging for "Small House of Uncle Thomas" in *The King and I*. Wise was distressed when *West Side Story* began running behind schedule due to Robbins' demands for perfection in the choreographed numbers, and after two-and-a-half months, Wise had Robbins removed. Both directors, however, shared credit, and both received Oscars, the first time the Academy Award went to co-directors.

Leonard Bernstein's score and Stephen Sondheim's lyrics seemed radical when audiences first heard them. The jazzy counterpoint in Bernstein's music at first sounded harsh to ears accustomed to singalong Broadway tunes, but Bernstein offered both, and gradually audiences embraced the music with warmth. Songs like "Maria," "Tonight," and "I Feel Pretty" helped balance the more syncopated numbers like "America" and "Gee, Officer Krupke!" The latter got a lyric-scrubbing for the screen—"My mother is a bastard; my pa's an s.o.b." became "My daddy beats my mommy, my mommy clobbers me." But both film and stage audiences knew that the song's closing line, "Gee, Officer Krupke, krup you!" had a euphemism for the "f" word, making this number quite popular among young people.

The film's executive producers, the Mirisch brothers, had originally wanted Elvis Presley as Tony, with gang members to be played by Frankie Avalon, Fabian, and Paul Anka. Fortunately, Jerome Robbins managed to convince them otherwise. For some actors, starring in the movie *West Side Story* became a fast rise to the top with nowhere to go from there. Richard Beymer as Tony did little else in what seemed a promising career; ditto George Chakiris, who won an award as Best Supporting Actor. Yet Natalie Wood (whose singing voice was dubbed by the ever-popular Marni Nixon) continued with an acting career that flourished until her tragic death in 1981. Rita Moreno, who also won an Oscar for her portrayal of Chakiris' Puerto Rican girlfriend, has added a Tony and an Emmy to her award collection as her career continues going strong.

Screenplay by Ernest Lehman

Based on the stage book by Arthur Laurents

From a conception by Jerome Robbins

Lyrics by Stephen Sondheim

Music by Leonard Bernstein

Produced by Robert Wise

Directed by Robert Wise and Jerome Robbins

CAST

Maria	Natalie Wood
Tony	Richard Beymer
Riff	Russ Tamblyn
Anita	Rita Moreno
Bernardo	George Chakiris

ACADEMY AWARD NOMINATIONS

11 nominations, 10 wins*

*Best Picture
*Best Director (Robert Wise and Jerome Robbins)
*Best Supporting Actor (George Chakiris)
*Best Supporting Actress (Rita Moreno)
 Best Screenplay Based on Material from Another Medium
*Best Cinematography, Color
*Best Art Direction-Set Decoration, Color
*Best Sound
*Best Scoring of a Musical Picture
*Best Film Editing
*Best Costume Design, Color

Jerome Robbins was awarded a statuette for "his brilliant achievements in the art of choreography on film."

THE GUNS OF NAVARONE
COLUMBIA
$13,000,000

"The only way to win a war is to be just as nasty as the enemy. One thing that worries me is that we're liable to wake up one morning and find out we're even nastier than they are."
—GREGORY PECK

COLUMBIA PICTURES hadn't had a hit since 1957, when *The Bridge on the River Kwai* provided that studio with a box office blockbuster. The war had helped them turn a huge profit, so why not try another war movie? *The Guns of Navarone* proved just the ticket. Written and produced by Carl Foreman (who had been on that infamous blacklist during the '50s but managed to rise above it with the screenplay for *High Noon*), the film was given the full "historical extravaganza" treatment: big budget ($6,000,000), big cast (Gregory Peck, David Niven, Anthony Quinn, and Anthony Quayle), big musical score (Dimitri Tiomkin), and big special effects that were so effective that they grabbed the Oscar.

For the location filming in the Aegean Sea, producer Foreman and crew spent a year scouring the Mediterranean and

Screenplay by Carl Foreman

Based on the novel by Alistair MacLean

Produced by Carl Foreman

Directed by J. Lee Thompson

CAST

Mallory	Gregory Peck
Miller	David Niven
Andrea	Anthony Quinn
Franklin	Anthony Quayle
Pappadimos	James Darren
Barnsby	Richard Harris

ACADEMY AWARD NOMINATIONS

7 nominations, 1 win*

Best Picture
Best Director (J. Lee Thompson)
Best Screenplay Based on Material from
   Another Medium
Best Sound
Best Scoring of a Dramatic or Comedy
   Picture (Dimitri Tiomkin)
Best Film Editing
*Best Special Effects

Aegean before selecting the 550-square-mile island of Rhodes for principal exterior work. Over a thousand Greek soldiers doubled as Germans invading the island. Access to the area selected to represent the "cliffs of Navarone" was by a two-hour overland donkey trek. The crew rounded up all the local donkeys plus others from 30 miles away, using the beasts to carry the camera and lighting equipment.

The efforts at reality paid off handsomely both at the box office and with the critics. *Time* commented: *"The Guns of Navarone*, a World War II military exercise of the those-poor-devils-haven't-got-a-chance school, is the most enjoyable consignment of baloney in months." *The New York Times* described the film as "one of those muscle-loaded pictures in the thundering tradition of DeMille . . . J. Lee Thompson has directed it with pace and has seen to it that the actors give the impression of being stout and bold." Audiences agreed, and gave *The Guns of Navarone* their nod of approval at the box office, where the film earned more than double what it cost.

④

EL CID
ALLIED ARTISTS
$12,000,000

"For God, Alfonso, and for Spain!"
—BATTLE CRY OF EL CID

DON RODRIGO Diaz de Vivar, Spain's great 11th-century military hero, became the subject of ballads and poems when he routed the Moors from Spanish soil after battling them for 30 years, earning the nickname "al Seid"—Arabic for "the Lord." Producer Samuel Bronston, who had produced *King of Kings* in 1960, figured it was time that modern audiences trembled before El Cid, too, and together with independent production company Allied Artists, produced a 70-millimeter Super Technirama spectacular to rival the original Spanish-Moorish confrontation.

Using the proven formula (Big Budget + Big Cast + Thousands of Extras + Big Screen + Big Score = Big Box office Bucks), Bronston won over moviegoers and critics alike. His budget was the biggest of any film that year—over $8,000,000, an enormous expenditure, but still yielding its backers a tidy profit. The cast? Big names like Charlton Heston, ranked number three at the box office by American

movie fans, and Sophia Loren, the Italian actress so popular with European audiences and whose presence guaranteed international success for the film.

Reviewers enjoyed the sense of the spectacle created by the film, though

---

Screenplay by Fredric M. Frank and Philip Yordan

Produced by Samuel Bronston

Directed by Anthony Mann

CAST

El Cid . . . . Charlton Heston
Chimene . . . . Sophia Loren
Ordonez . . . . Raf Vallone
Urraca . . . . Genevieve Page
Alfonso . . . . John Fraser

ACADEMY AWARD NOMINATIONS

2 nominations, no wins

Best Art Direction-Set Decoration, Color
Best Scoring of a Dramatic or Comedy
    Picture

---

most noted that the interaction between characters seemed to be its weak point. Wrote *Variety*: "'El Cid' is a fast-action, color-rich, corpse-strewn battle picture . . . the one reservation is that the action engages the eye rather than the mind." *The New York Times* agreed, noting that while the film was successful as spectacle, "only the human drama is still and dull in this narrative . . ." Perhaps the unkindest cut of all came from *Newsweek*, which griped that "the dramatics in it explode with all the force of a panful of popcorn. . . . [Anthony] Mann's direction is slow, stately, and confused, while Miss Loren and Heston spend much of the picture simply glaring at each other."

El Cid is occasionally run on independent movie channels, but does not hold the viewer's attention as well as it did in its theatrical release. The above reviews were fairly accurate in that they all made note of the film's main flaw—the lack of meaningful interaction between characters. Oftentimes, a film can get away with this on the big screen, but unfortunately, not on the small one.

THE ABSENT-MINDED PROFESSOR

WALT DISNEY PRODUCTIONS
$11,426,000

FLUBBER—It stood for flying rubber—and its formula brought laughs to the audience and dollars to the ailing Walt Disney Studios. The story line was a simple one: a college professor (Fred MacMurray) invents antigravity. He starts slowly, bouncing a perpetual-motion rubber ball, but quickly graduates to bigger objects—like the college basketball team, the film's villain (played by Keenan Wynn), and a clunky old Model-T automobile known as a flivver. The picture spelled fun for youngsters and their parents as well, which in turn spelled black ink once more for Disney.

Believe it or not, those Disney craftsmen, perfectionists all, hired a bona fide science professor as tech advisor. Among his tasks: create a formula for flubber that didn't sound like gibberish. See what you think of this formula, as described by the "Professor":

"The application of external thermal energy to two previously incompatible metastable compounds brought about fusion at high temperature, combustion, the release of explosive gasses and an accompanying residue—flubber. Never did I hope to find a metastable compound whose molecular configuration is such that the delivery of minute particles of energy to its surface would trigger a change in the configuration. This change in molecular configuration liberates enormous quantities of energy but they act only in a direction opposite of the force which triggered the molecular change. That's why we call it repulsive energy. The total effect is transient, and upon the shutting off of the externally applied energy, the elementary particles return to a state of pseudoequilibrium."

Got that? Good luck.

You might want to try this instead. Here is the recipe that the special-effects guys at Disney used to whip up the stuff that served as the prop for flubber:

To one pound saltwater taffy add one heaping tablespoon polyurethane foam, one cake of crumbled yeast. Mix till smooth, allow to rise. Then pour into saucepan over one cup cracked rice mixed with one cup water. Add topping of molasses. Boil till it lifts lid and says "Quirp."

Proceed at your own risk. Void where prohibited by law and parents!

The movie proved to be a huge hit for Disney. Fred MacMurray had been Tommy Kirk's father in *The Shaggy Dog*, and audiences eagerly welcomed them back with new identities for this Disney picture. And adding to the fun was the casting of three generations of Wynns—Keenan, playing the film's bad guy, his famous father Ed Wynn as the fire chief, and son Ned in a small role. It was the first time the trio had acted together.

It was evident that this film truly deserved a sequel, and within two years, *Son of Flubber* (1963) reunited the entire original cast for yet another romp. It did extremely well, narrowly missing the top five. Both movies appear from time to time on television or on Disney cable programming, and can also be rented (though they are difficult to locate).

Screenplay by Bill Walsh

Based on a story by Samuel W. Taylor

Produced by Walt Disney

Directed by Robert Stevenson

CAST

Prof. Ned Brainard ..... Fred MacMurray
Betsy Carlisle .... Nancy Olson
Alonzo Hawk .... Keenan Wynn
Bill Hawk .... Tommy Kirk
College President ...... Leon Ames
Fire Chief .... Ed Wynn

ACADEMY AWARD NOMINATIONS

3 nominations, no wins

Best Cinematography, Black and White
Best Art Direction-Set Decoration,
   Black and White
Best Special Effects

HOW THE WEST WAS WON
CINERAMA RELEASING CORPORATION/METRO-GOLDWYN-MAYER
$20,932,883

THE FIRST DRAMATIC Cinerama presentation arrived to trumpets and fanfare, ecstatic reviews, and box office frenzies as people stampeded to get seats. The movie, as sprawling as the great land itself, was the story of the push westward across the American plains in fulfillment of our "manifest destiny."

How the West Was Won was far from a documentary, however. The film was divided into three segments, with three different directors leaving their mark on this wonder: "The Civil War" was directed by John Ford; "The Railroad," by George Marshall; and "The Rivers, the Plains, the Outlaws" was under the command of Henry Hathaway. No less than *four* directors of photography were named in the credits.

Here was a Cinerama picture that, for the first time, was not made just for gawking, or as a showcase for effects like roller coaster rides. *How the West Was Won* was a remarkable achievement for a process which required a bank of three simultaneously-shooting cameras plus a three-projector system for exhibiting the finished product. Despite the difficulties of getting this epic on film, there were some fine cinematic moments, including lots of POV shots of shooting rapids and trains barrelling through tunnels.

As if that weren't enough, there's a real story. Narrated by Spencer Tracy, we follow the tale of Lilith Prescott (Debbie Reynolds) from youth through old age as our story unfolds across the continent. Along the way we meet nearly every working actor in Hollywood: James Stewart, Henry Fonda, Carroll Baker, Lee J. Cobb, Carolyn Jones, Karl Malden, Gregory Peck, George Peppard, Robert Preston, Eli Wallach, John Wayne, Richard Widmark, Walter Brennan, Andy Devine, Raymond Massey, Agnes Moorehead, Harry Morgan, Thelma Ritter, and Russ Tamblyn.

The film offered incomparable scenery, a star in its own right. Much of the location footage was shot by the Cinerama cameras (with second unit director Yakima Canutt in charge) in national parks and national forests from South Dakota to California.

There were singalong folk songs like "Erie Canal," "Shenandoah," "Poor Wayfaring Stranger," and "When Johnny Comes Marching Home." Some were sung, others were expertly woven into Alfred Newman's Academy Award–nominated score.

The film won the Oscar for Best Original Story and Screenplay, and it's easy to see why. Aside from an enjoyable story to tell, there were cleverly written bits and pieces of history, like the following:

"Have you seen San Francisco? It's ugly and it's small and it's full of fleas and it burns down about every five minutes, but each time they keep on rebuilding, it gets a little bigger and better than before. It's alive and kicking and nothing can stop it."

And this comment on our early mail service:

"The Pony Express—the most daring mail route in history. Eighty riders were in the saddle at all times, night and day, in all weather—half of them riding East, half riding West. Five dollars a letter the mail cost, and on thin paper, too."

We learned that "St. Louis [was] the busiest fur trading center in the world" and "California [was] named after a mythical island of pearls and gold in a 15th-century novel." The writing was both philosophical ("[The Civil War] ain't quite what I expected. There ain't much glory to looking at a man with his guts hanging out.") and poetic ("After Shiloh, the South never smiled"). Critical acclaim was unbridled. *The Hollywood Reporter* called the film "the best picture ever made in Cinerama" (and it was virtually the last). *Variety* labeled *How the West Was Won* a "blockbuster supreme, a magnificent and exciting spectacle which must inevitably dwarf the earnings of the travelogs in the three-screen process. It will, undoubtedly, run for several years, and will become one of the industry's all-time top grossers . . . Technically, there's a vast improvement in the process. The print joins are barely noticeable, and the wobble, which beset earlier productions, has been eliminated."

While *How the West Was Won* worked beautifully on the huge Cinerama screen, it suffers terribly when seen on videocassette or TV broadcast, the "seams" plainly visible as the TV editor was forced to pan from side to side trying to center the action for TV's square format, losing two-thirds of the picture in the process.

In 1978, ABC made a television series based on the original movie. It starred James Arness and Bruce Boxleitner, and had spectacular settings—location filming was done in Utah, Colorado, Arizona, and California. However, the mixture of Western and soap opera proved too costly, and ran only five months.

Written by James R. Webb

Produced by Bernard Smith

Directed by John Ford, George Marshall and Henry Hathaway

CAST

Linus Rawlings	James Stewart
Lilith Prescott	Debbie Reynolds
Eve Prescott	Carroll Baker
Zebulon Prescott	Karl Malden
Rebecca Prescott	Agnes Moorehead
Colonel Hawkins	Walter Brennan
Cleve van Valen	Gregory Peck
Roger Morgan	Robert Preston
Abraham Lincoln	Raymond Massey
General Sherman	John Wayne
Jethro Stuart	Henry Fonda

ACADEMY AWARD NOMINATIONS

8 nominations, 3 wins*

Best Picture
*Best Story and Screenplay Written Directly for the Screen (James R. Webb)
Best Cinematography, Color
Best Art Direction-Set Decoration, Color
*Best Sound
Best Original Score
*Best Film Editing
Best Costume Design, Color

Although released late in 1962, *How the West Was Won* was submitted for Academy Award consideration as a 1963 contender.

② LAWRENCE OF ARABIA
COLUMBIA
$19,000,000*

To WINSTON Churchill, he was "one of the greatest beings alive in our time." This was T(homas) E(dward) Lawrence, Englishman and honorary Arab sheikh, whose bravery in the desert, perched atop his camel with his burnoose flowing, made him a fit subject for what has become known as *the* classic epic film of our time.

In their first re-teaming since *The Bridge on the River Kwai*, producer Sam Spiegel and director David Lean selected a virtual unknown for the title role. Peter O'Toole, who would long thereafter be identified as Lawrence, had only one other movie credit to his name, a minor Disney production of *Kidnapped*. Lean's choice of the half-Scottish, half-Irish Shakespearean actor proved a fortuitous one, and the director later remarked in a Cable News Network interview, "He was frightfully good in the part." Shortly after the film's release, O'Toole began to have second thoughts. "There we were in the bloody desert doing a bloody drama," he told *Newsweek*. "Only one thing made me stick it out, and that was

Screenplay by Robert Bolt

Produced by Sam Spiegel

Directed by David Lean

CAST

Lawrence	. . . .	Peter O'Toole
Prince Feisal	. . . .	Alec Guinness
Auda Abu Tayi	. . . .	Anthony Quinn
Sherif Ali	. . . .	Omar Sharif
Turkish Bey	. . . .	Jose Ferrer

ACADEMY AWARD NOMINATIONS

10 nominations, 7 wins

*Best Picture
Best Actor (Peter O'Toole)
Best Supporting Actor (Omar Sharif)
*Best Director (David Lean)
Best Screenplay Based on Material from
   Another Source
*Best Cinematography, Color
*Best Art Direction-Set Decoration, Color
*Best Sound
*Best Original Score (Maurice Jarre)
*Best Film Editing

David Lean. Of all the principals, only he and I were in Jordan for the entire ten months. He carried the tripod, I the camera. After a horrible day I would see him sitting outside his tent, smoking a cigarette. I thought if he could do it, I could bloody well do it too."

The movie was shot on location in Spain as well as in the desert, and required thousands of extras, camels, and horses working in the 120-degree heat (only one day of interiors was shot on a London soundstage). Over 4,500 separate set-ups were used, and the total cost of the film ran over $12,000,000. Producer Sam Speigel was nervous before the movie premiered, remarking to *The New York Times*: "Good [pictures] can run for a long time, and over and over. I only hope the public also wants 'Lawrence' to do so."

He needn't have worried. The public and critics alike raved about the film. In 1971, it had its first re-release, but with nearly 20 minutes of Lean's masterpiece cut from its three hour, 40-minute length. Then, in 1989, *Lawrence of Arabia* was given another re-release, this time with all the missing footage personally restored by the director himself. Not only that, but when the original negative was discovered dam-

aged in parts, Peter O'Toole was called back to redub his lines. Since his voice had changed in the 26 years since he first spoke his lines, state-of-the-art electronic technology was employed to match his voice identically to that of the original recording.

The restored *Lawrence of Arabia* had a black-tie premiere in New York in February, 1989, followed by a limited engagement there, in Los Angeles, and in Washington. The experience of a beautifully restored print with the finest sound system in existence was greeted by thunderous applause with each screening. The *Los Angeles Times* called it "one of the seven wonders of the cinematic world" and *The New York Times* termed it "now more breathtaking than ever . . . a stirring and spectacularly beautiful epic."

Even with limited engagements, ticket sales for the re-released film brought in excellent returns for the exhibitors and justified the cost of the restoration. The picture continues to climb and may soon sit atop the list as a number-one hit. For Columbia Pictures, *Lawrence of Arabia* found a goldmine under all that sand.

*Estimated figure combining previous rental figure with early revenues for 1989 re-release.

THE LONGEST DAY
20TH CENTURY-FOX
$17,600,000

"Sometimes I wonder which side God's on." —JOHN WAYNE, COMPLAINING ABOUT THE RAIN

"I sometimes wonder whose side God is on." —GERMAN GENERAL, REALIZING THE GERMANS ARE ABOUT TO LOSE THE WAR

JUNE 6, 1944: D-Day. This was the *Longest Day* of the title, the day of the Allied invasion of Europe, and in re-creating it for this pseudo-documentary film, 20th Century-Fox's new studio boss Darryl F. Zanuck stopped just short of the real thing. His cast rivaled the original in its length—the Americans were headed by John Wayne (who else?), and included Robert Mitchum, Henry Fonda, Robert Ryan, Rod Steiger, Robert Wagner, Jeffrey Hunter, Red Buttons, George Segal, and Sal Mineo. Curiously, there was also a large collection of teen-idol recording stars like Paul Anka, Fabian, and Tommy Sands, appearing in their first dramatic roles. Richard Burton topped the list of British players, which also boasted Peter Lawford, Richard Todd, and Sean Connery. The Germans were played by Curt Jurgens, Gert Frobe (he later became "Goldfinger"), and a number of actors who were well-known in their homeland. Furthermore, all the German and the French actors spoke in their native language, subtitled in English. This added to the realism of the film, although it was demanding on

Screenplay by Cornelius Ryan

From the book by Cornelius Ryan

Additional episodes written by Romain Gary, James Jones, David Pursall, and Jack Seddon

Produced by Darryl F. Zanuck

American episodes directed by Andrew Marton

British episodes directed by Ken Annakin

German episodes directed by Bernhard Wicki

CAST

Lt. Col. Benjamin Vandervoort	John Wayne
Brig. Gen. Norman Cota	Robert Mitchum
Brig. Gen. Theodore Roosevelt	Henry Fonda
Brig. Gen. James M. Gavin	Robert Ryan
Pvt. John Steele	Red Buttons
Pvt. Flanagan	Sean Connery

ACADEMY AWARD NOMINATIONS

5 nominations, 2 wins*

Best Picture
*Best Cinematography, Black and White
Best Art Direction-Set Decoration, Black and White
Best Film Editing
*Best Special Effects

the audience. (Incidentally, this practically all-male cast had only one important female role, played by Irina Demich, Zanuck's girlfriend-du-jour.)

The film boasted 13 military advisors and 10 technical advisors, including an aging Frau Rommel. Many of the advisors were employed in the set-up of masterful special effects (which won the Academy Award). For the beach landing at Normandy, for example, 30 second assistant directors were put into uniform, each made a squadron leader in charge of a group of actors playing soldiers. It was up to these ADs to decide which ones would "die" and which would make it onto Omaha Beach. One hundred fifty "explosives" were set to be detonated by the effects personnel, but the smoke from the rigged devices was unpredictable and temporarily blinded some of the actors. Two of them missed their marks and inadvertently ran into some real explosives planted among the dummies; the accident blew them into the air (the footage remained in the movie) and very nearly killed them. Producer Darryl F. Zanuck halted production until the effects team was able to develop a white, non-blinding smoke.

The Longest Day is also one of the longest movies, three hours to the minute. The CinemaScope picture, which *TV Guide* calls "one of the great war films," is frequently run on independent movie stations.

4

IN SEARCH OF THE CASTAWAYS

WALT DISNEY PRODUCTIONS
$9,975,000

WALT DISNEY, who had had great success with *20,000 Leagues Under the Sea*, again turned to Jules Verne, this time for a tale that would take them around the world (not in 80 days) on a search for a missing sea captain. Along the way, Hayley Mills, Maurice Chevalier, Wilfrid Hyde-White, and others would encounter earthquakes, floods, fire, landslides (one effect looks like a prototype for a possible Disneyland ride), Andean condors, and crazed New Zealand Maori natives. It was a bit of fluff with great appeal for the younger set, but not too riveting for the adults whose hands they clutched throughout all the mayhem.

The film's meanderings are held firmly together by Hayley Mills, who at 16 was doing her third Disney film in four years. *Pollyana* and *The Parent Trap* had brought her international attention, and Uncle Walt couldn't wait to get her back up on the screen. With so much attention focused on the petite

star, Maurice Chevalier almost got lost in the shuffle. His talents are truly wasted, although he does get to sing a half-French/half-English song as they trek through the Andes.

Although *In Search of the Castaways* is by all counts a fantasy, for some reason Disney felt that a note of authenticity would be in order. Forty war-painted Maori dancers did their ancient ceremonial war dance, the

---

Screenplay by Lowell S. Hawley

From a story by Jules Verne

Produced by Walt Disney

Directed by Robert Stevenson

CAST

Professor Paganel ... Maurice Chevalier
Mary Grant .... Hayley Mills
Thomas Ayerton .... George Sanders
Lord Glenarvan ..... Wilfrid Hyde-White

Maori Haka, for the cameras at England's Pinewood Studios where the picture was filmed. The authentic dance culminates with the warriors sticking out their tongues to frighten their enemies. Today, these dances are performed mainly for tourists visiting New Zealand.

Critics were mostly favorable to the Disney yarn. *Variety* called it "a splendid piece of spectacular hokum, lavishly colored and packed with incident and special effects." *The New York Times* described the movie as "a whopping fable, more gimmicky than imaginative . . . it doesn't lack for lively melodrama that is more innocent and wholesome than much of the stuff the children see these days on television."

The movie appears on the Disney Channel from time to time, and is also available for rental. If you have small children, sit them down in front of the tube some rainy day, pop in the videocassette, and watch their faces light up.

THE MUSIC MAN

WARNER BROS.
$8,100,000

WHEN WARNER BROS. bought the rights to Meredith Willson's Broadway smash *The Music Man*, they thought they ought to use a "name" to star in the screen version, despite the fact that Tony-winning Robert Preston had appeared in 883 stage performances. Yet the studio still considered top-name actors for the part of the lovable rogue Harold Hill. Among those discussed: Cary Grant. Not a bad choice, considering he actually began his career as a song-and-dance man. Grant, however, would have no part of it. According to *The Guinness Book of Movie Facts and Feats*, he quipped, "Not only won't I play it, but unless Robert Preston plays it, I won't even go to see the picture." End of discussion.

Other members of the cast were of equally high caliber. Shirley Jones had been introduced in *Oklahoma!* back in 1955, and had since done *Carousel*, *April Love*, and, in a serious role, *Elmer Gantry*. She was a good casting choice, and *The Hollywood Reporter* commented: "Shirley Jones . . . is happily back in a milieu of her own, musical romance. She is lovely to look at, sings like a flesh-and-blood angel, and carries conviction in every gesture. She is the best singing actress of the screen in her own category, practically the only operetta singer we have."

Buddy Hackett and Hermione Gingold were somewhat bizarrely cast as small-town natives, but no one seemed to mind. Best of all was Ronny Howard as the lisping little Winthrop. Ronny was already a veteran of two years on TV's "The Andy Griffith Show," and he managed to charm critics with the best of them. Wrote *Variety*: "The little boy with the stammer and the bashful ways is a small gem as impersonated by Ronny Howard. He stays safely away from precociousness in all his scenes." And *The Hollywood Reporter* described Ronny, "a pint-sized kid whose talents know no dimension," as "a knockout."

Of course, this is the same talented person who, after appearing in umpteen seasons of Andy's show, starred in his own series, "Happy Days". Still, it wasn't until the '80s that Ron Howard found his true calling as a director, making such hit films as *Splash* and *Cocoon*.

But the title of the show says it all, and it is *music* that is the star of this movie. As we all know, "Seventy-Six Trombones" led the big parade, with "Marian the Librarian," "Till There Was You," "Trouble," and "Gary, Indiana" right behind.

The soundtrack, surprisingly enough, used only a dozen trombones, electronically amplified and multiplied (uh, 76 divided by 12 equals, hmm . . . each trombone represents six and one-third trombones?). Don't even think about the 110 cornets.

Screenplay by Marion Hargrove

From the musical comedy by Meredith Willson and Franklin Lacey

Music and lyrics by Meredith Willson

Produced and directed by Morton Da Costa

CAST

"Professor"
Harold Hill . . . . Robert Preston
Marian Paroo . . . . Shirley Jones
Mayor Shinn . . . . Paul Ford
Eulalie Shinn . . . . Hermione Gingold
Marcellus Washburn . . Buddy Hackett
Winthrop Paroo . . . . . Ronny Howard

ACADEMY AWARD NOMINATIONS

6 nominations, 1 win*

Best Picture
Best Art Direction-Set Decoration, Color
Best Sound
*Best Score, Adaptation or Treatment
  (Ray Heindorf)
Best Film Editing
Best Costume Design, Color

◢◣ 1 ◢◣
CLEOPATRA
20TH CENTURY-FOX
$26,000,000

THERE WERE romances, battles, clashes in leadership, fortunes spent, and fortunes lost—and that was what went on behind the scenes, not on the screen.

That *Cleopatra* would be a hit was a foregone conclusion. Audiences had been following the soap opera behind the scenes for nearly four years since the film's inception, and before it had even opened, Fox had pre-sold $14,000,000 worth of tickets. Most of the fans weren't history buffs interested in "the glory of Rome" or the fabled Egyptian queen who married her brother (and slept with everyone within earshot). What they came to see was not Cleopatra getting it on with Mark Antony, but Elizabeth Taylor being romanced by Richard Burton, staring passionately into each other's eyes, ignoring the director's pleas to "cut!" Their love affair, which had blossomed while in each other's professional arms, had fueled the hungry public's need for tabloid gossip, and now, wonder of wonders, there they were, and 25 feet high, too!

Yet *Cleopatra* had been termed an "unlucky" film early on by the press. Originally, production was to have taken place in London, but after nine months of shooting at a cost of $5,000,000, the producers had nothing to show for it. The film seemed plagued from the start. There had been a union row over Elizabeth Taylor's hairdresser; the star had had a string of illnesses, including a brush with death caused by double pneumonia requiring an emergency tracheotomy (a freshly healed scar is visible in close-ups); the original director, Rouben Mamoulian, resigned and was replaced by Joseph Mankiewicz; and the wretched English weather finally forced Fox to close down production in Britain and move to Rome for the duration.

The warm, sunny climate of Italy proved just the thing, and the romance between the two leads also began heating up. Although both Taylor and Burton each had a spouse, this seemed a minor problem—to them, at least. (As one anonymous critic put it: "Elizabeth Taylor is the first Cleopatra to

sail down the Nile to Las Vegas.") But the courtship presented problems for the crew. A visit from Burton's wife Sybil had thrown Liz into a tizzy, and after staying up all night crying, her eyes were too swollen to shoot the next day. The crew had to film around her scenes (although she voluntarily worked on a Saturday to make up for the lost time). On another occasion, the actress took advantage of the fine weather to sunbathe, tying up her yacht next to the barge set. Whenever she was needed for a shot, she would throw her costume on over her bikini. Lighting directors were driven nuts by her deepening suntan, and much of the footage had to be color-corrected to match her previously filmed interior shots.

The budget eventually ran close to a reported $44,000,000, making it the most expensive film to date (and in pre-

Screenplay by Joseph L. Mankiewicz, Ronald MacDougall, and Sidney Buchman

Based upon histories by Plutarch, Suetonius, and Appian and "The Life and Times of Cleopatra" by C. M. Franzero

Produced by Walter Wanger

Directed by Joseph L. Mankiewicz

CAST

Cleopatra	....	Elizabeth Taylor
Mark Antony	....	Richard Burton
Julius Caesar	....	Rex Harrison
Rufio	....	Martin Landau
Octavian	....	Roddy McDowall
Casca	....	Carroll O'Connor

ACADEMY AWARD NOMINATIONS

9 nominations, 4 wins*

  Best Picture
  Best Actor (Rex Harrison)
 *Best Cinematography, Color
 *Best Art Direction-Set Decoration, Color
  Best Sound
  Best Original Score
  Best Film Editing
 *Best Costume Design, Color
 *Best Special Visual Effects

inflation dollars, probably the most expensive film of all time). Of that, $130,000 was spent on Ms. Taylor's wardrobe of 65 costumes (and another 40 costumes costing $64,800 didn't appear after scenes were cut). The 24-carat gold-covered dress in which she makes her entry into Rome cost $6,500, a lot of moolah in the '60s. Ms. Taylor's salary reportedly also took a big chunk of the budget: the actress received $1,725,000 plus 10 percent of the gross above $7,500,000.

One way in which the studio was able to recoup some of its cash was to charge the highest admission price asked to that date. Audiences didn't seem to mind, and cheerily handed over their money to see the longest commercially-made American movie ever released (four hours, three minutes), figuring they were getting full value for their dollar. Zanuck, however, came under critics' fire for the length, and took an axe to twenty-two minutes within the first week. Later it was

shortened to three hours. The first network television run saw lost footage being restored and the production screened over two nights. Video-cassettes are in this longer format. And rumors still abound that there is even more "lost" footage, and that someday a six-hour version, shown over two successive days, may yet be edited together. Richard Burton would have been pleased: he always thought his best scenes ended up on the cutting room floor.

IT'S A MAD MAD MAD MAD WORLD

UNITED ARTISTS
$20,849,786

IF THERE WAS ONE characteristic of all '60s hits, it seemed to be that "bigger is better," and *It's a Mad Mad Mad Mad World* wrote the textbook. From its redundant title to its lengthy cast (nine stars, two co-stars, 29 also-stars, *and* "Jimmy Durante and a few surprises"), this movie screams "we're bigger!" and never lets up. Not only was it filmed in something called 70-millimeter Ultra Panavision, but it also boasted the new, seamless, single-lens Cinerama process. (One wonders why they bothered to call it "Cinerama," since it wasn't the three-camera, three-projector system with which audiences had grown familiar.)

Producer-director Stanley Kramer had a mad, mad time spending $9,400,000* of United Artists bucks getting the slapstick comedy on film. Virtually every comic available was rounded up and put on the screen: Sid Caesar, Milton Berle, Jonathan Winters, Buddy Hackett, Mickey Rooney, Phil Silvers—it looked like a Friars Club picnic. Also in the cast were Ethel Merman, Dorothy Provine, Edie Adams, Terry-Thomas, Dick Shawn, and, get this, Spencer Tracy!

The list of communities that had been disrupted during the location filming ran nearly as long as the cast. The

credits noted "Our thanks and apologies to the following California communities—Agoura, Kernville, Long Beach, Malibu, Oxnard, Palm Desert, Palm Springs, Palos Verdes Estates, San Pedro, Santas Ana, Barbara and Monica, 29 Palms, Universal City and

Original story and screenplay by William and Tania Rose
Produced and directed by Stanley Kramer

CAST

Capt. C. G. Culpepper .	Spencer Tracy
J. Russell Finch	Milton Berle
Melville Crump	Sid Caesar
Benjy Benjamin	Buddy Hackett
Mrs. Marcus	Ethel Merman
Ding Bell	Mickey Rooney
Sylvester Marcus	Dick Shawn
Otto Meyer	Phil Silvers
J. Algernon Hawthorne .	Terry-Thomas
Lennie Pike	Jonathan Winters

ACADEMY AWARD NOMINATIONS

6 nominations, 1 win*

Best Cinematography, Color
Best Sound
Best Song ("It's a Mad Mad Mad Mad World," music and words by Ernest Gold and Mack David)
Best Original Score
Best Film Editing
*Best Sound Effects

Yucca Valley." All aboard! But don't expect to see much of your hometown if it happens to appear on this list, since most of the film was spent inside cars, in wild chase scenes on the freeways and roads running through these cities.

What did the critics make of all this? *The Hollywood Reporter* termed it a "fun, fun, fun, fun film . . . it is not the story that matters, it is the development." *Variety* called it "a mad, mad, mad, mad picture, and it's going to make a lot of money . . . it is a throwback to the wild, wacky and wondrous time of the silent screen comedy, a kind of Keystone Kop Kaper with modern conveniences." But *Newsweek* labeled it "bad, bad, bad, bad," adding: "[It] is redundant, ridiculous, and too insistent . . . the title writer just didn't know when to stop; neither did the moviemaker Stanley Kramer . . . at the end of the long, long, long, long film one leaves in about as good a humor as a highway patrolman after a bad day on the freeway."

Yet despite commentary like the above, people still made a mad rush for the box office, and at $4.80 a ticket, they gobbled up the three-and-a-half hour picture like so much popcorn. The plot may have centered around a madcap treasure hunt for $350,000, but the real plot was United Artists' quest for box office gold. With this picture, they struck it rich to the tune of nearly $21,000,000.

*Kramer estimates it would cost at least three times that much to make the film today, mostly for stars' salaries.

TOM JONES
UNITED ARTISTS
$16,925,988

Bawdy, LUSTY, scandalous, rollicking, raucous, and veddy, veddy, British—these were the terms used to describe Tony Richardson's innovative film of the 18th-century classic novel by Henry Fielding. That *Tom Jones* should mark a milestone in filmmaking 200 years after the novel appeared is remarkable in itself; but that's just what it did, and audiences couldn't wait to be scandalized by it. Never again would the camera be banished to the hall; with this picture, the bedroom door had been left ajar, and we were all invited in.

Although it wasn't the clinical "this is how you do it" sex of the '80s, the beautiful rustic settings, the fox hunt, and other side stories were all basically foreplay for the movie's sexual *raison d'etre*. Even something as seemingly simple as eating a meal at a tavern became the most memorable scene of the film, each slavering bite, each downing of a morsel of chicken or lobster or oysters, becoming an allegory for s-e-x. Audiences would never look at a platter of chicken the same way again!

And the critics, pardon the expression, ate it up. *Newsweek* remarked:

Screenplay by John Osborne

From the novel by Henry Fielding

Produced and directed by Tony Richardson

CAST

Tom Jones . . . . Albert Finney
Sophie Western . . . . . . Susannah York
Squire Western . . . . Hugh Griffith
Miss Western . . . . Edith Evans
Lady Bellaston . . . . Joan Greenwood

ACADEMY AWARD NOMINATIONS

10 nominations, 4 wins*

*Best Picture
Best Actor (Albert Finney)
Best Supporting Actor (Hugh Griffith)
Best Supporting Actress (Diane Cilento)
Best Supporting Actress (Edith Evans)
Best Supporting Actress (Joyce Redman)
*Best Director (Tony Richardson)
*Best Screenplay Based on Material from Another Medium (John Osborne)
Best Art Direction-Set Decoration, Color
*Best Original Score (John Addison)

" 'Tom Jones' is a continually delightful, mercurially rhapsodic, and altogether breath-taking film. There is, in fact, no detail, however small, which does not merit unstinting admiration. 'Tom Jones,' an absolute triumph, is the best comedy ever made." *The New York Times'* reviewer admitted: "Perhaps there will be those who will be embarrassed by so much bawdiness on the screen. But I find it too funny to be tasteless, too true to be artistically false."

Tom Jones was re-released late in 1989, and the Academy Award–winning Best Picture of 1963 found a new audience succumbing to the charms of Albert Finney and Susannah York. The print was newly restored and re-edited by director Tony Richardson. The new version had been trimmed by seven minutes, which, Richardson told the *Los Angeles Times*, "I would have done then if I'd been smart enough. It's taken me 25 years to not be so dumb." *Tom Jones* has also been released on videocassette; you might want to rent the tape since, according to the *L. A. Times* reviewer, the film "holds up better than you might expect."

IRMA LA DOUCE

UNITED ARTISTS
$11,921,784

THE TEAMING OF director Billy Wilder with actors Jack Lemmon and Shirley MacLaine in 1960 had spelled magic in the highly acclaimed film *The Apartment*. Although it wasn't a box office blockbuster, it still earned a respectable $6,680,000 in North American rentals, placing it in the top 10 films of the year. What's more, it grabbed Oscars for Best Picture and Best Director, along with nominations for Lemmon and MacLaine. With a proven success formula like that, it was only a question of time before the Mirisch brothers, an independent production group, and United Artists, producer-distributor for *The Apartment*, gave it another go.

Irma La Douce had had a successful and lengthy run on the Paris and London stages when it was translated to Broadway in 1960. For the screen version, director Billy Wilder reunited his *Apartment*-mates Jack Lemmon and Shirley MacLaine, but decided to do the film as a comedy sans music. (The songs were eventually adapted as musical score minus the singing, and won an Oscar for composer Andre Previn.)

While the story concerns the life of a Paris streetwalker and her reluctant mentor, it is not raunchy in the sense that *Tom Jones* is; Irma is as matter-of-

---

Screenplay by Billy Wilder and I.A.L. Diamond

Based on the play by Alexandre Breffort

Produced and directed by Billy Wilder

CAST

Nestor	Jack Lemmon
Irma la Douce	Shirley MacLaine
Moustache	Lou Jacobi
Hippolyte	Bruce Yarnell
Inspector Lefevre	Herschel Bernardi
Kiki the Cossack	Grace Lee Whitney
Concierge	Howard McNear

ACADEMY AWARD NOMINATIONS

3 nominations, 1 win*

Best Actress (Shirley MacLaine)
Best Cinematography, Color
*Best Score—Adaptation or Treatment (Andre Previn)

---

fact about her career as the average office clerk. Although the subject matter is prostitution, the film is neither social commentary or a probing psychological study. There are, of course, business-related sexual jokes, like the client who, finding himself short of

cash, asks "Do you take traveler's checks?" and Irma's double-entendre remark to another customer, "I'm sorry. I never remember a face."

This was Shirley MacLaine's second important film role, and the critics lauded her. *Time* called her "an adorable golliwog in green lingerie and inky wig; her flamboyant self-assurance is the perfect foil for the bumbling Lemmon [character]." *Variety* took note of Lemmon's performance: "Lemmon plays his juicy role to the hilt, and there are moments when his performance brings to mind some of the great visual comedy of the classic silent film clowns."

Several minor roles in the cast were played by actors who would one day become famous. The desk clerk at the Hotel Casanova was played by Howard McNeer, who won fame as "Floyd" on "The Andy Griffith Show"; Grace Lee Whitney portrayed "Kiki the Cossack" and later went on to become "Yeoman Rand" on "Star Trek"; Bill Bixby, star of various TV shows including "The Incredible Hulk," had a bit part, and if you look closely, you'll see James Caan in a small walk-on. Caan later co-starred in *The Godfather I* and *II*. But that's another story . . .

THE SWORD IN THE STONE
WALT DISNEY PRODUCTIONS
$10,475,000

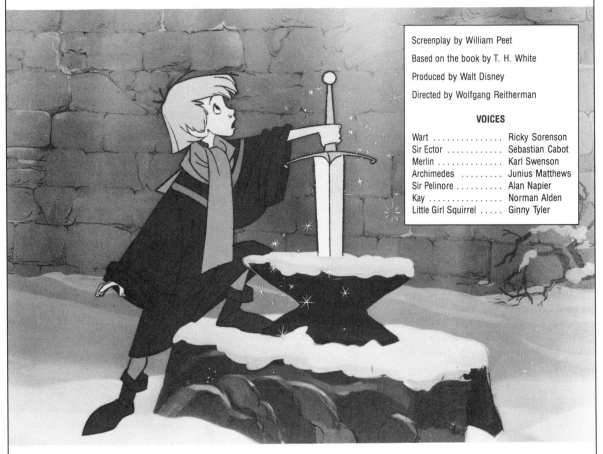

Screenplay by William Peet

Based on the book by T. H. White

Produced by Walt Disney

Directed by Wolfgang Reitherman

VOICES

Wart	Ricky Sorenson
Sir Ector	Sebastian Cabot
Merlin	Karl Swenson
Archimedes	Junius Matthews
Sir Pelinore	Alan Napier
Kay	Norman Alden
Little Girl Squirrel	Ginny Tyler

"Don't take gravity too lightly or it will pull you down."
—MERLIN

THEATERGOING audiences in 1960 were treated to *Camelot*, a hugely successful Broadway musical starring Richard Burton and Julie Andrews. It was based in part on English author T. H. White's Arthurian tetralogy *The Once and Future King*, but because of the magical elements inherent in *The Sword in the Stone*, most of the great storytelling in that book had to be omitted from *Camelot*. Enter Walt Disney.

The story concerns Merlin and his young charge Wart, the lad who would one day pull the sword from the stone and become the legendary King Arthur.

As Wart's tutor, Merlin gives the youngster a variety of transcendental experiences, transmuting him first into a fish, then a bird. (A similar effort at educating a future hero was used when Yoda attempted to train Jedi knight Luke Skywalker in the 1980 film *The Empire Strikes Back* [see page 272].) These moments were perfectly suited to animation, where anything is possible. Disney's first animated feature in two years was another box office success.

In typical Disney fashion, the studio hyped their latest hit with staggering facts, such as: "To paint the characters on celluloid, the backgrounds and all other color effects required 800 gallons of paint weighing nearly five tons, enough in liquid hues to dress the exteriors of 135 average-sized homes."

And: "Some 300 top Disney artists used up exactly 1,325,650 pencils before the three year job was done, enough to keep the New York Stock Exchange in business for a solid year, or redesign all the cities of the world."

For the voices, Disney selected some well-known talent. Veteran English actor Sebastian Cabot read the part of "Sir Ector," Norman Alden portrayed "Kay," and Alan Napier did the characterization of "Sir Pelinore." Napier later went on to co-star in TV's "Batman" series as the butler, Alfred.

Far from Disney's best, *The Sword in the Stone* is still an enjoyable bit of magic for the younger set. The videocassette is easily available for rental, and the movie can also frequently be found on cable's Disney Channel.

MARY POPPINS
WALT DISNEY PRODUCTIONS
$45,000,000

"Mary Poppins—practically perfect in every way."

So PROCLAIMS the tape measure that Mary Poppins carries with her, and there's no doubt that she measures up. Not only was she the perfect nanny, but the movie *Mary Poppins* was *perfect* in every way for Walt Disney and company. It was a box office smash, pulling in dollars by the bushel; it was a sensation at the Oscars, grabbing 13 nominations, the most ever for a Disney production and just one short of the record. And it won just about everyone's heart—critics, kids, their parents, grandparents. In a word, *Mary Poppins* was supercalifragilistic-expialidocious!

Walt Disney first became aware of P. L. Travers' "Mary Poppins" stories in 1948 when one of his daughters was reading them. But it wasn't until 1960 that he began to plan for a screen version. Much of the success must be attributed to the talented people that Walt brought together as the team for this movie. In-house director Robert Stevenson was given the assignment, having successfully directed 17 previous films at Disney Studios.

For the star herself, Walt chose Julie Andrews, whose success on Broadway in *My Fair Lady* and *Camelot* was legendary, but unfortunately not enough to sway the producers of the film version of *Fair Lady* to hire her. Warner Bros. selected Audrey Hepburn, and a bitterly disappointed Julie Andrews accepted what she felt was second prize as the lead in *Mary Poppins*. It proved to be the turning point in her career, and she was awarded the Oscar for Best Actress of 1964. It was an especially sweet victory, since her competition included many film veterans. Also up for Best Actress that year were Anne Bancroft, Sophia Loren, Debbie Reynolds, and Kim Stanley.

Co-starring with Ms. Andrews was Dick Van Dyke, who had just finished both stage and film versions of *Bye Bye Birdie* and was in the third season of his network TV series, "The Dick Van Dyke Show." Dick played the part of Mary's (very platonic) friend Bert, and later doubled as the old bank president.

Rounding out the fine cast were British comedian David Tomlinson as Mr. Banks, Glynis Johns as Mrs. Banks, Hermione Baddeley and Reta Shaw as the maids, Karen Dotrice and Matthew Garber as the Banks children, and special appearances by famed actors Ed Wynn (who appeared in a number of Disney films), Reginald Owen, Elsa Lanchester, and Arthur Treacher (later of Arthur Treacher's Fish and Chips fame).

Two Academy Awards went to the composers of the music for *Mary Poppins*. Richard M. and Robert B. Sherman were brothers who first came to the attention of Walt Disney when

---

Screenplay by Bill Walsh and Don DaGradi

Music and lyrics by Richard M. Sherman and Robert B. Sherman

Based on the books by P. L. Travers

Produced by Walt Disney

Directed by Robert Stevenson

CAST

Mary Poppins	Julie Andrews
Bert	Dick Van Dyke
Mr. Banks	David Tomlinson
Mrs. Banks	Glynis Johns
Uncle Albert	Ed Wynn

ACADEMY AWARD NOMINATIONS

13 nominations, 5 wins*

Best Picture
*Best Actress (Julie Andrews)
Best Director (Robert Stevenson)
Best Screenplay Based On Material from Another Medium
Best Cinematography, Color
Best Art Direction-Set Decoration, Color
Best Sound
*Best Song ("Chim Chim Cher-ee," music and words by Richard M. Sherman and Robert B. Sherman)
*Best Original Music Score (Richard M. Sherman and Robert B. Sherman)
Best Scoring of Music—Adaptation or Treatment
*Best Film Editing
Best Costume Design, Color
*Best Visual Effects

---

they wrote a 1958 tune called "Tall Paul." Disney wanted to turn blossoming Mouseketeer Annette into a recording star and bought the Shermans' song. They did a couple of other songs for Annette before Disney assigned them their first movie, *The Parent Trap*, with Hayley Mills. Their tune "Let's Get Together" became a hit and won them a cherished position on the Disney staff.

Mary Poppins was their crowning Disney achievement. Their memorable songs included the Award-winning "Chim Chim Cher-ee," "Feed the Birds," "A Spoonful of Sugar," "Jolly Holiday"—a total of 14 all together. But everybody's favorite always seemed to be the tongue-twisting "Supercalifragilisticexpialidocious." According to Richard Sherman, he and his brother first heard a similar word from the kids at their summer camp back in 1937. It was a test of one's verbal agility, something to impress the other kids with, and adults as well. When it came time to write a special song for the film, they recalled the nonsense word of their childhood, and the rest, as they say, is history.

One of the special treats in the movie is the combination of live action and animation. Disney had successfully used the process many times, beginning back in the '20s in something he called *Alice in Cartoonland*, and later in such Disney successes as *The Three Caballeros* and *Song of the South*. Many years after Walt Disney's death, the technique would be put to its most ambitious use in the studio's production of *Who Framed Roger Rabbit* (the producers of that film would even borrow the singing penguin waiters from *Mary Poppins!*).

So many elements were combined by the Disney magicians to make this film that it is impossible to single out one special reason for its success. It was the kind of magic that wouldn't happen again for a long time for that studio. Two years later, the producer of *Mary Poppins* was dead. It was the last feature which Walt Disney would complete, and for us, the perfect ending to a more than "practically perfect" career.

GOLDFINGER
UNITED ARTISTS
$22,997,706

HIS NAME WAS Bond, James Bond. He was brought to the attention of the moviegoing audience in 1962 with the first production of Ian Fleming's spy novels, *Dr. No*. It would become the most successful series of films in the history of the cinema: over $2,000,000,000 in worldwide rentals was reached with the 1987 release of *The Living Daylights*. In 1989, the 18th James Bond film, *Licence to Kill*, was released, and no end is in sight. There have been no less than four actors playing the sexy British secret agent*, but for many there can only be one—the original, Sean Connery.

The Scottish-born Connery had appeared seemingly from nowhere (he did have a part in 1959's *Darby O'Gill and the Little People*), and his mischievous grin and puppydog eyes would see a string of ladies—the "Bond Girls," as they later were called—finding their way into his industrial-strength bed.

The plot of *Goldfinger* involves a financier named Auric Goldfinger—played with panache by German actor Gert Frobe—who plans to corner the gold reserves of Britain and the United States.

Goldfinger was actually the third Bond picture released in the United States; *Dr. No* didn't make the top five list, but the second film, *From Russia With Love*, would become the fifth-

ranked 1964 movie. With *Goldfinger* in the number-two position, United Artists had a banner year.

Much of the popularity of the Bond series was due to its irreverence toward the sacred cows of cinematic "good taste." It was hard to omit Ian Fleming's frank sexual innuendos in translating the novels to the screen. To put it bluntly, James got laid a lot, and by women with names like Pussy Galore and Holly Goodhead—there was no doubt what Fleming had in mind.

But audiences also enjoyed watching Bond get out of cliffhanger situations. The man ate danger for breakfast, lunch, and dinner, aided by all sorts of special effects and mechanical gadgetry. *Goldfinger*, for example, had a

special smoke-screen-equipped, oil-slick-emitting, passenger-ejecting Aston Martin. Gimmicks, gals, guns—the formula worked.

The 007 "licence to kill" extended to the box office, where British producers Harry Saltzman and Albert "Cubby" Broccoli made a killing of their own. *Goldfinger's* budget was only $2,500,000. And while the film's villain didn't get to keep all the gold at Fort Knox, the producers certainly came close.

---

*Sean Connery (7), David Niven (1—*Casino Royale*), George Lazenby (1—*On Her Majesty's Secret Service*), Roger Moore (7) and Timothy Dalton (2 to date). And that's not counting Woody Allen as nephew Jimmy Bond in *Casino Royale*.

Screenplay by Richard Maibaum and Paul Dehn

Based on the novel by Ian Fleming

Produced by Harry Saltzman and Albert R. Broccoli

Directed by Guy Hamilton

CAST

James Bond	Sean Connery
Goldfinger	Gert Frobe
Pussy Galore	Honor Blackman
Jill Masterson	Shirley Eaton
Tilly Masterson	Tania Mallett

ACADEMY AWARD NOMINATIONS

*1 nomination, 1 win**

**Best Sound Effects

THE CARPETBAGGERS
PARAMOUNT
$15,500,000

JONAS (GEORGE PEPPARD): *What would you like to see on your honeymoon?*

MONICA (ELIZABETH ASHLEY): *Lots of lovely ceilings.*

NOBODY WOULD EVER call *The Carpetbaggers* a *film*. It was a *movie*, plain and simple, with dialogue like the above, straight out of the sizzling Harold Robbins novel. It didn't win any prizes, unless you can count $15,500,000 at the box office a prize. You can bet Paramount Pictures did. It was their first hit since 1956 and *The Ten Commandments* (a number of which were broken by this movie's characters). The ad copy stated that "it is unlikely that you will experience in a lifetime all that you will see in . . . *The Carpetbaggers*" and this was probably true, unless you happened to own an airplane factory *and* a movie studio. Come to think of it, Howard Hughes might have had a bone of contention with the ad copy. Although no mention is ever made of his name, there is an obvious parallel between the life of central character Jonas Cord, Jr. and that of the late billionaire.

George Peppard plays the ruthless central character who inherits megabucks from his father, then slashes and burns his way to further fortune, taking no prisoners in his greedy quest. He has difficulty in relating to those closest to him, and his wife Monica (Elizabeth Ashley) and friend/father-figure Nevada Smith (Alan Ladd) bear the brunt of his misguided psyche.

Many other talented actors appeared in this movie. In addition to the young George Peppard (later to star in many TV series, most recently "The A-Team"), the cast included Bob Cummings, Lew Ayres, Martin Balsam, and Carroll Baker. Ms. Baker had one of the most infamous scenes of the movie—she swings from a chandelier, sending it crashing to the floor.

Outstanding in the cast was Alan Ladd as Nevada Smith. It was his last picture; when a sequel (actually a prequel) was made based on the life of his character Nevada Smith, Steve McQueen starred in the title role.

Critics were puzzled. Was this to be taken seriously, or was it campy trash? *The Hollywood Reporter* seemed to enjoy the movie, praising its direction and casting. *Time* Magazine, however, called *The Carpetbaggers* "a swift, irresistibly vulgar compilation of all the racy stories anyone has ever heard about wicked old Hollywood of the '20s and '30s." And *The New York Times'* critic described it as "a sickly sour distillation of Harold Robbins' big-selling novel . . . Mr. Dmytryk has gone at this film . . . with a baseball bat. He has beaten it down to a square flat surface, without cinematic lift or style."

The New York Times predicted that "it will probably be seen by millions." The paper should have also mentioned that it would probably *make* millions— both would have been safe bets, since the public cared not a fig for the reviewers or their opinions. *The Carpetbaggers* bagged a bundle at the box office.

Screenplay by John Michael Hayes

Based on the novel by Harold Robbins

Produced by Joseph E. Levine

Directed by Edward Dmytryk

CAST

Jonas Cord, Jr.	George Peppard
Rina	Carroll Baker
Nevada Smith	Alan Ladd
Dan Pierce	Bob Cummings
Jennie Denton	Martha Hyer
Monica Winthrop	Elizabeth Ashley

MY FAIR LADY

WARNER BROS.
$12,000,000

It was *the* musical of the 20th century. Many a ticket scalper put his children through college thanks to this Broadway hit. And when Jack L. Warner paid $5,500,000 for the right to bring it to the screen, he thought he'd gotten a bargain. He was wrong, of course. He lost his shirt and a lot more after its production set him back another $17,000,000, and although it ranked as the number-four film for 1964, it failed to break even.

"It," of course, was *My Fair Lady*, the most eagerly awaited cinematic event since *Gone With the Wind*. The success of *My Fair Lady* was truly legendary. The Lerner and Loewe musical adaptation of George Bernard Shaw's *Pygmalion* bowed on Broadway in March, 1956, and its cast took their final bows six years and 2,717 performances later.

Its stars became legendary, too. Rex Harrison had performed the role in at least a thousand stage performances by the time he was signed to re-create Henry Higgins for the screen (although Jack L. Warner was still pushing for Cary Grant after he failed to get him into *The Music Man* [see page 165]). And everyone who had fallen in love with Eliza Doolittle had come to believe that Julie Andrews would re-create her part as well. But Jack Warner finally did prevail; he was convinced no one would come to see an "unknown" and signed Audrey Hepburn. Although Ms. Hepburn did an admiral acting job she couldn't sing a note, so Marni Nixon, already an established pro at this type of work, covered for her.

Rex Harrison could barely sing a note either, but he created a style of talking his way through a lyric that is still being emulated today. And what lyrics they were! Alan Jay Lerner managed to write some unbelievably clever rhymes. For example, Henry Higgins' patter in "You Did It" had "Budapest" rhymed with "a ruder pest." Brilliant lyrics, plus more familiar and singable tunes, helped make *My Fair Lady* the number-three-selling soundtrack album of 1964 (right behind The Beatles' *A Hard Day's Night* and *Mary Poppins)*. The disk contained all the Broadway favorites like "On the Street Where You Live," "Wouldn't It Be Lovely," "Get Me to the Church on Time," "I Could Have Danced All Night," and "The Rain in Spain."

One musical highlight, and certainly one of the most exquisite moments in the film, was "Ascot Gavotte." The entire number is a showcase for the talent of Academy Award–winning costume designer Cecil Beaton, who used gray, black, and white to dress the Edwardian ladies and gentlemen at the racetrack in what is an unforgettable panorama of elegance.

My Fair Lady is one of the real treats of the era when musicals were big box office, and has the rare distinction of becoming more enjoyable with each repeated viewing.

Screenplay by Alan Jay Lerner

Based on the play *Pygmalion* by George Bernard Shaw

Music and lyrics by Alan Jay Lerner and Frederick Loewe

Produced by Jack L. Warner

Directed by George Cukor

CAST

Eliza Doolittle	Audrey Hepburn
Prof. Henry Higgins	Rex Harrison
Alfred Doolittle	Stanley Holloway
Colonel Pickering	Wilfred Hyde-White
Mrs. Higgins	Gladys Cooper

ACADEMY AWARD NOMINATIONS

12 nominations, 8 wins*

*Best Picture
*Best Actor (Rex Harrison)
 Best Supporting Actor (Stanley Holloway)
 Best Supporting Actress (Gladys Cooper)
*Best Director (George Cukor)
 Best Screenplay Based on Material from Another Medium
*Best Cinematography, Color
*Best Art Direction-Set Decoration, Color
*Best Sound
*Best Score—Adaptation or Treatment (Andre Previn)
 Best Film Editing
*Best Costume Design, Color

FROM RUSSIA WITH LOVE

UNITED ARTISTS
$9,924,279

"My friends call me Tanya."
"Mine call me James Bond."

THIS WAS ONLY the second Bond film,* but already, eager fans of the Fleming novels, along with a whole new audience, had quickly warmed to the sexy British secret agent as portrayed by Sean Connery. *From Russia With Love* had the honor of being the first Bond movie to make it into the top five (later in the year, *Goldfinger* would go all the way to the number-two spot).

In comparison to the later films, this was one of the least gimmicky of the Bond series, which would progressively emphasize more and more action/adventure, eventually entering the realm of science fiction. *From Russia* also boasted one of the classiest of the Bond women—Italian actress Daniela Bianchi as Tatiana Romanova (whose friends, she tells Bond, call her "Tanya"). Her portrayal of the Russian spy-turned-counterspy is warm and realistic, compared with later films in the series, in which the ladies in Bondage are more like male fantasies than real women.

The story line is a complex one, with spies and counterspies abounding. James is sent to Istanbul to liberate a top-secret Russian decoding machine, and tangles with Tatiana—who is really a pawn of the sinister organization called SPECTRE, an international crime syndicate. There is good action in this, and without the complex and clever devices he would later come to depend upon from "Q" (aside from a trick briefcase), poor James is forced to

Screenplay by Richard Maibaum

Based on the novel by Ian Fleming

Produced by Harry Saltzman and Albert R. Broccoli

Directed by Terence Young

CAST

James Bond	....	Sean Connery
Tatiana Romanova	....	Daniela Bianchi
Kerim Bev	....	Pedro Armendariz
Rose Klebb	....	Lotte Lenya
Red Grant	....	Robert Shaw

actually use his fists and his wits to defeat the nasties. There's a great fight sequence with Robert Shaw, a chase by a helicopter, and a motorboat pursuit. Will Double-O-Seven escape? Are you kidding?

Early on, the critics seemed to know that a new phenomenon was afoot and gave the film unanimous praise, something of a phenomenon itself. *The New York Times* wrote: "Secret Agent 007 is very much with us again, and anyone who hasn't yet got to know him is urged to do so right away!" Other critics echoed its praises. *The Hollywood Reporter* called the movie "fast, funny entertainment . . . [James Bond's] further antics should provide a

strong boxoffice attraction as his movie fame grows and his appeal broadens."

Those who have followed the Bond series since its beginning have often said that the early movies were the best. Whether or not this is true is a matter of opinion, but it *is* true that *From Russia With Love* sticks closer than any of the others to the Ian Fleming novel. And for purists who prefer their Bond stirred, not shaken, there is no comparison.

*The first, *Dr. No* (1962), while not making it into the box office Top Five, turned a respectable profit and established the Bond films throughout the world. (In Japan, they translated the title into *We Don't Want a Doctor!*)

THE SOUND OF MUSIC

20TH CENTURY-FOX
$79,748,000

AFTER A YEAR in production (including 10 weeks on location in Austria and Germany) filming another hit Broadway show, Robert Wise and 20th Century-Fox gave a gift to the American public. *The Sound of Music* had children and dogs, singing nuns and Nazis, and gasp-for-breath scenery. The icing on this wonderful piece of sugar candy was "Mary Poppins" herself—Julie Andrews. She was no longer an unknown, thank you; for the second year in a row, she was the star of the number-one box office hit.

And, to coin a phrase, the box office was alive with the sound of money.

The dollars and yen and pounds and deutsche marks and francs came pouring in—you can bet these were a few of Fox's favorite things! And when the take was tallied, *The Sound of Music* had climbed every mountain to reach the top as the industry's all-time highest grossing film to date. Bye-bye, *Gone With the Wind*.

The movie is a three-hour adaptation of Rodgers and Hammerstein's hit musical about the Von Trapp Family Singers. It had all that glorious Salzburg scenery in color by DeLuxe on the wide, wide Todd-AO 70-millimeter screen, with some of the most easily remembered songs of any musical: "Maria," "The Sound of Music," "My Favorite Things," "Climb Every Mountain," the beautiful anthem "Edelweiss." Nothing's too musically complex or difficult to hum; even the tone-deaf can follow "Do-Re-Mi."

Julie Andrews herself modestly credits the mood of the movie with contributing to the film's phenomenal success. In an interview with *The New York Times* at the time of its release, she said, "It's very joyous. It's refreshing and not too complicated. A love story, with children and music. That word 'joyous' has an awful lot to do with it." Composer Richard Rodgers, when asked in the same *Times* piece to analyze the reasons for *The Sound of Music*'s success, commented, "It's irresistible if you like people and children."*

Originally, William Wyler was set to direct, but delays found him accepting another assignment, and Robert Wise,

The real Maria von Trapp meets Christopher Plummer as Robert Wise looks on.

Screenplay by Ernest Lehman

Based on the stage musical, book by Howard Lindsay and Russel Crouse

Music and lyrics by Richard Rodgers and Oscar Hammerstein II

Produced and directed by Robert Wise

CAST

Maria	Julie Andrews
Capt. Von Trapp . . .	Christopher Plummer
The Baroness	Eleanor Parker
Max Detweiler	Richard Haydn
Mother Abbess . . .	Peggy Wood
Sister Sophia	Marni Nixon

ACADEMY AWARD NOMINATIONS

*10 nominations, 5 wins**

*Best Picture
 Best Actress (Julie Andrews)
 Best Supporting Actress (Peggy Wood)
*Best Director (Robert Wise)
 Best Cinematography, Color
 Best Art Direction-Set Decoration, Color
*Best Sound
*Best Score—Adaptation or Treatment
*Best Film Editing
 Best Costume Design, Color

who had co-directed the hugely successful *West Side Story*, was called in, and won an Oscar for his work. Meanwhile, Fox wanted to cast Doris Day as Maria (the part had been played by Mary Martin on Broadway). Julie was still an unfamiliar face on movie screens, since *Mary Poppins* had yet to be released. The two cinematic roles would typecast her for nearly two decades.

Among the talented children playing the junior Von Trapps was a young actress who was well-known to TV audiences. When she was only four, Angela Cartwright had stolen the spotlight from Danny Thomas and company in "Make Room for Daddy." Robert

---

*Mrs. Myra Franklin of Cardiff, Wales, must like people and children a lot. She holds the Guinness world record as the patron who has seen the same film the highest number of times—as of 1988, she'd caught 940 British cinema screenings of *The Sound of Music*.

Wise, who had worked with her years earlier in *Somebody Up There Likes Me*, didn't remember her eight years later when he hired the 12-year-old for *The Sound of Music*, but never forgot her after it. "Angela was a real pro," he recalled to the *Los Angeles Times* recently, "and I cast her for the part because for one so young, she had so much experience on the screen already. She and the other children were easy to work with and they formed a very close-knit community. It has lasted, and they have stayed close throughout their lives."

And don't look now, but there's Marni Nixon as Sister Sophia! This marked the first on-screen appearance of the former ghost-singer. Also doing a walk-on was the real Baroness Maria Von Trapp, a.k.a. Maria, who visited the sets in Salzburg and landed a part as an extra.

When the film premiered at the beginning of March, critics lavished praise on it. *Variety* called it "one of the

top musicals to reach the screen," and went on to describe *The Sound of Music* as "a warmly-pulsating, captivating drama . . . magnificently mounted and with a brilliant cast." *The Hollywood Reporter* was ecstatic, with a headline proclaiming: " 'SOUND OF MUSIC' RESTORES FAITH IN THE ART OF MOTION PICTURES." What had caused us to lose faith was not made clear. But the trade paper made it perfectly clear that this was not a film to be missed: "Who says you can't buy happiness? As long as Robert Wise's 'The Sound of Music' is playing, you can. And that's going to be for a good long time. Don't, however, wait. Don't deprive yourself of the pleasure a moment longer than necessary. Run, do not walk, to the nearest boxoffice."

Good advice. And if it's been a while since you've seen it (or you've only caught one of the commercially-interrupted, abbreviated telecasts), run, do not walk, to your video store and rent a copy.

DOCTOR ZHIVAGO
METRO-GOLDWYN-MAYER
$47,116,811

THE SUCCESS of *Doctor Zhivago* was not an accidental piece of good fortune for MGM: it was a decidedly calculated hit. After acquiring the rights to Boris Pasternak's difficult-to-read Nobel-prize-winning novel, the studio set about securing the services of top industry talent, people like Italian producer Carlo Ponti (once and future spouse of Sophia Loren), and director David Lean, who had proven his mettle with *The Bridge on the River Kwai* and *Lawrence of Arabia.* Cast in important roles were two people already familiar to Lean from these films—Omar Sharif and Alec Guinness. As the film's centerpiece, "Lara," Lean selected a virtual unknown named Julie Christie. It ultimately became *her* picture, Ms. Christie's standout performance catching the attention of all.*

For this artfully conceived piece of movie merchandising, MGM planned a massive campaign, trumpeting the

Screenplay by Robert Bolt

Based on the novel by Boris Pasternak

Executive producer: Arvid L. Griffen

Produced by Carlo Ponti

Directed by David Lean

CAST

Yuri Zhivago	Omar Sharif
Lara	Julie Christie
Pasha Antipov	Tom Courtenay
Komarovsky	Rod Steiger
Tonya Gromeko	Geraldine Chaplin
Yevgraf Zhivago	Alec Guinness

ACADEMY AWARD NOMINATIONS

*10 nominations, 5 wins**

Best Picture
Best Supporting Actor (Tom Courtenay)
Best Director (David Lean)
*Best Screenplay Based on Material from Another Source
*Best Cinematography, Color
*Best Art Direction-Set Decoration, Color
Best Sound
*Best Original Musical Score (Maurice Jarre)
Best Film Editing
*Best Costume Design, Color

$11,000,000 production as the greatest thing since *Gone With the Wind.* Although the *Los Angeles Herald-Examiner* cried yes, indeed it was, most reviews were mixed, and a few critics were downright hostile. *Newsweek* shed tears, not for the film's highly emotional moments, but for what it decried as bad drama: "It is all too bad to be true: that so much has come to so little, that tears must be prompted by dashed hopes instead of enduring drama." Not exactly what the good folks at MGM were longing to hear. However, they probably took comfort in the review by *The Hollywood Reporter,* which praised the movie as "a majestic, magnificent picture of war and peace, on a national scale and scaled down to the personal. It has every element that makes a smash, long-run boxoffice hit."

Other reviewers took a stand somewhere between these two positions. All MGM could do was wait to see whether

they had a hit or a costly turkey on their hands.

Fortunately, audience word-of-mouth fulfilled the *Reporter's* predictions. Moviegoers bought their advance tickets, eager to sit through the three hour, 17-minute panorama of love and human drama played against the backdrop of the Russian Revolution and World War I. The excellent production values—exquisitely photographed scenery (filmed on location in Spain and Finland), a gripping narrative, striking sets, a moving score (Maurice Jarre's "Lara's Theme" helped push the *Dr. Zhivago* soundtrack album to number three for the year), and fine performances, all helped to make this MGM's second biggest moneymaker . . . right after you-know-what (*Gone With the Wind*).

---

*However, she won the Academy Award for a different film that year—*Darling.*

THUNDERBALL

UNITED ARTISTS
$28,621,434

"You don't think I enjoyed what we did this evening, do you? What I did tonight was for Queen and country!" —JAMES BOND, AFTER SEDUCING AN ENEMY AGENT

THE FOURTH in United Artists' by-now-successful James Bond series, *Thunderball* was the first Bond film to receive an Academy Award. It was also the most financially lucrative to date, firmly establishing this action/adventure saga as a genre in its own right.

What was different about this particular Bond film that found an even larger audience than had previous 007 movies? With spy films at their zenith in '65 (*The Ipcress Film*, *The Spy Who Came in from the Cold*, and *Our Man Flint* were just a few), United Artists wanted to take no chances with their hot property. In keeping with the old adage "it takes money to make money," the studio pumped $9,000,000 worth of gimmicks and special effects into *Thunderball* and established James Bond as the king of the gadgetry films. Also present were the traditional "Bond girls," the supervillainous agents from SPECTRE, and some of the most terrific underwater sequences ever

Screenplay by Richard Maibaum and John Hopkins

From an original story by Kevin McClory and Jack Whittingham

Based on the novel by Ian Fleming

Produced by Kevin McClory

Directed by Terence Young

CAST

James Bond	Sean Connery
Domino	Claudine Auger
Emilio Largo	Adolfo Celi
Fiona	Luciana Paluzzi
Felix Leiter	Rik Van Nutter

ACADEMY AWARD NOMINATIONS

1 nomination, 1 win*

*Best Special Visual Effects

filmed (location: the Bahamas).

The public was captured by the technology, the very dashing Sean Connery, and the lovely Brazilian co-star Fiona Volpe (the Queen would certainly be proud of her brave agent's success in her name). Even the critics seemed

to enjoy watching Bond swing for old England. Said *Variety:* " 'Thunderball' packs a wallop in its tongue-in-cheek treatment of agent-at-work." And *The Hollywood Reporter* proclaimed: "It's a bird! It's a plane! It's a Super-Bond! . . . [*Thunderball*] is sure to repeat the stream of gold that 'Goldfinger' unleashed." Indeed it did. With the success of the film came a relatively new phenomenon to the Industry, one that is an adjunct to all action/adventure films today—the licensing and merchandising of James Bond products. The likeness of Sean Connery or the "James Bond" copyrighted logo began appearing in department stores worldwide, on items like attaché cases, toys, sweaters, underwear, and dolls. Connery was appalled, complaining to *The New York Times*: "The whole thing has become a Frankenstein's monster. The merchandising, the promotion, the pirating—they're thoroughly distasteful."

In many ways, Connery was right, and there have always been those critical of the exploitation that seems to accompany hit films. But, as with most cult heroes, Connery eventually accepted the merchandising tie-ins in good spirit.

THOSE MAGNIFICENT MEN IN
THEIR FLYING MACHINES
20TH CENTURY-FOX
$14,000,000

According to *The Guinness Book of Movie Facts and Feats*, the seventh longest title ever given to a motion picture was *Those Magnificent Men in Their Flying Machines, or: How I Flew From London to Paris in 25 Hours and 11 Minutes.* Just getting the credits on the giant Todd-AO screen was itself a feat, so the producers devised a clever opening sequence that nearly steals the show. The film opens with a striking parallel to *This Is Cinerama*'s format—a pseudo-documentary beginning with historical black-and-white footage. We see classic shots of early attempts at flying—strange egg-beater-like aircraft, flying Venetian blinds with motors attached, and human wing-flappers are just some of the bizarre contraptions. And lest we think this all serious stuff, comedian Red Skelton is intercut throughout, camping it up in his inimitable style. Following this priceless montage, the actual credits are set forth in a cartoon sequence. It was one of the most cleverly done openings of any film to date.

Basically a slapstick comedy with plenty of sight gags and aerial chases, *Those Magnificent Men* was a British production supervised by American producer Stan Margulies. The only familiar American stars were Red Skelton, who vanished after the opening title sequence, and the Yank played by Stuart Whitman. Aside from the James

Bond films and a couple of others, there hadn't been much success at the box office for British fare in the United States. But the comedy was a smash hit on both sides of the Atlantic thanks to its great photography, straightforward storyline, and natural family appeal. It also boasted a top cast. Among the more familiar Britons in the picture were Sarah Miles, Robert Morley, Benny Hill, and the gap-toothed Terry-Thomas. Gert (*Goldfinger*) Frobe co-starred as a spiked-helmeted German cavalry officer intent upon bringing glory to the Fatherland, and there were also Italian, French, and Japanese stars to give the movie international appeal.

When the film was made in 1964, there were no airworthy examples of 1910 vintage planes in Britain, so small construction companies were pressed into service, building replicas of the early aircraft which are the real stars of the film.

In 1969, a re-teaming of writer-director Ken Annakin and actors Terry-Thomas and Gert Frobe resulted in a picture about vintage car racing called *Those Daring Young Men in Their Jaunty Jalopies* (British title: *Monte Carlo or Bust*). It was more like a spinoff than a true sequel, and featured Tony Curtis, Peter Cook, and Dudley Moore. It was cute, but couldn't muster the following of the prototype.

Following *Those Magnificent Men*, comic actor Terry-Thomas appeared in a number of comedy films, but by 1989, he was suffering from declining health due to Parkinson's disease. In April of that year, his show business friends learned his medical expenses had left him completely penniless; to repay the ailing star for all the years of laughter he had brought them, his colleagues staged a benefit, raising $170,000 to make his last days as comfortable as possible.

Screenplay by Jack Davies and Ken Annakin

Produced by Stan Margulies

Directed by Ken Annakin

CAST

Orvil Newton	Stuart Whitman
Patricia Rawnsley	Sarah Miles
Richard Mays	James Fox
Count Emilio Ponticelli	Alberto Sordi
Sir Percy War-Armitage	Terry-Thomas

ACADEMY AWARD NOMINATIONS

1 nomination, no wins

Best Writing—Original Story and Screenplay

THAT DARN CAT
WALT DISNEY PRODUCTIONS
$12,628,000

THAT DARN Walt Disney! There he was again with another hit. Animals and kids—it worked every time.

The animal in question was, of course, the title cat, "D. C." (for "Darn Cat"), played admirably by a scene-stealing sealpoint Siamese named Syn, who had also starred in Disney's *The Incredible Journey*. The nine-pound feline did most of his stuntwork, brave thing, using a double only 10 percent of the time; for his performance, he won the animal kingdom's highest honor for four-legged thespians—the "Patsy."

Syn was trained by Bill Koehler (Disney's chief animal trainer for 21 years, who had done likewise for Sam of *Shaggy Dog* fame) and partner Al Niemela. Most people are unaware of how difficult it is to train a cat—ever try to get your house pet to do a trick, like coming to you when called? These professional trainers used a bell signal and reward system to teach all the actions called for in the script to the bright Siamese (the Einstein of domestic cats).

Co-starring with Syn was Disney's favorite contract player, Hayley Mills. She was a veteran of five previous Disney films by now,* and at age 19, this would be her sixth and last for Walt. Two years later, she created a

mild scandal by doing a nude scene in the British film *The Family Way*, thereby shaking forever her Disney image.

The cast also included Dean Jones, who was quickly signed to a contract and became a fixture in the Disney firmament, later appearing in such films as *The Ugly Dachshund, The Love Bug*, and *The Shaggy D.A.* Elsa Lanchester appeared in *That Darn Cat*, her second Disney picture (she played an English nanny in *Mary Poppins*); William Demarest returned to the Disney soundstages following his work in *The Absent-Minded Professor* and *Son of Flubber*; former child star Roddy McDowall made his first Disney ap-

pearance in this movie and was later given the title role in the studio's *Bullwhip Griffin*; and Ed Wynn, whom Walt Disney considered his good luck charm and used in as many comedies as possible, popped up in *That Darn Cat* as a befuddled jeweler.

Walt's director of choice for the film was Britisher Robert Stevenson, who had already helmed ten successful Disney pictures, including *The Absent-Minded Professor, Old Yeller, In Search of the Castaways*, and his Academy Award–nominated *Mary Poppins*.

A classy title song was written by the brothers Sherman, Bob and Dick, and sung by Bobby Darin, whose popularity was at its zenith at that time. The Shermans' music for *Mary Poppins* had brought them two Oscars; "That Darn Cat," however, failed to become a musical hit.

The movie excelled at the box office, continuing in the tradition of Disney's wholesome family fare. Rhett Butler might have been allowed to say "damn" back in 1939, but in the wonderful world of Disney, frankly, my dear, it would always be that "darn" cat.

Screenplay by The Gordons and Bill Walsh

Based on the book *Undercover Cat* by The Gordons

Produced by Bill Walsh and Ron Miller

Directed by Robert Stevenson

CAST

Patti Randall	Hayley Mills
Zeke Kelso	Dean Jones
Ingrid Randall	Dorothy Provine
Gregory Benson	Roddy McDowall
Dan	Neville Brand

The Moon-Spinners, Summer Magic, In Search of the Castaways, The Parent Trap, and Pollyanna.

1

HAWAII
UNITED ARTISTS
$15,553,018

NINETEEN SIXTY-SIX was a financially lackluster year at the box office. The combined total of the top five films, $68,000,000, was lower than 1965's number-one *The Sound of Music* alone. Number-one film *Hawaii*'s figure of $15,500,000 was the lowest top amount since 1958, and the lowest for any number-one film since.

James A. Michener's novel *Hawaii* had been a blockbuster, and the same was expected of the film. But although all the elements were there—all-star cast, Panavision screen, lavish sets, costumes, and so on—the episodic Dalton Trumbo-Daniel Taradash script seemed as heavy as the layers of clothing worn in the tropics by the missionaries.

Although the company spent over four months filming in the Islands, there is very little of Hawaii in *Hawaii*. United Airlines does better in their commercials. Only the opening sequence of the ancient Hawaiian creation myth had the breathtaking scenery one might expect of this picture.

The New England village was also shot on location, in Old Sturbridge Village, Massachusetts (a historical replica of an early New England town). Before the missionaries, nicely played by Max Von Sydow and Julie Andrews, set out, we are given a foretaste of things to come for the poor heathen natives they're off to convert. The head of the family intones:

"Almighty God, look down with pity on this miserable company of sinners, conceived in lust, delivered in evil and slaves to every loathsome appetite the flesh is heir to. We have held fast against atheism, Romanism, Unitarianism and a score of lesser evils, and we thank thee that thou has chosen one of us to carry thy holy word and precious light of John Calvin to the wicked and benighted heathen of Hawaii. Amen."

Bye-bye to innocence in Paradise.

The harsh ocean voyage is one of the most dramatic and memorable scenes in the film. To get the right effect, the producers used a two-masted brigantine for the 1820 passenger ship Thetis, sailing her from Copenhagen to Honolulu on a 10,000-mile trip across the Atlantic and Pacific Oceans. The Cape Horn footage was actually shot in the Norwegian fjords 140 miles north of the Arctic Circle and doubled as the rugged Straits of Magellan. Even so, the producers didn't find the battering waves mountainous enough, and called upon effects expert Linwood Dunn to optically enhance the stormy seas. Dunn won an Oscar nomination for his efforts.

On arrival in the Hawaiian Islands, the long-suffering missionaries are greeted by the beautiful childlike natives and their Queen, memorably played by Jocelyne La Garde, a six-foot, 418-pound Tahitian of royal blood who had never acted before. In fact, she'd never even had to work for a living, and took the role of Malama only after she'd been convinced there was no one else available with the huge and regal physique which was required of an Alii Nui. She didn't speak English, either, memorizing her lines phonetically. What is most surprising is that the novice actress received the film's only acting nomination, for Best Supporting Actress.

The cast itself was a mini-United Nations. There were the leads, Julie Andrews and Max Von Sydow, an Englishwoman and a Swede, respectively, playing New Englanders (Von Sydow's two boys, ages seven and twelve, played his son); Englishman Richard Harris; mainland Americans Gene Hackman and Carroll O'Connor; a very young Bette Midler as a passenger aboard the Hawaii-bound ship; plus an assortment of actors of Hawaiian, Tonkinese, Tahitian, and Fijian blood.

One such member of the cast was Manu Tupou, a Tonkinese born in Fiji. Tupou, who plays the role of Keoki, the Hawaiian native whom the missionaries first "civilize," is a graduate of the University of Hawaii, with a Master's degree in sociology. Although Tupou made his film debut in *Hawaii*, the 6'4" actor admitted to having played a bit in his home island of Fiji in a Dinah Shore TV special called "Christmas Around the World."

The role of Neolani, a young free-loving Hawaiian, was portrayed by Elizabeth Logue, who was Hawaii's best-known model at the time the movie was made. She was considered a natural for the role, although it was necessary for her to make a slight physical change to win the part—she had to enhance her nose in order to look more like the producers' idea of a native Hawaiian.

Hawaiian location filming took four months, principally at Makua Beach on the Island of Oahu. A village consisting of 107 buildings was constructed and continuously aged during filming to accurately represent the village of Lahaina on Maui as it existed between 1820 and 1848. One of the most difficult scenes to film there was the burning of the missionary church. Tragedy was narrowly averted when Julie Andrew's dress, which was supposed to be scorched, actually caught fire.

The production was plagued by other troubles as well. During the location shooting, which lagged way behind

---

Screenplay by Dalton Trumbo and Daniel Taradash

Based on the novel by James Michener

Produced by Walter Mirisch

Directed by George Roy Hill

CAST

Jerusha Bromley	Julie Andrews
Abner Hale	Max Von Sydow
Rafer Hoxworth	Richard Harris
Charles Bromley	Carroll O'Connor
John Whipple	Gene Hackman

ACADEMY AWARD NOMINATIONS

7 nominations, no wins

Best Supporting Actress (Jocelyne La Garde)
Best Cinematography, Color
Best Sound
Best Song ("My Wishing Doll," music and words by Elmer Bernstein and Mack David)
Best Original Music Score (Elmer Bernstein)
Best Costume Design, Color
Best Special Visual Effects

schedule, there was one three-day period during which the film changed directors twice. One Friday afternoon, George Roy Hill was told he was to be removed from the picture, and the Mirisch Corporation announced that Arthur Hiller would be replacing him. No sooner had Hiller flown to Hawaii, however, then a number of Hawaiian bit players and extras announced they would strike, so the producers decided to reinstate Hill, who was back in the director's chair by Monday.

The production company spared no expense in ensuring an authentic look, importing thatch from Japan, since the pili leaves normally used for thatching huts in the story's era are no longer to be found in the Hawaiian Islands. Rooster feathers (for the colorful costumes) had to be imported from the Philippines. Red and gold royal cloaks came from Hong Kong, straw mattings from Mexico, boar's-teeth necklaces and bracelets from India, and silks from Taiwan.

Although *The Hollywood Reporter* predicted that "MIRISCH-UA 'HAWAII' LOOKS LIKE BOXOFFICE WINNER; AT LEAST 4 PERFORMANCES ARE OSCAR CONSIDERATION" (they weren't), most reviewers found *Hawaii* ponderous. *Time* likened the film to a "ten-ton mouse": "Whenever a dull moment threatens, [director George Roy] Hill rummages around in Michener's bottomless bag of epic tricks and comes up with windstorms, conflagrations, eruptions, street fights, breech births, shark attacks, luaus, lava-lavas and assorted shouts and muumuus . . . The spectator is rather too frequently allowed to feel that he is watching a rather small film on a very large screen . . . a 3½-hour story that could have been told just as well in two." *The New York Times* had a mixed reaction, enjoying the "eyepopping scenes of storm and seascape, of pomp and pestilence, all laid out in large strokes of brilliant DeLuxe color" while lamenting the fact that *Hawaii* seemed "as big and familiar as Diamond Head, and ultimately almost as heavy."

In 1970, the producers took advantage of the first film's previous location construction to make a sequel film, *The Hawaiians*. It starred Charlton Heston, Geraldine Chaplin, and John Phillip Law. This sequel had Heston returning to a Hawaii undergoing drastic evolutionary changes. The film drew upon the wealth of unused material in Michener's epic tome, involving such dramatic elements as family relationships, conflicts, business ventures, and even the lepers' colony on Molokai. Although cinematically well-crafted, the picture proved an enormous box office flop.

② THE BIBLE

20TH CENTURY-FOX
$15,000,000

ONCE AGAIN, here was a movie based on a book—a best-seller, in fact.

Actually, *The Bible* should really be called *The Book of Genesis*, since that's the only part of the Old Testament covered by the film. It was directed by John Huston, who also assumed the role of Noah (and the Voice of God).

Italian producer Dino De Laurentiis saw himself as a latter-day combination of Cecil B. DeMille and Mike Todd, and the self-appointed heir apparent spent an estimated $18,000,000 shooting in Sardinia, Sicily, North Africa, and at his studio in Rome. It was the most expensive film that year, and worldwide rentals saw it barely breaking even.

The requisite all-star cast was packed with many famous names, like George C. Scott as Abraham, Ava Gardner as Sarah, Michael Parks as Adam, Richard Harris as Cain, Stephen Boyd as Nimrod, and Peter O'Toole as all three Messengers of the Lord. The opening sequences depicting Adam and Eve are well-photographed by a very literal, unabashed camera. One blooper, however, was missed by the production staff. Since Adam is supposed to have been created from the elements, rather than born of a woman, he would not have a naval. In an otherwise effective piece of technical crafting, the post-production crew ne-

glected to airbrush Adam's belly button!

The would-be epic is probably best remembered for the Noah's Ark sequence, since Huston lavished most of his attention on that 45-minute-long segment. We're treated to a regular zoo parade as numerous animals board the giant ark set, two-by-two (although both elephants were female; bull elephants are generally untrainable, since they tend to be rambunctious). It looks very natural on the screen, but Huston once recounted how many months of work it took to train the animals to walk in formation, prey and predator alike, without the use of trick photography.

Huston's original choices for the part of Noah were Charlie Chaplin, who didn't want to work in someone else's film, and Alec Guinness, who had a schedule conflict. An avid animal lover himself, Huston had spent long hours talking to the various beasts, many of them brought from the wild, taming them so they were comfortable around him. In the end, he decided to take the part of Noah only because, as he recalled in his autobiography, *An Open Book,* "I began to realize how important it was that Noah should be on familiar terms with the animals—knowing them was as important as an actor's ability to play the role. So I decided to do the part myself."

Critics again had mixed opinions. *The Hollywood Reporter* proclaimed it a "Boxoffice Smash," adding: "It looks very much as if Dino De Laurentiis' production is going to be another in 20th-Fox's recent succession of landmark boxoffice smashes. The biblical film has been for so long a standard of Hollywood, and a cliché. It is one of Huston's major achievements that he has found fresh inspiration and vigor." *Time,* on the other hand, had great misgivings: "Unfortunately, it is a long way from The Beginning to the end. The Word is interpreted altogether literally, neither revitalized with the logic of drama nor illuminated by the magic of myth . . . There is somebody up there, all right, but who? A director, a Deity, or Our Man in Disneyland?" The reviewer summed up by saying, "Better read The Book."

Likewise the critic for *Newsweek,* who wrote that "the film vulgarizes a host of sublime images and metaphors by concretizing them and preserving them in the amber of mediocrity. The Gideons will not be leaving tickets for it in hotel rooms."

But for those who aren't looking for anything more than an entertaining film, *The Bible* is worth seeing, especially when all that went into the filmmaking process is taken into account.

Screenplay by Christopher Fry

Produced by Dino De Laurentiis

Directed by John Huston

CAST

Adam	Michael Parks
Eve	Ulla Bergryd
Cain	Richard Harris
Abel	Franco Nero
Noah	John Huston
Nimrod	Stephen Boyd
Abraham	George C. Scott
Sarah	Ava Gardner
The Three Angels	Peter O'Toole

ACADEMY AWARD NOMINATIONS

1 nomination, no wins

Best Original Music Score (Toshiro Mayuzumi)

WHO'S AFRAID OF VIRGINIA WOOLF?

WARNER BROS.
$14,500,000

1966

W**HEN LAST WE MET** Richard Burton and Elizabeth Taylor, they were making whoopee while making *Cleopatra.* The world's most watched couple were finally married in March, 1964, and from then on, the twosome made a string of film duets, including *The V.I.P.s* (1963) and *The Sandpiper* (1965). *Who's Afraid of Virginia Woolf?* marked their fourth joint venture.

The movie—if it can be called that, since it is virtually a stage play on film with a few exteriors of campus trees and such thrown in—is a four-person dialogue drama. George and Martha (the Burton-Taylor pairing) are sadomasochists who use words as weapons, aiming their barbs at a young professor and his wife (George Segal and Sandy Dennis) while indulging in an all-night orgy of booze and sexual innuendoes. The unsuspecting visitors gradually undergo a transformation and an eventual loss of innocence in this

Screenplay by Ernest Lehman

Based on the play by Edward Albee

Produced by Ernest Lehman

Directed by Mike Nichols

CAST

Martha	Elizabeth Taylor
George	Richard Burton
Nick	George Segal
Honey	Sandy Dennis

ACADEMY AWARD NOMINATIONS

13 nominations, 5 wins*

Best Picture
Best Actor (Richard Burton)
*Best Actress (Elizabeth Taylor)
Best Supporting Actor (George Segal)
*Best Supporting Actress (Sandy Dennis)
Best Director (Mike Nichols)
Best Screenplay Based on Material
  from Another Source
*Best Cinematography, Black and White
*Best Art Direction-Set Decoration,
  Black and White
Best Sound
Best Original Music Score (Alex North)
Best Film Editing
*Best Costume Design, Black and White

profoundly dark, moody, and occasionally depressing film. But the brilliant performances and likewise brilliant directing by first-time filmmaker Mike Nichols has made this a piece of cinematic literature.

As a mainstream film, *Who's Afraid of Virginia Woolf?* broke the old rules of censorship, pushing the Motion Picture Association of America and its production code to the limit. Language was the main barrier; the movie was reported to contain some of the most explicitly frank dialogue ever heard in an American film—by one tally, there were eleven "goddamn"s, five "son of a bitch"s, seven "bastard"s plus "screw you," "hump the hostess," "up yours," "monkey nipples," and other shocking expletives (but not the still risqué "f" word). Studio boss Jack L. Warner refused to soften on the subject, and the film eventually received an "R" rating, which at that time meant no one under age 18 would be admitted without parent or guardian, so becoming the first film under the new rating system to carry this designation. No doubt this added to the film's mystique and increased box office take.

The avant-garde production received widespread critical acclaim, particularly for its two principals. *Variety* wrote of Taylor: "Miss Taylor, who has proven she can act in response to sensitive direction, earned every penny of her reported million plus. Her characterization is at once sensual, spiteful, cynical, pitiable, loathsome, lustful and tender . . . the projection of three-dimensional reality requires talent which sustains the interest; the talent is here." And of Burton, the same trade paper wrote: "Burton . . . delivers a smash portrayal. He evokes sympathy during the public degradations to which his wife subjects him, and his outrage, as well as his deliberate vengeance, are totally believable."

The fact that Richard Burton did not win the Academy Award while Mrs. Burton did was a sore subject for Elizabeth for many years, since she felt (rightfully so) that his-and-hers Oscars were in order. It was Liz Taylor's second Oscar (the first was for *Butterfield 8* in 1960); that year, she aced out some interesting contenders, including Lynn and Vanessa Redgrave, Anouk Aimee, and Ida Kaminski.

④

A MAN FOR ALL SEASONS

COLUMBIA
$12,750,000

LIKE OTHER literate filmworks of 1966, *A Man for All Seasons* was a true screen gem for Columbia. The studio hadn't had a hit since 1962's *Lawrence of Arabia*, another historical epic. This time, it turned the clock back three centuries for a historical film that was actually more drama than epic, a serious work in which the production values were an adjunct to the picture and not the main attraction.

The story traces the life of Sir Thomas More as he rises through the ranks of 16th-century England to become one of the most important men in that country's history. The author, politician, humanist, scholar, and lawyer received the honor of being named Henry VIII's Lord Chancellor. Yet he refused to renounce the Pope and accept Henry's Protestant faith (which allowed for divorce, something Henry was very keen on)—with dire consequences.

Many of the English cast members were only recently familiar to American audiences . . . actors like Robert Shaw as King Henry VIII (he had been seen in *From Russia With Love*), Susannah

Screenplay by Robert Bolt

Based on the play by Robert Bolt

Executive Producer: William N. Graf

Produced and directed by Fred Zinnemann

CAST

Sir Thomas More	Paul Scofield
Alice More	Wendy Hiller
Thomas Cromwell	Leo McKern
King Henry VIII	Robert Shaw
Cardinal Wolsey	Orson Welles

ACADEMY AWARD NOMINATIONS

8 nominations, 6 wins*

*Best Picture
*Best Actor (Paul Scofield)
 Best Supporting Actor (Robert Shaw)
 Best Supporting Actress (Wendy Hiller)
*Best Director (Fred Zinnemann)
*Best Screenplay Based on Material
 from Another Medium
*Best Cinematography, Color
*Best Costume design, Color

York in the role of Margaret More (fresh from her part in *Tom Jones*) and, as Anne Boleyn, Vanessa Redgrave, whose sister had just hit the screens in *Georgy Girl*. A minor but important role ("Richard Rich") was played by John Hurt, known to audiences today for many fine performances, including *The Elephant Man*, although he was totally unknown in America back then. Orson Welles as Cardinal Wolsey was perhaps the most instantly recognizable actor in the cast.

But the title role went to the man who had created the part in screenwriter Robert Bolt's stage version. Paul Scofield's name was certainly not a household word in the U.S., yet his performance as the ill-fated More would win him an Oscar, one of only five Britons to receive Best Actor awards in 40 years.* Ironically, he would never again equal the success

afforded him in this picture.

The critics applauded this motion picture. *The New York Times* wrote that director Zinnemann "has crystallized the essence of this drama in such pictorial terms as to render even its abstractions vibrant . . . Mr. Scofield is brilliant . . . 'A Man for All Seasons' is a picture that inspires admiration, courage and thought." The *Hollywood Reporter* headlined: " 'A MAN FOR ALL SEASONS' IS RARE FILM 'FOR ALL TIMES.' " Indeed, it is well worth investing a few hours to watch the videocassette version, especially to see all those talented British performers who are somewhat more familiar to us today.

---

*Other winners were Charles Laughton, *The Private Life of Henry VIII*, 1933; Robert Donat, *Goodbye Mr. Chips*, 1939; Laurence Olivier, *Hamlet*, 1948, and Ben Kingsley, *Gandhi*, 1982.

LT. ROBIN CRUSOE, USN

WALT DISNEY PRODUCTIONS
$10,164,000

THERE HAVE BEEN 43 film versions (including two porno ones) of Daniel Defoe's shipwreck novel *Robinson Crusoe*. Walt Disney had already made a movie of *Swiss Family Robinson*, which is derivative of Defoe. Yet in 1966, Disney again turned to that classic tale, this time with one of TV's most popular actors—and his own "Bert" from *Mary Poppins*—in the title role.

The credits tell us that the movie was "based on a story by Retlaw Yensid." That's "Walter Disney" backwards—one of the few times Walt actually put his name in the credits. It might have been better if he hadn't. While pleasant enough, *Lt. Robin Crusoe* is one of the weakest of all the Disney films.

For Dick Van Dyke, this role is a *tour de force*, since he's onscreen virtually all the time. But his talents were wasted, as any Disney fan of *Mary Poppins* can

attest; there are no songs, no dances, and very few other characters with whom he can interact during most of the film. Later on in the picture, he gets his man Friday, or in this case, his girl Wednesday, played by Nancy Kwan, a Eurasian beauty who had made a name for herself in the films *The World of Suzie Wong* (1960) and *Flower Drum Song* (1961). She's fleeing from her overbearing papa, played by the great Russian character actor Akim Tamiroff, and trying to impersonate a superstitious South Seas islander. She's brought along a bunch of giggly beach bunnies, making this seem like a Disney version of the '60s bikini/beach pictures. Worst of all is a very un-Disney-like ending, in which Van Dyke gets rescued and leaves Kwan behind.

Why was this so-so film a hit, then? One big reason was Dick Van Dyke, whose charms were not lost on *The Hollywood Reporter:* "It isn't really the

story that counts . . . The comic spirit of the picture is provided by Dick Van Dyke, who has the happy faculty of appearing to compose his lines on the spur of the moment, and plays them with an economy of manner and certainty of timing that is always rewarding." Other reviewers weren't so eager to agree. *The New York Times* called *Lt. Robin Crusoe* a "silly, tired business that seems . . . bedraggled and synthetic . . . Most of the picture has Mr. Van Dyke mugging and tripping over the lush scenery." And those were the *favorable* comments.

The scenery was indeed lush—aside from shots of the aforementioned bikini-boppers, there was some glorious footage of the Hawaiian island of Kauai, but certainly not enough of it to send ticket-buyers dashing to their nearest box office. The success of this movie can only be attributed to two people: Retlaw Yensid and Ekyd Navkcid.

Screenplay by Bill Walsh and
    Don DaGradi

Produced by Bill Walsh and
    Ron Miller

Directed by Bryon Paul

CAST

Lt. Robin Crusoe	Dick Van Dyke
Wednesday	Nancy Kwan
Tanamashu	Akim Tamiroff
Umbrella Man	Arthur Malet
Captain	Tyler McVey

1

THE GRADUATE
AVCO/EMBASSY
$44,090,729

"Mrs. Robinson, you're trying to seduce me!"
—DUSTIN HOFFMAN, FRAMED BY
ANNE BANCROFT'S LEG

THERE COULDN'T have been a more fitting title for this film. Not only was it about Ben Braddock, college graduate about to enter the School of Life, but it could be applied to life in the late '60s in general. Film subject matter no longer held its earlier sexual taboos, and in a sense graduated into maturity. It also marked the graduation from obscurity to instant fame for director Mike Nichols. This was only his second film, after 1966's *Who's Afraid of Virginia Woolf?* (see page 187). Nichols' career continues unabated today, with such recent directorial achievements as

Silkwood (1983), *Heartburn* (1986), and *Working Girl* (1988).

The Graduate wasn't Hoffman's first film. The young man who began his acting career as an automobile-commercial pitchman had made a couple of low-budget movies that no one ever heard of—no one, it seems, except Mike Nichols, who screen-tested Hoffman after Robert Redford turned the part down, and paid him $750 a week to be in the film (Hoffman earned $20,000 in the role but afterward signed up for much-needed unemployment benefits). The huge box office success of *The Graduate*—it was soon to be ranked the third highest grossing film of all time, right behind *The Sound of Music* and *Gone With the Wind*—launched Hoffman into instant stardom. This

short Jewish kid from L.A. and New York was not Robert Redford/drop-dead gorgeous, but he could *act*. Twenty-three years later, he continues to prove this, making hit after hit, garnering Oscar after Oscar.

Of his performance in *The Graduate*, *Newsweek* wrote: "It is Dustin Hoffman in his first motion-picture performance [sic] who turns Benjamin into an endearing, enduring hero. He never seems sure of what his voice, eyes or hands are doing, or whose orders they are following. He wears the world like a new pair of shoes. He nods his head whenever he doesn't quite know what he means, which is often. He is wrenchingly simple and vividly intelligent, even with his self-doubts, and his bumbling seduction scenes with the

wife of his father's law partner . . . are as funny as anything ever committed to film."

While it was definitely Hoffman's picture, the others in the cast were also superb. Anne Bancroft was elegantly seductive in a Lauren Bacall-"come hither" sort of way. Director Nichols had originally offered the part to Patricia Neal, but that actress felt she hadn't recovered sufficiently from a stroke she suffered in 1965. Doris Day also rejected it as offensive to her values, so the part went to Ms. Bancroft by default. She won an Academy Award nomination for her portrayal of Mrs. Robinson, and her acting talents have taken her from an Oscar-winning performance in *The Miracle Worker* to a number of comedic roles for her husband, Mel Brooks.

It was also graduation time for Katharine Ross, for whom this was a first film appearance. She captured the eye of a number of critics (as well as grabbing an Oscar nomination). *Time* described her as "one of the freshest new faces in Hollywood," and *Variety* predicted that "Miss Ross, an exciting fresh actress from the Universal stable . . . has a long career ahead of her."

Co-scripter Buck Henry's filmwriting

Screenplay by Calder Willingham and Buck Henry

Based on the novel by Charles Webb

Produced by Lawrence Turman

Directed by Mike Nichols

CAST

Mrs. Robinson	Anne Bancroft
Ben Braddock	Dustin Hoffman
Elaine Robinson	Katharine Ross
Mr. Braddock	William Daniels
Mr. Robinson	Murray Hamilton

ACADEMY AWARD NOMINATIONS

7 nominations, 1 win*

Best Picture
Best Actor (Dustin Hoffman)
Best Actress (Anne Bancroft)
Best Supporting Actress (Katharine Ross)
*Best Director (Mike Nichols)
Best Screenplay Based on Material from Another Medium
Best Cinematography

Beginning with 1967, separate "Color" and "Black and White" divisions were eliminated for the Best Cinematography award.

career was also launched by this movie. During the '60s, he came to prominence as a television writer for such talents as Steve Allen and Gary Moore. He followed *The Graduate* with *Candy* (1968), *Catch-22* (1970), and *What's Up Doc?* (1972). Henry is a true Hollywood "hyphenate," with a long list of writing, directing, and acting credits. He was nominated (along with Warren Beatty) for Best Director for *Heaven Can Wait* (1978). Watch for him in *The Graduate* as the hotel desk clerk. (Keep your eyes peeled also for Mike Farrell in the hotel lobby, and Richard Dreyfuss in the Berkeley rooming house.)

One star of the film has to be the music of Simon & Garfunkel, which, surprisingly, didn't win any nominations. Their tune "The Sounds of Silence" had been a number-one hit for two weeks back in January, 1966, and was familiar to audiences by the time it was used as part of the score in *The Graduate*. The other popular song to emerge from the movie was "Mrs. Robinson," which was a number-one song for three weeks, beginning June 1, 1968. Rounding out the album (which was the best-selling soundtrack of 1967) were "Scarborough Fair/Canticle" and "April Come She Will."

THE JUNGLE BOOK
WALT DISNEY PRODUCTIONS
$39,500,000

THE LAST ANIMATED feature to be personally produced by Walt Disney, who died eight months before its initial release, was *The Jungle Book*. The film was based on Rudyard Kipling's stories of a boy raised by wolves, and appeared exactly 30 years after Disney's first animated feature, *Snow White and the Seven Dwarfs*. It was a financial success from the start, right up there with Disney's all-time greatest hits like *Bambi*, *Pinocchio*, and *Fantasia*.

Wolfgang "Woolie" Reitherman, Disney's favorite animation director, was at the helm, working with a team of 70 animators and 200 artists for over three years to get the story of Mowgli and his jungle pals on film. Many of these animals were created in response to the personality of the actor who supplied its voice. Phil Harris played Baloo the Bear, and some of the famous performer's own mannerisms were incorporated by the animators. Sebastian Cabot gave voice to the panther Bagheera. He worked on other Disney films, including *Winnie the Pooh* and *The Sword in the Stone*, but is probably best remembered as "Mr. French" in TV's "Family Affair." Jazz musician Louis Prima spoke the part of King Louie, the swinging ape. Academy Award–winner George Sanders (*All About Eve*) provided the voice for the tiger, Shere Khan. Sterling Holloway

played Kaa, the lisping hypnotic snake; he was a veteran of many Disney films, appearing as "The Cheshire Cat" in *Alice in Wonderland* and also the voice of "Winnie the Pooh" in many of those cartoons. Woolie Reitherman's son Bruce did the voice of Mowgli the Man-Cub; Clint Howard (Ronny's brother and also a child actor at the time) played his baby elephant friend, and a Beatles soundalike—reportedly Chad Stuart, of Chad and Jeremy—played the vulture with the Ringo haircut.

Walt's favorite musical team, the Sherman Brothers, were also called in. They composed five original songs: "I Wanna Be Like You," "Kaa's Song," "My Own Home," and two others. Another songwriter, Terry Gilkyson, contributed the catchy "Bare Necessities," which won the film's only Oscar nomination.

It had been four years since the last Disney animated feature (*The Sword in the Stone*), and a new crop of kids and their parents eagerly welcomed this latest offering. Its success at the box office might also be attributed to enthusiasm on the part of the critics. *The New York Times* wrote on December 25: "Merry Christmas right back to the Walt Disney studio! A perfectly dandy cartoon feature, 'The Jungle Book,' scooted into local theatres yesterday just ahead of the big day, and it's ideal for the children . . . this glowing little picture should be grand fun for all ages . . . the Disney picture is simple, uncluttered, straight-forward fun."

The Walt Disney Company planned to re-release *The Jungle Book* in the summer of 1990, and following that, it will probably become available on home video.

Screenplay by Larry Clemmons, Ralph Wright, Ken Anderson, and Vance Gerry

Based on the book by Rudyard Kipling

Produced by Walt Disney

Directed by Wolfgang Reitherman

VOICES

Baloo	Phil Harris
Bagheera	Sebastian Cabot
King Louie	Louis Prima
Shere Khan	George Sanders
Kaa	Sterling Holloway

ACADEMY AWARD NOMINATIONS

1 nomination, no wins

Best Song ("The Bare Necessities," music and words by Terry Gilkyson)

GUESS WHO'S COMING TO DINNER
COLUMBIA
$25,500,000

"You're two wonderful people who happened to fall in love and happen to have a pigmentation problem."
—SPENCER TRACY

THE TIMES, they were a-changing. Sexual taboos in the movies had been overcome for the most part by the late '60s, and it was time to tackle other barriers. The racial intermarriage theme may be dated today, but *Guess Who's Coming to Dinner* was a landmark film in its time. There had been an earlier picture dealing with miscegenation—1959's *Island in the Sun*, which dealt with two interracial romances (John Justin and Dorothy Dandridge, Harry Belafonte and Joan Fontaine). But it took the teaming of Katharine Hepburn and Spencer Tracy to make the theme a box office hit.

Through the years, Hepburn and Tracy had made eight movies together; *Guess Who* was their ninth and last. Ms. Hepburn hadn't made a film in five years, and everyone had assumed she had retired. Not so Stanley Kramer, at whose urging she reunited with her old partner Spencer Tracy. He hadn't

worked in four years, and producer-director Kramer thought it might be therapeutic for him. But Tracy was ill throughout the production, and it proved a challenge to Kramer and the rest of the crew to schedule the shooting around the rapidly weakening actor. Ten days after the last take, Spencer Tracy died.

The story involved a wealthy white couple's daughter bringing home her fiancé, played by charming and handsome Sidney Poitier. So what was all the fuss about? This black man was a parent's dream come true; in the words of *Harper's* reviewer, he was "a world-famous expert on international hygiene problems and in terms of character . . . a near-perfect mixture of Albert Schweitzer, Louis Pasteur and Ralph Bunche, while looking like Sidney Poitier, who plays the role. Who could resist that?"

Many people, unfortunately, for back in 1967, it was considered a *crime* for people of different races to marry. When Tracy says, "In 16 or 17 states, you'd be breaking the law," he wasn't exaggerating—at one time, 41 states

barred mixed marriages. Back in 1959, for example, a racially mixed couple in Virginia was sentenced to a year in jail. Their name, ironically, was "Loving." The Lovings appealed to the Supreme Court, which overturned their conviction in June, 1967, just six months before the release of *Guess Who's Coming to Dinner*. But people's attitudes weren't so quick to change, and although the laws were struck from the books, the acceptance of racially mixed marriages is far from universal even today.

In March, 1989, 22 years after *Guess Who's Coming to Dinner* premiered, the NBC television network aired its first interracial soap opera, "Generations." In order to compete with other networks' soaps, which were now concerning themselves with once-controversial or taboo subjects like homosexuality, AIDS, child abuse, and alcoholism, NBC gambled that since 20 percent of the daytime audience was black, this drama might boost their ratings. Initially, the show seemed to be doing well, remaining in the top twenty daytime drama listings.

Screenplay by William Rose

Produced and directed by Stanley Kramer

CAST

Matt Drayton	Spencer Tracy
John Prentice	Sidney Poitier
Christina Drayton . . .	Katharine Hepburn
Joey Drayton	Katharine Houghton

ACADEMY AWARD NOMINATIONS

10 nominations, 2 wins*

Best Picture
Best Actor (Spencer Tracy)
*Best Actress (Katharine Hepburn)
Best Supporting Actor (Cecil Kellaway)
Best Supporting Actress (Beah Richards)
Best Director (Stanley Kramer)
*Best Story and Screenplay Written Directly for the Screen
Best Art Direction
Best Scoring of Music—Adaptation or Treatment
Best Film Editing

BONNIE AND CLYDE
WARNER BROS.
$22,800,000

*"They're young. They're in love.
They rob banks."*
—ADVERTISING COPY FOR
BONNIE AND CLYDE

WARREN BEATTY, brother of Shirley MacLaine, hadn't had much success with his movie career since he'd acted in two films back in 1961 (*Splendor in the Grass, The Roman Spring of Mrs. Stone*). He figured if he could produce his own vehicle, he could get his career back on track, so he purchased the script for *Bonnie and Clyde* for $75,000. The investment paid off— what began as a film full of little-knowns became the sleeper of the year and Warner Bros.' most financially successful picture of the decade.

Stylish, classy, innovative in its special effects (the overcranked slo-mo footage of their death scene has become a classic), *Bonnie and Clyde* was outwardly a fact-based story of two outlaws of the '30s, a sort of Mr. and Mrs. Jesse James, folk heroes (in this

Screenplay by David Newman and Robert Benton

Produced by Warren Beatty

Directed by Arthur Penn

CAST

Clyde Barrow . . . . Warren Beatty
Bonnie Parker . . . . Faye Dunaway
C. W. Moss . . . . Michael J. Pollard
Buck Barrow . . . . Gene Hackman
Blanche . . . . Estelle Parsons
Eugene Grizzard . . . . . Gene Wilder

ACADEMY AWARD NOMINATIONS

10 nominations, 2 wins*

Best Picture
Best Actor (Warren Beatty)
Best Actress (Faye Dunaway)
Best Supporting Actor (Gene Hackman)
Best Supporting Actor (Michael J. Pollard)
*Best Supporting Actress (Estelle Parsons)
Best Director (Arthur Penn)
Best Screenplay Written Directly for the Screen
*Best Cinematography
Best Costume Design

movie, at least) in the Robin Hood tradition—they robbed banks, we are told, because the banks foreclosed on poor people. But in addition to action and graphic violence set to banjo-plunkin' bluegrass music, this movie had a *love story*. Audiences were as drawn to the two central figures as they would have been to any two well-drawn, sympathetically portrayed characters, criminal or otherwise.

Beatty's future was sealed with this picture; after it, he'd never have to beg for financing of his other projects. He not only brought the film in on time, but for a mere $2,500,000—earning back its cost nearly tenfold.

Newcomer Faye Dunaway also established her credibility as an actress after *Bonnie and Clyde*. It was her first major motion picture, and her first Oscar nomination as well. Critics were

entranced by her winsome ways. The actress also made the pages of top fashion magazines as the "Bonnie Parker" look (V-neck sweater, maxiskirt, beret) became an international craze.

Other outstanding performances were turned in by the rest of the cast, as evidenced by their all receiving nominations for Oscars. Gene Hackman and Estelle Parsons made for a memorable couple, and both went on to successful film careers. Michael J. Pollard as C. W. Moss, the goofy moon-faced creature who signs on with the Parker gang, seemed to find equally offbeat roles, playing everything from an alien child in an episode of TV's "Star Trek," to a half-witted psychopath in *Dirty Little Billy* (1972), to his most recent role as a sadistic father in *Season for Fear* (1989).

THE DIRTY DOZEN

METRO-GOLDWYN-MAYER
$20,403,826

1967

BACK DURING World War II, MGM built its reputation as the studio that made the big musicals, lots of songs and dances with stars like Judy Garland, Fred Astaire, Ginger Rogers. So what was the studio thinking when they turned out a war picture in 1967, at a time when no studio in town was doing war? For one thing, they obviously had a corner on the market. And war wasn't far from our daily thoughts as the Vietnam "living room war" was escalating. Given the right cast and script, the studio knew there was box office money to be made.

The picture was indeed a grim and dirty portrayal of war (yes, it's hell) as we follow a group of convicts on a suicide mission—they're given a choice of death, or death. Crafted almost as a suspense/thriller, the film's well-written script is further enhanced by the chemistry of the dozen assorted types making up the cast.

Lee Marvin stars as the leader of the squad, a no-nonsense guy we're glad is on our side. His hand-picked "dirties" include John Cassavetes as a psychotic hustler, former football star Jim Brown as an anti-white militant, Trini Lopez, a popular singer (he sang the theme song, "The Bramble Bush") as a young Puerto Rican, Telly Savalas as a Bible-quoting sex maniac, and Clint Walker as a psychopath. Other members of the mostly all-male cast included Charles Bronson, Ernest Borgnine, George Kennedy, and Donald Sutherland.

Word-of-mouth was a big plus in selling this picture to a war-weary public, since it received very mixed notices in the press. *Time* put it this way: *"The Dirty Dozen* is the definitive enlisted man's picture. In its view, World War II was a private affair in which officers were hypocritical, stupid or German, and only the dogfaced soldier was gutsy enough to be great. In this film, the lopsided interpretation works largely because of a fine cast and a taut plot that closes the credibility gap . . . Director Robert Aldrich gets convincingly raw, tough performances in even the smallest roles."

Even *The Hollywood Reporter* had trouble being 100 percent positive about this movie: " 'The Dirty Dozen' . . . is the beneficiary of extensive advance publicity and excitement and has a strong, virile cast to deliver both the brutalizing violence and grotesque comedy which will make it one of MGM's big money pictures of the year. It is overlong, uneven and frequently obscure, but will succeed by virtue of its sustained action, even though what it attempts to say, if anything, remains elusive."

The public seemed unaffected by these "good news/bad news" reviews and afforded the picture cult status. A series of TV movies followed: *The Dirty Dozen: The Next Mission* (1985), *The Dirty Dozen: The Deadly Mission* (1987), *The Dirty Dozen: The Fatal Mission* (1988). Some included original cast members like Ernest Borgnine, Telly Savalas, and the late Lee Marvin. A short-lived TV series ran on the Fox Network from April to July, 1988.

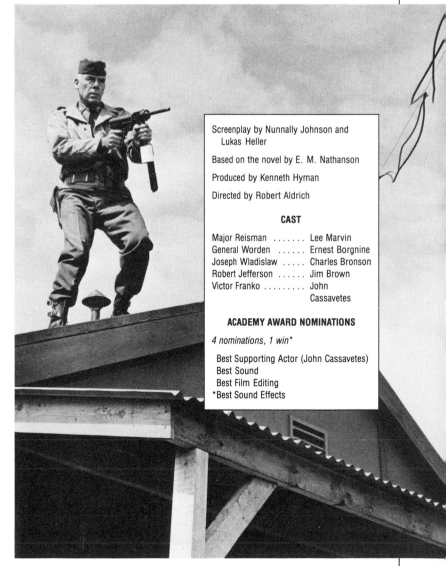

Screenplay by Nunnally Johnson and Lukas Heller

Based on the novel by E. M. Nathanson

Produced by Kenneth Hyman

Directed by Robert Aldrich

CAST

Major Reisman	Lee Marvin
General Worden	Ernest Borgnine
Joseph Wladislaw	Charles Bronson
Robert Jefferson	Jim Brown
Victor Franko	John Cassavetes

ACADEMY AWARD NOMINATIONS

4 nominations, 1 win*

Best Supporting Actor (John Cassavetes)
Best Sound
Best Film Editing
*Best Sound Effects

FUNNY GIRL

COLUMBIA
$26,325,000

As the '60s drew to a close, the decade of hit Broadway musicals had two more aces left up its sleeve, and both were held by a movie unknown. But after *Funny Girl* and *Hello, Dolly!* the name of Barbra Streisand would become one of the best-known monikers in the industry.

The young Jewish girl from Brooklyn had set her sights on a show business career since childhood, when she would sit in her room singing all the songs on the Broadway original-cast albums she lovingly collected. By her early teens, she was making her own demo records, and later held down jobs as a theater usherette and switchboard operator while she pursued her career. At 19,

she was finally signed for a role in the short-lived musical *I Can Get It for You Wholesale*.

The play didn't last, but Barbra did. She was spotted by composer Jule Styne, who had been working on a musical based on the life of comedienne Fanny Brice. Producer Ray Stark had several other screen personalities in mind for his production, like Anne Bancroft, Carol Burnett, Kaye Ballard, Mitzi Gaynor, or possibly Eydie Gorme. But Styne was pre-sold on Streisand, and insisted that Stark consider her, especially as her recording career began to take off. Fortunately, Stark agreed to a contract, and the play opened in March, 1964. It played to

packed houses for 1,348 performances before heading for Hollywood and the movie screen.

Filming began in May, 1967, but with a reluctant Ms. Streisand. She had always been self-conscious about her appearance and now feared that the facial features she considered her worst would be exaggerated by the hugeness of the movie screen. Her main concern was her nose, which many found larger than "standard," whatever that is. Fortunately, she never underwent cosmetic surgery, for it is her slightly flawed nose that reminds us that this woman with the exceptional set of vocal chords is human after all. Nevertheless, she generally prefers to be photographed in left profile, her "better side," as they say in showbiz.

Co-starring with Barbra Streisand was Omar Sharif, perhaps the casting coup of the century. Here was an Egyptian matinee idol, as dashing a male as there could be—an Arab named Omar—cast in the role of Jewish Fanny Brice's Jewish husband, Nick Arnstein. Sharif's credentials were certainly impeccable; he'd actually played an Arab in *Lawrence of Arabia*, and the title Russian in *Doctor Zhivago*. Now he was to kiss a Jewish princess on a 20-foot-high screen. It was only weeks before that the Arab-Israeli Six-Day War had taken place. The Egyptian press denounced him as a traitor, and there was talk of revoking his citizenship. But Sharif had a job to do, and fortunately, he ignored politics.

Others in the cast included Anne Francis as Fanny Brice's friend Georgia, and Walter Pidgeon as Florenz Ziegfeld. The two had appeared together in one other film, back in 1956, as father and daughter in the science fiction movie *Forbidden Planet*.

There are some truly great musical numbers in *Funny Girl*, most notably "People," Streisand's first recording hit and now her theme song; "Don't Rain on My Parade," "Second Hand Rose" (which was added for the movie version), "You Are Woman, I Am Man," and the title song, which was also written for the film and nominated for an Oscar.

Nearly every reviewer had enormous praise for Ms. Streisand. *Newsweek*, for example, described her screen debut as "the most accomplished, original and enjoyable musical-comedy performance that has ever been captured on film." Columbia Pictures charged a six-dollar top for tickets to the New York and Los Angeles engagements, an unheard-of amount in those days. But nobody seemed to mind. The film played at one Times Square theater for over a year and became the highest grossing film musical since *The Sound of Music*.

In 1975, Columbia produced a sequel called *Funny Lady*, again with Barbra Streisand and Omar Sharif, plus James Caan as her second husband. Ben Vereen and Roddy McDowall co-starred. It pulled in $19,300,000 in North American rentals, not as much as its predecessor, but certainly a respectable amount. It's worth watching once you've seen the first film.

Screenplay by Isobel Lennart

Based on the play and book by Isobel Lennart

Music by Jule Styne

Lyrics by Bob Merrill

Produced by Ray Stark

Directed by William Wyler

CAST

Fanny Brice	Barbra Streisand
Nick Arnstein	Omar Sharif
Rose Brice	Kay Medford
Georgia James	Anne Francis
Florenz Ziegfeld	Walter Pidgeon

ACADEMY AWARD NOMINATIONS

8 nominations, 1 win*

Best Picture
*Best Actress (Barbra Streisand)
Best Supporting Actress (Kay Medford)
Best Cinematography
Best Sound
Best Song ("Funny Girl," music by Jule Style, words by Bob Merrill)
Best Score of a Musical Picture
Best Film Editing

For the first time in the history of the Academy, there was a tie for Best Actress. Co-winner was Katharine Hepburn for *A Lion in Winter*.

2

2001: A SPACE ODYSSEY

METRO-GOLDWYN-MAYER
$25,521,917

Two THOUSAND and one. The first year of the 21st century. The promise of things to come.

With Stanley Kubrick's masterpiece, filmmaking entered the future, literally leaping galaxies ahead from where it had been. With its sophisticated special effects, the film anticipated the age of high-tech movies such as *Star Wars*, *Close Encounters of the Third Kind*, and *Alien*. Like the film's black monolith, Kubrick was pointing the way.

To many, especially the younger generation, *2001* was not just a movie—it was the ultimate sensory experience. Humans were just beginning to take their first teetering steps out of cradle Earth; within a year, Neal Armstrong would leave rippled footprints on the moon. Yet here was a movie that zoomed ahead in time and said, "That's ancient history!" And if you sat in the front row of the balcony—theaters had balconies back then—and gazed across the dark void between you and the screen as the orbital space station turned in perfect rhythm to "The Blue Danube" and Pan Am's shuttle prepared to dock . . . wow! Your heart soared, and you were a space voyager, too.

While much of the film was left open to interpretation by audiences and critics, the movie's strong man vs. machine theme was one aspect of the storyline

that was clear to nearly everyone. In the 21st century, it seems, artificial intelligence will be an everyday fact of life. The "protagonist" of *2001* (if there really is one) is the spaceship's on-board computer, HAL 9000*, whose malfunction precipitates a life-or-death struggle for the two hero-astronauts—the major *human* drama in the story.

Although science fiction aficionados eagerly embraced *2001*, mainstream audiences were confused by the story and message. What *was* the black monolith, anyhow? And what did the ending mean? Were there real chimp babies among the costumed actors? Did our ancestors evolve because of alien intervention, or did the aliens intervene because our ancestors were evolving? How did they shoot the Pan Am hostess walking upside down? (Answer: the same way they shot Fred Astaire's "dancing on the ceiling" scene in *Royal Wedding*—with a turning room and synchronized camera.) And just how *do* you use the zero-G toilet?

2001 was also prophetic in that it shows us to be on speaking terms with our Cold War enemies, actually cooperating with the Russians by the 21st century. Unthinkable back in 1968, yet by 1989, with the next century only slightly more than a decade away, the

unthinkable was already happening.

But back then, the only people who talked about peace and détente were hippies. This movie was a turn-on for them, and not just because toking up before the "Jupiter and Beyond the Infinite" sequence made it the greatest trip since Dorothy left Kansas and ended up in Oz. *2001* struck a chord in a generation with little hope for a future. It said "Hang on! Humans will survive . . . and evolve into Future Humans . . . and in *only 33 years!*"

The film's final moments were among the most controversial of all. Many likened the powerful visual image of the fetal "Star Child" approaching the ancient planet Earth to the images painted on the Sistine Chapel ceiling, in which God reaches out and gives the spark of life to Adam. Perhaps if Michelangelo had been alive in 1968, he would have used the motion picture screen as his medium. And in the tradition of Michelangelo, there is really only one word for the combined genius of Stanley Kubrick, Arthur C. Clarke, and special effects wizard Douglas Trumbull's efforts—masterpiece.

---

*"HAL," fans are delighted to point out, is a parody of "IBM," one letter of the alphabet lower for each initial.

Screenplay by Stanley Kubrick and
  Arthur C. Clarke

Produced and directed by Stanley Kubrick

CAST

Bowman	Keir Dullea
Poole	Gary Lockwood
Dr. Heywood Floyd	William Sylvester
Moonwatcher	Dan Richter
HAL 9000	Douglas Rain

ACADEMY AWARD NOMINATIONS

*4 nominations, 1 win**

  Best Director (Stanley Kubrick)
  Best Story and Screenplay Written
    Directly for the Screen
  Best Art Direction-Set Decoration
*Best Special Visual Effects

THE ODD COUPLE
PARAMOUNT
$20,000,000

"I've been sitting here breathing cleaning fluid and ammonia for three hours. Nature didn't intend for poker to be played like that."
—WALTER MATTHAU

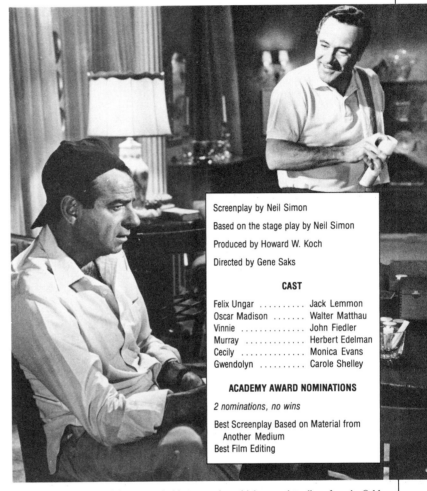

BACK IN THE '50s, most of the hit movies were translated to the screen from best-selling novels; yet in the '60s, a goodly number of Broadway shows made their way up onto the screen. 1968 was a perfect example of that trend. Three out of the five top movies were plays: a musical, a comedy, and a Shakespearean tragedy. But despite the possibility of experiencing déjà vu, audiences were more than willing to go with what were already proven successes.

Neil Simon's *The Odd Couple* had been a Broadway hit for more than two years, and it was only a question of time before it became a screen hit as well. Its story line was so basic that nearly everyone in the audience could relate to it (translation: box office success). Quite simply, it's the story of two estranged husbands who are now roomies—Oscar Madison, a happy-as-a-clam slob, and Felix Ungar, your basic compulsive neatnik. Put 'em together and what have you got? In the hands of Neil Simon, non-stop laughs; for Paramount Pictures, non-stop bucks.

Walter Matthau was signed to reprise his Broadway role as the cigar-chomping sportswriter Oscar, a man so messy he should be voted "most likely to be condemned" by the Board of Health. His onstage partner had been Art Carney, but those nervous folks in Hollywood didn't think he would be a big enough draw for the screen version,* so they signed Jack Lemmon for the part of Oscar's neurotic apartment-mate. The team had appeared together in *The Fortune Cookie* (1966), and Lemmon was eager to work with his cohort again.

The movie met with audience approval as well as critical acclaim. *The Hollywood Reporter* predicted a smash box office hit, writing: "Jack Lemmon as the Saran-wrapped, fanatical argu-

*Carney had the last laugh, of course, when he walked off with an Academy Award six years later in *Harry and Tonto* (1974).

Screenplay by Neil Simon

Based on the stage play by Neil Simon

Produced by Howard W. Koch

Directed by Gene Saks

CAST

Felix Ungar	Jack Lemmon
Oscar Madison	Walter Matthau
Vinnie	John Fiedler
Murray	Herbert Edelman
Cecily	Monica Evans
Gwendolyn	Carole Shelley

ACADEMY AWARD NOMINATIONS

2 nominations, no wins

Best Screenplay Based on Material from Another Medium
Best Film Editing

ment against toilet training turns in his best performance since 'The Apartment,' and Walter Matthau eclipses his achievement in 'The Fortune Cookie' . . . Paramount has a hit and laughs will ring to the sound of coin . . ."

The formula of *The Odd Couple*—two mismatched people unwittingly paired for bad or for worse—readily lends itself to derivations. At least four TV shows owe their existence, in whole or in part, to *The Odd Couple.* Paramount launched a situation comedy based on the film, starring Tony Randall and Jack Klugman as Felix and Oscar; the show had a successful five-year run on ABC. Later, Paramount created a

series which was virtually a female *Odd Couple*: "Laverne and Shirley" was spun off of the studio's hit, "Happy Days." In 1982–83 they tried it again, this time with two black men as "The New Odd Couple"—Ron Glass played Felix to Demond Wilson's Oscar. Then there's ABC's show, "Perfect Strangers"—an American and his Euro-peasant cousin living in Chicago. And Neil Simon himself wrote a female version of his stage play, with Rita Moreno as *Olive* Madison and Sally Struthers as *Florence* Ungar. The combinations and possibilities are endless. Let's see . . . in 1988 there was *Rain Man*, and *Twins* . . .

BULLITT
WARNER BROS.
$19,000,000

"With you, living with violence is a way of life, living with violence and death."

—JACQUELINE BISSET
TO STEVE MCQUEEN

ESCAPISM RULED at the box office, and *Bullitt* was escapism at its best. A police melodrama with Steve Mc-Queen, an exciting, hot star (fans voted him number two in popularity for the year, right behind Barbra Streisand), this film couldn't miss. The former star of TV's "Wanted—Dead or Alive" as well as films like *The Great Escape* and *The Sand Pebbles* was back for more action as a renegade cop single-handedly taking on corruption in San Francisco. This was no martini-sipping James Bond character either—the aptly named Lieutenant Bullitt (does anyone remember his first name?*) was a down-and-dirty cop who didn't mind mussing his hair.

Yet at first, McQueen was dubious about accepting the role which would

become one of his most famous. According to William F. Nolan's *McQueen*, he once said: "I'd never expected to play a cop. As a kid, running the streets, I'd been hassled a lot by the police and I'd always figured that they were on one side of the fence with me on the other. I never felt easy around cops. But here in 'Frisco,' I saw the other side of police work, and it was a real eye-opener." To prepare for the role, McQueen spent weeks driving around in a squad car with actual police detectives. "They really won my respect," the actor said.

But what this picture is best remembered for is the free-wheeling chase scene through the streets of San Francisco. It was this sequence that kept moviegoers coming back to the box office again and again. What *Ben-Hur* had done for the chariot, *Bullitt* did for the car. This roller coaster ride (some people actually got physically sick) ran a full eleven minutes with no music, just the sounds of gears grinding, wheels squeeling, sirens blaring. Months had been spent in the planning, rigging the cars for the beating they would take, and the scene required weeks to stage and shoot. An accomplished driver, McQueen insisted on

doing his own stunt driving. Eight cameras were used to record the action—two mounted inside the cars. At one point, one of the cars slammed into a camera platform (similar to what happened in *Ben-Hur*) and blew it up. The footage was left in the picture. The final sequence was edited well enough to impress the Motion Picture Academy members, who nominated the film for an Oscar for Best Film Editing.

Bullitt's main adversary is played by Robert Vaughn in the first of his many "dignified heavy" roles to follow. Until now, fans knew him mostly as "Napoleon Solo," the star of "The Man From U.N.C.L.E.," one of the most popular television series of the '60s (and still in syndication today). Jacqueline Bissett had a brief but effective role as *Bullitt*'s girlfriend in one of her first screen appearances.

Viewing the movie on your television monitor cannot possibly be as exciting as it was on the big screen. By now, we've all been subjected to car chases as almost nightly fare, so it is important to remember that this was one of the first—and is still one of the best.

———————————
*Bullitt's first name is Frank.

Screenplay by Alan R. Trustman and Harry Kleiner

Based on the novel *Mute Witness* by Robert L. Pike

Executive Producer: Robert E. Relyea

Produced by Philip D'Antoni

Directed by Peter Yates

CAST

Bullitt	Steve McQueen
Chalmers	Robert Vaughn
Cathy	Jacqueline Bisset
Delgetti	Don Gordon
Weissberg	Robert Duvall

ACADEMY AWARD NOMINATIONS

2 nominations, 1 win*

Best Sound
*Best Film Editing

ROMEO AND JULIET
PARAMOUNT
$17,473,000

THE STORY of the two star-crossed lovers of Verona is supposedly based on an actual historical occurrence in 1303; the account was first published by Bandello in 1554, translated into French in 1559, and eventually arrived in England in 1562. William Shakespeare's play of *Romeo and Juliet* was first performed in 1597 by the Globe Theatre Company, with the part of Juliet played by a boy, as was the custom, since it was considered inappropriate for women to appear on the stage.

This first of Shakespeare's great tragedies has been filmed 32 times, mostly in silent or ballet renditions. Among the most famous screen versions were a 1935 MGM film starring Norma Shearer and Leslie Howard, directed by George Cukor, and a J. Arthur Rank production from England, with Laurence Harvey and Susan Shentall. And don't forget Robert Wise's production of *West Side Story* (see page 156).

But there were variations that made Franco Zeffirelli's version unique, and subsequently drew audiences to see this highly acclaimed film. For one thing, the casting was historically accurate—both stars were the proper age. Director Zeffirelli is reported to have first offered the role of Romeo to

Screenplay by Franco Brusati and
Masolino D'Amico

Based on the play by William Shakespeare

Produced by Anthony Havelock-Allan

Directed by Franco Zeffirelli

CAST

Romeo	Leonard Whiting
Juliet	Olivia Hussey
Friar Laurence	Milo O'Shea
Tybalt	Michael York
Mercutio	John McEnery

ACADEMY AWARD NOMINATIONS

4 nominations, 2 wins*

Best Picture
Best Director (Franco Zeffirelli)
*Best Cinematography
*Best Costume Design

Beatle Paul McCartney, who refused because he was afraid of acting in a classic for what would have been his first screen role. The part eventually went to Leonard Whiting, an unknown 17-year-old English teenager without much acting experience. An even younger teen won the role of Juliet—15-year-old ingenue Olivia Hussey, who went on to become a film and TV star, appearing in such movies as *Death on the Nile* (1978) and a remake of *The Cat and the Canary* (1978). She continues to be active in film and TV today. Ironically, most people recall her name while forgetting that of Leonard Whiting. He appeared in one other major film, *Royal Hunt of the Sun* (1969), but the much-predicted major acting career failed to materialize.

One of the reasons for the movie's box office success was that it was the right film for the time. Here was a story about young people who bucked the system, idealists who stood up to the Establishment in the era of "turn on, tune in, drop out." It was the time of hippies and flower children, and Romeo and Juliet were their 16th-century equivalents. *Hair* was letting it all hang out on Broadway, and a non-offensive nude scene for the two lovers was almost obligatory. However, so

tastefully done was this scene that most parents weren't offended; even those in charge of bestowing the all-important letter rating gave *Romeo and Juliet* a PG (parental guidance). Exhibitors sighed their relief as most parents happily guided their youngsters straight to the box office.

Purists were disappointed, however, since Zeffirelli took a lot of liberties with the Bard's words; Shakespeare was substantially edited as scenes got shifted around and speeches were given to different characters. But the director must be credited for the outstanding production values he insisted upon for this film. Authentic Italian locations were used; costumes were made from only the finest French velvets and brocades; dialogue coaches, fencing, riding, and dancing lessons were the order of the day for the cast; and cameramen rode horseback to get important handheld shots.

Special mention must also be made of the music by Nino Rota. His soundtrack album was number four for the year, and so impressed Henry Mancini that he did his own arrangement of the theme. Mancini's instrumental recording on RCA of "The Love Theme from Romeo and Juliet" was number one for the week of June 28, 1969.

BUTCH CASSIDY AND THE SUNDANCE KID
20TH CENTURY-FOX
$46,039,000

"The Hole in the Wall Gang led by Butch Cassidy and the Sundance Kid are all dead now. But once they ruled the World! Most of what follows is true." —OPENING CARDS

WITH WARNER BROS.' *Bonnie and Clyde* serving as a successful blueprint, Fox produced its biggest blockbuster since *The Sound of Music*. Based on historical fact, *Butch Cassidy and the Sundance Kid* is a tragicomedy—we laugh ourselves silly right up until the end, when they're sprayed with bullets. But unlike *Bonnie and Clyde*, the final death scene is (mercifully) not revealed to us, since the camera freezes frame and our heroes never die before our eyes.

Fifty years before director George Roy Hill (*Hawaii*) brought us this movie, Harry Longabaugh, a.k.a. The Sundance Kid, teamed up with Robert Leroy Parker, a.k.a. Butch Cassidy, and enjoyed a spree of train holdups and bank robberies. As in the movie, the pair, along with former school-teacher Etta Place, fled to South America with Pinkerton detectives giving chase. But contrary to the film's ending, there is evidence to support the fact that Sundance may have escaped, returned to the United States, and led the remainder of his life under an assumed identity.

This story fascinated writer William Goldman, who spent more than six years researching Butch's and Sundance's exploits, discovering along the way that they weren't your typical outlaws who shot first, took the money, and ran. His findings showed that they didn't like to shoot or otherwise harm people they were holding up, making the duo likely candidates for a motion picture. Richard Zanuck (son of Darryl F.) at 20th Century-Fox agreed, and paid Goldman a record $400,000 for his script.

Casting for the right twosome proved a chore. Goldman envisioned Paul Newman as Sundance and Jack Lemmon playing Butch. Zanuck disagreed, believing Steve McQueen would make a better Butch. But Newman and McQueen had an ongoing

billing feud dating back to the '50s with *Somebody Up There Likes Me*, and when Newman demanded top billing, McQueen refused to sign on. Enter Robert Redford, whose career was barely getting underway. His fortuitous teaming with Newman provided the chemical magic that moviemakers dream about—heaven couldn't have provided a better match. (They would be re-teamed four years later in *The Sting*, for Universal.)

Goldman kept his script light, and audiences just adored two handsome actors who played so well off each other. One of the most remembered scenes has the two cornered by the law with nowhere to go, except to the river hundreds of feet below:

> BUTCH
> I'll jump first.
>
> SUNDANCE
> No.
>
> BUTCH
> Then you jump first.
>
> SUNDANCE
> No, I said.
>
> BUTCH
> What's the matter with you?
>
> SUNDANCE
> I can't swim!
>
> BUTCH
> (laughing)
> Why, you're crazy! The fall will probably kill you!

And then, in this most famous bit, the two gather their courage, and with a whoop, leap to the waters below. Even if Butch and Sundance thought they were done for, the audience knew they'd get out of this cliffhanger—there were still several more reels to go.

Another delightful number is the bicycle-riding sequence with Butch and Etta Place (Katharine Ross). Two-wheel bikes were just making their appearance at that time, and there is historical evidence to support the possibility that Butch learned to ride one. In this scene, Newman aptly did his own stunts, like riding on his stomach, and standing with one foot on the seat

and one in the air. Burt Bacharach's accompanying tune "Raindrops Keep Falling on My Head" couldn't have suited the number better. Sung by B. J. Thomas, the song climbed to the top of the charts and remained at number one for four weeks in January, 1970. It produced gold for composers Bacharach and Hal David in the form of an Oscar, as well as a Best Score Oscar.

In 1979, director Richard Lester did a prequel, *Butch and Sundance—The Early Days*, starring Tom Berenger and William Katt. This movie about how Butch and Sundance met and teamed up had mild success. But nothing has ever topped the original *Butch Cassidy and the Sundance Kid*, which holds the record as the highest earning Western of all time.*

---

*According to *The Guinness Book of Movie Facts and Feats*. However, the book also states that if figures are adjusted for inflation, *Duel in the Sun* (1947) would actually surpass *Butch Cassidy*.

Screenplay by William Goldman

Executive Producer: Paul Monash

Produced by John Foreman

Directed by George Roy Hill

CAST

Butch Cassidy	Paul Newman
The Sundance Kid	Robert Redford
Etta Place	Katharine Ross
Percy Garris	Strother Martin
Bike Salesman	Henry Jones

ACADEMY AWARD NOMINATIONS

7 nominations, 4 wins

Best Picture
Best Director (George Roy Hill)
*Best Story and Screenplay Based on Material Not Previously Published or Produced (William Goldman)
*Best Cinematography
Best Sound
*Best Song ("Raindrops Keep Fallin' on My Head," music by Burt Bacharach, words by Hal David)
*Best Original Score—Non-Musical (Burt Bacharach)

THE LOVE BUG
WALT DISNEY PRODUCTIONS
$23,150,000

WALT WAS GONE, but many of those who were part of his studio roster were determined to carry on the tradition of family entertainment. The first true success to proudly bear the Disney name was a delightful fantasy that would have made the Old Man proud.

The title had a double entendre (a non-sexual one; this is Disney we're talking about). One reference is to the commonly used expression "bitten by the love bug." But the title also describes the film's star car—a Volkswagen Beetle, i.e., "bug." What is really strange, however, is that at no time in the movie (or in any of the Disney press material, for that matter) does anyone ever refer to Herbie as "a Volkswagen" or "a VW." He is *always* "the Little Car." The reasoning behind this is simple: if you're going to personify an automobile, don't call it by a commonplace designation. People should think "little car," not "hunk of metal from Germany."

Bill Walsh was the producer filling Walt's shoes, and he also handled the writing chores on *Love Bug.* Walsh had certainly paid his dues at the Disney factory, having worked there for 22 years on such Disney classics as *The Shaggy Dog, The Absent-Minded Professor, Son of Flubber, Mary Poppins,* and *That Darn Cat.* And Robert Stevenson was back in the director's chair after a successful track record that included such Disney winners as *Mary Poppins, That Darn Cat, The Absent-Minded Professor, In Search of the Castaways,* and many others.

Also returning to the Disney fold was Dean Jones, appearing as the lead in his

sixth film for the studio (other films included *That Darn Cat, Blackbeard's Ghost,* and *The Horse in the Gray Flannel Suit*). His love interest was played by Michele Lee, whose career was just beginning to blossom then. But if there is a scene-stealer (aside from the cutesy car) in the picture, comedian Buddy Hackett fits the bill. Most noted for his appearances on the nightclub circuit, Hackett had also made some top box office hits, including *The Music Man* and *It's a Mad Mad Mad Mad World.* His teaming with Herbie was a bit of inspired casting— there's real chemistry here.

Shot on location in the Bay Area, the film is full of wild street chases through San Francisco—a sort of "Disney Does *Bullitt*," right down to the obligatory run down twisty Lombard Street (also in *Bullitt*). Fisherman's Wharf, Chinatown, the Golden Gate Bridge, the Monterey Peninsula, and even Virginia City, Nevada, all figured prominently in the location shooting. Most of the location work was done by a second unit, with the cast doing the majority of their scenes on a Disney soundstage or at the nearby Paramount Ranch.

Racing sequences dominate a good

deal of *The Love Bug,* with over 40 stunt drivers credited. These scenes were filmed at Willow Springs and Riverside Raceway.

Much of the stuntwork involved "Herbie," who had to appear to be doing the driving himself. (It's hard not to think of the car as a "he.") To accomplish this, an assemblage of specially rigged identical VWs were provided by effects expert Eustace Lycett. One was fitted with a Porsche engine for high-speed scenes; another was rigged for blind driving (as in *The Shaggy Dog*); yet another ran on three wheels; one ran on only two; one was cut in half with front and rear sections running on their own; one shook and trembled with fear; and one acted drunk. A number were created for the purpose of totalling them in crash/stunt situations.

Herbie has proved himself a perennial Disney star, and to date, three sequels have been made: *Herbie Rides Again* (1974), *Herbie Goes to Monte Carlo* (1977), and *Herbie Goes Bananas* (1980). In addition, there has been a limited television series based on the further adventures of the Little Car, now appearing on the Disney Channel.

Screenplay by Bill Walsh and Don DaGradi

Based on a story by Gordon Buford

Produced by Bill Walsh

Directed by Robert Stevenson

CAST

Jim	Dean Jones
Carole	Michele Lee
Thorndyke	David Tomlinson
Tennessee	Buddy Hackett
Havershaw	Joe Flynn

MIDNIGHT COWBOY

UNITED ARTISTS
$20,499,282

THE SORDID, depressing tale of a male hustler himself being hustled in New York City and his buddy and part-time pimp "Ratso" Rizzo, *Midnight Cowboy* had the dubious honor of being awarded a Motion Picture Association of America rating of "X." While today's audiences have come to think of the "X" designation mainly in connection with pornography, back in the '60s this film, which contained an explicit (albeit very brief) sex act plus a lot of blue language, could receive nothing less than a scarlet-letter "X." What's more, members of the prestigious Academy of Motion Picture Arts and Sciences—those folks who brought you the Oscar—shocked the world by voting *Midnight Cowboy* the Best Picture of 1969 (as well awarding the film Oscars for Best Director and Best Screenplay), thereby legitimizing the film. A few years later, the MPAA reconsidered (after a few nips and tucks with an editor's scissor) and changed the rating to an "R," thereby increasing the number of potential ticket buyers.

Dustin Hoffman, the naive *Graduate* we had all found so sweet and innocent only two years before, was superb in the about-face role of the gimpy, begrimed Ratzo. Hoffman told *The New York Times* in a 1982 interview that early rejections in his acting career provided him with a powerful resource for acting roles such as this. "Ratso Rizzo was not character acting," said Hoffman. "That was just an autobiography of subjective feelings about oneself." Hoffman's salad days as an

actor were over, however; he could say goodbye to the unemployment line that he'd been on since *The Graduate* (which left him with little cash), since he was paid a cool $250,000 for his work in *Midnight Cowboy*.

Critics applauded his acting abilities but reserved most of the praise for newcomer Jon Voight. A month after the film opened, *Newsweek* wrote: "It was Jon Voight, a sparkling-blue-eyed and moon-faced amalgam of Tab Hunter and early Brandon de Wilde, who captured the imagination of moviegoers. On the strength of his Candide-like portrayal of Midnight Cowboy Joe Buck, the Texas stud turned Times Square hustler, Voight has emerged as one of the industry's new breed of 'instant successes.'"

The Academy agreed, and bestowed an Oscar nomination on the promising actor. Like Dustin Hoffman, Voight had paid his dramatic dues. When he was quite young, he spent six months on Broadway singing "Sixteen Going on Seventeen" in *The Sound of Music*, worked in a few off-Broadway plays, and had one minor movie role before landing *Midnight Cowboy*. Voight then went on to a prosperous career, starring in such films as *Deliverance* (1972), *Coming Home* (1978), *The Champ* (1979), and *Runaway Train* (1985).

Screenplay by Waldo Salt

Based on the novel by James Leo Herlihy

Produced by Jerome Hellman

Directed by John Schlesinger

CAST

Ratso Rizzo	Dustin Hoffman
Joe Buck	Jon Voight
Cass	Sylvia Miles
Mr. O'Daniel	John McGiver
Shirley	Brenda Vaccaro

ACADEMY AWARD NOMINATIONS

7 nominations, 3 wins*

*Best Picture
  Best Actor (Dustin Hoffman)
  Best Actor (Jon Voight)
  Best Supporting Actress (Sylvia Miles)
*Best Director (John Schlesinger)
*Best Screenplay Based on Material from Another Medium
  Best Film Editing

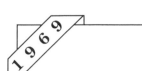

EASY RIDER
COLUMBIA
$19,100,000

"A man went looking for America.
And couldn't find it anywhere."
—ADVERTISING COPY
FOR *EASY RIDER*

ON THE SURFACE, *Easy Rider* appears to be about two drug dealers who chuck it all and become two for the road. Looking for America? Go East, young men—on Harleys, not horses. Terms like "counterculture" are frequently used when describing the film that was more a statement than a movie.

This labor of love was mounted by Dennis Hopper, who co-wrote, directed, and starred in the picture. He was partnered with another young rebel, Peter Fonda, son of Henry and an actor in his own right. The triumvirate was completed by Jack Nicholson as the Texas lawyer who joins up with the bikers along the way and learns a thing or two about the real world, like how to smoke dope, but more importantly, how to feel really free. While his character is in the film for only a short time, Jack Nicholson created a sensation in the role and garnered an Oscar nomination. He almost didn't get the part; Hopper had signed Rip Torn, but the deal fell through and Nicholson signed on. It proved to be the turning point in a career that still finds him at the top of the box office today.

One other performance is worth mentioning here. Look for Robert Walker, Jr. as Jack, the Hippie com-

---

Screenplay by Peter Fonda, Dennis Hopper, and Terry Southern

Produced by Peter Fonda

Directed by Dennis Hopper

CAST

Wyatt/Capt. America ...	Peter Fonda
Billy	Dennis Hopper
George Hanson	Jack Nicholson
Rancher	Warren Finnerty
Karen	Karen Black

ACADEMY AWARD NOMINATIONS

2 nominations, no wins

Best Supporting Actor (Jack Nicholson)
Best Original Story and Screenplay

---

mune leader. He is the spitting image of his father (his mother was Jennifer Jones). Adding to the confusion, he billed himself without the "Jr." designation. ("Star Trek"-kers will remember his performance in an early episode, "Charlie X.")

This Cinderella film was made on the unbelievable budget of $555,000 and grossed over $60,000,000 worldwide, earning more than all of Henry Fonda's films combined (pre-*On Golden Pond*). Shot in only seven weeks, the picture had a limited script, with many of the scenes being enacted by locals who ad-libbed according to Hopper's brief directions. The 127,000 feet of film took Hopper a full year to edit into a completed picture. He premiered it at the Cannes Film Festival in May, 1969, and went on to take the honors as "Best Film by a New Director."

A contemporary rock soundtrack made use of songs by current rock artists and rose to the top of the charts. The best-selling soundtrack album of 1969 featured "Born to Be Wild," the film's theme, recorded by Steppenwolf, plus songs by The Byrds, The Band, and Jimi Hendrix.

Today, *Easy Rider* is sometimes regarded as a cult film, marking the death of the decade of the '60s and the end of an era. Expressions like "groovy," "I'm getting my thing together," and "you do your own thing in your own time" have taken their place as part of our cultural history—a new generation with its own slang expressions has grown up since the premiere of this picture. But there are still some things to be learned from viewing the film, and it's certainly worthwhile watching when it appears on TV, hopefully in an uncut version.

Peter Fonda has continued to act (although not as prolifically as his sister, Jane), and Dennis Hopper has continued to direct. But Hopper's dream is to do a sequel to *Easy Rider*. Back in 1983, he had agreed to co-star in a Fonda-produced sequel called *Biker Heaven*, but it failed to materialize. Now drug-free and hard at work, he hopes to shoot an *Easy Rider* for the '90s. Meanwhile, his first one has earned the right to be termed "classic."

HELLO, DOLLY!
20TH CENTURY-FOX
$15,200,000

"**E**XPENSIVE" IS THE best word to describe Fox's lavish production of the Broadway musical success *Hello, Dolly!* Despite the early returns from *Butch Cassidy and the Sundance Kid*, Fox was having a terrible year, and was verging on bankruptcy. The first three quarters of 1969 saw the studio posting a net loss of $21,978,000, yet they continued to pour money into a last-ditch effort at pumping new life into the Big Screen Musical genre. *Hello, Dolly!* cost Fox $26,400,000 and lost them nearly as much. For Fox (and virtually every other studio), Big Screen Musicals were dead, and it would be several years before the studio would be out of the red.

The Broadway version of *Hello, Dolly!* starred Carol Channing as the exuberant matchmaker Dolly Levi, and was an instant hit. (Originally, the producers had wanted Ethel Merman in the part, but she turned it down.*) The title song was a hit as well, landing at the top of the charts in May, 1964, with 63-year-old Louis Armstrong becoming the oldest artist ever to have a number-one song. Five years later, a special role was created for him in the film, and he sang a duet with the film's star, Barbra Streisand.

After viewing *Thoroughly Modern Millie*, producer Ernest Lehman decided he didn't want Carol Channing for the screen version, finding her personality too dominating. He considered Lucille Ball and Elizabeth Taylor, but settled on Streisand, whose *Funny Girl* hadn't yet been released but was certain to be a hit. Walter Matthau was set to co-star, and Gene Kelly, star of many a musical himself, was signed to direct.

All the ingredients were in place— the lavish costumes, fantastic sets (the reconstruction of New York's Fifth Avenue in the 1890s cost $2,000,000 alone), huge cast, great musical numbers, and the memorable title song. So what caused this to be the most lavish flop in musical history?

In conducting the post mortem, it is easy to point to this or that element,

but it was a combination of many elements that rang the death knell for this film as well as the genre. As had been discovered with pictures like *The Graduate* and *Easy Rider*, the moviegoing audience was comprised of mostly under-30s, and young people just weren't impressed with lavish musicals. Also, many felt that Barbra Streisand, at age 27, was miscast as the matronly Dolly. Costs seemed to escalate out of control. Fox took a gamble, and lost.

Watch closely the young man playing Cornelius Hackl. British actor Michael Crawford, seen here in one of his few appearances in American films, went on to become the star of the biggest theatrical musical hit of the '80s, Andrew Lloyd Webber's *Phantom of the Opera*. Four years after the play opened in London (1986), he was still playing to SRO crowds in the American touring company.

---

*In 1970, Ethel Merman finally assumed the role that had been created for her, and several songs which had been dropped for the Channing version were reinstated. Additionally, there had been an all-black cast version (1967) starring Pearl Bailey.

Screenplay by Ernest Lehman

Based on the stage play by Michael Stewart

Adapted from the play *The Matchmaker* by Thorton Wilder

Music & lyrics by Jerry Herman

Produced by Ernest Lehman

Directed by Gene Kelly

CAST

Dolly Levi . . . . Barbra Streisand
Horace
Vandergelder . . . . . . Walter Matthau
Cornelius Hackl . . . . Michael Crawford
Orchestra Leader . . Louis Armstrong
Irene Molloy . . . . . . Marianne McAndrew

ACADEMY AWARD NOMINATIONS

7 nominations, 3 wins

Best Picture
Best Cinematography
*Best Art Direction-Set Decoration
*Best Sound
*Best Score of a Musical Picture
Best Film Editing
Best Costume Design

1970–1979

The Seventies were a mixed movie bag. Gone were most of the extravaganzas, the musicals, and the religious epics. Replacing them was a brand-new genre—the disaster film. People now went to the movies to live out their worst fears—burning to death in a high-rise, drowning in tragic sea disasters, falling from the sky and crashing to earth in airplanes. Even the earth under our feet was suspect and might at any moment open up and swallow us. And if these disasters didn't get us, there was always the Mafia, giant apes, giant sharks, out-of-control trains, and that old '50s standby, invaders from space.

If our national anxiety was reflected in the types of films we craved, there were also moments of reprieve from all the terror. Comic relief came in the form of pictures like *M*A*S*H*, *What's Up Doc?*, and *Blazing Saddles*.

Perhaps the greatest inspiration for films of the Seventies came from outer space. Towards the end of the decade, the promises made by the film technology of *2001: A Space Odyssey* were fulfilled with the arrival of *Star Wars* and other features involving special effects. These movies heralded a new age of film, and audiences were the lucky beneficiaries.

The movie ratings system was overhauled in this decade, in keeping with the rapidly growing population of under-30 moviegoers. "G," "M," "R," and "X" were replaced by "G" (all ages admitted), "GP" (general patronage), "R" (now allowing under-17-year-olds to be admitted if accompanied by adults), and "X" (no one under 17 admitted). In 1975, "GP" was changed to "PG" (parental guidance suggested).

1

LOVE STORY
PARAMOUNT
$50,000,000

"What can you say about a 25-year-old girl who died? That she was beautiful and brilliant. That she loved Mozart and Bach. And the Beatles. And me."
—OPENING NARRATION

WHAT CAN YOU SAY about a movie that made $50,000,000? That it was the biggest hit Paramount had ever had. That it made stars of its leading players. That it caused whole forests to be felled so tons of Kleenex could be produced.

The novelization alone could have done that. Even as this movie about two lovers from opposite sides of the tracks was being filmed, screenwriter Erich Segal was at work cranking out a novel with virtually the same dialogue, adding a few "he said"s and "she said"s, priming the public for the upcoming tear-jerker of all time. Until now, movies were made from books that were already on the bestseller list. Beginning with *Love Story*, a whole new genre of fiction was created—the motion picture novelization. Nearly 418,000 hardcover editions and 4,350,000 paperback copies were printed for the first edition—the largest in history. Millions more were sold in later editions. Everyone, it seemed, loved *Love Story*.

Robert Evans loved the script when Segal's agent William Morris first showed it to him. Although the project had been turned down by six other studios, Paramount's production chief thought that *Love Story* would be the perfect vehicle for his own romantic interest, Ali MacGraw.

Ali (née Alice) MacGraw was born on April Fool's Day in 1938 in Pound Ridge, New York. The daughter of artists, she graduated from Wellesley College, where she studied art history. Before entering films, she was an editorial assistant on *Harper's Bazaar*, an assistant to a fashion photographer, and a model whose wholesome looks kept her in frequent demand as a cover girl on women's magazines. Ali was catapulted to stardom in her second movie role as an 18-year-old Jewish Princess/college girl (she was 30 at the time) in *Goodbye, Columbus* (1968). At the time

of *Love Story*, she was married to Paramount studio boss Robert Evans; they were later divorced, and she subsequently married the late actor Steve McQueen. Since *Love Story*, her film appearances have been sporadic, among them *The Getaway* (1972), and *Just Tell Me What You Want* (1980). During the '80s, MacGraw found new life in television, appearing as a regular on "Dynasty."

Segal's script was loosely based on fact. The associate professor of classics at Yale combined the story of an old girlfriend with a story he had been told by one of his graduate students. Evans had the script rewritten (thirty times), and along the way Jenny was changed from a Brooklyn Jewish girl to an Italian Roman Catholic from Rhode Island.

Several different actors were considered as potential Oliver Barretts. The role of the perennial preppy was turned down by Jon Voight, Michael Sarrazin, Michael York, Beau Bridges, and Michael Douglas. But Ryan O'Neal had just finished a long stint as Rodney Harrington on TV's "Peyton Place" and was anxious to begin a big-screen

career. O'Neal, twice married at the time, with three children (and a prison record), seemed an unlikely candidate for the role of the Ivy Leaguer. But with his looks, charm, and 519 episodes of "Peyton Place" under his belt, Paramount decided to take a chance.

Critics delighted in alternately exalting and slashing this movie soap opera. Wrote *Time*: "Ali MacGraw promises to become the closest thing to a movie star of the '40s . . . When a Radcliffe girl chooses to die on-screen, the Academy Awards can be heard softly rustling like Kleenexes in the background . . . Ryan O'Neal gives the character of the neon scion a warmth and vulnerability."

Most people agreed, and lines snaked around the block wherever it played. Soon everyone was quoting the movie's famous slogan, "Love means never having to say you're sorry." For Paramount Pictures, *Love Story* meant never having to say you're sorry, regardless of what the critics might have to say. The studio couldn't care less about *Newsweek*'s comments: "The ersatz score put together by Francis Lai is so perfectly schmaltzy that one suspects the film was set to music first and then written. . . . 'Love Story' is very much [an] exploitation movie, cashing in on crying the way other movies cash in on sex." Critic Roger Ebert, in his *Movie Home Companion*'s "Glossary of Movie Terms," defined "Ali MacGraw's Disease" as a "movie illness in which [the] only symptom is that the sufferer grows more beautiful as death approaches." *Variety*, on the other hand, found the film "outstanding," and praised it as "another rare breath of fresh air in the smog of contemporary cinema psychoneurosis."

The huge success of *Love Story* prompted Erich Segal to devise a sequel (how could he resist?), and in 1977 he published *Oliver's Story*, in which the widower discovers that there *is* life after Jenny. In the 1978 film version, Ryan O'Neal reprised his role, with Candice Bergen as his new love interest. But audiences thought him a two-timer, wanting him to mourn his true love the rest of his life. Pass the Kleenex.

Screenplay by Erich Segal

Based on the novel by Erich Segal

Executive Producer: David Golden

Produced by Howard G. Minsky

Directed by Arthur Hiller

CAST

Jenny	Ali MacGraw
Oliver Barrett IV	Ryan O'Neal
Phil	John Marley
Oliver Barrett III	Ray Milland
Dean	Russell Nype

ACADEMY AWARD NOMINATIONS

7 nominations, 1 win*

Best Picture
Best Actor (Ryan O'Neal)
Best Actress (Ali MacGraw)
Best Supporting Actor (John Marley)
Best Director (Arthur Hiller)
Best Original Story and Screenplay
*Best Original Score

AIRPORT
UNIVERSAL
$45,220,118

THE "SPECTACULAR" was dead; long live the disaster film. In making Ross Hunter's *Airport*, Universal combined the best of the epic spectaculars from the '50s with this new genre by leaving in the traditional all-star cast, adding the "We're all going to die!" element of terror plus '70s state-of-the-art special effects. The disaster film was based on a formula that guaranteed success throughout the decade.

The basic premise of *Airport* was simple, which is why it was so easily imitated. Create your own scenario: A (plane/building/shark/ship/giant ape) is about to (crash/burn/eat the humans/ sink) and everyone will die unless (George Kennedy/Paul Newman/Steve McQueen/Roy Scheider/Gene Hackman/Jeff Bridges) can figure out a way to save them. See? You, too, can be a movie producer.

Airport, the original disaster movie, had many things going for it, such as a huge cast of really good actors. Among those featured were such names as Burt Lancaster (the airport manager), Dean Martin (strangely cast as an airline pilot—would *you* fly with him?), Jacqueline Bisset (a stewardess), Helen Hayes (a shifty old stowaway), and George Kennedy (he saves the day).

Screenplay by George Seaton

Based on the novel by Arthur Hailey

Produced by Ross Hunter

Directed by George Seaton

CAST

Mel Bakersfeld	Burt Lancaster
Vernon Demerest	Dean Martin
Tanya Livingston	Jean Seberg
Gwen Meighen	Jacqueline Bisset
Patroni	George Kennedy
Ada Quonsett	Helen Hayes

ACADEMY AWARD NOMINATIONS

10 nominations, 1 win*

Best Picture
*Best Supporting Actress (Helen Hayes)
Best Supporting Actress (Maureen Stapleton)
Best Screenplay Based on Material from Another Medium
Best Cinematography
Best Art Direction-Set Decoration
Best Sound
Best Original Score
Best Film Editing
Best Costume Design

Also rounded up for this *Grand Hotel*ish roll call were Van Heflin, Maureen Stapleton, Barry Nelson, Dana Wynter, Lloyd Nolan, and Barbara Hale.

Critics were cautious in their assessment. *The Hollywood Reporter* wrote: " 'Airport,' with its superb line-up of talent and already known title should give Universal one of its more popular films of the year . . . The one place it may find limited appeal will be on transoceanic flights." *Variety* was not quite as optimistic about the film's moneymaking prospects, noting: "This jet age 'Grand Hotel' might do good business for exhibitors, but it's doubtful there will be the kind of stampede necessary to bail out Universal's investment of around $10,000,000."

Wrong. Universal was bailed out many times over by this most successful film they had done to date. Sequel-mania also swept the studio, and there were three more *Airport* films, all with the same basic formula: *Airport 1975*, *Airport '77*, and *Airport '79—The Concorde*. None of these did as well as the original, nor, for that matter, as well as the Paramount spoofs *Airplane!* (1980) and *Airplane II: The Sequel* (1982).

M*A*S*H

20TH CENTURY-FOX
$36,720,000

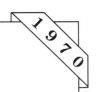

"I now close my military career and just fade away, an old soldier who tried to do his duty as God gave him the light to see that duty."
—GEN. DOUGLAS MACARTHUR, QUOTED IN OPENING CARD

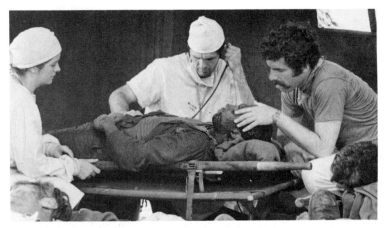

IT WAS OFFICIALLY called the Korean "Police Action." The State Department never admitted we were in a war, since Congress had never declared war. Yet every day, hundreds of young men gave their blood and their lives in this civil conflict, many of them not even out of their teens yet. It was a nasty little war which propelled World War II hero General Dwight Eisenhower into the presidency in 1952, when he promised to bring an end to the undeclared war.

The unsung heroes of this, as in any battle, were the doctors and nurses who patched the soldiers together so they could live to fight another day. Ernest Hemingway had written of gruesome front lines and ambulance drivers of World War I with deadly seriousness. Who could ever imagine finding *humor* in such circumstances?

One doctor could, and did. His name was Richard Hooker, and his first-hand experience became the basis of a novel which had the honor of being rejected by no less than 17 publishers before it became a modest seller. There had never been a blockbuster film about the Korean War, yet Fox saw possibilities in making a film of the *M*A*S*H* novel. With growing unrest and dissatisfaction with the Vietnam "Police Action," this was the right film for the time, and it became a huge success.

The doctors are about as irreverent as they could be without being court-martialed. We never see actual combat as the doctors in a *M*obile *A*rmy *S*urgical *H*ospital wage their battles with the U.S. military. The film is episodic in style; there are many memorable moments, such as the scene with "Hot Lips" and the hidden mike, the re-enactment of the Last Supper, the Hot-Lips-in-the-shower scene, the trip to Tokyo, and the no-holds-barred football game. Elliot Gould (former husband of Barbra Streisand) co-starred with Canadian actor Donald Sutherland, who rocketed to stardom following this picture. The film also served to introduce John Schuck and Gary Burghoff.*

For Ring Lardner, Jr., it was the high point in what had been a career marked by tragedy. In 1947, he had been subpoenaed by the House Committee on Un-American Activities and convicted of contempt of Congress as one of the "Hollywood Ten." He served 10 months of a one-year sentence in Federal prison and was blacklisted in the entertainment industry for 15 years. *M*A*S*H* brought him the second of two Academy Awards the gifted writer earned (the other was for *Woman of the Year* in 1942).

The movie itself was a milestone picture which premiered at the Cannes Film Festival and won the coveted "Palme d'Or" for Best Film of 1970. Most critics agreed with the public that it was unique, so it was bewildering when Fox announced that *M*A*S*H* would become a *television* show for the 1972 fall season. At first, the series seemed like a true flop, as had been so many other attempts at translating hit movies to TV. But the studio and network stuck with it, and gradually the ratings began to climb. Eventually "M*A*S*H" (starring Alan Alda as Hawkeye, the role Donald Sutherland had created) became number one in TV ratings. And a rare phenomenon occurred: the series actually *surpassed* the movie in popularity. "M*A*S*H" 's longevity was due for the most part to the creative genius of Alda, who later wrote and directed several episodes. After nine years, the program was still on top when Alda convinced Fox to end the show. But high ratings in syndication continue to this day, making "M*A*S*H" one of the truly great properties of all time.

Screenplay by Ring Lardner, Jr.

From the novel by Richard Hooker

Produced by Ingo Preminger

Directed by Robert Altman

CAST

Trapper John	....	Elliott Gould
Hawkeye	....	Donald Sutherland
Duke	....	Tom Skerritt
Major Hot Lips	......	Sally Kellerman
Lt. Dish	....	Jo Ann Pflug
Radar O'Reilly	......	Gary Burghoff

ACADEMY AWARD NOMINATIONS

*5 nominations, 1 win**

Best Picture
Best Supporting Actress
  (Sally Kellerman)
Best Director (Robert Altman)
*Best Screenplay Based on Material from
  Another Medium (Ring Lardner, Jr.)
Best Film Editing

---

*When *M*A*S*H* was translated to TV, Burghoff was the only member of the original cast to make the transition.

PATTON
20TH CENTURY-FOX
$28,100,000

"Compared to war, all other forms of human endeavor shrink to insignificance." —GEORGE S. PATTON, QUOTED IN *PATTON*

BEFORE 20th Century-Fox released *M*A*S*H*, the studio had produced a true war film in the tradition of its highly successful *The Longest Day*. Desperately in need of a hit after gigantic losses in 1969 with the failure of *Hello, Dolly!*, Fox was not disappointed. While *M*A*S*H* proclaimed war was hell, *Patton*'s title general vowed otherwise.

"Old Blood and Guts," as he became known, was a firm believer in reincarnation; he had distinct feelings of déjà

Screenplay by Francis Ford Coppola and Edmund H. North

Based on factual material from *Patton: Ordeal and Triumph* by Ladislas Farago and *A Soldier's Story* by Omar N. Bradley

Produced by Frank McCarthy

Directed by Franklin J. Schaffner

CAST

Gen. George S. Patton, Jr.	George C. Scott
Gen. Omar N. Bradley	Karl Malden
Field Marshal Montgomery	Michael Bates
Field Marshal Rommel	Karl Michael Vogler
Gen. Bedell Smith	Edward Binns

ACADEMY AWARD NOMINATIONS

10 nominations, 7 wins*

* *Best Picture
* *Best Actor (George C. Scott)
* *Best Director (Franklin J. Schaffner)
* *Best Original Story and Screenplay (Francis Ford Coppola and Edmund H. North)
* Best Cinematography
* *Best Art Direction-Set Decoration
* *Best Sound
* Best Original Score
* *Best Film Editing
* Best Special Visual Effects

vu on the battlefields of Europe, and used ancient strategies to his advantage. Born into a military family, Patton attended West Point and was one of the first American tank commanders in World War I. By the Second World War, he was in charge of the Third Army. He loved war more than life itself, as these words from the film prove: "There's only one proper way for a professional soldier to die. That's from the last bullet of the last battle of the last war."

Patton is portrayed in this movie as a megalomaniac, a human war machine who could be a merciless sadist one minute, a gentle poet the next. He appears as an inadvertent screw-up who makes us believe we won the war in spite of him. When the war ends, a German remarks, "He's an anachronism, a pure warrior. Lack of war will kill him." General Patton never had a chance to find out: he was killed in an auto accident in Germany in 1945.

George C. Scott's portrayal of George S. Patton has become legendary since this film's release. The six-minute-long opening, as he stands at attention addressing the troops in front of what has to be the world's largest American flag, is an image not easily forgotten. All of this takes place before the opening credits—a departure from the previously standard format—adding to the feeling that we are watching a real event. Later in the film, actual Fox Movietone News footage gives us a further sense of authenticity.

The role of Patton had originally been offered to Lee Marvin; when he refused it, Rod Steiger was sought for the part, but he turned it down on the grounds that it glorified militarism (anti-Vietnam War fever was running high at the time). Scott, whose last big picture had been *The Bible*, accepted the part—but refused the Oscar for Best Actor, becoming the first actor ever to do so. No definitive reason was ever given, but Scott was known to be dissatisfied with the film and especially his performance in it. *Academy Awards Illustrated* quotes him as remarking, "I was much better playing Shylock in a Central Park performance."

In 1986, George C. Scott reprised his Oscar-winning role as Patton in a made-for-television movie called "The Last Days of Patton." It co-starred Eva Marie Saint, Richard Dysart, and Murray Hamilton, and is re-run from time to time on the CBS network.

THE ARISTOCATS

WALT DISNEY PRODUCTIONS
$26,462,000

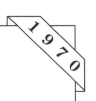

T HE DEATH of Walt Disney in 1966 left a void in that famous studio and saw others attempting to duplicate his uncanny talent for spotting potential hit properties. "What would Walt do?" became an oft-asked question. In an effort to hit on a formula for success, his heirs decided on *The Aristocats*. The project had been on the drawing boards at the time of Walt's death, and he had given his blessing on the basis of a few sketches. It proved to have what it takes at the box office, especially in France, where they delighted in the animation of the French settings. Two releases (the initial one in 1970, plus one in 1987) have helped secure a place in the top five for the animated feature.

The plot was hardly original. In many ways it was derivative of *101 Dalmations*, with adorable kittens being kidnapped this time instead of adorable puppies. But it is certainly good entertainment, and children as well as parents can easily sit through the one hour, 18-minute musical.

Celebrity voices add a great deal to the enjoyment, particularly Phil Harris as Thomas O'Malley, the Alley Cat. Also unforgettable are vocalizations by Eva Gabor as Duchess, Sterling Holloway (remember him as The Cheshire Cat and Winnie the Pooh?) as Roquefort the Mouse, Paul Winchell as the Chinese Cat, Nancy Kulp as Frou-Frou, Pat Buttram (Gene Autry's ex-sidekick) as Napoleon, Hermione Baddeley as Madame, and Monica Evans and Carole Shelley as the geese,

Abigail and Amelia. If these last two voices sound familiar, you may remember them as the "Pigeon Sisters" in *The Odd Couple*.

The Academy Award–winning Sherman Brothers were pressed back into service to write most of the songs for *The Aristocats*, including the title song (sung by Maurice Chevalier), "Scales and Arpeggios," and "She Never Felt Alone." Phil Harris sings "Thomas O'Malley Cat," written by Terry Gilkyson. But the show-stopper is a jazz number headed up by the late Scatman Crothers as "Scat Cat" called "Ev'rybody Wants to Be a Cat," by Floyd Huddleston and Al Rinker. It's truly the best moment in the movie, as Scat Cat leads a group of hippie-cats on

a parade over the rooftops of Paris.

The latest Disney studio Christmas package was well received by *The New York Times*, which wrote: "Bless the Walt Disney organization for 'The Aristocats,' as funny, warm and sweet an animated cartoon package as ever gave a movie marquee a Christmas glow . . . The real beauty of the picture, which is as amusing, smoothly machined and beautifully colored as any Disney should be, is in the characterizations, sustained within a sprightly but simple format."

Since there has been only one re-release, it seems likely that Disney Studios will probably try one more reissue before making *The Aristocats* available for home video.

Screenplay by Larry Clemmons

Based on a story by Tom McGowan and Tom Rowe

Produced by Wolfgang Reitherman and Winston Hibler

Directed by Wolfgang Reitherman

VOICES

O'Malley	Phil Harris
Duchess	Eva Gabor
Roquefort	Sterling Holloway
Abigail	Monica Evans
Amelia	Carole Shelley

FIDDLER ON THE ROOF

UNITED ARTISTS
$38,251,196

EVERYONE HAD assumed that musicals were dead, but *Fiddler on the Roof* proved there was life in the genre yet. The successful show (which bowed on Broadway in 1964 and was still running at the time the film version was released) spawned the biggest musical hit movie in many a year, and while still an echo of the '60s screen musicals, *Fiddler* could be counted among the best.

That the story of Tevye the milkman from the Jewish *shtetl* in pogrom-plagued tsarist Russia could become a popular American hit was something of a miracle itself. Based on the "Tevye" stories of Sholen Aleichem, one of the most popular Yiddish-language writers of all time, *Fiddler on the Roof* was steeped in Jewish culture and tradition, yet also appealed to a broader audience because of its dealings with universal concepts and emotions of love, joy, sorrow, family, and tradition. The film, set in a Ukrainian village, tells the plight of Tevye, his wife, and the three daughters he's trying to marry off. The violin music of Isaac Stern is featured throughout the soundtrack.

The movie was shot on location at Pinewood Studios, just outside of London, where the village of Anatevka was re-created, with exteriors filmed in the countryside of Yugoslavia. It had a budget of $9,000,000, modest by the standards of some musicals, and used a cast of mostly unknowns, at least to the American audience.

Israeli stage performer Topol (born Chaim Topol) had played Tevye in the London stage version of *Fiddler*, performing the part exactly 430 times—he admitted to taking six days off for the Arab-Israeli Six Day War in 1967. (When he was nominated for the Oscar in the film version, he had to secure permission from his Army superiors to attend, since his reservist unit was on active duty at the time.) The Tel Aviv–born actor first began performing with the Israeli Army entertainment unit and later did several films in his native country. In the late '60s, he worked in British films, including *Before Winter Comes* (1969), with David Niven, before landing the part of Tevye.

Another plum role went to actress Molly Picon, as Yente the Matchmaker.

Miss Picon was well known to patrons of Yiddish theater, and the late actress was 72 years old when she appeared in the most famous role of her film career. She saw her work as a chance to perform in a document of historical significance. "It's part of a world that's gone," she said in a 1971 interview with *The New York Times*. "There's such a joy and tenderness about this. There's a sadness, too. The world that we're portraying has been destroyed."

Most of the rest of the cast have remained relatively unknown to Amer-

lywood Reporter wrote: " 'Fiddler on the Roof' is a lavish, carefully made, splendidly designed musical film. It demonstrates once again that ample amounts of time and money, intelligently employed, can indeed buy perfection."

The timeless story of parents watching their flock grow into young adulthood is beautifully captured in the music and lyrics of Jerry Bock and Sheldon M. Harnick. Although the two have collaborated on other projects, *Fiddler* is by far their most successful musical achievement. The songs have just the right feeling of sadness that pervades most Jewish folk music, giving an authentic feeling to the score while still managing to reach a general audience. Songs like "If I Were A Rich Man," "Sunrise, Sunset," "Matchmaker, Matchmaker," and "Tradition," plus Isaac Stern's violin solos (his playing was used to dub the film's opening fiddler) helped make this the number-two-selling soundtrack album of the year.

Screenplay by Joseph Stein

Adapted from stage play by Joseph Stein

Based on the stories of Sholem Aleichem

Music by Jerry Bock

Lyrics by Sheldon Harnick

Produced and directed by Norman Jewison

CAST

Tevye .... Topol
Golde .... Norma Crane
Motel .... Leonard Frey
Yente .... Molly Picon
Lazar Wolf .... Paul Mann

ACADEMY AWARD NOMINATIONS

8 nominations, 3 wins*

Best Picture
Best Actor (Topol)
Best Supporting Actor (Leonard Frey)
Best Director (Norman Jewison)
*Best Cinematography
Best Art Direction-Set Decoration
*Best Sound
*Best Scoring, Adaptation

ican audiences in the ensuing years, but one name stands out. Fans of "Starsky and Hutch" will recognize Paul Michael Glaser (now mostly known as a television director), billed as Michael Glaser, in the part of Perchik.

Critical accolades were showered on *Fiddler on the Roof*. *Variety* said: "Sentimental in a theatrical way, romantic in the old-fashioned way, nostalgic of immigration days, affirmative of human decency, loyalty, bravery and folk humor, . . . 'Fiddler on the Roof' is a powerhouse attraction." And *The Hol-*

BILLY JACK

WARNER BROS.
$32,500,000

"Once in a generation, a hero becomes a legend."
—OPENING STATEMENT

Tom LAUGHLIN'S masterful performance as vigilante for the rights of Native Americans made Billy Jack an unlikely candidate for box office hit status. The producer, director, writer, and star of the film, which was made on a shoestring budget of $800,000, turned it into the sleeper of the decade. It is a simplistic tale of good and evil, youth verses the Establishment, and it reached exactly the audience for which it was intended—the disillusioned young people trying to express their horror over war in general and Vietnam in particular.

The low budget is very apparent in the home-movie-like quality of the film, which is what director Laughlin was seeking. It is part student film, part docudrama, part improvisation. The audience is given the status of out-worlders, privy to sacred Indian tribal rituals like the "Indian Snake Ceremony" and the "Wovoka Friendship Dance." With authentic locations and Native Americans in the cast, Laughlin quickly gains the audience's sympathy for the heretofore overlooked and exploited aboriginal population of our land.

Yet there is something disturbing about *Billy Jack* and its pessimistic attitude. A sample of the dialogue tells why. When one of the characters, tired of being subjected to racist violence and humiliation, says, "We'll go some place else, some place where it doesn't have to be like this," another retorts: "Oh really? Tell me, where is that place? In what remote corner of this country—no the entire goddamn planet—is there such a place where men really care about one another and really love each other? *Just one place!*"

Laughlin produced the film independently, found he couldn't get the distribution he had been promised by AIP, and struck a deal with Warner Bros. Yet promotion by the distributor was not forthcoming, and *Billy Jack* might have all but disappeared were it not for the persistence of its creator. Laughlin sued Warners for $51,000,000, settled out of court, and eventually won re-release status for the film in 1974, when it proceeded to double its 1971 grosses. Heavy saturation advertising in a TV blitz campaign turned the trick. Once the enemy of theatrically-distributed movies, television was now harnessed as distributors' most powerful weapon.

Critics failed to predict the success that was forthcoming. *The Hollywood Reporter* said: "Most of the time, the picture seems attenuated and flat, because it's a complicated, tricked-up story that needed a steady pace and strong characterizations to work—neither of which it has . . . Its boxoffice possibilities look slim."

On that last subject, the trade paper was incorrect. Yet although the film was vastly successful in the early '70s, today the incongruity of an ex-Green beret who preaches non-violence, then karate-chops his way through half the Southwest makes this picture difficult to watch except as a curiosity piece. Still, the film has remained a cult classic nearly 20 years later.

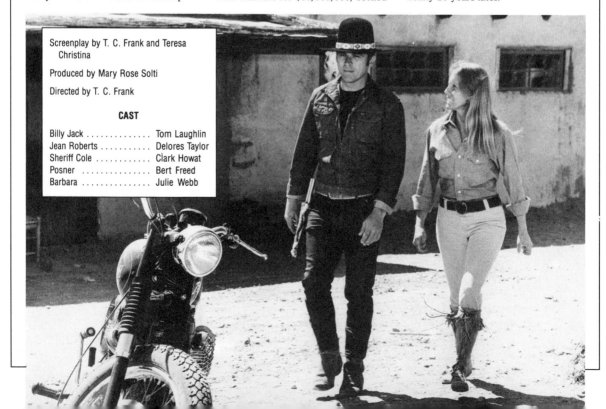

Screenplay by T. C. Frank and Teresa Christina

Produced by Mary Rose Solti

Directed by T. C. Frank

CAST

Billy Jack	Tom Laughlin
Jean Roberts	Delores Taylor
Sheriff Cole	Clark Howat
Posner	Bert Freed
Barbara	Julie Webb

THE FRENCH CONNECTION

20TH CENTURY-FOX
$26,315,000

Screenplay by Ernest Tidyman

Based on the novel by Robin Moore

Produced by Philip D'Antoni

Directed by William Friedkin

CAST

Jimmy "Popeye" Doyle ..	Gene Hackman
Alain Charnier	Fernando Rey
Buddy Russo	Roy Scheider
Sal Boca	Tony LoBianco
Pierre Nicoli	Marcel Bozzuffi

ACADEMY AWARD NOMINATIONS

*8 nominations, 5 wins**

*Best Picture
*Best Actor (Gene Hackman)
 Best Supporting Actor (Roy Scheider)
*Best Director (William Friedkin)
*Best Screenplay Based on Material from
 Another Medium (Ernest Tidyman)
 Best Cinematography
 Best Sound
*Best Film Editing

BASICALLY NOTHING MORE than a jazzed-up cops-and-robbers movie with a *Bullitt*-derived* car-chase sequence, *The French Connection* somehow won Best Picture over complex productions like *Fiddler on the Roof, Nicholas and Alexandra, A Clockwork Orange*, and *The Last Picture Show*—all nominees for 1971 and all equally worthy of the number-one prize. Seldom had a movie with such a simple premise garnered so much attention and been so well received.

The French Connection, shot almost entirely in and around Manhattan, was based on a novel by Robin Moore, which in turn was based on the true-life exploits of two tough New York cops— Eddie "Popeye" Egan, and Sonny Grosso, both of whom appear briefly as other characters in the film. Gene Hackman starred as Jimmy "Popeye"

---
*Highly likely, since Philip D'Antoni was producer on both pictures.

Doyle, and Grosso, now renamed "Buddy Russo," was played by Roy Scheider. The critics and public found their performances so convincing and natural that *Time* seemed certain that the dialogue must have been ad-libbed rather than scripted, commenting that "the actors who play the cops are so well cast that they seem to have grown up next door to the precinct house."

Gene Hackman, who had been nominated as Best Supporting Actor for his roles in *Bonnie and Clyde* (1967) and *I Never Sang For My Father* (1970), was as astonished as anyone when he walked off with the Best Actor award. According to *Academy Awards Illustrated*, Hackman said: "I had no idea . . . that *Connection* would [be a runaway hit]. I thought it would either be well-received by critics and stand as an example of that kind of film, or that it would be an audience movie. I didn't think it would be both."

There is no doubt that all else paled

in the film when compared to that spectacular, superbly-edited chase sequence. Plenty of point-of-view shots coupled with expert editing had moviegoers literally on the edge of their seats, and despite an "R" rating— which theoretically should have hurt box office potential—the film was a huge financial success thanks to the repeat business from patrons anxious to take additional rides on this Cinerama-like roller coaster.

In 1975, there was the inevitable sequel, which also had a chase sequence (on foot, this time). It failed to live up to both the quality and financial success of the first. There was also a 1986 movie-for-television, *Popeye Doyle*.

In 1989, the original suspect sought as the head of the street-distribution network for the drug ring portrayed in the film was captured in Los Angeles— 17 years after he fled investigators probing his ties to the narcotics underworld. The saga continues.

BENJIE (OLIVER CONANT): *My mother and father never did that.*

HERMIE (GARY GRIMES): *Why not?*

BENJIE: *Because it's stupid.*

MANY A YOUNGSTER, especially in the protective era of the '40s, felt as aghast and confused as Benjie and Hermie when they learned the truth about sex and where they came from. Now that films were becoming more sexually permissive, it is easy to see why so many people found *Summer of '42* such a meaningful film, making the "R" rating inconsequential in terms of box office repeat business.

The film was the first of the many modern "coming of age" pictures that would follow. These were especially prevalent in the early '80s when the "how to lose your virginity" genre really came into its own with films like *Little Darlings* (1980) and *Porky's* (1982).

The nostalgic look at the war years was enhanced by the director's attention to the most minute detail. Nothing was overlooked, from the totally authentic set decoration, to the price of movie tickets at the box office (adults 25 cents, children 10 cents), to Bette Davis up on the screen uttering her famous ending to *Now Voyager* ("Don't let's ask for the moon—we have the stars") while the boys played grope-and-tickle with their dates.

It was such a well-crafted film that most critics found little fault in it, except perhaps for some protracted scenes with Hermie, the adolescent protagonist, taking long walks and staring into the sunset. *Newsweek* praised director Mulligan's "knack for drawing natural, charming and, at the same time, complicated performances from young people, and a gentleness and warmth that, when they work, tightrope their way across sentiment to genuinely touch us." Jennifer O'Neill, former model and cover girl, gives a sensitive portrayal as the "older woman," a war widow who initiates Hermie into the art of love while she herself uses the young man for consolation over her grief. Although O'Neill had appeared in minor roles in films since 1968, her performance in *Summer of '42* propelled her to stardom.

One of the film's best and most remembered scenes was Hermie's embarrassing attempt to purchase "rubbers" (condoms). It is important for modern audiences to bear in mind the utter humiliation that young men were made to feel back in those days, when purchasing what was then the common form of birth control was a hush-hush affair. In fact, this classic scene was recently parodied in a British award-winning television commercial which has a young man discretely trying to purchase condoms while the insensitive druggist blurts out on the loudspeaker, "Stockroom, do we have any condoms left?"

Two years following the success of *Summer of '42*, the studio brought out the sequel, *Class of '44*. It wasn't bad, as sequels go, but it couldn't touch the original's success.

Screenplay by Herman Raucher

Produced by Richard A. Roth

Directed by Robert Mulligan

CAST

Dorothy . . . . Jennifer O'Neill
Hermie . . . . Gary Grimes
Oscy . . . . Jerry Houser
Benjie . . . . Oliver Conant
Aggie . . . . Katherine Allentuck

ACADEMY AWARD NOMINATIONS

4 nominations, 1 win*

Best Original Story and Screenplay
Best Cinematography
*Best Original Dramatic Score
 (Michel Legrand)
Best Film Editing

DIAMONDS ARE FOREVER
UNITED ARTISTS
$19,726,829

"My name is Bond. James Bond."

THOSE WORDS WERE music to the execs at United Artists, who could always count on the superspy to save the day for them at the box office with the same panache with which he saved England.

Diamonds Are Forever was the eighth Bond movie, the seventh to be produced by Albert "Cubby" Broccoli and Harry Saltzman, and the sixth to star Sean Connery. Many thought it the best, although most were just grateful to see Connery back in the harness again, even if he was beginning to gray at the temples. It had been four years since his last Bond picture (*You Only Live Twice*, 1967), and the actor hadn't been able to shake the typecasting. Oh well, why not put the image to good use?

This time, Bond was trying to expose an elaborate diamond smuggling operation, tangling along the way with his old nemesis, Blofeld (played here by Charles Gray). The movie included the usual assortment of Bond girls, such as Jill St. John as Tiffany Case, and Lana Wood (sister of Natalie) as Plenty O'Toole. "M" (Bernard Lee), "Q" (Desmond Llewelyn), Miss Money-penny (Lois Maxwell), and Felix Leiter (Norman Burton became the fourth actor to play the part) were by now

Screenplay by Richard Maibaum and
  Tom Mankiewicz

Based on the novel by Ian Fleming

Produced by Harry Saltzman and
  Albert R. Broccoli

Directed by Guy Hamilton

CAST

James Bond	Sean Connery
Tiffany Case	Jill St. John
Blofeld	Charles Gray
Plenty O'Toole	Lana Wood
Willard Whyte	Jimmy Dean

ACADEMY AWARD NOMINATIONS

1 nomination, no wins

Best Sound

standard fixtures in any Bond film and favorites with the audience. "Willard Whyte," the billionaire kidnapped by Blofeld, is played by Jimmy Dean, the country singer from Texas who gained later fame with Jimmy Dean Sausages.

By this time, the Bond films were getting bigger and better budgets, and much of the money went toward authentic locations. *Diamonds* was filmed in England (Pinewood Studios), Germany, Holland, France, and the United States. Direction was by the same person who did *Goldfinger*—Guy Hamilton—but he brought a much lighter touch to *Diamonds*, emphasizing high camp rather than danger. For example, in the screen's second big chase scene of the year (see *The French Connection*, page 219), Tiffany's Mustang is pitted against the Las Vegas police, with 20 cars totalled in the sequence.

While the audience was obviously happy to have Sean Connery back as James Bond, critics seemed to have mixed feelings. *Time* remarked that "Bond looks better than ever, partly because Sean Connery has returned to play him. During Connery's one-picture absence, some fellow named Lazenby filled the role—the way concrete fills a hole." Yet *Newsweek* wrote: "Connery himself looks a bit long in the tooth to be running around the world scaling buildings, racing cars and generally cutting up."

The actor must have agreed, and loudly proclaimed, "Never again!" But in 1983, the same year Roger Moore played James Bond in *Octopussy*, Sean Connery decided to have another go at male Bonding, with his final (?) venture—*Never Say Never Again*.

1

THE GODFATHER
PARAMOUNT
$86,275,000

"I'm gonna make him an offer he can't refuse." —MARLON BRANDO

THERE HAD BEEN nothing like it in years. In fact, this was the long-awaited pretender to the box office throne which had been retained by that blockbuster of all time, *Gone With the Wind*. *The Godfather* handily surpassed the champion to become the reigning king of the box office, netting a phenomenal $86,275,000, nearly double the amount of Paramount's previous biggest hit, *Love Story* (1970).

Back in 1966, Paramount had bought a story from Mario Puzo, paying $7,500 for the 20-page outline. They then made the writer an offer he couldn't refuse—even before the book was published, the studio paid him another $80,000, gave him an office and secretary on the lot, and had him finish the novel. The book went on to become one of the best-sellers of all time: 500,000 copies in hardcover, 10,000,000 paperback copies in print.

Gleefully, Paramount announced plans for filming *The Godfather*. Almost immediately, there was a backlash from the Italian-American Civil Rights League, a group reportedly headed by Joseph Columbo, the reputed don of one of New York City's five Mafia families. The group held an anti-*Godfather*-movie rally in Madison Square Garden, raising $600,000 for their cause. According to reports in *Time*, the offices of Gulf and Western, Paramount's parent company in New York, had to be evacuated twice because of bomb threats. In the end, the League was only successful in getting the producers to substitute all references to "the Mafia" with "the family."

The first order of business was the proper casting of the plum role of Don Vito Corleone, the Godfather himself. Marlon Brando was Coppola's first choice, but many at the studio were skeptical. Actors who were given consideration were George C. Scott, Laurence Olivier, and even Italian producer Carlo Ponti. Melvin Belli, the flamboyant San Francisco attorney and aspiring actor, offered his services.* Most of the opposition to Brando centered on the character sketch of the Don as a man in his sixties, short, stout, graying hair; Brando was in his mid-forties. The decision was finalized one afternoon when Coppola hosted a screening of an actor test for the execs. They nodded approval, then inquired about the vaguely familiar actor. Coppola beamed as he announced it was Brando in full make-up.

Critic Rex Reed commented on Brando's portrayal of the Don, "Most of the time he sounds like he has a mouth full of wet toilet paper," and indeed it was once reported that Brando did stuff his mouth with cotton balls. But it is impossible to imagine anyone else in this role, any more than one can imagine someone other than Clark Gable as Rhett Butler. Brando was simply fated to be Don Corleone.

In a characteristic move, the eccentric Brando refused the Academy's award for Best Actor, sending his proxy to the ceremony in the form of a Native American named Sacheen Littlefeather, who dolefully walked on stage to refuse the Oscar while bemoaning the treatment of Indians in Hollywood. The Academy didn't seem to mind, and later nominated the two-fold winner for his eighth chance at Oscar, for *Last Tango in Paris* (1973).

The others in the film were also well-cast. Coppola's sister, Talia Shire, played Vito Corleone's daughter Connie. She had had limited acting experience, but later became a star in her own right (primarily as Mrs. Rocky Balboa in the *Rocky* movies). Al Pacino, a New York stage actor who had won both an Obie and a Tony, landed the pivotal role of Michael even though he had only one previous film credit, *Panic in Needle Park* (1971). He received a nod from the Academy with a nomination for Best Supporting Actor, as did James Caan, who portrayed the explosive Sonny. Recording and nightclub star Al Martino played the part of Johnny Fontane, whom many saw as a parallel to Frank Sinatra (although this was vigorously denied by that singer-actor).

Ninety percent of the movie was shot on the streets of New York City and its suburbs, with the remaining ten percent filmed on a soundstage in the Bronx. Additional footage was shot in Sicily.

Although the violence and language of the *Godfather* mandated an "R" rating, public and critical acclaim made this one of the most successful films of all time, and Paramount immediately began preparing a sequel, *The Godfather, Part II*, which reached the screen in 1974. A special release from Paramount Home Video called *The Godfather Saga* is an edited videocassette version that combines elements of both films but rearranges them into chronological order.

Fifteen years later, in 1989, the studio decided to revive the property with a new sequel, *The Godfather, Part III*, which began filming in November on location in New York and Italy. Release was scheduled for summer, 1990.

Screenplay by Mario Puzo and Francis Ford Coppola

Based on the novel by Mario Puzo

Produced by Albert S. Ruddy

Directed by Francis Ford Coppola

CAST

Don Vito Corleone . . . . . . Marlon Brando
Michael Corleone . . . . Al Pacino
Sonny Corleone . . . . James Caan
Tom Hagen . . . . Robert Duvall
Kay Adams . . . . Diane Keaton

ACADEMY AWARD NOMINATIONS

*10 nominations, 3 wins**

*Best Picture
*Best Actor (Marlon Brando)
 Best Supporting Actor (James Caan)
 Best Supporting Actor (Robert Duvall)
 Best Supporting Actor (Al Pacino)
 Best Director (Francis Ford Coppola)
*Best Screenplay Based on Material from Another Medium (Mario Puzo and Francis Ford Coppola)
 Best Sound
 Best Film Editing
 Best Costume Design

---

*Belli had once guest starred on TV's original "Star Trek" series. To this day, he continues to offer his services.

THE POSEIDON ADVENTURE
20TH CENTURY-FOX
$42,000,000

"At midnight on New Year's Eve, the S.S. Poseidon, enroute from New York to Athens, met with disaster and was lost. There were only a handful of survivors. This is their story." —OPENING CARD

AS WITH THAT other ill-fated ship, *The Titanic*, there was no question in the audience's mind that this was going to be a disaster film and that most of the characters we were about to meet were doomed. Here was the basic premise of all disaster films: the audience, safely noshing in their seats, would calmly bet on who would survive and who would not. If the formula was always the same, so was the predicted box office success.

Screenplay by Stirling Silliphant and Wendell Mayes

Based on the novel by Paul Gallico

Produced by Irwin Allen

Directed by Ronald Neame

CAST

Rev. Frank Scott	Gene Hackman
Mike Rogo	Ernest Borgnine
James Martin	Red Buttons
Monnie Parry	Carol Lynley
Acres	Roddy McDowall
Linda Rogo	Stella Stevens
Belle Rosen	Shelley Winters

ACADEMY AWARD NOMINATIONS

8 nominations, 1 win*

Best Supporting Actress (Shelley Winters)
Best Cinematography
Best Art Direction-Set Decoration
Best Sound
*Best Song ("The Morning After," music and words by Al Kasha and Joel Hirschhorn)
Best Original Dramatic Score (John Williams)
Best Film Editing
Best Costume Design

The category of Best Special Visual Effects was dropped for 1972. Instead, *The Poseidon Adventure* was given the "Special Achievement Award" for visual effects.

What *Airport* had done for the unfriendly skies, *The Poseidon Adventure* did for the high seas. Academy Award–winner Gene Hackman (*The French Connection*) played the minister who keeps his cool while all about are losing theirs; others in the star-studded cast were Ernest Borgnine, Red Buttons, Carol Lynley, Roddy McDowall, Stella Stevens, Shelley Winters (probably the most remembered performance—she won an Oscar nomination), Jack Albertson, Pamela Sue Martin (in her pre-"Dallas" days), Arthur O'Connell, Fred Sadoff, Bob Hastings, and Leslie Nielsen as the Captain.

The film was made all the more convincing with the use of visual effects, which won the Academy's Special Achievement Award for effects designers L. B. Abbott and A. D. Flowers. The *Queen Mary*, berthed in Long Beach, was used for exteriors of the ship, while miniatures were set afloat in a tank on the Fox lot in which the storm effects were created. Most ingenious of all was the Grand Salon

set, built to tilt 30 degrees with the camera also tilting. To simulate the overturned ship, an upside-down set was also created, with the "ceiling" underfoot and the "floor" carpeted overhead (tables were bolted to it).

The movie's theme song, "The Morning After," won an Oscar as Best Original Song. Maureen McGovern's single of this love theme became a number-one gold record, remaining in that position on the *Billboard* charts for two weeks in August, 1973.

Scoring of "The Morning After" was done by John Williams, earning him an Oscar nomination. Producer Irwin Allen had worked with Williams before— when he was producing a television show called "Lost in Space." Williams wrote the theme to the TV series, billed as "Johnny" Williams in the credits.

There was a sequel, of course. *Beyond the Poseidon Adventure* (1979) found Telly Savalas, Sally Field, Michael Caine, and others attempting a salvage operation on the infamous ship. But the film itself couldn't be salvaged. It was plainly a disaster.

WHAT'S UP DOC?

WARNER BROS.
$28,000,000

"Once upon a time, there was a plaid overnight case."
—OPENING NARRATION

THUS BEGINS Peter Bogdanovich's homage to the screwball comedies so popular in the '30s. Teaming Barbra Streisand and Ryan O'Neal in this irreverent piece of slapstick, Bogdanovich includes every sight gag known to humankind, beginning with the mix-up of four pieces of luggage that opens the film.

If the movie seems derivative of *Bringing Up Baby*, the 1938 Cary Grant–Katharine Hepburn screwball comedy which defined the genre for all time, it is not entirely accidental, since the Howard Hawks–directed classic served as the blueprint for *What's Up Doc?*

During rehearsals, Bogdanovich shot tests of his two stars and showed the footage to Howard Hawks. According to Shaun Considine's *Barbra Streisand*, Hawks told the young director that Streisand had the same problem Hepburn had had. She was trying too hard to be funny. "Tell them to just read the lines. They've got to play off each other and get the laughs from their attitudes," Hawks instructed. He also thought it was wrong for Bogdanovich to admit the plot's source. "You made a mistake telling 'em where you stole it from," Hawks told him. "I never said who I stole it from."

What a breath of fresh air this was for audiences in a year heavy with deadly-serious films like *The Godfather*, *The Poseidon Adventure*, and *Deliverance*. There were no lessons to be

learned, no social commentary. Like the Cole Porter tune says, "Anything Goes" (the film makes heavy use of Porter's songs, including the Streisand-O'Neal duet of "You're the Top" sung over opening credits).

The movie has the second-most-popular California location for its setting, San Francisco, and there was the by-now-obligatory car chase through its hilly streets. Only seven or eight cars get totaled this time, though; after all, this is not *Bullitt*.

Reviews were mixed, with critics uncertain of what to make of this salute to *Bringing Up Baby*—tampering with classics usually doesn't sit well with critics. But *Variety* termed the comedy "terrific" and predicted gold at the box office: "This picture is a total smash. The script and cast are excellent; the direction and comedy staging are outstanding; and there are literally reels of pure, unadulterated and sustaining laughs . . . mature audiences haven't seen a new film like this in a generation . . . The Warner Bros. release has nothing in sight but money, by the carload . . . Buck Henry, David Benton and Robert Newman have fashioned a great screenplay."

The film's ending pokes fun at *Love Story*, Ryan O'Neal's most famous film to that time:

JUDY
Love means never having to say you're sorry.

HOWARD
That's the dumbest thing I ever heard!

Maybe so, but there was certainly chemistry between the pair—they were reunited in 1979 for another romp in *The Main Event*.

Screenplay by Buck Henry, David Newman, and Robert Benton

From a story by Peter Bogdanovich

Produced and directed by Peter Bogdanovich

CAST

Judy Maxwell . . . . Barbra Streisand
Howard Bannister . . . . . Ryan O'Neal
Hugh Simon . . . . Kenneth Mars
Eunice Burns . . . . Madeline Kahn
Frederick Larrabee . . . . Austin Pendleton

④
DELIVERANCE
WARNER BROS.
$22,600,000

WHEN IT CAME TIME to translate erstwhile poet James Dickey's 1970 best-seller to the screen, Dickey himself was put in charge of writing the screenplay for *Deliverance*, something rarely done in Hollywood. In fact, Dickey managed to get himself cast in a minor part as well, as "Sheriff Bullard."

This suspenseful, beautifully photographed film about four Atlanta businessmen off on a weekend of pitting their skills against nature is hardly a joy cruise. Their survivalist, man-against-the-elements white-water canoeing trip turns to tragedy and death, while the river flows angrily, noisily onward. It is almost as if the visitors to this pristine wilderness have themselves raped the virginal forests and landscapes. There is also a profound sense of sadness pervading the latter half of the film, one which lingers even after the lights come up.

The drama is riveting, and audiences obviously related to the gang of four in the film, projecting themselves into each treacherous situation from the safety of their theater seats. John Boorman's first venture into this all-location film would certainly not be his last, and the style of *Deliverance*—in which the trees and river become characters themselves—is one Boorman would again draw upon for *The Emerald Forest* (1985).

Location shooting used up half of the film's extremely low $2,000,000 budget. Boorman selected a northern Georgia county bisected by the Chattooga River. The location crew filmed there for two months, with most of the budget going to local carpenters, truck drivers, food, and lodging. Boorman filmed in sequence, which is rarely done in filmmaking, and the four stars—Burt Reynolds, Jon Voight, Ned Beatty (in his screen debut), and Ronny Cox (ditto)—did all of their own, sometimes very dangerous, stunts. Following the release and ultimate success of *Deliverance*, Rabun County had a sudden influx of tourists, eager to see the film's location with their own eyes, and three companies began running guided canoe tours down the river. In order to lure more movie companies and their dollars to avail themselves of the locations, the state of Georgia promptly set up a Film Commission—something virtually every state in the Union has today.

Burt Reynolds may have been one of the main reasons so many people came to see *Deliverance*. Only three months before the film's release, the handsome Floridian had posed in the buff for *Cosmopolitan* Magazine, and the publicity hadn't exactly hurt him at the box office. (His other feature of 1972 was Woody Allen's *Everything You Always Wanted to Know About Sex but Were Afraid to Ask*—as far as one can tell, there was no intended correlation between his centerfold and that film's title.)

One of the best-remembered scenes in this movie is the musical interlude of "Dueling Banjos," a lively bluegrass number. Released as a single, the tune became a pop hit, climbing into *Billboard's* top ten.

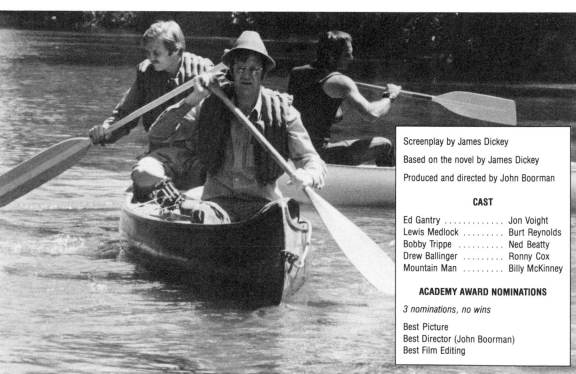

Screenplay by James Dickey

Based on the novel by James Dickey

Produced and directed by John Boorman

CAST

Ed Gantry	Jon Voight
Lewis Medlock	Burt Reynolds
Bobby Trippe	Ned Beatty
Drew Ballinger	Ronny Cox
Mountain Man	Billy McKinney

ACADEMY AWARD NOMINATIONS

3 nominations, no wins

Best Picture
Best Director (John Boorman)
Best Film Editing

1972

JEREMIAH JOHNSON
WARNER BROS.
$21,900,000

Screenplay by John Milius and
Edward Anhalt

Based on the novel *Mountain Man* by
Vardis Fisher and the story "Crow
Killer" by Raymond W. Thorp and
Robert Bunker

Produced by Joe Wizan

Directed by Sydney Pollack

CAST

Jeremiah Johnson	Robert Redford
Bear Claw	Will Geer
Del Gue	Stefan Gierasch
Swan	Delle Bolton
Caleb	Josh Albee

*"His name was Jeremiah Johnson,
and he wanted to be a mountain
man."* —OPENING NARRATION

NINETEEN SEVENTY-TWO was a very good year for Warner Bros. The film studio had three of the top five films for a combined total of $72,500,000 in domestic rentals. Their comedy *What's Up Doc?* was the only one of that genre in the top five. Aside from this exception, we liked our films violent that year, although *Jeremiah Johnson* had less violence than the others. There were some similarities between *Deliverance* and *Jeremiah Johnson*: both featured a return to the wilderness way of life, a remote dream in a country that was in a recession and entangled in a war nobody wanted.

"Ride due West as the sun sets; turn left at the Rocky Mountains," he was told, and Jeremiah was off on his back-to-nature trek. Along the way we learned that life was hard back in 1825,

and maybe things weren't so bad for us after all. "I wanted this film to be an antidote to the general feeling in the States today that getting away from civilization is such a terrific thing and is so romantic," Redford told a reporter at the Cannes Film Festival in 1972, where the film had its world premiere. "I wanted to show the kids what it is really like going it on your own in the wilderness and thoroughly deromanticize it for them." Director Sydney Pollack, soon to become a much-sought-after director, agreed, telling *The New York Times*: "You cannot live totally selfishly and be completely independent in the world. You must adjust to the needs of nature or of man." *The Hollywood Reporter* noted: "Sydney Pollack's control of the movie's rich detail is thorough and steady. He knows exactly what he wants and with unusual relaxation and confidence moves from episode to episode with a musical, rhythmic pace which avoids the senti-

mental and obvious consistently."

Some saw Robert Redford miscast as the rugged mountaineer who inadvertently marries a Flathead Indian woman, then launches a personal vendetta against the dreaded Crows he despises when they kill his family. According to co-scripter Edward Anhalt, "The real Jeremiah Johnson killed 247 Crow Indians and then ate their livers." Fortunately, Redford doesn't have to eat Crow, or this might not have been the box office hit it was. In fact, it is probably his very miscasting that worked so well for Warners. The public voted him number three at the box office, and climbing rapidly.

The old adage about never working with children and dogs should be appended to include "and Utah" as well, since Redford's only real co-star, aside from by Will Geer (Grandpa Zeb in TV's "The Waltons"), is the beautiful scenery of Utah's National Forests and Zion National Park.

1

THE EXORCIST

WARNER BROS.
$89,000,000

"Have you ever heard of exorcism? It's a stylized ritual in which the rabbi or the priest tries to drive out the so-called invading spirit."
—REGAN'S DOCTOR TO MRS. MACNEIL

WILLIAM PETER BLATTY's novel *The Exorcist* became one of the hottest sellers of all time, and by the time the film version was released the day after Christmas, 1973, nearly everyone in the country *had* heard of exorcism. The author claimed to have based his story on fact: when he was a college student at Georgetown University in 1949, the case of a "possessed" 14-year-old boy had hit the newspapers. Catholic priests apparently exorcised the boy's demon, after which the child grew up, married, and led a normal life. The story stayed with the impressionable, Jesuit-trained Blatty, who changed his story's victim to a 12-year-old girl.

The film quickly soared to the top of the box office charts and all hell broke loose as reports of audience reactions (sympathetic vomiting, fainting, miscarriages, heart attacks, and the like) spread like wildfire, fanned by the gleeful Warner Bros. publicity department. Actually, the book was scarier by far, since the reader's imaginative mind knew no bounds, while the film was limited to special effects, trick photography, and sound effects to tap into people's deepest fears and superstitions. It worked, though, and audiences lined up around the block to be frightened and repulsed by the "R"-rated film.

The rating itself came as something of a shock to many unsuspecting moviegoers, who were suddenly assaulted with every four-letter Anglo-Saxon-derived expression ever conceived, emanating from the mouth of 14-year-old Linda Blair (the expletives were dubbed, however, by the more mature actress Mercedes Mc-Cambridge). Despite the "R" rating by the Motion Picture Association of America, many City Fathers decided to restrict the audience to over 17s only. In Los Angeles, the film's young star herself was forbidden to buy a ticket unless accompanied by an adult. As quoted in *Films of the Seventies*, Jack

Valenti, president of the MPAA, defended his organization's position: "Ratings come from what viewers see, not what they imagine they see. In *The Exorcist* there is *no* overt sex. There is *no* excessive violence. There *is* some strong language, but it is rationally related to the film's theme and is kept to a minimum."

Amazing what could be seen on the screen only four years after *Midnight Cowboy* and not get an "X." If you were under 17, and your parents didn't have a babysitter, they might have taken you to see little Linda spewing forth streams of vomit and obscenities with equal gusto, not to mention masturbating with a crucifix.

The film had expertly crafted special effects and make-up. Oatmeal and pea soup were pumped through a tube concealed in an appliance on Linda's lower lip. (After learning the secret of this trick, many people swore off pea soup for life.) The 360-degree headspin that the possessed child supposedly does was filmed with a full-scale mechanical double of Linda, complete with radio-controlled eyes that blinked. Audiences ate it up.

Critics and film analysts found enough material in this film to keep their columns filled for months. Some saw it as a sign of a depraved society; others attributed its popularity not to a bloodthirsty population, but to the audience's need to see a film in which Good eventually triumphs over Evil (your basic morality play); while still others thought people were simply curious to learn what all the fuss was about.

For Warner Bros., it didn't matter, as they tallied up the receipts of their top film to date, and quickly plotted the sequel. *Exorcist II* arrived in 1977, directed by John Boorman (*Deliverance*), and starred Richard Burton, Louise Fletcher, James Earl Jones, Ned Beatty, and, of course, the Devil's pet possessee, Linda Blair. The movie had a devil of a time at the box office, where even recutting by the director couldn't exorcise the film's problems. The original is still the best, especially when rented intact at the video store, not sanitized and hacked to pieces as it is on local channels.

Screenplay by William Peter Blatty

Based on the novel by William Peter Blatty

Executive Producer: Noel Marshall

Produced by William Peter Blatty

Directed by William Friedkin

CAST

Mrs. MacNeil	Ellen Burstyn
Regan MacNeil	Linda Blair
Father Merrin	Max von Sydow
Lt. Kinderman	Lee J. Cobb
Sharon	Kitty Winn
Father Karras	Jason Miller

ACADEMY AWARD NOMINATIONS

*10 nominations, 2 wins**

Best Picture
Best Actress (Ellen Burstyn)
Best Supporting Actor (Jason Miller)
Best Supporting Actress (Linda Blair)
Best Director (William Friedkin)
*Best Screenplay Based on Material from Another Medium (William Peter Blatty)
Best Cinematography
Best Art Direction-Set Decoration
*Best Sound
Best Film Editing

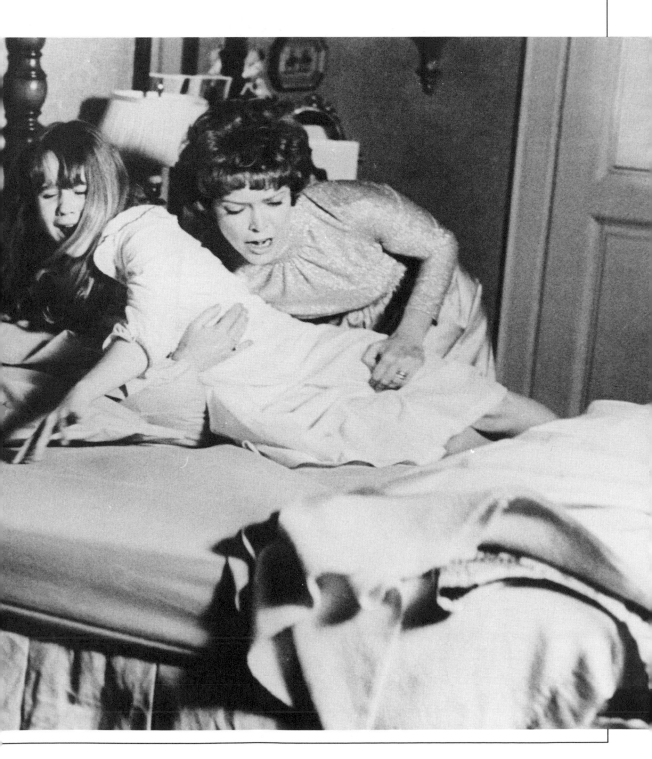

② THE STING
UNIVERSAL
$78,212,000

FROM THE VERY FIRST shot of the old Universal logo, with the single-engine plane putt-putting around the globe, audiences knew they were in for a treat. George Roy Hill, re-teamed here with Paul Newman and Robert Redford—Butch and Sundance—couldn't have selected a more appropriate piece of theme music either: "The Entertainer" aptly describes the director and his picture. *The Sting* is prime entertainment—it doesn't get much better than this.

Hill successfully transports us in a cinematic time machine back to the days of the '30s con artists by never letting any anachronisms slip into this period piece. Each scenic transition is introduced with that '30s technique, "the wipe," as if an invisible hand sweeps across the screen and leads us to the next number. In order to stress this technique, each segment is introduced with a slide telling us what this act will be about. We see:

> THE SET UP
> THE HOOK
> THE TALE
> THE WIRE
> THE SHUT-OFF
> THE STING

The plot is so well developed and intricately woven that it takes considerable concentration from the audience to follow all its entanglements, one of the reasons for the film's great success, as people returned repeatedly to try to catch what they'd missed the first time. And it didn't hurt that Redford and Newman, the picture's two stars, were also the number-one and number-two box office favorites in the polls.

The movie had opened barely a week before the year's top hit, *The Exorcist*, and part of its popularity had to be due to the comic relief audiences needed after that film's intensity. People were swept along by the whole mystique of *The Sting*, right down to the '30s wardrobe. What Faye Dunaway had done for the beret and maxiskirt in *Bonnie and Clyde*, Redford and Newman did for men's fashions. Lapels broadened and pin-striped gangster suits became the rage. Edith Head also got a lot of mileage out of that old

---

Screenplay by David S. Ward

Produced by Tony Bill, Michael Phillips, and Julia Phillips

Directed by George Roy Hill

CAST

Henry Gondorff	Paul Newman
Johnny Hooker	Robert Redford
Doyle Lonnegan	Robert Shaw
Lt. Snyder	Charles Durning
Singleton	Ray Walston
Billie	Eileen Brennan

ACADEMY AWARD NOMINATIONS

10 nominations, 7 wins*

*Best Picture
 Best Actor (Robert Redford)
*Best Director (George Roy Hill)
*Best Original Story and Screenplay
  (David S. Ward)
 Best Cinematography
*Best Art Direction-Set Decoration
 Best Sound
*Best Scoring: Original Song Score and/or
  Adaptation (Marvin Hamlisch)
*Best Film Editing
*Best Costume Design

---

standby, the T-shirt. "Whenever I wanted Paul Newman to look mean, I allowed his T-shirt to show," the costume designer said, as quoted in *The Hollywood Reporter Magazine*.

The Sting wasn't just a big hit with the fans. The Academy found the picture a winner in the old tradition and showered it with ten Oscar nominations and seven wins (although it seems an inequity that only one of the two leads, Robert Redford, received a Best Actor nod).

Critics were unanimous in their enthusiasm for the movie. Wrote *Variety*: "Paul Newman and Robert Redford are superbly reteamed . . . George Roy Hill's outstanding direction of David S. Ward's finely-crafted story of multiple deception and surprise ending will delight both mass and class audiences." *The Hollywood Reporter* called it "a disciplined, delightful film." *Newsweek* said: "Like its heroes, the film succeeds on charm and con. Newman and Redford radiate a charismatic appeal that tilts the movie in their favor." And *The New York Times* described *The Sting* as "a variation on the old Dr. Gillespie-Dr. Kildare relationship, with a bit of Laurel and Hardy thrown in. It is also apparently very good box office."

Indeed it was. Having cost only $5,500,000 million to make (with a reported $1,000,000 each for Redford and Newman), the take at Universal proved that the chemistry was still there.

Not so successful, however, was the inevitable sequel, *The Sting II* (1983). Audiences just didn't fall for Jackie Gleason and Mac Davis in the Newman/Redford roles, and it was Universal that got stung this time.

AMERICAN GRAFFITI
UNIVERSAL
$55,128,175

"Where were you in '62?"
—ADVERTISING COPY FOR
AMERICAN GRAFFITI

"Without exception, all players fit perfectly into the concept and execution, and all the young principals and featured players have a bright and lengthy future. And so does Lucas." —VARIETY

INDEED THEY ALL DID. George Lucas had one legitimate film credit to his name—*THX-1138*—and $1,500 in total personal assets in 1973 when he convinced Universal executive Ned Tanen to finance his pet project, a nostalgic look at the early '60s, heavily based on Lucas' own teen years. The young exec reluctantly agreed and gave the 26-year-old Lucas the miniscule budget of $750,000, plus another $500,000 for prints and advertising.* No one could have predicted the kind of phenomenal success *American Graffiti* would become. The film's rental take at the box office returned *fifty* times the investment. The future director of the legendary *Star Wars* was on his way.

Variety was certainly correct about the future of the young players, too. The cast list read like a "who will be who." Ronny Howard, still only 18,

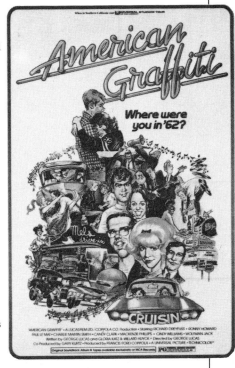

would soon become the lead in a hit TV series called "Happy Days," which was very much derivative of *American Graffiti*; Mackenzie Phillips, 12-year-old daughter of musician John Phillips, would go on to co-star in TV's "One Day At A Time"; Richard Dreyfuss, who had played only a few walk-ons in some obscure movies, would become one of the major stars of the decade; Cindy Williams, not yet known as half of "Laverne and Shirley," would become the co-star of one of TV's hottest hits; Suzanne Somers, the elusive blonde in the white T-Bird, a former model in her first professional acting job, went on to a TV career also, starring in "Three's Company" and "She's the Sheriff"; and Harrison Ford, who was then supplementing his ailing acting career with part-time carpentry jobs, would eventually star in some of the biggest blockbuster films of all time.

Technically unsophisticated, *American Graffiti* was nevertheless a major hit because of its realistic quality. Lucas shot entirely on location in San Rafael and Petaluma, small Northern California towns. Between the hours of 9:00 P.M. when it was just dark enough, and 5:00 A.M., before the sun would come up, the main streets of these towns were cordoned off for the night shoot. It was grueling work, but there were lighter moments as well. Locals for miles around were encouraged to rent their vintage hot rods for the film at $25 a night, and they really got into the spirit of things, drag racing between takes, having themselves one last fling at the '60s. Over 400 cars were eventually used, among them the yellow dragster driven by Paul Le Mat's character "John." Look closely at its unusual license plate—THX 138—an obvious inside joke and reference to the Lucas film (but with only three numerals, as permitted by California law).

Further enhancing the nostalgia was the soundtrack, which contained no fewer than 43 rock-and-roll hits from the '50s and '60s. Used basically as "source music" (music emanating from radios or other sources, rather than deliberately orchestrated background), the music was relentless. There was

seldom a silent interlude, even during dialogue, and this seemed to propel the essentially plotless film along.

The movie's climactic drag race was based on Lucas own high school experiences. Shy, shorter than average, and looking younger than his true age, the teenager found thrills in hot rodding, and nearly killed himself in a serious accident. A lucky break for him, and us, that he wasn't. George Lucas has since become the most successful producer-director in motion picture history, reportedly earning over one billion dollars.

In 1979, a sequel, *More American Graffiti*, reunited Clark, Phillips, Williams, and Howard in an episodic film covering the years 1964–67. Lucas did not direct.

---

*Tanen wanted to change the title to *Another Slow Night in Modesto*, afraid audiences would think it was an Italian film, or a movie about feet. Producer Francis Coppola suggested *Rock Around the Block*. But Lucas liked his own title, which he felt evoked memories of a bygone civilization, and refused to change it.

Screenplay by George Lucas, Gloria Katz, and Willard Huyck

Produced by Francis Ford Coppola

Directed by George Lucas

CAST

Curt	....	Richard Dreyfuss
Steve	....	Ronny Howard
John	....	Paul Le Mat
Terry	....	Charles Martin Smith
Laurie	....	Cindy Williams
Bob Falfa	....	Harrison Ford

ACADEMY AWARD NOMINATIONS

5 nominations, no wins

Best Picture
Best Supporting Actress (Candy Clark)
Best Director (George Lucas)
Best Original Story and Screenplay
Best Film Editing

PAPILLON
ALLIED ARTISTS
$22,500,000

HENRI CHARRIERE was a Frenchman who spent 13 years in captivity for a murder he swore he didn't commit. The court didn't buy it, and sentenced him to life in prison, but he made good his escape time and again. Eventually, he was sentenced to Devil's Island off French Guiana in South America, a supposedly "escape-proof" prison. Not for Charriere. Nicknamed "Papillon"— The Butterfly, for a tattoo on his chest, plus his need to soar freely, like a butterfly itself—Charriere became the first man in history to escape from that dreaded penal colony, improvising a raft of dried coconut husks. After many years as a refugee in Venezuela, he went public and did what anyone would do under the circumstances—he wrote his memoirs, and the book became a best-seller.

The property was acquired by independent film company Allied Artists, and the late Franklin J. Schaffner (*Patton*) was signed as director. He chose Steve McQueen for the title role, but felt that the story lacked human interaction. Thus was created the part of Louis Dega, for which he signed the chameleon-like Dustin Hoffman, who was by now becoming an actor's actor. Another "odd couple" was created.

The movie was shot on location in Spain and Jamaica, the latter nearly as

Screenplay by Dalton Trumbo and Lorenzo Semple, Jr.

Based on the book by Henri Charriere

Executive Producer: Ted Richmond

Produced by Robert Dorfmann and Franklin J. Schaffner

Directed by Franklin J. Schaffner

CAST

Papillon	Steve McQueen
Dega	Dustin Hoffman
Indian Chief	Victor Jory
Julot	Don Gordon
Leper Colony Chief	Anthony Zerbe

ACADEMY AWARD NOMINATIONS

1 nomination, no wins

Best Original Dramatic Score

punishing as the real Devil's Island for which it doubled, with searing heat, mosquitoes, and crocodiles. Hoffman claims to have lost 20 pounds during the ordeal, and Charriere himself thought the setting so real he kept scanning the horizon for guards who might at any second come and grab him.

The film opened to less than enthusiastic reviews at Christmastime, 1973. Critics complained about its length (150 minutes) and its pessimistic feeling. *Newsweek* wrote: "*Papillon* offers torture as entertainment but winds up making entertainment a form of torture . . . the dispiriting, grim tone of the film and its sensational interest in atrocities speak only of the futility of rebellion . . ." *The Hollywood Reporter* called the film "a long, difficult and grim experience which does not do backflips to engage the audience . . . the screenplay by Trumbo and Semple has awkward expository dialogue, little humor, and except for two major roles, no characterizations." *Variety*'s review seemed ambiguous: "The atmosphere

bores into the brain like it does to its victims, leaving them as well as an audience stunned, disoriented, incredulous and nearly catatonic. It takes literally hours to come out of 'Papillon.'"

Reviews like these piqued moviegoers' curiosity. Surprisingly, the film became a hit, almost doubling its financial outlay of $12,000,000. One reason may be the "PG" rating, which meant more take at the box office from the younger crowd. The rating originally had been an "R," but the distributor argued that the feature was tasteful, discrete and restrained, so persuading the Motion Picture Association of America to make the change. Nevertheless, this is an extremely intense film, and certainly isn't for most young teens.

While emphasis is on the McQueen/Hoffman pairing (and their characters' implied homosexual attraction), others in the cast worth noting are Victor Jory as the Indian Chief, Bill Mumy (former child actor on TV's "Lost in Space"), and co-screenwriter Dalton Trumbo as the Commandant.

THE WAY WE WERE

COLUMBIA
$22,457,000

"Can I ask you a question? Do you smile all the time?"
—STREISAND TO REDFORD

OF COURSE he smiled all the time. Wouldn't you if you were the number-one box office star of the year, with two hit movies in a row—*Jeremiah Johnson, The Sting*, and now *The Way We Were*? Make that *three* hit movies.

The pollsters' highest-ranking female star, Barbra Streisand, was cleverly paired opposite Robert Redford—*goy meets girl*, joked some—but it was a chemical combination that ought to have come with a warning label. Hormones stirred in theaters across the land as we watched these two actors, as odd a couple as ever there was, fall in love in this rather improbable story of a golden boy novelist-turned-Hollywood screenwriter and the idealistic, socialistic, even Communistic object of his affections.

Newsweek cleverly dubbed the couple Miss Left and Mr. Right, then added: "This is one of a vanishing breed of movies in which the stars, by their

very presence, alter the story. In a way, they *are* the story." This was pretty much the truth, and provoked *Time*'s reviewer to near rage: "This ill-written, wretchedly performed and tediously directed film . . . does not actually have anything on its mind except to bring together two hot properties in a period setting for which there is currently a lot of nostalgia." Despite less-than-kind reviews like these, word of mouth helped make *The Way We Were* a box office sensation.

Although Streisand doesn't sing in the picture, her recording of the title song became even more popular than the movie. It first appeared on the charts in November, 1973, shortly after the film's release, and by February, "The Way We Were" had steadily climbed to the number-one position, which it held for three weeks. It was also Barbra's first number-one hit. And for composer Marvin Hamlisch, the song brought him one of *three* Academy Awards he took home the night of the 1973 ceremony—one for *The Sting* and two for *The Way We Were*.

Screenplay by Arthur Laurents

Based on the novel by Arthur Laurents

Produced by Ray Stark

Directed by Sydney Pollack

CAST

Katie	Barbra Streisand
Hubbell	Robert Redford
J. J.	Bradford Dillman
Carol Ann	Lois Chiles
George Bissinger	Patrick O'Neal

ACADEMY AWARD NOMINATIONS

6 nominations, 2 wins*

Best Actress (Barbra Streisand)
Best Cinematography
Best Art Direction-Set Decoration
*Best Song ("The Way We Were," music by Marvin Hamlisch, words by Alan and Marilyn Bergman)
*Best Original Dramatic Score
Best Costume Design

THE TOWERING INFERNO

20TH CENTURY-FOX/WARNER BROS.
$52,000,000

"To those who give their lives so that others might live . . . to the fire fighters of the world . . . This picture is gratefully dedicated."
—OPENING CARD

THIS IS ONE of those rare films that saw two studios cooperating in a co-production—sort of like Coke and Pepsi collaborating on a new soft drink. Producer Irwin Allen, the man behind 1972's successful *The Poseidon Adventure*, had the blessings of 20th Century-Fox to pursue his forte and do another disaster film. But the property which commanded their attention, a novel called *The Tower*, by Richard Martin Stern, was already owned by Warner Bros. Meanwhile, 20th and Allen obtained the rights to a similar book, *The Glass Inferno*, by Tom Scortia and Frank Robinson. Not wanting any competition from Warners, they approached that studio with the idea of a co-production. Thus was born the child of this unusual mating, *The Towering Inferno*.

It was no secret what the plot concerned; by now, audiences were wildly enthusiastic about disaster films and could recite the formula with little difficulty. This time, the film's mega-stars weren't on a doomed airliner, or in a topsy-turvy steamship, but in a situation much closer to our everyday experiences—trapped inside a burning skyscraper—and the public approbation in the form of box office dollars was the greatest yet. Of course, there were now *two* leading actors there to save the day: Steve McQueen and Paul Newman. Ever since Newman had starred in *Somebody Up There Likes Me* and received top billing, McQueen had been trying to get one up on him, even turning down the co-starring role in *Butch Cassidy and the Sundance Kid* because his name would come after Newman's. But *The Towering Inferno* appeased his ego once and for all, with *both* men's names appearing simultaneously on the screen, McQueen's positioned higher than Newman's.

For McQueen, the role of the fire captain was a windfall. In his 1956 screen debut as a bit player in *Somebody Up There Likes Me*, he had earned $19 a day. His share of the gross profits in *The Towering Inferno* came to 7.5

percent. This, coupled with his up-front payment, eventually brought him a whopping $12,000,000. Even by today's standards, this is a staggering amount. Renowned *Los Angeles Times* critic Charles Champlin, however, rushed to McQueen's defense: "McQueen's fire captain in *Towering Inferno* left no doubt why he was worth every penny of the millions he earned. He brought to that role an authority that few other actors could touch."

In August, 1974, three months before the *Towering Inferno*'s release, and as part of the advance publicity in connection with the picture, 20th Century-Fox was able to arrange for Steve McQueen to be named an "honorary Los Angeles fire fighter," complete with an official City Hall ceremony.

Screenplay by Stirling Silliphant

Based on the novels *The Tower* by Richard Martin Stern and *The Glass Inferno* by Thomas N. Scortia and Frank M. Robinson

Produced by Irwin Allen

Directed by John Guillermin

Action scenes directed by Irwin Allen

CAST

Fire Chief
O'Hallorhan . . . . . . Steve McQueen
Doug Roberts . . . . Paul Newman
Jim Duncan . . . . . . William Holden
Susan . . . . Faye Dunaway
Harlee Claiborne . . . Fred Astaire
Simmons . . . . Richard Chamberlain
Lisolette . . . . Jennifer Jones

ACADEMY AWARD NOMINATIONS

8 nominations, 3 wins*

Best Picture
Best Supporting Actor (Fred Astaire)
*Best Cinematography
Best Art Direction-Set Decoration
Best Sound
*Best Song ("We May Never Love Like This Again," music and words by Al Kasha and Joel Hirschhorn)
Best Original Dramatic Score (John Williams)
*Best Film Editing

The rest of the all-star cast (ingredient number two for any disaster-movie recipe) was a true cross section of famous names and faces, some old-timers as well as newcomers, sports figures, and even soap stars. Appearing as those hapless folks whose lives were about to be changed were William Holden, Faye Dunaway, Fred Astaire, Susan Blakely, Richard Chamberlain, Jennifer Jones, O. J. Simpson, Robert Vaughn, Robert Wagner, and Susan Flannery. According to *Inside Oscar*, Paul Newman, still fuming over his credits feud, cracked, "Hell, we all know who the real star of this movie is—that damned fire."

But the film's special effects were probably closer to the real "star"— visuals that made us believe for a harrowing 165 minutes that we were actually watching a burning, 138-story skyscraper. Fox built a four-story section of a building for the elevator sequence, with matte paintings and miniatures inserted into the shot for added realism. The exterior of the Hyatt Regency in San Francisco doubled for the skyscraper itself. Dummies were substituted for people being blown out of windows. In all, a team comprised of 25 stuntmen and stunt-women, under the supervision of coordinator Paul Stader, performed more than 200 individual stunts during the filming.

Paul D. Zimmerman of *Newsweek* loathed the film, yet for some unknown reason, the last paragraph of his review sounds like a course in Film Analysis 101: "The glass tower becomes a combustible symbol of American affluence, built precariously on rotten foundations. 'Towering Inferno' senses that beneath the best of everything lurks the worst of everything. And its torrential climax, when a roomful of enormous top-floor water tanks is blown up, can be read as an apocalyptic ritual cleansing of all that is decayed in our society."

Was this really true? Did anybody really care? Here's what really happened: a big building caught fire, some people died, some lived, audiences loved it, and Fox and Warners made off with a lot of loot—nearly quadruple their $14,000,000 investment. No covert symbolism in that.

BLAZING SADDLES
WARNER BROS.
$47,800,000

"I must have killed more men than Cecil B. DeMille."—GENE WILDER

MEL BROOKS' humor is a lot like the ads they used to run for Levy's Rye Bread—you don't have to be Jewish to enjoy it (but it couldn't hurt). The man is simply off-the-wall *meshugge*, and his send-up of the Western genre in *Blazing Saddles* has become a classic in a very short time. The laughs, puns, and surprises come so fast and furious that if you don't already have one, it's worth buying a VCR for this film alone, just so you can reverse-scan for the quickies you're bound to miss on first viewing. There's the sign proclaiming "Howard Johnson's Ice Cream Parlor— 1 flavor;" star Cleavon Little's Gucci-emblazoned saddlebags; and Mel Brooks as the Jewish Indian Chief speaking Yiddish to Cleavon's wagon train. Brooks also wrote three songs for the soundtrack—"I'm Tired," "The French Mistake," and "The Ballad of Rock Ridge."

Outstanding comedy casting by Brooks, who directed and co-scripted, enhances the fun: Cleavon Little as the new black sheriff, Harvey Korman as Hedy—oops!—that's *Hedley* Lamarr,

Screenplay by Mel Brooks, Norman Steinberg, Andrew Bergman, Richard Pryor, and Alan Uger

Based on a story by Andrew Bergman

Produced by Michael Hertzberg

Directed by Mel Brooks

CAST

Bart	Cleavon Little
Jim	Gene Wilder
Gov. Leoetomane, Indian Chief	Mel Brooks
Hedley Lamarr	Harvey Korman
Lili von Shtupp	Madeline Kahn

ACADEMY AWARD NOMINATIONS

3 nominations, no wins

Best Supporting Actress (Madeline Kahn)
Best Song ("Blazing Saddles," music by John Morris, words by Mel Brooks)
Best Film Editing

and Gene Wilder and Madeline Kahn, a team Brooks would use separately and together in future comedies. Kahn has perhaps the best role in the film, lisping her way through a Marlene Dietrich

take-off as Lili von Shtupp (the name is a Yiddish vulgarism, just like it sounds). Only Brooks could get away with having her spout lines like "I'm not a wabbit—I need some west," and her appreciative glee after sizing up Cleavon Little and discovering that he's *not*: "It's twue, it's twue!"

The hilarious comedy was a huge hit at the box office, and with the critics as well. *Newsweek* proclaimed the picture an "insane take-off on the classic Western . . . triggering laughs that measure a full ten on the Richter scale." *Variety's* reviewer, although he found the R-rated language "incessant," wrote that "if comedies are measured solely by the number of yocks they generate from audiences, then Mel Brooks' 'Blazing Saddles' must be counted a success . . . Few viewers will have time between laughs to complain that pic is essentially a raunchy, protracted version of a television comedy skit."

In fact, *Blazing Saddles* generated almost a cultlike following with the college crowd, and continues to find an audience today whenever it is shown on TV. Rent the uncut version on video-cassette so you won't miss out on some of the decidedly adult humor.

YOUNG FRANKENSTEIN

20TH CENTURY-FOX
$38,823,000

"Pardon me boy, is this the Transylvania Station?"
"Ya, ya—Track 29. Can I give you a shine?" —DIALOGUE EXCHANGE

THE ABOVE NONSENSE is typical of Mel Brooks humor: audiences groan with mock disdain but love every second of it. 1974 was definitely the Year of Mel Brooks. After the success of *Blazing Saddles* earlier that year, Brooks' *Young Frankenstein* ("That's Fr*ah*nkenst*ee*n") fired the second salvo of irreverent humor. Having given us his send-up of the Western genre, Brooks now tackled the classic horror film of the '30s—the original chiller simply titled *Frankenstein*.

The idea of remaking *Frankenstein* was certainly not a new one. The same year would also see a campy 3-D bomb called *Andy Warhol's Frankenstein*, and there have been at least 15 other films about the monster first described by 19th-century novelist Mary Shelley.

Brooks' *Young Frankenstein* is certainly the most financially successful of them all, since he chose to parody the two original (and best) of the lot, *Frankenstein* and *Bride of Frankenstein*. Brooks carefully duplicated the look and feel of the black-and-white

classic, right down to the use of the original Frankenstein laboratory equipment borrowed from Universal Studios, complete with discharging bolts of electricity and skyward rising platform. Film techniques such as "wipes" and "irising" for scene transitions make this

---

Screenplay by Gene Wilder and
  Mel Brooks

Based on characters created by Mary
  Shelley

Produced by Michael Gruskoff

Directed by Mel Brooks

CAST

Dr. Frankenstein	Gene Wilder
Monster	Peter Boyle
Igor	Marty Feldman
Elizabeth	Madeline Kahn
Frau Blucher	Cloris Leachman
Blind Man	Gene Hackman

ACADEMY AWARD NOMINATIONS

2 nominations, no wins

Best Screenplay Adapted from
  Other Material
Best Sound

---

a true parody of the original.

Superb casting heightened the fun of the film. *Newsweek*'s comments summed it up best: "The poodle-haired [Gene] Wilder, in his finest performance to date, is aided by a puckish, addled Igor (Marty Feldman), whose hump keeps shifting shoulders, as well as by the scary Frau Blucher (Cloris Leachman), whose very name makes horses rear. But when [Peter] Boyle takes life, so does the movie, leading to two of the great scenes in screen comedy." The scenes referred to were the musical "Puttin' on the Ritz" number, in which Wilder and his monster, dressed to the nines, break into a tap dance, and the encounter with the blind hermit (Gene Hackman), a klutz who keeps injuring the poor creature.

Another fine performance, often overlooked and underrated, was that of Teri Garr as the German girl, Inga. Known mostly as a television actress prior to this movie (she had guest-starred on a "Star Trek" episode, "Assignment: Earth," when she was only 19, and later became a regular on *The Sonny and Cher Show*), Teri went on to a prosperous career as a character actress in the '70s and '80s, and continues making movies today.

4

EARTHQUAKE
UNIVERSAL
$35,849,994

"This used to be a helluva town!"
—LLOYD NOLAN

IN THE CONTINUING saga of the disaster film genre, so far there had been tragedy in the skies, on the sea, and in a towering edifice. With *Earthquake*, we were now told that we didn't have to leave home to experience the ultimate in terror—even the very ground under our feet wasn't safe anymore. And this film went them all one better by adding a new dimension of *audience participation*, thanks to a sound system Universal Studios termed "Sensurround." Linked to one of the sound tracks, the low-frequency vibrations made theaters appear to experience "tremors" during the actual earthquake footage; although any stereo buff (and his next-door neighbor) knows you can achieve the same effect at home by turning up the bass on your hi-fi. For this privilege, exhibitors were charged an additional $500 a week by the distributor, while signs in the lobby as well as an on-screen disclaimer warned the squeamish to beware.

It was an added gimmick that more than paid off as moviegoers returned

Screenplay by George Fox and Mario Puzo

Executive Producer: Jennings Lang

Produced and directed by Mark Robson

CAST

Graff	Charlton Heston
Remy Graff	Ava Gardner
Patrolman Slade	George Kennedy
Royce	Lorne Greene
Denise	Genevieve Bujold

ACADEMY AWARD NOMINATIONS

4 nominations, 1 win*

Best Cinematography
Best Art Direction-Set Decoration
*Best Sound
Best Film Editing

This year there were no nominations per se for "Best Visual Effects," but the Academy singled out *Earthquake* for a "Special Achievement Award for Visual Effects."

several times for the experience. (*Midway*, a war movie using the same system, failed to produce the same financial results.) The "star" of the show, the actual quake itself, doesn't appear for quite some time, although there are a few "foreshocks." First, we must meet our all-star cast. Let's see . . . this time we have Charlton Heston (you just know he's going to make it to the end), Ava Gardner as his bitchy wife, George Kennedy, Lorne Greene, Genevieve Bujold, Richard Roundtree, Marjoe Gortner as The Bad Guy, Barry Sullivan, Lloyd Nolan, Victoria Principal, and Walter Matthau as The Drunk (a cameo billed under his real name, Walter Matuschanskayasky). When the film was recut for TV, 18 minutes of new material was included, which added a character played by Debralee Scott.

The title disaster is supposedly a 9.9 on the Richter scale. All told, we experience 11 actual minutes of shaking, during which time we see the total wasting of Los Angeles (the helluva town mourned by Lloyd Nolan above). Landslides, crumbling skyscrapers, dam bursts, floods, flames, collapsing bridges, ground fissures opening—you name it, this film's got it. The effects combined mattes, miniatures, and real footage of L.A. very convincingly, although it is obvious when "camera shakes" were used, and one carload of plastic toy cows going over the side of a bridge leaves much to be desired. There was potential danger from all the falling debris and trick shots, providing work for 141 stuntpeople, a Hollywood record.

In 1988, the movers and shakers at Universal Studios decided to incorporate the experience into their world-famous Universal Tour, capitalizing on California's current paranoia as residents awaited the predicted "Big One." One morning in early June of 1989, Los Angeles actually experienced a minor (4.5) quake. Tourists at Universal just figured it was part of the ride.

THE TRIAL OF BILLY JACK

WARNER BROS.
$31,100,000

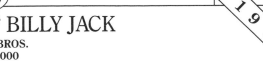

WHEN LAST WE SAW Billy Jack, he was being hauled off to prison, even though we, the audience, knew he was right. Could a situation like this go unresolved? Not for Tom Laughlin, who had turned that first low-budget "protest" film (see p. 218) into a $32,500,000 winner. It was a sleeper of a picture, one which seemed the most unlikely candidate for a sequel, and a successful one at that. Nevertheless, that's exactly what happened.

Tom and his wife Delores (Taylor) were back, re-creating their previous roles (actually, Laughlin had originated the character of Billy Jack in a 1967 motorcycle gang "B" movie), and not much else is new. Billy's out of jail now, but there are still battles to be fought on behalf of the American Indians and his wife's progressive Freedom School. And again, the message is "non-violence," meaning that violence should be used only when absolutely necessary, which is about once every five minutes in this film. A Kent State–type mas-sacre by National Guardsmen drives this point home at the picture's climax.

Why were these films so popular? Obviously, there were no big all-star casts. Actors included Laughlin, his wife, his 16-year-old daughter Teresa, director William Wellman's son, Bill Jr., plus an assortment of Native American actors such as Buffalo Horse, Rolling Thunder, Guy Greymountain, Oshannah Fastwolf, and Sacheen Littlefeather (Marlon Brando's proxy at the 1972 Oscar ceremony). There was no Big Name director, either. Tom's son Frank handled those chores. About the biggest name in *The Trial of Billy Jack*'s credits was Elmer Bernstein, the renowned composer, who did the soundtrack.

One theory for the success of this movie was offered by *Variety*, which thought it was due to the "deliberate pitch [it] made to attract youth and 'rebel' audiences." Were there really that many rebels out there? *The New York Times*' reviewer had a different theory: "The average American is a sucker for anything described as home-made. Slap that label on candy, cookies, ice cream, canned soups and . . . [the American consumer] will buy it, no matter what it tastes like . . . In at least one respect, 'The Trial of Billy Jack' really is home-made . . . the only thing the Laughlins aren't doing is making the popcorn being sold in the theaters."

Most reviewers had trouble making sense out of the movie's huge following. This mattered not at all to the Laughlin Family Filmmakers, who followed with yet another sequel, *Billy Jack Goes to Washington* (1977). Like that other man who went to Washington back in 1939*, writer-director-star Tom Laughlin takes on corruption in the Senate in this film. But many thought he had overstepped his bounds this time, and *Billy Jack Goes to Washington* bombed.

---

*Jimmy Stewart in *Mr. Smith Goes to Washington* (see page 21).

Screenplay by Frank and Teresa Christina

Produced by Joe Cramer

Directed by Frank Laughlin

CAST

Billy Jack	Tom Laughlin
Jean Roberts	Delores Taylor
Doc	Victor Izay
Carol	Teresa Laughlin
National Guardsman	William Willman, Jr.

WHAT DO A nude girl, a boy on a raft, a dog, a pier, and a fisherman all have in common? Yes, the answer is: shark food. But not for just any shark. These individuals and objects were all on the menu for *Jaws*, the first megahit for Steven Spielberg. The picture had the honor of being the first film to break the $100,000,000 mark in rentals, becoming the highest grossing film to that date and surpassing previous record-holders *The Godfather*, *The Sound of Music*, and *Gone With the Wind* (if inflation is not taken into account).

The novel had been a best-seller, so it was only a matter of time before it became a movie. The Peter Benchley novel had five and a half million copies in print at the time the rights were purchased by Richard Zanuck and his partner David Brown for a paltry $175,000. Benchley was signed to write the script as well, but it underwent five drafts before completion, including a final polish by Carl Gottlieb, who received co-credit. (Watch for Benchley as a reporter.)

Steven Spielberg was only 26 when he was assigned director's chores on this $12,000,000 picture. At age 20, the young man had bluffed his way onto the Universal lot, acting as if he be-

Screenplay by Peter Benchley and Carl Gottlieb

Based on the novel by Peter Benchley

Produced by Richard D. Zanuck and David Brown

Directed by Steven Spielberg

CAST

Chief Martin Brody .... Roy Scheider
Quint .... Robert Shaw
Matt Hooper .... Richard Dreyfuss
Ellen Brody .... Lorraine Gary
Mayor Vaughn .... Murray Hamilton

ACADEMY AWARD NOMINATIONS

4 nominations, 3 wins*

  Best Picture
*Best Sound
*Best Original Score (John Williams)
*Best Film Editing

longed there by setting up shop in an empty office. Pretty soon studio executives began to accept him, and after viewing some of his clever student film efforts, he was handed some TV directing assignments, including episodes of the series "Night Gallery." His early

film credits included a thriller called *Duel* (a movie-of-the-week pitting Dennis Weaver against a crazed truck driver) and his only feature, *The Sugarland Express*, a technically difficult picture which convinced the execs at Universal that he was right for *Jaws*.

Spielberg insisted that the film be shot on location rather than in a tank to give it the realism he wanted. "I could have shot the movie in the tank, or even in a protected lake somewhere, but it would not have looked the same," the director told *Time*. Martha's Vineyard was finally selected as the fictional village of Amity, although the residents were less than thrilled at the prospect of having 150 members of a movie crew despoiling their lovely island. Greed won out, however, when they realized the boost this would give local businesses.

Since it's hard to find 20-foot white sharks who can take direction well, the company hired special effects expert Robert A. Mattey to construct a mechanical shark (Mattey had once created the giant squid for Walt Disney's *20,000 Leagues Under the Sea*). Actually, Mattey whipped up three pseudosharks, collectively dubbed "Bruce." Each hydraulically-operated plastic creature weighed a ton and a half and cost $150,000. It took 13 scuba-geared technicians to operate the Bruces, which broke down with regularity.

Despite the problems, the film was a huge sensation when it hit the screens just in time for summer. Enormous blocklong lines were commonplace wherever it was shown—thanks to word of mouth and the publicity department at Universal, which hyped every shark sighting up and down both the Atlantic and Pacific coasts. Shark hysteria reached an all-time high as the poor, mostly inoffensive creatures were hunted and strung up like Nazi war criminals.

The success of *Jaws* and the baby-faced Spielberg was aided by three human stars as well. Richard Dreyfuss, who had made a couple of moderately successful hits like *American Graffiti*

and *The Apprenticeship of Duddy Kravitz*, was certain he was starring in what would turn out to be "the turkey of the year." Fortunately he was wrong, and the actor, who is the same age as Spielberg, was later given the starring role in one of Spielberg's biggest hits, *Close Encounters of the Third Kind*. Actor Robert Shaw, who had appeared in top hits such as *From Russia With Love* and *The Sting*, was also reluctant to play opposite a shark, terming the story "a piece of shit." Fortunately, his wife disagreed, and convinced him to take the part of the crusty old salt who goes after the shark with a vengeance. Rounding out the cast was Roy Scheider (Oscar-nominated in *The French Connection*) as the local sheriff, a role he would repeat in *Jaws*equels.

An unusual star was born from this film, but was never actually seen on camera. Composer John Williams, who

had been nominated for an Oscar for his *Towering Inferno* score, won his first Academy Award for his driving music in *Jaws*. The oft-parodied theme brilliantly underscores the anticipatory danger the audience feels well before the shark is ever seen.

Jaws spawned a school of sequels and imitation films plus piles of merchandise all bearing the familiar open-mouthed shark logo, while making piles of money for Universal. A few years later, the studio added a lake to its tour attraction, complete with full-scale town and billboard proclaiming "Amity Island Welcomes You." On cue, Bruce the Shark swims directly toward the tour tram and leaps at the visitors sitting on the *right* side. Most of the time, that is: there are those rare occasions when the tour shark is "on a break" (read: break*down*), just like his movie counterpart, Bruce.

ONE FLEW OVER THE CUCKOO'S NEST

UNITED ARTISTS
$59,939,701

It took 13 years for Ken Kesey's 1962 cult novel about life in a mental ward and a victim of the system to be made into a film. In 1963, the book had been brought to the Broadway stage by Kirk Douglas; after 11 weeks, the play closed (although it did have a successful run off-Broadway starting in March, 1971, with William Devane in the lead role). Douglas attempted to bring it to the screen for years. He eventually turned his option over to son Michael Douglas, then the star of the TV series "The Streets of San Francisco." By "packaging" the property to include Jack Nicholson in the lead, Douglas the younger, now co-producer, was able to raise the $3,000,000 in backing that he needed to make his film. The results proved spectacular, helping to put United Artists (who wisely agreed to release the independent production) on top of the box office in the year following its release.

The icing on the cake came at Oscar time, when the Academy blessed

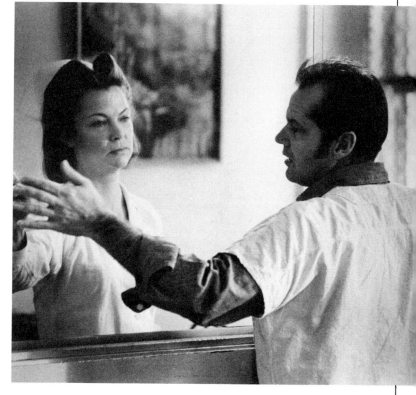

Screenplay by Lawrence Hauben and
Bo Goldman

From the novel by Ken Kesey

Produced by Saul Zaentz and Michael
Douglas

Directed by Milos Forman

CAST

Randel P. McMurphy . Jack Nicholson
Nurse Ratched ...... Louise Fletcher
Harding .... William Redfield
Orderly Turkle .... Scatman Crothers
Martini .... Danny De Vito

ACADEMY AWARD NOMINATIONS

9 nominations, 5 wins*

*Best Picture
*Best Actor (Jack Nicholson)
*Best Actress (Louise Fletcher)
  Best Supporting Actor (Brad Dourif)
*Best Director (Milos Forman)
*Best Screenplay Adapted from Other
  Material (Lawrence Hauben and
  Bo Goldman)
  Best Cinematography
  Best Original Score
  Best Film Editing

Cuckoo's Nest with the "Big Five" Awards—Best Picture, Actor, Actress, Director, and Screenplay—the first time this feat had been achieved since 1934's *It Happened One Night*. This shot in the arm saw the take at the box office increase by 70 percent as moviegoers came to see what all the fuss was about.

They weren't disappointed. The counterculture novel adapted well to the screen, with Nicholson giving the performance of his life. *The New York Times* wrote that he "slips into the role of Randel [McMurphy] with such easy grace that it's difficult to remember him in any other film." *Newsweek* went even further, proclaiming that "McMurphy is the ultimate Nicholson performance—the last angry crazy profane wise-guy rebel, blowing himself up in the shrapnel of his own liberating laughter."

Louise Fletcher, in the role of the detestable Nurse Ratched, received equal acclaim. It was only her second feature; she had concentrated on TV in her early career and later took time out to raise a family. Her performance caught the attention of both the press and her peers in the Academy. When she received her Oscar for Best Actress, she gave an acceptance speech in deaf sign language, the first person ever to do so (both her parents had been deaf from childhood and she was raised "bilingual").

The production was filmed on location at the Oregon State Mental Hospital, with many of the patients playing minor parts and helping the crew. The only mishap occurred when one of the grips (men in charge of setting up equipment) accidentally left a protective screen open on a window after running in cable from the outside, and a patient jumped through the window backwards, falling three floors and fracturing his shoulder. The Salem, Oregon newspaper headlined: "ONE FLEW *OUT* OF THE CUCKOO'S NEST."

THE ROCKY HORROR PICTURE SHOW

20TH CENTURY-FOX
$26,000,000

"I wanna go to the late night double feature picture show, by RKO."
—LYRIC TO "SCIENCE FICTION/ DOUBLE FEATURE"

IT WAS BORN in the mind of Richard O'Brien as *They Came From Denton High,* but by the time British producer Michael White (*Sleuth, Oh! Calcutta*) had brought it to the stage, it had been rechristened *The Rocky Horror Show.* The musical spoof of '50s monster movies was spotted by American producer and director Lou Adler, who booked it into his Roxy Theatre on the Sunset Strip in L.A. Even as the play was enjoying a line-around-the-block run, Adler was negotiating the film deal with 20th Century-Fox. What emerged is the biggest cult film of all time.

The Rocky Horror Picture Show opened to very negative reviews by very confused critics. What *was* this weird thing on the screen about a singing transsexual transvestite from Transylvania in kinky underwear? Both *The Hollywood Reporter* and *Variety* faulted the film for lacking the excitement and sparkle of the stage version; if the critics were to be believed, this was the turkey of all time.

Over at Fox they were about to conduct the post mortem and use the film as a tax write-off, when something happened. Like the very monsters the film was sending up, the film seemed to rise from the freshly-dug grave and take on a life of its own. Theater owners who were filling only 50 seats

in their 800-seat venues noticed that the *same* 50 people were returning every week, seeing the picture again and again. In the Westwood area of Los Angeles, the theater was selling out every night, not to a new crowd, but to the *same* audience. And the people were singing the songs along with the characters on the screen. The songs were simple enough for a ten-year-old to mimic, admitted the producers. Songs like "Dammit Janet," "Sweet Transvestite," and "Time Warp" had both catchy lyrics and lively rock music. But it wasn't *The Sound of Music,* so why were there so many repeats? Something was happening here.

The film was kept alive by an underground following which refused to let it die. Soon it broke into the midnight circuit in New York City, and in a few weeks word of mouth had produced a flood of exhibitors' requests in Fox's distribution offices begging for a print in Cleveland, Austin, Toronto, Philadelphia . . . the list goes on and on, and so does the picture. Even in 1990, there were midnight showings being held in Los Angeles and New York, as well as dozens of other cities.

But this *is* a film of a different color. The key to the phenomenon is audience participation. Fans attend the

Saturday midnight show prepared for an evening of fun. They arrive in costume, dressed as their favorite on-screen character, many wearing Tim Curry drag make-up, she-bitch hose, and garter belts. During the next hour and a half, they will *become* that person. Others come armed with rice to throw in the film's early wedding sequence, squirt guns to shoot during the rainy scene, toast for the "toast," flashlights, Scott toilet paper, and playing cards. Everyone knows and recites every line and song lyric of the film, often talking back to the actors as if fusing with the fantasy. For a "virgin," it is often difficult to know what's going on.

Some say the craze has peaked; many theater owners are tired of sweeping up rice and toilet paper streamers every Sunday morning at 2:00 A.M. and have forbidden attendees to interact with the movie. There is talk of a release on videocassette (underground copies have been around for years) and private parties are sure to continue the tradition in living rooms. For its fans numbering in the millions, and for 20th Century-Fox, too, there is life after premature celluloid death has been pronounced, and *The Rocky Horror Picture Show* is living proof.

Screenplay by Jim Sharman and Richard O'Brien

Based on the stage musical by Richard O'Brien

Executive Producer: Lou Adler

Produced by Michael White

Directed by Jim Sharman

CAST

Frank N. Furter . . . . Tim Curry
Janet Weiss . . . . Susan Sarandon
Brad Majors . . . . Barry Bostwick
Riff Raff . . . . Richard O'Brien
Dr. Everett Scott . . . . . . Jonathan Adams

SHAMPOO

COLUMBIA
$23,822,000

"November 4, 1968. Election eve."
—OPENING CARD

DON'T LET the opening card mislead you. This film about a male beauty operator (in the literal sense) had very little to do with the election. If it's about the eve of anything, it's the start of the sexual revolution, and Warren Beatty fires the first shot. What's more, he takes no prisoners in this farcical, triangular romp through the bedrooms of Southern California.

There is certainly nothing new in the story line about a swinging bachelor in the pre-AIDS years of promiscuity. So producer-writer-star Beatty found a way to turn the standard plot into a sure-fire winner at the box office and pick up a few Oscar nominations along the way—he chose beautiful and talented leading ladies with appeal to both sexes. Goldie Hawn had won a Best Supporting Actress Oscar for *Cactus Flower* in 1969; Julie Christie won Best Actress in 1965's *Darling*, as well as another nomination in *McCabe and Mrs. Miller* (1971); and Lee Grant had won an Emmy for her role in TV's "Peyton Place" and one for a TV movie, *The Neon Ceiling* (1971).

Beatty excelled at spotting future star talent, a gift he used successfully in the film. Carrie Fisher, then 17-year-old offspring of Eddie Fisher and Debbie Reynolds, played a minor role in *Shampoo*—her first film appearance. She would be selected by George Lucas a few years later to play Princess Leia, the only female role in his *Star Wars* saga. And it was during the music scoring sessions of this film that Carrie met her future ex-husband, Paul Simon, when Beatty selected that half of the erstwhile Simon & Garfunkel team to do the music.

Another fine performer in a lead role was Jack Warden. He received an Oscar nomination also, and television viewers will probably best remember him as the star of "Crazy Like a Fox," which ran on CBS during the early 1980s.

Watch for a walk-on by Howard Hessman, another future TV star. Hessman co-starred in "WKRP in Cincinnati" and later starred in his own show, "Head of the Class."

When *Shampoo* was released in 1975, it was not well received by the critics, despite its fine cast and script. As *Variety* said, "All the excellent creative components do not add up to a whole," and *The Hollywood Reporter* termed the film "slick, hip entertainment, but also pretty shallow and cynical." *Shampoo* seems dated when you watch it today: the '70s seem very, very long ago, and the '60s time frame makes this film even more like ancient history.

Screenplay by Robert Towne and
   Warren Beatty

Produced by Warren Beatty

Directed by Hal Ashby

CAST

George	....	Warren Beatty
Jackie	....	Julie Christie
Jill	....	Goldie Hawn
Felicia	....	Lee Grant
Lester	....	Jack Warden
Johnny Pope	....	Tony Bill
Lorna	....	Carrie Fisher

ACADEMY AWARD NOMINATIONS

4 nominations, 1 win*

  Best Supporting Actor (Jack Warden)
**Best Supporting Actress (Lee Grant)
  Best Original Screenplay
  Best Art Direction-Set Decoration

DOG DAY AFTERNOON

WARNER BROS.
$22,500,000

"I'm a Catholic and I don't want to hurt anybody." —AL PACINO (SONNY)

"How beautiful you were when you were a baby." —JUDITH MALINA (SONNY'S MOTHER)

WERE IT NOT for the fine acting, fine directing, fine scripting, fine . . . everything, this would be just another police-crime drama about a bank robbery on a hot afternoon in Brooklyn. Although the line is never said, the only cliché that is missing is the familiar "We've got the place surrounded—come out with your hands up."

What makes this different is that we're shown the robbery from the POV of the *robber*. Al Pacino is Sonny, a "nice boy" to his family, a bisexual loved by both his wives, female and male, who keeps digging himself in deeper and deeper, taking us along with him. It is a study in madness, the same kind of madness that once saw Patty Hearst joining her captors. We, the audience, are made to feel the pressures Sonny feels and not the fears of the hostages that are so typical of this sort of film. It might seem like

Based on a magazine article by P. F. Kluge and Thomas Moore

Screenplay by Frank Pierson

Produced by Martin Bregman and Martin Elfand

Directed by Sidney Lumet

CAST

Sonny	Al Pacino
Sal	John Cazale
Moretti	Charles Durning
Leon	Chris Sarandon
Jenny	Carol Kane

ACADEMY AWARD NOMINATIONS

6 nominations, 1 win*

Best Picture
Best Actor (Al Pacino)
Best Supporting Actor (Chris Sarandon)
Best Director (Sidney Lumet)
*Best Original Screenplay (Frank Pierson)
Best Film Editing

fantastic fiction were it not reality-based. At the beginning of the film we are told: "What you are about to see is true—It happened in Brooklyn, New York on August 22, 1972." There ought to be another mention later in the picture, since one tends to forget this could really have taken place. Only at the end are we reminded this was a factual story, when we learn that Sonny was sentenced to 20 years. With an early parole, he should be out by now.

Al Pacino gives a powerful performance so effective it seems almost ad-libbed. His acting technique—the nuances, the gestures, a look here, a nervous tic there—rightfully earned him the Oscar nomination. (He also received nominations for *Godfather I* and his other Lumet-directed film, *Serpico*.) *Godfather I* and *II* made him a

star; *Dog Day Afternoon* showcased him as an actor. The intensity of his performance was not without a price—about halfway through the production, Pacino collapsed from exhaustion and had to be hospitalized for a short time. He swore off movies for a while, returning to his first love, the Broadway stage.

John Cazale gives a memorable performance as Sal, Sonny's partner-in-crime. Cazale had also worked in both *Godfather* pictures, playing Pacino's brother Fredo.

One of the hostages, a young actress named Carol Kane, is worth noting. Ms. Kane received a nomination for Best Actress in 1975 for her starring role in *Hester Street*. She went on to costar in TV's "Taxi" as well as numerous other films and television series.

1

ROCKY

UNITED ARTISTS
$56,524,972

HOLLYWOOD LOVES a rags-to-riches tale almost as much as it loves a film about a successful underdog. With *Rocky*, audiences got both and United Artists helped reap the profits. Everyone was a winner.

It almost didn't happen. Thirty-year-old Sylvester Stallone had already written and received rejections on 32 scripts. With a pregnant wife and $106 in his bank account, he sat down to write script number 33. He called it *Rocky*, and within three days the fact-based account of a has-been fighter who stages a comeback and winds up heavyweight boxing champ of the world was completed. It was grabbed by producers Irwin Winkler and Robert Chartoff, who saw it as a star vehicle for the likes of Burt Reynolds or Robert Redford (everyone, it seems, automatically thought of Redford for everything). But Stallone would have no part of a deal that didn't include himself in the lead. He had been a struggling actor even before he was a struggling writer, plus he had the right bod for the role. With a budget just slightly under $1,000,000, the company completed principal photography in 28 days ("the gestation time for a water bug," Stallone pointed out to *The New York Times*), shooting on location in Philadelphia and Los Angeles.

Rocky became the sleeper of the decade and established the formula for the film's Roman-numeraled sequels. Rocky is down and out, but circumstances beyond his control compel him into just one more fight, a fight there's no way in hell he can win. We see him training like an automaton, with lots of sweat and tears (the blood comes later in the ring when he's punished beyond belief). Yes, he wins the bout, but by that time, we've been suckered in and cheered him on like one of our own family, so that when he wins against all the odds, it's practically an orgasmic moment. Audiences almost always cheer wildly, breaking into spontaneous applause, because *Rocky* and the sequels are inspiring, uplifting, stand-up-and-cheer pictures. Rocky Balboa is a hero, a man of the people, and we needed heroes in that decade of Nixon and Watergate. Stallone was quoted by

Academy Awards Illustrated as saying: "It was never a script about boxing. It was always about a man simply fighting for his dignity. People require symbols of humanity and heroism."

Like Rocky himself, this picture came from behind to take the top prize of the Motion Picture Academy—the Oscar for Best Picture. And the contenders were all heavyweights: *All the President's Men, Bound for Glory, Network,* and *Taxi Driver.* Clearly, *Rocky* captured the hearts of Academy members as well as their highest award.

Stallone himself personally made it into the record books as a double Oscar nominee (as actor and screenwriter), a

---

Screenplay by Sylvester Stallone

Executive Producer: Gene Kirkwood

Produced by Irwin Winkler and Robert Chartoff

Directed by John G. Avildsen

CAST

Rocky Balboa .... Sylvester Stallone
Adrian .... Talia Shire
Paulie .... Burt Young
Apollo Creed .... Carl Weathers
Mickey .... Burgess Meredith

ACADEMY AWARD NOMINATIONS

10 nominations, 3 wins*

*Best Picture
Best Actor (Sylvester Stallone)
Best Actress (Talia Shire)
Best Supporting Actor
  (Burgess Meredith)
Best Supporting Actor (Burt Young)
*Best Director (John G. Avildsen)
Best Screenplay Written Directly
  for the Screen
Best Sound
Best Original Song ("Gonna Fly Now,"
  music by Bill Conti, words by Carol
  Connors and Ayn Robbins)
*Best Film Editing

While not winning the Oscar, the single version of "Gonna Fly Now, The Theme from *Rocky*" rose to number-one on the *Billboard* charts for the week of July 2, 1977.

---

rare feat accomplished at the time by only two others—Charles Chaplin, for *The Great Dictator* (1940), and Orson Welles, for *Citizen Kane* (1941).

Stallone's co-stars were more like props supporting the centerpiece, but their performances were admirable. Burgess Meredith had become popular back in the late '60s when he played "The Penguin" on TV's "Batman." As Rocky's trainer, Mickey, he found another continuing character he would play in two films to come. The 68-year-old veteran of over 100 films received a Best Supporting Actor nomination, his first recognition by the Academy. He had co-starred in many popular films, including *Advise and Consent* (1962), *The Cardinal* (1963), *Hurry Sundown* (1967), *The Day of the Locust* (1975), and *The Hindenburg* (1975). According to the book *Inside Oscar,* the attention at the Awards ceremony night caused him to comment: "Believe it or not, *Rocky* is my first smash hit out of 120 films. I had many successes artistically, but nothing like *Rocky.*"

Talia Shire played Rocky's lady-love (and later his wife), the only woman's part of any consequence; she's a subservient non-feminist type, whom audiences met before in the two *Godfather* movies (Shire is Francis Coppola's sister). She appeared in several Roger Corman "B" movies under her maiden name of Talia Coppola before her break in her brother's film. *The New York Times* reserved what little praise it had for Talia Shire: "She's a real actress, genuinely touching and funny as an incipient spinster who comes late to sexual life. She's so good, in fact, that she almost gives weight to Mr. Stallone's performance, which is the large hole in the center of the film." The remainder of the review went on to trash Stallone's performance in no uncertain terms. Did "Sly" (his friends' nickname for him) mind? Not in the least. He had 10 percent of the profits in his contract . . . for a man who began with $106 in his pocket, that's a lot of money. And he thought of this picture as a one-shot—his next role, he hoped, might be the upcoming movie of *Superman.* But he was never offered that part; it went to another underdog.

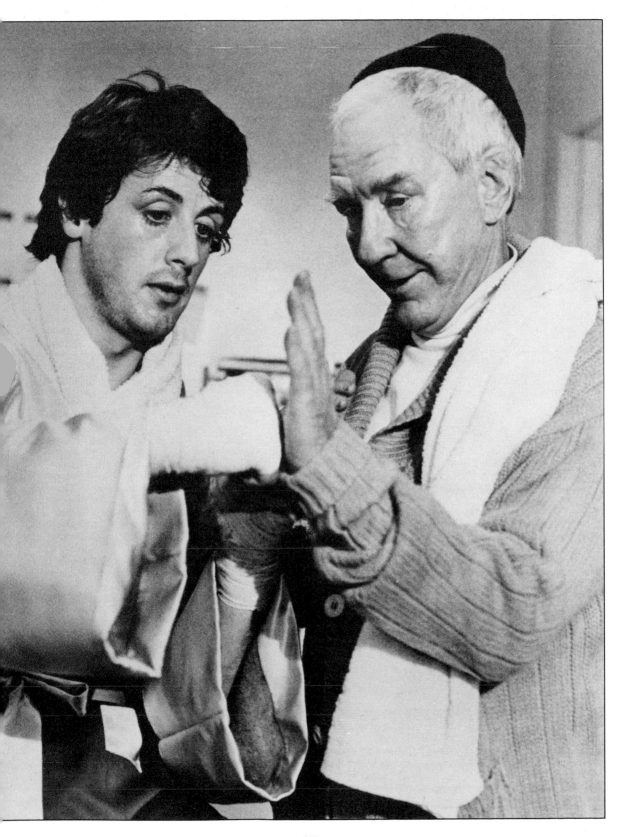

A STAR IS BORN
WARNER BROS.
$37,100,000

Rᴇᴍᴀᴋᴇs are commonplace in the movie industry. The feeling seems to be that if a story is good, it is worth retelling. Even Shakespeare was known to rework a classic story or two. And in Hollywood, a successful remake can often top its predecessor. Such was the case of *The Ten Commandments* (see page 122), *Ben-Hur* (see page 140), and *Cleopatra* (see page 166). All had been successful films of the '20s, yet the remakes surpassed the original in both scope and financial success.

This was the thought of Barbra Streisand and her First Artists production company when they acquired the rights to *A Star Is Born*. But this was not a simple remake of a classic film; it was already a thrice-told tale. The first version, directed by George Cukor, was called *What Price Hollywood* back in 1932, and starred Constance Bennett as the ingenue who rises to the top at the expense of others. It served as the blueprint for the original film titled *A Star Is Born*, the Janet Gaynor-Frederic March 1937 version which is

Screenplay by John Gregory Dunne, Joan Didion, and Frank Pierson

Based on a story by William Wellman and Robert Carson

Executive Producer: Barbra Streisand

Produced by Jon Peters

Directed by Frank Pierson

CAST

Esther Hoffman	Barbra Streisand
John Norman Howard	Kris Kristofferson
Brian	Paul Mazursky
Bobby Ritchie	Gary Busey
Gary Danziger	Oliver Clark
Photographer	Sally Kirkland

ACADEMY AWARD NOMINATIONS

4 nominations, 1 win*

Best Cinematography
Best Sound
*Best Song ("Evergreen, Love Theme from *A Star Is Born*," music by Barbra Streisand, words by Paul Williams)
Best Original Song Score (Roger Kellaway)

termed a "classic" today. Then, in 1954, Cukor again directed *A Star Is Born*, starring Judy Garland (in what many believe to her best acting performance) and James Mason.

Screenwriters John Gregory Dunne and Joan Didion had originally conceived of a way for an updated version of the familiar story to find its modern audience by taking their "star" out of Hollywood for her "birth" and placing her in the world of rock music instead of Screenland. Their first choices for the roles were Carly Simon and James Taylor, who passed on the project. Next they considered Liza Minnelli and Elvis Presley, Mick and Bianca Jagger, and even Sonny and Cher. Eventually Jon Peters, Barbra Streisand's hairdresser-turned-producer, obtained the property, and she agreed to star in it. Her co-star choices ranged from Marlon Brando (who *had* done the musical *Guys and Dolls*) to Elvis Presley. Brando declined, and Presley was already on the way down—the King didn't want this to be the movie he would be remembered for, even if the

two men who had previously played the role had been nominated for Oscars. (Less than a year after the movie's release, Elvis was gone.) Barbra's final choice for co-star was Kris Kristofferson, a singer who could act, an actor who could sing.

Barbra executive-produced this virtual one-woman show as a vehicle for her talents (even her wardrobe was spotlighted—the credit reads: "Ms. Streisand's clothes from her closet"). She obviously has as many fans as the heroine of her story, since the film did incredibly well at the box office, easily surpassing the combined totals of all three previous versions. And while it wasn't the Oscar powerhouse of its forerunners, Streisand managed to pull down an Academy Award for the film's theme song, "Evergreen." The song rose to the top of the *Billboard* charts, where it reached number one in March, 1977, remaining there for three weeks. It also won a Grammy for "Song of the Year," while Streisand was voted a Grammy for Best Pop Vocal Performance, Female.

KING KONG
PARAMOUNT
$36,915,000

"I'm a Libra. What sign are you?"
—JESSICA LANGE
TO KING KONG

KING KONG, that swinging single ape we all knew and loved in the '30s, was back, still the perennial bachelor, size 52-foot (loose) and fancy free. This time, the studio promised, Kong was bigger and badder (and meaner than a junkyard dog).

It was the second remake of the year (see *A Star Is Born*, page 248), and like the *Kong* of old, this, too, was a real crowd pleaser. It was updated, of course. The original Merian C. Cooper version had a movie crew stumbling across the giant anthropoid in the South Seas; the spectacular $24,000,000 Dino DeLaurentiis remake saw an oil company searching for black gold, the hottest commodity of the '70s. And for Kong's demise, the Big Apple's Empire State Building was deemed too puny for the Mighty Ape—only the twin towers of the World Trade Center

Screenplay by Lorenzo Semple, Jr.

Based on a story by Edgar Wallace and Merian C. Cooper

Executive Producers: Federico De Laurentiis and Christian Ferry

Produced by Dino De Laurentiis

Directed by John Guillermin

CAST

Jack Prescott . . . . Jeff Bridges
Fred Wilson . . . . Charles Grodin
Dawn . . . . Jessica Lange
Capt. Ross . . . . John Randolph
Bagley . . . . Rene Auberjonois

ACADEMY AWARD NOMINATIONS

2 nominations, no wins

Best Cinematography
Best Sound

King Kong received a Special Achievement Award for Visual Effects (Carlo Rambaldi, Glen Robinson, and Frank Van Der Veer). Since this was not a contested category, the Academy also gave the same award to another film that year, *Logan's Run*.

would do for his downfall. (Movie posters rather obscenely depicted the hairy beast astride the two 110-story buildings.)

Purists were horrified, not by the creature himself, but at the very thought of tampering with one of the classic horror films of all time. The film took a tongue-in-cheek, campy attitude one minute, a serious one the next, making audiences uncertain as to the film's intent. Was the inane dialogue, like the above parody of '70s singles-bar ice-breaking chitchat, meant to be taken seriously? Jessica Lange, a former fashion model introduced in this film, was saddled with lines like "You goddamn chauvinist pig ape!" and "Oh, come on, Kong. Forget about me. This thing is never gonna work."

Instead of the miniature stop-motion animation invented by Willis O'Brien, this new Kong used a combination of effects to achieve what O'Brien had done on a tabletop back in the pioneering days of 1933. First there was make-up man Rick Baker in a monkey suit with five different facially expressive

masks, depending on Kong's mood. Then there was a 40-foot-high mechanical ape weighing six-and-a-half tons, capable of wiggling his arm, rolling his neck, twitching his ears, rotating his hips, and smiling. There was also a hydraulically-operated arm with a hand six feet across in which the gentle giant holds and caresses Ms. Lange. The genius behind this mechanical miracle was Carlo Rambaldi, who would go on to become one of the most sought after effects men in Hollywood, later working on *Close Encounters of the Third Kind* and *E.T.*.

While *King Kong* has not replaced the 1933 version in the hearts and minds of its enduring fan following around the world, the remake nevertheless did well at the box office and more than made back its initial outlay. In 1986, a sequel was attempted (*King Kong Lives*), but did poorly.

Perhaps movie makers have now learned that bigger is not always better. In the case of the remakes of *King Kong*, to paraphrase an old expression, " 'Twas booty killed the beast."

SILVER STREAK
20TH CENTURY-FOX
$30,018,000

"In ten minutes you're going to have two hundred tons of locomotive smashing its way through Central Station on its way to Marshall Field!" —CHIEF OF POLICE TO AN "AMROAD" OFFICIAL

THE PRODUCERS of *Silver Streak* (and there were quite of few of them) didn't seem completely certain just what type of genre this film was. More a recipe than a film, it was one part love story, one part action-adventure, one part murder mystery, one part comedy, and one part disaster film (see above dialogue). With something for everyone, one thing was certain—it did well at the box office, although early reviews predicted doom for more than just the runaway train. *Newsweek* called the movie "Train of Fools" and wrote: "It's a sluggish adventure movie about an L.A.-to-Chicago train trip that wastes two considerable talents . . . when Richard Pryor finally puts in an appearance, well over an hour into the story, his frantic timing and good-natured vulgarity are welcome."

Part of the film's problem for the critics—certainly not with the audience, who returned often enough to push the movie into the year's top

five—was that Gene Wilder wasn't doing the sort of comedy we'd come to expect from him. After his screen debut as a nervous undertaker in *Bonnie and Clyde*, he had hit his stride playing cuddly, frenetic types in Mel Brooks movies like *Blazing Saddles* and *Young Frankenstein*. With *Silver Streak*, we were asked to believe he was a serious lover one minute, a

---

Screenplay by Colin Higgins

Executive Producers: Frank Yablans and Martin Ransohoff

Produced by Edward K. Milkis and Thomas L. Miller

Directed by Arthur Hiller

CAST

George Caldwell	. . . . .	Gene Wilder
Hilly Burns	. . . .	Jill Clayburgh
Grover Muldoon	. . . . .	Richard Pryor
Roger Devereau	. . . . .	Patrick McGoohan
Sweet	. . . .	Ned Beatty

ACADEMY AWARD NOMINATIONS

1 nomination, no wins

Best Sound

---

comedian the next. Only when Richard Pryor appears on the scene and the two begin to do *schtick* does Wilder's true humor come through.

The critics loved Pryor. Before his role in *Silver Streak*, the black comedian had worked mostly as a nightclub and TV entertainer. He had a small but important role in *Lady Sings the Blues* (1972), but mostly appeared in mediocre films like *The Bingo Long Traveling All-Stars and Motor Kings* (1976) and *Car Wash* (1976). Pryor himself was lukewarm about his participation in *Silver Streak*, describing it to *The New York Times* as "a 'business decision.'"

Others in the cast included Patrick McGoohan as a villain, an interesting departure for the British actor who had a huge following on both sides of the Atlantic for his '60s portrayal of spies in TV's "Secret Agent" and "The Prisoner." Actor Richard Kiel, who would later become known as "Jaws" in the James Bond film series, makes an appearance as Reace/Goldtooth, his character's name derived from the toothy grin that became his trademark.

Happily for fans of the Wilder/Pryor pairing, the two were again teamed in the 1980 film, *Stir Crazy*. It too became a box office hit (see page 275).

ALL THE PRESIDENT'S MEN
WARNER BROS.
$30,000,000

POLITICAL FILMS usually don't go over well with moviegoers. So when Robert Redford paid $450,000 to option Bob Woodward and Carl Bernstein's best-seller about their exposé of the Watergate cover-up, he had difficulty convincing potential backers that this picture would be a money-maker. Didn't he know how angered television viewers had been during the hearings when their soaps were pre-empted? No one wanted to see more about Watergate, Redford was told, even with him in the lead role. Eventually, he was able to convince Warner Bros. to budget the film at a modest $8,500,000, still a considerable gamble for a political film.

It was not easy bringing such a controversial subject to the screen. Redford, who selected Dustin Hoffman for his co-star, turned to William Goldman for a screenplay adaptation. Goldman had written *Butch Cassidy and the Sundance Kid*, and Redford didn't want to take chances (no problem, as Goldman proved when he won the Best Screenplay Oscar). "We stuck very

---

Screenplay by William Goldman

Based on a book by Carl Bernstein and Bob Woodward

Produced by Walter Coblenz

Directed by Alan J. Pakula

CAST

Carl Bernstein	Dustin Hoffman
Bob Woodward	Robert Redford
Harry Rosenfeld	Jack Warden
Howard Simons	Martin Balsam
Deep Throat	Hal Holbrook
Ben Bradlee	Jason Robards

ACADEMY AWARD NOMINATIONS

*8 nominations, 4 wins**

Best Picture
*Best Supporting Actor (Jason Robards)
Best Supporting Actress (Jane Alexander)
Best Director (Alan J. Pakula)
*Best Screenplay Based on Material from Another Medium (William Goldman)
*Best Art Direction-Set Decoration
*Best Sound
Best Film Editing

---

close to the book," says Redford on the back of the videocassette version's box. "The story is itself such a thriller that there was no need to resort to literary license or fictionalization."

Shot with the cooperation of the *Washington Post* (Woodward and Bernstein's employing newspaper), there is a documentary feeling to the film. This is because *All the President's Men* is done as "docudrama," combining elements of both documentary and drama. It begins with actual footage of Richard Nixon about to address Congress, and ends with his taking the Presidential Oath of Office, followed by a montage of headlines leading to his resignation. Intercut throughout the entire film are real news reports, adding to the feeling of authenticity.

The newspaper was also instrumental in aiding the production designers in duplicating the newsroom down to the last detail, including authentic trash. Such attention to minutiae won an Oscar for the art directors and set designers.

There were two Best Supporting Actor/Actress nominations—Jason Robards as *Post* editor Ben Bradlee, and Jane Alexander as a bookkeeper on Nixon's staff who provides key background data. But it is surprising that neither of the principals, Redford and Hoffman, were nominated for Best

Actor, while Sylvester Stallone was nominated for his first major film role that year in *Rocky*. So was an obscure Italian named Giancarlo Giannini, for *Seven Beauties*—another unusual move for the Academy, which rarely nominated foreign actors for the top award.

Others noteworthy in *All the President's Men* were Jack Warden, Martin Balsam, Ned Beatty (he received a nomination from the Academy that year, but for another film—*Network*), and Hal Holbrook as the informant, "Deep Throat." A few future television stars were in other roles: Stephen Collins as Hugh Sloan (he co-starred in the film *Star Trek: The Motion Picture* [1979] and several TV shows); Robert Walden as Donald Segretti (he was in "Lou Grant" and the Showtime series "Brothers"); and a dark-haired Meredith Baxter as Mrs. Sloan (who later added her married name of Birney to her billing when she co-starred as the blonde mom on the TV series "Family Ties").

Critics called it "ingenious" (*Variety*), "spellbinding . . . the thinking man's 'Jaws' " (*The New York Times*), and "a superb movie" (*Leonard Maltin's TV Movies and Video Guide*). When it's listed in *TV Guide*, *All the President's Men* is given four stars, a must-see. Good advice; catch it next time it's on.

1

STAR WARS
20TH CENTURY-FOX
$193,500,000

"A long time ago, in a galaxy far, far away. . . ."
—OPENING CRAWL

PART SATURDAY afternoon matinee, part *Wizard of Oz*, part *Star Trek* (even the title was obviously derivative), part Buck Rogers, part Flash Gordon, part Knights of the Round Table—and *all* George Lucas. That was the magic loosed upon an unsuspecting public in the summer of 1977. The movie which had begun as a germ of an idea in the fertile mind of George Lucas back in 1973 ended up being the sleeper of the century. Movies would never be the same again.

George Lucas had difficulty convincing people to listen to him when, following the success of his first hit, *American Graffiti*, he wrote an outline for what would be his loving tribute to the serials he'd enjoyed so much as a youth, originally entitled *The Star Wars*. No studio in town would give him a tumble. Science fiction films weren't successful, appealing only to a handful of freaks and weirdos, the studios said, and Lucas pounded on several doors before receiving the considerable backing of $9,500,000 he needed when 20th Century-Fox agreed to finance the project.

Actually, it was more fantasy than science fiction. Lucas created an imaginary world of princesses and knights, fighters with movable wings (not necessary in the vacuum of space), and anthropomorphic robots. The plot was as old as fiction itself—the forces of good (Luke Skywalker, all in white) versus the forces of evil (Darth, as in "dark," Vader, all in black). Yet as derivative as it was, *Star Wars* was also the most imaginative use of cinemagic ever, with the finest technical effort ever given any picture, sci-fi or otherwise. Computerized and digitally-timed special effects, layer upon layer of stars, ships, backgrounds, animation, humans, and so on made us believe, no matter how shaky the science. Above all, it was *entertainment*. Virtually every second of the picture was filled with excitement, action, or visual interest of some sort. Cliffhangers occurred every ten minutes or so, without the "tune in next week to find out if our

heroes live": the spellbound audience knew immediately.

The critics knew immediately that they were not only looking into the future (or past, as it were), but into the very future of the motion picture industry itself. *The Hollywood Reporter* sized up the situation: " 'Star Wars' will undoubtedly emerge as one of the true classics in the genre of science fiction/ fantasy films. In any event, it will be thrilling audiences of all ages for a long time to come." *Newsweek* called the movie "pure sweet fun all the way . . . [George Lucas] says it's a movie for children—what he means is that he wants to touch the child in all of us . . . *Star Wars* brims with adventure,. charm

---

Screenplay by George Lucas

Produced by Gary Kurtz

Directed by George Lucas

CAST

Luke Skywalker	Mark Hamill
Han Solo	Harrison Ford
Princess Leia	Carrie Fisher
Grand Moff Tarkin	Peter Cushing
Obi-Won (Ben) Kenobi . .	Alec Guinness
C3PO	Anthony Daniels
R2D2	Kenny Baker

ACADEMY AWARD NOMINATIONS

10 nominations, 6 wins*

  Best Picture
  Best Supporting Actor (Alec Guinness)
  Best Director (George Lucas)
  Best Screenplay Written Directly
    for the Screen
*Best Art Direction-Set Decoration
*Best Sound
*Best Original Score (John Williams)
*Best Film Editing
*Best Costume Design
*Best Visual Effects

A Special Achievement Award for Sound Effects went to Benjamin Burtt, Jr., for the creation of the alien, creature, and robot voices in *Star Wars*.

A single of the theme and Cantina number by Meco hit the number-one spot on Billboard charts in October, 1977, remaining there for two weeks.

---

and marvels . . . Lucas makes fun a sparkling pop metaphor for the sheer joy of goodness that could even make friends out of men, mutations and machines."

By now, there's hardly a person alive in *this* galaxy who does not think of characters like C3PO, R2D2, and Chewbacca as close friends. Fans of the film adored the 'droids (short for "androids," of course) and the eight-foot-tall Wookie, Chewbacca, a cross between a walking dog and animal-like human. Even Chewie's growling vocalizations were endearing, having been electronically created from mixing the sounds of a bear and a lion.

The public couldn't get enough of *Star Wars* in any form, eagerly embracing the merchandise that poured forth. T-shirts, lunchboxes, bedsheets (one store dubiously advertised, "Now you can have scenes of Luke in action on your mattress!")—the theme song became a number-one hit, and John Williams' music became the bestselling soundtrack of all time, with over 3,000,000 copies sold.

The film's ending unintentionally left the story open for sequels. Originally, *Star Wars* was meant as a one-shot, a film complete in itself. But as soon as three-hour-long lines began forming at the box office, Fox executives knew they were on to something. Suddenly, George Lucas and his newly-formed company Lucasfilm were busy creating a *Star Wars* saga. The film was given a new opening crawl with its next release. Instead of starting with the receding crawl proclaiming simply, "A long time ago, in a galaxy far, far away," the opening slide began with EPISODE IV—A NEW HOPE. (All prints now in release have this beginning title.)

Huh? What about Episodes I, II, and III? Had we slept through them? No, these were (and still are) *prequels*, awaiting the spark of life from their creator, Lucas. Meanwhile, he began prepping Episode V (which is actually only the second in the series), *The Empire Strikes Back*, and Episode VI, *The Return of the Jedi*.

Fans of the series are ever hopeful that Mr. Lucas will come out of semi-retirement and complete the proposed nine-part series.

CLOSE ENCOUNTERS OF THE THIRD KIND

COLUMBIA
$82,750,000

Close Encounter of the First
Kind: sighting of a UFO

Close Encounter of the Second
Kind: physical evidence

Close Encounter of the Third
Kind: contact

—COLUMBIA PICTURES
SCREENING PROGRAM

THE SIGHTING OF UFOs (unidentified
flying objects) was not a new phenomenon. Sightings began appearing with
regularity following the Second World
War, when people's eyes were focused
skyward, looking for enemy aircraft
that might at any minute rain down
death and destruction. Whether due to
mass hysteria or some unexplained
mystery, there was definitely *something*
being seen, and even the U.S. Air
Force began keeping files on reported
sightings. During that time, the term
"close encounter" was coined to describe the degree to which the sighting
was experienced. And although Steven
Spielberg originally wanted to call his
movie on the subject *Watch the Skies*,
he eventually settled on the more
technical title of *Close Encounters of the
Third Kind.*

There had been a spate of "alien
encounter" films during the '50s, when
UFO sightings were at their zenith. In

many ways, *CE3K* (as the film is
frequently abbreviated) was somewhat
derivative of those movies: a touch of
The Day the Earth Stood Still, a little
War of the Worlds, a tiny bit of *Earth
Versus the Flying Saucers, It Came from
Outer Space*, and so on. But unlike the
latter two "B" movies, *CE3K* was done
with a big budget, technical advice,
lavish special effects, and a fantastic
script written by the director himself,
Steven Spielberg.

Like *Star Wars, CE3K* was a technical marvel. Doug Trumbull, the FX
genius behind *2001: A Space Odyssey*,
worked his spells on this Spielberg
production, converting his 13,500-
square-foot building into a complete
movie studio, with special rooms for
developing, optical printing and editing,
"dolly" tracks for camera passes at the
models of space ships (expertly crafted
by another fine talent, Greg Jein),
construction shops, paint shops, and
hundreds of thousands of dollars worth
of special equipment—much of it designed by Trumbull as the need arose.

The live action was shot in various
worldwide locations. The crowd sequences in India took weeks and thousands of extras—DeMille himself
couldn't have done better. And the
largest indoor set ever used in a film
was built in a dirigible hangar in Mobile,

Alabama—it was equal to six times the
size of the largest soundstage in Hollywood. Here they shot the movie's
climax when the chandelier-like "Mothership" arrives.

Wyoming's Devil's Tower, a unique
mountain setting in a desolate area near
Huelot, Wyoming, also saw weeks of
camera crews trudging through the
wilderness. Columbia originally wanted
Spielberg to film this on a Burbank
soundstage, but the director insisted on
authentic location backgrounds.

In 1980, Steven Spielberg did the
unheard of—he re-edited his already
successful picture, cutting scenes that
he felt slowed down the film (e.g., the
shots of Richard Dreyfuss obsessively
digging up the yard) and adding others,
including an all-new ending in which we
are actually treated to a look inside the
Mothership. The feature was even
given a new title: *Close Encounters of
the Third Kind: The Special Edition.*
Box office earnings again soared. And
for Columbia and Spielberg (as well as
the audience), it was indeed special.

Screenplay by Steven Spielberg

Produced by Julia and Michael Phillips

Directed by Steven Spielberg

CAST

Roy Neary .... Richard Dreyfuss
Claude Lacombe ...... Francois Truffaut
Ronnie Neary .... Teri Garr
Jullian Guiler .... Melinda Dillon
Barry Guiler .... Cary Guffey

ACADEMY AWARD NOMINATIONS

8 nominations, 1 win*

Best Supporting Actress (Melinda Dillon)
Best Director (Steven Spielberg)
*Best Cinematography
Best Art Direction-Set Decoration
Best Sound
Best Original Score
Best Film Editing
Best Visual Effects

Close Encounters of the Third Kind
received a Special Achievement Award for
Sound Effects Editing (to Frank Warner,
sound effects editor)

SATURDAY NIGHT FEVER
PARAMOUNT
$74,100,000

"**T**RIBAL RITES of the New Saturday Night." That was the name of the cover story article by Nik Cohn appearing in *New York Magazine*'s June, 1976 issue. It dealt with kids in Brooklyn, New York, who lived from Saturday to Saturday, "exploding" on the weekends at the local disco. The main character of this fact-based story was "Vincent," a third-generation Italian-American who "owned fourteen floral shirts, five suits, eight pairs of shoes, three overcoats, and had appeared on *American Bandstand* . . . When Saturday night came round and he walked into 2001 Odyssey [sic], all the other Faces [sic] automatically fell back before him, cleared a space for him to float in, right at the very center of the dance floor."

Producer Robert Stigwood found the story a movie natural and acquired the screen rights for Paramount. Stigwood had a young man under a three-picture-deal contract, and the lead role seemed a natural for him. John Travolta had only been in two movies up until that time, *The Devil's Rain* (1975) and *The Boy in the Plastic Bubble* (made-for-TV, 1976). But audiences were familiar with him from his weekly appearances as "Barbarino" on TV's "Welcome Back, Kotter." And *Fever*'s main character, "Tony Manero," was an unintentional clone of Barbarino, making this the ideal vehicle for launching Travolta into mainstream features.

Screenplay by Norman Wexler

Based on a story by Nik Cohn

Executive Producer: Kevin McCormick

Produced by Robert Stigwood

Directed by John Badham

CAST

Tony Manero . . . . John Travolta
Stephanie . . . . Karen Lynn Gorney
Bobby C . . . . Barry Miller
Joey . . . . Joseph Cali
Annette . . . . Donna Pescow

ACADEMY AWARD NOMINATIONS

1 nomination, no wins

Best Actor (John Travolta)

The soundtrack became one of the best-sellers of all time, with over 35,000,000 copies sold worldwide. Bee Gees (for "*Brothers Gibb*") hit songs included "How Deep Is Your Love,"* "Night Fever,"* "Staying Alive,"* "More Than a Woman," "If I Can't Have You"* (performed by Yvonne Elliman), and "You Should Be Dancing."** Amazingly, none of these tunes was nominated for Best Song, nor was the score nominated by the Academy.

The film captured the imaginations of young people who turned disco dancing into a national craze while emulating the fashions worn in the film. By 1978, white three-piece polyester leisure suits with black shirts and Cuban heels were all the rage, along with Travolta look-alike and "Spanish hustle" contests. John Travolta himself emerged as a cult hero, and the charismatic young performer would soon emerge as Paramount/Stigwood's hottest contract player in decades.

The original 1977 release received an "R" rating, which eliminated much of the young audience who could not be admitted unless accompanied by an adult. Many potential ticket-buyers wanted to enjoy this musical film with wonderful dance numbers by the multi-talented young star, but there were some sex scenes and a lot of blue language the MPAA rightly termed inappropriate for young teens. So in 1979, Paramount re-edited the feature, deleting seven minutes of offensive footage and, as required by the MPAA, withdrew all copies of the "R"-rated version from circulation. The newly recut edition received a "PG" rating and went on to enjoy a whole new audience.

*Became a number-one hit and was written especially for *Saturday Night Fever*.

**Became a number-one hit prior to inclusion in *Saturday Night Fever*.

SMOKEY AND THE BANDIT
UNIVERSAL
$58,949,939

CAR CHASES, when well done, can usually pull any ailing studio out of the doldrums. Toss in a hunky good-ol'-boy type like Burt Reynolds, plus the current fad, whatever it may be, and the lucky studio can count its box office take to the happy tune of plunkin' banjo music from here to Georgia.

For Universal, which hadn't had a top-five hit since 1975's *Jaws*, *Smokey and the Bandit* saw the studio making out like bandits. Burt Reynolds had proved he could act in *Deliverance* (1972), and polls placed him squarely atop the list of box office favorites in 1977, his fourth year in the top ten. The screenplay about hauling a truckload of bootlegged beer from Texas to Georgia was a textbook on how many different ways to crash a car, with the clichéd Southern redneck potbellied sheriff (played by Jackie Gleason) in hot pursuit. It seems like formula writing at its most generic—except that this is the picture that invented the formula.

The CB craze had peaked while the film was in production in 1976, with the biggest fad since the hula hoop bringing in over $2 billion in sales. So just for good measure, the producers tossed in a heavy dose of CB jive, like "That's a big 10-4, good buddy" (translation: over and out), "What's your handle?" (code name), and "There's a Smokey up the

road taking pictures" (a highway patrolman is using radar up ahead).

Along with Burt Reynolds, there was co-star Sally Field, known mostly as the cutesy star of the '60s "Gidget" and "The Flying Nun" TV series. The unnunlike Ms. Field would go on to co-star as his female sidekick in a number of other Reynolds movies, as well as in real life, when the couple became an "item" for a number of years. She had won an Emmy for her work in the TV movie *Sybil*, and would later shine in films such as *Norma Rae* (1979), for which she received the Oscar, and *Places in the Heart* (1984), another Award–winning role ("You like me! Right now you *like* me!" she crowed on Oscar night in 1984).

Several reviewers crowed as well. *Time* found that *Smokey and the Bandit* "deals in broad comedy and simple emotions . . . between crashes, Reynolds is given a series of wisecracks

that establish his basic screen character—shrewd, laid-back, a tad reckless and a devil with women . . . the whole enterprise is fairly tacky, but it is also rather jaunty fun." *The Hollywood Reporter* wrote: "There are a number of amusing sequences which are combined with some exciting road action to provide a mildly entertaining—and totally mindless—film . . . Reynolds performs with an offhand, easy style and he creates an engaging character."

Reynolds parlayed his success into two less successful sequels, *Smokey and the Bandit II* (1980), again with Field and Gleason, and *Smokey and the Bandit 3** (1983), with Jackie Gleason and Paul Williams, but not Sally Field, who by then had split with Reynolds for good.

---

*There was an unexplained switch from Roman to Arabic numerals in the second sequel.

Screenplay by James Lee Barrett, Charles Shyer, and Alan Mandel

Based on a story by Hal Needham

Executive Producer: Robert L. Levy

Produced by Mort Engelberg

Directed by Hal Needham

CAST

Bandit	Burt Reynolds
Carrie	Sally Field
Cledus	Jerry Reed
Sheriff Justice	Jackie Gleason
Little Enos	Paul Williams
Big Enos	Pat McCormick

ACADEMY AWARD NOMINATIONS

1 nomination, no wins

Best Film Editing

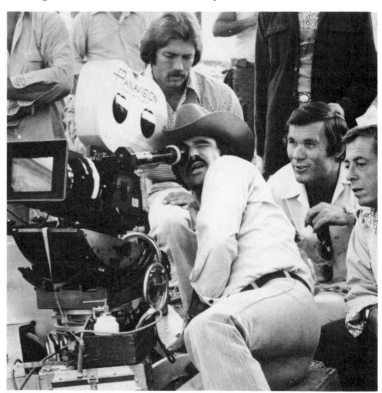

Burt Reynolds grabs a look through the camera lens before the next scene is filmed.

THE GOODBYE GIRL
METRO-GOLDWYN-MAYER/WARNER BROS.
$41,839,170

"Oh God, please let me get hit by a rich man in a Rolls Royce."
—MARSHA MASON

IN A RARE DEPARTURE from his usual method, Neil Simon created a play directly for the screen rather than for live theater. Writing *The Goodbye Girl* mainly as a starring vehicle for his then-wife Marsha Mason, he chose the medium after careful consideration. "Any idea ordinarily says to me, 'I'm a play' or 'I'm a movie,'" the playwright commented to *The New York Times*. "But an integral character was a 10-year-old girl. I didn't want to face the difficulty of having to get a performance from a child night after night."

The Goodbye Girl is in many ways reminiscent of Simon's earlier hit film, *The Odd Couple*. Like Felix and Oscar, this movie's two protagonists are thrown together in a New York apartment where their personalities clash like plaids and stripes. But unlike the roomies in the first hit, these two are of *opposite* sexes and inevitably wind up in love with each other. And the rest is pure Neil Simon at his best.

Another rare departure was the fact that this was a co-production of two studios, Metro-Goldwyn-Mayer and Warner Bros., with Warner Bros. acting as the releasing company and

Screenplay by Neil Simon

Produced by Ray Stark

Directed by Herbert Ross

CAST

Elliot Garfield	Richard Dreyfuss
Paula McFadden	Marsha Mason
Lucy McFadden	Quinn Cummings
Mark	Paul Benedict
Donna	Barbara Rhoades

ACADEMY AWARD NOMINATIONS

5 nominations, 1 win*

Best Picture
**Best Actor (Richard Dreyfuss)
Best Actress (Marsha Mason)
Best Supporting Actress
  (Quinn Cummings)
Best Screenplay Written Directly for the
  Screen

---

handling distribution.

Although the film was intended as a showcase for Marsha Mason, a.k.a. Mrs. Simon, most of the accolades went to Richard Dreyfuss. Although the actor failed to be nominated for his hit picture of the year, *Close Encounters of the Third Kind*, or his earlier achievement in *Jaws* (1975), he walked off with the prize for Best Actor in *The Goodbye Girl*. The role of Elliot Garfield was as good a role as any actor dared hope for: an actor playing an actor. Critics were agog over Dreyfuss' performance. According to *Time*, "he gets the girl in the end, but he gets the audience first." And *Newsweek*, while noting that Dreyfuss might appear to be an unlikely romantic lead, praised him as "charmingly, abrasively funny, perfectly setting the manic rhythm for Simon's confrontational comedy." The compliment was echoed by Dreyfuss'

peers at the Motion Picture Academy, who voted him the Oscar for Best Actor over the likes of Richard Burton (*Equus* marked his seventh nomination—and loss), John Travolta (*Saturday Night Fever*), Woody Allen (*Annie Hall*), and Marcello Mastroianni (*A Special Day*).

The highlight of the film for many was the portrayal by Dreyfuss' character of Shakespeare's Richard III as gay. This outlandish sequence is probably the scene that clinched the Oscar for him. Several reviewers likened it to the "Springtime for Hitler" send-up in Mel Brooks' *The Producers* (1968).

Young actress Quinn Cummings surprised many as a Best Supporting Actress nominee in her first film performance. The child star was quickly added to the cast of TV's "Family," in which she co-starred from 1978 until the show's demise in 1980.

GREASE
PARAMOUNT
$96,300,000

"If you can't be an athlete, be an athletic supporter."

—EVE ARDEN
(PRINCIPAL McGEE)

NOSTALGIA FOR the '50s was at an all-time high back in 1972, when off-Broadway first became home to a new musical called *Grease*. The production caught on, in the words of one of its songs, like "Greased Lightning," racking up 3,388 performances before closing in 1980, one of the longest running productions in Broadway history. Even as Robert Stigwood began shooting his Paramount production back in 1977, the road company was playing an appearance in Los Angeles. But there was never a question about who would play the lead—already under contract in a three-picture deal was the star of Stigwood's *Saturday Night Fever* success of the previous year, John Travolta. Ironically, the star had appeared in *Grease* on Broadway prior to his being signed as "Vinnie Barbarino" in "Welcome Back, Kotter."

Selected as Travolta's co-star was popular Australian recording artist Olivia Newton-John in her American film debut (her Aussie accent is never explained in the movie). There was an unusual chemistry between the virginal character of "Sandy," played by Newton-John, and the tough on the outside/soft on the inside, greasy-hood-your-mother-warned-you-about character of "Danny," played by Travolta. Musicals may have been essentially dead in this "special effects" decade, but thanks to these two, *Grease* proved there was still a last gasp left in the genre.

Stockard Channing, who would later star in her own TV show and make numerous guest appearances on others, played "Rizzo," leader of the girl gang "The Pink Ladies." Jeff Conaway, who eventually co-starred on TV's "Taxi," appeared as "Kenickie"; Didi Conn, star of the movie *You Light Up My Life*, played "Frenchie"; and Lorenzo Lamas, later of TV's "Falcon Crest," appeared as "Tom Chisum." There were cameo appearances as well by Frankie Avalon, Eve Arden, Edd "Kookie" Byrnes, Joan Blondell, Sid Caesar, Dody Goodman, and a real

greaser rock group, Sha Na Na (they, too, would get their own TV show).

Most of the box office excitement, however, was generated by the animal magnetism of John Travolta. The man knew his way around a dance floor, disco, gymnasium, or even stadium bleachers, as one of the film's big production numbers would have it. This would be his biggest box office hit; although his next film for Paramount, 1980's *Urban Cowboy*, would earn $23,000,000 in domestic rentals, it couldn't touch the success of either *Saturday Night Fever* or *Grease*.

With 17 musical numbers, *Grease* is one of the most ambitious musicals ever to hit the screen. The soundtrack album became the number-two best-seller with 24,000,000 copies, right behind *Saturday Night Fever* and all those Bee Gees tunes. Two of the songs climbed the charts as singles and made it to the number-one spot—"You're the One That I Want," a duet by Travolta and Newton-John, and Frankie Valli's rendition of the title song. Other memorable tunes, each sung in elaborate production numbers, included "Summer Nights," sung by Travolta and Newton-John; "Look at Me, I'm Sandra Dee," performed by

---

Screenplay by Bronte Woodard

Adaptation by Allan Carr

From the Broadway musical by Jim Jacobs and Warren Casey

Produced by Robert Stigwood and Allan Carr

Directed by Randal Kleiser

CAST

Danny . . . . John Travolta
Sandy . . . . Olivia Newton-John
Rizzo . . . . Stockard Channing
Kenickie . . . . Jeff Conaway
Frenchy . . . . Didi Conn

ACADEMY AWARD NOMINATIONS

1 nomination, no wins

Best Song ("Hopelessly Devoted to You," music and words by John Farrar)

Stockard Channing; "Greased Lightning," done by Travolta and Jeff Conaway; "Beauty School Dropout," a fantasy number by Frankie Avalon; and the finale "We Go Together," again with Travolta and Newton-John.

For the movie, *Grease*'s Broadway score was supplemented by a selection of golden oldies from the '50s, as well as by original songs new to the film. The movie version also differed from the stage version by taking advantage of the possibilities offered by location shooting. Venice High School represented the exteriors of Rydell, with two other local high schools used for the dance contest and the carnival-finale.

"Grease is the word," proclaimed the title song, while reviewers tended towards the word "slick." *Variety* pronounced *Grease* "slick as a ducktail hairdo," commenting: " 'Grease' has got it, from the outstanding animated titles of John Wilson all the way through the rousing finale as John Travolta and Olivia-Newton John ride off into pre-Vietnam era teenage happiness. The Robert Stigwood–Allan Carr production values compliment superbly the broad comedy-drama, zesty choreography and very excellent new plus revived music." *The New York Times* saw *Grease* paying homage to '50s films like *Don't Knock the Rock* and *Rock Around the Clock*, in the manner in which *Close Encounters of the Third Kind* acknowledged a debt to the '50s science fiction "B" films. They, too, termed the film "slick." The title didn't translate too well into other languages, though. In Spanish, the word for "grease" is "grasa," which literally means "fat" or "oil," so in Spain the movie was released under the title *Brilliantina/Brilliantine* and in Venezuela as *Vaselina/Vaseline*.

Believe it or not, a non-Travolta sequel was released in 1982. Didi Conn, Eve Arden, Sid Caesar, and Dody Goodman all returned, plus new additions Lorna Luft (daughter of Judy Garland and Sid Luft), Connie Stevens, Maxwell Caulfield, Adrian Zmed, and Tab Hunter. The chemistry didn't work, the tunes weren't catchy, and the film bombed, earning only $6,500,000. Ramalamadingdong.

SUPERMAN
WARNER BROS.
$82,800,000

You will believe a man can fly.
—ADVERTISING COPY
FOR *SUPERMAN*

BACK DURING the Depression, two teenagers named Jerry Siegel and Joe Shuster created a comic book hero that has survived for generations. "Superman" first flew across the pages of comic books back in 1938, and has been brought to the screen, big and small, many times. There was an early animated cartoon, followed by '40s serials with Kirk Alyn donning cape and tights for Saturday afternoon cliffhangers. In the '50s, an acclaimed television series starred George Reeves and broke ground by filming in color as early as 1954, thus assuring it a place even today in syndicated rerun heaven. But in the '70s, with movie technology soaring even higher than the Man of Steel, the time was right to give

Screenplay by Mario Puzo, David Newman, Leslie Newman, and Robert Benton

Story by Mario Puzo

Based on characters created by Jerry Siegel and Joel Shuster

Executive Producer: Ilya Salkind

Produced by Pierre Spengler

Directed by Richard Donner

CAST

Jor-El . . . . Marlon Brando
Lex Luthor . . . . Gene Hackman
Superman/Clark Kent . Christopher Reeve
Otis . . . . Ned Beatty
Perry White . . . . Jackie Cooper
Lois Lane . . . . Margot Kidder

ACADEMY AWARD NOMINATIONS

3 nominations, no wins

Best Sound
Best Original Score (John Williams)
Best Film Editing

Superman received the "Special Achievement Award" for Visual Effects (Les Bowie, Colin Chilvers, Denys Coop, Foy Field, Derek Meddings, and Zoran Perisic)

Superman a big-budget treatment.

First order of business: finding the right man for the job. Faster than you can say "speeding bullet," there were muscled hopefuls auditioning at the Warner Bros. lot. Sly Stallone made no secret of the fact he wanted a big "S" on his chest. Another early contender was Bruce Jenner, Olympic decathlon winner. Athlete, yes . . . actor, no. He kept his day job. Two hundred interviews later, the role was landed by 24-year-old Christopher Reeve (ironically, a name very similar to TV's man from Krypton, although no relation). "We wanted a relative unknown," director Richard Donner told *The New York Times*, "so the public wouldn't think of an established personality pretending he was flying and performing great feats of strength."

The film was budgeted at $25,000,000, but before they finished getting the bugs out (like finding ways to hide the apparatus used in the flying sequences) the cost had escalated to a reported $55,000,000—some claimed even higher. This would make the movie the second most expensive *ever*, right behind 1988's *Rambo III*.

One reason for the huge success was the characterization. Although certainly

a bigger-than-life comic hero, Reeve's Superman was vulnerable, and not just to Kryptonite. When he falls in love with Lois Lane (played by Margot Kidder), there is something very human about it. Superman becomes Everyman for just a moment, and audiences can identify with that. When she dies, he grieves and disobeys his prime directive by interfering with the laws of nature to bring her back to life. Would we do no less if we could? Men identified strongly with a superhero with human flaws, while women sighed at the looks of Chris Reeve, whose smile could melt hearts faster than his heat vision could melt steel. Kids also adored the PG-rated film, making this the perfect box office draw for families, singles, kids, science fiction and fantasy buffs, and just about everyone else looking for an enjoyable time at the movies.

Three sequels have been made to date. Each time Chris Reeve says it's the last, not wishing to become typecast as Superman or his alter ego, Clark Kent. And while he has continued to broaden the scope of his acting career with many other fine film credits, to many he will always be *the* incarnation of Superman.

NATIONAL LAMPOON'S ANIMAL HOUSE

UNIVERSAL
$70,826,000

PART RITES of passage, part slapstick comedy with a touch of "slob humor" tossed in for good measure, *National Lampoon's Animal House* nostalgically harkens back to the year of 1962. This, you may remember, was also the year zeroed in on by George Lucas in *American Graffiti* (1973), but unlike that earlier depiction of tribal rites, *Animal House* pulled very few punches. Food fights, toga parties, sexual hijinks, demolition derbies—this picture had it all. It also had an excellent cast and talented production team, which helped push the movie over the top with the young adult crowd.

Chief party animal was John Belushi, the late actor-comedian who achieved fame on television's popular "Saturday Night Live." Although much of his acting in *Animal House* is limited to grunting or raising eyebrows before letting loose his special brand of humor, it was his name that was the main drawing card. When he crams his

mouth with mashed potatoes, then slaps both bulging cheeks and announces "I'm a zit. Get it?," audiences got it, and loved it, and came back for more. Of Belushi's performance, *Newsweek* said: "John Belushi is the movie's heavy slugger. As the oxlike Blutarsky, a fellow given to crunching beer cans on his brutish forehead, Belushi looks as if he'd just taken the first step up the evolutionary ladder . . . he unleashes his epic appetite on the school's lunch counter, hilariously demonstrating man's genetic link to the industrial vacuum cleaner."

The film's director, John Landis, then only 27 years old, had his finger on the pulse of his equally young audience. He described this kind of comedy to *Newsweek* as "behavioral humor of outrage. It's definitely offensive. It's antagonistic. But it's all in good fun."

As with *American Graffiti*, the cast boasted a long line of future movie and TV stars: Tim Matheson (*1941*), Tom Hulce (*Amadeus*), Karen Allen (*Raiders*

of the Lost Ark), Martha Smith ("Scarecrow and Mrs. King"), and Kevin Bacon (*Footloose*). Donald Sutherland as pothead Professor Jennings was the biggest "name" at the time, although he was given last billing. And as in *American Graffiti*, we are given an epilogue of character destinies, in case we care "what ever became of . . .?" The humor continues right through the credits as we learn that one of the characters, a "Nixon aide, was raped in prison," and that another went on to glory as "a Universal Tour guide—ask for Babs" (the inevitable plug given at the time for the studio's other moneymaker, the Universal Tour).

The movie was co-produced by Ivan Reitman and co-scripted by Harold Ramis. Ramis and Belushi worked together in "Second City," a comedy forerunner to "Saturday Night Live." And six years later, Ramis and Reitman were reunited in *Ghostbusters*, with Reitman directing that picture and Ramis co-starring.

Screenplay by Harold Ramis, Douglas Kenney, and Chris Miller

Produced by Matty Simmons and Ivan Reitman

Directed by John Landis

CAST

John Blutarsky (Bluto)	John Belushi
Eric Stratton (Otter) ..	Tim Matheson
Dean Wormer	John Vernon
Marion Wormer	Verna Bloom
Katy	Karen Allen
Babs Jensen	Martha Smith
Chip Diller	Kevin Bacon
Prof. Jennings	Donald Sutherland
Larry Kroger (Pinto) ..	Thomas Hulce

EVERY WHICH WAY BUT LOOSE
WARNER BROS.
$51,900,000

Screenplay by Jeremy Joe Kronsberg

Produced by Robert Daley

Directed by James Fargo

CAST

Phil Beddoe . . . . Clint Eastwood
Lynn Halsey-Taylor . . . . Sondra Locke
Orville . . . . Geoffrey Lewis
Echo . . . . Beverly D'Angelo
Ma . . . . Ruth Gordon

THERE WAS no doubt about it—we liked our movies light in 1978. There were heavy hitters, to be sure: films like *The Deer Hunter* and *Coming Home* reminded us of the Vietnam War and did well at the Oscars, but not at the box office. What we wanted was *escapism*, and if that meant musicals, fantasy, and "low" humor, so be it.

Every Which Way But Loose, like other popular films of 1978, didn't pick up a single Academy Award nomination. But the statuette wasn't vital to this film's success. What the public wanted was beer, girls, and fist fights, and this movie had all three—with an average of one fight scene every ten minutes. This Warner Bros. release also featured a number of country & western tunes which were fashionable with the latent CB crowd, some of the songs becoming crossover hits on pop or middle-of-the-road radio stations. Charlie Rich's "Behind Closed Doors" and two songs by Mel Tillis set toes tapping in movie theaters across the land. *Every Which Way But Loose* made

money every which way you turned.

There were two main attractions in the feature, one human, one not. Clint Eastwood was the human star, and his pairing with Clyde the Orangutan was the most talked-about human/ape pairing since Ronald Reagan co-starred with a chimp in *Bedtime for Bonzo* (1951). According to *Hollywood Anecdotes*, when Eastwood was elected mayor of Carmel, California, Reagan exclaimed, "Can you imagine that? What makes him think a middle-aged movie actor who's played with a chimp could have a future in politics?"

The movie soon became a favorite target of critics. *Variety* claimed: "This film is way off the mark. If people line up for this one—and they probably will—they'll line up for any Clint Eastwood picture . . . for Eastwood fans, the essential elements are there. Lots of people get beat up." *Newsweek*'s review was as subtle as King Kong: "They say that if a million monkeys sat down at typewriters, one of them would eventually produce 'War and

Peace.' Well, one of them—bearing the name of Jeremy Joe Kronsberg— seems to have written *Every Which Way But Loose*, a Clint Eastwood 'comedy' that could not possibly have been created by human hands. The proof is that the only decent part is played by an orangutan . . . James Fargo directed, every which way but well."

No one else had a fondness for the film either—no one else except the public. Moviegoers enjoyed the chemistry between the bizarre ménage à trois of Clint, Clyde, and Sondra Locke, Clint's love interest in the film and in real life. In 1989, however, that relationship ended, and Sondra Locke brought a palimony suit against Eastwood after the couple had lived together for 13 years. Before separating, however, the pair managed a sequel film, *Any Which Way You Can* (see page 277), and it did surprisingly well, unusual for most sequels. Both pictures are frequently run on television cable channels; for some reason, the sequel appears more often than the original.

JAWS 2
UNIVERSAL
$50,431,964

"Just when you thought it was safe to go back in the water . . ."
—ADVERTISING COPY FOR *JAWS 2*

Summertime and the fish are scarce. What's a hungry shark to do? Why, chow down on Amity, of course, that resort of choice for discriminating great whites. Lots of people too dumb to get out of the water. Mmm, mmm!

You'd think the good folks of Amity would know by now that when Chief Brody (Roy Scheider) blows his whistle, he means business. Unfortunately, not too many people are inclined to listen. And not just people get chomped upon: this shark even takes on boats and helicopters for a second course. Jaws, 2, Amity, 0.

In the summer of '78, just when you thought it was safe to go back to the theater, *Jaws 2* hit the movie screens. Hoping to take a bite out of the box office dollars, this sequel was a mere minnow compared to the original *Jaws* (page 240), but it still managed a solid fifth place for the year, proving there was life in the old fish yet.

Most of the original human stars were not in the movie, nor did director Steven Spielberg return. But Amity was again saved by Roy Scheider, who admitted to *The New York Times* that he was reluctant to return to the role: *"Jaws* is the best damn movie *ever* made. *Jaws 2* is a contractual commitment that I will fulfill as best I can." Rejoining Scheider were Lorraine Gary as his wife, Murray Hamilton as the

nearsighted mayor ("Shark? What shark?"), and Jeffrey Kramer as the deputy.

Bruce, the mechanical shark-trio from the first film, had gone to that great feeding frenzy in the sky, so designer Bob Mattey had a completely redesigned model built at the cost of about $2,250,000. Bruce II had new skin and two new sets of teeth, plus more valves and hoses to increase his repertoire of movements. Fifteen shark operators were required to put the mechanical marvel through its paces, which included lashing its tail from side to side, opening and closing its jaws, moving its fins, and rolling its eyes.

The critics were not impressed, however. Only *The Hollywood Reporter* genuinely seemed to like the movie: "It's a spin-off, not a rip-off. It promises thrills, and it delivers—in abundance.

It's obviously as meticulously produced as its predecessor, right down to the throbbing John Williams score."

Yet *Time* called the film "the work of a computer that has been programmed by the same drones who used to manufacture Universal Pictures' disaster movies," and *Newsweek* complained that "the new shark has no personality—it's just a set of motorized choppers, a buzz saw with fins."

But if the reviewers weren't happy, the audience certainly was, and so were the brass at Universal. Based on the box office success of *Jaws 2*, there were two additional sequels—*Jaws 3-D* (1983; shown on TV and videocassette as *Jaws III*, in normal 2-D) and *Jaws: The Revenge* (1987), the fourth, and so far final, chapter. Or could it be? Just when you thought you were safe from sequels . . .

Screenplay by Carl Gottlieb and
  Howard Sackler

Based on characters created by
  Peter Benchley

Produced by Richard D. Zanuck and
  David Brown

Directed by Jeannot Szwarc

CAST

Brody	Roy Scheider
Ellen Brody	Lorraine Gary
Mayor Vaughn	Murray Hamilton
Peterson	Joseph Mascolo
Hendricks	Jeffrey Kramer

The crew of *Jaws 2* get "Bruce" ready for a shot.

KRAMER VS. KRAMER

COLUMBIA
$59,986,335

"I'd like to know what law is it that says that a woman is a better parent simply by virtue of her sex?"
—DUSTIN HOFFMAN

DIVORCE WAS at an all-time high as the decade of the '70s ended; the decline of the family unit saw more and more single-parent situations become the rule rather than the exception. With courts across the land kept busy in deciding child custody cases, *Kramer vs. Kramer* was the right film at the right time.

For once, Dustin Hoffman did not play another unusual character like a con man, a prisoner, or a super reporter, but a role that many people could relate to: an average hard-working parent, trying to make a success of his career while inadvertently neglecting his family. When his wife leaves him, even the women in the audience sided with Ted Kramer and his plight in trying to raise, then retain custody of, his young son.

Still, the character portrayed by Meryl Streep is by no means a loathsome bitch. She's a troubled woman who belatedly "discovers herself" in that first full decade of women's liberation. While it's true she leaves her home and son, she is an accurate portrait of many confident, self-dependent women. It was the realistic aspects of *Kramer vs. Kramer*, plus the fine performances of two of Hollywood's top actors, that assured this picture a place at the top of the box office.

The film marked the directorial debut of 47-year-old Robert Benton. Benton adapted the screenplay from Avery Corman's novel, and producer Stanley Jaffe planned to have Francois Truffaut handle the directing chores. But Benton balked and insisted that he himself be allowed to direct. Jaffe relented, but it soon became a free-for-all, with Hoffman assisting with rewrites on the script and in the editing, while Streep wrote most of her own dialogue. In between, there were feuds on the set as the two personalities jockeyed for scene dominance. Yet what emerged was an astonishingly coherent film.

Critics overwhelmingly proclaimed it

a smash. *The Hollywood Reporter* wrote: *"Kramer vs. Kramer* may not be what is termed in contemporary usage an 'event' movie. It has no earthquakes, no towering infernos, no colossal meteorites on a collision course with old Manhattan. What this Stanley R. Jaffe production does have is wisdom, insight, compassion, and an extraordinary sensitivity to present-day problems and pain . . . *Kramer vs. Kramer* is not an 'event'—it's an *event.*" *Variety* also praised the "powerhouse drama" as "a perceptive, touching, intelligent film about one of the raw sores of contemporary America, the dissolution of the family unit . . . 'Kramer' is about people, not abstract stereotypes."

Both Dustin Hoffman and Meryl Streep were congratulated by the press for their outstanding performances, and both were duly nominated for, and received, Academy Awards. Ms. Streep chose to enter the Best Supporting Actress category, however, raising an eyebrow or two in Hollywood gossip columns about her motivation.

Screenplay by Robert Benton

Based on the novel by Avery Corman

Produced by Stanley R. Jaffe

Directed by Robert Benton

CAST

Ted Kramer	Dustin Hoffman
Joanna Kramer	Meryl Streep
Margaret Phelps	Jane Alexander
Billy Kramer	Justin Henry
John Shaunessy	Howard Duff

ACADEMY AWARD NOMINATIONS

9 nominations, 5 wins*

*Best Picture
*Best Actor (Dustin Hoffman)
 Best Supporting Actor (Justin Henry)
 Best Supporting Actress (Jane Alexander)
*Best Supporting Actress (Meryl Streep)
*Best Director (Robert Benton)
*Best Screenplay Based on Material from
 Another Medium (Robert Benton)
 Best Cinematography
 Best Film Editing

Many felt she thought she'd have a better chance against the competition, including Jane Alexander, another nominated star from the film. Others argued that the role of Joanna Kramer was not a dominant one, with her actual on-screen appearance very limited (*Variety* called her part "a 'minor' role she manages to make 'major'").

There is no doubt, however, that the Best Picture competition was formidable. *Kramer vs. Kramer* was up against the likes of *All That Jazz, Apocalypse Now, Breaking Away*, and *Norma Rae* (which won the Best Actress award for Sally Field). The New York Film Critics earlier had also given the film their highest award, and proclaimed Dustin Hoffman their choice for Best Actor. And the Hollywood Foreign Press Service, which annually presents the Golden Globe Awards, also selected Hoffman as their choice for Best Actor. At that ceremony, the actor, while noting that he thought awards made more sense when given for lifetime achievement to men like Henry Fonda or Jack Lemmon, nevertheless seemed grateful and quipped, "I'd like to thank divorce."

The most interesting Academy Award nomination, however, went to the youngster who was at the center of it all. Justin Henry was just six years old and a novice actor when he was signed for the part of Billy Kramer. He was selected from a field of over 200 candidates, with Dustin Hoffman helping to make the final selection for the right boy to play his son, even screen-testing with 40 finalists before choosing Justin. The senior actor spent much time coaching the boy for their scenes together. "The first few days his concentration was terrible," said Hoffman, according to *Inside Oscar*. "He kept looking at the camera . . . by the third week, he was becoming an actor." So much so that the Academy nominated him for an Oscar (the youngest person ever to receive that honor).

As the decade of the '70s drew to a close, it left us with the legacy of *Kramer vs. Kramer*. This final Best Picture of the '70s is still timely even today as we enter the '90s and is worth catching on HBO or Showtime, which frequently run this neo-classic.

STAR TREK: THE MOTION PICTURE

PARAMOUNT
$56,000,000

"The Human Adventure Is Just Beginning."
—ADVERTISING COPY, FROM A QUOTE BY GENE RODDENBERRY

"Star Trek Lives!"
—RALLYING CRY OF "TREKKERS"

FOR TEN YEARS there had been a void in the world of "Star Trek" fans, commonly called "Trekkies" (although the fans themselves prefer the designation "Trekkers"). The legendary television program, which ran on NBC from 1966 to 1969, had been unceremoniously cancelled by the network back in '69, even after it had been saved for two seasons by an unprecedented letter-writing campaign. Banished to rerun oblivion, its popularity soared to intergalactic heights during the ensuing years, and the clamor for a

---

Screenplay by Harold Livingston

Based on a story by Alan Dean Foster

Produced by Gene Roddenberry

Directed by Robert Wise

CAST

Captain Kirk	William Shatner
Spock	Leonard Nimoy
Dr. McCoy	DeForest Kelley
Scotty	James Doohan
Sulu	George Takei

ACADEMY AWARD NOMINATIONS

3 nominations, no wins

Best Art Direction-Set Decoration
Best Original Score (Jerry Goldsmith)
Best Visual Effects

---

reunion assaulted the executive offices of the copyright holder, Paramount Pictures, like so many Klingons attacking the Federation.

In 1975, the studio announced a modest film would at last be made, at a budget of $4,000,000. Trekkers were elated. Then Paramount dropped the other spaceboot—a "name" would be sought to sit in Captain Kirk's chair, someone with box office potential, like Robert Redford.

More letters, and intervention from the show's creator, Gene Roddenberry, saved the starship Enterprise once again, and the original cast was signed. By now Trekkers knew the roll call: William Shatner (Captain James T. Kirk); Leonard Nimoy (Mr. Spock); DeForest Kelley (Dr. Leonard "Bones" McCoy); James Doohan (Lt. Commander Montgomery "Scotty" Scott); Nichelle Nichols (Lt. Uhura); George Takei (Lt. Sulu); and Walter Koenig (Lt. Chekov).

Work began on a script, but over the next four years, the format shifted with regularity between the big and little screen, as the studio heads tried to find the proper format for what was, after all, *only* a TV series. New series were planned, then abruptly scrapped; films were on drawing boards only to be abandoned. Eventually, convinced that a science fiction film *could* be successful after witnessing what should have been *Star Trek*'s audience marching to the beat of the *Star Wars* drummer, the studio gave the go-ahead to producer Roddenberry. Robert Wise was signed as director, and the budget was upped to $15,000,000.

Astronomical problems arose during production. There were constant script revisions*; there were special effects promised but not delivered by the originally contracted firm, Robert Abel and Associates, at a loss of $5,000,000 (Doug Trumbull, the wiz behind *2001*, was pressed into last-minute service). With deadlines approaching, editing became a nightmare, some editors even bringing sleeping bags to the studio so round-the-clock shifts could get the film to its exhibitors by the promised delivery date. Costs escalated, with the final price tag reaching $44,000,000, nearly three times the original budget.

For all the *Star Trek: The Motion Picture*-bashing engaged in as new films in the series emerge (last count: five), in reality, the first one was the most successful. Only two *Trek* movies have made it into the top five: *Star Trek: The Motion Picture* (number two for 1979), and *Star Trek IV: The Voyage Home* (number five for 1986). The latter film made only $820,000 more in domestic rentals than the first movie; with inflation and higher ticket costs taken into account, the most financially successful of the five films in the series remains *Star Trek: The Motion Picture*.

The original release ran 132 minutes and omitted some expository footage; subsequent releases and TV runs have added an additional ten minutes, much to the delight of Trekkers.

---

*The script was the brainchild of Gene Roddenberry, based on his original story, "Robot's Return," which in turn became the basis for credited writer Alan Dean Foster's story. The final script, however, was basically a committee effort, and Roddenberry eventually decided to let others take the credit for it.

THE JERK

UNIVERSAL
$42,989,656

1979

"I was born a poor black child."
—STEVE MARTIN
(NAVIN JOHNSON)

STEVE MARTIN was a former TV writer who moved on to a successful career as stand-up comic and television performer. During the '70s, he had garnered a loyal following, and it was his fans' support he was counting on when he co-scripted *The Jerk* with Carl Gottlieb and Michael Elias. His admirers weren't disappointed. Although the film has a lot of vulgar language and was rated "R," it still did surprisingly well, proving that under-17s are a

Screenplay by Steve Martin, Carl Gottlieb, and Michael Elias

Based on a story by Steve Martin and Carl Gottlieb

Produced by David V. Picker and William E. McEuen

Directed by Carl Reiner

CAST

Navin Johnson . . . . Steve Martin
Marie . . . . Bernadette Peters
Patty Bernstein . . . . . . Catlin Adams
Mother . . . . Mabel King
Harry Hartounian . . . . . Jackie Mason

resourceful group who can easily find a way around the MPAA's rating system.

The character Martin creates in this picture, a white goofus who discovers he's not the natural child of black parents and sets out to seek his fortune, offers a plum role for the talented actor-comedian. He plays the lovable but unlikely moron to the hilt. Sight gags, puns, even tongue twisters—everything is fair game for this Jerry Lewis-like oddball character. He is ably assisted by Bernadette Peters, who plays the perfect straight woman to Martin's character. Typical dialogue:

MARIE
I'm a cosmetologist.

NAVIN
It must be tough to handle weightlessness.

Naturally, the two become romantically involved, leading to more funny dialogue. For example, after making love, he announces: "I slit the sheet. The sheet I slit. And on the slitted sheet I sit . . . I've never been relaxed enough around anyone to be able to say that."

Some of the best sequences in this Carl Reiner–directed movie are the spoofs of other hit pictures, among them *2001: A Space Odyssey, The Exorcist,* and *Saturday Night Fever.* Reiner also makes a cameo appearance

as a director. Martin himself makes an appearance in another role—that of "Pig Eye Johnson," the man who juggles cats (don't worry, they're not real, despite the convincing sound effects).

Reviews were mixed, and some papers, like *The Hollywood Reporter,* were downright hostile: "Going the full distance on a feature film is clearly beyond [Steve Martin], and he receives precious little help from Carl Reiner's flat, head-on direction. . . . there are all those Steve Martin fans who turned [his book] 'Cruel Shoes' into a best-seller and his record albums into pure Platinum; they may also rally to the support of his movie. But I doubt it. Any picture that calls itself 'The Jerk' deserves what it gets."

What it got was a heaping helping of box office gold, dispelling this critic's gloomy predictions. *Newsweek* was somewhat more favorable, remarking that "if Martin ever finds the proper vehicle, he could become a first-rate screen comedian. 'The Jerk' is a promising warm-up."

Martin and Peters re-teamed in 1981 for *Pennies from Heaven,* and although the movie was not a box office blockbuster, each performer has since gone on to enjoy separate, highly successful careers in film, TV, and theater. *The Jerk* had the last laugh after all.

④ ROCKY II
UNITED ARTISTS
$42,169,387

"I'm officially retired now."
—"ROCKY BALBOA"

WANNA MAKE a bet? Rocky Balboa, that hunk of a punching machine we all cheered to victory in 1976's number-one film and Best Picture, *Rocky* (hereinafter known as *Rocky I*), began this sequel with the above announcement. It didn't take much intelligence or guesswork to realize that there was still an hour and fifty-nine or so minutes of movie to fill, and that *something* was going to happen up there on the screen.

Of course, that something was part of what was now the standard *Rocky* formula: the Champ has sworn off boxing with a "never again" promise; he's coerced into "just this one last fight"; his challenger is a cross between Superman and a 20-megaton bomb; he trains his brains out; he fights an excruciating and nearly deadly fight, and—cue the Oscar-winning "Gonna Fly Now" music—it's a miracle! "This is the greatest day in the history of my life!" exclaims the re-crowned human punching bag as he staggers to his feet and waves his arms in the air, victorious yet again.

Not a film filled with surprises. Yet audiences adored this boxing wonder, created, acted, written, and directed by

Sylvester Stallone. If *Rocky I* had taken Hollywood and the world-at-large by storm, then at first it would seem that *Rocky II* took it by drizzle. No trumpets, no Oscars (not even one nomination) for the previously acclaimed hero, making this even more of an underdog. But audiences *love* an underdog, with both film and hero proving there was plenty of life left in old Rocky yet.

Joining Sly Stallone again were Talia Shire as his devoted wife and Burgess Meredith as his devoted trainer. His devoted opponent, "Apollo Creed," was also back for more punishment at the fists of Rocky Balboa. As *The New York Times* commented: "Though the Count de Sade gets no screen credit, it must have been he who refereed both fights;

anybody else would have stopped the first, and there wouldn't have been a sequel."

Stallone attributes the realism to diligent research. "I studied a lot of fight films and borrowed ideas for *Rocky*," he told *The New York Times*. "Real fights, I mean—Marcel Cerdan, Rocky Marciano, Joe Louis, Rocky Graziano . . . Muhammad Ali." The creator of a legend added, "I like Rocky. [He's] a nice guy. Not smart. I see him with a man's body and the mind of a 15-year-old . . . he relates to people. I hope audiences still can relate to him."

Time's reviewer had difficulty finding anything to relate to. "There might have been fun in *Rocky II*," he wrote, "but not with Stallone serving as writer and director." The critic added: "The movie's obligatory set piece, a reprise of Rocky's triumphal jog up the steps of the Philadelphia Museum of Art, now looks like a tableau out of Cecil B. DeMille . . . one almost expects him to wrap himself in the flag; perhaps he is saving that *piece de resistance* for *Rocky III*."

Whether the *Time* reviewer was psychic or Stallone took a cue from this scathing review is not known, but two sequels later, in *Rocky IV* (1985), that's *exactly* what the fighter did.

Screenplay by Sylvester Stallone

Produced by Irwin Winkler and Robert Chartoff

Directed by Sylvester Stallone

CAST

Rocky Balboa . . . . Sylvester Stallone
Adrian . . . . Talia Shire
Paulie . . . . Burt Young
Apollo Creed . . . . Carl Weathers
Mickey . . . . Burgess Meredith

ALIEN
20TH CENTURY-FOX
$40,300,000

PURPORTEDLY a story about deep space and a group of seven astronauts—five men and two women—working on a battered commercial space-tug, *Alien* was actually a basic "gotcha!" suspense/terror film, more closely aligned to *Psycho* or *Jaws* than to classic science-fiction films like *2001* or *Star Trek*. The first patrons of this summer release entered the theaters unaware of what to expect; they left in a shaken state, nervously watching every dark shadow, every flutter of a leaf, checking their cars carefully before entering the unknown void of their dark interiors to begin the uncertain drive home.

The film tapped into our deepest nightmares of "something" hiding down the dark, unseen corridors of our minds, lurking there from our childhood. Scary—that was the word most used to describe *Alien*. People screamed, and returned to theaters to scream again. *Variety* sized up the movie's potential instantly, proclaiming: "Another hot summer at the Fox-office."*

Even more interesting than the film's suspenseful plot about an alien "monster" intent on using human bodies as hosts for its next generation, was the fact that the film gave birth to the next generation of movie makers, important names we'd be hearing from in the next decade or two. Although only given

second billing, the most successful person aboard the space-tug *Nostromo* would also be the most successful actor in the cast.

Sigourney Weaver ("Ripley") had only one other film to her credit (a minor role in 1977's *Annie Hall*) when she was signed to co-star in *Alien*. She has continued her promising career with such '80s hits as *Ghostbusters* (1984); *Aliens* (the 1986 pluralized sequel to *Alien*); *Working Girl* (1988); *Gorillas in the Mist* (1988); and *Ghostbusters II* (1989). Along the way, she has picked up several Academy Award nominations, including one for *Aliens* (1986).

The other star to emerge from *Alien* was a man well-known to his native British audiences, although only vaguely familiar to Americans—mostly aficionados of Public Television. John Hurt, who plays Kane, the *Nostromo*'s executive officer, has received many accolades, including the British "Best TV Actor of the Year" Award for his 1975 performance as Quentin Crisp in *The Naked Civil Servant*, and critical acclaim for his portrayal of Caligula in

the PBS series *I, Claudius*. But his most well-known performance to date has been the lead in the 1980 film *The Elephant Man*, for which Hurt received an Oscar nomination.

The film is also noteworthy for its visual effects, which grabbed the second Oscar for Carlo Rambaldi (his first had been for *King Kong*). Rambaldi had worked on Spielberg's *Close Encounters of the Third Kind*, and his name would soon become a household word with the 1982 hit, *E. T. The Extra-Terrestrial*.

So effective were *Alien*'s mechanical and puppet effects that the film's director of photography, Derek Vanlint, became nauseous during "dailies" (viewing of previous day's footage) showing the "birth" sequence, and had to leave the projection room. He spent the rest of the shoot trying to live that moment down.

---

*While the picture cost a mere $11,000,000 to produce, the advertising campaign totalled a whopping $16,000,000—more than the film itself—and it took nearly a year for *Alien* to turn a profit.

Screenplay by Dan O'Bannon

Executive Producer: Ronald Shusett

Produced by Gordon Carroll, David Giler, and Walter Hill

Directed by Ridley Scott

CAST

Dallas . . . . Tom Skerritt
Ripley . . . . Sigourney Weaver
Lambert . . . . Veronica Cartwright
Brett . . . . Harry Dean Stanton
Kane . . . . John Hurt

ACADEMY AWARD NOMINATIONS

2 nominations, 1 win

Best Art Direction-Set Decoration
*Best Visual Effects

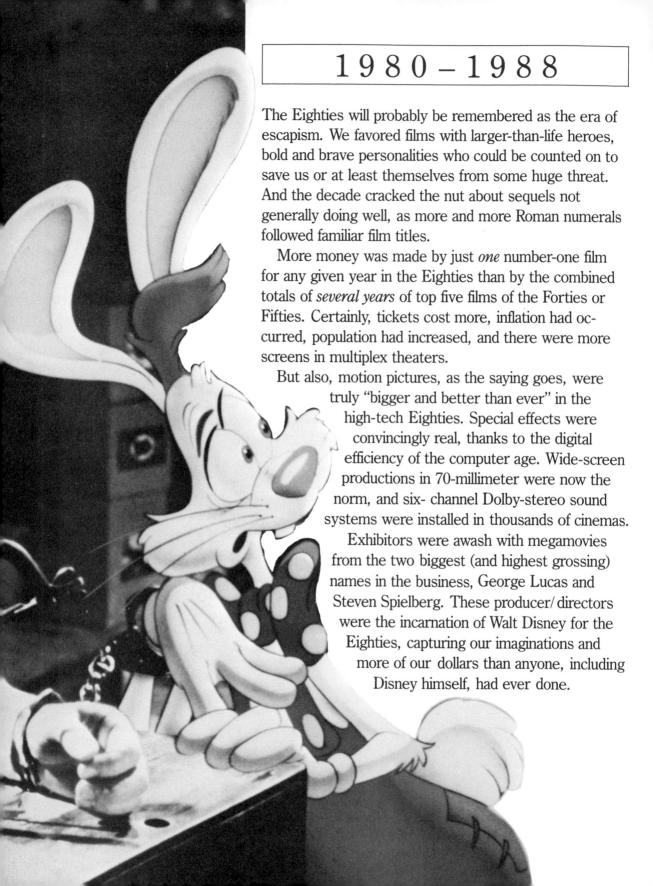

1980 – 1988

The Eighties will probably be remembered as the era of escapism. We favored films with larger-than-life heroes, bold and brave personalities who could be counted on to save us or at least themselves from some huge threat. And the decade cracked the nut about sequels not generally doing well, as more and more Roman numerals followed familiar film titles.

More money was made by just *one* number-one film for any given year in the Eighties than by the combined totals of *several years* of top five films of the Forties or Fifties. Certainly, tickets cost more, inflation had occurred, population had increased, and there were more screens in multiplex theaters.

But also, motion pictures, as the saying goes, were truly "bigger and better than ever" in the high-tech Eighties. Special effects were convincingly real, thanks to the digital efficiency of the computer age. Wide-screen productions in 70-millimeter were now the norm, and six- channel Dolby-stereo sound systems were installed in thousands of cinemas.

Exhibitors were awash with megamovies from the two biggest (and highest grossing) names in the business, George Lucas and Steven Spielberg. These producer/directors were the incarnation of Walt Disney for the Eighties, capturing our imaginations and more of our dollars than anyone, including Disney himself, had ever done.

Forget the old "line around the block" cliché—the mere whisper of the name "Spielberg" or "Lucas" was enough to send scores of sleeping-bag-toting fans down to makeshift campsites in front of box offices as early as two days before the picture ever opened.

At the beginning of the decade, a new invention was poised to turn the movie business upside down. Called the videocassette recorder, or VCR for short, it revolutionized the industry by bringing the theater into our homes. But rather than hurt business, the VCR seemed to make no difference whatsoever to exhibitors whose patrons wanted to see these "events" on the big screen first.

Initially, only a small minority of die-hard movie buffs owned these new gadgets, which frequently cost upwards of $1,000. In 1980, 1 percent of all households had a VCR, but by 1989, the demand for these wonders pushed prices down to under $200, and the ownership figure had jumped to more than 60 percent. In the long run, this meant huge profits for film studios, whose coffers were further swollen with royalties for videocassette sales. Actors, directors, writers, and other filmmakers threw picket lines around studios demanding their fair share of these profits, and strikes occasionally beset the film industry as this situation sorted itself out. In the end, everyone was happy: filmgoers, cassette buyers, talent, and studio executives. The Eighties were Hollywood's most successful decade ever.

THE EMPIRE STRIKES BACK

20TH CENTURY-FOX
$141,600,000

"EPISODE V
THE EMPIRE STRIKES BACK
*It is a dark time for the
Rebellion . . .*"

THUS BEGINS another chapter in
George Lucas' own private Saturday
matinee, the one he was kind enough
to invite us all to attend with him.
"Episode V" was actually only the
second look at our friends from *Star
Wars* in this first of a promised multitude of sequels from that number-one
box office hit. And while it didn't
surpass its predecessor financially,
many thought it equal to or better than
the original in content.

All the Star Warriors were back, of
course—Luke Skywalker, his evil
nemesis Darth Vader, Princess Leia
and Han Solo (whose romance begins
to emerge in this film), Chewbacca the
Wookie, Droids R2D2 and C3PO, plus
some new additions to the gallery of
space people. Most innovative was the
centuries-old Jedi knight and Luke's
reluctant trainer, Yoda. He's sort of a
cross between Walter Cronkite and
Peter Lorre, with a touch of Burgess
Meredith's "Mickey" to "Rocky" counterpart Luke, with his "What am I
going to do with this kid?" attitude (a
formula that would later become the
basis of three *Karate Kid* pictures).
Urged on by a disembodied Obi-Won
Kenobi (Alec Guinness), Yoda (performed by Muppeteer Frank Oz) is the
closest thing to a philosopher we'll ever
find in a science fiction movie, and he
gets the best lines in the film:

LUKE
(observing Yoda levitate his ship)
I don't believe it!

YODA
That is why you fail.

Later, he exhorts Luke to "Try not!
Do! Or do not. There is no *try*."
Definitely words of wisdom for anyone,
not necessarily a Jedi-in-training. We
learn more about the mysterious
"Force" that was with us in that first
film: "Life creates it and makes it
grow," the elfin Yoda explains, "its
energy surrounds us and binds us."
And Yoda's urging Luke to "feel the

flow, feel the Force around you" had
mystics and ministers alike busily ana-
lyzing the religious overtones inherent
in this central philosophy.

Another welcome addition to the cast
was the first black character* in what
so far had seemed to be an all-white
universe. Near the end of the picture,
we are introduced to Lando Calrissian
(Billy Dee Williams), Cloud City's black
ruler (with an unexplained, vaguely
Armenian-sounding surname), who sets
the movie's denouement into motion.

As in the first film, the action never
stops, as our eyes are constantly
dazzled with optical magic—walking
cameloid tanks (homage to *Lawrence of
Arabia*, say some interpretations), hair-
raising forays through an asteroid field,
plus monsters and creatures of all
sizes. Inventive crew members of the
executive producer's own company, Industrial Light and Magic, devised optical printers capable of combining layer
upon layer of elements to achieve a
nearly three-dimensional image in sequences such as the asteroid-dodging
scene.

Like its predecessor, *The Empire
Strikes Back* was shot at the EMI
Elstree Studios outside of London.
Scenes of the ice planet Hoth were
shot on a real glacier at Finse, Norway,
where Scott trained for his expedition
to the South Pole.

The hugely successful film was not
financed by 20th Century-Fox, but only
released through that distributor. Although the studio had supplied the
$11,000,000 needed to film *Star Wars*,
for *Empire* George Lucas put up
$18,000,000 of his own money while
retaining all worldwide rights to the
property for his company, Lucasfilm.
This risk caused him to be temporarily
overextended and although he received
much criticism from well-meaning
friends, the producer eventually made
it all back, plus. The Force was certainly with him as, fortunately for us,
George Lucas struck back.

---

*The only other regular black cast member
was James Earl Jones, the unseen provider
of the voice of Darth Vader (Vader was
played by English actor David Prowse).

Screenplay by Leigh Brackett and
Lawrence Kasdan

Based on a story by George Lucas

Executive Producer: George Lucas

Produced by Gary Kurtz

Directed by Irvin Kershner

CAST

Luke Skywalker . . . . . . Mark Hamill
Han Solo . . . . Harrison Ford
Princess Leia . . . . Carrie Fisher
Darth Vader . . . . David Prowse
Yoda . . . . Frank Oz
Lando Calrissian . . . . . Billy Dee Williams
Obi-Won (Ben) Kenobi . Alec Guinness

ACADEMY AWARD NOMINATIONS

3 nominations, 1 win*

Best Art Direction-Set Decoration
*Best Sound
Best Original Score (John Williams)

With no other nominees in the category,
The Empire Strikes Back was given the
Academy's Special Achievement Award for
Visual Effects (Brian Johnson, Richard
Edlund, Dennis Muren, and Bruce
Nicholson)

9 TO 5

20TH CENTURY-FOX
$59,100,000

WOMEN'S LIB had been with us for nearly a decade when *9 to 5* appeared on the scene. It was the perfect film for the '80s, which saw women in every aspect of the work force. Here was a film with three female leads, like that box office hit of the '50s, *How to Marry a Millionaire*. But unlike that earlier movie, *9 to 5* was aimed not at an audience of leering and gawking males, but at today's working woman. And women all over the country could certainly relate to this trio and their male chauvinist boss.

The three actresses were especially convincing as secretaries, although Dolly Parton, receiving only third billing, outshone her other two co-stars, since she seemed the most natural of the bunch. This was her first movie appearance, and *Newsweek* called her "a sweet and easy comic presence, a natural actress." The country-and-western singer wrote the title song as well, and it climbed the *Billboard* charts to reach number one by February, only two months after the picture's release. The singer also picked up an Oscar nomination for Best Song.

Jane Fonda and Lily Tomlin played the other two secretaries with whom audiences identified. The picture was produced solely by Jane's production company, IPC, but she certainly didn't select the best role for herself. Although she received top billing, she was relegated to playing straight-

woman. Lily Tomlin shines in her part, and has the film's best fantasy sequence. Dressed in "Snow White" costume and wig, surrounded by a Disney gallery of adorable bunnies and bluebirds chirping their hearts out, Tomlin chirps gaily back at the critters in this hilarious send-up of *Snow White*, *Song of the South*, and *Bambi*.

Cast as their male chauvinist pig of a boss with no redeeming traits whatsoever, Dabney Coleman excels in playing this cardboard-cutout role. During the years that followed, Coleman has

---

Screenplay by Colin Higgins and Patricia Resnick

Based on a story by Patricia Resnick

Produced by Bruce Gilbert

Directed by Colin Higgins

CAST

Judy Bernly	Jane Fonda
Violet Newstead	Lily Tomlin
Doralee Rhodes	Dolly Parton
Franklin Hart, Jr.	Dabney Coleman
Tinsworthy	Sterling Hayden

ACADEMY AWARD NOMINATIONS

1 nomination, no wins

Best Original Song ("9 to 5," music and words by Dolly Parton)

---

played similar characters many times; his own TV show, "Buffalo Bill," had him portraying a sleazy type.

Was the film realistic in its depiction of life at the office? An article which appeared in *The New York Times* two weeks after the film's release noted that "a secretary must be a waitress who serves coffee and snacks to the boss; a personal shopper who buys birthday presents for the wife; a nurse, who administers his eyedrops; a maid, who tends plants and dusts . . . 'We were brought up to do these things,' [an interviewed secretary] said, 'and I guess it seemed a natural extension to do them in the office. But today many more women are demanding to be treated as full-fledged human beings. The movie reflects this.' "

However, the film drew in more than just harassed office workers. No boss could ever be the complete ass depicted by Coleman, so no boss ever recognized himself in that caricature. This gave the picture its wide appeal, and gave Fox the number-two box office hit of the year.

In March, 1982, "9 to 5" debuted as an ABC television series. Dolly Parton's sister Rachel Dennison co-starred with Rita Moreno and Valerie Curtin; Jane Fonda co-produced. The show was cancelled by ABC in October, 1983, but was later resurrected for syndication with James Komack producing and Sally Struthers as one of the stars.

STIR CRAZY
COLUMBIA
$58,364,420

"One hundred and twenty five years?! I'll be one hundred and sixty-nine when I get out!"
—RICHARD PRYOR

WILDER WAS BACK, and Pryor got him for the second pairing of this "odd couple." Unlike their earlier duet, *Silver Streak*, there were few other characters to get in their way; the screen was all theirs, as was most of this picture, turned over to the twosome's ad-libs by actor-turned-director Sidney Poitier. What emerged was a semi-funny, semi-serious film that seemed to lose its sense of direction and the love of critics along the way, but never the pair's loyal fans. Wilder and Pryor together were demographically appealing, making for box office dollars and placing the Columbia picture strongly among the year's top five. As *Time* Magazine put it: "Recipe for a popular movie: take a series of stock situations, two gifted farceurs, and stir. Crazy!"

The recipe worked. And it didn't hurt that there were some other clichés folded in, like a barroom brawl, a corrupt prison system and warden, the "great" escape, and that favorite gag when all else fails: two grown men in chicken suits. This, more than any of the other gimmicks, did the most to sell the film. Everywhere you looked that Christmas, there were ads and TV promos for *Stir Crazy* with Wilder and Pryor dressed in feathery regalia. For some reason, people found this irresistible and (pardon the pun) flocked to the theaters.

Although audiences enjoyed the tried-but-true formula, *The Hollywood*

Reporter found it tough to swallow: "Although Gene Wilder and Richard Pryor again demonstrate that they make excellent foils for each other . . . it's difficult to avoid the feeling that its Bruce Jay Friedman script . . . should either have been shot straight or not at all. . . . But Pryor, even when working with minimal comic material, manages to give the film liveliness and color."

Pryor seemed to catch the attention of more than one critic. While *Variety* termed the film "saleable," most of the credit also went to Pryor: "His pained look into the camera when he's sentenced to jail, his hopeless reactions to Wilder's eccentricities and his overall stance as the famed fool make a flimsy

feature like 'Stir Crazy' worth seeing. To quote an often used line, 'that takes talent.' "

In 1985, a television series was assayed based on the movie, but like many other attempts at translating films into TV shows, it was short-lived.

Wilder and Pryor were reunited again in 1989 for another on-screen romp in the movie *See No Evil, Hear No Evil*. The comedy received rave reviews from "The Today Show"'s supercritic, Gene Shalit, who exclaimed, "You could die laughing." Not many people did, however, and the film failed to become a blockbuster. Like the other Wilder/Pryor pictures, this one is now available on video.

Screenplay by Bruce Jay Friedman

Produced by Hannah Weinstein

Directed by Sidney Poitier

CAST

Skip Donahue	Gene Wilder
Harry Monroe . . .	Richard Pryor
Rory Schultebrand	Georg Stanford Brown
Meredith	Jobeth Williams
Deputy Ward Wilson	Craig T. Nelson

4

AIRPLANE!
PARAMOUNT
$40,610,000

"Thank God it's only a motion picture!" —ADVERTISING COPY FOR *AIRPLANE!*

AMONG THE films parodied by this zany send-up to end all send-ups were *Airport*, the *Airport* sequels, *Jaws*, *From Here to Eternity*, and *Saturday Night Fever*. In many ways, *Airplane!* seems like an hour-and-a-half-long "Saturday Night Live" sketch, with the nonstop puns, satire, and looniness never abating.

Back in 1976, Paramount Pictures made their first attempt at satirizing the wave of disaster films popping up all over movie screens in the '70s. The picture was called *The Big Bus*, but it was a big *bust* instead. It involved a sort of "superbus," but audiences generally preferred their disasters and disaster take-offs to, well, take off.

The film opens with John Williams' driving *Jaws* theme as a plane's tailfin bisects a cloudbank. This is going to be fun, promises Paramount, and the studio keeps its word. Like the disaster-genre films it parodies, *Airplane!* has an all-star cast, including basketball great Kareem Abdul-Jabbar as a co-pilot, Lloyd Bridges as the troubled troubleshooter, Peter Graves as Captain Oveur, Robert Hays as the former pilot who turns fear of flying into an art form (and of course saves the day), Julie Hagerty as his girlfriend-cum-stewardess, plus a dozen or so television stars like Leslie Nielsen, Robert Stack, Barbara Billingsley (from "Leave it to Beaver"), Jimmie Walker ("Good Times"), and Jill Whelan ("The Love Boat").

But that's not all, folks! Ethel Mer-

Screenplay by Jim Abrahams, David Zucker, and Jerry Zucker

Produced and directed by Jim Abrahams, David Zucker, and Jerry Zucker

CAST

Ted Striker	Robert Hays
Elaine	Julie Hagerty
Murdock	Kareem Abdul-Jabbar
McCroskey	Lloyd Bridges
Captain Oveur	Peter Graves
Dr. Rumack	Leslie Nielsen

man plays a *man*—a shell-shocked soldier who's deluded into believing he's Ethel Merman. David Leisure ("Joe Isuzu" and co-star of "Empty Nest") can be seen in an early role as the shaven-head Hare Krishna passenger. And then there's the late Howard Jarvis, author of California's Proposition 13 (a property tax-reform bill), playing a passenger stuck in a taxicab throughout the whole picture! If you watch closely, you'll catch the film's writer-exec producers Jim Abrahams, David Zucker, and Jerry Zucker as Religious Zealot #6, Ground Crewman #2, and Ground Crewman #1, respectively.

Airplane! was based on a '50s Paramount drama called *Zero Hour*, in which the pilot and co-pilot of an

airliner are stricken by food poisoning, and one of the passengers, a former fighter pilot who blames himself for the deaths of several of his comrades, assumes command and is "talked" down. Combine this thread of a plot with your basic *Airport* picture, and voilà: a surefire comedy hit.

Two years later, Paramount was back with a sequel, *Airplane II: The Sequel*. It starred William Shatner plus returnees Robert Hays, Julie Hagerty, Peter Graves, and Lloyd Bridges, with cameos by Raymond Burr, Chuck Connors, and Sonny Bono. It wasn't as successful as the original *Airplane!*, but is still quite funny. Both movies appear frequently on TV, and are also available for rental on videocassette.

ANY WHICH WAY YOU CAN

WARNER BROS.
$40,500,000

CLINT EASTWOOD has managed to make a career out of playing three basic characters: the loner cowboy of the *Fistful of Dollars* films, "Dirty Harry" from the series of films about that self-styled vigilante, and "Philo Beddoe," the easy-going westerner who has orangutan, will travel. His second appearance in the *Every Which Way/Any Which Way* saga saw him reunited with his pal Clyde (*Time* immediately dubbed the film *Philo and Clyde*) and significant other Sondra Locke.

Fistfights are one of the main elements fans have come to expect from any Clint Eastwood movie, and fights aplenty arrive like clockwork, averaging about one every 20 minutes. This time, there are a bunch of neo-Nazi bikers who are the baddies, but of course they get their comeuppance.

North Hollywood's Palomino Club (a real-life country-and-western nightclub) is again the setting for the musical scenes, with plenty of tunes to help produce a soundtrack album from this urban cowboy watering hole. Fats Domino performs "Whiskey Heaven," and the soundtrack is further enhanced by source music like Glen Campbell doing the title song, "Beers to You" sung by Ray Charles and Clint Eastwood, and "Cow Patti" by Jim Stafford.

There's not much of a guest cast, but the late Ruth Gordon does a memorable job as Clint's crotchety old mother who feistily takes on the neo-Nazi bikers. There's also a funny parody of the movie *10*, with Ruth's face superimposed over that of Bo Derek.

The original orangutan who played Clyde was not available for this sequel, so an orang named "Buddha" was substituted. According to an article by Jill Donner in the Writers Guild of America West *Journal* for April, 1989, this ape was so mistreated on the set and at its home compound that the instrument designed to hit the poor creature was named a "Buddha club" after him. Donner writes that the club, still in wide use in the movie and TV industry, can be either a metal pipe disguised in a newspaper wrapper or a basic three-and-a-half foot axe handle.

Clyde/Buddha apparently misbehaved on the set of *Any Which Way* one afternoon, and was "disciplined" on arrival back at his compound. Two weeks after the movie wrapped, Buddha was found dead of a reported cerebral hemorrhage. Whether or not the story of his beating is true, there has been much controversy lately in Hollywood regarding the American Humane Association and its on-set representatives. Hopefully, the animals themselves will be the beneficiaries of all the attention now focused on this aspect of the industry.

Screenplay by Stanford Sherman

Based on characters created by Jeremy Joe Kronsberg

Executive Producer: Robert Daley

Produced by Fritz Manes

Directed by Buddy Van Horn

CAST

Philo Beddoe . . . . Clint Eastwood
Lynne Halsey-Taylor . . . . Sondra Locke
Orville . . . . Geoffrey Lewis
James Beekman . . . . Harry Guardino
Ma . . . . Ruth Gordon

RAIDERS OF THE LOST ARK

PARAMOUNT
$115,598,000

Steven Spielberg and George Lucas: their very names above the title guaranteed (a) a good time at the movies and (b) a huge take at the box office. And that was *separately*. Together, the package ought to come with a warning label, the combination was so explosive. Lucky the studio that had such a pairing. Lucky the audience, too.

Paramount Pictures couldn't have been happier. They would get to release the Lucasfilm production, financed by the successful producer of the two (so far) *Star Wars* epics. The idea for *Raiders* dated back to 1977, when George Lucas was vacationing in Hawaii with Steven Spielberg a week before *Star Wars* opened. "George had gone to Hawaii to get away from what he thought would be a monumental disaster," said Spielberg in a press release at the time. "At dinner one night, when George got the news that the film was a hit the first week, and he was suddenly laughing again, he told me the story of these movies he wanted to make, a series of archeology films. . . . I've always wanted to bring a serial to life that blends Lash LaRue, Spy Smasher, Masked Marvel and Tailspin Tommy with elements from Edgar Rice Burroughs and George's great imagination." Lucas, too, had always wanted to make that kind of serial, but had to put the ideas on the shelf while doing *Star Wars*.

Synchronicity finally happened in 1980, as production on *Raiders* began at EMI Elstree Studios near London, plus on location in France, Tunisia, and Hawaii. Lucas co-wrote the story with Phil Kaufman (who had once written a draft for *Star Trek: The Motion Picture* and later went on to write and direct *The Right Stuff*). At the same time, he sketched out two additional chapters—*Indiana Jones and the Temple of Doom* (1984) and *Indiana Jones and the Last Crusade* (1989). They set the story in 1936 in order to use some true facts about Adolf Hitler, a student of religious doctrine, artifacts, and the occult. The tale centers around the adventures of a larger-than-life archeology professor who spends his summers hunting for artifacts . . . in this case, the mythical Ark of the Covenant,

which, according to Biblical lore and the film's storyline, contains the broken tablets of the Ten Commandments. It was a film worthy of DeMille himself, with exotic locations, lost cities, power-crazed villains, romantic interludes, and brushes with certain death.

Harrison Ford was selected to portray Indiana Jones, popularly called "Indy" (like the 500 car race of the same name). It was Ford's fourth film for George Lucas—*American Graffiti* and the two *Star Wars* pictures preceded this. He became much more of a sex symbol after playing Indy than he did in the role of Han Solo, and has since gone on to play the dashing archaeologist in the film's two sequels. He has also moved on to straight dramatic roles, in films such as *The Mosquito Coast* and *Witness*. But in a recent interview for the Lucasfilm Fan Club newsletter, the actor was quoted as saying, "I think *Raiders of the Lost Ark* was probably the most fun I've had on a film."

Karen Allen played the ballsy "Marion Ravenwood" whom he meets and later beds (not on screen, of course; this is "PG"). Her only other major film credit had been in John Landis' *National Lampoon's Animal House* (see page 261).

The other star of the film is the memorable music score by the top motion picture composer of our time, John Williams. Currently serving as conductor of the Boston Pops Orchestra, the musician has composed scores for more than 50 films, including *The Poseidon Adventure, The Towering Inferno, Earthquake, Jaws, Close Encounters of the Third Kind, Superman,* and the *Star Wars* pictures. Try to hear him conducting his own music in a live performance; it's an experience you'll never forget. Occasionally, you can catch him performing on PBS.

The critics were blown away by *Raiders of the Lost Ark*; there were no dissenters among all the top reviewers. *The Hollywood Reporter* gushed: "If George Lucas were to say that he could make a terrific entertainment out of Chairman Mao's Little Red Book, at this point I'd be inclined to believe him*—this point being just a few hours after seeing his 'Raiders of the Lost Ark.' And if he wanted to bring along Steven Spielberg to direct, I'd believe him even more." Of all that has been written by critics, Roger Ebert, in his *Movie Home Companion*, seems to have captured the film's feeling the best: "*Raiders of the Lost Ark* is an out-of-body experience, a movie of glorious imagination and breakneck speed that grabs you in the first shot, hurtles you through a series of incredible adventures, and deposits you back in reality two hours later—breathless, dizzy, wrung-out, and with a silly grin on your face."

Your friendly local video store will be only too happy to rent you a tape. If you haven't seen it lately, check it out and be prepared to experience the fun all over again.

Screenplay by Lawrence Kasdan

Story by George Lucas and Philip Kaufman

Executive Producers: George Lucas and Howard Kazanjian

Produced by Frank Marshall

Directed by Steven Spielberg

CAST

Indiana Jones . . . . Harrison Ford
Marion . . . . Karen Allen
Dietrich . . . . Wolf Kahler
Belloq . . . . Paul Freeman
Toht . . . . Ronald Lacey

ACADEMY AWARD NOMINATIONS

8 nominations, 4 wins*

  Best Picture
  Best Director (Steven Spielberg)
  Best Cinematography
 *Best Art Direction
 *Best Sound
  Best Original Score (John Williams)
 *Best Film Editing
 *Best Visual Effects

A Special Achievement Award for Sound Effects Editing went to Benjamin P. Burtt, Jr. and Richard L. Anderson.

---

*This was, of course, before Lucas' major misstep, *Howard the Duck*.

SUPERMAN II

WARNER BROS.
$65,100,000

HEROES WERE IN. Luke Skywalker, Indiana Jones, even James Bond had captured our hearts and our imaginations. And ever since 1978, fans of the hit movie *Superman* had been patiently awaiting the promised return of their larger-than-life hero. They were not disappointed. When *Superman II* leaped onto the screen this year, the public again sent the movie soaring to box office heights, and like the first opus, it landed squarely in the number-two position, proving that the Man from Krypton still had plenty of bounce left in him.

There were some returnees, of course. Back again were Gene Hackman as Lex Luthor (given top billing over Chris Reeve's title character), Ned Beatty as the bumbling Otis, Jackie Cooper as Perry White, Margot Kidder as Lois Lane, Marc McClure as Jimmy Olsen (a virtual non-role, considering the importance of the character in the comics and TV series), plus a pack of new villains. Most outstanding among these is Sarah Douglas, who seems born to play evil personified. As Ursa, the dominatrix from Krypton with her two greaser cohorts, she creates one of the most charming villainesses since *101 Dalmatians'* "Cruella De Vil." (The English actress followed her performance in *Superman II* with a fiendish role in the TV movie *V: The Final Battle* and a recurring part on "Falcon Crest" from 1983 to 1985). When the space trio arrives on Earth hell-bent on stirring up trouble, they land in a small town, and are immediately sized up by the locals: "From the look of them, I'd bet $10 they're from Los Angeles," says one. It's campy, and great fun.

But even better, for the romantics in the audiences, this is the film where Superman and Lois finally get it on. He first gives up his super powers and becomes—horror of horrors—mortal. Clark Kent shows us unexpected warmth and vulnerability, a tribute to the fine acting of Reeve, whose charac-

terizations must constantly change for his dual role. One of the reasons for the huge success of this sequel is the chance to see our hero in love. Audiences eagerly returned to the theater to see what had never before happened to the Man of Steel.*

Superman II won not only the heart of Lois Lane, but the support of the critics as well. *Newsweek* proclaimed: "*Superman II* is a success, a stirring sequel to the smash of ['78 and] '79. Whether you will prefer it to the original is like choosing between root beer and Fresca. They're both bubbly, but the flavor is different."

The film credits Richard Lester (*A Hard Day's Night, The Three Musketeers*) as director, but it also includes

footage shot by Richard Donner when he directed *Superman I* back in 1977. At that time, there were plans to do at least two movies, and the crew immediately segued into *Superman II*. (Some of Lester's shots were likewise included in Donner's picture.)

Superman II was actually released worldwide in December, 1980, but it was six months before Warner Bros. released it in the United States, earning a pile of money overseas during the winter months in countries like Australia, South Africa, and Brazil, before allowing the Man of Steel to migrate for the warm North American summer. The reception at the box office proved warm indeed; we'd be seeing more of Superman in years to come.

---

*In the "Superman" TV series, there was an episode in which Superman and Lois get married ("The Wedding of Superman"), but alas, it was only Lois' dream.

Screenplay by Mario Puzo, David Newman, and Leslie Newman

Story by Mario Puzo

Executive Producer: Ilya Salkind

Produced by Pierre Spengler

Directed by Richard Lester

CAST

Lex Luthor	Gene Hackman
Superman/Clark Kent	Christopher Reeve
Otis	Ned Beatty
Perry White	Jackie Cooper
Lois Lane	Margot Kidder

ON GOLDEN POND

UNIVERSAL
$61,174,744

presented Hank with Spence's "lucky" hat, which he then wore as part of his *Golden Pond* wardrobe.

"I'm living on borrowed time as it is," gripes Norman Thayer, Henry Fonda's character, all the while Fonda knowing that he himself was doing just that. But he gave it his all, and in the process gave the performance of his life. The film was released in November, 1981, and the following spring's Academy Awards ceremony saw Oscars going to Katharine Hepburn as Best Actress (now she had a record *four* statuettes) and—at last—to Henry Fonda. At ages 76 and 74, respectively, they were the oldest Best Actor and Actress winners in the Academy's history. For Fonda, the Award was long overdue. But sadly, he was too ill to attend the ceremony, so daughter Jane (herself a nominee, although not the winner) accepted for her ailing dad. Five months later, on August 12, 1982, Henry Fonda passed away.

THERE IS a distinct possibility that today's young generation of filmgoers might have remembered Henry Fonda as "the father of Jane Fonda" had it not been for his final screen performance. The actor had been making movies in Hollywood for 45 years, memorable pictures like *Jesse James, The Grapes of Wrath, Mister Roberts,* and *12 Angry Men.* Yet surprisingly, with over 60 films to his credit, Henry Fonda had never been honored with an Academy Award for Best Actor.*

On the other hand, Katharine Hepburn was one of Hollywood's most honored actresses. In 48 years, she had managed to rack up 12 nominations, more than any other performer, and had already won a record three

Oscars: for *Morning Glory* (1933), *Guess Who's Coming to Dinner* (1967), and *The Lion in Winter* (1968).

Jane Fonda's company had optioned *On Golden Pond,* Ernest Thompson's play about the trauma of facing old age, as a starring vehicle for her father, but also as what would assuredly be her only opportunity to appear together in a film with him. With the Katharine Hepburn/Henry Fonda co-star combination, the company struck pay dirt. Between them, the two venerable performers had a combined 95 years of motion picture acting in 129 films, plus countless stage and television appearances.

On Golden Pond will always be remembered as special for a number of reasons. Surprisingly, Hepburn and Fonda, Sr. had never worked together in all their years in the same industry. She'd made nine films with Spencer Tracy, but had never even met Hank Fonda. The first day on the set, Kate

*In 1980, the Academy presented an Honorary Award to "Henry Fonda, the consummate actor, in recognition of his brilliant accomplishments and enduring contribution to the art of motion pictures."

Screenplay by Ernest Thompson

Based on the play by Ernest Thompson

Produced by Bruce Gilbert

Directed by Mark Rydell

CAST

Ethel Thayer	Katharine Hepburn
Norman Thayer, Jr. ..	Henry Fonda
Chelsea	
Thayer Wayne	Jane Fonda
Billy Ray	Doug McKeon
Bill Ray	Dabney Coleman

ACADEMY AWARD NOMINATIONS

*10 nominations, 3 wins**

  Best Picture
*Best Actor (Henry Fonda)
*Best Actress (Katharine Hepburn)
  Best Supporting Actress (Jane Fonda)
  Best Director (Mark Rydell)
*Best Screenplay Based on Material from
    Another Medium (Ernest Thompson)
  Best Cinematography
  Best Sound
  Best Original Score (Dave Grusin)
  Best Film Editing

ARTHUR
WARNER BROS.
$42,000,000

"Isn't this fun? Don't you wish you were me? I know I do."
—DUDLEY MOORE

At FIVE-FOOT-THREE, puppy-eyed, sheepishly grinning, tousled-haired Dudley Moore is the closest thing to a living teddy bear the screen has ever seen. He could never, for example, play a crazed killer, or a truck driver. And he is certainly an unlikely candidate for a romantic lead. Yet this pint-sized cherub from England has landed some of the screen's choicest roles opposite babes like Bo Derek in Blake Edwards' movie *10*, which catapulted the composer/pianist/comedian/British TV personality into international stardom. In 1981, his second major American film, *Arthur*, saw him playing opposite Liza Minnelli, the gifted singer/actress daughter of Judy Garland and Vincente Minnelli, plus Jill Eikenberry, still basically an unknown, but soon to become a familiar face after co-starring in TV's "L.A. Law."

In *Arthur*, "Cuddly Dudley," as he was dubbed by nearly every female who saw him, plays what could have been the most repulsive of creatures— a sot, a perpetually plastered drunk.

Dudley manages to make alcoholism almost cute. He is bolstered by his faithful retainer, a latter-day "Jeeves" to Arthur's "Bertie"—both P. G. Wodehouse characters of the '30s to whom the film's lead characters bear more than passing resemblance. Jeeves, or in this case "Hobson," is the rock on whom Arthur frequently rests his weary but very wealthy head. Sir John Gielgud was 78 when he played the role of Hobson. His career in show business has spanned 65 years, including recognition by the Motion Picture Academy for his role in *Arthur*, which won him the Oscar for Best Supporting Actor.

Newsweek missed the limousine on this one when its reviewer announced: "*Arthur* is not the best comedy of the season." The fact is that *Arthur* amassed over $42,000,000 in rentals, better than most comedies in several years. There was simple humor, to be sure, like Arthur announcing, "I think I'll take a bath," and Hobson retorting, "I'll alert the media." There was even the old "walk this way" routine, still getting laughs after all these years. Mostly, though, people just came to enjoy the film's star, and to pull for the

poor little rich guy of the film's title.

"Arthur's Theme (The Best That You Can Do)" was also a hit, sung by Christopher Cross. It climbed to the top of the *Billboard* charts by October, 1981, remaining there for three weeks. It was the odds-on favorite for an Oscar, the eighth number-one "rock era" song to win the top prize.

In 1988, the sequel, *Arthur 2: On the Rocks*, attempted to recapture the feeling of the first picture. But the more recent audiences had trouble finding the appeal of a character like Arthur, an overgrown man-child whose alcoholism had still not been properly addressed. If he was cute and funny in the first picture, seven years later he was pathetic and obnoxious. Even Dudley's brilliant performance was not enough to sustain interest in the sequel. With more public awareness of the disease of alcoholism, plus ad campaigns like MADD (Mothers Against Drunk Driving), Nancy Reagan's "Just Say No" program, and the valuable services performed by the Betty Ford Center, the public had had enough of "the hilarious drunk" as central character. The sequel was a huge fiasco.

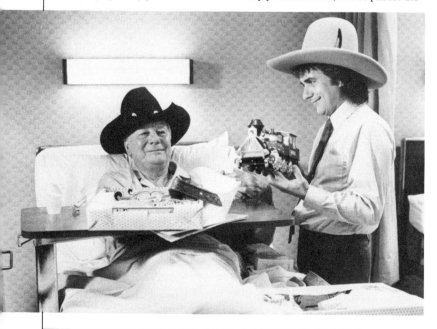

Screenplay by Steve Gordon

Produced by Robert Greenhut

Directed by Steve Gordon

CAST

Arthur Bach	Dudley Moore
Linda Marolla	Liza Minnelli
Hobson	John Gielgud
Martha Bach	Geraldine Fitzgerald
Susan Johnson	Jill Eikenberry

ACADEMY AWARD NOMINATIONS

4 nominations, 2 wins*

Best Actor (Dudley Moore)
*Best Supporting Actor (John Gielgud)
Best Screenplay Written Directly
 for the Screen
*Best Original Song ("Arthur's Theme
 [Best That You Can Do]," music and
 words by Burt Bacharach, Carole Bayer
 Sager, Christopher Cross, and
 Peter Allen)

STRIPES

COLUMBIA
$40,886,589

"An army without leaders is like a foot without a big toe."
—BILL MURRAY

IN 1980, GOLDIE HAWN scored a hit in *Private Benjamin*, the story of a Jewish princess who joins the Army. It barely missed the top five, but with $36,000,000 in rentals, the uproariously funny comedy was a huge success. A year later, actor-comedian Bill Murray became a male counterpart to Hawn's Benjamin with a theme that had been widely pursued over the years, beginning with Charlie Chaplin in *Shoulder Arms* (1918) and continuing through Abbott and Costello in *Buck Privates*, (1941), Bob Hope in *Caught in the Draft* (1941), Danny Kaye in *Up in Arms* (1944), and Jerry Lewis in *At War With the Army* (1951). Completed less than a year after Goldie's movie, *Stripes* had audiences laughing even harder, making this film even more successful at the box office.

Co-produced and directed by Ivan Reitman, who had showcased Murray's talents in his previous film *Meatballs* (1980), *Stripes* was the surprise comedy hit of the summer of '81. Harold Ramis, who had co-written both Reitman's *National Lampoon's Animal House* and *Meatballs*, worked on the script for *Stripes* as well as co-starred in it. (The trio of Reitman-Murray-

Ramis would be at it again in three years for *Ghostbusters*; see page 296.)

Ivan Reitman's m.o. was to give Murray pretty much free rein, since the actor is at his best when working improvisationally. "Directors might think, 'Oh, here comes that wild and wacky guy. I'll just turn on the camera, and he'll do funny things,' " said Reitman in an interview in *Premiere* magazine. "I start from a premise of his being a gifted actor who's right for a part that he plays, and I try to help him as much as I can. I think I have a sense of his range. And I'm always looking for him to do his best, to top himself."

Still, Murray was reluctant to do

Screenplay by Len Blum, Dan Goldberg, and Harold Ramis

Produced by Ivan Reitman and Dan Goldberg

Directed by Ivan Reitman

CAST

John	....	Bill Murray
Russell	....	Harold Ramis
Sgt. Hulka	....	Warren Oates
Louise	....	Sean Young
Ox	....	John Candy
Capt. Stillman	....	John Larroquette

Stripes—he had also felt the same way before he agreed to do *Meatballs*—and Reitman had a hard time convincing him of the movie's potential. At first it was "out of the question," but Reitman enlisted Ramis as a co-star (his first picture), which turned the trick for Murray. "The fact that he put Harold in it was kind of a cheap shot," Murray admitted to *Premiere*. "If I said no, I said no to Harold, to his screen debut."

The Hollywood Reporter's Robert Osborne had mostly pleasant commentary on the movie: "Private Benjamin, make way for Private Winger. Columbia, get set for some tall summer grosses . . . 'Stripes' consistently rolls along with good humor, solid laughs and a tail-wagging air." *Variety* called the picture "The new Army as frat house & summer camp," adding: " 'Stripes' is a cheerful, mildly outrageous and mostly amiable comedy . . . there's little in the way of art or comic subtlety here, but the film really seems to work. . . ."

Watch for appearances by some actors who would go on to success in the '80s: John Larroquette, who became a co-star on TV's "Night Court"; John Candy, who starred on "SCTV" and in many movies; actress Sean Young, who appeared in *Blade Runner*, *Dune*, *No Way Out*, and *Batman*; and Judge Reinhold, who appeared in *Beverly Hills Cop I* and *II*.

E.T. THE EXTRA-TERRESTRIAL

UNIVERSAL
$228,618,939

He is afraid.
He is totally alone.
He is 3,000,000 light
years from home.
—ADVERTISING COPY
FOR *E.T.*

" 'Jaws,' 'Close Encounters of the Third Kind,' 'Raiders of the Lost Ark.' And now, 'E.T. The Extra-Terrestrial.' Steven Spielberg has done it again. He has created another instant American classic."
—THE HOLLYWOOD REPORTER

IF THERE IS a person alive on this planet who has not yet seen or heard of *E.T. The Extra-Terrestrial*, then they are, in a sense, very lucky. Lucky, because they can still experience seeing *E.T.* for the first time. It's like your first taste of ice cream in the summer, the first time you saw the vast ocean, or the first ray of sunshine after a three-day downpour.

Nineteen eighty-two was the summer we went to the movies and fell in love with a creature from another world: a short, squat, huggable, wrinkly little guy that looked like a shell-less, upright turtle, who touched the innocent child on the screen and the one within our hearts. Just about everyone was caught up in the emotional experience, critic and cynic, child and adult alike. Only those with the hardest of hearts could have refused to like the wondrous alien.

The film itself seems almost to have been directed *by* a child, and that is part of the genius of Steven Spielberg. As an adult, he still has one foot in the world of children. That he is gifted when working with children is an understatement: he understands kids even better than that other full-grown child, Walt Disney, had understood them, and his ease in directing them is readily apparent. "Their inexperience allows the honesty to come out," he told *Newsweek.* "They *can't* censor. And I *am* a kid."

So at home is Spielberg in the world of children that the story is told entirely from the story's youngsters' point of view, right down to the low angles suggesting the height of a child. When we do meet adults, they are almost

invariably antagonistic; even Dee Wallace as the mother, while a sympathetic character, isn't in on the erratic behavior of her kids until the end. In fact, the film was banned in Sweden for children under eleven because the censors there felt it showed parents in a poor light.

No problem in America, however, where *E.T.* gave a whole new definition to the term "blockbuster." It wasn't unheard of for people to spend up to two hours waiting patiently in the hot sun for a first (or second or third) chance to catch the on-screen magic. A spate of bumperstickers appeared, urging "E.T. Phone Home!"; Neil Diamond recorded a hit song "Turn on Your Heart Light" (a reference to the glowing red heart of the creature; the song has since become a hit at Diamond's concerts, where audience members turn on pocket flashlights); people named puppies and kittens "E.T."; and Halloween would never be the same, as thousands of junior E.T.'s waddled door-to-door looking for Reese's Pieces (the merchandising tie-in propelled the

---

Screenplay by Melissa Matheson

Produced by Steven Spielberg and Kathleen Kennedy

Directed by Steven Spielberg

CAST

Mary	Dee Wallace
Elliott	Henry Thomas
Kays	Peter Coyote
Michael	Robert MacNaughton
Gertie	Drew Barrymore

ACADEMY AWARD NOMINATIONS

9 nominations, 3 wins*

Best Picture
Best Director (Steven Spielberg)
Best Screenplay Written Directly
  for the Screen
Best Cinematography
Best Sound
*Best Original Score (John Williams)
Best Film Editing
*Best Visual Effects
*Best Sound Effects Editing

---

candy to an 85 percent increase in revenue).

The creature at the center of all this was a mechanical marvel created by Carlo Rambaldi, the Italian puppet-master behind King Kong and the *CE3K* aliens. In addition to Rambaldi's astonishingly realistic electronic puppet, which had a wide range of facial expressions, there were also live-acted E.T.'s, including one by the shortest adult performer in film. At 2'7", Tamara de Treaux, a little person weighing 40 pounds, was one of three actors playing E.T. Tamara, according to *The Guinness Book of Movie Facts and Feats*, is the shortest adult performer in movies. The San Francisco-born actress and singer did what she called her "Daffy Duck waddle" in the scene when the alien toddles up the ramp into its spacecraft. Other actors were Pat Bilson, 2' 10", and a legless schoolboy named Matthew de Merritt, who played the drunk scene while walking on his hands inside an E.T. suit. And the voice of the creature was provided by actress Debra Winger (star of the number-four box office hit of the year, *An Officer and a Gentleman*).

The film was termed "an enchanted fantasy" by *The New York Times* and "an instant American classic" by *The Hollywood Reporter, Variety* proclaimed simply, "*E.T.* equals B.O. [box office]." The latter statement in particular was a prophetic one. Before E.T. was able to phone home and head for his own planet, he managed to haul away enough loot to keep him in Reese's Pieces for the next several millennia. The movie went on to become the number-one box office hit of all time, grossing over $700,000,000 worldwide, with nearly $229,000,000 in domestic rentals (although many are quick to point out that if inflation is taken into account, *Gone With The Wind* is still number-one). In 1988, the video-cassette was released for home video, and it also quickly rocketed to the top; with 15,000,000 units sold, it was the best-selling videocassette in history, returning another $225,000,000 to MCA (parent company of Universal). Their promotional campaign declared "E.T. Home!", and so at long last he was.

TOOTSIE
COLUMBIA
$96,292,736

Ever since he had won an Oscar for *Kramer vs. Kramer*, Dustin Hoffman had been exploring the idea of what it would be like to be a member of the opposite gender. "The great scripts don't drop out of the sky," the actor told *Time*. "You have to invent them." He kicked the theme of "what is a man/what is a woman?" around for many years, eventually arriving at an early draft of the script to what would be Columbia's biggest hit to that date.

Tootsie began with a script draft by Murray Schisgal, followed by input from seven other writers, including an original script by Don McGuire, rewrites, polishes, and new drafts by Robert Kaufman, Larry Gelbart, Elaine May, Valerie Curtin, Barry Levinson, and Robert Garland. A Writers' Guild arbitration awarded final credit to Larry Gelbart and Murray Schisgal (screenplay) from a story by Don McGuire. But it was pure Dustin Hoffman all the way, with the actor creating the character of Dorothy Michaels from untapped corners of his talented psyche.

Hoffman was the one mainly responsible for the development of Dorothy. Determined to make the character convincing as a woman and not just appear to be another man in drag, Hoffman practiced through a succession of screen tests. In one test Dorothy/Dustin was asked how she felt about

having a baby. "I think it's a little late in the day for that," she said, then suddenly burst into tears. "I felt so terrible I would never have that experience," Hoffman related to *The New York Times*. The father of several children explained, "Nothing like that has ever happened to me. I've been acting for nearly 30 years and I've never had a moment like that before in my life."

It was a great year for films about cross-dressing. While Dustin was proving to audiences that he made a convincing woman, Barbra Streisand portrayed a young man in *Yentl*, while Julie Andrews proved she could do the same in *Victor/Victoria*. But the public's choice was clearly *Tootsie*, at least in terms of box office.

The Academy showered the film with 10 Oscar nominations. Jessica Lange, whose last leading man had been King Kong, welcomed the chance to play opposite Dustin Hoffman, even if he was dressed as a woman for most of their scenes together. The Academy nominated her for two Awards that year—Best Actress, for *Frances*, and Best Supporting Actress, for *Tootsie*, the first time since 1942 that an actress had been nominated in two categories simultaneously. (She won for *Tootsie*.) And Dustin Hoffman was nominated for Best Actor, with his role as Dorothy Michaels rather than the ne'er-do-well

actor Michael Dorsey catching the Academy's, and the public's, eye.

Other noteworthy performances in the movie are Teri Garr as Michael's befuddled girlfriend; Dabney Coleman in his typically lecherous role as the soap opera director; Bill Murray in a rather minor part as Michael's roommate; and Geena Davis as a soap actress, one of her earliest film appearances (both she and Hoffman would be Oscar winners in 1988).

Time knew immediately that *Tootsie* was on a roll, when it noted: "It is not just the best comedy of the year; it is popular art on the way to becoming cultural artifact." And *Newsweek* summed it up quite concisely: "*Tootsie* will make you very happy."

Frequently shown uncut on premium cable channels like Showtime and HBO, *Tootsie* shouldn't be missed.

Screenplay by Larry Gelbart and Murray Schisgal

From a story by Don McGuire and Larry Gelbart

Executive Producer: Charles Evans

Produced and directed by Sydney Pollack

CAST

Dorothy Michaels	Dustin Hoffman
Julie	Jessica Lange
Sandy	Teri Garr
Ron	Dabney Coleman
Les	Charles Durning
Jeff	Bill Murray

ACADEMY AWARD NOMINATIONS

10 nominations, 1 win*

Best Picture
Best Actor (Dustin Hoffman)
*Best Supporting Actress (Jessica Lange)
Best Supporting Actress (Teri Garr)
Best Director (Sydney Pollack)
Best Screenplay Written Directly for the Screen
Best Cinematography
Best Sound
Best Song ("It Might Be You," music by Dave Grusin, words by Alan and Marilyn Bergman)
Best Film Editing

Director Sydney Pollack (left) appears as Dustin Hoffman's high-powered agent.

ROCKY III

UNITED ARTISTS
$66,262,796

J UST WHEN YOU thought it was safe to go back into the boxing ring, along came *Rocky III*, the third outing for irrepressible prize fighter Rocky Balboa, a.k.a. the Italian Stallion a.k.a. Sylvester Stallone. This time, the writer-director-star added a few new twists, like a black opponent named Clubber Lang, menacingly played by Mr. T. (né Lawrence Tero), the mohawk-sporting former bodyguard of Leon Spinks. Burgess Meredith returned as his trainer, but only long enough to do a dying scene (and receive a Jewish funeral—surprising audiences who thought he was supposed to be Irish for two movies). Rocky's former nemesis, Apollo Creed, was now his trainer, guaranteed to turn the champ back into a lean, mean fighting machine.

One of the new additions to the cast was wrestling personality Hulk Hogan, whose career was just beginning to take off in 1982. He is seen here in what is billed as a charity match between Rocky and himself, a must-see for all fans.

Not much is new, however. Stallone slyly stayed with his tried and true formula, the one audiences by now had come to eagerly anticipate. The

Buildup to the Big Fight is the basic plot, yet audiences still delighted in this magic moment, and *Rocky III* made more money than either of its two predecessors (inflation not taken into account). *Newsweek* commented that "just as Sinatra can endlessly reprise 'My Way' and still raise goosebumps, so Stallone can turn out shameless

---

Screenplay by Sylvester Stallone

Produced by Irwin Winkler and
   Robert Chartoff

Directed by Sylvester Stallone

CAST

Rocky Balboa	Sylvester Stallone
Adrian	Talia Shire
Paulie	Burt Young
Apollo Creed	Carl Weathers
Mickey	Burgess Meredith
Clubber Lang	Mr. T

ACADEMY AWARD NOMINATIONS

1 nomination, no wins

Best Song ("Eye of the Tiger," music and
   words by Jim Peterik and Frankie
   Sullivan III)

---

variations on his Believe-in-Yourself miracle play and still get the old adrenaline pumping." *Time* hailed *Rocky III* as "Winner and Still Champion," describing Stallone's character as a "meat-and-potatoes exemplar of the American dream, a working stiff's contender who battles for his dignity against odds that seem overwhelming."

While *Rocky III* was champion at the box office, the new theme song, "Eye of the Tiger," quickly rose to number one on the *Billboard* charts; the recording by the rock group Survivor (who also did the theme for *Rocky IV*) remained champ for a phenomenal six weeks. The Academy thought "Eye of the Tiger" a good contender for Best Song and awarded the song an Oscar.

Sylvester Stallone, like the character he portrayed, announced that *Rocky III* was the last chapter in what he had always thought of as a trilogy. Originally, he had planned to set this final episode of his opus in the Roman Colosseum, with Rocky slugging it out with a Russian opponent. Alas, he settled for Mr. T. But there was still plenty of life left in old Rocky B., as audiences were learning with regularity every three years or so.

To be continued . . .

AN OFFICER AND A GENTLEMAN

PARAMOUNT
$55,223,000

1982

MUCH OF THE SIZZLE of an *Officer and a Gentleman* had to do with the on-screen romance between the two leads, Richard Gere and Debra Winger. This summer movie, which began as a sleeper and emerged as a blockbuster, focuses on sexual attraction, leaving very little to the audience's imagination. While blue-haired ladies gasped at the picture's unabashed eroticism, others in the audience had by now come to accept almost anything as perfectly allowable on screen as long as it enhanced the story—which is what directors had been fighting for lo these many years.

Aside from the hot relationship between Gere and Winger, and the B-story about his Navy buddy, played by David Keith (similarly involved with a local girl), there was a fine performance by Louis Gossett, Jr. as the tough drill instructor whose job it is to turn out officers. *Variety* cited the contribution of one of the screen's finest black actors by noting: " 'Officer' belongs to Louis Gossett Jr . . . [he] takes a near-cliché role of the tough, unrelenting drill instructor and makes him a sympathetic hero without ever softening a whit. Gossett does more with his eyes

and a facial reaction than others can accomplish with pages of dialogue."

The sparks between Gere and Winger flew right off the screen, and the public, which had only recently fallen in love with an extra-terrestrial, immediately took the officer candidate and his ambitious girlfriend into their hearts. Yet it was interesting to watch the critics argue over whether or not this physical attraction worked. *The Hollywood Reporter* proclaimed in no uncertain terms that the picture didn't have what it took: "If Paramount's 'An Officer and a Gentleman' fails as a motion picture (and it does, regrettably), one reason is because it painfully lacks the singular ingredient most necessary to successfully orchestrate a romantic motion picture theme: chemistry between its two principals, Richard Gere and Debra Winger."

Could he have seen the same movie as the critic for *Newsweek*? "These days good love stories are almost as

hard to come by on screen as off. One problem is chemical; some of our young actors and actresses . . . don't know how to strike romantic sparks . . . Debra Winger and Richard Gere know how in 'An Officer and a Gentleman.' When they're on together the screen exudes a palpable sexuality, a bona fide romantic ache. And it's not just two actors the audience is responding to, but the plight of two well-drawn characters."

Obviously, the audience was more in agreement with the latter critique, if they even bothered to read reviews at all. Most went just because it was good escapist summer fare. The theme song from the film, "Up Where We Belong," sung by Joe Cocker and Jennifer Warnes, climbed the pop charts to land up where it belonged, in the number-one spot, holding that position for three weeks. It also won the Oscar for Best Song, and the music was later used by Continental Airlines as their theme song.

Screenplay by Douglas Day Stewart

Produced by Martin Elfand

Directed by Taylor Hackford

CAST

Zack Mayo	Richard Gere
Paula Pokrifki	Debra Winger
Sid Worley	David Keith
Byron Mayo	Robert Loggia
Sgt. Emil Foley	Louis Gossett, Jr.

ACADEMY AWARD NOMINATIONS

6 nominations, 2 wins*

Best Actress (Debra Winger)
*Best Supporting Actor (Louis Gossett, Jr.)
Best Screenplay Written Directly for the Screen
*Best Song ("Up Where We Belong," music by Jack Nitzsche and Buffy Sainte-Marie, words by Will Jennings)
Best Original Score (Jack Nitzsche)
Best Film Editing

PORKY'S
20TH CENTURY-FOX
$54,000,000

W ERE TEENAGERS really sex-crazed in the '50s? The answer supplied by the 20th Century-Fox release *Porky's* seems to be yes, yes, yes. Another in a long line of sexual coming-of-age films, this one caught the public's attention in the spring of '82 (after a pre-release in 1981), a time when young people's fancies seemed likely to turn to thoughts of . . . pictures like this.

As tasteful as *American Graffiti* had been, its imitators, such as *National Lampoon's Animal House* and *Meatballs*, had become progressively raunchier, culminating in this first of several films consisting mainly of one long dirty joke as storyline. Yet the public adored the "R"-rated picture, and word of mouth, plus an advertising campaign depicting leering youths at a peephole in the girls' locker room, propelled this Canadian-made picture to box office success. The movie seemed to be particularly popular among the members of the under-17 set, the impressionable teens the "R" rating was supposed to be protecting—who somehow managed to produce the requisite "parent or guardian."

Critics sharpened their tongues and let fly their barbs with the same carefree abandonment as the high-schoolers on screen. *Variety* lamented: "[*Porky's*] is undoubtedly one of the grossest [films] ever released by a major studio under an R rating. It also boasts a cast larger than 'The Ten Commandments,' and proceeds to break nearly every one of them. Bob Clark's exposé of teenaged tomfoolery so aggressively wallows in bad taste that it nearly transcends it, and commercial prospects are an open question . . . hard to say if gross equals grosses." *The Hollywood Reporter* wrote: "In lieu of originality, scripter-director-co-producer Bob Clark unleashes a virtual wall-to-wall avalanche of four-letter words, and all related synonyms, as well as graphic depictions of everything happening in the groin area . . . everyone at Angel Street [High] is horny, apparently 24 hours a day . . . under Clark's direction and via his scripting, the kids all come off less like good-spirited hell-raisers and more like mental defectives . . . the picture was filmed in Florida and should be an embarrassment to all involved."

Two of those involved, who certainly were not embarrassed, were among the only ones receiving critical approval. Susan Clark and her husband Alex Karras are known to today's TV viewers as the adoptive parents of "Webster," but their roles in this picture were far from parental. Ms. Clark played a backwoods hooker in a short sequence, while her spouse played an exasperated sheriff in another scene. Porky himself was played by Chuck Mitchell, who has continued to appear as the porcine owner of the redneck bawdy house in sequels.

Yes, there were sequels, two at last count. The astonishing success at the box office prompted Fox to follow up with *Porky's II: The Next Day* (1983) and *Porky's Revenge* (1985). About the only thing that had changed was Porky himself, having slimmed down quite a bit. While the teens were as sex-crazed as ever, audiences were not as enthusiastic, and the series appears (mercifully to some) to have run its course.

Screenplay by Bob Clark

Executive Producers: Harold Greenberg and Melvin Simon

Produced by Don Carmody and Bob Clark

Directed by Bob Clark

CAST

Honeywell	. . . .	Kim Cattrall
Brian Schwartz	. . . .	Scott Colomby
Wendy	. . . .	Kaki Hunter
Balbricker	. . . .	Nancy Parsons
Cherry Forever	. . . .	Susan Clark
Sheriff Wallace	. . . .	Alex Karras

RETURN OF THE JEDI

20TH CENTURY-FOX
$168,002,414

Je'di (n) 1: an ancient order of Knights of the Empire 2: a member of that order; a Jedi Knight

Re'turn of the Je'di (n) 1: title of the third movie in the *Star Wars* trilogy 2: the amount of money earned at the box office by that film, as in "The return of *The Jedi* was millions and millions of dollars."

ORIGINALLY, IT WAS to be called *The Revenge of the Jedi.* Paramount Pictures, however, had another film in progress at that time with "revenge" in its title, a sequel to *Star Trek I* with the working title of *Star Trek II: The Revenge of Khan.* Lucasfilm's future with Paramount called for a sequel to *Raiders of the Lost Ark*, while *Star Trek* was considered one of the studio's crown jewels. Each creative team desperately tried persuading the other to switch titles. Eventually, *The Revenge of Khan* became *The Vengeance of Khan*, and finally *The Wrath of Khan*, and since Jedi Knights were supposed to be peace-loving types, it was decided that the word "revenge" was unbecoming a knight anyway, and the Lucasfilm project was redubbed *Return of the Jedi.*

But what's in a name? They could easily have used the deliberately misleading "nom de screen" the crew was given for secrecy purposes—*Blue Harvest*—and it would still have made oodles of money. *Star Wars* fans were a loyal lot, and the business generated at the box office for this summer release was enough to propel the film into hyperspace sooner than you could say "Millenium Falcon." In fact, this second sequel did better than the first (*The Empire Strikes Back*), a rarity in the film industry. In overall box office standings, *E.T.* phones in at number one, *Star Wars* is number two, and *Return of the Jedi* is the number three moneymaker of all time, one ahead of *Empire*, at number four (inflation not taken into account).

It would certainly have helped to have seen one of the films two predecessors. Anyone going to see *Return of the Jedi* "cold" would probably have felt like Alice falling down the rabbit hole to Wonderland. And one of the reasons for the film's unfaltering success had to be the fan following for the *Star Wars* gang. A cult had quickly formed around the characters, with many fans emulating their favorites at the numerous *Star Wars*/"Star Trek"/ science fiction conventions held regularly throughout the United States and in many countries overseas. Princess Leias, Han Solos, Luke Skywalkers, Darth Vaders, and acrylic-clad wookies abounded at these affairs, as did the films' gadgetry, such as light sabers and other role-playing aids. Dealers sold every conceivable tie-in product available, as well as newsletters and "fanzines" (fan-created magazines) for those who craved the printed word on their heroes. Prizes were awarded for the best costume. Many youngsters could not remember a time *without* the *Star Wars* characters. There was a phenomenon afoot here, and this instantly propelled this long-awaited sequel to the sequel over the top.

Still, a lot of people were surprised at the picture's success, including a number of critics, who panned the film

---

Screenplay by Lawrence Kasdan and George Lucas

Based on a story by George Lucas

Executive Producer: George Lucas

Produced by Howard Kazanjian

Directed by Richard Marquand

CAST

Luke Skywalker ...... Mark Hamill
Han Solo .... Harrison Ford
Princess Leia .... Carrie Fisher
Landro Carissian ..... Billy Dee Williams
Yoda .... Frank Oz

ACADEMY AWARD NOMINATIONS

4 nominations, no wins

Best Art Direction-Set Decoration
Best Sound
Best Original Score (John Williams)
Best Sound Effects Editing

Return of the Jedi received a Special Achievement Award for Visual Effects.

---

when it first opened. *The New York Times* wrote: " 'Return of the Jedi' . . . doesn't really end the trilogy as much as it brings it to a dead stop. The film . . . is by far the dimmest adventure of the lot. All the members of the old 'Star Wars' gang are back doing what they've done before, but this time with a certain evident boredom." The reviewer for *The Hollywood Reporter* wasn't thrilled either: "Unfortunately, it conveys the sense that the machinery has already begun to wear down, and the inventiveness to wear thin . . . there's a kind of desperation about it, a feeling that Lucas and co-writer Lawrence Kasdan are simply trying to figure out what they can do next to amuse the kiddies."

Newsweek, on the other hand, seemed to have mixed feelings: "At $32.5 million it is certainly the most expensive of the three. With more special effects per minute than its predecessors, it's definitely the busiest. Also the most battle-ridden, the most cartoony, and let's just spit it right out—the most disappointing . . . There's no doubt that 'Jedi' gives you your money's worth; it's so packed with wonders you may feel like an oversated child who's just been presented with the entire inventory of F. A. O. Schwarz for his birthday."

This movie was no disappointment act. And the reference to the famous toystore F.A.O. Schwarz was an appropriate one, since the merchandising of cuddly creatures like the "Ewoks" from Endor, plus the usual assortment of models, laser swords, lunchboxes, bedsheets, and so on, would eventually serve to more than double any profits at the box office. George Lucas' final tribute to the Jedi was profitable for all: Luke was reunited with his father and sister; Han Solo got the girl, and Lucas got the loot.

"I look upon the three *Star Wars* films as chapters in one book," Lucas told *Time* Magazine. "Now the book is finished, and I have put it on the shelf."

(Left to right): George Lucas, Harrison Ford, C3PO, Carrie Fisher, Mark Hamill, Chewbacca, R2D2, and director Richard Marquand.

②

TERMS OF ENDEARMENT

PARAMOUNT
$50,250,000

"Have you come to Terms *yet?"*
—ADVERTISING COPY
FOR *TERMS OF ENDEARMENT*

A LOT OF people did come to *Terms*. This was another "audience picture"— like *Love Story, On Golden Pond,* and even any of the *Rocky* movies, a film which attracts audiences not because of special effects or energetic action, or because of hot-and-cold running bimbos, but simply because there is a story to which audiences can relate.

The picture was virtually a one-man showcase for writer-producer-director James L. Brooks. Brooks began his career as a lowly copy boy at CBS News in New York, later moving to the West Coast, where he formed a profitable partnership with fellow writer Allan Burns. Together, the pair created the beloved "Mary Tyler Moore Show"; Brooks and Burns won four Emmies for their work during the show's seven-year run. While working at Paramount under a development deal, Larry McMurtry's novel, *Terms of Endearment,* crossed Brooks' path. He was so enthralled by the possibilities that he asked Paramount to option the book for him, reserving the right to direct it himself. "I was overwhelmed by the fact that I was going to take on directing," confessed Brooks in the film's production handbook. "I could absolutely visualize where I'd screw up.

But I was secure about working with actors, and I do have experience as a producer. Everything else I've learned has been by some kind of osmosis."

Brooks was blessed with a winning cast, one of the reasons for the film's huge success. Shirley MacLaine had

---

Screenplay by James L. Brooks

Produced and directed by James L. Brooks

CAST

Emma Horton	Debra Winger
Aurora Greenway	Shirley MacLaine
Garrett Breedlove	Jack Nicholson
Flap Horton	Jeff Daniels
Sam Burns	John Lithgow
Vernon Dahlart	Danny DeVito

ACADEMY AWARD NOMINATIONS

11 nominations, 5 wins*

*Best Picture
*Best Actress (Shirley MacLaine)
 Best Actress (Debra Winger)
 Best Supporting Actor (John Lithgow)
*Best Supporting Actor (Jack Nicholson)
*Best Director (James L. Brooks)
*Best Screenplay Based on Material from
 Another Medium (James L. Brooks)
 Best Art Direction-Set Decoration
 Best Sound
 Best Original Score (Michael Gore)
 Best Film Editing

---

been in demand constantly since her last top-five film at the box office, *Irma La Douce* (see page 170). She had worked in such popular films as *Woman Times Seven, Sweet Charity,* and *Two Mules for Sister Sara.* During much of the '70s, she was politically active, and led the first woman's delegation to China in 1973. She also began a career as a writer of controversial autobiographical books. In 1977, she returned to the screen and received an Oscar nomination for *The Turning Point.* With *Terms of Endearment,* the oft-nominated MacLaine finally received her Award.

Jack Nicholson co-stars as the letch next door, a role he seemed born to. The actor had had six Oscar nominations and one win (*One Flew Over the Cuckoo's Nest*; see page 242) when he accepted the part of former astronaut Garrett Breedlove, Aurora Greenway's (MacLaine's) horny neighbor.

Others in the superlative cast included Debra Winger as Emma Horton, Aurora's daughter; Danny DeVito in an early film role (he had worked with director Brooks on TV's "Taxi"); and John Lithgow, who has worked constantly through the ensuing years.

The film, while dealing with a depressing theme, is also comedic, touching, and ultimately uplifting. Stock up on Kleenex when you watch it, but be prepared for smiles, too.

TRADING PLACES
PARAMOUNT
$40,600,000

"When I was growing up and we wanted a Jacuzzi, we had to fart in the tub." —EDDIE MURPHY

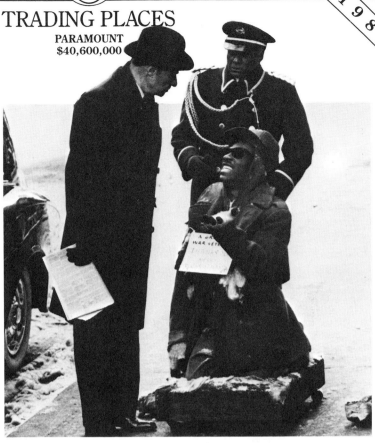

EDDIE MURPHY became a household name at the age of 21, when he emerged as a bona fide star from the ranks of TV's "Saturday Night Live" in the early '80s. His first feature, *48 HRS.* (1982), saw the young actor/comedian on the road to further success, and he was signed to a multiple-picture deal with Paramount Pictures. *Trading Places*, a comedy based on a simple premise (remember Mark Twain's *The Prince and the Pauper?*), is up there with the best of Murphy's subsequent films.

Dan Aykroyd and Eddie Murphy play two men whose paths were never meant to cross. Aykroyd is a wealthy investment broker, Murphy a poor but clever survivor of the ghetto. They are thrown together in a scheme devised by the conniving Duke Brothers, played by Ralph Bellamy and Don Ameche (together on the screen for the first time in this film). Suddenly, Murphy is given carte blanche at the Dukes' investment firm, while Aykroyd must learn to cope with being a "street person."

The John Landis–directed picture featured some of Murphy's old "Saturday Night Live" buddies in a variety of roles. Murphy actually received second billing in the credits (the last time that would ever happen), with Dan Aykroyd as "Louis Winthorpe III" listed at the top of the cast. Al Franken, another "Saturday Night Live" alumnus, played

the minor part of a "Baggage Handler," while John Belushi's brother Jim was listed as "Harvey." There were a number of well-known names in the cast as well, such as veteran actors Ralph Bellamy (this was his 99th film) and Don Ameche (this was his 49th). When Eddie Murphy found out their combined totals, he quipped, "That means that between the three of us, we've made 150 movies!" Other "names" in the cast included Jamie Lee Curtis as "Ophelia" the hooker, Frank Oz as the "Corrupt Cop" (you may recall Oz as a Muppeteer and the wizard behind *The Empire Strikes Back*'s "Yoda"), and rock and roll oldie Bo Diddley as the "Pawnbroker."

While the film loosely addresses racial and cultural prejudices, the emphasis is still on comedy, and the summer release found a wide audience eager for comic relief. Critics also discovered what audiences knew all along—Eddie Murphy was one funny guy. *Newsweek* didn't have much favorable comment for the picture itself, but Murphy captured the reviewer's complete atten-

tion: "John Landis' movie confirms what '48 HRS.' suggested: Murphy is the most dynamic new comic talent around, a quicksilver quick-change artist whose rapport with the audience is instantaneous . . . Murphy is the movie's hottest—and funniest—commodity." *Time* concurred: "*Trading Places* [is] one of the most emotionally satisfying and morally gratifying comedies of recent times . . . *Trading Places* also makes Eddie Murphy a force to be reckoned with . . . [He] demonstrates the powers of invention that signal the arrival of a major comic actor, and possibly a great star. He makes *Trading Places* something more than a good-hearted comedy. He turns it into an event." *The New York Times* predicted: "The film's pleasures are unequivocal, beginning with the lithe, graceful, uproarious performance of Mr. Murphy . . . A terrific career is in store."

All those predicting a successful career for Eddie Murphy, please raise your hands. In the words of one of Murphy's "Saturday Night Live" characters, "Can you say *very, very rich?*"

Screenplay by Timothy Harris and Herschel Weingrod

Executive Producer: George Folsey, Jr.

Produced by Aaron Russo

Directed by John Landis

CAST

Louis Winthorpe III	Dan Aykroyd
Billy Ray Valentine	Eddie Murphy
Randolph Duke	Ralph Bellamy
Mortimer Duke	Don Ameche
Coleman	Denholm Elliott
Ophelia	Jamie Lee Curtis

④

WARGAMES
METRO-GOLDWYN-MAYER/UNITED ARTISTS
$38,519,833

"Shall we play a game?"—COMPUTER

"Let's play Global Thermonuclear War." —MATTHEW BRODERICK

VIDEO GAMES and computer technology had reached a fever pitch in the early '80s. The country was in the throes of "Pac-Man" fever, the symptoms of which included young people gluing themselves to joysticks and monitor screens for hours at a time while little creatures gobbled up mazes of small dots. Virtually every red-blooded teenage boy in the country was thus afflicted, along with a goodly number of equally red-blooded young females. (And, lest the games become too sexist, some clever person devised the oxymoronic *"Ms.* Pac-Man.")

WarGames targeted this youthful audience and struck home with a 100-megaton hit. It began with a simple "what if . . ." premise. What if a teenage hacker/gamester were to accidentally launch World War III? Simple, but very scary. The kid thinks he's still playing a game as the countdown to oblivion begins. Eventually it's the youngsters (and the audience, who is in on it from the start) versus. the superintelligence of our government.

Screenplay by Lawrence Lasker and Walter F. Parkes

Produced by Harold Schneider

Directed by John Badham

CAST

David .... Matthew Broderick
McKittrick .... Dabney Coleman
Falken .... John Wood
Jennifer .... Ally Sheedy
General Beringer .... Barry Corbin

ACADEMY AWARD NOMINATIONS

3 nominations, no wins

Best Screenplay Written Directly for the Screen
Best Cinematography
Best Sound

Guess who's right all along?

John Badham's tight direction keeps this premise from becoming improbable.* There is suspense aplenty, making the film an "edge of the seat"-er. The director of the 1978 hit *Saturday Night Fever*, Badham also turned out another exciting action-adventure film, *Blue Thunder*, in the summer of '83.

Much of the film's success must go to the young stars. Matthew Broderick and Ally Sheedy were two promising young actors in the early '80s. They have both continued in prosperous careers through the decade, and will no doubt be major actors of the '90s. *The New York Times* wrote: "Young Mr. Broderick, a Tony nominee for his current Broadway performance in Neil Simon's 'Brighton Beach Memoirs,' is very serious and grave—and thus very appealing—as the unassuming computer wizard . . . Miss Sheedy . . . here succeeds in being distinctive in an ordinary role."

Rounding out the cast was Dabney Coleman, again typed as the baddie, in this case a computer defense specialist who thinks David (Broderick) is a Commie spy. Coleman can play "obnoxious" quite well; by now, he'd become the man audiences loved to hate.

WarGames was released domestically in early May, 1983, coinciding with the Cannes Film Festival. It was given the honor of appearing as the final film at that annual world-famous event.

---

*At least we'd all like to *think* it's improbable. Recently, hackers successfully implanted "viruses" in sensitive computer networks.

SUPERMAN III

WARNER BROS.
$37,200,000

Screenplay by David Newman and
Leslie Newman

Executive Producer: Ilya Salkind

Produced by Pierre Spengler

Directed by Richard Lester

CAST

Superman/Clark Kent	Christopher Reeve
Gus Gorman	Richard Pryor
Perry White	Jackie Cooper
Ross Webster	Robert Vaughn
Lois Lane	Margot Kidder

IT'S HARD TO KNOW which came first—Richard Pryor, or the egg laid by *Superman III*. In a severe departure from the format established in the first two *Superman* films, this one plays it for laughs. It may be humorous, and the talented Richard Pryor may have a huge fan following, but somehow this picture isn't on target. Most audiences thought it just didn't *feel* right.

For one thing, there are two leading actors: Chris Reeve, appearing as Superman for the third time, and Pryor, somehow turning the film into "The Richard Pryor Show" whenever he's on screen. It was as if the producers first signed Pryor, then tried to create a movie around him. He certainly was a big box office draw. And Chris Reeve also had a legion of loyal fans who, if need be, would turn up at the box office to watch Superman recite Chaucer for two hours. Still, this film only pulled in half the amount of *Superman II*, and at $37,200,000, it was the lowest-grossing top-five film since 1976.

Pryor plays Gus Gorman, a com-puter whiz snapped up by the movie's villain, Robert Vaughn, playing a power-hungry bigwig à la *Bullitt* (see page 200), but on a grander scale—he plans to rule the Earth. Along the way, Supe (Pryor actually calls him this!) gets zapped by a strain of Kryptonite, and, in a sequence guaranteed to send Freudians rushing down to the local Bijou, our superhero does battle with himself! Seems this Kryptonite actually splits his superpersonality into "good" and "bad" halves. Under the influence of the "bad" self, he becomes a wom-anizing, beer-slurping, five-o'clock-shadowed superbum who snuffs out the Olympic flame and straightens up the Leaning Tower of Pisa just for spite.

There also isn't much action with his leading lady of the past two films, Margot Kidder as Lois Lane, although she does put in an appearance. This time, Clark Kent returns to his Small-ville High reunion, where he attracts the attention of Lana Lang, his onetime high school crush. In the film's most original development, she actually falls for Clark, and not his superalterego.

Critics weren't certain what to write about this film. Most seemed to enjoy Pryor's performance, unaware of any problems Superman purists might have been suffering. *Variety* commented that "virtually none of the film's set action and spectacle pieces . . . has the scope or the technical imagination of either of the previous pics," and *The New York Times* wrote that "anyone who has been following the 'Superman' saga will find this installment enjoyable enough, but some of the magic is missing."

Most true Superman fans agreed, which is why this sequel failed to take off like the others. It was also an em-barrassment to Christopher Reeve, who swore off the character. He was eventually persuaded to do one more, *Superman IV: The Quest for Peace* (1987), a return to the style of first two *Superman* movies. Unfortunately, it fared poorly, earning only $8,000,000 in domestic returns. It seems poor writ-ing, not Kryptonite, has finally done in Superman.

1

GHOSTBUSTERS
COLUMBIA
$130,211,324

"Are you troubled by strange noises in the night? Do you experience feelings of dread in your basement or attic? Have you or your family actually seen a spook, spectre or ghost? If the answer is yes, then don't wait another minute. Just pick up the phone and call the professionals—GHOSTBUSTERS!"
—"COMMERCIAL" IN
GHOSTBUSTERS

MONTHS BEFORE the public ever heard of *Ghostbusters*, billboards around the country showed a Casper-like apparition popping through the universal symbol for something forbidden—a red circle with a diagonal slash. The message below read "Coming to save the world this summer." It might just as easily have read "Coming to save Columbia Pictures this summer," for that is exactly what it did. The studio had had a big hit back in 1982 with *Tootsie*, but nothing could have prepared Columbia for the huge success that was about to materialize from *Ghostbusters*. Before the year was over, it would become the *fifth* highest-grossing picture of all time.

Some called it a comedy, since the plot involved a "Three Musketeers-ish group (Bill Murray, Dan Aykroyd, Harold Ramis) camping it up in New York while in pursuit of some really whimsical supernatural beings (one cute little green ghost's favorite pastime is gorging on hotel food). Others saw this spoof as a fantasy—it does take a bit of imagination to believe that otherworldly creatures live in Sigourney Weaver's fridge, or that she and co-star Rick Moranis can turn into gargoyle-ish red-eyed dogs. Actually, it doesn't matter. It's innovative and entertaining, and audiences ate it up.

The movie was originally conceived as a John Belushi–Dan Aykroyd vehicle called *Ghostsmashers* before Belushi's untimely death from a drug overdose in 1982, and the "eating and drinking ghost" is actually producer-director Ivan Reitman's tribute to that late comedian's character "Bluto" from his previous hit, *National Lampoon's Animal House* (see page 261). With the screenplay by principals Aykroyd and

Screenplay by Dan Aykroyd and Harold Ramis

Executive Producer: Bernie Brillstein

Produced and directed by Ivan Reitman

CAST

Dr. Peter Venkman ...	Bill Murray
Dr. Raymond Stantz ..	Dan Aykroyd
Dana Barrett	Sigourney Weaver
Dr. Egon Spengler ...	Harold Ramis
Louis Tully	Rick Moranis

ACADEMY AWARD NOMINATIONS

2 nominations, no wins

Best Song ("Ghostbusters," music and words by Ray Parker, Jr.)
Best Visual Effects

Ramis presenting many opportunities for ad-libbing, director Reitman encouraged improvisation in his actors. And he himself did a cameo as the Mercedes McCambridge-like voice of "possessed" Sigourney Weaver rising on the bed Linda Blair–fashion, as well as providing all the alien voices except that of "Gozer," the Sumerian demigod with designs on planet Earth.

A catchy title song did much to promote the film. "Who you gonna call? GHOSTBUSTERS!" became the sensation of the summer. Ray Parker, Jr. was presented with a dilemma when he was asked by Reitman to compose a title song. Said Parker to *USA Today*: "It's hard to write a song where your main objective is to use the word 'ghostbusters' . . . I wanted to make a simple, easy song people could sing along with and not have to think about." The song became a number-one hit for three weeks in August, 1984. It was again used as the theme of the 1989 sequel, *Ghostbusters II*, with Run-DMC's version as well as the Ray Parker one appearing in that film.

Time's reviewer really got caught up in the fun: "These spectacular confrontations are well handled by Director Reitman, who always finds the time for the funny aside, the wittily telling detail. . . . But praise is due to everyone connected with *Ghostbusters* for thinking on a grandly comic scale and delivering the goofy goods, neatly timed and perfectly packaged."

The Stay-Puft Marshmallow Man, appearing in one of the film's silliest moments, required a man wearing a suit to stomp through a miniature set of New York City. There were three Fiberglas heads used, each with a different facial expression—smiling, surprised, and grimacing.

Over at Columbia, only smiles were in abundance. The profitable picture ultimately spawned a sequel, *Ghostbusters II*, and it seemed to be doing fairly well in early box office returns, although not quite as well as its predecessor.

Producer/director Ivan Reitman (left) confers with Dan Aykroyd and Bill Murray about a scene from *Ghostbusters*.

2

INDIANA JONES AND THE TEMPLE OF DOOM

PARAMOUNT
$109,000,000

"If adventure has a name, it must be Indiana Jones!"

—ADVERTISING COPY FOR *INDIANA JONES AND THE TEMPLE OF DOOM*

THREE YEARS AFTER their highly acclaimed *Raiders of the Lost Ark*, Steven Spielberg and George Lucas brought out the next installment of the adventures of the famous fictional archeologist who matches wits with the forces of evil. Actually a prequel to *Raiders* set three years prior to that movie, *Indiana Jones and the Temple of Doom* has one of the most memorable openings of any film. The Paramountain, the logo seen at the beginning of all Paramount Pictures, suddenly transforms into a gong as the credits are introduced (homage to George Steven's 1939 epic *Gunga Din*). We never actually see the movies title, which unfolds behind "Willie Scott" (Kate Capshaw), performer at the "Obi Wan" Club (get it?), singing "Anything Goes" in Mandarin Chinese, followed by a Busby Berkeley–type production number. All this in the first reel!

A dizzying pace is set in the ensuing sequences, with Spielberg never letting up for a moment. Indy fights for his life in the search for a poison antidote; we meet his newest sidekick, a 10-year-old lad named Short Round (Ke Huy Quan), who drives their getaway car;

the threesome wind up in an airplane (a scene which pays homage to the films of the '30s with the old "line across the map" technique of following a plane's progress); followed by a plane crash, a toboggan ride, and an elephant trek through the jungle. And we've still got most of the picture to go!

Despite all this action, many people now believe this to be the weakest of the three *Indiana Jones* movies. Even director Spielberg acknowledged the film's dark and somber feeling. With

---

Screenplay by Willard Huyck and Gloria Katz

Executive Producers: George Lucas and Frank Marshall

Produced by Robert Watts

Directed by Steven Spielberg

CAST

Indiana Jones	Harrison Ford
Willie Scott	Kate Capshaw
Short Round	Ke Huy Quan
Mola Ram	Amrish Purl
Chattar Lal	Roshan Seth

ACADEMY AWARD NOMINATIONS

2 nominations, 1 win*

Best Original Score (John Williams)
*Best Visual Effects

---

much of the plot centering on children who have been kidnapped into torturous slavery, plus beatings, devil-worship, human sacrifices, and heart-snatching—not fun subjects for youngsters—there was little of the light, uplifting tone of the first picture.

Newsweek called it "pure cinematic energy encumbered with as little soul food as possible," but the reviewer tempered his praise with reservations: "Now I enjoy human sacrifice as much as the next American youth, but at this point the movie loses its stylish integration of violence and humor and becomes a careening juggernaut of beatings, gougings and crunchings . . . in 'Indiana Jones' Spielberg and Lucas have let their genius for probing deep into us with their mastery of movie rhythms get out of hand."

Audiences didn't pay the least bit of attention to detractors like the above. They paid their money, they took their ride, and came back again for more. *Indiana Jones and the Temple of Doom* took its place as the eighth highest-grossing film of all time, right behind *Raiders of the Lost Ark*.

In 1989, the third (and everyone involved swears, the final) Indy film, *Indiana Jones and the Last Crusade*, hit the summer box office. It was well on its way to the Spielberg-Lucas hall of fame as another top moneymaker as the summer drew to a close.

BEVERLY HILLS COP

PARAMOUNT
$108,000,000

IT WAS A GREAT year for Paramount. In addition to their success with *Indiana Jones and the Temple of Doom*, the studio still had another trump card to play. Eddie Murphy had co-starred in that studio's highly lucrative movie, *Trading Places*, in 1983. While critics enjoyed the film in general, most of them saved their superlatives for its second-billed star, Eddie Murphy, predicting a phenomenal career for the comedy actor. With *Beverly Hills Cop*, that prediction became a reality.

Murphy stars as Axel Foley, a Detroit policeman tracking the killer of a friend in Beverly Hills. He is certainly more laid back than his California counterparts as he locks horns with the Beverly Hills Police Department. You get the feeling that Murphy could talk his way out of hell itself if called upon to do so, and leave the Devil muttering apologies. He gets excellent support from Judge Reinhold as Detective Billy Rosewood and John Ashton as Sergeant Taggart; these well-scripted characters are perfect foils for Murphy's style and humor. (Believe it or not, the part of Axel Foley was originally written for more of an action picture, with Sylvester Stallone in mind.)

Screenplay by Daniel Petrie, Jr.

Based on a story by Danilo Bach and Daniel Petrie, Jr.

Executive Producer: Mike Moder

Produced by Don Simpson and Jerry Bruckheimer

Directed by Martin Brest

CAST

Axel Foley	Eddie Murphy
Detective Billy Rosewood	Judge Reinhold
Sergeant Taggart	John Ashton
Jenny Summers	Lisa Eilbacher
Lieutenant Bogomil	Ronny Cox
Serge	Bronson Pinchot

ACADEMY AWARD NOMINATIONS

1 nomination, no wins

Best Screenplay Written Directly for the Screen

It didn't take long for the critics to heap their praises upon this sure-fire Christmas release. *The Hollywood Reporter* heralded both the film and Murphy's performance: "This lickety-split action comedy is distinguished by the wry, character-conscious direction of Martin Brest, who coaxes a silver-bullet performance from star Eddie Murphy that's practically criminal in its accuracy."

One of the most memorable minor roles in the film went to a then-unknown named Bronson Pinchot. *Newsweek*'s reviewer was quick to spot the actor's potential: "Oddest of all is a salesman in the villain's art gallery who goes by the name of Serge and is of God-knows-what nationality; as played by a singular actor named Bronson Pinchot, Serge is the most unexpectedly and unusually hilarious bit role

within recent memory. The unknown Pinchot may be one of the few people alive who could steal a scene from Eddie Murphy." Pinchot continued that character and accent when he was selected to star in a popular TV series, "Perfect Strangers"; on that show he plays "Balki," the Balkan bumpkin, a character not unlike Serge in *Beverly Hills Cop.*

With the success of *Beverly Hills Cop*, Eddie Murphy's position atop Paramount's roster of talent was assured. The studio eagerly extended his contract, gave him a whole building for his production company, plus practically any perk the superstar might request (his electric golf cart, for example, boasts a Rolls Royce front grill).

Sequels? Of course. Three years later, *Beverly Hills Cop II* was back for more fun and bullets (see page 316).

GREMLINS
WARNER BROS.
$79,500,000

"Keep him out of the light . . .
"Don't get him wet . . .
"And never, never feed him after
midnight."

—WARNING TO HOYT AXTON
WHEN HE PURCHASES A "MOGWAI"

NATURALLY, all of the above rules about the care and feeding of a "mogwai" are about to be broken, or there'd be no picture. That bit of business having been established before the opening credits, the audience, who had probably seen all kinds of publicity about the film before purchasing their tickets, had only to settle back in their chairs and wait for the fun to unfold.

The movie *Gremlins* is "presented" by Steven Spielberg, a name synonymous with "big box office" (he executive-produced this one), but some began to doubt his sense of humor, wondering if the wunderkind's dark side was beginning to force its way through. The picture begins innocently enough: it's Christmastime in a Frank Capra-esque town (movie send-ups abound); the local theater marquee reads *A Boy's Life* and *Watch the Skies*—early titles of two of Spielberg's biggest hits, *E.T. The Extra-Terrestrial* and *Close Encounters of the Third Kind.* Dad's been out Christmas shopping, and he brings home an unusual gift for son Billy: a mogwai, a cuddly, Disney-eyed creature who sings to himself. What child wouldn't want one for a pet?

But Gizmo, as he's quickly named by Billy's inventor father, isn't just your average mogwai. When he's inadvertently moistened, all hell breaks loose, literally. The Gremlins which eventually

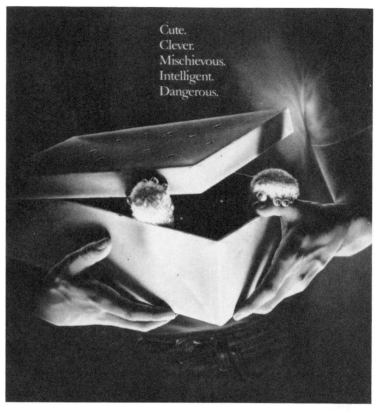

Cute.
Clever.
Mischievous.
Intelligent.
Dangerous.

Screenplay by Chris Columbus

Executive Producers: Steven Spielberg, Frank Marshall, and Kathleen Kennedy

Produced by Michael Finnell

Directed by Joe Dante

CAST

Billy	Zach Galligan
Kate	Phoebe Cates
Rand Peltzer	Hoyt Axton
Lynn Peltzer	Frances Lee McCain
Mrs. Deagle	Polly Holliday

materialize as offspring of Gizmo aren't your garden-variety pets at all, and thereby hangs a tale. When these creatures are turned loose on the town, the film goes from cute to grim.

Cute: Gremlins in earmuffs and ski caps, caroling through the town. Gremlins arm-wrestling in the local saloon. Gremlins taking in the local cinema—the film's been changed to Disney's *Snow White*—singing "Heigh-ho" along with the Seven Dwarfs, like kids at a matinee.

Grim: Billy's mom nuking a gremlin in the microwave. Gremlins trashing the town and offing the town grouch.

"Gremlins are not good," admitted director Joe Dante. to *Time.* "You can't trust them. You don't want one for a pet. You don't want your daughter to marry one." Steven Spielberg noted that "if they could speak English, they'd probably say, 'Let's party!' It's how they party that can be hazardous

to your health."

Audiences took quite freely to these party animals. In a year filled with fantasies and imaginative action films (*Ghostbusters* and *Indiana Jones and the Temple of Doom* were the top two moneymakers for the year), this picture was in the right place at the right time. The public didn't mind the evil critters, even cheering them on. And since Gizmo remained wide-eyed and innocent throughout the movie, we always knew everything would turn out all right.

In 1989, Warner Bros. and Amblin Entertainment (Spielberg's production company) began filming a sequel, *Gremlins II.* The same creative talents—Joe Dante as director, Michael Finnell as producer, Spielberg, Kathleen Kennedy, and Frank Marshall as executive producers—as well as stars Zach Galligan and Phoebe Cates, returned for more merry mayhem.

THE KARATE KID

COLUMBIA
$43,432,881

SLEEPER: that's what people were calling *The Karate Kid*, 1984's entry into the "feel good" school of movies. The summer release concerned a young 98-pound wimp who gets a dose of Oriental wisdom, along with some practical pointers in the fine art of crunching your aggressor's bones, from a mysterious janitor, superbly played by Pat Morita. Pat was somewhat familiar to audiences as "Arnold," the owner of the drive-in on TV's "Happy Days." Little did audiences suspect that the erstwhile hamburger-slinger was a philosopher. And no one was more surprised by his acting career than Morita himself. "I can't even imagine how I ever got into the entertainment business," the actor told the *San Francisco Chronicle*. "I don't sing, I don't dance, I don't juggle, I don't have an animal act and I can't even do karate, to tell you the truth." Not exactly fighting words from a karate master. "Karate really mystifies me," he continued. "All that stuff about breaking bricks. Why don't they just pick up the brick and hit 'em over the head with it?"

Luckily, none of this attitude came across on the screen. Mr. Miyagi's 17-year-old charge Daniel, played by

---

Screenplay by Robert Mark Kamen

Executive Producer: R. J. Louis

Produced by Jerry Weintraub

Directed by John G. Avildsen

CAST

Daniel . . . . Ralph Macchio
Miyagi . . . . Noriyuki "Pat" Morita
Ali . . . . Elisabeth Shue
Kreese . . . . Martin Kove
Lucille . . . . Randee Heller

ACADEMY AWARD NOMINATIONS

1 nomination, no wins

Best Supporting Actor (Noriyuki "Pat" Morita)

---

then-21-year-old Ralph Macchio, captured the hearts of the underdog-loving public. Sound familiar? Not surprising, since the film's director also made the original *Rocky*. He even referred to this picture jokingly as *The Karocky Kid*. *The Hollywood Reporter* saw a further parallel: "Put 'Rocky' in 'Alice Doesn't Live Here Anymore,' set it in the Valley and you've got 'The Karate Kid.' . . .

[the film] will have an uphill battle all the way if it is to be a contender in this summer's heavyweight box office division." The critical bash-fest continued with *Time* noting the picture's similarities to *Flashdance*, *Rocky*, and even *Star Wars*: "[The film provides Daniel] with a Yoda-like mentor full of gnomic instruction and inspiration in his struggle against evil. In short, *The Karate Kid* presents the smallest imaginable variations on three well-tested formulas for movie success." *The New York Times*' reviewer was one of the few reviewers who saw the potential in *The Karate Kid*: "[The film] has the makings of a genuinely heart-warming two-man drama, with Mr. Morita a charming cut-up and Mr. Macchio gently likable."

The film's popularity in the theaters has been matched only by its popularity in various formats. First, there were the sequels—two of them, *The Karate Kid, Part II* (1986; see page 312) and *The Karate Kid, Part III* (1989). There is also a new DIC Enterprises animated series on NBC's Saturday morning schedule. Pat Morita provides the voice for his Miyagi character, who continues to dispense "Miyagi-isms."

BACK TO THE FUTURE
UNIVERSAL
$104,408,738

FIVE WEEKS into the shooting of *Back to the Future*, executive producer Steven Spielberg had the leading actor replaced. He had already spent $4,000,000 and had to reshoot a number of scenes. But Spielberg was unhappy with Eric Stoltz in the role of Marty McFly, and demanded that he be removed from the cast. His choice for a replacement was a well-known TV actor who had unwittingly turned "Family Ties" into what could easily have been called "The Michael J. Fox Show." The young actor made no bones about the fact that he was "just one of the players" and disliked being the constant center of that show's spotlight. Spielberg had no trouble spotting Fox's talent, though, and nabbed him for his ailing production.

Michael J. Fox* began his TV career in his native Canada at the age of 14, and became an overnight sensation in Paramount's hit TV show, "Family Ties," which ran on NBC for seven seasons. Like Ralph Macchio in *The Karate Kid*, Fox was either blessed or cursed, depending on how one looks at it, with appearing much younger than his actual age. In "Family Ties," he played teenager Alex P. Keaton well into his '20s; in *Back to the Future*, he was 24 years old playing 17. Nevertheless, Fox's charisma probably helped turn this cute picture into a real winner.

It wasn't an easy job for Fox, either. He was still working on "Ties," and for six weeks he'd work all day at the Paramount lot, then hop in his black Jeep and head over to the Universal lot for shooting from 6:00 P.M. till midnight, go home for a quick sleep, then do it all again the next day.

The teaming of Fox with another television actor, Christopher Lloyd ("Reverend Jim" from "Taxi") as the kookie mad-professor type, made for beautiful chemistry. Fox plays Marty McFly, a modern teen whose pal Dr. Emmett Brown (Lloyd) sends the lad back to that nostalgic year 1955, just in time for him to meet up with his parents, who were then teens themselves. (Worse, his own future mother develops a crush on him!) There's an old adage in science fiction time-travel stories: If you so much as kill a bug, you may also be destroying the future as we know it. This sort of premise has been a staple of science fiction ever since the genre was invented, and of course, in *Back to the Future*, the chain of events that is set up has exactly the results predicted.

Watch closely for some of the neat touches that director Zemeckis has incorporated into the setting for the film. The little town, for example, shows subtle changes over the decades. A theater marquee in 1955 that had been showing Ronald Reagan in *Cattle Queen of Montana* now exhibits porn films, the Studebaker dealership now sells Toyotas, and the malt shop has become an aerobics gymnasium.

Screenplay by Robert Zemeckis and Bob Gale

Executive Producers: Steven Spielberg, Kathleen Kennedy, and Frank Marshall

Produced by Bob Gale and Neil Canton

Directed by Robert Zemeckis

CAST

Marty McFly	Michael J. Fox
Dr. Emmett Brown	Christopher Lloyd
George McFly	Crispin Glover
Lorraine Baines	Lea Thompson
Jennifer Parker	Claudia Wells

ACADEMY AWARD NOMINATIONS

*4 nominations, 1 win**

Best Screenplay Written Directly for the Screen
Best Sound
Best Song ("Power of Love," music by Chris Hayes and Johnny Colla, words by Huey Lewis)
*Best Sound Effects Editing

Those visitors to Southern California who take the famed Universal Studios Tour have an opportunity to see this town square as part of the "tram tour."

Robert Zemeckis directed his co-written (with Bob Gale) script, but it was a long struggle getting it made. *Back to the Future* was rejected by all the major studios because, according to Zemeckis, "it wasn't raunchy enough." Spielberg finally gave the 33-year-old Zemeckis a chance; he'd also been the first to recognize Zemeckis' talent when he gave him his first break on *I Wanna Hold Your Hand*, a movie about the Beatles. Zemeckis is also noted for his popular movie *Romancing the Stone* (1984).

A spoof of '50s rock and roll is one of the highlights of the film, right down to Fox's impression of Chuck Berry. One of the musical numbers, "The Power of Love," by Huey Lewis and the News, received an Academy Award nomination, rose to number one on the pop charts for two weeks in August, 1985, and became the fifth best-selling song of the year. (Watch for Huey Lewis in a cameo appearance as a high school teacher.)

In 1989, Universal and Amblin Entertainment announced the production of the long-awaited sequel(s) to *Back to the Future*. *Back to the Future II* and *III* were lensed back-to-back, with the first released in time for Christmas, 1989, and the second one due in the summer of 1990. Both films re-team Michael J. Fox and Chris Lloyd, with Bob Zemeckis again at the helm. One of the reasons for this unusual move was the availability of both Fox and Zemeckis (director of 1988's hit movie *Who Framed Roger Rabbit*—see page 322), popular talents who might not be available at a later date. *Future II*'s plot involves sending Fox's character Marty McFly into the 21st century, to the year 2015, where he must confront his own future and set things aright. The film promises to become as much a hit as its predecessor.

Meanwhile, the final episode of "Family Ties" was filmed in the spring of 1989, so at least Michael J. Fox was able to get some sleep during these film productions.

---

*When he first joined the Screen Actors Guild, there was already an actor named Michael Fox. Regulations prohibit two actors from belonging to the Guild with the same stage name, so Michael decided to add a middle initial. His own middle initial, "A," would have made him "Michael A. Fox," and he cringed at the prospects of plays upon his name. He finally selected "J," after an actor he admired, Michael J. Pollard.

RAMBO: FIRST BLOOD PART II
TRI-STAR
$78,919,250

VIOLENCE LOVERS, unite! Your hero is alive and well and living on the big screen. He's a superman-turned-soldier, a robotic, superbly muscled human who can do one thing well: kill. Already the center of a film called *First Blood*, Sylvester Stallone's character of John Rambo is back and bigger than life once again. This time, there are some MIAs in need of rescuing in Vietnam, and only one man can save them. Machine-gunning, grenading, and sweating his way through the jungles of Southeast Asia, ex-Green Beret John Rambo proves it's brawn, not brains, that counts when you've got right on your side.

Like G.I. Joe of the cartoons, this macho killing machine was a comic-book hero come to life. Fans of Stallone, including President Reagan, all contributed to Rambomania in the summer of '85. In June, following the release of 39 American hostages by Lebanese terrorists, our former President remarked, "Boy, I saw *Rambo* last night. I know what to do the next time this happens!"

"This time do we get to win?" implores the muscled Rambo when given this assignment. Yes, we do, but why did the film have to be so gratuitously violent? According to the National Coalition of Television Violence (which also monitors big-screen features, since they eventually land on the small one), Rambo averaged 161 brutally violent acts per hour. Yet many saw this film as a paean to American patriotism. "People have been waiting for a chance to express their patriotism," said Stallone during the height of the film's popularity. "*Rambo* triggered long-suppressed emotions that had been out of vogue." A few years later, according to *The Cable Guide* Magazine, the actor had tired of the "stigma people have put on [Rambo] as a symbol of right-wing aggressiveness . . . [Rambo's] really Oriental. He thinks more in terms of Muslim or Eastern philosophies. He has no sense of the self. He doesn't stand outside and observe war—he becomes war . . . Rambo is Zen-like. He's a disenfranchised samurai."

Newsweek, after describing the three *Rocky* films as "bloodbaths," stated that *Rambo*'s violence "makes the 'Rockys' look like 'Winnie-the-Pooh.' It's crunch, slash, ratatat all the way." *The Hollywood Reporter* had similar comments: "Stallone proves his prowess with a knife, a machine gun, a composite bow (complete with explosive heads), a Russian antitank gun and a Russian fighter helicopter . . . In the orgy of destruction that follows, the audience merely looking for action will have its appetite sated and its prejudices catered to. And these days, for a large segment of the population, that is what is considered entertainment. As a result, look for 'Rambo' to do big business and no doubt 'Rambo 2–First Blood 3' will be on its way soon."

Actually, the sequel was simply called *Rambo III* (1988), and it turned out to be the most expensive film in movie history, costing a reported $63,000,000 to make. Rambo and Rocky may have made Sly Stallone a wealthy man*, but *Rambo III* lost a bundle.

---

*Stallone's fee is said to be $20,000,000 per picture. *Forbes* has estimated Stallone's total worth at $650,000,000, making him the wealthiest star in the history of motion pictures.

Screenplay by Sylvester Stallone and James Cameron

Based on a story by Kevin Jarre

Based on characters created by David Morrell

Executive Producers: Mario Kassar and Andrew Vajna

Produced by Buzz Feitshans

Directed by George P. Cosmatos

CAST

Rambo	....	Sylvester Stallone
Trautman	....	Richard Crenna
Murdock	....	Charles Napier
Co Bao	....	Julia Nickson
Podovsky	....	Steven Berkoff

ACADEMY AWARD NOMINATIONS

1 nomination, no wins

Best Sound Effects Editing

ROCKY IV
METRO-GOLDWYN-MAYER/UNITED ARTISTS
$76,023,246

"It's suicide! You can't win!"
—WARNING TO ROCKY BALBOA

ROCKY BALBOA was back for more, in a year that seemed to be dominated by Sly Stallone. His second- and third-place pictures for 1985, *Rambo* and *Rocky IV*, together totalled $155,000,000 in rentals. One might think the public would have had enough by now of this writer-director-actor and his tough-guy characters; not so. In *Rocky IV*, Rocky fulfills the earlier prophecy of one *Rocky II* reviewer by literally wrapping himself in the American flag, after he overcomes the best fighter the Soviet Union has to offer. Following the Big Fight, the triumphant pugilist exclaims: "In here there were two guys killing each other, but I guess that's better than twenty million. I can change, you can change, everybody can change."

Of course, Rocky does more in this film than conjugate the verb "to change." Again, the film opens with the has-been Rocky on the brink of no-where. He's been married to Adrian (Talia Shire) for nine years now—and it feels like it to us, too. Somehow he's

persuaded to do just "one more fight"—this time against a Russian from hell. The Big Bad Commie trains; Rocky trains, again with old foe Apollo Creed (Carl Weathers); Rocky runs outdoors; the Russian trains in a high-tech gym. Eventually Rocky climbs a mountain, culminating in the now-familiar fists-over-head gesture from the first *Rocky*.

It's the "fight of his life," of course.

Screenplay by Sylvester Stallone

Executive Producers: James D. Brubaker and Arthur Chobanian

Produced by Irwin Winkler and Robert Chartoff

Directed by Sylvester Stallone

CAST

Rocky Balboa	Sylvester Stallone
Drago	Dolph Lundgren
Apollo Creed	Carl Weathers
Adrian	Talia Shire
Paulie	Burt Young
Ludmilla	Brigitte Nielsen

The audience is again suckered into thinking maybe Rocky *won't* win this one. But there is good character development, and we've really come to care about Rocky, his wife, and even little Rocky, Jr. Of course, he wins, and even the Russians can't help cheering for our man. (Don't miss the smiling ringside Gorbachev lookalike.)

The most adversarial role went to Brigitte Nielsen as the Russian trainer, Ludmilla. At six feet tall, the Scandinavian beauty walked off with the biggest prize of all—she ended up with Stallone himself, in what proved to be a "rocky" marriage which ended in divorce a few years later.

Rocky IV proved to be a huge success, earning even more money than 1982's *Rocky III*. Naturally there were plans for a *Rocky V*, which had just begun filming in Los Angeles and Philadelphia late in 1989. Of course, the film includes a spectacular fight, and a spectacular budget to match. *Rocky IV* cost around $31,000,000, and the next sequel is budgeted at $30,000,000. Get a ringside seat early—if past history means anything, it, too, will be a knockout.

THE COLOR PURPLE
WARNER BROS.
$47,900,000

"Omission impossible."
—THE NEW YORK POST

"Purple 11, Spielberg 0"
—THE LOS ANGELES
HERALD-EXAMINER

STEVEN SPIELBERG's first attempt at a totally serious film was *The Color Purple*. The man who had won fame as a director of action, fantasy, and supernatural films made a beautiful piece of cinema based on a difficult-to-film book—Alice Walker's diary-style, Pulitzer Prize–winning novel about the metamorphosis of a young black woman. The movie was breathtaking, from the first opening shots, to the well-integrated music, to the splendid tone and texture it established. Spielberg brought "Celie," "Mister," "Shug Avery," and all of Alice Walker's characters to life with a good deal of faithful attention to the novel.

Not surprisingly, *The Color Purple* was showered with Oscar nominations, 11 in all, yet not one was offered to the film's director. Rarely is a film nominated for Best Picture without the director being nominated in his category as well: after all, pictures don't

put themselves together. Word of Spielberg's snubbing generated an audible response throughout the Hollywood film community the day after the Academy Awards were announced. Spielberg could not be reached for comment, but Warner Bros. wasted no time in buying an ad in the trades proclaiming that "the company is shocked and dismayed that the movie's primary creative force—Steven Spielberg—was not recognized." Spielberg did, however, win the Director's Guild Award, viewed by many as a consolation prize. Ironic, too, since it is directors who nominate directors in the Academy. His peers failed to reward him in one organization, while lauding him in another.

The film was noteworthy in another area, too. Both first-time actresses Whoopi Goldberg (née Caryn Johnson) and Oprah Winfrey were nominated for Oscars. Whoopi was best known as a stand-up comic, and many doubted she could handle the role. (She's been disproving such talk ever since.) And Oprah Winfrey was most noted as a talk-show host who had started with a small morning show in Baltimore and had only recently moved on to Chicago.

She would soon hit the big time with a top nationally-syndicated TV talk show.

More disappointment followed on Oscar night. With 11 Award nominations, *The Color Purple* received not a single Oscar. Although the NAACP accused the Academy of a deliberate shut-out, this is highly unlikely, due to the strict controls of secret balloting. Financially, the film wasn't a true blockbuster, but at least there was some compensation in its success at the box office.

If you rent the videocassette, try to see this film on a big-screen TV so you can enjoy the breathtaking cinematography.

Screenplay by Steven Spielberg

Based on the novel by Alice Walker

Executive Producers: John Peters and Peter Guber

Produced by Steven Spielberg, Kathleen Kennedy, Frank Marshall, and Quincy Jones

Directed by Steven Spielberg

CAST

Albert	Danny Glover
Celie	Whoopi Goldberg
Shug Avery	Margaret Avery
Sofia	Oprah Winfrey
Harpo	Willard Pugh

ACADEMY AWARD NOMINATIONS

11 nominations, no wins

Best Picture
Best Actress (Whoopi Goldberg)
Best Supporting Actress (Margaret Avery)
Best Supporting Actress (Oprah Winfrey)
Best Screenplay Based on Material from Another Medium
Best Cinematography
Best Art Direction-Set Decoration
Best Song ("Miss Celie's Blues [Sister]," music by Quincy Jones and Rod Temperton, words by Quincy Jones, Rod Temperton, and Lionel Richie)
Best Original Score (Quincy Jones and 11 others)
Best Costume Design
Best Make-up

OUT OF AFRICA
UNIVERSAL
$43,103,469

"I had a farm in Africa . . ."
—OPENING TO ISAK DINESEN'S
BOOK *OUT OF AFRICA*

DANISH WRITER Isak Dinesen emigrated to colonial Africa in the early 20th century. Her real name was Karen Blixen, and she did indeed have a farm. This loosely biographical picture is primarily a tragic love story starring two of the decade's top-drawing names, Meryl Streep and Robert Redford. They make a classy pair, and audiences were moved to fall in love along with them. Set against splendid scenery of Kenya, the picture follows the young Karen in her loveless marriage to Bror Blixen (Klaus Maria Brandauer) in this episodic film about her affair with Great White Hunter Denys Finch-Hatton.

It's more a tapestry than a movie, with wondrous expanses of the African landscape as seen from Finch-Hatton's airplane, set to soaring music from John Barry (winner of Best Original Score). Other colorful characters from Blixen/Dinesen's books are woven throughout the picture. At 153 minutes, some thought the movie overly long, but not the romantics in the audience, many of whom returned more than once, giving the picture an additional boost at the box office. It was needed, as this was an expensive film to produce, costing a reported $31,000,000.

Sydney Pollack directed Robert Red-

Screenplay by Kurt Luedtke

Based on the following:
Out of Africa and other writings by Isak Dinesen
Isak Dinesen: The Life of a Storyteller by Judith Thurman
Silence Will Speak by Errol Trzebinski

Executive Producer: Kim Jorgensen

Produced and directed by Sydney Pollack

CAST

Karen	Meryl Streep
Denys	Robert Redford
Bror	Klaus Maria Brandauer
Berkeley	Michael Kitchen
Farah	Malick Bowens

ACADEMY AWARD NOMINATIONS

11 nominations, 7 wins*

*Best Picture
Best Actress (Meryl Streep)
Best Supporting Actor (Klaus Maria Brandauer)
*Best Director (Sydney Pollack)
*Best Screenplay Based on Material from Another Medium (Kurt Luedtke)
*Best Cinematography
*Best Art Direction-Set Decoration
*Best Sound
*Best Original Score (John Barry)
Best Film Editing
Best Costume Design

ford in *Jeremiah Johnson* and again in this movie. He had also directed the popular hit of 1982, *Tootsie* (see page 286). With *Out of Africa*, the director finally received an Academy Award.

The film was made on location during an African drought. Just as the crew was considering a move, the rains finally came. Many of the crew fell victim to malaria. And filming of the animals posed many problems as the crew camped in the bush. Sometimes it was necessary to wait hours for the wild herds to move to the right spot in the shot (it's illegal to touch or maneuver any wild animal). The film featured three dogs, an eagle, and five lions. All these animals had to be imported from California: seems there were no trained lions on their native continent.

Critics praised the picture. *The Hollywood Reporter* called it "a splendid, beautifully composed love story, a resplendent holiday film . . . Compositionally masterful, 'Out of Africa' moves with carefully modulated visual rhythms . . . In the leads, Streep and Redford are certain to garner Oscar nominations for their intelligent, gifted portrayals. Brandauer also brings distinction to his role."

Meryl Streep did indeed receive a nomination (her sixth), but oddly enough, Redford did not. And Brandauer, as predicted, was nominated for Best Supporting Actor.

1

TOP GUN
PARAMOUNT
$79,400,000

Screenplay by Jim Cash and Jack Epps, Jr.

Executive Producer: Bill Badalato

Produced by Don Simpson and
Jerry Bruckheimer

Directed by Tony Scott

CAST

Maverick	....	Tom Cruise
Charlie	....	Kelly McGillis
Ice	....	Val Kilmer
Goose	....	Anthony Edwards
Viper	....	Tom Skerritt

ACADEMY AWARD NOMINATIONS

4 nominations, 1 win*

Best Sound
*Best Song ("Take My Breath Away,"
  music by Giorgio Moroder, words by
  Tom Whitlock)
Best Film Editing
Best Sound Effects Editing

THEY COULD HAVE called it *Top Movie*. This number-one hit film had all the ingredients for success: handsome male lead, sexy female to play opposite him, plenty of action for those so inclined, and beautiful machinery—in this case, a fleet of Navy fighter planes. Yet preliminary marketing tests showed that audiences were not completely satisfied. Fearing the worst, producers Don Simpson and Jerry Bruckheimer (the team responsible for *Beverly Hills Cop*) called their principals back for additional photography six months after they had wrapped. Seems the audiences wanted more passion between Maverick (Tom Cruise) and Charlie (Kelly McGillis). That actress, who had appeared as a blonde in the film, had already cropped and darkened her hair for another movie, so in one scene, an encounter in an elevator, she had to wear a military cap.

The story of Maverick and his Radar Intercept Officer, "Goose" (Anthony Edwards), training to become the elitest of the elite—the best fighter pilots in the world—captured the imagination of the public. There was plenty of action and technical accuracy. The Navy gave its full support to the picture; there is much footage of real Top Gun pilots in evidence. Eight naval F-l4 pilots' names are listed in the credits, as well as 16 Top Gun instructors and "MIG" pilots (played by Americans with nicknames like "Horse," "Circus," "Sunshine," "Hollywood," "Tex," "Rat," and "Jaws").

Producers Simpson and Bruckheimer got the idea for the film from a May, 1983 article entitled "Top Guns" which ran in *California* magazine. The creative pair thought there was great potential for a film in the article. "Not only did we like the title and strong aerial photography which accompanied the article," recalled Simpson in the *Top Gun* production handbook, "but we were attracted to this uncommon environment, with its own terminology and its bigger-than-life characters." Bruckheimer added: "The pilots that attend the actual Top Gun school are a combination of Olympic athletes in the sky and rock and roll heroes. We immediately saw a movie."

Part of the thrill for audiences was the true feeling of sitting in the cockpit of an F-l4 "pulling G's." It was a Disneyland ride on screen, complete with stomach-wrenching rolls and turns. The film's star, Tom Cruise, spent several months commuting between Los Angeles and the Miramar Naval Air Station north of San Diego, attending Top Gun classes and learning about what it takes to be a pilot. "A Top Gun instructor once told me," said Cruise, quoted in Jolene Anthony's *Tom Cruise*, "that there are only four occupations worthy of a man: actor, rock star, jet fighter pilot, or President of the United States." Cruise's pre-production training was capped by a spectacular ride in the back seat of a TA-4, part of the famous Blue Angels squadron.

Kelly McGillis, Cruise's movie love interest, also did extensive research for her role. "Last year I was studying the Amish people for *Witness*, and the next year, I'm learning about negative Gs and inverted flight tanks for *Top Gun*," she said during filming, according to the *Top Gun* production handbook.

As part of the location shooting, 35 crew members spent four days at sea aboard the carrier USS *Enterprise*. Tom Cruise brought his own camera to record the events on the flight deck, and found himself being taught by an enlisted man to taxi the airplanes on the flight line. It was any young man's dream come true. The star of such popular films as *Taps*, *The Outsiders*, and *Risky Business* joined the ranks of superstardom with the popularity of *Top Gun*, soaring to the top of box office polls as the year's number-one performer.

The film's theme song, "Take My Breath Away" (and this picture certainly did just that for a lot of people), became a number-one hit the week of September l3, 1986, and went on to collect Oscars for its composers, Giorgio Moroder and Tom Whitlock. The team wrote two more popular songs for the film, "Danger Zone" and "Lead Me On," plus a number of other soundtrack songs.

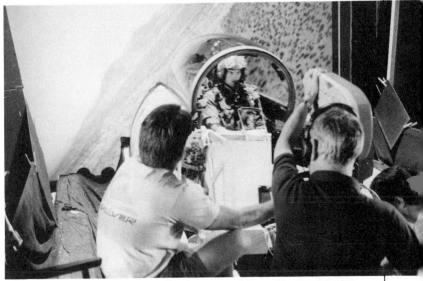

Much of *Top Gun*'s aerial action was filmed on a soundstage with rear projection.

"CROCODILE" DUNDEE
PARAMOUNT
$70,227,000

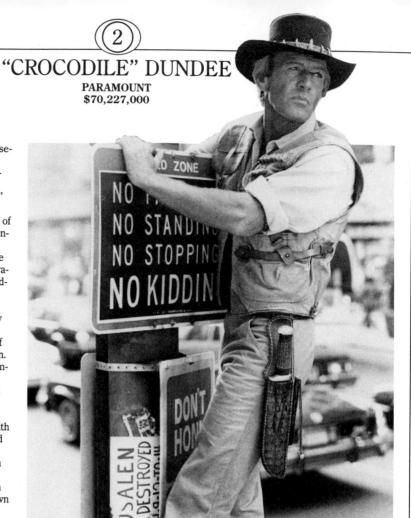

PAUL HOGAN was not exactly a household word in America. The former rigger on the Sydney, Australia, Harbour Bridge, who had gone on to become the Aussie "Johnny Carson," had been seen by only a handful of Yanks who might have caught reruns of his variety show on late-night independent TV channels. So when his Australian hit film *Crocodile Dundee* came to America, the releasing studio, Paramount Pictures, decided (after considering 250 alternate titles) to put quotation marks around the word "Crocodile" lest Americans stay away from what they might suspect was a nature film on the care and feeding of reptiles. It was an unfounded concern. Americans took one look at the charming and sexy Mr. Hogan and couldn't have cared less whether the picture's title had quotes around it or not.

Suddenly, Aussie was chic. It was trendy to toss down a few Fosters with your mates (pronounced "mites") and even plan a trip Down Under. In fact, after this picture's release, Australian tourism increased by 40 percent. Hogan himself had been a spokesman for "the land of Wonder, the land Down Under" for years, promising all of us he'd "slip an extra shrimp on the barbie."*

What Paul Hogan did was create a character in the James Bond tradition—

Screenplay by Paul Hogan, Ken Shadie, and John Cornell

Produced by John Cornell

Directed by Peter Faiman

CAST

Mick "Crocodile"
Dundee . . . . Paul Hogan
Sue Charlton . . . . Linda Kozlowski
Walter Reilly . . . . John Meillon
Neville Bell . . . . David Gulpilil
Con . . . . Ritchie Singer

ACADEMY AWARD NOMINATIONS

1 nomination, no wins

Best Screenplay Written Directly for the Screen

---

a hero who could handle himself in any situation—except that this guy was an Aussie babe in the woods. The woods, in this case, was the jungle called New York City, and Hogan as Mick "Crocodile" Dundee proved you can take the Aussie out of the bush, but you can't take the bush out of the Aussie. In the film's story, Dundee is "adopted" by an American reporter, Sue Charlton (Linda Kozlowski), who persuades the croc hunter to journey back to the Big Apple with her so she can finish her story. His childlike reaction to everyday things we take for granted is what gives this story its main appeal.

Some changes in vocabulary had to be made for Americans to understand the Aussie colloquialisms, and several minutes were cut entirely. One scene, however, remained unchanged, although most Americans didn't understand the reference. At the end of the film, Mick is in the New York subway,

fighting his way through the crowd, trying frantically to reach his girlfriend, Sue. In a sequence which parallels the familiar sheepdogs walking across the backs of the sheep in Australia (the world's leading sheep-breeding country), Mick climbs over the backs of subway patrons. Australians roared with laughter at this sight gag, while most Americans didn't catch on.

Paul Hogan's popularity rocketed with this film's surprising success, and Paramount ordered an immediate sequel (see page 324). The actor was inundated with offers, but continued to patriotically promote his native country, as well as its products, including Foster's Lager. Many of these commercials are still on TV today.

---

*Chances are your Australian hosts would give you blank stares if you request one. "Shrimps" are called "prawns" there, and anyway, they usually barbecue steaks and chicken like the rest of us.

PLATOON

ORION
$69,742,143

"Dedicated to the men who fought and died in the Vietnam War."
—TITLE CARD

WAR MOVIES have always been box office hits. In the '40s we had *Sergeant York, A Yank in the R.A.F., 30 Seconds Over Tokyo*, and others. In the '50s, there were the "funny" war films, like *Mister Roberts* and *Operation Petticoat*, as well as the dramatic stories of *Battle Cry, From Here to Eternity*, and *The Bridge on the River Kwai*. In the late '80s, with film technology perfected to an art form, war movies reached new heights, culminating in Oliver Stone's masterpiece, *Platoon*.

Never had war been portrayed this realistically. Actor Mickey Rooney was so disturbed by the film that he thought they should have a sign outside theaters banning women, a sexist point of view that may well be merited. *Platoon* is a paean to the insanity that we call war, neither glorifying nor trivializing it. This is humanity at its lowest element, the animal brain stem in control, the cerebrum somehow on hiatus. The film

is frightening and depressing, and yes, superb filmmaking. Above all else, the viewer must constantly remind himself that he or she has not dropped into some jungle during a war, but is still sitting comfortably (by now, uncomfortably) in a theater or living-room chair. It's not the shoot-'em-up-and-let's-hear-a-cheer *Rambo* school of filmmaking violence, but a much more painful, stomach-turning, blood-and-guts movie. Not too many people visited the concession stand during this one.

Oliver Stone had a personal interest in doing this film. He had served for 15 months in Vietnam when, at the age of 21, he dropped out of Yale and joined the infantry. The experiences of his hero, Chris (Charlie Sheen), directly parallel Stone's own wartime hell. Stone spent 10 years trying to get the feature made, meanwhile writing such

films as *Midnight Express* (1978) and *Scarface* (1983), and writing and directing *Salvador*. He finally persuaded Orion Productions to make *Platoon*, which he brought in on a budget of only $6,000,000.

It turned out to be the biggest film Orion ever had, returning their investment tenfold. Publicity and word of mouth helped increase the audience for this picture. Besides its harsh realism, there is attention to fine details. Listen for the voice of the real Adrian Cronauer in the background, blaring out "Gooood Morning Vietnam!" This was not added as an inside joke; that hit film wouldn't even be released for another year.

This picture appears uncut, with all its violence and language intact, on many cable channels. Send the kids to bed early.

Screenplay by Oliver Stone

Executive Producers: John Daly and Derek Gibson

Produced by Arnold Kopelson

Directed by Oliver Stone

CAST

Sergeant Barnes	Tom Berenger
Sergeant Elias	Willem Dafoe
Chris	Charlie Sheen
Big Harold	Forest Whitaker
Rhah	Francesco Quinn

ACADEMY AWARD NOMINATIONS

8 nominations, 4 wins*

**Best Picture
 Best Supporting Actor (Tom Berenger)
 Best Supporting Actor (Willem Dafoe)
*Best Director (Oliver Stone)
 Best Screenplay Written Directly
  for the Screen
 Best Cinematography
*Best Sound
Best Film Editing

THE KARATE KID, PART II
COLUMBIA
$58,362,026

IN DIRECT contrast to violent films like *Platoon, Rambo: First Blood Part II*, and even *Top Gun, The Karate Kid, Part II* was a kinder, gentler type of picture for war-weary audiences. Reprising their original roles were Ralph Macchio as the downtrodden teenaged Daniel (Macchio was now 24 years old) and Pat Morita as his sage advisor/ mentor/trainer. Like the first film, this one was a sleeper: no one expected it to do much business. But like its inspiration, *Rocky*, the Roman-numeraled sequel brought in many of the film's original fans, along with many newcomers. This picture actually made more than its predecessor.

Critics immediately took sides. Some thought the movie was merely a rip-off of a rip-off, as if someone at Columbia had perhaps demanded, "Send in the clones!" The Hollywood trade paper *Daily Variety* called the film "a pokey and hokey sequel to the 1984 chop socky kidpic"; yet *The Hollywood Reporter* considered the sequel "a gentle yet exciting film—even rarer, a sequel that's better than the original."

The sequel certainly had more story to it than did its predecessor. Accompanied by his young charge, Miyagi (Morita) returns to his native Okinawa, where his father is dying. Back home, he meets up with an old nemesis and an old girlfriend, while Daniel finds a new nemesis and new girlfriend. Morita has the juicier role here, as noted by *The Hollywood Reporter*. " 'The Karate Kid, Part II' is most certainly Morita's story, and his performance is the film's highlight. It is measured, tender and completely winning. Morita seems a certain bet for Academy consideration as the wise and comical martial arts sage." However, although the actor was nominated for his part in the first *Karate Kid*, the Academy chose to ignore Morita's critically praised performance this time around. The only nomination received was for "Glory of Love" as Best Song. The recording by co-composer Peter Cetera shot to the top of the *Billboard* charts, remaining at number one for two weeks.

In the summer of 1989, yet another installment was released, *The Karate Kid, Part III*. The 27-year-old Macchio was still baby-faced enough to play teenage karate student Daniel LaRusso, but was beginning to fear typecasting. "I guess the thing I want most is to be perceived as a versatile actor who does many things," Macchio told the *Los Angeles Times*. "The challenge is breaking through the mold of being the angelic, identifiable 'Karate Kid' character." *Kid III* completes Macchio's three-picture deal. Says the actor, "My instinct is to move on to other things . . . I can't feasibly foresee myself just playing this kid getting beat up again and prevailing in the end."

Sylvester Stallone couldn't have put it better.

Screenplay by Robert Mark Kamen

Executive Producer: R. J. Louis

Produced by Jerry Weintraub

Directed by John G. Avildsen

CAST

Daniel	Ralph Macchio
Miyagi	Noriyuki "Pat" Morita
Yukie	Nobu McCarthy
Sato	Danny Kamekona
Chozen	Yuji Okumoto

ACADEMY AWARD NOMINATIONS

1 nomination, no wins

Best Song ("Glory of Love," music by Peter Cetera, and David Foster, words by Peter Cetera and Diane Nini)

STAR TREK IV: THE VOYAGE HOME

PARAMOUNT
$56,820,071

THERE had been two sequels to the successful *Star Trek: The Motion Picture* (1979; see page 266). In *Star Trek II: The Wrath of Khan*, Ricardo Montalban, as the nefarious "Khan," a character created in one of the TV episodes, attacks the Enterprise and kills the beloved character of Mr. Spock. Trekkers were furious. Paramount, realizing they may have killed the goose that lays golden eggs for them on a regular basis, found a way to resurrect the popular Vulcan in the third picture in the series, appropriately titled *Star Trek III: The Search for Spock* (they found him, in case you're wondering). For this third movie, Leonard Nimoy, the actor who had fleshed out Gene Roddenberry's creation of the half-Vulcan, half-human Mr. Spock, promised to return only if given directorial chores. The picture did well, and he was given another assignment: *Star Trek IV: The Voyage Home.*

This fourth *Trek* did slightly better financially than *Star Trek I* (but not if inflation is taken into account), since it found a wider audience. The picture has to do with the Enterprise crew trying to return to Earth without their beloved Enterprise (they had trashed the starship a picture or two back)— oh, and while they were at it, they have

to find a way to save the planet from Destruction by Strange Aliens from Space. The aliens, it seems, are searching for their old pals, the whales from centuries past, but none exist in the 24th century, so Kirk and Company set out to return to an earlier time on Earth when whales hadn't been hunted to extinction. It's a nice thought, if a bit hokey.

Some of the best scenes are not, as one might expect, in space, but on 20th-century Earth—San Francisco, to be exact. There are some delightful numbers with our spacepeople of the future trying to figure out how to use money, operate computers which must be museum pieces to them, take a bus (in a clever bit with Leonard Nimoy's assistant Kirk Thatcher as a punker with a boombox), and mix with the population without arousing suspicion as to who they really are.

There are shades of *"Crocodile" Dundee* in the "Man from Mars" shtick,

but it's all good fun, and mainstream audiences, as well as the hardcore Trekkers and science fiction fans, made this another big hit for Paramount. (The studio, in fact, had three of the top five hits for the year, totalling nearly $200,000,000 in rentals.)

In 1989, Paramount released *Star Trek V: The Final Frontier*. Since Leonard Nimoy had directed *two* of the popular films, it seemed only fair, argued William Shatner, that he be allowed to direct at least one sequel. In fact, his *Star Trek IV* contract already provided for that. In 1988, he drafted a story which became the basis for *Star Trek V*. The picture opened in the summer of 1989, and although it showed early signs of being a hit, box office take was off dramatically by the end of the summer. It was quickly released on videocassette, and the studio planned to take a "wait and see" attitude before deciding the fate of the Enterprise crew and a *Star Trek VI*.

Screenplay by Steve Meerson, Peter Krikes, Harve Bennett, and Nicholas Meyer

Executive Producer: Ralph Winter

Produced by Harve Bennett

Directed by Leonard Nimoy

CAST

Kirk . . . . William Shatner
Spock . . . . Leonard Nimoy
McCoy . . . . DeForest Kelley
Scotty . . . . James Doohan
Sulu . . . . George Takei

ACADEMY AWARD NOMINATIONS

4 nominations, no wins

Best Cinematography
Best Sound
Best Original Score
Best Sound Effects Editing

1

THREE MEN AND A BABY
TOUCHSTONE PICTURES (WALT DISNEY PRODUCTIONS)
$81,313,000

*"I think it's your turn to change
her."* —STEVE GUTTENBERG

*"I'll give you a thousand dollars if
you do it."* —TOM SELLECK

IT WAS every leading lady's dream.
Imagine sharing co-credit with Tom
Selleck, Ted Danson, and Steve Guttenberg, having them fuss over you,
sing to you, share their penthouse with
you. Then, imagine you're their six-
month-old baby. That's the set-up for
Three Men and a Baby. And the old
warning about never acting with children and animals goes triple here . . .
in what borders on armed robbery,
the little infant girl steals every scene
she's in.

Screenplay by James Orr and
Jim Cruickshank

Based on the film *Trois Hommes et un
Couffin* written by Coline Serreau

Executive Producer: Jean Francois Lepetit

Produced by Ted Field and Robert W. Cort

Directed by Leonard Nimoy

CAST

Peter . . . . Tom Selleck
Michael . . . . Steve Guttenberg
Jack . . . . Ted Danson
Sylvia . . . . Nancy Travis
Rebecca . . . . Margaret Colin

The Walt Disney Company made out
like bandits at the box office with this
Touchstone release*. Ever since the
creative team from Paramount, consisting of Michael Eisner, Jeffrey Katzenberg, and Richard Frank, defected to
Disney, the company, which had been
ailing since Walt's death, had begun a
turnaround which put Disney Studios
once more among the serious contenders in Hollywood's film industry.

Three Men and a Baby was a delight
for several reasons. It was based on a
popular French film, *Trois Hommes et
un Couffin* (*Three Men and a Cradle*,
1985). *Trois Hommes* broke box office
records in France and was nominated in
the U.S. for an Academy Award as the
Best Foreign Film of 1985. It was also

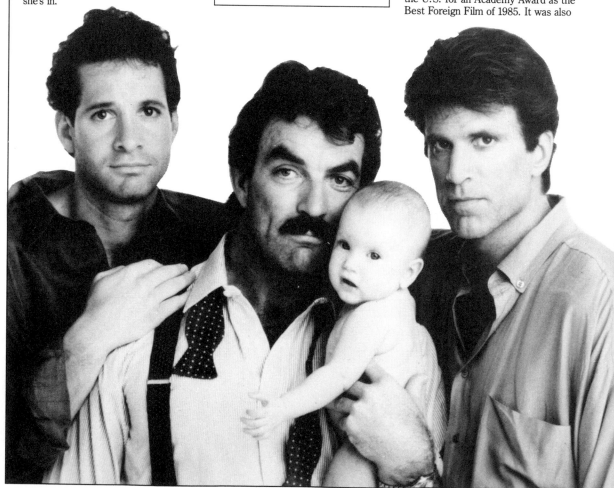

the highest-grossing foreign language film in the U.S. in 1986. Both films have basically the same plot: three bachelors-about-town are suddenly saddled with fatherhood when a baby is abandoned on their doorstep. There's a subplot about drugs and some hoods who mistakenly think our heroes are their contacts, but all that's not really important. Some of the most delightful moments for audiences are whenever the baby (actually twin girls, Lisa and Michelle Blair) is on screen.

The film was shot in Toronto, Canada, with Leonard Nimoy, fresh from his directing successes on two *Star Trek* films, handling his first non-Trek assignment. Nimoy proves that he knows his way around kids (he's a

---

*Walt Disney Productions uses the Disney name mostly for the "G"-rated pictures the studio releases; a subsidiary company, Touchstone, is used for the more adult "PG" and "R" releases. Buena Vista (named after the street the studio is on in Burbank) is the name for Disney's distribution arm. for reasons of simplification, Touchstone and Disney productions in this book are all referred to in charts as "Disney" releases.

grandfather) as well as around a starship. For the film's huge box office take, Nimoy, in a press release at the time, credited his fine cast: "I think that the relationship between the three actors is palpable on screen. I am particularly sensitive to the importance of this because *Star Trek* was an example of a situation where the chemistry between the performers was crucial to the project's success."

The *Three Men* were popular '80s stars from film and TV. Tom Selleck was best known for his continuing TV series, "Magnum, P.I.," which ran for eight seasons on CBS; many have hailed him as a modern Clark Gable. During his summer hiatuses from "Magnum," he starred in a number of action-adventure films, including *High Road to China*, *Runaway*, and *Lassiter*. But his most successful feature so far has been *Three Men and a Baby*, quite a departure for the macho idol.

Steve Guttenberg had an impressively long list of film credits, including the hit fantasy film *Cocoon* (1985), directed by Ron Howard; *Police Academy 1, 2, 3,* and *4* (1984, 1985, 1986, and 1987, respectively); and

Short Circuit (1986). While he had more film credits than his two male co-stars, he admitted his lack of any experience when it came to handling babies. According to *Three Men*'s press release, "this was one time . . . that not having experience was actually a plus because it made my character all the more believable."

Bachelor number three in the film, Ted Danson, is best known as the perennial bachelor Sam Malone on the hit TV series "Cheers."

To prepare for their roles, Danson, Selleck, and Guttenberg hit the Toronto singles scene. "We went out eating and dancing and had a great time," recalled Danson in the same press release. "Of course, it was all in the name of research and role preparation." (Can you imagine these three guys showing up in a singles bar?)

Both *Three Men and a Cradle*, the original French film, and *Three Men and a Baby*, are delightfully funny; the French version is subtitled, rather than dubbed, but if reading subtitles is a chore, these can easily be ignored and you'll still get the picture. A sequel is scheduled to begin filming in 1990.

BEVERLY HILLS COP II
PARAMOUNT
$80,857,776

Eddie Murphy's name is so entwined with the comic genre that's it's easy to classify *Beverly Hills Cop II* as a comedy. Certainly, there are some hilarious moments in this picture. But there is a serious undertone to this film, as Axel Foley returns to help his Beverly Hills pals, Billy (Judge Reinhold) and Taggart (John Ashton), when their police captain (again played by Ronny Cox) is critically wounded. Dean Stockwell (once a cute child star) plays the heavy, with Brigitte Nielsen (Sly Stallone's former lady) as his hitwoman.

If not for Murphy, this film might just be another Beverly Hills cops-and-robbers picture. For example, there's that old standby, the car chase—this time a demolition derby with a cement truck. Murphy's quick improvisational wit, however, saves the picture from becoming anything close to routine. "I never had aspirations to be in the movie business," admitted Murphy in a Paramount production handbook. "I was always a stand-up comedian, and that's what I am more than anything."

Screenplay by Larry Ferguson and Warren Skaaren

From a story by Eddie Murphy and Robert D. Wachs

Based on characters created by Danilo Bach and Daniel Petrie, Jr.

Executive Producers: Robert D. Wachs and Richard Tienken

Produced by Don Simpson and Jerry Bruckheimer

Directed by Tony Scott

CAST

Axel Foley	Eddie Murphy
Billy Rosewood	Judge Reinhold
Maxwell Dent	Jurgen Prochnow
Andrew Bogomil	Ronny Cox
John Taggart	John Ashton

ACADEMY AWARD NOMINATIONS

1 nomination, no wins

Best Song ("Shakedown," music by Harold Faltermeyer and Keith Forsey, words by Harold Faltermeyer, Keith Forsey, and Bob Seger)

Could be, but the winner of the People's Choice Awards for 1985 can always be counted on to turn a routine picture into a smash.

Reviews were less than kind for the film. *Variety* complained: " 'Beverly Hills Cop II' is a noisy, numbing, unimaginative, heartless remake of the original film. Everything that was funny and appealing the first time has been attempted again here, but has all gone sour and cold . . . but none of this will matter at the boxoffice, as Murphy, Simpson, Bruckheimer, et al., will once again laugh all the way to the bank."

Count on it. Eddie Murphy became the highest-paid black film star in history when he banked $7,000,000 for his latest ride down Rodeo Drive. Since then, his Paramount contract has been renegotiated at an undisclosed figure. He recently completed producing and directing a Paramount film in which he also stars, *Harlem Nights*. (No doubt this will put enough money in Murphy's account for him to buy that studio.)

The soundtrack for *Beverly Hills Cop* had produced a successful single, "The Heat Is On," which peaked at number two in March, 1985. With the release of *Cop II*, a new song was added to the charts: "Shakedown." The Bob Seger recording climbed the pop charts to number one, where it remained during the first week in August, 1987. It also became a Best Song contender, the movie's only Academy Award nomination.

Eddie Murphy's vocabulary is quite colorful, in addition to the violence and nudity this picture contains. The "R" rating didn't seem to hurt it any at the box office, but it is *not* a family comedy. *Beverly Hills Cop II* can be seen frequently on cable channels, and while not as much fun as the first, it's still an Eddie Murphy showcase, and he doesn't have all those fans for nothing.

FATAL ATTRACTION

PARAMOUNT
$70,000,000

"**I** WAS ALWAYS interested in lust," said Michael Douglas in *Cable Guide* Magazine. "Everybody has someone they've lusted for." If that is true, then this would be the reason behind the huge success of the summer of '87's hit film, *Fatal Attraction*.

In this case, Douglas is the lustee, not the lustor. What starts as a simple little weekend tryst turns into a nightmare for Dan Gallagher (Douglas) when the object of his affections, Alex Forrest (Glenn Close), becomes obsessed, then maniacal, about her one-night-stand lover. Douglas says he is happily married, but Close isn't buying it. When he spurns her attentions, she stalks him like a quarry. Soon we learn this is not a triangular romance picture, but a deadly game of cat and mouse.

Much of this movie's suspense owes a debt to Alfred Hitchcock and the *Psycho* school of filmmaking. It is not a mystery—we know Close is stalking Douglas and terrorizing his family, and she gives new meaning to the words "insanely jealous." The question is, when will she next strike, and how? It is a psychological-suspense thriller/romance, not for the squeamish, although certainly predictable in outcome.

Newsweek provided something of a warning label for its readers, when its reviewer wrote: "Alex is a figure designed to send men rushing off to their shrinks, aquiver with sexual paranoia . . . What Freddy or Jason is to horny teens, Alex may become to the Yuppie male contemplating an extramarital fling."

Indeed, business was brisk on psychiatric couches across the country, while at the same time declining at singles bars following the film's release. Glenn Close researched her role by taking the script to three psychiatrists, one of whom helped her construct a detailed emotional and psychiatric history for the character. She described Alex to *Newsweek* as "between being a total child and a femme fatale. Her sexuality has been all screwed up, and she has no sense of self-worth. She tries to provoke people to hate her as much as she hates herself."

Most of the audience wasn't interested in psychoanalyzing Douglas' unfortunate choice of a bed partner. According to statistics, a high percentage of the married public are either involved in or contemplating extramarital affairs; many men were reluctantly escorted to this picture by their concerned significant others, who would not believe that the plural of "spouse" is "spice." It became the most talked-about film of the summer, and gave Paramount yet another great box office year, with three films in the top five (*Beverly Hills Cop II, Fatal Attraction, The Untouchables*) for a total take of close to $187,000,000 in domestic rentals.

Screenplay by James Dearden

Produced by Stanley R. Jaffe and Sherry Lansing

Directed by Adrian Lyne

CAST

Dan Gallagher	Michael Douglas
Alex Forrest	Glenn Close
Beth Gallagher	Anne Archer
Jimmy	Stuart Pankin
Hildy	Ellen Foley
Arthur	Fred Gwynne

ACADEMY AWARD NOMINATIONS

6 nominations, no wins

Best Picture
Best Actress (Glenn Close)
Best Supporting Actress (Anne Archer)
Best Director (Adrian Lyne)
Best Screenplay Based on Material from Another Medium
Best Film Editing

GOOD MORNING, VIETNAM
TOUCHSTONE PICTURES (WALT DISNEY PRODUCTIONS)
$58,103,000

ROBIN WILLIAMS is always a risk when signed to a picture: a risk in the best sense of the word, since that producer is generally likely to get more than he bargained for. That is precisely what makes Robin Williams so desirable. He is one of the quickest natural wits in the business, a perpetual ad-libber who is virtually always "on," even when relaxing with friends.

As Adrian Cronauer in *Good Morning, Vietnam*, Williams hits his stride. Cronauer was a real Vietnam DJ on the local Armed Forces Radio network. As portrayed by Robin Williams, at least, he was to radio what Hawkeye Pierce was to *M*A*S*H*—a cut-up who refused to take war, or orders, seriously. His instructions were to read propaganda, but Cronauer, as marvelously ad-libbed by Williams, had his own idea about what the soldiers wanted to hear. And of course he was right. Producer Mark Johnson noted in a press release at the time: "Nobody else works with the inventiveness, the quickness and the zaniness of Robin Williams. When he sat down in the control booth to do the scenes involving Cronauer's broadcasts, we just let the cameras roll. He managed to create something new for every single take."

Robin Williams was born in a Chicago suburb in 1952. In Robin's high school years, his father retired to Marin County, California, where Williams was voted "Most Humorous" and "Most Likely to Succeed" by his classmates.

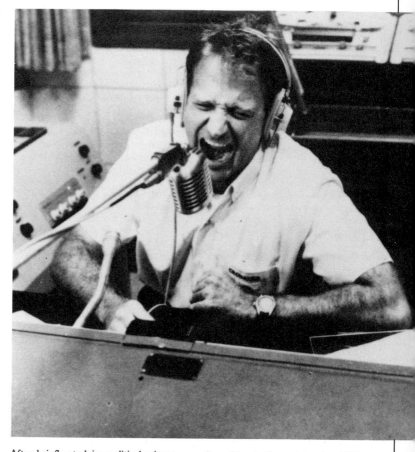

Screenplay by Mitch Markowitz

Produced by Mark Johnson and
  Larry Brezner

Directed by Barry Levinson

CAST

Adrian Cronauer ...	Robin Williams
Edward Garlick	Forest Whitaker
Tuan	Tung Thanh Tran
Trinh	Chintara Sukapatana
Lt. Steven Hauk ...	Bruno Kirby

ACADEMY AWARD NOMINATIONS

1 nomination, no wins

Best Actor (Robin Williams)

After briefly studying political science, Williams entered Marin College as a theater major, but soon enrolled at New York's famed Juilliard Academy (Chris Reeve was a classmate), where he spent three years under the tutelage of actor John Houseman, among other notables. After college, he performed on the California nightclub circuit, eventually landing at the Los Angeles Comedy Store. He was spotted by casting agents there, and appeared on TV in what was supposed to be a one-shot performance as "Mork from Ork" on the popular "Happy Days" show. Viewer response encouraged Paramount to spin off his own show, *Mork and Mindy* (1978 premiere), which showcased his outrageous antics. (Lucky studio audiences got to see an even better show than what was actu-

ally written in the script, when Williams ad-libbed non-stop at tapings.) He was soon starring in films such as *Popeye* and *The World According to Garp*, but *Good Morning, Vietnam* was his first true hit. In 1989, Williams starred in another Touchstone hit, *Dead Poets Society*, well on its way to becoming a top moneymaker.

Good Morning, Vietnam was more than a Robin Williams laugh fest; it had a serious side as well. The story marks a departure from many of the recent Vietnam stories like *Platoon* in that its format is a new genre called "dramedy"—drama/comedy. Williams has us clutching our sides in laughter one minute, then director Barry Levinson throws in something from the serious side of war to sober us. It's fine adult entertainment.

THE UNTOUCHABLES
PARAMOUNT
$36,866,530

A HIGHLY successful TV show that ran on ABC from 1959 to 1963, "The Untouchables" starred Robert Stack as Eliot Ness, the no-nonsense "Fed" who took a bite out of crime in the days of Prohibition. People who had Stack's portrayal in their minds as they headed for theaters emerged two hours later from the "R"-rated film with a new hero. As Eliot Ness, Kevin Costner created a whole new image for a character that had been mere cardboard for an earlier generation.

"The biggest challenge of Eliot Ness," Costner said during filming, according to the movie's production handbook, "is that he's not a flashy character, and the trick is to try not to make him flashy. He's a really steady character, a homebody with a real sense of what's right and wrong . . . and he's kind of courageous." Costner found offers pouring in after *The Untouchables*, his first starring role. His 1988 hit *Bull Durham* and 1989 *Field of Dreams* landed him on the cover of *Time*. In two short years, his price tag had risen to $5,000,000, and many were calling the handsome, intelligent actor a cross between Jimmy Stewart and Gary Cooper.

Under the direction of Brian De Palma, generally noted for blood-spurting thrillers like *Carrie, Dressed to Kill,* and *Scarface, The Untouchables* focuses on the pursuit of gangster Al Capone (played magnificently by Robert De Niro) by Ness and his cronies, a select team of investigators who couldn't be bought or bribed—hence the designation "untouchables." The team includes "George Stone" (Andy Garcia), an Italian rookie cop, and "Oscar Wallace" (Charles Martin Smith), a government accountant sent by Washington to get the goods on Capone. The plum role, though, went to Sean Connery, as Jimmy Malone, a seasoned cop who tests Ness' abilities to take on Capone. Connery proved he had outgrown the James Bond image with his Oscar win for Best Supporting Actor.

Although the picture is violent, as is to be expected with most De Palma films, there are fine production values, and *The Untouchables* received praise from critics. *Daily Variety* called the crime drama "a beautifully crafted portrait of Prohibition-era Chicago" in which "script, directing, characterization, wardrobe, art direction and score jointly evoke the celebrated conflict between gangster bootleggers and Federal agents." The reviewer had special praise for Connery, Costner, and especially De Niro, "a compelling figure who stops just short of caricature. With the addition of 30 pounds and the legendary facial scar, De Niro is quite convincing—perhaps never more so than during one powerful scene in which he wields a baseball bat while philosophizing about business with his lieutenants."

Anyone who has seen this picture will instantly recall this scene, brutal yet wonderfully directed. Like the man said, this is a study in good filmmaking, and incidentally, entertainment on a very adult level.

Kevin Costner (on balcony) awaits the next shot on the set of *The Untouchables*.

Screenplay by David Mamet

Produced by Art Linson

Directed by Brian De Palma

CAST

Eliot Ness . . . . Kevin Costner
Jim Malone . . . . . . Sean Connery
Oscar Wallace . . . . Charles Martin Smith
George Stone . . . . . Andy Garcia
Al Capone . . . . Robert De Niro

ACADEMY AWARD NOMINATIONS

4 nominations, 1 win*

**Best Supporting Actor (Sean Connery)
Best Art Direction-Set Decoration
Best Original Score (Ennio Morricone)
Best Costume Design

1

RAIN MAN

METRO-GOLDWYN-MAYER/UNITED ARTISTS
$80,000,000*

A SEEMINGLY unlikely candidate for the top moneymaker of 1988, *Rain Man*, released just in time for the Christmas crowd, immediately began grabbing the public's and critics' attention. The subject matter was autism, a neurological handicap which affects four in 10,000 and is characterized by isolated compulsive behavior, lack of emotional contact with others, and frequently, an extreme sensitivity to sounds and touch. As Raymond Babbitt, Dustin Hoffman portrays a man with this disability who is not only an autistic but also a "savant"—that one percent of autistics who have uncanny abilities to do extraordinary things like multiply huge numbers instantly, or memorize half the phone book at one sitting.**

Such is not usually the stuff of box office blockbusters. But Hoffman's remarkable performance, together with numerous Oscars and Oscar nominations, saw word of mouth bringing in a brisk business. By mid-'89, the film had passed 1988's box office leader, *Who Framed Roger Rabbit*, in a tortoise-and-hare race across the finish line.

Hoffman's performance is nothing short of brilliant. The actor plays Raymond Babbitt (an early childhood trauma caused him to confuse the sound of his own name with the words "rain man"), who is heir to the family fortune left by a father who had the boy institutionalized. All this comes as a shock to his brother, Charlie (Tom Cruise, proving he can do a serious role), who feels cheated of his inheritance and abducts Raymond for a cross-country trip which will find both men considerably changed by journey's end. It's literally an "Odd Couple" syndrome.

While autism might not sound like a subject befitting comedy, it is the film's lighthanded treatment of the disorder that is one of the main reasons for the wide appeal. In one of *Rain Man's* most humorous sequences, we learn that Raymond is terrified of flying. His brother is frantic to get him on a plane to California, but Raymond throws a tantrum. It seems there is only one airline that doesn't give Raymond nightmares—"Qantas," he says. "Qantas never crashes." Although Australia's

national airline doesn't fly from U.S. domestic routes, ticket sales have been rising handsomely ever since this commercial plug.

To prepare for the role of Raymond, Dustin Hoffman intensively studied autism, consulting with experts and autistics and their families. A major source was the UCLA Neuropsychiatric Institute and Hospital. One of their subjects, a young man named Joe Sullivan, was the study of a documentary film. Hoffman viewed the film, then pored over 15 hours of unedited outtakes. "The documentary really moved me," Hoffman told *People* Magazine. "Joe's a lovely guy, and if you look closely enough there is a very healthy soul there." Hoffman based his characterization of Raymond on Joe and another autistic person.

Steven Spielberg turned down an offer of $5,000,000 to direct *Rain Man*, citing other commitments. A deal

---

Screenplay by Ronald Bass and Barry Morrow

Based on story by Barry Morrow

Executive Producers: Peter Guber and Jon Peters

Produced by Mark Johnson

Directed by Barry Levinson

CAST

Raymond Babbitt	Dustin Hoffman
Charlie Babbitt	Tom Cruise
Susanna	Valeria Golino
Dr. Bruner	Jerry Molen
John Mooney	Jack Murdock

ACADEMY AWARD NOMINATIONS

8 nominations, 4 wins

*Best Picture
*Best Actor (Dustin Hoffman)
*Best Director (Barry Levinson)
*Best Original Screenplay (Ronald Bass, Barry Morrow, screenplay; Barry Morrow, story)
Best Art Direction-Set Decoration
Best Cinematography
Best Film Editing
Best Original Score (Hans Zimmer)

---

with Sydney Pollack also fell through, opening the way for Barry Levinson. Levinson had scored a hit with 1987's *Good Morning, Vietnam*, and *Rain Man* was his sixth picture. His first film, *Diner*, was to his career what *American Graffiti* had been to George Lucas: it launched him as a major film director (and coincidentally, launched the acting careers of Steve Guttenberg, Mickey Rourke, and Kevin Bacon, as Lucas' film did for an earlier generation of actors). Although it would be easy to grab credit for *Rain Man's* success, Levinson is quick in his generosity. "In the best sense of the word," he said in a recent television interview, "I think it was a terrific collaborative piece. We all knew what we had to ultimately accomplish." In the same interview, co-star Tom Cruise praised his director: "He likes actors, and he allowed Dustin to work, and me to work, and to play around. If you have an idea, he addresses it." To top it all off, Levinson brought the picture in at $2,500,000 *under* budget.

While certainly not made as a public service, the film has nevertheless been widely acclaimed by people working in the field of autism. Brad Tatum, director of the Washington, D.C., chapter of the Autism Association of America, himself the father of an autistic child, told *The Hollywood Reporter*: "The film lets people know that in most cases it is hopeless and that an autistic person stays autistic in the end—there is no cure. But it also shows many of the things autistics can do . . . the movie gave out the kind of information that we like to give out as an organization . . . that they are not crazy or dangerous—they just think differently."

It's too soon to gain a proper perspective on this film, but it will almost assuredly be looked upon as a landmark picture by the end of the '90s.

---

*Rental figure is approximate and is based on combined published rentals plus projected figure extrapolated from film's 1988–89 grosses.

**In *Rain Man*, Dustin Hoffman's character memorizes a phone book up to the names Marsha and William Gottsegen, Hoffman's real-life in-laws.

1988

WHO FRAMED ROGER RABBIT
TOUCHSTONE PICTURES (WALT DISNEY PRODUCTIONS)
$78,000,000

"A laugh can be a very powerful thing. Why, sometimes in life, it's the only weapon we have."
—ROGER RABBIT

THE WORLD according to Roger Rabbit can be a very wonderful thing, as this enormous hit for Touchstone/Disney proved. It was one of the cleverest, funniest, happiest films to come along in many a year, a picture Walt himself would have been proud of, to say the least. And no wonder—look who was behind it: none other than Disney's self-appointed heir-apparent, Steven Spielberg. For the first time, Spielberg's Amblin Entertainment combined forces with the best talents at the Disney factory for what is billed as a "Spielberg Presents" film, directed by *Back to the Future*'s Robert Zemeckis.

The Disney production notes list 11 pages of names of talent who went into this picture, all of whom should be proud to be associated with this superb film combining animation with live action. The concept isn't new, of course.

Walt himself used it in early "Alice" cartoons, and in *Song of the South*. But modern computer technology has made this state-of-the-art live/animated movie a wonder to behold.

Credit Bob Hoskins for interactive believability. As Eddie Valiant, he had to play to empty space most of the time, or at best to Charles Fleischer, the voice of Roger, who often appeared on the set in a full bunny suit to give Hoskins something to relate to.

The vocalizations were right on, too. Fleischer is the perfect rabbit, while an unbilled Kathleen Turner gives just the right throatiness to the voice of sexy Jessica Rabbit.

The story was based on the Gary K. Wolf book, *Who Censored Roger Rabbit?*, although it was changed a great deal. The plot involves the "Toons," stars of cartoons who commute from "Toontown," and their interaction with human actors in Hollywood. Roger's honeybunny, Jessica, is photographed with a man who is later murdered, and Roger becomes the prime suspect. Chris Lloyd as the villainous "Judge Doom" plots and schemes against our heroes. It's up to detective Eddie Valiant to set things right for the hapless Roger Rabbit.

There is so much going on here, though, that the story is almost incidental. Second and third viewings were not uncommon for moviegoers, who

tried to spot new things and pick up on missed dialogue with each return to the theater. There are tributes and send-ups all over the place. To wit:

Every item is called "Acme," as in the old Chuck Jones "Road Runner" cartoons.

A "cattle call" at the studio has preening cartoon cows standing in line.

Dumbo flutters by a window, and the studio boss mutters, "He works for peanuts."

When Detective Valiant enters his office, he hangs his hat on a Maltese Falcon.

Then there are the "inside" jokes about Los Angeles:

"Who needs a car in L.A.?" asks Eddie. "We've got the best public transportation system in the world."

"What's a freeway?" someone asks. "Eight lanes . . . smooth, fast . . . traffic jams will be a thing of the past."

In 1989, Disney released a new Roger Rabbit cartoon, *Tummy Trouble* (the studio's first new cartoon in many years). Meanwhile, *Who Framed Roger Rabbit* is now available on videocassette. Go ahead, treat yourself to it.

Screenplay by Jeffrey Price and Peter S. Seaman

Based on the book *Who Censored Roger Rabbit?* by Gary K. Wolf

Executive Producers: Steven Spielberg and Kathleen Kennedy

Produced by Robert Watts and Frank Marshall

Directed by Robert Zemeckis

CAST

Eddie Valiant .... Bob Hoskins
Judge Doom .... Christopher Lloyd
Dolores .... Joanna Cassidy
Marvin Acme .... Stubby Kaye
Voice of Roger Rabbit . Charles Fleischer

ACADEMY AWARD NOMINATIONS

6 nominations, 3 wins*

Best Art Direction-Set Decoration
Best Cinematography
*Best Film Editing
Best Sound
*Best Sound Effects Editing
*Best Visual Effects

COMING TO AMERICA
PARAMOUNT
$65,000,000

FOR PARAMOUNT Pictures, the two sweetest words in the English language are "Eddie Murphy." The man can virtually write his own ticket with that studio, and in *Coming to America*, that's just about what he did. As story writer, producer, and star, the triple threat again proved that his name is synonymous with big box office. But it's more than just his name; it's his talent that can turn an ordinary property into a megahit.

Case in point: *Coming to America*. As a royal prince of the mythical African country of Zamunda, Murphy and his devoted friend, played by newcomer Arsenio Hall (Paramount liked Hall's performance so much they gave him his own talk show after this film) set out for America, where the prince hopes to find an old-fashioned girl to be his bride. Naturally, a series of sight gags and *"Crocodile" Dundee*–type mishaps ensues as our rich but naive royal pair stumbles through the Big Apple.

Highlighting the film are the many characters played by Murphy and Hall, who showcase their talents with a number of characterizations—including Murphy as an old Jewish man, complete with thick accent (incredible make-up actually has him looking like an elderly *white* man). Part of the fun for audiences was trying to spot where Murphy and Hall would pop up next, a gimmick good for repeat business at the box office. In one instance, Murphy plays a cantankerous old New York barber named Clarence, and in yet another he's entertainer Randy Watson. Not to be outdone by Murphy, Arsenio Hall shows his range of comedic abilities in diverse roles. In addition to his first starring role as Semmi, Murphy's African pal, Hall crops up as a fiery preacher and an elderly barber named Morris. Special make-up by two-time Oscar winner Rick Baker, plus some clever optical/photographic work, allowed the two actors to portray six characters within the same scene.

Baker had previously collaborated with director John Landis on *An American Werewolf in London* and *Michael Jackson's Thriller*. His work for *Coming to America* required him to create "life masks" of Murphy's and Hall's faces, from which he could sculpt the necessary appliances. In one of his best jobs ever, Baker made up Murphy as the aforementioned elderly Jewish man, then had one of the film's producers introduce Murphy to the Paramount brass who had known him for years. No one recognized him.

Reviews bordered on scathing. *The Hollywood Reporter* lamented: "Eddie Murphy's latest 'Coming' is likely to leave the wreath-bearers, the frantic faithful, the crowd herders, and the legions of line-waiters in numbed disbelieving disappointment . . . Distressingly, the film flops into the blandest of sitcom formats . . . except for the effervescent Murphy, this very common comedy doesn't have much more to strut than your average network re-run. Box office will undoubtedly be gargantuan at first, but Paramount's gold mine has been shortshafted by 'Coming to America''s dullwitted screenplay . . ."

Did Murphy's fans notice? Did they even read *The Hollywood Reporter*? *Variety*, too, called the film a "true test for loyal [Murphy] fans."

Eddie Murphy must have millions of them, since they made this the numberthree film of the year.

Screenplay by David Sheffield and Barry W. Blaustein

Based on a story by Eddie Murphy

Executive Producers: Mark Lipsky and Leslie Belzberg

Produced by George Folsey, Jr. and Robert D. Wachs

Directed by John Landis

CAST

Prince Akeem	Eddie Murphy
Semmi	Arsenio Hall
Cleo McDowell	John Amos
King Jaffe Joffer	James Earl Jones
Lisa McDowell	Shari Headley

ACADEMY AWARD NOMINATIONS

2 nominations, no wins

Best Costume Design
Best Make-up

"CROCODILE" DUNDEE II

PARAMOUNT
$57,300,000

THE SUCCESS of Paul Hogan's first film, the Australian-made *"Crocodile" Dundee,* saw Paramount Pictures eagerly signing the actor to a contract for a sequel. This time, he wouldn't have to put up his own money for the movie, then try to market it in America. This time, Paramount gave him carte blanche. And with both Eddie Murphy and Paul Hogan in its fold, Paramount had a very good year.

Hogan wrote his own screenplay with assistance from his son, Brett, for whom it was a first experience. Hogan père commented in a Paramount production handbook: "Brett's enthusiasm and contributions made the movie happen sooner than it would have otherwise. He brought a fresh outlook, imaginative dialogue and some great gags to the film."

This story of Michael J. "Crocodile" Dundee (call him "Mick") picks up where the first one left off, with our Aussie living with girlfriend Sue in New York City. A series of adventures eventually lands the characters back Down Under, where the famous crocodile hunter is really in his element. Aborigines, crocs, and a water buffalo all cross paths with our hero, who must do battle with . . . Latino drug dealers? Oh well. Hogan is an old-fashioned man's man, and his popularity is as legendary as his screen counterpart's croc-fighting escapades.

The studio was banking on that (literally) when they opened the picture on an unprecedented number of screens—2,837 North American ven-

ues—on May 25, 1988. Lines immediately formed, and *The Hollywood Reporter* predicted: "Paramount should be able to stride right past the Labor Day weekend with sizeable print offerings of this engaging, likeable sequel. While star Paul Hogan's enjoying a long cool one with his real-life mates, the studio will be savoring a long hot one at the ticket windows; when the summer glut clears, 'Croc II' will likely have put all its box office competition down under."

Although big box office was taken for granted, it wasn't helped any by many of the less than favorable reviews of the film. *Variety* called it "a disappointing followup to the disarmingly charming first feature . . . too slow to constitute an adventure and has too few laughs to be a comedy . . . initial box office probably will be good until word of mouth gets out."

Or until people read that review. Which, it would appear, they did not. The picture did about three-fourths the business of the first, which is excellent for a sequel and made for happy executives at Paramount.

Paul Hogan has admitted to being burned out on the crocodile hunter, though. He has sworn off ever playing Mick Dundee again, apparently preferring to do promos for the Australian Tourist Commission (600,000 additional tourists thanks to the TV ads) and commercials for Foster's Lager ("That's Australian for beer, mate!"). But in the words of another man who also claimed to have had enough of his alter ego, "Never say never again."

Screenplay by Paul Hogan and Brett Hogan

Executive Producer: Paul Hogan

Produced by John Cornell and Jane Scott

Directed by John Cornell

CAST

Mick "Crocodile" Dundee	Paul Hogan
Sue Charlton	Linda Kozlowski
LeRoy Brown	Charles Dutton
Rico	Hechter Ubarry
Miguel	Juan Fernandez

"Actually, I hate violence."
—ARNOLD SCHWARZENEGGER

"But you're so good at it!"
—DANNY DEVITO

IVAN REITMAN directed this outrageous comedy, which hit movie screens during the Christmas rush and was, amazingly, still running in a few theaters by late summer of 1989, even after the picture had been released on home video. It was definitely a last-minute entry into the top five race for 1988, pulling away from a pack that included big hits like *Big*, *Beetlejuice*, *A Fish Called Wanda*, and *The Naked Gun*, any of which might have ended up in the top film list of the year. But there was something enduring and endearing about this story of *Twins*, separated from birth and reunited again at age 35. Something . . . familiar.

For one thing, there were similarities to the number-one film of the year, *Rain Man*. Obviously, since these were simultaneous releases, the parallels were not intentional. But the stories of both films involve brothers, separated in childhood, reunited later in adult life. And, as in the case of *Rain Man*, one brother is bent on exploitation of the other. There are still further analogies in that they travel cross-country together on a quest. In both instances, we have the familiar "Odd Couple" syndrome.

But there are differences, since this is an Ivan Reitman (*National Lampoon's Animal House*; *Ghostbusters*) comedy. An odder couple you couldn't find.

Schwarzenegger plays Julius Benedict, a genetic experiment gone right. When he learns that he has an unknown twin brother, also part of that long-ago experiment, his superbly conditioned heart leaps as he leaves his lifelong island habitat in search of his long-lost sibling in the Big Orange (L.A.). Lots of crowd-pleasing "Man from Mars" shtick à la *"Crocodile" Dundee* when Arnold discovers the other half of that experiment, a genetic boo-boo played by Danny DeVito. "It's like looking in a mirror!" wisecracks DeVito (Vincent) when confronted by the brother whose kneecaps he barely clears.

It's played strictly for laughs, and as such, critics found very little to criticize. *Variety* described the pairing of Schwarzenegger and DeVito as inspired, praising the film's "near-perfect execution in Reitman's hands" and its "lively mix of sight gags and fresh, topical jokes."

One of the best sight gags finds Schwarzenegger stopping in front of a *Rambo* poster to compare musculature. And on that subject, check out the physique of Hugh O'Brian, who at the age of 65 never looked better. O'Brian rose to popularity in the '50s as the star of TV's "The Life and Legend of Wyatt Earp"; he appears in *Twins* as one of the guys' fathers.

*Rental figure is approximate and is based on combined published rentals plus projected figure extrapolated from film's 1988–89 grosses.

Screenplay by William Davies,
 William Osborne, Timothy Haris,
 and Herschel Weingrod

Executive Producers: Joe Medjuck and
 Michael C. Gross

Produced and directed by Ivan Reitman

CAST

Julius Benedict	Arnold Schwarzenegger
Vincent Benedict	Danny DeVito
Marnie Mason	Kelly Preston
Linda Mason	Chloe Webb
Mary Ann Benedict	Bonnie Bartlett

Only their mother can tell them apart.

1989 AND THE 1990s

The summer of 1989 was often referred to as the Summer of the Sequels. *Indiana Jones and the Last Crusade* (Paramount, 3rd in series), *Star Trek V: The Final Frontier* (Paramount, 5th in series), *Ghostbusters II* (Columbia), *The Karate Kid III* (Columbia), *Lethal Weapon II* (Warner Bros.), *Licence to Kill* (United Artists, 16th or 18th in the Bond series, depending on which ones are included), *Nightmare on Elm Street V: The Dream Child* (New Line International), *Friday the 13th Part VIII: Jason Takes Manhattan* (Paramount), all vied for their share of the box office bucks.

Re-released *Peter Pan* (Disney) continued to do well, adding even more to that film's previous success, while the new Disney pictures *Dead Poets Society* and *Honey, I Shrunk the Kids* also grabbed a share of the summer box office for that studio.

But it was a new contender dressed in a black cape who made off with most of the loot. The summer of '89's megahit, destined to soar to the top of the all-time great chart, was Warner Bros.' *Batman*, directed by little-known Tim Burton and starring Michael Keaton as the Caped Crusader from Gotham, with Jack Nicholson as his archrival, The Joker. No jokes at the box office, where the picture cleaned up and even began threatening top moneymaker *E.T. The Extra-Terrestrial*. An Oscar nomination for Jack Nicholson seemed almost inevitable. Also inevitable, it seems, are *Batman II*, *Batman III*, and so on—sequels which will keep the Batdollars pouring into Warners' bank account well into the Nineties.

The only other new potential hit was Tri-Star's *Look Who's Talking*, starring John Travolta and Kirstie Alley (with Bruce Willis as the voice of a baby!), which many felt might be the year's sleeper. Time will tell.

As the Nineties draw near, high-technology films continue to entice the computer-age audience into theaters. The number of films appearing with Roman numerals attached to their titles is growing, of course. But there is also a trend toward "people" pictures, basic dramas and comedies with the types of stories audiences loved back in the Thirties and Forties. Video stores do a brisk rental business in cassettes of the earlier films; nostalgia seems to be at an all-time high. There are more and more re-releases—in 1989, business was assured for theaters offering "50th Anniversary" showings of the hit 1939 films. And television cable channels like American Movie Classics, which show the oldies, have added thousands of subscribers in recent years.

But whatever the Nineties and the years beyond bring, the real winners will be us—the movie audience.

APPENDIXES

FILMS BY YEAR

GONE WITH THE WIND	1939	MGM	77,641,106
THE WIZARD OF OZ	1939	MGM	4,544,851
THE HUNCHBACK OF NOTRE DAME	1939	RKO	1,500,000
JESSE JAMES	1939	Fox	1,500,000
MR. SMITH GOES TO WASHINGTON	1939	Columbia	1,500,000
PINOCCHIO	1940	Disney	32,957,000
FANTASIA	1940	Disney	28,660,000
BOOM TOWN	1940	MGM	4,586,415
REBECCA	1940	Selznick	1,500,000
SANTA FE TRAIL	1940	Warner Bros.	1,500,000
SERGEANT YORK	1941	Warner Bros.	6,135,707
DIVE BOMBER	1941	Warner Bros.	*1,500,000
HONKY TONK	1941	MGM	*1,500,000
THE PHILADELPHIA STORY	1941	MGM	*1,500,000
A YANK IN THE R.A.F.	1941	Fox	*1,500,000
BAMBI	1942	Disney	47,265,000
MRS. MINIVER	1942	MGM	5,390,009
YANKEE DOODLE DANDY	1942	Warner Bros.	4,719,681
RANDOM HARVEST	1942	MGM	4,665,501
CASABLANCA	1942	Warner Bros.	4,145,178
THIS IS THE ARMY	1943	Warner Bros.	8,301,000
FOR WHOM THE BELL TOLLS	1943	Paramount	7,100,000
THE OUTLAW	1943	RKO	5,075,000
THE SONG OF BERNADETTE	1943	Fox	5,000,000
STAGE DOOR CANTEEN	1943	United Artists	4,339,532
GOING MY WAY	1944	Paramount	6,500,000
MEET ME IN ST. LOUIS	1944	MGM	5,132,202
SINCE YOU WENT AWAY	1944	United Artists	4,924,756
30 SECONDS OVER TOKYO	1944	MGM	4,471,080
WHITE CLIFFS OF DOVER	1944	MGM	4,045,250
THE BELLS OF ST. MARY'S	1945	RKO	8,000,000
LEAVE HER TO HEAVEN	1945	Fox	5,500,000
SPELLBOUND	1945	United Artists	4,970,583
ANCHORS AWEIGH	1945	MGM	4,778,679
THE VALLEY OF DECISION	1945	MGM	4,566,374
SONG OF THE SOUTH	1946	Disney	29,228,717
THE BEST YEARS OF OUR LIVES	1946	RKO	11,300,000
DUEL IN THE SUN	1946	Selznick	11,300,000
THE JOLSON STORY	1946	Columbia	7,600,000
BLUE SKIES	1946	Paramount	5,700,000

WELCOME STRANGER	1947	Paramount	6,100,000
THE EGG AND I	1947	Universal	5,500,000
UNCONQUERED	1947	Paramount	5,250,000
LIFE WITH FATHER	1947	Warner Bros.	5,057,000
FOREVER AMBER	1947	Fox	5,000,000
THE RED SHOES	1948	Archers/Eagle-Lion	5,000,000
RED RIVER	1948	United Artists	4,506,825
THE PALEFACE	1948	Paramount	4,500,000
THE THREE MUSKETEERS	1948	MGM	4,306,876
JOHNNY BELINDA	1948	Warner Bros.	4,266,000
SAMSON AND DELILAH	1949	Paramount	11,500,000
BATTLEGROUND	1949	MGM	5,051,143
JOLSON SINGS AGAIN	1949	Columbia	5,000,000
THE SANDS OF IWO JIMA	1949	Republic	5,000,000
I WAS A MALE WAR BRIDE	1949	Fox	4,100,000
CINDERELLA	1950	Disney	41,087,000
KING SOLOMON'S MINES	1950	MGM	5,586,000
ANNIE GET YOUR GUN	1950	MGM	4,919,394
CHEAPER BY THE DOZEN	1950	Fox	4,425,000
FATHER OF THE BRIDE	1950	MGM	4,054,405
QUO VADIS?	1951	MGM	11,901,662
ALICE IN WONDERLAND	1951	Disney	7,196,000
SHOW BOAT	1951	MGM	5,533,000
DAVID AND BATHSHEBA	1951	Fox	4,720,000
THE GREAT CARUSO	1951	MGM	4,531,000
THIS IS CINERAMA	1952	CRC	15,400,000
THE GREATEST SHOW ON EARTH	1952	Paramount	14,000,000
THE SNOWS OF KILIMANJARO	1952	Fox	6,500,000
IVANHOE	1952	MGM	6,258,000
HANS CHRISTIAN ANDERSEN	1952	RKO	6,000,000
PETER PAN	1953	Disney	24,532,000
THE ROBE	1953	Fox	17,500,000
FROM HERE TO ETERNITY	1953	Columbia	12,200,000
SHANE	1953	Paramount	9,000,000
HOW TO MARRY A MILLIONAIRE	1953	Fox	7,300,000
WHITE CHRISTMAS	1954	Paramount	12,000,000
20,000 LEAGUES UNDER THE SEA	1954	Disney	11,267,000
REAR WINDOW	1954	Paramount	9,812,271
THE CAINE MUTINY	1954	Columbia	8,700,000
THE GLENN MILLER STORY	1954	Universal	7,590,994
LADY AND THE TRAMP	1955	Disney	40,249,000
CINERAMA HOLIDAY	1955	CRC	12,000,000
MISTER ROBERTS	1955	Warner Bros.	8,500,000
BATTLE CRY	1955	Warner Bros.	8,100,000
OKLAHOMA!	1955	Magna	7,100,000

THE TEN COMMANDMENTS	1956	Paramount	43,000,000
AROUND THE WORLD IN 80 DAYS	1956	United Artists/WB	23,120,000
GIANT	1956	Warner Bros.	14,000,000
SEVEN WONDERS OF THE WORLD	1956	CRC	12,500,000
THE KING AND I	1956	Fox	8,500,000
THE BRIDGE ON THE RIVER KWAI	1957	Columbia	17,195,000
PEYTON PLACE	1957	Fox	11,500,000
SAYONARA	1957	Warner Bros.	10,500,000
OLD YELLER	1957	Disney	10,050,000
RAINTREE COUNTY	1957	MGM	5,962,839
SOUTH PACIFIC	1958	Fox	17,500,000
AUNTIE MAME	1958	Warner Bros.	9,300,000
CAT ON A HOT TIN ROOF	1958	MGM	8,785,162
NO TIME FOR SERGEANTS	1958	Warner Bros.	7,500,000
GIGI	1958	MGM	7,321,423
BEN-HUR	1959	MGM	36,992,088
SLEEPING BEAUTY	1959	Disney	21,998,000
THE SHAGGY DOG	1959	Disney	12,317,000
OPERATION PETTICOAT	1959	Universal	9,321,555
DARBY O'GILL AND THE LITTLE PEOPLE	1959	Disney	8,336,000
SWISS FAMILY ROBINSON	1960	Disney	20,178,000
PSYCHO	1960	Universal	11,200,000
SPARTACUS	1960	Universal	10,300,454
EXODUS	1960	United Artists	8,331,582
THE ALAMO	1960	United Artists	7,918,776
101 DALMATIANS	1961	Disney	38,562,000
WEST SIDE STORY	1961	United Artists	19,645,570
GUNS OF NAVARONE	1961	Columbia	13,000,000
EL CID	1961	Allied Artists	12,000,000
THE ABSENT-MINDED PROFESSOR	1961	Disney	11,426,000
HOW THE WEST WAS WON	1962	CRC/MGM	20,932,883
LAWRENCE OF ARABIA	1962	Columbia	*19,000,000
THE LONGEST DAY	1962	Fox	17,600,000
IN SEARCH OF THE CASTAWAYS	1962	Disney	9,975,000
THE MUSIC MAN	1962	Warner Bros.	8,100,000
CLEOPATRA	1963	Fox	26,000,000
IT'S A MAD MAD MAD MAD WORLD	1963	MGM	20,849,786
TOM JONES	1963	United Artists	16,925,988
IRMA LA DOUCE	1963	United Artists	11,921,784
THE SWORD IN THE STONE	1963	Disney	10,475,000
MARY POPPINS	1964	Disney	45,000,000
GOLDFINGER	1964	United Artists	22,997,706
THE CARPETBAGGERS	1964	Paramount	15,500,000
MY FAIR LADY	1964	Warner Bros.	12,000,000
FROM RUSSIA WITH LOVE	1964	United Artists	9,924,279

THE SOUND OF MUSIC	1965	Fox	79,748,000
DOCTOR ZHIVAGO	1965	MGM	47,116,811
THUNDERBALL	1965	United Artists	28,621,434
THOSE MAGNIFICENT MEN IN THEIR FLYING MACHINES	1965	Fox	14,000,000
THAT DARN CAT	1965	Disney	12,628,000
HAWAII	1966	United Artists	15,553,018
THE BIBLE	1966	Fox	15,000,000
WHO'S AFRAID OF VIRGINIA WOOLF?	1966	Warner Bros.	14,500,000
A MAN FOR ALL SEASONS	1966	Columbia	12,750,000
LT. ROBIN CRUSOE, USN	1966	Disney	10,164,000
THE GRADUATE	1967	Avco/Embassy	44,090,729
THE JUNGLE BOOK	1967	Disney	39,500,000
GUESS WHO'S COMING TO DINNER	1967	Columbia	25,500,000
BONNIE AND CLYDE	1967	Warner Bros.	22,800,000
THE DIRTY DOZEN	1967	MGM	20,403,826
FUNNY GIRL	1968	Columbia	26,325,000
2001: A SPACE ODYSSEY	1968	MGM	25,521,917
THE ODD COUPLE	1968	Paramount	20,000,000
BULLITT	1968	Warner Bros.	19,000,000
ROMEO AND JULIET	1968	Paramount	17,473,000
BUTCH CASSIDY AND THE SUNDANCE KID	1969	Fox	46,039,000
THE LOVE BUG	1969	Disney	23,150,000
MIDNIGHT COWBOY	1969	United Artists	20,499,282
EASY RIDER	1969	Columbia	19,100,000
HELLO, DOLLY!	1969	Fox	15,200,000
LOVE STORY	1970	Paramount	50,000,000
AIRPORT	1970	Universal	45,220,118
M*A*S*H	1970	Fox	36,720,000
PATTON	1970	Fox	28,100,000
THE ARISTOCATS	1970	Disney	26,462,000
FIDDLER ON THE ROOF	1971	United Artists	38,251,196
BILLY JACK	1971	Warner Bros.	32,500,000
THE FRENCH CONNECTION	1971	Fox	26,315,000
SUMMER OF '42	1971	Warner Bros.	20,500,000
DIAMONDS ARE FOREVER	1971	United Artists	19,726,829
THE GODFATHER	1972	Paramount	86,275,000
THE POSEIDON ADVENTURE	1972	Fox	42,000,000
WHAT'S UP DOC?	1972	Warner Bros.	28,000,000
DELIVERANCE	1972	Warner Bros.	22,600,000
JEREMIAH JOHNSON	1972	Warner Bros.	21,900,000
THE EXORCIST	1973	Warner Bros.	89,000,000
THE STING	1973	Universal	78,212,000
AMERICAN GRAFFITI	1973	Universal	55,128,175
PAPILLON	1973	Allied Artists	22,500,000
THE WAY WE WERE	1973	Columbia	22,457,000

THE TOWERING INFERNO	1974	Fox/Warner Bros.	52,000,000
BLAZING SADDLES	1974	Warner Bros.	47,800,000
YOUNG FRANKENSTEIN	1974	Fox	38,823,000
EARTHQUAKE	1974	Universal	35,849,994
THE TRIAL OF BILLY JACK	1974	Warner Bros.	31,100,000
JAWS	1975	Universal	129,549,325
ONE FLEW OVER THE CUCKOO'S NEST	1975	United Artists	59,939,701
THE ROCKY HORROR PICTURE SHOW	1975	Fox	26,000,000
SHAMPOO	1975	Columbia	23,822,000
DOG DAY AFTERNOON	1975	Warner Bros.	22,500,000
ROCKY	1976	United Artists	56,524,972
A STAR IS BORN	1976	Warner Bros.	37,100,000
KING KONG	1976	Paramount	36,915,000
SILVER STREAK	1976	Fox	30,018,000
ALL THE PRESIDENT'S MEN	1976	Warner Bros.	30,000,000
STAR WARS	1977	Fox	193,500,000
CLOSE ENCOUNTERS OF THE THIRD KIND	1977	Columbia	82,750,000
SATURDAY NIGHT FEVER	1977	Paramount	74,100,000
SMOKEY AND THE BANDIT	1977	Universal	58,949,939
THE GOODBYE GIRL	1977	MGM/Warner Bros.	41,839,170
GREASE	1978	Paramount	96,300,000
SUPERMAN	1978	Warner Bros.	82,800,000
NATIONAL LAMPOON'S ANIMAL HOUSE	1978	Universal	70,826,000
EVERY WHICH WAY BUT LOOSE	1978	Warner Bros.	51,900,000
JAWS 2	1978	Universal	50,431,964
KRAMER VS. KRAMER	1979	Columbia	59,986,335
STAR TREK: THE MOTION PICTURE	1979	Paramount	56,000,000
THE JERK	1979	Universal	42,989,656
ROCKY II	1979	United Artists	42,169,387
ALIEN	1979	Fox	40,300,000
THE EMPIRE STRIKES BACK	1980	Fox	141,600,000
9 TO 5	1980	Fox	59,100,000
STIR CRAZY	1980	Columbia	58,364,420
AIRPLANE!	1980	Paramount	40,610,000
ANY WHICH WAY YOU CAN	1980	Warner Bros.	40,500,000
RAIDERS OF THE LOST ARK	1981	Paramount	115,598,000
SUPERMAN II	1981	Warner Bros.	65,100,000
ON GOLDEN POND	1981	Universal	61,174,744
ARTHUR	1981	Warner Bros.	42,000,000
STRIPES	1981	Columbia	40,886,589
E.T. THE EXTRA-TERRESTRIAL	1982	Universal	228,618,939
TOOTSIE	1982	Columbia	96,292,736
ROCKY III	1982	MGM/United Artists	66,262,796
AN OFFICER AND A GENTLEMAN	1982	Paramount	55,223,000
PORKY'S	1982	Fox	54,000,000

RETURN OF THE JEDI	1983	Fox	168,002,414
TERMS OF ENDEARMENT	1983	Paramount	50,250,000
TRADING PLACES	1983	Paramount	40,600,000
WARGAMES	1983	MGM/United Artists	38,519,833
SUPERMAN III	1983	Warner Bros.	37,200,000
GHOSTBUSTERS	1984	Columbia	130,211,324
INDIANA JONES AND THE TEMPLE OF DOOM	1984	Paramount	109,000,000
BEVERLY HILLS COP	1984	Paramount	108,000,000
GREMLINS	1984	Warner Bros.	79,500,000
THE KARATE KID	1984	Columbia	43,432,881
BACK TO THE FUTURE	1985	Universal	104,408,738
RAMBO: FIRST BLOOD PART II	1985	Tri-Star	78,919,250
ROCKY IV	1985	MGM/United Artists	76,023,246
THE COLOR PURPLE	1985	Warner Bros.	47,900,000
OUT OF AFRICA	1985	Universal	43,103,469
TOP GUN	1986	Paramount	79,400,000
"CROCODILE" DUNDEE	1986	Paramount	70,227,000
PLATOON	1986	Orion	69,742,143
THE KARATE KID, PART II	1986	Columbia	58,362,026
STAR TREK IV: THE VOYAGE HOME	1986	Paramount	56,820,071
THREE MEN AND A BABY	1987	Disney	81,313,000
BEVERLY HILLS COP II	1987	Paramount	80,857,776
FATAL ATTRACTION	1987	Paramount	70,000,000
GOOD MORNING, VIETNAM	1987	Disney	58,103,000
THE UNTOUCHABLES	1987	Paramount	36,866,530
RAIN MAN	1988	MGM/United Artists	*80,000,000
WHO FRAMED ROGER RABBIT	1988	Disney	*78,000,000
COMING TO AMERICA	1988	Paramount	65,000,000
"CROCODILE" DUNDEE II	1988	Paramount	57,300,000
TWINS	1988	Universal	*55,000,000

*Figures are informed estimates.

FILMS BY TITLE

ABSENT-MINDED PROFESSOR, THE	1961	Disney	11,426,000
AIRPLANE!	1980	Paramount	40,610,000
AIRPORT	1970	Universal	45,220,118
ALAMO, THE	1960	United Artists	7,918,776
ALICE IN WONDERLAND	1951	Disney	7,196,000
ALIEN	1979	Fox	40,300,000
ALL THE PRESIDENT'S MEN	1976	Warner Bros.	30,000,000
AMERICAN GRAFFITI	1973	Universal	55,128,175
AN OFFICER AND A GENTLEMAN	1982	Paramount	55,223,000
ANCHORS AWEIGH	1945	MGM	4,778,679
ANNIE GET YOUR GUN	1950	MGM	4,919,394
ANY WHICH WAY YOU CAN	1980	Warner Bros.	40,500,000
ARISTOCATS, THE	1970	Disney	26,462,000
AROUND THE WORLD IN 80 DAYS	1956	United Artists/WB	23,120,000
ARTHUR	1981	Warner Bros.	42,000,000
AUNTIE MAME	1958	Warner Bros.	9,300,000
BACK TO THE FUTURE	1985	Universal	104,408,738
BAMBI	1942	Disney	47,265,000
BATTLE CRY	1955	Warner Bros.	8,100,000
BATTLEGROUND	1949	MGM	5,051,143
BELLS OF ST. MARY'S, THE	1945	RKO	8,000,000
BEN-HUR	1959	MGM	36,992,088
BEST YEARS OF OUR LIVES, THE	1946	RKO	11,300,000
BEVERLY HILLS COP	1984	Paramount	108,000,000
BEVERLY HILLS COP II	1987	Paramount	80,857,776
BIBLE, THE	1966	Fox	15,000,000
BILLY JACK	1971	Warner Bros.	32,500,000
BLAZING SADDLES	1974	Warner Bros.	47,800,000
BLUE SKIES	1946	Paramount	5,700,000
BONNIE AND CLYDE	1967	Warner Bros.	22,800,000
BOOM TOWN	1940	MGM	4,586,415
BRIDGE ON THE RIVER KWAI, THE	1957	Columbia	17,195,000
BULLITT	1968	Warner Bros.	19,000,000
BUTCH CASSIDY AND THE SUNDANCE KID	1969	Fox	46,039,000
CAINE MUTINY, THE	1954	Columbia	8,700,000
CARPETBAGGERS, THE	1964	Paramount	15,500,000
CASABLANCA	1942	Warner Bros.	4,145,178
CAT ON A HOT TIN ROOF	1958	MGM	8,785,162
CHEAPER BY THE DOZEN	1950	Fox	4,425,000
CINDERELLA	1950	Disney	41,087,000
CINERAMA HOLIDAY	1955	CRC	12,000,000
CLEOPATRA	1963	Fox	26,000,000
CLOSE ENCOUNTERS OF THE THIRD KIND	1977	Columbia	82,750,000
COLOR PURPLE, THE	1985	Warner Bros.	47,900,000
COMING TO AMERICA	1988	Paramount	65,000,000

"CROCODILE" DUNDEE	1986	Paramount	70,227,000
"CROCODILE" DUNDEE II	1988	Paramount	57,300,000
DARBY O'GILL AND THE LITTLE PEOPLE	1959	Disney	8,336,000
DAVID AND BATHSHEBA	1951	Fox	4,720,000
DELIVERANCE	1972	Warner Bros.	22,600,000
DIAMONDS ARE FOREVER	1971	United Artists	19,726,829
DIRTY DOZEN, THE	1967	MGM	20,403,826
DIVE BOMBER	1941	Warner Bros.	*1,500,000
DOCTOR ZHIVAGO	1965	MGM	47,116,811
DOG DAY AFTERNOON	1975	Warner Bros.	22,500,000
DUEL IN THE SUN	1946	Selznick	11,300,000
E.T. THE EXTRA-TERRESTRIAL	1982	Universal	228,618,939
EARTHQUAKE	1974	Universal	35,849,994
EASY RIDER	1969	Columbia	19,100,000
EGG AND I, THE	1947	Universal	5,500,000
EL CID	1961	Allied Artists	12,000,000
EMPIRE STRIKES BACK, THE	1980	Fox	141,600,000
EVERY WHICH WAY BUT LOOSE	1978	Warner Bros.	51,900,000
EXODUS	1960	United Artists	8,331,582
EXORCIST, THE	1973	Warner Bros.	89,000,000
FANTASIA	1940	Disney	28,660,000
FATAL ATTRACTION	1987	Paramount	70,000,000
FATHER OF THE BRIDE	1950	MGM	4,054,405
FIDDLER ON THE ROOF	1971	United Artists	38,251,196
FOR WHOM THE BELL TOLLS	1943	Paramount	7,100,000
FOREVER AMBER	1947	Fox	5,000,000
FRENCH CONNECTION, THE	1971	Fox	26,315,000
FROM HERE TO ETERNITY	1953	Columbia	12,200,000
FROM RUSSIA WITH LOVE	1964	United Artists	9,924,279
FUNNY GIRL	1968	Columbia	26,325,000
GHOSTBUSTERS	1984	Columbia	130,211,324
GIANT	1956	Warner Bros.	14,000,000
GIGI	1958	MGM	7,321,423
GLENN MILLER STORY, THE	1954	Universal	7,590,994
GODFATHER, THE	1972	Paramount	86,275,000
GOING MY WAY	1944	Paramount	6,500,000
GOLDFINGER	1964	United Artists	22,997,706
GONE WITH THE WIND	1939	MGM	77,641,106
GOOD MORNING, VIETNAM	1987	Disney	58,103,000
GOODBYE GIRL, THE	1977	MGM/Warner Bros.	41,839,170
GRADUATE, THE	1967	Avco/Embassy	44,090,729
GREASE	1978	Paramount	96,300,000
GREAT CARUSO, THE	1951	MGM	4,531,000
GREATEST SHOW ON EARTH, THE	1952	Paramount	14,000,000
GREMLINS	1984	Warner Bros.	79,500,000
GUESS WHO'S COMING TO DINNER	1967	Columbia	25,500,000
GUNS OF NAVARONE	1961	Columbia	13,000,000
HANS CHRISTIAN ANDERSEN	1952	RKO	6,000,000
HAWAII	1966	United Artists	15,553,018

HELLO, DOLLY!	1969	Fox	15,200,000
HONKY TONK	1941	MGM	*1,500,000
HOW THE WEST WAS WON	1962	CRC/MGM	20,932,883
HOW TO MARRY A MILLIONAIRE	1953	Fox	7,300,000
HUNCHBACK OF NOTRE DAME, THE	1939	RKO	1,500,000
I WAS A MALE WAR BRIDE	1949	Fox	4,100,000
IN SEARCH OF THE CASTAWAYS	1962	Disney	9,975,000
INDIANA JONES AND THE TEMPLE OF DOOM	1984	Paramount	109,000,000
IRMA LA DOUCE	1963	United Artists	11,921,784
IT'S A MAD MAD MAD MAD WORLD	1963	MGM	20,849,786
IVANHOE	1952	MGM	6,258,000
JAWS	1975	Universal	129,549,325
JAWS 2	1978	Universal	50,431,964
JEREMIAH JOHNSON	1972	Warner Bros.	21,900,000
JERK, THE	1979	Universal	42,989,656
JESSE JAMES	1939	Fox	1,500,000
JOHNNY BELINDA	1948	Warner Bros.	4,266,000
JOLSON SINGS AGAIN	1949	Columbia	5,000,000
JOLSON STORY, THE	1946	Columbia	7,600,000
JUNGLE BOOK, THE	1967	Disney	39,500,000
KARATE KID, THE	1984	Columbia	43,432,881
KARATE KID, PART II, THE	1986	Columbia	58,362,026
KING AND I, THE	1956	Fox	8,500,000
KING KONG	1976	Paramount	36,915,000
KING SOLOMON'S MINES	1950	MGM	5,586,000
KRAMER VS. KRAMER	1979	Columbia	59,986,335
LADY AND THE TRAMP	1955	Disney	40,249,000
LAWRENCE OF ARABIA	1962	Columbia	*19,000,000
LEAVE HER TO HEAVEN	1945	Fox	5,500,000
LIFE WITH FATHER	1947	Warner Bros.	5,057,000
LONGEST DAY, THE	1962	Fox	17,600,000
LOVE BUG, THE	1969	Disney	23,150,000
LOVE STORY	1970	Paramount	50,000,000
LT. ROBIN CRUSOE, USN	1966	Disney	10,164,000
M*A*S*H	1970	Fox	36,720,000
MAN FOR ALL SEASONS, A	1966	Columbia	12,750,000
MARY POPPINS	1964	Disney	45,000,000
MEET ME IN ST. LOUIS	1944	MGM	5,132,202
MIDNIGHT COWBOY	1969	United Artists	20,499,282
MISTER ROBERTS	1955	Warner Bros.	8,500,000
MR. SMITH GOES TO WASHINGTON	1939	Columbia	1,500,000
MRS. MINIVER	1942	MGM	5,390,009
MUSIC MAN, THE	1962	Warner Bros.	8,100,000
MY FAIR LADY	1964	Warner Bros.	12,000,000
NATIONAL LAMPOON'S ANIMAL HOUSE	1978	Universal	70,826,000
9 TO 5	1980	Fox	59,100,000
NO TIME FOR SERGEANTS	1958	Warner Bros.	7,500,000
ODD COUPLE, THE	1968	Paramount	20,000,000

OFFICER AND A GENTLEMAN, AN	1982	Paramount	55,222,000
OKLAHOMA	1955	Magna	7,100,000
OLD YELLER	1957	Disney	10,050,000
ON GOLDEN POND	1981	Universal	61,174,744
ONE FLEW OVER THE CUCKOO'S NEST	1975	United Artists	59,939,701
101 DALMATIANS	1961	Disney	38,562,000
OPERATION PETTICOAT	1959	Universal	9,321,555
OUT OF AFRICA	1985	Universal	43,103,469
OUTLAW, THE	1943	RKO	5,075,000
PALEFACE, THE	1948	Paramount	4,500,000
PAPILLON	1973	Allied Artists	22,500,000
PATTON	1970	Fox	28,100,000
PETER PAN	1953	Disney	24,532,000
PEYTON PLACE	1957	Fox	11,500,000
PHILADELPHIA STORY, THE	1941	MGM	*1,500,000
PINOCCHIO	1940	Disney	32,957,000
PLATOON	1986	Orion	69,742,143
PORKY'S	1982	Fox	54,000,000
POSEIDON ADVENTURE, THE	1972	Fox	42,000,000
PSYCHO	1960	Universal	11,200,000
QUO VADIS?	1951	MGM	11,901,662
RAIDERS OF THE LOST ARK	1981	Paramount	115,598,000
RAIN MAN	1988	MGM/United Artists	*80,000,000
RAINTREE COUNTY	1957	MGM	5,962,839
RAMBO: FIRST BLOOD PART II	1985	Tri-Star	78,919,250
RANDOM HARVEST	1942	MGM	4,665,501
REAR WINDOW	1954	Paramount	9,812,271
REBECCA	1940	Selznick	1,500,000
RED RIVER	1948	United Artists	4,506,825
RED SHOES, THE	1948	Archers/Eagle-Lion	5,000,000
RETURN OF THE JEDI	1983	Fox	168,002,414
ROBE, THE	1953	Fox	17,500,000
ROCKY	1976	United Artists	56,524,972
ROCKY HORROR PICTURE SHOW, THE	1975	Fox	26,000,000
ROCKY II	1979	United Artists	42,169,387
ROCKY III	1982	MGM/United Artists	66,262,796
ROCKY IV	1985	MGM/United Artists	76,023,246
ROMEO AND JULIET	1968	Paramount	17,473,000
SAMSON AND DELILAH	1949	Paramount	11,500,000
SANDS OF IWO JIMA, THE	1949	Republic	5,000,000
SANTA FE TRAIL	1940	Warner Bros.	1,500,000
SATURDAY NIGHT FEVER	1977	Paramount	74,100,000
SAYONARA	1957	Warner Bros.	10,500,000
SERGEANT YORK	1941	Warner Bros.	6,135,707
SEVEN WONDERS OF THE WORLD	1956	CRC	12,500,000
SHAGGY DOG, THE	1959	Disney	12,317,000
SHAMPOO	1975	Columbia	23,822,000
SHANE	1953	Paramount	9,000,000
SHOW BOAT	1951	MGM	5,533,000
SILVER STREAK	1976	Fox	30,018,000

SINCE YOU WENT AWAY	1944	United Artists	4,924,756
SLEEPING BEAUTY	1959	Disney	21,998,000
SMOKEY AND THE BANDIT	1977	Universal	58,949,939
SNOWS OF KILIMANJARO, THE	1952	Fox	6,500,000
SONG OF BERNADETTE, THE	1943	Fox	5,000,000
SONG OF THE SOUTH	1946	Disney	29,228,717
SOUND OF MUSIC, THE	1965	Fox	79,748,000
SOUTH PACIFIC	1958	Fox	17,500,000
SPARTACUS	1960	Universal	10,300,454
SPELLBOUND	1945	United Artists	4,970,583
STAGE DOOR CANTEEN	1943	United Artists	4,339,532
STAR IS BORN, A	1976	Warner Bros.	37,100,000
STAR TREK: THE MOTION PICTURE	1979	Paramount	56,000,000
STAR TREK IV: THE VOYAGE HOME	1986	Paramount	56,820,071
STAR WARS	1977	Fox	193,500,000
STING, THE	1973	Universal	78,212,000
STIR CRAZY	1980	Columbia	58,364,420
STRIPES	1981	Columbia	40,886,589
SUMMER OF '42	1971	Warner Bros.	20,500,000
SUPERMAN	1978	Warner Bros.	82,800,000
SUPERMAN II	1981	Warner Bros.	65,100,000
SUPERMAN III	1983	Warner Bros.	37,200,000
SWISS FAMILY ROBINSON	1960	Disney	20,178,000
SWORD IN THE STONE, THE	1963	Disney	10,475,000
TEN COMMANDMENTS, THE	1956	Paramount	43,000,000
TERMS OF ENDEARMENT	1983	Paramount	50,250,000
THAT DARN CAT	1965	Disney	12,628,000
30 SECONDS OVER TOKYO	1944	MGM	4,471,080
THIS IS CINERAMA	1952	CRC	15,400,000
THIS IS THE ARMY	1943	Warner Bros.	8,301,000
THOSE MAGNIFICENT MEN IN THEIR FLYING MACHINES	1965	Fox	14,000,000
THREE MEN AND A BABY	1987	Disney	81,313,000
THREE MUSKETEERS, THE	1948	MGM	4,306,876
THUNDERBALL	1965	United Artists	28,621,434
TOM JONES	1963	United Artists	16,925,988
TOOTSIE	1982	Columbia	96,292,736
TOP GUN	1986	Paramount	79,400,000
TOWERING INFERNO, THE	1974	Fox/Warner Bros.	52,000,000
TRADING PLACES	1983	Paramount	40,600,000
TRIAL OF BILLY JACK, THE	1974	Warner Bros.	31,100,000
20,000 LEAGUES UNDER THE SEA	1954	Disney	11,267,000
TWINS	1988	Universal	*55,000,000
2001: A SPACE ODYSSEY	1968	MGM	25,521,917
UNCONQUERED	1947	Paramount	5,250,000
UNTOUCHABLES, THE	1987	Paramount	36,866,530
VALLEY OF DECISION, THE	1945	MGM	4,566,374
WARGAMES	1983	MGM/United Artists	38,519,833
WAY WE WERE, THE	1973	Columbia	22,457,000
WELCOME STRANGER	1947	Paramount	6,100,000

WEST SIDE STORY	1961	United Artists	19,645,570
WHAT'S UP DOC?	1972	Warner Bros.	28,000,000
WHITE CHRISTMAS	1954	Paramount	12,000,000
WHITE CLIFFS OF DOVER	1944	MGM	4,045,250
WHO FRAMED ROGER RABBIT	1988	Disney	*78,000,000
WHO'S AFRAID OF VIRGINIA WOOLF?	1966	Warner Bros.	14,500,000
WIZARD OF OZ, THE	1939	MGM	4,544,851
YANK IN THE R.A.F., A	1941	Fox	*1,500,000
YANKEE DOODLE DANDY	1942	Warner Bros.	4,719,681
YOUNG FRANKENSTEIN	1974	Fox	38,823,000

---

*Figures are informed estimates.

FILMS BY STUDIO

EL CID	1961	Allied Artists	12,000,000
PAPILLON	1973	Allied Artists	22,500,000
THE RED SHOES	1948	Archers/Eagle-Lion	5,000,000
THE GRADUATE	1967	Avco/Embassy	44,090,729
THE BRIDGE ON THE RIVER KWAI	1957	Columbia	17,195,000
THE CAINE MUTINY	1954	Columbia	8,700,000
CLOSE ENCOUNTERS OF THE THIRD KIND	1977	Columbia	82,750,000
EASY RIDER	1969	Columbia	19,100,000
FROM HERE TO ETERNITY	1953	Columbia	12,200,000
FUNNY GIRL	1968	Columbia	26,325,000
GHOSTBUSTERS	1984	Columbia	130,211,324
GUESS WHO'S COMING TO DINNER	1967	Columbia	25,500,000
GUNS OF NAVARONE	1961	Columbia	13,000,000
JOLSON SINGS AGAIN	1949	Columbia	5,000,000
THE JOLSON STORY	1946	Columbia	7,600,000
THE KARATE KID	1984	Columbia	43,432,881
THE KARATE KID, PART II	1986	Columbia	58,362,026
KRAMER VS. KRAMER	1979	Columbia	59,986,335
LAWRENCE OF ARABIA	1962	Columbia	*19,000,000
A MAN FOR ALL SEASONS	1966	Columbia	12,750,000
MR. SMITH GOES TO WASHINGTON	1939	Columbia	1,500,000
SHAMPOO	1975	Columbia	23,822,000
STIR CRAZY	1980	Columbia	58,364,420
STRIPES	1981	Columbia	40,886,589
TOOTSIE	1982	Columbia	96,292,736
THE WAY WE WERE	1973	Columbia	22,457,000
CINERAMA HOLIDAY	1955	CRC	12,000,000
SEVEN WONDERS OF THE WORLD	1956	CRC	12,500,000
THIS IS CINERAMA	1952	CRC	15,400,000
HOW THE WEST WAS WON	1962	CRC/MGM	20,932,883
THE ABSENT-MINDED PROFESSOR	1961	Disney	11,426,000
ALICE IN WONDERLAND	1951	Disney	7,196,000
THE ARISTOCATS	1970	Disney	26,462,000
BAMBI	1942	Disney	47,265,000
CINDERELLA	1950	Disney	41,087,000
DARBY O'GILL AND THE LITTLE PEOPLE	1959	Disney	8,336,000
FANTASIA	1940	Disney	28,660,000
GOOD MORNING, VIETNAM	1987	Disney	58,103,000
IN SEARCH OF THE CASTAWAYS	1962	Disney	9,975,000
THE JUNGLE BOOK	1967	Disney	39,500,000
LADY AND THE TRAMP	1955	Disney	40,249,000
THE LOVE BUG	1969	Disney	23,150,000
LT. ROBIN CRUSOE, USN	1966	Disney	10,164,000

MARY POPPINS	1964	Disney	45,000,000
OLD YELLER	1957	Disney	10,050,000
101 DALMATIONS	1961	Disney	38,562,000
PETER PAN	1953	Disney	24,532,000
PINOCCHIO	1940	Disney	32,957,000
THE SHAGGY DOG	1959	Disney	12,317,000
SLEEPING BEAUTY	1959	Disney	21,998,000
SONG OF THE SOUTH	1946	Disney	29,228,717
SWISS FAMILY ROBINSON	1960	Disney	20,178,000
THE SWORD IN THE STONE	1963	Disney	10,475,000
THAT DARN CAT	1965	Disney	12,628,000
THREE MEN AND A BABY	1987	Disney	81,313,000
20,000 LEAGUES UNDER THE SEA	1954	Disney	11,267,000
WHO FRAMED ROGER RABBIT	1988	Disney	*78,000,000
ALIEN	1979	Fox	40,300,000
THE BIBLE	1966	Fox	15,000,000
BUTCH CASSIDY AND THE SUNDANCE KID	1969	Fox	46,039,000
CHEAPER BY THE DOZEN	1950	Fox	4,425,000
CLEOPATRA	1963	Fox	26,000,000
DAVID AND BATHSHEBA	1951	Fox	4,720,000
THE EMPIRE STRIKES BACK	1980	Fox	141,600,000
FOREVER AMBER	1947	Fox	5,000,000
THE FRENCH CONNECTION	1971	Fox	26,315,000
HELLO, DOLLY!	1969	Fox	15,200,000
HOW TO MARRY A MILLIONAIRE	1953	Fox	7,300,000
I WAS A MALE WAR BRIDE	1949	Fox	4,100,000
JESSE JAMES	1939	Fox	1,500,000
THE KING AND I	1956	Fox	8,500,000
LEAVE HER TO HEAVEN	1945	Fox	5,500,000
THE LONGEST DAY	1962	Fox	17,600,000
M*A*S*H	1970	Fox	36,720,000
9 TO 5	1980	Fox	59,100,000
PATTON	1970	Fox	28,100,000
PEYTON PLACE	1957	Fox	11,500,000
PORKY'S	1982	Fox	54,000,000
THE POSEIDON ADVENTURE	1972	Fox	42,000,000
RETURN OF THE JEDI	1983	Fox	168,002,414
THE ROBE	1953	Fox	17,500,000
THE ROCKY HORROR PICTURE SHOW	1975	Fox	26,000,000
SILVER STREAK	1976	Fox	30,018,000
THE SNOWS OF KILIMANJARO	1952	Fox	6,500,000
THE SONG OF BERNADETTE	1943	Fox	5,000,000
THE SOUND OF MUSIC	1965	Fox	79,748,000
SOUTH PACIFIC	1958	Fox	17,500,000
STAR WARS	1977	Fox	193,500,000
THOSE MAGNIFICENT MEN IN THEIR FLYING MACHINES	1965	Fox	14,000,000
THE TOWERING INFERNO	1974	Fox/Warner Bros.	52,000,000
A YANK IN THE R.A.F.	1941	Fox	*1,500,000
YOUNG FRANKENSTEIN	1974	Fox	38,823,000
OKLAHOMA!	1955	Magna	7,100,000

ANCHORS AWEIGH	1945	MGM	4,778,679
ANNIE GET YOUR GUN	1950	MGM	4,919,394
BATTLEGROUND	1949	MGM	5,051,143
BEN-HUR	1959	MGM	36,992,088
BOOM TOWN	1940	MGM	4,586,415
CAT ON A HOT TIN ROOF	1958	MGM	8,785,162
THE DIRTY DOZEN	1967	MGM	20,403,826
DOCTOR ZHIVAGO	1965	MGM	47,116,811
FATHER OF THE BRIDE	1950	MGM	4,054,405
GIGI	1958	MGM	7,321,423
GONE WITH THE WIND	1939	MGM	77,641,106
THE GREAT CARUSO	1951	MGM	4,531,000
HONKY TONK	1941	MGM	*1,500,000
IT'S A MAD MAD MAD MAD WORLD	1963	MGM	20,849,786
IVANHOE	1952	MGM	6,258,000
KING SOLOMON'S MINES	1950	MGM	5,586,000
MEET ME IN ST. LOUIS	1944	MGM	5,132,202
MRS. MINIVER	1942	MGM	5,390,009
THE PHILADELPHIA STORY	1941	MGM	*1,500,000
QUO VADIS?	1951	MGM	11,901,662
RAINTREE COUNTY	1957	MGM	5,962,839
RANDOM HARVEST	1942	MGM	4,665,501
SHOW BOAT	1951	MGM	5,533,000
30 SECONDS OVER TOKYO	1944	MGM	4,471,080
THE THREE MUSKETEERS	1948	MGM	4,306,876
2001: A SPACE ODYSSEY	1968	MGM	25,521,917
THE VALLEY OF DECISION	1945	MGM	4,566,374
WHITE CLIFFS OF DOVER	1944	MGM	4,045,250
THE WIZARD OF OZ	1939	MGM	4,544,851
RAIN MAN	1988	MGM/United Artists	*80,000,000
ROCKY III	1982	MGM/United Artists	66,262,796
ROCKY IV	1985	MGM/United Artists	76,023,246
WARGAMES	1983	MGM/United Artists	38,519,833
THE GOODBYE GIRL	1977	MGM/Warner Bros.	41,839,170
PLATOON	1986	Orion	69,742,143
AIRPLANE!	1980	Paramount	40,610,000
BEVERLY HILLS COP	1984	Paramount	108,000,000
BEVERLY HILLS COP II	1987	Paramount	80,857,776
BLUE SKIES	1946	Paramount	5,700,000
THE CARPETBAGGERS	1964	Paramount	15,500,000
COMING TO AMERICA	1988	Paramount	65,000,000
"CROCODILE" DUNDEE	1986	Paramount	70,227,000
"CROCODILE" DUNDEE II	1988	Paramount	57,300,000
FATAL ATTRACTION	1987	Paramount	70,000,000
FOR WHOM THE BELL TOLLS	1943	Paramount	7,100,000
THE GODFATHER	1972	Paramount	86,275,000
GOING MY WAY	1944	Paramount	6,500,000
GREASE	1978	Paramount	96,300,000
THE GREATEST SHOW ON EARTH	1952	Paramount	14,000,000
INDIANA JONES AND THE TEMPLE OF DOOM	1984	Paramount	109,000,000
KING KONG	1976	Paramount	36,915,000

LOVE STORY	1970	Paramount	50,000,000
THE ODD COUPLE	1968	Paramount	20,000,000
AN OFFICER AND A GENTLEMAN	1982	Paramount	55,223,000
THE PALEFACE	1948	Paramount	4,500,000
RAIDERS OF THE LOST ARK	1981	Paramount	115,598,000
REAR WINDOW	1954	Paramount	9,812,271
ROMEO AND JULIET	1968	Paramount	17,473,000
SAMSOM AND DELILAH	1949	Paramount	11,500,000
SATURDAY NIGHT FEVER	1977	Paramount	74,100,000
SHANE	1953	Paramount	9,000,000
STAR TREK: THE MOTION PICTURE	1979	Paramount	56,000,000
STAR TREK IV: THE VOYAGE HOME	1986	Paramount	56,820,071
THE TEN COMMANDMENTS	1956	Paramount	43,000,000
TERMS OF ENDEARMENT	1983	Paramount	50,250,000
TOP GUN	1986	Paramount	79,400,000
TRADING PLACES	1983	Paramount	40,600,000
UNCONQUERED	1947	Paramount	5,250,000
THE UNTOUCHABLES	1987	Paramount	36,866,530
WELCOME STRANGER	1947	Paramount	6,100,000
WHITE CHRISTMAS	1954	Paramount	12,000,000
THE SANDS OF IWO JIMA	1949	Republic	5,000,000
THE BELLS OF ST. MARY'S	1945	RKO	8,000,000
THE BEST YEARS OF OUR LIVES	1946	RKO	11,300,000
HANS CHRISTIAN ANDERSEN	1952	RKO	6,000,000
THE HUNCHBACK OF NOTRE DAME	1939	RKO	1,500,000
THE OUTLAW	1943	RKO	5,075,000
DUEL IN THE SUN	1946	Selznick	11,300,000
REBECCA	1940	Selznick	1,500,000
RAMBO: FIRST BLOOD PART II	1985	Tri-Star	78,919,250
THE ALAMO	1960	United Artists	7,918,776
DIAMONDS ARE FOREVER	1971	United Artists	19,726,829
EXODUS	1960	United Artists	8,331,582
FIDDLER ON THE ROOF	1971	United Artists	38,251,196
FROM RUSSIA WITH LOVE	1964	United Artists	9,924,279
GOLDFINGER	1964	United Artists	22,997,706
HAWAII	1966	United Artists	15,553,018
IRMA LA DOUCE	1963	United Artists	11,921,784
MIDNIGHT COWBOY	1969	United Artists	20,499,282
ONE FLEW OVER THE CUCKOO'S NEST	1975	United Artists	59,939,701
RED RIVER	1948	United Artists	4,506,825
ROCKY	1976	United Artists	56,524,972
ROCKY II	1979	United Artists	42,169,387
SINCE YOU WENT AWAY	1944	United Artists	4,924,756
SPELLBOUND	1945	United Artists	4,970,583
STAGE DOOR CANTEEN	1943	United Artists	4,339,532
THUNDERBALL	1965	United Artists	28,621,434
TOM JONES	1963	United Artists	16,925,988
WEST SIDE STORY	1961	United Artists	19,645,570
AROUND THE WORLD IN 80 DAYS	1956	United Artists/WB	23,120,000

AIRPORT	1970	Universal	45,220,118
AMERICAN GRAFFITI	1973	Universal	55,128,175
BACK TO THE FUTURE	1985	Universal	104,408,738
E.T. THE EXTRA-TERRESTRIAL	1982	Universal	228,618,939
EARTHQUAKE	1974	Universal	35,849,994
THE EGG AND I	1947	Universal	5,500,000
THE GLENN MILLER STORY	1954	Universal	7,590,994
JAWS	1975	Universal	129,549,325
JAWS 2	1978	Universal	50,431,964
THE JERK	1979	Universal	42,989,656
NATIONAL LAMPOON'S ANIMAL HOUSE	1978	Universal	70,826,000
ON GOLDEN POND	1981	Universal	61,174,744
OPERATION PETTICOAT	1959	Universal	9,321,555
OUT OF AFRICA	1985	Universal	43,103,469
PSYCHO	1960	Universal	11,200,000
SMOKEY AND THE BANDIT	1977	Universal	58,949,939
SPARTACUS	1960	Universal	10,300,454
THE STING	1973	Universal	78,212,000
TWINS	1988	Universal	*55,000,000
ALL THE PRESIDENT'S MEN	1976	Warner Bros.	30,000,000
ANY WHICH WAY YOU CAN	1980	Warner Bros.	40,500,000
ARTHUR	1981	Warner Bros.	42,000,000
AUNTIE MAME	1958	Warner Bros.	9,300,000
BATTLE CRY	1955	Warner Bros.	8,100,000
BILLY JACK	1971	Warner Bros.	32,500,000
BLAZING SADDLES	1974	Warner Bros.	47,800,000
BONNIE AND CLYDE	1967	Warner Bros.	22,800,000
BULLITT	1968	Warner Bros.	19,000,000
CASABLANCA	1942	Warner Bros.	4,145,178
THE COLOR PURPLE	1985	Warner Bros.	47,900,000
DELIVERANCE	1972	Warner Bros.	22,600,000
DIVE BOMBER	1941	Warner Bros.	*1,500,000
DOG DAY AFTERNOON	1975	Warner Bros.	22,500,000
EVERY WHICH WAY BUT LOOSE	1978	Warner Bros.	51,900,000
THE EXORCIST	1973	Warner Bros.	89,000,000
GIANT	1956	Warner Bros.	14,000,000
GREMLINS	1984	Warner Bros.	79,500,000
JEREMIAH JOHNSON	1972	Warner Bros.	21,900,000
JOHNNY BELINDA	1948	Warner Bros.	4,266,000
LIFE WITH FATHER	1947	Warner Bros.	5,057,000
MISTER ROBERTS	1955	Warner Bros.	8,500,000
THE MUSIC MAN	1962	Warner Bros.	8,100,000
MY FAIR LADY	1964	Warner Bros.	12,000,000
NO TIME FOR SERGEANTS	1958	Warner Bros.	7,500,000
SANTA FE TRAIL	1940	Warner Bros.	1,500,000
SAYONARA	1957	Warner Bros.	10,500,000
SERGEANT YORK	1941	Warner Bros.	6,135,707
A STAR IS BORN	1976	Warner Bros.	37,100,000
SUMMER OF '42	1971	Warner Bros.	20,500,000
SUPERMAN	1978	Warner Bros.	82,800,000
SUPERMAN II	1981	Warner Bros.	65,100,000

SUPERMAN III	1983	Warner Bros.	37,200,000
THIS IS THE ARMY	1943	Warner Bros.	8,301,000
THE TRIAL OF BILLY JACK	1974	Warner Bros.	31,100,000
WHAT'S UP DOC?	1972	Warner Bros.	28,000,000
WHO'S AFRAID OF VIRGINIA WOOLF?	1966	Warner Bros.	14,500,000
YANKEE DOODLE DANDY	1942	Warner Bros.	4,719,681

*Figures are approximate.

BUT WHAT ABOUT . . . ?

A number of important films fail to appear on the list of the top five hits of each year. Many will be surprised that these aren't number-ones, or at least runners-up. While generally box office success is a measure of quality, this is not always the case. The following motion pictures are generally remembered by audiences as successful, if not financially, then in emotional impact and/or quality of production (these are alphabetically listed and not ranked according to gross or rental dollars):

1 9 3 9

DARK VICTORY
DESTRY RIDES AGAIN
ELIZABETH AND ESSEX
GOODBYE, MR. CHIPS
NINOTCHKA
STAGECOACH

1 9 4 0

THE GRAPES OF WRATH
THE GREAT DICTATOR
NORTHWEST MOUNTED POLICE
NORTHWEST PASSAGE
OUR TOWN
THE ROAD TO SINGAPORE
STRIKE UP THE BAND

1 9 4 1

CITIZEN KANE
DR. JEKYLL & MR. HYDE
DUMBO*
HOW GREEN WAS MY VALLEY
THE MALTESE FALCON

1 9 4 2

HOLIDAY INN
NOW, VOYAGER
THE PRIDE OF THE YANKEES
THE ROAD TO MOROCCO

1 9 4 3

CABIN IN THE SKY
A GUY NAMED JOE
LASSIE COME HOME
THE PHANTOM OF THE OPERA

1 9 4 4

ARSENIC AND OLD LACE
THE CANTERVILLE GHOST
GASLIGHT
NATIONAL VELVET
TO HAVE AND HAVE NOT

1 9 4 5

THE CORN IS GREEN
THE LOST WEEKEND
MILDRED PIERCE
SARATOGA TRUNK
A TREE GROWS IN BROOKLYN

1 9 4 6

THE BIG SLEEP
GILDA
GREAT EXPECTATIONS
IT'S A WONDERFUL LIFE
NOTORIOUS
THE POSTMAN ALWAYS RINGS TWICE
THE RAZOR'S EDGE
THE YEARLING

*Although Dumbo earned $4,000,000, it is
not included among the top five of 1941
since it runs only 64 minutes, not long
enough to qualify as a feature.

1 9 4 7

THE BACHELOR AND THE BOBBY-SOXER
THE FARMER'S DAUGHTER
GENTLEMAN'S AGREEMENT
THE GHOST AND MRS. MUIR
MIRACLE ON 34TH STREET
THE ROAD TO RIO

1 9 4 8

HAMLET
KEY LARGO
THE SNAKE PIT
TREASURE OF SIERRA MADRE

1 9 4 9

ADAM'S RIB
ALL THE KING'S MEN
LITTLE WOMEN
THE THIRD MAN
TWELVE O'CLOCK HIGH

1 9 5 0

ALL ABOUT EVE
THE ASPHALT JUNGLE
BORN YESTERDAY
HARVEY
SUNSET BOULEVARD

1 9 5 1

THE AFRICAN QUEEN
AN AMERICAN IN PARIS
THE DAY THE EARTH STOOD STILL
DEATH OF A SALESMAN
A PLACE IN THE SUN
A STREETCAR NAMED DESIRE

1 9 5 2

COME BACK, LITTLE SHEBA
HIGH NOON
THE MEMBER OF THE WEDDING
MOULIN ROUGE
THE QUIET MAN
SINGING IN THE RAIN

1 9 5 3

CALL ME MADAM
GENTLEMEN PREFER BLONDES
MOGAMBO
ROMAN HOLIDAY
STALAG 17
WAR OF THE WORLDS

1 9 5 4

THE COUNTRY GIRL
THE HIGH AND THE MIGHTY
ON THE WATERFRONT
SEVEN BRIDES FOR SEVEN BROTHERS
A STAR IS BORN
THREE COINS IN THE FOUNTAIN

1 9 5 5

EAST OF EDEN
LOVE IS A MANY-SPLENDORED THING
MARTY
PICNIC
REBEL WITHOUT A CAUSE
TO CATCH A THIEF

1 9 5 6

BUS STOP
CAROUSEL
FRIENDLY PERSUASION
HIGH SOCIETY
SOMEBODY UP THERE LIKES ME

1 9 5 7

A FAREWELL TO ARMS
FUNNY FACE
SILK STOCKINGS
12 ANGRY MEN
THE THREE FACES OF EVE
WITNESS FOR THE PROSECUTION

1 9 5 8

THE BROTHERS KARAMAZOV
DAMN YANKEES
THE DEFIANT ONES
THE OLD MAN AND THE SEA
VERTIGO

1 9 5 9

ANATOMY OF A MURDER
THE DIARY OF ANNE FRANK
THE FIVE PENNIES
NORTH BY NORTHWEST
THE NUN'S STORY
PILLOW TALK
PORGY AND BESS
SOME LIKE IT HOT

1 9 6 0

THE APARTMENT
BUTTERFIELD 8
ELMER GANTRY
THE MAGNIFICENT SEVEN
NEVER ON SUNDAY

1 9 6 1

BREAKFAST AT TIFFANY'S
LA DOLCE VITA
FANNY
FLOWER DRUM SONG
JUDGEMENT AT NUREMBERG
LOVER COME BACK
THE PARENT TRAP

1 9 6 2

THE DAYS OF WINE AND ROSES
DR. NO
GYPSY
THE MIRACLE WORKER
MUTINY ON THE BOUNTY
TO KILL A MOCKINGBIRD
WHAT EVER HAPPENED TO BABY JANE?

1 9 6 3

THE BIRDS
BYE BYE BIRDIE
THE GREAT ESCAPE
HUD
LILIES OF THE FIELD
SON OF FLUBBER

1 9 6 4

BECKET
DR. STRANGELOVE
A HARD DAY'S NIGHT
THE PINK PANTHER
A SHOT IN THE DARK
THE UNSINKABLE MOLLY BROWN
ZORBA THE GREEK

1 9 6 5

THE AGONY AND THE ECSTASY
CAT BALLOU
DARLING
THE GREATEST STORY EVER TOLD
HELP!
THE SANDPIPER
SHIP OF FOOLS
A THOUSAND CLOWNS

1 9 6 6

ALFIE
GEORGY GIRL
A MAN AND A WOMAN
THE RUSSIANS ARE COMING,
     THE RUSSIANS ARE COMING
THE SAND PEBBLES

1 9 6 7

CAMELOT
DOCTOR DOLITTLE
IN THE HEAT OF THE NIGHT
THOROUGHLY MODERN MILLIE
VALLEY OF THE DOLLS
YOU ONLY LIVE TWICE

1 9 6 8

THE LION IN WINTER
OLIVER!
PLANET OF THE APES
ROSEMARY'S BABY
STAR!
YELLOW SUBMARINE

1969

ANNE OF THE THOUSAND DAYS
BOB & CAROL & TED & ALICE
CACTUS FLOWER
GOODBYE, COLUMBUS
ON HER MAJESTY'S SECRET SERVICE
PAINT YOUR WAGON
THEY SHOOT HORSES, DON'T THEY?
TRUE GRIT

1970

CATCH-22
FIVE EASY PIECES
LITTLE BIG MAN

1971

CARNAL KNOWLEDGE
A CLOCKWORK ORANGE
DIRTY HARRY
THE LAST PICTURE SHOW
NICHOLAS AND ALEXANDRA

1972

CABARET
DEEP THROAT
LADY SINGS THE BLUES
SOUNDER

1973

DAY FOR NIGHT
LAST TANGO IN PARIS
LIVE AND LET DIE
MAGNUM FORCE
PAPER MOON
ROBIN HOOD
SERPICO
A TOUCH OF CLASS

1974

AIRPORT 1975
CHINATOWN
THE GODFATHER PART TWO
HARRY AND TONTO
THE LONGEST YARD
THE THREE MUSKETEERS

1975

FUNNY LADY
THE MAN WHO WOULD BE KING
NASHVILLE
THE SUNSHINE BOYS
THREE DAYS OF THE CONDOR

1976

BOUND FOR GLORY
CARRIE
NETWORK
THE OMEN
SILENT MOVIE
TAXI DRIVER

1977

ANNIE HALL
THE DEEP
JULIA
OH GOD!
THE SPY WHO LOVED ME
THE TURNING POINT

1978

THE BUDDY HOLLY STORY
COMING HOME
THE DEER HUNTER
HEAVEN CAN WAIT
UP IN SMOKE

1979

ALL THAT JAZZ
THE AMITYVILLE HORROR
. . . AND JUSTICE FOR ALL
APOCALYPSE NOW
THE CHINA SYNDROME
MANHATTAN
MOONRAKER
NORMA RAE

1980

COAL MINER'S DAUGHTER
THE ELEPHANT MAN
ORDINARY PEOPLE
PRIVATE BENJAMIN
URBAN COWBOY

1 9 8 1

ABSENCE OF MALICE
THE CANNONBALL RUN
CHARIOTS OF FIRE
THE FOX AND THE HOUND
THE GODS MUST BE CRAZY
MOMMIE DEAREST
REDS

1 9 8 2

ANNIE
GANDHI
POLTERGEIST
SOPHIE'S CHOICE
STAR TREK II: THE WRATH OF KHAN
THE VERDICT

1 9 8 3

THE BIG CHILL
FANNY AND ALEXANDER
FLASHDANCE
THE RIGHT STUFF
RISKY BUSINESS
SILKWOOD
YENTL
ZELIG

1 9 8 4

AMADEUS
FOOTLOOSE
THE KILLING FIELDS
A PASSAGE TO INDIA
PLACES IN THE HEART
POLICE ACADEMY
ROMANCING THE STONE
A SOLDIER'S STORY
SPLASH
STAR TREK III: THE SEARCH FOR SPOCK
2010

1 9 8 5

AGNES OF GOD
COCOON
THE JEWEL OF THE NILE
KISS OF THE SPIDER WOMAN
PRIZZI'S HONOR
RUNAWAY TRAIN
WITNESS

1 9 8 6

ALIENS
CHILDREN OF A LESSER GOD
DOWN AND OUT IN BEVERLY HILLS
FERRIS BUELLER'S DAY OFF
THE FLY
HANNAH AND HER SISTERS
THE MISSION
STAND BY ME

1 9 8 7

BROADCAST NEWS
CRY FREEDOM
DIRTY DANCING
HOPE AND GLORY
THE LAST EMPEROR
LETHAL WEAPON
MOONSTRUCK
WALL STREET
THE WITCHES OF EASTWICK

1 9 8 8

THE ACCIDENTAL TOURIST
BEETLEJUICE
BIG
COCKTAIL
DANGEROUS LIAISONS
A FISH CALLED WANDA
GORILLAS IN THE MIST
MISSISSIPPI BURNING
THE NAKED GUN
OLIVER AND COMPANY
SCROOGED
WILLOW
WORKING GIRL

BIBLIOGRAPHY

Anthony, Jolene M. *Tom Cruise*. New York: St. Martin's Press, 1988.

Balaban, Bob. *Close Encounters of the Third Kind Diary*. A Paradise Press Book, 1978.

Benson, Raymond. *The James Bond Bedside Companion*. New York: Dodd, Mead & Co., 1984.

Bergan, Ronald, Graham Fuller, and David Malcolm. *Academy Award Winners*. New York: Crescent Books, 1986.

Boller, Paul F., Jr. and Ronald L. Davis. *Hollywood Anecdotes*. New York: Ballantine Books, 1987.

Bookbinder, Robert. *The Films of The Seventies*. Secaucus, N.J.: Citadel Press, 1980.

Brode, Douglas. *The Films of the Fifties*. Secaucus, N.J.: Citadel Press, 1976.

Brode, Douglas. *The Films of the Sixties*. Secaucus, N.J.: Citadel Press, 1980.

Brodsky, Jack and Nathan Weiss. *The Cleopatra Papers*. New York: Simon & Schuster, 1963.

Bronson, Fred. *The Billboard Book of Number One Hits*. New York: Billboard Books, 1988.

Brooks, Tim and Earle Marsh. *The Complete Directory to Prime Time Network TV Shows*. New York: Ballantine Books, 1979.

Cagin, Seth and Philip Dray. *Hollywood Films of The Seventies*. New York: Harper & Row, 1984.

Callan, Michael Feeney. *Sean Connery*. New York: Stein & Day, 1983.

Considine, Shaun. *Barbra Streisand*. New York: Delacorte Press, 1985.

Culhane, John. *Special Effects in the Movies*. New York: Ballantine Books, 1981.

Eames, John Douglas. *The MGM Story*. New York: Crown Publishers, 1977.

Ebert, Roger. *Roger Ebert's Movie Home Companion, 1989 Edition*. Kansas City: Andrews & McMeel, 1988.

Edwards, Anne. *Early Reagan*. New York: William Morrow & Co., 1987.

Ewen, David. *The New Complete Book of the American Musical Theater*. New York: Holt, Rinehart and Winston, 1970.

Finch, Christopher. *The Art of Walt Disney*. New York: Harry N. Abrams, 1975.

Finler, Joel. *All-Time Box-Office Hits*. New York: Gallery Books, 1985.

Finler, Joel W. *The Hollywood Story*. New York: Crown Publishers, 1988.

Fitzgerald, Michael G. *Universal Pictures*. New York: Arlington House, 1977.

Friedrich, Otto. *City of Nets*. New York: Harper & Row, 1986.

Grossman, Gary. *Superman, Serial to Cereal*. New York: Popular Library, 1977.

Guiles, Fred Lawrence. *Jane Fonda*. New York: Doubleday & Co., 1982.

Halliwell, Leslie. *The Filmgoer's Companion, Sixth Edition*. New York: Hill & Wang, 1977.

Harmetz, Aljean. *The Making of The Wizard of Oz*. New York: Limelight Editions, 1984.

Henkin, Bill. *The Rocky Horror Picture Show Book*. Hawthorn Books, 1979.

Huston, John. *An Open Book*. New York: Alfred A. Knopf, 1980.

Kaplan, Mike. *Variety Who's Who in Show Business*. New York: Garland Publishing, 1983.

Katz, Ephraim. *The Film Encyclopedia*. New York: A Perigee Book, 1979.

Klain, Jane; British Ed., William Pay; Canadian Ed., Patricia Thompson. *International Motion Picture Almanac, 60th Edition*. New York: Quigley Publishing Company, 1989.

Kobal, John. *John Kobal Presents The Top 100 Movies*. New York: New American Library, 1988.

Koehler, William R. *The Wonderful World of Disney Animals*. New York: Howell Book House, 1979.

Koszarski, Richard. *Hollywood Directors*. Oxford: Oxford University Press, 1977.

Lasky, Michael S. and Robert A. Harris. *The Films of Alfred Hitchcock*. Secaucus, N.J.: Citadel Press, 1976.

Lenburg, Jeff. *Dustin Hoffman*. New York: St. Martin's Press, 1983.

Lloyd, Ann and Graham Fuller. *The Illustrated Who's Who of the Cinema*. New York: Portland House, 1987.

Lyon, Richard Sean. *The 1989 Investor's Guide to Films*. West Los Angeles: LyonHeart Publishers, 1989.

Maltin, Leonard. *The Disney Films, New Updated Edition*. New York: Crown Publishers, 1984.

Maltin, Leonard. *Leonard Maltin's TV Movies And Video Guide, 1989 Edition*. New York: NAL Penguin, 1988.

Martin, Mick and Marsha Porter. *Video Movie Guide*. New York: Ballantine Books, 1987.

Morella, Joe, Edward Z. Epstein, and John Griggs. *The Films of World War II*. Secaucus, N.J.: Citadel Press, 1980.

Nolan, William F. *McQueen*. New York: Congdon & Weed, 1984.

Osborne, Robert. *Academy Awards Illustrated*. La Habra, Cal.: ESE California, 1977.

Parish, James Robert. *The Fox Girls*. New York: Arlington House, 1971.

Preminger, Otto. *Preminger*. New York: Doubleday & Co., 1977.

Robbins, Jhan. *Yul Brynner*. New York: Dodd, Mead & Co., 1987.

Robertson, Patrick. *The Guinness Book Of Movie Facts And Feats*. Great Britain: Guinness Books, 1988.

Sackett, Susan and Gene Roddenberry. *The Making Of Star Trek: The Motion Picture*. New York: Pocket Books, 1980.

Scheuer, Steven H. *Movies on TV And VideoCassette*. New York: Bantam Books, 1989.

Sennett, Ted. *Great Movie Directors*. New York: Harry N. Abrams, 1986.

Sharif, Omar, with Marie-Therese Guinchard. *The Eternal Male*. New York: Doubleday & Co., 1977.

Spoto, Donald. *Stanley Kramer, Film Maker*. New York: Putnam, 1978.

Taylor, Elizabeth. *Elizabeth Takes Off*. New York: G. P. Putnam's Sons, 1987.

Terrace, Vincent. *The Complete Encyclopedia of Television Programs, Vols. 1 & 2*. New Jersey: A. S. Barnes & Co., 1976.

Thomas, Bob. *Walt Disney*. New York: Pocket Books, 1976.

Thomas, Tony. *The Films of The Forties*. Secaucus, N.J.: Citadel Press, 1975.

Wiley, Mason and Damien Bona. *Inside Oscar*. New York: Ballantine Books, 1987.

Wilkerson, Tichi and Marcia Borie. *Hollywood Legends*. Los Angeles: Tale Weaver Publishing, 1988.

PHOTO CREDITS

Courtesy of Marvin Paige's Motion Picture & TV Research Service.

FIDDLER ON THE ROOF © 1971 Mirisch Productions, Inc. and Cartier Productions, Inc. All Rights Reserved.

FOR WHOM THE BELL TOLLS Copyright © by Universal Pictures, a Division of Universal City Studios, Inc. Courtesy of MCA Publishing Rights, A Division of MCA Inc. Courtesy of Marvin Paige's Motion Picture & TV Research Service.

FOREVER AMBER © 1947, renewed 1974 Twentieth Century-Fox Film Corporation. All rights reserved. Courtesy of Marvin Paige's Motion Picture & TV Research Service.

THE FRENCH CONNECTION © 1971 Twentieth-Century-Fox Film Corporation. All Rights Reserved.

FROM HERE TO ETERNITY © 1953 Columbia Pictures Industries, Inc. All Rights Reserved. Courtesy of Marvin Paige's Motion Picture & TV Research Service.

FROM RUSSIA WITH LOVE © 1963 Danjaq S.A. All Rights Reserved.

FUNNY GIRL © 1968 Columbia Pictures Industries, Inc. All Rights Reserved. Courtesy of the Academy of Motion Picture Arts and Sciences.

GHOSTBUSTERS © 1984 Columbia Pictures Industries, Inc. All Rights Reserved.

GIANT © 1956 Giant Productions. Renewed 1984 Warner Bros. Inc., George Stevens, Jr. and Jess S. Morgan. All Rights Reserved.

GIGI © 1958 Loew's Inc. and Arthur Freed Productions, Inc. Ren. 1986 MGM/UA Entertainment Co. and Arthur Freed Productions, Inc. Courtesy of Marvin Paige's Motion Picture & TV Research Service.

THE GLENN MILLER STORY Copyright © by Universal Pictures, a Division of Universal City Studios, Inc. Courtesy of MCA Publishing Rights, A Division of MCA Inc. Courtesy of Marvin Paige's Motion Picture & TV Research Service.

THE GODFATHER Copyright © 1972 by Paramount Pictures Corporation. All Rights Reserved.

GOING MY WAY Copyright © by Universal Pictures, a Division of Universal City Studios, Inc. Courtesy of MCA Publishing Rights, a Division of MCA Inc.

GOLDFINGER © 1964 Danjaq S.A. All Rights Reserved.

GONE WITH THE WIND © 1939 Selznick International Pictures, Inc. Ren. 1967 Metro-Goldwyn-Mayer Inc. Page 19: Courtesy of Marvin Paige's Motion Picture & TV Research Service.

GOOD MORNING, VIETNAM © Touchstone Pictures.

THE GOODBYE GIRL © 1977 Metro-Goldwyn-Mayer Inc. and Warner Bros.

Inc. All Rights Reserved.

GREASE Copyright © 1977 by Paramount Pictures Corporation. All Rights Reserved.

THE GREATEST SHOW ON EARTH Copyright © 1952 by Paramount Pictures Corporation. All Rights Reserved.

GREMLINS © 1984 Warner Bros. Inc. All Rights Reserved.

GUESS WHO'S COMING TO DINNER © 1967 Columbia Pictures Industries, Inc. All Rights Reserved.

THE GUNS OF NAVARONE © Columbia Pictures Industries, Inc. All Rights Reserved.

HAWAII © 1966 The Mirisch Corporation. Assigned © 1985 United Artist Corporation. All Rights Reserved.

HELLO, DOLLY! © 1969 Chenault Productions, Inc. and Twentieth Century-Fox Film Corporation. All Rights Reserved.

HONKY TONK © 1941 Loew's Inc. Ren. 1968 Metro-Goldwyn-Mayer Inc.

HOW THE WEST WAS WON © 1962 Metro-Goldwyn-Mayer Inc., and Cinerama, Inc.

THE HUNCHBACK OF NOTRE DAME © 1939 RKO Radio Picture, Inc. Ren. 1967 RKO General, Inc. Courtesy of the Academy of Motion Picture Arts and Sciences.

I WAS A MALE WAR BRIDE © 1949, renewed 1977 Twentieth Century-Fox Film Corporations. All Rights Reserved.

IN SEARCH OF THE CASTAWAYS © The Walt Disney Company.

INDIANA JONES AND THE TEMPLE OF DOOM © Lucasfilm Ltd. 1983. All Rights Reserved.

IRMA LA DOUCE © 1963 The Mirisch Company, Inc. Assigned © 1985 United Artists Corporation. All Rights Reserved.

IT'S A MAD MAD MAD MAD WORLD © 1963 Casey Productions, Inc. All Rights Reserved.

IVANHOE © 1952 Loew's Inc. Ren. 1980 Metro-Goldwyn-Mayer Inc.

JAWS Copyright © by Universal Pictures, a Division of Universal City Studios, Inc. Courtesy of MCA Publishing Rights, a Division of MCA Inc.

JAWS 2 Copyright © by Universal Pictures, a Division of Universal City Studios, Inc. Courtesy of MCA Publishing Rights, A Division of MCA Inc.

JEREMIAH JOHNSON © 1972 Warner Bros. Inc. and Sanford Productions, Inc.

THE JERK Copyright © by Universal Pictures, a Division of Universal Studios, Inc. Courtesy of MCA Publishing Rights, A Division of MCA Inc.

JESSE JAMES © 1939, renewed 1966 Twentieth Century-Fox Film Corporation. All Rights Reserved. Courtesy of Marvin Paige's Motion Picture & TV Research Service.

JOHNNY BELINDA © 1948 Warner Bros. Pictures, Inc. Ren. 1975 United Artists Television, Inc. Courtesy of Marvin Paige's Motion Picture & TV Research Service.

JOLSON SINGS AGAIN © 1949 Columbia Pictures Industries, Inc. All Rights Reserved.

THE JOLSON STORY © 1946 Columbia Pictures Industries, Inc. All Rights Reserved. Courtesy of Marvin Paige's Motion Picture & TV Research Service.

THE JUNGLE BOOK © The Walt Disney Company.

THE KARATE KID © 1984 Columbia Pictures Industries, Inc. All Rights Reserved.

THE KARATE KID, PART II © 1985 Columbia Pictures Industries, Inc. All Rights Reserved.

THE KING AND I © 1956, renewed 1984 Twentieth Century-Fox Film Corporation. All rights reserved.

KING KONG © 1976 by Dino De Laurentiis Corporation. All Rights Reserved.

KING SOLOMON'S MINES © 1950 Loew's Inc. Ren. 1977 Metro-Goldwyn-Mayer Inc.

KRAMER VS. KRAMER © 1979 Columbia Pictures Industries, Inc. All Rights Reserved.

LADY AND THE TRAMP © The Walt Disney Company.

LAWRENCE OF ARABIA © 1962 Columbia Pictures Industries, Inc. All Rights Reserved.

LEAVE HER TO HEAVEN © 1946, renewed 1973 Twentieth Century-Fox Film Corporation. All Rights Reserved. Courtesy of Marvin Paige's Motion Picture & TV Research Service.

LIFE WITH FATHER © 1947 Katherine B. Day, Howard Lindsay and Russell Crouse. All Rights Reserved.

THE LONGEST DAY © 1962 Darryl F. Zanuck Productions, Inc., & Twentieth Century-Fox Film Corporation. All Rights Reserved.

THE LOVE BUG © The Walt Disney Company.

LOVE STORY Copyright © 1970 by Paramount Pictures Corporation. All Rights Reserved.

LT. ROBIN CRUSOE, USN © The Walt Disney Company.

M*A*S*H* © Aspen Productions, Inc. and Twentieth Century-Fox Film Corporation. All Rights Reserved.

A MAN FOR ALL SEASONS © 1966 Columbia Pictures Industries, Inc. All Rights Reserved.

MARY POPPINS © The Walt Disney Company. Courtesy of the Academy of Motion Picture Arts and Sciences.

MEET ME IN ST. LOUIS © 1944 Loew's Inc. Ren. 1971 Metro-Goldwyn-Mayer Inc.

MIDNIGHT COWBOY © 1969 Jerome

INDEX